Beginning Microsoft SQL Server® 2008 Programming

Beginning
Microsoft SQL Server® 2008 Programming

Beginning
Microsoft SQL Server® 2008 Programming

Robert Vieira

WILEY

Wiley Publishing, Inc.

Beginning Microsoft SQL Server® 2008 Programming

Published by
Wiley Publishing, Inc.
10475 Crosspoint Boulevard
Indianapolis, IN 46256
www.wiley.com

Copyright © 2009 by Wiley Publishing, Inc., Indianapolis, Indiana

Published simultaneously in Canada

ISBN-13: 978-0-470-25701-2

Manufactured in the United States of America

10 9 8 7 6 5 4 3 2 1

Library of Congress Cataloging-in-Publication Data:

Vieira, Robert.
 Beginning SQL server 2008 programming / Robert Vieira.
  p. cm.
 Includes index.
 ISBN 978-0-470-25701-2 (paper/website) 1. SQL server. 2. Database management. 3. Relational databases.
I. Title.
 QA76.9.D3V5254 2008
 005.75'85--dc22
                                    2008033212

For over 10 years now, and through what is now 5 books (6 when I finish the Pro title this time around), I've dedicated my books to my daughters (well, it was a single daughter when I wrote my first one). I don't see any reason to change that now.

Things in life have changed a great deal for me over the years, and the oldest daughter didn't have to sacrifice as much time with me this time around (college life means she doesn't want to see that much of me anyway — I hate kids growing up!). The younger one regularly asks me when I'm going to be done, so I guess she's noticed time lost, and, frankly, so have I.

And so it is, once again, that I dedicate this book to my two daughters, and promise that at least some portion of the proceeds of this book will help pay for a nice trip to Disney World so we can make up a little time!

About the Author

Experiencing his first infection with computing fever in 1978, **Rob Vieira** knew right away that this was something "really cool." In 1980 he began immersing himself in the computing world more fully — splitting time between building and repairing computer kits, and programming in Basic as well as Z80 and 6502 assembly. In 1983, he began studies for a degree in Computer Information Systems, but found the professional mainframe environment too rigid for his tastes, and dropped out in 1985 to pursue other interests. Later that year, he caught the "PC bug" and began the long road of programming in database languages from dBase to SQL Server. Rob completed a degree in Business Administration in 1990, and since has typically worked in roles that allow him to combine his knowledge of business and computing. Beyond his Bachelor's degree, he has been certified as a Certified Management Accountant as well as Microsoft Certified as a Solutions Developer (MCSD), Trainer (MCT), and Database Administrator (MCDBA).

Rob is currently the DBA Team Lead for the Stockamp practice of The Huron Consulting Group in Portland, Oregon, and makes occasional speaking appearances on database development, business intelligence, and other topics.

He resides with his youngest daughter Adrianna (aka Addy, aka Trillian, aka "T") in Vancouver, WA.

Credits

Executive Editor
Bob Elliott

Development Editor
Sydney Jones

Technical Editor
John Mueller

Production Editor
Daniel Scribner

Copy Editor
Kim Cofer

Editorial Manager
Mary Beth Wakefield

Production Manager
Tim Tate

Vice President and Executive Group Publisher
Richard Swadley

Vice President and Executive Publisher
Joseph B. Wikert

Project Coordinator, Cover
Lynsey Stanford

Compositor
Craig Johnson, Happenstance Type-O-Rama

Proofreaders
Justin Neely, Word One
Kathy Pope, Word One
Josh Chase, Word One

Indexer
Ron Strauss

Acknowledgments

Over the years, there have been so many that deserve a note of thanks. Some long ago earned a permanent place in my acknowledgment list, and others are new to the scene but have done their own special things along the way.

Kate Hall, who, although she was probably ready to kill me by the end of each of my first two books, somehow guided me through the edit process to build a better book each time. I have long since fallen out of touch with Kate, but she will always be the most special to me as someone who really helped shape my writing career. I continue to hold this first dedication spot for you — wherever you are Kate, I hope you are doing splendidly.

Adaobi Obi Tulton, who has had to put up with yet another trialing year of dealing with my life and what that has sometimes meant to delivery schedules. If I ever make it rich, I may hire Adaobi as my spiritual guide. While she can be high stress about deadlines, she has a way of displaying a kind of "peace" in just about everything else I've seen her do. I need to learn that. (I said the same thing in my last book, but I don't seem to have made much progress.)

Dominic Shakeshaft, who got me writing in the first place (then again, given some nights filled with writing instead of sleep lately, maybe it's not thanks I owe him…).

Catherine Alexander, who played Kate's more than able-bodied sidekick for my first title, and was central to round two. Catherine was much like Kate in the sense she had a significant influence on the shape and success of my first two titles.

Greg Jackson, who saved me some sleepless nights by taking over some of the copy-edit phase duties for this title, so I could increase my focus on finishing the Professional title without messing up the schedule. The trials of late changes to the product and troubles in the editing process wound up making things substantially more frustrating than I imagine Greg thought he was signing up for, and I appreciate his willingness to keep sorting things out until I stepped back in.

A few other honorable mentions are deserved for past or present contributions (forgive me if I leave someone out): Richard Waymire, Gert Drapers, Bill Ramos, Dan Jones, and Bob Elliott.

Contents

Contents

Contents

Contents

Contents

Contents

Contents

Contents

Contents

Introduction

And so the journey continues, and, as I've said before, what a long, strange trip it's been. When I first wrote *Professional SQL Server 7.0 Programming* in early 1999, the landscape of both books and the development world was much different than it is today. At the time, .NET was as yet unheard of, and while Visual Studio 98 ruled the day as the most popular development environment, Java was coming on strong and alternative development tools, such as Delphi, were still more competitive than they typically are today. The so-called "dot com" era was booming, and the use of database management systems (DBMS), such as SQL Server, was growing exponentially.

There was, however, a problem. While one could find quite a few books on SQL Server, they were all oriented toward the administrator. They spent tremendous amounts of time and energy on things that the average developer did not give a proverbial hoot about. Something had to give, and as my development editor and I pondered the needs of the world, we realized that we could not solve world hunger or arms proliferation ourselves, but we could solve the unrealized need for a new kind of SQL book — one aimed specifically at developers.

At the time, I wrote *Professional SQL Server 7.0 Programming* to be everything to everyone. It was a compendium. It started at the beginning and progressed to a logical end. The result was a very, very large book that filled a void for a lot of people (hooray!).

With SQL Server 2005, SQL Server was in its second revision since I released my first book and, as we did the planning for that round of books, we realized that we once again had a problem — the Professional title was too big to fit in a single book. The new features of SQL Server 2005 created a situation where there was simply too much content to squeeze into one book (we literally exceeded the bindery limits for a book), and so we made the choice to split the old Professional series title into a Beginning and a more targeted Professional pair of titles. A lot of work was put into the split, but, in the end, there was still a significant degree of overlap. SQL Server 2008 adds yet another stack of new features, provides me the opportunity to take the Professional title even more toward the advanced reader, and allows me to round out the Beginning title more cleanly.

My hope is that, in this book, you find something that covers all of the core elements of SQL Server with the same success that we had in the original Professional SQL Server Programming titles. When we're done, you should be set to be a highly functional SQL Server 2008 programmer and, when you need it, be ready to move on to the more advanced Professional title.

Who This Book Is For

It is almost sad that the word "beginner" is in the title of this book. Don't get me wrong; if you are a beginner, then this title is for you. But it is designed to last you well beyond your beginning days. What is covered in this book is necessary for the beginner, but there is simply too much information for you to remember all of it all the time, and so it is laid out in a fashion that should make a solid review and reference item even for the more intermediate, and, yes, even advanced user.

The beginning user will want to start right at the beginning. Things are designed such that just about everything in this book is a genuine "need to know" sort of thing. With the possible exception of the chapters on XML, Reporting Services, and Integration Services, every item in this book is fundamental to you having the breadth of understanding you need to make well-informed choices on how you approach your SQL Server problems. Even these three topics are increasingly fundamental to being a serious SQL Server developer.

For the intermediate user, you can probably skip perhaps as far as Chapter 7 or 8 for starting. While I would still recommend scanning the prior chapters for holes in your skills or general review, you can probably skip ahead with little harm done and get to something that might be a bit more challenging for you.

Advanced users, in addition to utilizing this as an excellent reference resource, will probably want to focus on Chapter 12 and beyond. Virtually everything from that point forward should be of some interest (the new debugging, transactions, XML, Reporting Services, Integration Services, and more!).

What This Book Covers

Well, if you've read the title, you're probably not shocked to hear that this book covers SQL Server 2008 with a definite bent toward the developer's perspective.

SQL Server 2008 is the latest incarnation of a database management system that has now been around for about two decades. It builds on the base redesign that was done to the product in version 7.0 — finally providing us separate date and time data types, as well as geospatial support. This book focuses on core development needs of every developer, regardless of skill level. The focus is highly oriented to just the 2008 version of the product, but there is regular mention of backward-compatibility issues as they may affect your design and coding choices.

How This Book Is Structured

The book is designed to become increasingly more advanced as you progress through it, but, from the very beginning, I'm assuming that you are already an experienced developer — just not necessarily with databases. In order to make it through this book, you do need to already have understanding of programming basics such as variables, data types, and procedural programming. You do not have to have ever seen a query before in your life (though I suspect you have).

The focus of the book is highly developer-oriented. This means that we will, for the sake of both brevity and sanity, sometimes gloss over or totally ignore items that are more the purview of the database administrator than the developer. We will, however, remember administration issues as they either affect the developer or as they need to be thought of during the development process — we'll also take a brief look at several administration-related issues in Chapter 19.

The book makes a very concerted effort to be language independent in terms of your client-side development. VB, C#, C++, Java, and other languages are generally ignored (we focus on the server side of the equation) and treated equally where addressed.

In terms of learning order, we start by learning the foundation objects of SQL, and then move on to basic queries and joins. From there, we begin adding objects to our database and discuss items that are important to the physical design — then it is on to the more robust code aspects of SQL Server scripting, stored procedures, user-defined functions, and triggers. We then look at a few of the relatively peripheral features of SQL Server. Last but not least, we wrap things up with a discussion of administration meant to help you keep the databases you develop nice and healthy.

What You Need to Use This Book

In order to make any real, viable use of this book, you will need an installation of SQL Server. The book makes extensive use of the actual SQL Server 2008 management tools, so I highly recommend that you have a version that contains the full product, rather than just using SQL Server Express. That said, the book is focused on the kind of scripting required for developers, so even SQL Server Express users should be able to get the lion's share of learning out of most of the chapters. You will also need the AdvenureWorks2008 sample database, as well as a few custom databases installed. Instructions for accessing these databases can be found in the ReadMe file on this book's Web site (www.wrox.com).

A copy of Visual Studio is handy for working with this book, but most of the Visual Studio features needed are included in the Business Intelligence Studio that comes along with the SQL Server product.

Conventions

To help you get the most from the text and keep track of what's happening, we've used a number of conventions throughout the book.

Try It Out
The Try It Out is an exercise you should work through, following the text in the book.

1. They usually consist of a set of steps.
2. Each step has a number.
3. Follow the steps through with your copy of the database.

How It Works
After each Try It Out, the code you've typed will be explained in detail.

> **Boxes like this one hold important, not-to-be forgotten information that is directly relevant to the surrounding text.**

Tips, hints, tricks, and asides to the current discussion are offset and placed in italics like this.

As for styles in the text:

❑   We *highlight* new terms and important words when we introduce them.

❑   We show keyboard strokes like this: Ctrl+A.

❏   We show file names, URLs, and code within the text like so: `persistence.properties`.

❏   We present code in two different ways:

> In code examples we highlight new and important code with a gray background.

> The gray highlighting is not used for code that's less important in the present context, or has been shown before.

Source Code

As you work through the examples in this book, you may choose either to type in all the code manually or to use the source code files that accompany the book. All of the source code used in this book is available for download at `http://www.wrox.com`. Once at the site, simply locate the book's title (either by using the Search box or by using one of the title lists) and click the Download Code link on the book's detail page to obtain all the source code for the book. You can also find a copy of the downloads at `http://www.professionalsql.com`.

> *Because many books have similar titles, you may find it easiest to search by ISBN; this book's ISBN is 978-0-470-25701-2.*

Once you download the code, just decompress it with your favorite compression tool. Alternatively, you can go to the main Wrox code download page at `http://www.wrox.com/dynamic/books/download.aspx` to see the code available for this book and all other Wrox books.

Errata

We make every effort to ensure that there are no errors in the text or in the code. However, no one is perfect, and mistakes do occur. If you find an error in one of our books, like a spelling mistake or faulty piece of code, we would be very grateful for your feedback. By sending in errata you may save another reader hours of frustration and at the same time you will be helping us provide even higher quality information.

To find the errata page for this book, go to `http://www.wrox.com` and locate the title using the Search box or one of the title lists. Then, on the book details page, click the Book Errata link. On this page you can view all errata that have been submitted for this book and posted by Wrox editors. A complete book list, including links to each book's errata, is also available at `www.wrox.com/misc-pages/booklist.shtml`.

If you don't spot "your" error on the Book Errata page, go to `www.wrox.com/contact/techsupport.shtml` and complete the form there to send us the error you have found. We'll check the information and, if appropriate, post a message to the book's errata page and fix the problem in subsequent editions of the book.

p2p.wrox.com

For author and peer discussion, join the P2P forums at p2p.wrox.com. The forums are a Web-based system for you to post messages relating to Wrox books and related technologies and interact with other readers and technology users. The forums offer a subscription feature to e-mail you topics of interest of your choosing when new posts are made to the forums. Wrox authors, editors, other industry experts, and your fellow readers are present on these forums.

At http://p2p.wrox.com you will find a number of different forums that will help you not only as you read this book, but also as you develop your own applications. To join the forums, just follow these steps:

1. Go to p2p.wrox.com and click the Register link.

2. Read the terms of use and click Agree.

3. Complete the required information to join as well as any optional information you wish to provide and click Submit.

4. You will receive an e-mail with information describing how to verify your account and complete the joining process.

You can read messages in the forums without joining P2P but in order to post your own messages, you must join.

Once you join, you can post new messages and respond to messages other users post. You can read messages at any time on the Web. If you would like to have new messages from a particular forum e-mailed to you, click the Subscribe to this Forum icon by the forum name in the forum listing.

For more information about how to use the Wrox P2P, be sure to read the P2P FAQs for answers to questions about how the forum software works as well as many common questions specific to P2P and Wrox books. To read the FAQs, click the FAQ link on any P2P page.

www.professionalsql.com

Limited support for the book and occasional blog entries can also be found at http://www.professionalsql.com. While formal support requests should be sent through the p2p.wrox.com website, professionalsql.com provides a mirror of the key downloads, as well as occasional commentary from me on the general state of the development world. You can contact me at robv@professionalsql.com — my sole requests for questions or contacts are:

❑ Please don't send me the questions from your take-home mid-term or other school quizzes/tests (and yes, people really have done that).

❑ Focus questions to those not readily answered from general sources (Google, the p2p.wrox.com website, the many popular SQL Server websites, or a simple Books Online query).

❏ Understand that, while I try, I cannot always respond to every request for help, advice, or other questions.

❏ Recognize that the exposure of my e-mail address in this book represents a certain degree of trust in you, the reader, that you will not abuse that openness.

I am always happy to hear about people's SQL experiences, so please feel free to drop me a line and brag about the wonderful things you've managed to do with SQL Server.

RDBMS Basics: What Makes Up a SQL Server Database?

What makes up a database? Data for sure. (What use is a database that doesn't store anything?) But a *Relational Database Management System* (*RDBMS*) is actually much more than data. Today's advanced RDBMSs not only store your data, they also manage that data for you, restricting the kind of data that can go into the system, and facilitating getting data out of the system. If all you want is to tuck the data away somewhere safe, you could use just about any data storage system. RDBMSs allow you to go beyond the storage of the data into the realm of defining what that data should look like, or the *business rules* of the data.

Don't confuse what I'm calling the "business rules of data" with the more generalized business rules that drive your entire system (for example, preventing someone from seeing anything until they've logged in, or automatically adjusting the current period in an accounting system on the first of the month). Those types of rules can be enforced at virtually any level of the system (these days, it's usually in the middle or client tier of an n-tier system). Instead, what we're talking about here are the business rules that specifically relate to the data. For example, you can't have a sales order with a negative amount. With an RDBMS, we can incorporate these rules right into the integrity of the database itself.

The notion of the database taking responsibility for the data within, as well as the best methods to input and extract data from that database, serve as the foundation of what this book is all about. This chapter provides an overview of the rest of the book. Most items discussed in this chapter are covered again in later chapters, but this chapter is intended to provide you with a road map or plan to bear in mind as we progress through the book. With this in mind, we'll take a high-level look into:

❑   Database objects

❑   Data types

❑   Other database concepts that ensure data integrity

An Overview of Database Objects

An instance of an RDBMS such as SQL Server contains many *objects*. Object purists out there may quibble with whether Microsoft's choice of what to call an object (and what not to) actually meets the normal definition of an object, but, for SQL Server's purposes, the list of some of the more important database objects can be said to contain such things as:

- The database itself
- The transaction log
- Indexes
- Filegroups
- Diagrams
- Views
- Stored procedures
- User-defined functions

- Users
- Roles
- Assemblies
- Tables
- Reports
- Full-text catalogs
- User-defined data types

The Database Object

The database is effectively the highest-level object that you can refer to within a given SQL Server. (Technically speaking, the server itself can be considered to be an object, but not from any real "programming" perspective, so we're not going there.) Most, but not all, other objects in a SQL Server are children of the database object.

If you are already familiar with SQL Server you may now be saying, "What? What happened to logins or SQL Agent tasks?" SQL Server has several other objects (as listed previously) that exist in support of the database. With the exception of linked servers, and perhaps Integration Services packages, these are primarily the domain of the database administrator and, as such, we generally don't give them significant thought during the design and programming processes. (They are programmable via something called the SQL Management Objects (SMO), which is beyond the scope of this book.) While there are some exceptions to this rule, I generally consider them to be advanced in nature, and thus save them for the Professional version of this book.

A database is typically a group of constructs that include at least a set of table objects and, more often than not, other objects, such as stored procedures and views that pertain to the particular grouping of data stored in the database's tables.

What types of tables do we store in just one database and what goes in a separate database? We discuss that in some detail later in the book, but for now we'll take the simple approach of saying that any data that is generally thought of as belonging to just one system, or is significantly related, will be stored in a single database. An RDBMS, such as SQL Server, may have multiple databases on just one server, or it may have only one. The number of databases that reside on an individual SQL Server depends on such factors as capacity (CPU power, disk I/O limitations, memory, and so on), autonomy (you want one person to have management rights to the server this system is running on, and someone else to have admin rights to a different server), and just how many databases your company or client has. Some servers have only one production database; others may have many. Also, keep in mind that with any version of SQL Server that you're likely to find in production these days (SQL Server 2000 was already five years old by the time it was replaced, so we'll assume most shops have that or higher), we have the ability to have multiple instances of SQL Server — complete with separate logins and management rights — all on the same physical server.

I'm sure many of you are now asking, "Can I have different versions of SQL Server on the same box — say, SQL Server 2005 and SQL Server 2008?" The answer is yes. You can mix SQL Server 2005 and 2008 on the same box. Personally, I am not at all trusting of this configuration, even for migration scenarios, but, if you have the need, yes, it can be done.

When you first load SQL Server, you start with at least four system databases:

❑   `master`

❑   `model`

❑   `msdb`

❑   `tempdb`

All of these need to be installed for your server to run properly. (Indeed, without some of them, it won't run at all.) From there, things vary depending on which installation choices you made. Examples of some of the databases you may see include the following:

❑   ReportServer (the database that serves Reporting Server configuration and model storage needs)

❑   ReportServerTempDB (the working database for Reporting Server)

❑   AdventureWorks2008 (the sample database)

❑   AdventureWorksLT2008 (a new, "lite" version of the sample database)

❑   AdventureWorksDW2008 (sample for use with Analysis Services)

In addition to the system-installed examples, you may, when searching the Web or using other tutorials, find reference to a couple of older samples:

❑   `pubs`

❑   `Northwind`

In the previous edition of this book, I made extensive use of the older examples. Unfortunately, there is little guarantee how long those examples will remain downloadable, and, as such, I made the choice to switch over to the new examples. The newer AdventureWorks2008 database is certainly a much more robust example and does a great job of providing examples of just about every little twist and turn you can make use of in SQL Server 2008. There is, however, a problem with that — complexity. The Adventure-Works2008 database is excessively complex for a training database. It takes features that are likely to be used only in exceptional cases and uses them as a dominant feature. So, with that said, let me make the point now that AdventureWorks2008 should not necessarily be used as a template for what to do in other similar applications.

The master Database

Every SQL Server, regardless of version or custom modifications, has the master database. This database holds a special set of tables (system tables) that keeps track of the system as a whole. For example, when you create a new database on the server, an entry is placed in the sysdatabases table in the master database. All extended and system-stored procedures, regardless of which database they are intended for use with, are stored in this database. Obviously, since almost everything that describes your server is stored in here, this database is critical to your system and cannot be deleted.

The system tables, including those found in the master database, were, in the past, occasionally used in a pinch to provide system configuration information, such as whether certain objects existed before you performed operations on them. Microsoft warned us for years not to use the system tables directly, but, since we had few other options, most developers ignored that advice. Happily, Microsoft began giving us other options in the form of system and information schema views; we can now utilize these views to get at our systems' metadata as necessary with Microsoft's full blessing. For example, if you try to create an object that already exists in any particular database, you get an error. If you want to force the issue, you could test to see whether the table already has an entry in the sys.objects table for that database. If it does, you would delete that object before re-creating it.

> If you're quite cavalier, you may be saying to yourself, "Cool, I can't wait to mess around in those system tables!" *Don't go there!* Using the system tables in any form is fraught with peril. Microsoft makes absolutely no guarantees about compatibility in the master database between versions. Indeed, they virtually guarantee that they will change. Fortunately, several alternatives (for example, system functions, system stored procedures, and information_schema views) are available for retrieving much of the metadata that is stored in the system tables.
>
> All that said, there are still times when nothing else will do, but, in general, you should consider them to be evil cannibals from another tribe and best left alone.

The model Database

The model database is aptly named, in the sense that it's the model on which a copy can be based. The model database forms a template for any new database that you create. This means that you can, if you wish, alter the model database if you want to change what standard, newly created databases look like. For example, you could add a set of audit tables that you include in every database you build. You could also include a few user groups that would be cloned into every new database that was created on the system. Note that since this database serves as the template for any other database, it's a required database and must be left on the system; you cannot delete it.

There are several things to keep in mind when altering the model database. First, any database you create has to be at least as large as the model database. That means that if you alter the model database to be 100MB in size, you can't create a database smaller than 100MB. There are several other similar pitfalls. As such, for 90 percent of installations, I strongly recommend leaving this one alone.

The msdb Database

msdb is where the SQL Agent process stores any system tasks. If you schedule backups to run on a database nightly, there is an entry in msdb. Schedule a stored procedure for one-time execution, and yes, it has an entry in msdb. Other major subsystems in SQL Server make similar use of `msdb`. SSIS packages and policy-based management definitions are examples of other processes that make use of msdb.

The tempdb Database

`tempdb` is one of the key working areas for your server. Whenever you issue a complex or large query that SQL Server needs to build interim tables to solve, it does so in tempdb. Whenever you create a temporary table of your own, it is created in tempdb, even though you think you're creating it in the current database. (An alias is created in the local database for you to reference it by, but the physical table is created in tempdb). Whenever there is a need for data to be stored temporarily, it's probably stored in tempdb.

tempdb is very different from any other database. Not only are the objects within it temporary, the database itself is temporary. It has the distinction of being the only database in your system that is completely rebuilt from scratch every time you start your SQL Server.

> **Technically speaking, you can actually create objects yourself in tempdb. I strongly recommend against this practice. You can create temporary objects from within any database you have access to in your system — they will be stored in tempdb. Creating objects directly in tempdb gains you nothing, but adds the confusion of referring to things across databases. This is another of those "Don't go there!" kind of things.**

ReportServer

This database will only exist if you installed ReportServer. (It does not necessarily have to be the same server as the database engine, but note that, if it is a different server, then it requires a separate license.) The ReportServer database stores any persistent metadata for your Reporting Server instance. Note that this is purely an operational database for a given Reporting Server instance, and should not be modified or accessed other than through the Reporting Server.

ReportServerTempDB

This serves the same basic function as the ReportServer database, except that it stores nonpersistent data (such as working data for a report that is running). Again, this is a purely operational database, and you should not access or alter it in any way except through the Reporting Server.

AdventureWorks2008

SQL Server included samples long before this one came along. The old samples had their shortcomings, though. For example, they contained a few poor design practices. In addition, they were simplistic and focused on demonstrating certain database concepts rather than on SQL Server as a product, or even databases as a whole. I'll hold off the argument of whether AdventureWorks2008 has the same issues or not. Let's just say that AdventureWorks2008 was, among other things, an attempt to address this problem.

From the earliest stages of development of SQL Server 2005, Microsoft knew they wanted a far more robust sample database that would act as a sample for as much of the product as possible. Adventure-Works2008 is the outcome of that effort. As much as you will hear me complain about its overly complex nature for the beginning user, it is a masterpiece in that it shows it *all* off. Okay, so it's not really *everything*, but it is a fairly complete sample, with more realistic volumes of data, complex structures, and sections that show samples for the vast majority of product features. In this sense, it's truly terrific.

AdventureWorks2008 will be something of our home database — we use it extensively as we work through the examples in this book.

AdventureWorksLT2008

The "LT" in this stands for lite. This is just an extremely small subset of the full AdventureWorks2008 database. The idea is to provide a simpler sample set for easier training of basic concepts and simple training. While I've not been privy to the exact reasoning behind this new sample set, my suspicion is that it is an effect to try and kill the older, Northwind and pubs sample sets, which have been preferred by many trainers over the newer AdventureWorks2008 set, as the AdventureWorks2008 database is often far too complex and cumbersome for early training.

AdventureWorksDW2008

This is the Analysis Services sample. (The DW stands for Data Warehouse, which is the type of database over which most Analysis Services projects will be built.) Perhaps the greatest thing about it is that Microsoft had the foresight to tie the transaction database sample with the analysis sample, providing a whole set of samples that show the two of them working together.

Decision support databases are well outside the scope of this book, and you won't be using this database, but keep it in mind as you fire up Analysis Services and play around. Take a look at the differences between the two databases. They are meant to serve the same fictional company, but they have different purposes: Learn from it.

The pubs Database

Ahhhh, pubs! It's almost like an old friend. pubs is one of the original example databases and was supplied with SQL Server as part of the install prior to SQL Server 2005. It is now only available as a separate download from the Microsoft Website. You will still find many training articles and books that refer to pubs, but Microsoft has made no promises regarding how long they will continue to make it available. pubs has absolutely nothing to do with the operation of SQL Server. It is merely there to provide a consistent place for your training and experimentation. You do not need pubs to work the examples in this book, but you may want to download and install it to work with other examples and tutorials you may find on the Web.

The Northwind Database

If your past programming experience has involved Access or Visual Basic, then you should already be somewhat familiar with the Northwind database. Northwind was added to SQL Server beginning in version 7.0, but was removed from the basic installation as of SQL Server 2005. Much like pubs, it can, for now, be downloaded separately from the base SQL Server install. (Fortunately, it is part of the same sample download and install as pubs is.) Like pubs, you do not need the Northwind database to work the examples in this book, but it is handy to have available for work with various examples and tutorials you will find on the Web.

The Transaction Log

Believe it or not, the database file itself isn't where most things happen. Although the data is certainly read in from there, any changes you make don't initially go to the database itself. Instead, they are written serially to the *transaction log*. At some later point in time, the database is issued a *checkpoint*; it is at that point in time that all the changes in the log are propagated to the actual database file.

The database is in a random access arrangement, but the log is serial in nature. While the random nature of the database file allows for speedy access, the serial nature of the log allows things to be tracked in the proper order. The log accumulates changes that are deemed as having been committed, and then writes several of them at a time to the physical database file(s).

We'll take a much closer look at how things are logged in Chapter 14, but for now, remember that the log is the first place on disk that the data goes, and it's propagated to the actual database at a later time. You need both the database file and the transaction log to have a functional database.

The Most Basic Database Object: Table

Databases are made up of many things, but none is more central to the make-up of a database than tables are. A table can be thought of as equating to an accountant's ledger or an Excel spreadsheet. It is made up of what is called *domain* data (columns) and *entity* data (rows). The actual data for the database is stored in the tables.

Each table definition also contains the *metadata* (descriptive information about data) that describes the nature of the data it is to contain. Each column has its own set of rules about what can be stored in that column. A violation of the rules of any one column can cause the system to reject an inserted row, an update to an existing row, or the deletion of a row.

Let's take a look at the Production.Location table in the AdventureWorks2008 database. (The view presented in Figure 1-1 is from the SQL Server Management Studio. This is a fundamental tool and we will look at how to make use of it in the next chapter.)

	LocationID	Name	CostRate	Availability	ModifiedDate
1	1	Tool Crib	0.00	0.00	1998-06-01 00:00:00.000
2	2	Sheet Metal Racks	0.00	0.00	1998-06-01 00:00:00.000
3	3	Paint Shop	0.00	0.00	1998-06-01 00:00:00.000
4	4	Paint Storage	0.00	0.00	1998-06-01 00:00:00.000
5	5	Metal Storage	0.00	0.00	1998-06-01 00:00:00.000
6	6	Miscellaneous Storage	0.00	0.00	1998-06-01 00:00:00.000
7	7	Finished Goods Storage	0.00	0.00	1998-06-01 00:00:00.000
8	10	Frame Forming	22.50	96.00	1998-06-01 00:00:00.000
9	20	Frame Welding	25.00	108.00	1998-06-01 00:00:00.000
10	30	Debur and Polish	14.50	120.00	1998-06-01 00:00:00.000
11	40	Paint	15.75	120.00	1998-06-01 00:00:00.000
12	45	Specialized Paint	18.00	80.00	1998-06-01 00:00:00.000
13	50	Subassembly	12.25	120.00	1998-06-01 00:00:00.000
14	60	Final Assembly	12.25	120.00	1998-06-01 00:00:00.000

Figure 1-1

The table in Figure 1-1 is made up of five columns of data. The number of columns remains constant regardless of how much data (even zero) is in the table. Currently, the table has fourteen records. The number of records will go up and down as we add or delete data, but the nature of the data in each record (or row) is described and restricted by the *data type* of the column.

Indexes

An *index* is an object that exists only within the framework of a particular table or view. An index works much like the index does in the back of an encyclopedia. There is some sort of lookup (or "key") value that is sorted in a particular way and, once you have that, you are provided another key with which you can look up the actual information you were after.

An index provides us ways of speeding the lookup of our information. Indexes fall into two categories:

❑ **Clustered** — You can have only one of these per table. If an index is clustered, it means that the table on which the clustered index is based is physically sorted according to that index. If you were indexing an encyclopedia, the clustered index would be the page numbers (the information in the encyclopedia is stored in the order of the page numbers).

❑ **Non-clustered** — You can have many of these for every table. This is more along the lines of what you probably think of when you hear the word "index." This kind of index points to some other value that will let you find the data. For our encyclopedia, this would be the keyword index at the back of the book.

Note that views that have indexes — or *indexed views* — must have at least one clustered index before they can have any non-clustered indexes.

Triggers

A *trigger* is an object that exists only within the framework of a table. Triggers are pieces of logical code that are automatically executed when certain things (such as inserts, updates, or deletes) happen to your table.

Triggers can be used for a great variety of things, but are mainly used for either copying data as it is entered, or checking the update to make sure that it meets some criteria.

Constraints

A *constraint* is yet another object that exists only within the confines of a table. Constraints are much like they sound; they confine the data in your table to meet certain conditions. Constraints, in a way, compete with triggers as possible solutions to data integrity issues. They are not, however, the same thing: Each has its own distinct advantages.

Filegroups

By default, all your tables and everything else about your database (except the log) are stored in a single file. That file is, by default, a member of what's called the *primary filegroup*. However, you are not stuck with this arrangement.

SQL Server allows you to define a little over 32,000 *secondary files*. (If you need more than that, perhaps it isn't SQL Server that has the problem.) These secondary files can be added to the primary filegroup or created as part of one or more *secondary filegroups*. While there is only one primary filegroup (and it is actually called "Primary"), you can have up to 255 secondary filegroups. A secondary filegroup is created as an option to a CREATE DATABASE or ALTER DATABASE command.

Diagrams

We will discuss database diagramming in some detail when we discuss normalization and database design. For now, suffice it to say that a database diagram is a visual representation of the database design, including the various tables, the column names in each table, and the relationships between tables. In your travels as a developer, you may have heard of an *entity-relationship diagram (ERD)*. In an ERD the database is divided into two parts: entities (such as "supplier" and "product") and relations (such as "supplies" and "purchases").

> *The included database design tools are, unfortunately, a bit sparse. Indeed, the diagramming methodology the tools use does not adhere to any of the accepted standards in ER diagramming. Still, these diagramming tools really do provide all the "necessary" things, so they are at least something of a start.*

Figure 1-2 is a diagram that shows some of the various tables in the `AdventureWorks2008` database. The diagram also (though it may be a bit subtle since this is new to you) describes many other properties about the database. Notice the tiny icons for keys and the infinity sign. These depict the nature of the relationship between two tables. We'll talk about relationships extensively in Chapters 6 and 8, and we'll look further into diagrams later in the book.

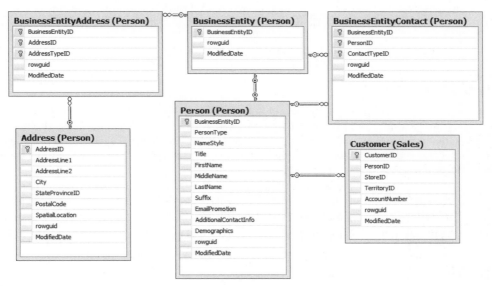

Figure 1-2

Views

A *view* is something of a virtual table. A view, for the most part, is used just like a table, except that it doesn't contain any data of its own. Instead, a view is merely a preplanned mapping and representation of the data stored in tables. The plan is stored in the database in the form of a query. This query calls for data from some, but not necessarily all, columns to be retrieved from one or more tables. The data retrieved may or may not (depending on the view definition) have to meet special criteria in order to be shown as data in that view.

Until SQL Server 2000, the primary purpose of views was to control what the user of the view saw. This has two major impacts: security and ease of use. With views you can control what the users see, so if there is a section of a table that should be accessed by only a few users (for example, salary details), you can create a view that includes only those columns to which everyone is allowed access. In addition, the view can be tailored so that the user doesn't have to search through any unneeded information.

In addition to these most basic uses for views, you also have the ability to create what is called an *indexed view*. This is the same as any other view, except that you can now create an index against the view. This results in a couple of performance impacts (some positive, one negative):

❑ Views that reference multiple tables generally have *much* better read performance with an indexed view, because the join between the tables is preconstructed.

❑ Aggregations performed in the view are precalculated and stored as part of the index; again, this means that the aggregation is performed one time (when the row is inserted or updated), and then can be read directly from the index information.

❑ Inserts and deletes have higher overhead because the index on the view has to be updated immediately; updates also have higher overhead if the key column or the cluster key of the index is affected by the update.

We will look into these performance issues more deeply in Chapter 10.

Stored Procedures

Stored procedures (or *sprocs*) are the bread and butter of programmatic functionality in SQL Server. Stored procedures are generally an ordered series of Transact-SQL (the language used to query Microsoft SQL Server) statements bundled up into a single logical unit. They allow for variables and parameters, as well as selection and looping constructs. Sprocs offer several advantages over just sending individual statements to the server in the sense that they:

❑ Are referred to using short names, rather than a long string of text, therefore less network traffic is required in order to run the code within the sproc.

❑ Are pre-optimized and precompiled, saving a small amount of time each time the sproc is run.

❑ Encapsulate a process, usually for security reasons or just to hide the complexity of the database.

❑ Can be called from other sprocs, making them reusable in a somewhat limited sense.

While sprocs are the core of programmatic functionality in SQL Server, be careful in their use. They are often a solution, but they are also frequently not the only solution. Make sure they are the right choice before selecting a sproc as the option you go with.

User-Defined Functions

User-Defined Functions (UDFs) have a tremendous number of similarities to sprocs, except that they:

❑ Can return a value of most SQL Server data types. Excluded return types include `text`, `ntext`, `image`, `cursor`, and `timestamp`.

❑ Can't have side effects. Basically, they can't do anything that reaches outside the scope of the function, such as changing tables, sending e-mails, or making system or database parameter changes.

UDFs are similar to the functions that you would use in a standard programming language such as VB.NET or C++. You can pass more than one variable in, and get a value out. SQL Server's UDFs vary from the functions found in many procedural languages, in that *all* variables passed into the function are passed in by value. If you're familiar with passing in variables By Ref or passing in pointers, sorry, there is no equivalent here. There is, however, some good news in that you can return a special data type called a table. We'll examine the impact of this in Chapter 13.

Users and Roles

These two go hand in hand. *Users* are pretty much the equivalent of logins. In short, this object represents an identifier for someone to log in to the SQL Server. Anyone logging in to SQL Server has to map (directly or indirectly, depending on the security model in use) to a user. Users, in turn, belong to one or more *roles*. Rights to perform certain actions in SQL Server can then be granted directly to a user or to a role to which one or more users belong.

Rules

Rules and constraints provide restriction information about what can go into a table. If an updated or inserted record violates a rule, then that insertion or update will be rejected. In addition, a rule can be used to define a restriction on a *user-defined data type*. Unlike constraints, rules aren't bound to a particular table. Instead they are independent objects that can be bound to multiple tables or even to specific data types (which are, in turn, used in tables).

Rules have been considered deprecated by Microsoft for several releases now. They should be considered there for backward compatibility only and should be avoided in new development.

> *Given that Microsoft has introduced some new deprecation-management functionality in SQL Server 2008, I suspect that features (such as rules) that have been deprecated for several versions may finally be removed in the next version of SQL Server. As such, I feel the need to stress again that rules should not be utilized for new development. Indeed, it is probably long past time to actively migrate away from them.*

Defaults

There are two types of defaults. There is the default that is an object unto itself, and the default that is not really an object, but rather metadata describing a particular column in a table (in much the same way that we have rules, which are objects, and constraints, which are not objects, but metadata). They both serve the same purpose. If, when inserting a record, you don't provide the value of a column and that column has a default defined, a value will be inserted automatically as defined in the default. You will examine both types of defaults in Chapter 6.

User-Defined Data Types

User-defined data types are either extensions to the system-defined data types or complex data types defined by a method in a .NET assembly. The possibilities here are almost endless. Although SQL Server 2000 and earlier had the idea of user-defined data types, they were really limited to different filtering of existing data types. With releases since SQL Server 2005, you have the ability to bind .NET assemblies to your own data types, meaning you can have a data type that stores (within reason) about anything you can store in a .NET object. Indeed, the new spatial data types (`Geographic` and `Geometric`) that have been added in SQL Server 2008 are implemented using a user-defined type based on a .NET assembly. .NET assemblies are covered in detail in *Professional SQL Server 2008 Programming*.

Careful with this! The data type that you're working with is pretty fundamental to your data and its storage. Although being able to define your own thing is very cool, recognize that it will almost certainly come with a large performance cost. Consider it carefully, be sure it's something you need, and then, as with everything like this, TEST, TEST, TEST!!!

Full-Text Catalogs

Full-text catalogs are mappings of data that speed the search for specific blocks of text within columns that have full-text searching enabled. Prior to SQL Server 2008, full-text catalogs were stored external to the database (thus creating some significant backup and recovery issues). As of SQL Server 2008, full-text catalogs have been integrated into the mail database engine and storage mechanisms. Full text indexes are beyond the scope of this text, but are covered extensively in *Professional SQL Server 2008 Programming*.

SQL Server Data Types

Now that you're familiar with the base objects of a SQL Server database, let's take a look at the options that SQL Server has for one of the fundamental items of any environment that handles data — data types. Note that, since this book is intended for developers, and that no developer could survive for 60 seconds without an understanding of data types, I'm going to assume that you already know how data types work, and just need to know the particulars of SQL Server data types.

SQL Server 2008 has the intrinsic data types shown in the following table:

Data Type Name	Class	Size in Bytes	Nature of the Data
Bit	Integer	1	The size is somewhat misleading. The first `bit` data type in a table takes up 1 byte; the next 7 make use of the same byte. Allowing nulls causes an additional byte to be used.
Bigint	Integer	8	This just deals with the fact that we use larger and larger numbers on a more frequent basis. This one allows you to use whole numbers from -2^{63} to $2^{63}-1$. That's plus or minus about 92 quintillion.
Int	Integer	4	Whole numbers from −2,147,483,648 to 2,147,483,647.

Data Type Name	Class	Size in Bytes	Nature of the Data
SmallInt	Integer	2	Whole numbers from –32,768 to 32,767.
TinyInt	Integer	1	Whole numbers from 0 to 255.
Decimal or Numeric	Decimal/ Numeric	Varies	Fixed precision and scale from $-10^{38}-1$ to $10^{38}-1$. The two names are synonymous.
Money	Money	8	Monetary units from -2^{63} to 2^{63} plus precision to four decimal places. Note that this could be any monetary unit, not just dollars.
SmallMoney	Money	4	Monetary units from –214,748.3648 to +214,748.3647.
Float (also a synonym for ANSI Real)	Approximate Numerics	Varies	Accepts an argument (for example, Float(20)) that determines size and precision. Note that the argument is in bits, not bytes. Ranges from –1.79E + 308 to 1.79E + 308.
DateTime	Date/Time	8	Date and time data from January 1, 1753, to December 31, 9999, with an accuracy of three hundredths of a second.
DateTime2	Date/Time	Varies (6–8)	Updated incarnation of the more venerable DateTime data type. Supports larger date ranges and large time-fraction precision (up to 100 nanoseconds). Like DateTime, it is not time zone aware, but does align with the .NET DateTime data type.
SmallDateTime	Date/Time	4	Date and time data from January 1, 1900, to June 6, 2079, with an accuracy of one minute.
DateTimeOffset	Date/Time	Varies (8–10)	Similar to the DateTime data type, but also expects an offset designation of –14:00 to +14:00 offset from UTC time. Time is stored internally as UTC time, and any comparisons, sorts, or indexing will be based on that unified time zone.

Continued

13

Data Type Name	Class	Size in Bytes	Nature of the Data
Date	Date/Time	3	Stores only date data from January 1, 0001, to December 31, 9999, as defined by the Gregorian calendar. Assumes the ANSI standard date format (YYYY-MM-DD), but will implicitly convert from several other formats.
Time	Date/Time	Varies (3–5)	Stores only time data in user-selectable precisions as granular as 100 nanoeconds (which is the default).
Cursor	Special Numeric	1	Pointer to a cursor. While the pointer takes up only a byte, keep in mind that the result set that makes up the actual cursor also takes up memory. Exactly how much will vary depending on the result set.
Timestamp/ rowversion	Special Numeric (binary)	8	Special value that is unique within a given database. Value is set by the database itself automatically every time the record is either inserted or updated, even though the timestamp column wasn't referred to by the UPDATE statement (you're actually not allowed to update the timestamp field directly).
UniqueIdentifier	Special Numeric (binary)	16	Special Globally Unique Identifier (GUID) is guaranteed to be unique across space and time.
Char	Character	Varies	Fixed-length character data. Values shorter than the set length are padded with spaces to the set length. Data is non-Unicode. Maximum specified length is 8,000 characters.
VarChar	Character	Varies	Variable-length character data. Values are not padded with spaces. Data is non-Unicode. Maximum specified length is 8,000 characters, but you can use the "max" keyword to indicate it as essentially a very large character field (up to 2^31 bytes of data).
Text	Character	Varies	Legacy support as of SQL Server 2005. Use varchar(max) instead!

Data Type Name	Class	Size in Bytes	Nature of the Data
NChar	Unicode	Varies	Fixed-length Unicode character data. Values shorter than the set length are padded with spaces. Maximum specified length is 4,000 characters.
NVarChar	Unicode	Varies	Variable-length Unicode character data. Values are not padded. Maximum specified length is 4,000 characters, but you can use the "max" keyword to indicate it as essentially a very large character field (up to 2^31 bytes of data).
Ntext	Unicode	Varies	Variable-length Unicode character data. Like the Text data type, this is legacy support only. In this case, use nvarchar(max).
Binary	Binary	Varies	Fixed-length binary data with a maximum length of 8,000 bytes
VarBinary	Binary	Varies	Variable-length binary data with a maximum specified length of 8,000 bytes, but you can use the "max" keyword to indicate it as essentially a LOB field (up to 2^31 bytes of data).
Image	Binary	Varies	Legacy support only as of SQL Server 2005. Use varbinary(max) instead!
Table	Other	Special	This is primarily for use in working with result sets, typically passing one out of a User-Defined Function or as a parameter for stored procedures. Not usable as a data type within a table definition (you can't nest tables).
HierarchyID	Other	Special	Special data type that maintains hierarchy-positioning information. Provides special functionality specific to hierarchy needs. Comparisons of depth, parent/child relationships, and indexing are allowed. Exact size varies with the number and average depth of nodes in the hierarchy.

Continued

Data type Name	Class	Size in Bytes	Nature of the Data
Sql_variant	Other	Special	This is loosely related to the Variant in VB and C++. Essentially, it is a container that allows you to hold most other SQL Server data types in it. That means you can use this when one column or function needs to be able to deal with multiple data types. Unlike VB, using this data type forces you to *explicitly* cast it in order to convert it to a more specific data type.
XML	Character	Varies	Defines a character field as being for XML data. Provides for the validation of data against an XML Schema as well as the use of special XML-oriented functions.
CLR	Other	Varies	Varies depending on the specific nature of the CLR object supporting a CLR based custom data type.

Most of these have equivalent data types in other programming languages. For example, an int in SQL Server is equivalent to a Long in Visual Basic, and, for most systems and compiler combinations in C++, is equivalent to a signed int.

SQL Server has no concept of unsigned numeric data types.

In general, SQL Server data types work much as you would expect given experience in most other modern programming languages. Adding numbers yields a sum, but adding strings concatenates them. When you mix the usage or assignment of variables or fields of different data types, a number of types convert *implicitly* (or automatically). Most other types can be converted explicitly. (You specifically say what type you want to convert to.) A few can't be converted between at all. Figure 1-3 contains a chart that shows the various possible conversions:

Why would we have to convert a data type? Well, let's try a simple example. If I wanted to output the phrase, Today's date is ##/##/####, where ##/##/#### is the current date, I could write it like this:

```
SELECT 'Today''s date is ' + GETDATE()
```

We will discuss Transact-SQL statements such as this in much greater detail later in the book, but the expected result of the previous example should be fairly obvious to you.

The problem is that this statement would yield the following result:

```
Msg 241, Level 16, State 1, Line 1
Conversion failed when converting date and/or time from character string.
```

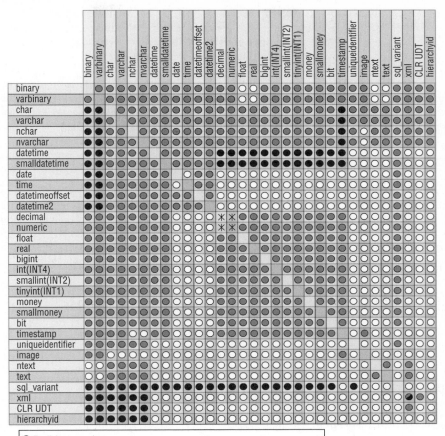

● Explicit conversion
◉ Implicit conversion
○ Conversion not allowed
✳ Requires explicit CAST to prevent the loss of precision or scale that
   might occur in an implicit conversion.
◕ Implicit conversions between xml data types are supported only if the
   source or target is untyped xml. Otherwise, the conversion must be explicit.

Figure 1-3

Not exactly what we were after, is it? Now let's try it with the CONVERT() function:

```
SELECT 'Today''s date is ' + CONVERT(varchar(12), GETDATE(),101)
```

Using CONVERT like this yields something like:

```
-----------------------------------
Today's date is 01/01/2008

(1 row(s) affected)
```

17

Date and time data types, such as the output of the GETDATE() function, aren't implicitly convertible to a string data type, such as Today's date is, yet we run into these conversions on a regular basis. Fortunately, the CAST and CONVERT() functions enable us to convert between many SQL Server data types. We will discuss the CAST and CONVERT() functions more in a later chapter.

In short, data types in SQL Server perform much the same function that they do in other programming environments. They help prevent programming bugs by ensuring that the data supplied is of the same nature that the data is supposed to be (remember 1/1/1980 means something different as a date than as a number) and ensures that the kind of operation performed is what you expect.

NULL Data

What if you have a row that doesn't have any data for a particular column — that is, what if you simply don't know the value? For example, let's say that we have a record that is trying to store the company performance information for a given year. Now, imagine that one of the fields is a percentage growth over the prior year, but you don't have records for the year before the first record in your database. You might be tempted to just enter a zero in the PercentGrowth column. Would that provide the right information though? People who didn't know better might think that meant you had zero percent growth, when the fact is that you simply don't know the value for that year.

Values that are indeterminate are said to be NULL. It seems that every time I teach a class in programming, at least one student asks me to define the value of NULL. Well, that's a tough one, because by definition a NULL value means that you don't know what the value is. It could be 1. It could be 347. It could be –294 for all we know. In short, it means *undefined* or perhaps *not applicable*.

SQL Server Identifiers for Objects

Now you've heard all sorts of things about objects in SQL Server. Let's take a closer look at naming objects in SQL Server.

What Gets Named?

Basically, everything has a name in SQL Server. Here's a partial list:

- Stored procedures
- Tables
- Columns
- Views
- Rules
- Constraints
- Defaults
- Indexes
- Filegroups
- Triggers
- Databases
- Servers
- User-defined functions
- Logins
- Roles
- Full-text catalogs
- Files
- User-defined types

And the list goes on. Most things I can think of except rows (which aren't really objects) have a name. The trick is to make every name both useful and practical.

Rules for Naming

As I mentioned earlier in the chapter, the rules for naming in SQL Server are fairly relaxed, allowing things like embedded spaces and even keywords in names. Like most freedoms, however, it's easy to make some bad choices and get yourself into trouble.

Here are the main rules:

❑   The name of your object must start with any letter, as defined by the specification for Unicode 3.2. This includes the letters most Westerners are used to: A–Z and a–z. Whether "A" is different than "a" depends on the way your server is configured, but either makes for a valid beginning to an object name. After that first letter, you're pretty much free to run wild; almost any character will do.

❑   The name can be up to 128 characters for normal objects and 116 for temporary objects.

❑   Any names that are the same as SQL Server keywords or contain embedded spaces must be enclosed in double quotes ("") or square brackets ([]). Which words are considered keywords varies depending on the compatibility level to which you have set your database.

Note that double quotes are only acceptable as a delimiter for column names if you have SET QUOTED_IDENTIFIER ON. *Using square brackets (* [*and*] *) avoids the chance that your users will have the wrong setting.*

These rules are generally referred to as the rules for identifiers and are in force for any objects you name in SQL Server, but may vary slightly if you have a localized version of SQL Server (one adapted for certain languages, dialects, or regions). Additional rules may exist for specific object types.

> **I'm going to take this as my first opportunity to launch into a diatribe on the naming of objects. SQL Server has the ability to embed spaces in names and, in some cases, to use keywords as names. Resist the temptation to do this! Columns with embedded spaces in their name have nice headers when you make a** SELECT **statement, but there are other ways to achieve the same result. Using embedded spaces and keywords for column names is literally begging for bugs, confusion, and other disasters. I'll discuss later why Microsoft has elected to allow this, but for now, just remember to associate embedded spaces or keywords in names with evil empires, torture, and certain death. (This won't be the last time you hear from me on this one.)**

Summary

Like most things in life, the little things do matter when thinking about an RDBMS. Sure, almost anyone who knows enough to even think about picking up this book has an idea of the *concept* of storing data in columns and rows, even if they don't know that these groupings of columns and rows should be called tables. But a few tables seldom make a real database. The things that make today's RDBMSs great are the extra things — the objects that enable you to place functionality and business rules that are associated with the data right into the database with the data.

Database data has *type*, just as most other programming environments do. Most things that you do in SQL Server are going to have at least some consideration of type. Review the types that are available, and think about how these types map to the data types in any programming environment with which you are familiar.

Tools of the Trade

Now that we know something about the many types of objects that exist in SQL Server, we probably should get to know something about how to find these objects, and how to monitor your system in general.

In this chapter, we will look into the tools that serve SQL Server's base engine (the relational database engine — tools for managing the add-on services in the chapters where we cover each of those services). Some of them offer only a small number of highly specialized tasks; others do many different things. Most of them have been around in SQL Server in one form or another for a long time.

The tools we will look at in this chapter will be:

- ❏ SQL Server Books Online
- ❏ SQL Server Configuration Manager
- ❏ SQL Server Management Studio
- ❏ SQL Server Integration Services (SSIS), including the Import/Export Wizard
- ❏ Database Engine Tuning Advisor
- ❏ Reporting Services Configuration Manager
- ❏ Bulk Copy Program (bcp)
- ❏ Profiler
- ❏ sqlcmd
- ❏ PowerShell

Books Online

Is *Books Online* a tool? I think so. Let's face it. It doesn't matter how many times you read this or any other book on SQL Server; you're not going to remember everything you'll ever need to know about SQL Server. SQL Server is one of my mainstay products, and I still can't remember it all. Books Online is simply one of the most important tools you're going to find in SQL Server.

My general philosophy about books or any other reference materials related to programming is that I can't have enough of them. I first began programming in 1980 or so, and back then it was possible to remember most things (but not everything). Today it's simply impossible. If you have any diversification at all (something that is, in itself, rather difficult these days), there are just too many things to remember, and the things you don't use every day get lost in dying brain cells.

Here's a simple piece of advice: Don't even try to remember it all. Remember what you've seen is possible. Remember what is an integral foundation to what you're doing. Remember what you work with every day. Then remember to build a good reference library (starting with this book) and keep a healthy list of good SQL Server sites in your favorites list to fill in information on subjects you don't work with every day and may not remember the details of.

As you see in Figure 2-1, Books Online in SQL Server uses the updated .NET online help interface, which is replacing the older standard online help interface used among the Microsoft technical product line (Back Office, MSDN, Visual Studio).

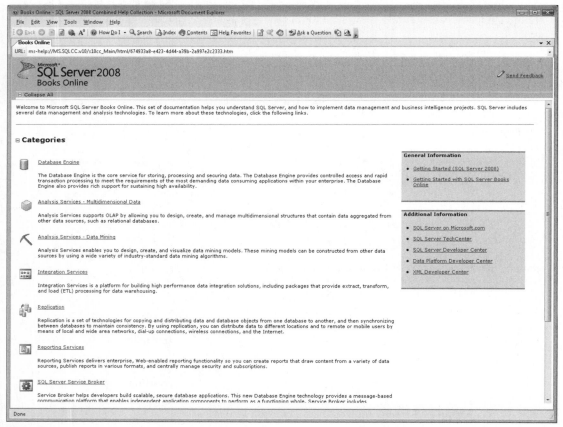

Figure 2-1

Everything works pretty much as one would expect here, so I'm not going to go into the details of how to operate a help system. Suffice it to say that SQL Server Books Online is a great quick reference that follows you to whatever machine you're working on at the time.

> Technically speaking, it's quite possible that not every system you move to will have Books Online (BOL) installed. This is because you can manually deselect BOL at the time of installation. Even in tight space situations, however, I strongly recommend that you always install BOL. It really doesn't take up all that much space when you consider cost per megabyte these days, and having that quick reference available wherever you are running SQL Server can save you a fortune in time. (On my machine, Books Online takes up roughly 110MB of space.)

SQL Server Configuration Manager

Administrators who configure computers for database access are the main users of this tool, but it's still important to understand what this tool is about.

The SQL Server Configuration Manager combines some settings that were, in earlier releases, spread across multiple tools into one spot. The items managed in the Configuration Manager fall into two areas:

❑ Service Management

❑ Network Configuration

Note that, while I'm only showing two major areas here, the Configuration Manager splits the Network Configuration side of things up into multiple nodes.

Service Management

SQL Server is a large product and the various pieces of it utilize a host of services that run in the background on your server. A full installation will encompass nine different services, and seven of these can be managed from this part of the SQL Server Configuration Manager (the other two are services that act as background support).

The services available for management here include:

❑ **Integration Services** — This powers the Integration Services engine that you look at in Chapter 18.

❑ **Analysis Services** — This powers the Analysis Services engine.

❑ **Reporting Services** — The underlying engine that supports Reporting Services.

❑ **SQL Server Agent** — The main engine behind anything in SQL Server that is scheduled. Utilizing this service, you can schedule jobs to run on a variety of different schedules. These jobs can have multiple tasks to them and can even branch into different tasks depending on the outcome of some previous task. Examples of things run by the SQL Server Agent include backups, as well as routine import and export tasks.

❑ **SQL Server** — The core database engine that works on data storage, queries, and system configuration for SQL Server.

❑ **SQL Server Browser** — This supports advertising your server so those browsing your local network can identify that your system has SQL Server installed.

Network Configuration

A fair percentage of the time, any connectivity issues discovered are the result of client network configuration, or how that configuration matches with that of the server.

SQL Server provides several of what are referred to as *Net-Libraries* (network libraries), or *NetLibs*. These are dynamic-link libraries (DLLs) that SQL Server uses to communicate with certain network protocols. NetLibs serve as something of an insulator between your client application and the network protocol, which is essentially the language that one network card uses to talk to another, that is to be used. They serve the same function at the server end, too. The NetLibs supplied with SQL Server 2008 include:

❑ Named Pipes

❑ TCP/IP (the default)

❑ Shared Memory

❑ VIA (a special virtual interface that your storage-hardware vendor may support)

> *VIA is a special network library that is made for use with some very special (and expensive) hardware. If you're running in a VIA environment, you'll know about the special requirements associated with it. For those of you that aren't running in that environment, it suffices to say that VIA offers a very fast but expensive solution to high-speed communication between servers. It would not usually be used for a normal client.*

The same NetLib must be available on both the client and server computers so that they can communicate with each other via the network protocol. Choosing a client NetLib that is not also supported on the server will result in your connection attempt failing with a `Specified SQL Server Not Found` error.

Regardless of the data access method and kind of driver used (SQL Native Client, ODBC, OLE DB), it will always be the driver that talks to the NetLib. The process works as shown in Figure 2-2. The steps in order are:

1. The client app talks to the driver (SQL Native Client, ODBC).

2. The driver calls the client NetLib.

3. This NetLib calls the appropriate network protocol and transmits the data to a server NetLib.

4. The server NetLib then passes the requests from the client to SQL Server.

> In case you're familiar with TCP/IP, the default port that the IP NetLib will listen on is 1433. A port can be thought of as being like a channel on the radio — signals are bouncing around on all sorts of different frequencies, but they only do you any good if you're *listening* on the right channel. Note that this is the default, so there is no guarantee that the particular server you're trying to connect to is listening to that particular port — indeed, most security experts recommend changing it to something nonstandard.

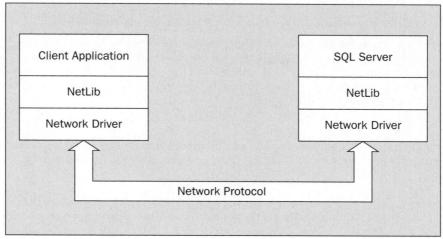

Figure 2-2

Replies from SQL Server to the client follow the same sequence, only in reverse.

The Protocols

Let's start off with that "What are the available choices?" question. If you run the Configuration Management utility and open the Server Network Configuration tree, you'll see something like Figure 2-3.

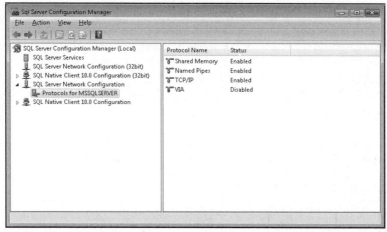

Figure 2-3

How many nodes are shown here will vary depending on your installation. In Figure 2-3, there are duplicate nodes for Network and Client configuration to allow for separate treatment of 32bit vs. 64bit libraries. There will only be one node for each if you're running a 32bit installation.

> For security reasons, only Shared Memory is enabled at installation time.
>
> You'll want to leave Shared Memory enabled for when you're accessing the machine locally. (It works only when the client is on the same physical server as the SQL Server installation.) But you need to enable at least one other NetLib if you want to be able to contact your SQL Server remotely (say, from a Web server or from different clients on your network).

Keep in mind that, in order for your client to gain a connection to the server, the server has to be listening for the protocol with which the client is trying to communicate and, in the case of TCP/IP, on the same port.

At this point, you might be tempted to say, "Hey, why don't I just enable every NetLib? Then I won't have to worry about it." This situation is like anything you add onto your server — more overhead. In this case, it would both slow down your server (not terribly, but every little bit counts) and expose you to unnecessary openings in your security. (Why leave an extra door open if nobody is supposed to be using that door?)

OK, now let's take a look at what we can support and why we would want to choose a particular protocol.

Named Pipes

Named Pipes can be very useful when TCP/IP is not available, or there is no Domain Name Service (DNS) server to allow the naming of servers under TCP/IP.

> Technically speaking, you can connect to a SQL Server running TCP/IP by using its IP address in the place of the name. This works all the time, even if there is no DNS service, as long as you have a route from the client to the server. (If it has the IP address, then it doesn't need the name.) Keep in mind, however, that if your IP address changes for some reason, you'll need to change what IP address you're accessing (a real pain if you have a bunch of config files you need to go change!).

TCP/IP

TCP/IP has become something of the de facto standard networking protocol and is also the only option if you want to connect directly to your SQL Server via the Internet, which, of course, uses only IP.

Don't confuse the need to have your database server available to a Web server with the need to have your database server directly accessible to the Internet. You can have a Web server that is exposed to the Internet, but also has access to a database server that is not directly exposed to the Internet. (The only way for an Internet connection to see the data server is through the Web server.)

Connecting your data server directly to the Internet is a security hazard in a big way. If you insist on doing it (and there can be valid reasons for doing so, rare though they may be), then pay particular attention to security precautions.

Shared Memory

Shared memory removes the need for inter-process marshaling — a way of packaging information before transferring it across process boundaries — between the client and the server, if they are running on the same box. The client has direct access to the same memory-mapped file where the server is storing data. This removes a substantial amount of overhead and is *very* fast. It's only useful when accessing the server locally (say, from a Web server installed on the same server as the database), but it can be quite a boon performance-wise.

On to the Client

Now we've seen all the possible protocols and we know how to choose which ones to offer. Once we know what our server is offering, we can go and configure the client. Most of the time, the defaults are going to work just fine, but let's take a look at what we've got. Expand the Client Network Configuration tree and select the Client Protocols node, as shown in Figure 2-4.

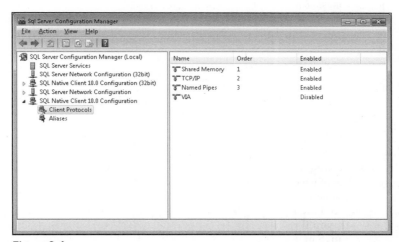

Figure 2-4

SQL Server has the ability for the client to start with one protocol, then, if that doesn't work, move on to another. In Figure 2-4, I am first using Shared Memory, then trying TCP/IP, and finally going to Named Pipes if TCP/IP doesn't work as defined by the Order column. Unless you change the default (changing the priority by using the up and down arrows), Shared Memory is the NetLib that is used first for connections to any server not listed in the aliases list (the next node under Client Network Configuration), followed by TCP/IP and so on.

> If you have TCP/IP support on your network, configure your server to use it for any remote access. IP has less overhead and just plain runs faster; there is no reason not to use it, unless your network doesn't support it. It's worth noting, however, that for local servers (where the server is on the same physical system as the client), the Shared Memory NetLib will be quicker, as you do not need to go through the network stack to view your local SQL Server.

The Aliases list is a listing of all the servers on which you have defined a specific NetLib to be used when contacting that particular server. This means that you can contact one server using IP and another using Named Pipes — whatever you need to get to that particular server. Figure 2-5 shows a client configured to use the Named Pipes NetLib for requests from the server named HOBBES and to use whatever is set up as the default for contact with any other SQL Server.

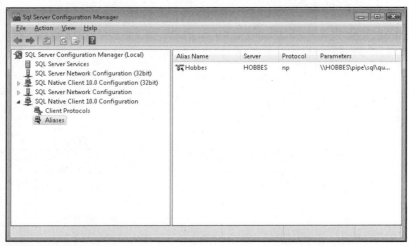

Figure 2-5

Again, remember that the Client Network Configuration setting on the network machine must have a default protocol that matches one supported by the server, or it must have an entry in the Aliases list to specifically choose a NetLib supported by that server.

If you are connecting to your SQL Server over the Internet (which is a very bad idea from a security standpoint, but people do it), you'll probably want to use the server's actual IP address, rather than the name of the server. This gets around some name resolution issues that may occur when dealing with SQL Server and the Internet. Keep in mind, however, that you'll need to change the IP address manually if the server gets a new IP; you won't be able to count on DNS to take care of it for you.

SQL Server Management Studio

The *SQL Server Management Studio* is pretty much home base when administering a SQL Server. It provides a variety of functionality for managing your server using a relatively easy-to-use graphical user interface. Branched off of the Visual Studio IDE environment's code base, it combines a myriad of functionality that used to be in separate tools.

For the purposes of this book, we're not going to cover everything that the Management Studio has to offer, but let's make a quick run down of the things you can do:

❑   Create, edit, and delete databases and database objects

❑   Manage scheduled tasks, such as backups and the execution of SSIS package runs

❑   Display current activity, such as who is logged on, what objects are locked, and from which client they are running

❑   Manage security, including such items as roles, logins, and remote and linked servers

❑   Initiate and manage the Database Mail Service

❑   Create and manage full-text search catalogs

❑   Manage configuration settings for the server

❑   Initiate an instance of the new PowerShell console

❑   Create and manage publishing and subscribing databases for replication

We will be seeing a great deal of the Management Studio throughout this book, so let's take a closer look at some of the key functions Management Studio serves.

Getting Started with the Management Studio

When you first start the Management Studio, you are presented with a Connection dialog box similar to the one in Figure 2-6.

Figure 2-6

Your login screen may look a little bit different from this, depending on whether you've logged in before, what machine you logged into, and what login name you used. Most of the options on the login screen are pretty self-explanatory, but let's look at a couple in more depth.

Server Type

This relates to which of the various subsystems of SQL Server you are logging in to (the normal database server, Analysis Services, Report Server, or Integration Services). Since these different types of servers can share the same name, pay attention to this to make sure you're logging in to what you think you're logging in to.

Server Name

As you might guess, this is the SQL Server in to which you're asking to be logged. In Figure 2-6, we have chosen ".". This doesn't mean that there is a server named period, but rather that we want to log in to the default instance of SQL Server that is on this same machine, regardless of what this machine is named. Selecting "." (local) not only automatically identifies which server (and instance) you want to use, but also how you're going to get there. You can also use "(local)" as another option that has the same meaning as ".".

> **SQL Server allows multiple *instances* of SQL Server to run at one time. These are just separate loads into memory of the SQL Server engine running independently from each other.**

Note that the default instance of your server will have the same name as your machine on the network. There are ways to change the server name after the time of installation, but they are problematic at best, and deadly to your server at worst. Additional instances of SQL Server will be named the same as the default (HOBBES or KIERKEGAARD in many of the examples in this book) followed by a dollar sign, and the instance name, for example, SIDDARTHA$SHRAMANA.

If you select "." or (local), your system uses the Shared Memory NetLib regardless of which NetLib you selected for contacting other servers. This is a bad news/good news story. The bad news is that you give up a little bit of control. (SQL Server will always use Shared Memory to connect; you can't choose anything else.) The good news is that you don't have to remember which server you're on and you get a high-performance option for work on the same machine. If you use your local PC's actual server name, your communications will still go through the network stack and incur the overhead associated with that, just as if you were communicating with another system, regardless of the fact that it is on the same machine.

Now what if you can't remember what the server's name is? Just click the down arrow to the right of the server box to get a list of recently connected servers. If you scroll down, you'll see a Browse for More option. If you choose this option, SQL Server will poll the network for any servers that are advertising to the network; essentially, this is a way for a server to let itself be known to other systems on the network. You can see from Figure 2-7 that you get two tabs: one that displays local servers (all of the instances of SQL Server on the same system you're running on) and another that shows other SQL Servers on the network.

You can select one of these servers and click OK.

Figure 2-7

Watch out when using the Server selection dialog box. Although it's usually pretty reliable, there are ways of configuring a SQL Server so that it doesn't broadcast. When a server has been configured this way, it won't show up in the list. Also, servers that are only listening on the TCP/IP NetLib and don't have a DNS entry will not show up. You must, in this case, already know your IP address and refer to the server using it.

Authentication

You can choose between Windows Authentication and SQL Server Authentication. Windows Authentication will always be available, even if you configured it as SQL Server Authentication. Logins using usernames and passwords that are local to SQL Server (not part of a larger Windows network) are acceptable to the system only if you specifically turn on SQL Server Authentication.

Windows Authentication

Windows Authentication is just as it sounds. You have Windows users and groups. Those Windows users are mapped into SQL Server logins in their Windows user profile. When they attempt to log in to SQL Server, they are validated through the Windows domain and mapped to roles according to the login. These roles identify what the user is allowed to do.

The best part of this model is that you have only one password. (If you change it in the Windows domain, then it's changed for your SQL Server logins, too.) You don't have to fill in anything to log in; it just takes the login information from the way you're currently logged in to the Windows network. Additionally, the administrator has to administer users in only one place. The downside is that mapping this process can get complex and, to administer the Windows user side of things, you must be a domain administrator.

SQL Server Authentication

The security does not care at all about what the user's rights to the network are, but rather what you explicitly set up in SQL Server. The authentication process doesn't take into account the current network login at all; instead, the user provides a SQL Server–specific login and password.

This can be nice because the administrator for a given SQL Server doesn't need to be a domain administrator (or even have a username on your network, for that matter) to give rights to users on the SQL Server. The process also tends to be somewhat simpler than under Windows Authentication. Finally, it means that one user can have multiple logins that give different rights to different things.

Try It Out   **Making the Connection**

Let's get logged in.

1. Choose the (local) option for the SQL Server.
2. Select SQL Server Authentication.

3. Select a login name of sa, which stands for System Administrator. Alternatively, you may log in as a different user, as long as that user has system administrator privileges.

4. Enter the same password that was set when you installed SQL Server. On case-sensitive servers, the login is also case sensitive, so make sure you enter it in lowercase.

If you're connecting to a server that has been installed by someone else, or where you have changed the default information, you need to provide login information that matches those changes. After you click OK, you should see the Object Explorer window screen shown in Figure 2-8.

> Be careful with the password for the sa user. This and any other user who is a sysadmin is a super-user with full access to everything.

Figure 2-8

How It Works

The Login dialog gathers all the information needed to create the connection. Once it has that, it assembles the connection information into a single connection string and sends that to the server. The connection is then either accepted or rejected and, if it is accepted, a connection handle is given to the Query window so that the connection information can be used over and over again for many queries, as long as you do not disconnect.

Again, many of the items here (New, Open, Save, Cut, Paste, and so on) are things that you have seen plenty of times in other Windows applications and should be familiar with, but there's also a fair amount that's specific to SQL Server. The main thing to notice for now is that the menus in the Management Studio are context sensitive — that is, different menus are available and what they contain changes based on which window is active in the Studio. Be sure to explore the different contextual menus you get as you explore different parts of the Management Studio.

Query Window

This part of the Management Studio takes the place of what was, at one time, a separate tool that was called *Query Analyzer*. The Query window is your tool for interactive sessions with a given SQL Server. It's where you can execute statements using *Transact-SQL* (T-SQL). I lovingly pronounce it "Tee-Squeal," but it's supposed to be "Tee-Sequel." T-SQL is the native language of SQL Server. It's a dialect of Structured Query Language (SQL), and is largely compliant with modern ANSI/ISO SQL standards. You'll find that most RDBMS products support basic ANSI/ISO SQL compatibility.

Because the Query window is where we will spend a fair amount of time in this book, let's take a more in-depth look at this tool and get familiar with how to use it.

Getting Started

Well, I've been doing plenty of talking about things in this book, and it's high time we started doing something. To that end, open a new Query window by clicking the New Query button towards the top-left of the Management Studio, or choosing File ⇨ New ⇨ New Query With Current Connection from the File menu. When the Query window opens, you'll get menus that largely match those in Query Analyzer back when that was a separate tool. We will look at the specifics, but let's get our very first query out of the way.

Start by selecting `AdventureWorks2008` in the database drop-down box on the SQL Editor toolbar, then type the following code into the main window of the Query window:

```
SELECT * FROM Person.Address;
```

Notice several things happen as you type:

❑ The coloring of words and phrases changes as you type.

❑ As you type, the Management Studio guesses at what you're trying to do (as shown in Figure 2-9). Utilizing *IntelliSense*, much like Visual Studio, SQL Server will give you hints as to what probably should come next in your code.

Statement keywords should appear in blue. Unidentifiable items, such as column and table names (these vary with every table in every database on every server), are in black. Statement arguments and connectors are in red. Pay attention to how these work and learn them. They can help you catch many bugs before you've even run the statement (and seen the resulting error).

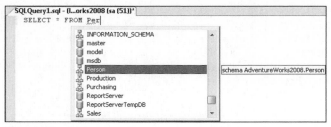

Figure 2-9

Note that IntelliSense is new with SQL Server 2008. While they have done a terrific job with it, it is not without some peculiarities created by the nature of SQL versus other languages. Of particular importance is what help you can get when you're adding columns to be selected. We'll see more about the syntax of this in later chapters, but SQL syntax calls for column names before the names of the tables those columns are sourced from. The result is problematic for IntelliSense as, when you are typing your column names, the tool has no way of knowing what tables you're trying to get those columns from (and therefore no way of giving you appropriate hints). If you're desperate, you can get around this by skipping ahead to add the table names, then coming back to fill in the column names.

The check-mark icon (Parse) on the SQL Editor toolbar represents another simple debugging item that quickly parses the query for you without actually attempting to run the statement. If there are any syntax errors, this should catch them before you see error messages. A debugger is available as another way to find errors. We'll look at that in depth in Chapter 12.

Now click the Execute button (with the red exclamation point next to it) on the toolbar. The Query window changes a bit, as shown in Figure 2-10.

Notice that the main window has been automatically divided into two panes. The top is your original query text; the bottom is called the *results pane*. In addition, notice that the results pane has a tab at the top of it. Later on, after we've run queries that return multiple sets of data, you'll see that we can get each of these results on separate tabs; this can be rather handy, because you often don't know how long each set of data, or *result set*, is.

> **The terms result set and recordset are frequently used to refer to a set of data that is returned as a result of some command being run. You can think of these words as interchangeable.**

Now change a setting or two and see how what we get varies. Take a look at the toolbar above the Query window and check out a set of three icons, highlighted in Figure 2-11.

These control the way you receive output. In order, they are Results to Text, Results to Grid, and Results to File. The same choices can also be made from the Query menu under the Results To submenu.

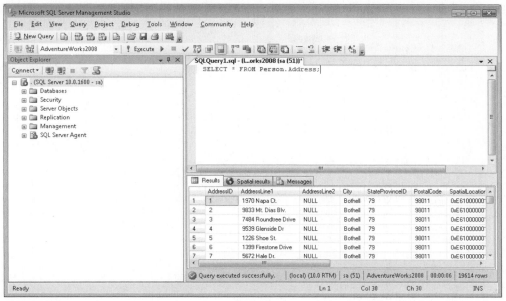

Figure 2-10

Figure 2-11

Results to Text

The Results to Text option takes all the output from your query and puts it into one page of text results. The page can be of virtually infinite length (limited only by the available memory in your system).

Before discussing this further, rerun that previous query using this option and see what you get. Choose the Results to Text option and rerun the previous query by clicking Execute, as shown in Figure 2-12.

The data that you get back is exactly the same as before. It's just given to you in a different format. I use this output method in several scenarios:

❏ When I'm only getting one result set and the results have only fairly narrow columns

❏ When I want to be able to save my results in a single text file

❏ When I'm going to have multiple result sets, but the results are expected to be small, and I want to be able to see more than one result set on the same page without dealing with multiple scrollbars

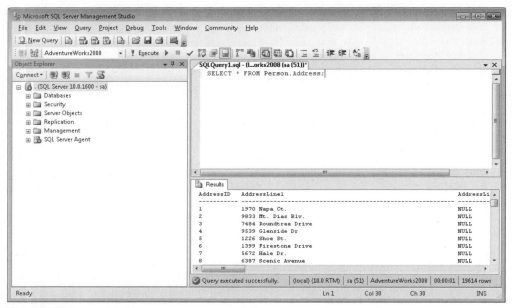

Figure 2-12

Results to Grid

This option divides the columns and rows into a grid arrangement. Following is a list of specific things that this option gives you that the Results to Text doesn't:

❑ You can resize the column by hovering your mouse pointer on the right border of the column header, then clicking and dragging the column border to its new size. Double-clicking the right border results in the autofit for the column.

❑ If you select several cells, then cut and paste them into another grid (say, Microsoft Excel), they will be treated as individual cells. (Under the Results to Text option, the cut data is pasted all into one cell.)

❑ You can select just one or two columns of multiple rows. (Under Results to Text, if you select several rows, all the inner rows have every column selected; you can select only in the middle of the row for the first and last row selected.)

I use this option for almost everything because I find that I usually want one of the benefits I just listed.

Results to File

Think of this one as largely the same as Results to Text, but instead of to screen, it routes the output directly to a file. I use this one to generate files I intend to parse using some utility or that I want to easily e-mail.

sqlcmd Mode

We will discuss sqlcmd a bit more shortly. For now, suffice it to say that it is a tool that helps us run queries from a Windows command line. It has some special scripting abilities that are meant specifically for command-line scripting. By default, these special script commands are not available in the Query window. Turning sqlcmd mode on activates the special sqlcmd scripting options even in the Query window.

> **Be aware that the Query window always utilizes the** `SQLNativeClient` **connection method (even when operating in sqlcmd mode), whereas the actual sqlcmd utility will use an OLE DB connection. The result is that you may see slight differences in behavior between running a script using sqlcmd versus using sqlcmd from the Query window. These tend to be corner case differences, and are rarely seen and generally innocuous.**

Show Execution Plan

Every time you run a query, SQL Server parses your query into its component parts and then sends it to the *query optimizer*. The query optimizer is the part of SQL Server that figures out the best way to run your query to balance fast results with minimum impact to other users. When you use the Show Estimated Execution Plan option, you receive a graphical representation and additional information about how SQL Server plans to run your query. Similarly, you can turn on the Include Actual Execution Plan option. Most of the time, this will be the same as the estimated execution plan, but you will occasionally see differences here due to changes that the optimizer decides to make while running the query, as well as changes in the actual cost of running the query versus what the optimizer *thinks* is going to happen.

Let's see what a query plan looks like in our simple query. Click the Include Actual Execution Plan option, and execute the query again, as shown in Figure 2-13.

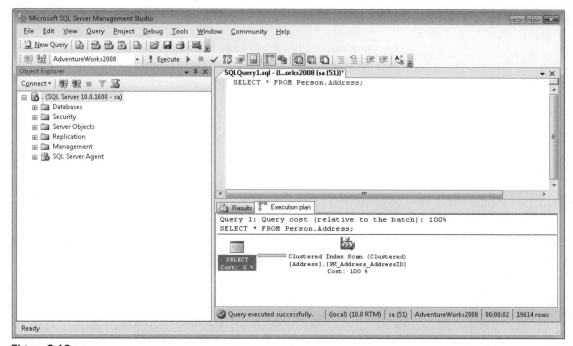

Figure 2-13

Note that you have to actually click the Execution Plan tab for it to come up and that your query results are still displayed in the way you selected. The Show Estimated Execution plan option gives you the same output as an Include Actual Execution Plan does with two exceptions:

❏ You get the plan immediately rather than after your query executes.

❏ Although what you see is the actual *plan* for the query, all the cost information is estimated and the query is not actually run. Under Include Actual Execution, the query is physically executed and the cost information you get is actual rather than estimated.

Note that the plan in Figure 2-13 is an extremely simple execution plan. More complex queries may show a variety of branching and parallel operations.

The Available Databases Combo Box

Finally, take another look at the Available Databases combo box. In short, this is where you select the default database that you want your queries to run against for the current window (we changed AdventureWorks2008 to be our default database earlier). Initially, the Query window will start with whatever the default database is for the user that's logged in (for sa, that is the master database unless someone has changed it on your system). You can then change it to any other database that the current login has permission to access. Since we're using the sa user ID, every database on the current server should have an entry in the Available Databases combo box.

The Object Explorer

This useful little tool enables you to navigate your database, look up object names, and even perform actions like scripting and looking at the underlying data.

In the example in Figure 2-14, I've expanded the database node all the way down to the listing of tables in the AdventureWorks2008 database. You can drill down even farther to see individual columns (including data type and similar properties) of the tables — a very handy tool for browsing your database.

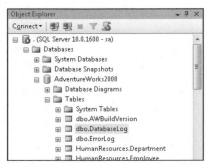

Figure 2-14

SQL Server Integration Services (SSIS)

Your friend and mine — that's what *SSIS* (formerly known as Data Transformation Services or DTS) is. I simply sit back in amazement every time I look at this feature of SQL Server. To give you a touch of perspective here, I've done a couple of Decision Support Systems (DSS) projects over the years. (These are usually systems that don't have online data going in and out, but instead pull data together to help management make decisions.) A DSS project gathers data from a variety of sources and pumps it into one centralized database to be used for centralized reporting.

These projects can get very expensive very quickly, as they attempt to deal with the fact that not every system calls what is essentially the same data by the same name. There can be an infinite number of issues to be dealt with. These can include data integrity (what if the field has a NULL and we don't allow NULLs?) or differences in business rules (one system deals with credits by allowing a negative order quantity, another doesn't allow this and has a separate set of tables to deal with credits). The list can go on and on, and so can the expense.

With SSIS a tremendous amount of the coding, usually in some client-side language, that had to be done to handle these situations can be eliminated or, at least, simplified. SSIS enables you to take data from any data source that has an OLE DB or .NET data provider and pump it into a SQL Server table.

> Be aware that there is a special OLE DB provider for ODBC. This provider allows you to map your OLE DB access directly to an ODBC driver. That means anything that ODBC can access can also be accessed by OLE DB (and, therefore, SSIS).
>
> While we're at it, it's also worth pointing out that SSIS, although part of SQL Server, can work against any OLE DB source and any OLE DB destination. That means that SQL Server doesn't need to be involved in the process at all other than to provide the data pump. You could, for example, push data from Oracle to Excel, or even DB/2 to MySQL.

While transferring your data, we can also apply what are referred to as transformations to that data. *Transformations* essentially alter the data according to some logical rule(s). The alteration can be as simple as changing a column name, or as complex as an analysis of the integrity of the data and application of rules to change it if necessary. To think about how this is applied, consider the example I gave earlier of taking data from a field that allows NULLs and moving it to a table that doesn't allow NULLs. With SSIS you can automatically change any NULL values to some other value you choose during the transfer process. (For a number, that might be zero or, for a character, it might be something like unknown.)

Bulk Copy Program (bcp)

If SSIS is your friend and mine, then the *Bulk Copy Program*, or *bcp*, would be that old friend that we may not see that much anymore, but really appreciate when we do.

bcp is a command-line program whose sole purpose in life is to move formatted data in and out of SQL Server en masse. It was around long before what has now become SSIS was thought of, and while SSIS is replacing bcp for most import/export activity, bcp still has a certain appeal for people who like command-line utilities. In addition, you'll find an awful lot of SQL Server installations out there that still depend on bcp to move data around fast.

SQL Server Profiler

I can't tell you how many times this one has saved my bacon by telling me what was going on with my server when nothing else would. It's not something a developer (or even a DBA, for that matter) tends to use every day, but it's extremely powerful and can be your salvation when you're sure nothing can save you.

SQL Server Profiler is, in short, a real-time tracing tool. Whereas Performance Monitor is all about tracking what's happening at the macro level — system configuration stuff — the Profiler is concerned with tracking specifics. This is both a blessing and a curse. The Profiler can, depending on how you configure your trace, give you the specific syntax of every statement executed on your server. Now imagine that you are doing performance tuning on a system with 1000 users. I'm sure you can imagine the reams of paper that would be used to print the statements executed by so many people in just a minute or two. Fortunately, the Profiler has a vast array of filters to help you narrow things down and track more specific problems, such as long-running queries, or the exact syntax of a query being run within a stored procedure. This is nice when your procedure has conditional statements that cause it to run different things under different circumstances.

sqlcmd

As I mentioned back when we were talking about the Management Console, SQL Server has a tool to use when you want to include SQL commands and management tasks in command-line batch files — sqlcmd. You won't see sqlcmd in your SQL Server program group. Indeed, it's amazing how many people don't even know that this utility is around; that's because it's a console application rather than a Windows program.

Prior to version 7.0 and the advent of what was then called DTS (now SSIS), sqlcmd was often used in conjunction with the Bulk Copy Program (bcp) to manage the import of data from external systems. This type of use is decreasing as administrators and developers everywhere learn the power and simplicity of SSIS. Even so, there are occasionally items that you want to script into a larger command-line process. sqlcmd gives you that capability.

sqlcmd can be very handy, particularly if you use files that contain scripts. Keep in mind, however, that there are tools that can accomplish much of what sqlcmd can more effectively and with a user interface that is more consistent with the other things you're doing with your SQL Server. You can find full coverage of sqlcmd in *Professional SQL Server 2008 Programming*.

> *Once again, just for history and being able to understand if people you talk SQL Server with use a different lingo, sqlcmd is yet another new name for this tool of many names. Originally, it was referred to as ISQL. In SQL Server 2000 and 7.0, it was known as osql.*

PowerShell

PowerShell is a new feature with SQL Server 2008. PowerShell serves as an extremely robust scripting and server-navigation engine. Using PowerShell, the user can navigate all objects on the server as though they were part of a directory structure in the file system. (You even use the `dir` and `cd` style commands you use in a command window.)

PowerShell is well outside the scope of a beginning title, but it is important to realize that it's there. It is covered in more depth in *Professional SQL Server 2008 Programming*.

Summary

Most of the tools that you've been exposed to here aren't ones you'll use every day. Indeed, for the average developer, only SQL Server Management Studio will get daily use. Nevertheless it's important to have some idea of the role that each one can play. Each has something significant to offer you. We will see each of these tools again in our journey through this book.

Note that there are some other utilities available that don't have shortcuts on your Start menu (connectivity tools, server diagnostics, and maintenance utilities), which are mostly admin related.

The Foundation
Statements of T-SQL

At last! We've finally disposed of the most boring stuff. It doesn't get any worse than basic objects and tools, does it? Unfortunately, we have to lay down a foundation before we can build a house. The nice thing is that the foundation is now down. Having used the clichéd example of building a house, I'm going to turn it all upside down by talking about the things that let you enjoy living in it before we've even talked about the plumbing. You see, when working with databases, you have to get to know how data is going to be accessed before you can learn all that much about the best ways to store it.

In this chapter, we will discuss the most fundamental *Transact-SQL (T-SQL)* statements. T-SQL is SQL Server's own dialect of Structured Query Language (SQL). The T-SQL statements that we will learn in this chapter are:

- ❏   SELECT
- ❏   INSERT
- ❏   UPDATE
- ❏   DELETE

These four statements are the bread and butter of T-SQL. We'll learn plenty of other statements as we go along, but these statements make up the basis of T-SQL's *Data Manipulation Language* (*DML*). Because you'll generally issue far more commands meant to manipulate (that is, read and modify) data than other types of commands (such as those to grant user rights or create a table), you'll find that these will become like old friends in no time at all.

In addition, SQL provides many operators and keywords that help refine your queries. We'll learn some of the most common of these in this chapter.

While T-SQL is unique to SQL Server, the statements you use most of the time are not. T-SQL is largely ANSI/ISO compliant (The standard was originally governed by ANSI, and was later taken over by the ISO. It was ANSI long enough that people generally still refer to it as ANSI compliance.), which means that, by and large, it complies with a very wide open standard. What this means to you as a developer is that much of the SQL you're going to learn in this book is directly transferable to other SQL-based database servers such as Sybase (which long ago used to share the same code base as SQL Server), Oracle, DB2, and MySQL. Be aware, however, that every RDBMS has different extensions and performance enhancements that it uses above and beyond the ANSI/ISO standard. I will try to point out the ANSI vs. non-ANSI ways of doing things where applicable. In some cases, you'll have a choice to make — performance versus portability to other RDBMS systems. Most of the time, however, the ANSI way is as fast as any other option. In such a case, the choice should be clear: Stay ANSI compliant.

Getting Started with a Basic SELECT Statement

If you haven't used SQL before, or don't feel like you've really understood it yet, pay attention here! The SELECT statement and the structures used within it form the basis of the lion's share of all the commands we will perform with SQL Server. Let's look at the basic syntax rules for a SELECT statement:

```
SELECT [ALL|DISTINCT] [TOP (<expression>) [PERCENT] [WITH TIES]] <column list>
[FROM <source table(s)/view(s)>]
[WHERE <restrictive condition>]
[GROUP BY <column name or expression using a column in the SELECT list>]
[HAVING <restrictive condition based on the GROUP BY results>]
[ORDER BY <column list>]
[[FOR XML {RAW|AUTO|EXPLICIT|PATH [(<element>)]}][, XMLDATA][, ELEMENTS][, BINARY
base 64]]
[OPTION (<query hint>, [, ...n])]
```

Wow — that's a lot to decipher, so let's look at the parts.

Note that the parentheses around the TOP expression are, technically speaking, optional. Microsoft refers to them as "required," then points out that a lack of parentheses is actually supported, but for backward compatibility only. This means that Microsoft may pull support for that in a later release, so if you do not need to support older versions of SQL Server, I strongly recommend using parentheses to delimit a TOP expression in your queries.

The SELECT Statement and FROM Clause

The verb — in this case a SELECT — is the part of the overall statement that tells SQL Server what we are doing. A SELECT indicates that we are merely reading information, as opposed to modifying it. What we are selecting is identified by an expression or column list immediately following the SELECT. You'll see what I mean by this in a moment.

Next, we add in more specifics, such as where we are getting this data. The FROM statement specifies the name of the table or tables from which we are getting our data. With these, we have enough to create a basic SELECT statement. Fire up the SQL Server Management Studio and let's take a look at a simple SELECT statement:

```
SELECT * FROM INFORMATION_SCHEMA.TABLES;
```

Let's look at what we've asked for here. We've asked to SELECT information; you can also think of this as requesting to display information. The * may seem odd, but it actually works pretty much as * does everywhere: It's a wildcard. When we say SELECT *, we're saying we want to select every column from the table. Next, the FROM indicates that we've finished saying what items to output and that we're about to say what the source of the information is supposed to be — in this case, INFORMATION_SCHEMA.TABLES.

> INFORMATION_SCHEMA **is a special access path that is used for displaying metadata about your system's databases and their contents.** INFORMATION_SCHEMA **has several parts that can be specified after a period, such as** INFORMATION_SCHEMA.SCHEMATA **or** INFORMATION_SCHEMA.VIEWS. **These special access paths to the metadata of your system have been put there so you won't have to use system tables.**

Try It Out   The SELECT Statement

Let's play around with this some more. Change the current database to be the AdventureWorks2008 database. Recall that to do this, you need only select the AdventureWorks2008 entry from the combo box in the toolbar at the top of the Query window in the Management Studio, as shown in Figure 3-1.

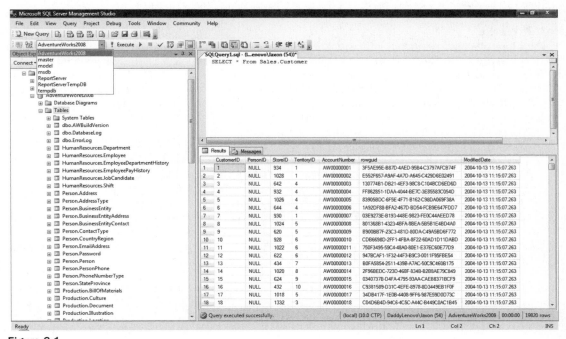

Figure 3-1

If you're having difficulty finding the combo box that lists the various databases, try clicking once in the Query window. The SQL Server Management Studio toolbars are context sensitive — that is, they change by whatever the Query window thinks is the current thing you are doing. If you don't have a Query window as the currently active window, you may have a different set of toolbars up (one that is more suitable to some other task). As soon as a Query window is active, it should switch to a set of toolbars that are suitable to query needs.

Now that we have the `AdventureWorks` database selected, let's start looking at some real data from our database. Try this query:

```
SELECT * FROM Sales.Customer;
```

After you have that in the Query window, just click Execute on the toolbar and watch SQL Server give you your results. This query will list every row of data in every column of the `Sales.Customer` table in the current database (in our case, AdventureWorks2008). If you didn't alter any of the settings on your system or the data in the AdventureWorks2008 database before you ran this query, then you should see the following information if you click on the Messages tab:

```
(19820 row(s) affected)
```

For a `SELECT` statement, the number shown here is the number of rows that your query returned. You can also find the same information on the right-hand side of the status bar (found below the results pane), with some other useful information, such as the login name of the user you're logged in as, the current database as of when the last query was run (this will persist, even if you change the database in the database drop-down box, until you run your next query in this query window), and the time it took for the query to execute.

How It Works

Let's look at a few specifics of your `SELECT` statement. Notice that I capitalized `SELECT` and `FROM`. This is not a requirement of SQL Server — we could run them as `SeLeCt` and `frOM` and they would work just fine. I capitalized them purely for purposes of convention and readability. You'll find that many SQL coders will use the convention of capitalizing all commands and keywords, while using mixed case for table, column, and non-constant variable names. The standards you choose or have forced upon you may vary, but live by at least one rule: Be consistent.

OK, time for one of my world famous soapbox diatribes. Nothing is more frustrating for a person who has to read your code or remember your table names than lack of consistency. When someone looks at your code or, more important, uses your column and table names, it shouldn't take him or her long to guess most of the way you do things just by experience with the parts that he or she has already worked with. Being consistent is one of those incredibly simple things that has been missed to at least some degree in almost every database I've ever worked with. Break the trend: Be consistent.

The `SELECT` is telling the Query window what we are doing and the `*` is saying what we want (remember that `*` = every column). Then comes the `FROM`.

A `FROM` clause does just what it says — that is, it defines the place from which our data should come. Immediately following the `FROM` will be the names of one or more tables. In our query, all of the data came from a table called `Customer`.

Now let's try taking a little bit more specific information. Let's say all we want is a list of all our customers by last name:

```
SELECT LastName FROM Person.Person;
```

Your results should look something like:

```
Achong
Abel
Abercrombie
...
He
Zheng
Hu
```

Note that I've snipped rows out of the middle for brevity. You should have 19,972 rows. Since the last name of each customer is all that we want, that's all that we've selected.

*Many SQL writers have the habit of cutting their queries short and always selecting every column by using a * in their selection criteria. This is another one of those habits to resist. While typing in a * saves you a few moments of typing out the column names that you want, it also means that more data has to be retrieved than is really necessary. In addition, SQL Server must figure out just how many columns "*" amounts to and what specifically they are. You would be surprised at just how much this can drag down your application's performance and that of your network. In short, a good rule to live by is to select what you need — that is, exactly what you need. No more, no less.*

Let's try another simple query. How about:

```
SELECT Name FROM Production.Product;
```

Again, assuming that you haven't modified the data that came with the sample database, SQL Server should respond by returning a list of 504 different products that are available in the AdventureWorks database:

```
Name
----------------------------------------
Adjustable Race
Bearing Ball
BB Ball Bearing
...
...
Road-750 Black, 44
Road-750 Black, 48
Road-750 Black, 52
```

The columns that you have chosen right after your SELECT clause are known as the SELECT list. In short, the SELECT list is made up of the columns that you have requested be output from your query.

> **The columns that you have chosen right after your SELECT clause are known as the SELECT list.**

The WHERE Clause

Well, things are starting to get boring again, aren't they? So let's add in the WHERE clause. The WHERE clause allows you to place conditions on what is returned to you. What we have seen thus far is unrestricted information, in the sense that every row in the table specified has been included in our results. Unrestricted queries such as these are very useful for populating things like list boxes and combo boxes, and in other scenarios where you are trying to provide a *domain listing*.

> For our purposes, don't confuse a domain with that of a Windows domain. A domain listing is an exclusive list of choices. For example, if you want someone to provide you with information about a state in the U.S., you might provide them with a list that limits the domain of choices to just the 50 states. That way, you can be sure that the option selected will be a valid one. We will see this concept of domains further when we begin talking about database design, as well as entity versus domain constraints.

Now we want to try looking for more specific information. We don't want a listing of product names. We want information on a specific product. Try this: See if you can come up with a query that returns the name, product number, and reorder point for a product with the ProductID 356.

Let's break it down and build the query one piece at a time. First, we're asking for information to be returned, so we know that we're looking at a SELECT statement. Our statement of what we want indicates that we would like the product name, product number, and reorder point, so we're going to have to know what the column names are for these pieces of information. We're also going to need to know from which table or tables we can retrieve these columns.

Now we'll take a look at the tables that are available. Since we've already used the Production.Product table once before, we know that it's there. The Production.Product table has several columns. To give us a quick listing of our column options we can study the Object Explorer tree of the Production.Product table from Management Studio. To open this screen in the Management Studio, click Tables underneath the AdventureWorks2008 database, then expand the Production.Product and Columns nodes. As in Figure 3-2, you will see each of the columns along with its data type and nullability options. Again, we'll see some other methods of finding this information a little later in the chapter.

We don't have a column called product name, but we do have one that's probably what we're looking for: Name. (Original eh?) The other two columns are, save for the missing space between the two words, just as easy to identify.

Therefore, our Products table is going to be the place we get our information FROM, and the Name, ProductNumber, and ReorderPoint columns will be the specific columns from which we'll get our information:

```
SELECT Name, ProductNumber, ReorderPoint
FROM Production.Product
```

This query, however, still won't give us the results that we're after; it will still return too much information. Run it and you'll see that it still returns every record in the table rather than just the one we want.

If the table has only a few records and all we want to do is take a quick look at it, this might be fine. After all, we can look through a small list ourselves, right? But that's a pretty big if. In any significant system, very few of your tables will have small record counts. You don't want to have to go scrolling through 10,000 records. What if you had 100,000 or 1,000,000? Even if you felt like scrolling through them all, the time before the results were back would be increased dramatically. Finally, what do you do when you're designing this into your application and you need a quick result that gets straight to the point?

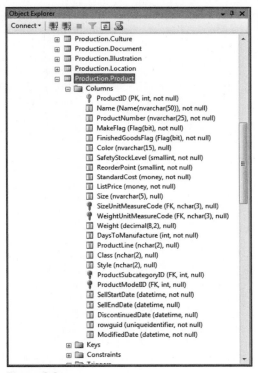

Figure 3-2

What we're after is a conditional statement that will limit the results of our query to just one product identifier — 356. That's where the WHERE clause comes in. The WHERE clause immediately follows the FROM clause and defines what conditions a record has to meet before it will be shown. For our query, we would want the ProductID to be equal to 356, so let's finish our query:

```
SELECT Name, ProductNumber, ReorderPoint
FROM Production.Product
WHERE ProductID = 356
```

Run this query against the AdventureWorks2008 database and you should come up with:

```
Name                                ProductNumber        ReorderPoint
---------------------------------   ------------------   ------------
LL Grip Tape                        GT-0820                   600

(1 row(s) affected)
```

This time we've gotten back precisely what we wanted — nothing more, nothing less. In addition, this query runs much faster than the first query.

Let's take a look at all the operators we can use with the WHERE clause:

Operator	Example Usage	Effect
=, >, <, >=, <=, <>, !=, !>, !<	`<Column Name> = <Other Column Name>` `<Column Name> = 'Bob'`	Standard comparison operators, these work as they do in pretty much any programming language with a couple of notable points: 1. What constitutes "greater than," "less than," and "equal to" can change depending on the collation order you have selected. (For example, `"ROMEY" = "romey"` in places where case-insensitive sort order has been selected, but `"ROMEY" < > "romey"` in a case-sensitive situation.) 2. `!=` and `<>` both mean "not equal." `!<` and `!>` mean "not less than" and "not greater than," respectively.
AND, OR, NOT	`<Column1> = <Column2> AND <Column3> >= <Column 4>` `<Column1> != "MyLiteral" OR <Column2> = "MyOtherLiteral"`	Standard boolean logic. You can use these to combine multiple conditions into one WHERE clause. NOT is evaluated first, then AND, then OR. If you need to change the evaluation order, you can use parentheses. Note that XOR is not supported.
BETWEEN	`<Column1> BETWEEN 1 AND 5`	Comparison is TRUE if the first value is between the second and third values inclusive. It is the functional equivalent of A>=B AND A<=C. Any of the specified values can be column names, variables, or literals.
LIKE	`<Column1> LIKE "ROM%"`	Uses the % and _ characters for wildcarding. % indicates a value of any length can replace the % character. _ indicates any one character can replace the _ character. Enclosing characters in [ ] symbols indicates any single character within the [ ] is OK. ([a-c] means a, b, and c are OK. [ab] indicates a or b are OK). ^ operates as a NOT operator, indicating that the next character is to be excluded.
IN	`<Column1> IN (List of Numbers)` `<Column1> IN ("A", "b", "345")`	Returns TRUE if the value to the left of the IN keyword matches any of the values in the list provided after the IN keyword. This is frequently used in subqueries, which we will look at in Chapter 16.

Operator	Example Usage	Effect

ALL,
ANY,
SOME
	`<column|expression>`
	`(comparision operator)`
	`<ANY|SOME> (subquery)`
		These return TRUE if any or all (depending on which you choose) values in a subquery meet the comparison operator's (e.g., <, >, =, >=) condition. ALL indicates that the value must match all the values in the set. ANY and SOME are functional equivalents and will evaluate to TRUE if the expression matches any value in the set.

EXISTS	`EXISTS (subquery)`	Returns TRUE if at least one row is returned by the subquery. Again, we'll look into this one further in Chapter 16.

Note that these are not the only operators in SQL Server. These are just the ones that apply to the WHERE clause. There are a few operators that apply only as assignment operators (rather than comparison). These are inappropriate for a WHERE clause.

ORDER BY

In the queries that we've run thus far, most have come out in something resembling alphabetical order. Is this by accident? It will probably come as somewhat of a surprise to you, but the answer to that is yes. If you don't say you want a specific sorting on the results of a query, then you get the data in the order that SQL Server decides to give it to you. This will always be based on what SQL Server decided was the lowest-cost way to gather the data. It will usually be based either on the physical order of a table, or on one of the indexes SQL Server used to find your data.

Microsoft's samples have a nasty habit of building themselves in a manner that happen to lend themselves to coming out in alphabetical order (long story as to why, but I wish they wouldn't do that!), but most data won't work that way. The short rendition as to why has to do with the order in which Microsoft inserts their data. Since they typically insert it in alphabetical order, the ID columns are ordered the same as alphabetical order (just by happenstance). Since most of these tables happen to be physically sorted in ID order (we'll learn more about physical sorting of the data in Chapter 9), the data wind up appearing alphabetically sorted. If Microsoft inserted the data in a more random name order — as would likely happen in a real-life scenario — then the names would tend to come out more mixed up unless you specifically asked for them to be sorted by name.

Think of an ORDER BY clause as being a sort by. It gives you the opportunity to define the order in which you want your data to come back. You can use any combination of columns in your ORDER BY clause, as long as they are columns (or derivations of columns) found in the tables within your FROM clause.

Let's look at this query:

```
SELECT Name, ProductNumber, ReorderPoint
FROM Production.Product;
```

This will produce the following results:

```
Name                            ProductNumber        ReorderPoint
-----------------------------   ----------------     ------------
Adjustable Race                 AR-5381                       750
Bearing Ball                    BA-8327                       750
...

...
Road-750 Black, 48              BK-R19B-48                     75
Road-750 Black, 52              BK-R19B-52                     75

(504 row(s) affected)
```

As it happened, our query result set was sorted in ProductID order. Why? Because SQL Server decided that the best way to look at this data was by using an index that sorts the data by ProductID. That just happened to be what created the lowest-cost (in terms of CPU and I/O) query. Were we to run this exact query when the table has grown to a much larger size, SQL Server might have choose an entirely different execution plan, and therefore might sort the data differently. We could force this sort order by changing our query to this:

```sql
SELECT Name, ProductNumber, ReorderPoint
FROM Production.Product
ORDER BY Name;
```

Note that the WHERE clause isn't required. It can either be there or not depending on what you're trying to accomplish. Just remember that if you do have a WHERE clause, it goes before the ORDER BY clause.

Unfortunately, that previous query doesn't really give us anything different, so we don't see what's actually happening. Let's change the query to sort the data differently — by the ProductNumber:

```sql
SELECT Name, ProductNumber, ReorderPoint
FROM Production.Product
ORDER BY ProductNumber;
```

Now our results are quite different. It's the same data, but it's been substantially rearranged:

```
Name                            ProductNumber             ReorderPoint
-----------------------------   ------------------------  ------------
Adjustable Race                 AR-5381                            750
Bearing Ball                    BA-8327                            750
LL Bottom Bracket               BB-7421                            375
ML Bottom Bracket               BB-8107                            375
...

...
Classic Vest, L                 VE-C304-L                            3
Classic Vest, M                 VE-C304-M                            3
Classic Vest, S                 VE-C304-S                            3
Water Bottle - 30 oz.           WB-H098                              3

(504 row(s) affected)
```

SQL Server still chose the least-cost method of giving us our desired results, but the particular set of tasks it actually needed to perform changed somewhat because the nature of the query changed.

We can also do our sorting using numeric fields (note that we're querying a new table):

```
SELECT Name, SalesPersonID
FROM Sales.Store
WHERE Name BETWEEN 'g' AND 'j'
  AND SalesPersonID > 283
ORDER BY SalesPersonID, Name DESC;
```

This one results in:

```
Name                                               SalesPersonID
-------------------------------------------------- -------------
Inexpensive Parts Shop                             286
Ideal Components                                   286
Helpful Sales and Repair Service                   286
Helmets and Cycles                                 286
Global Sports Outlet                               286
Gears and Parts Company                            286
Irregulars Outlet                                  288
Hometown Riding Supplies                           288
Good Bicycle Store                                 288
Global Bike Retailers                              288
Instruments and Parts Company                      289
Instant Cycle Store                                290
Impervious Paint Company                           290
Hiatus Bike Tours                                  290
Getaway Inn                                        290

(15 row(s) affected)
```

Notice several things in this query: We've made use of many of the things that we've talked about up to this point. We've combined multiple WHERE clause conditions and also have an ORDER BY clause in place. In addition, we've added some new twists in our ORDER BY clause. First, we now have an ORDER BY clause that sorts based on more than one column. To do this, we simply comma delimited the columns we wanted to sort by. In this case, we've sorted first by SalesPersonID and then added a sub-sort based on Name. Second, the DESC keyword tells SQL Server that our ORDER BY should work in descending order for the Name sub-sort, rather than the default of ascending. (If you want to explicitly state that you want it to be ascending, use ASC.)

> While we usually sort the results based on one of the columns that we are returning, it's worth noting that the ORDER BY clause can be based on any column in any table used in the query, regardless of whether it is included in the SELECT list.

Aggregating Data Using the GROUP BY Clause

With ORDER BY, we have kind of taken things out of order compared with how the SELECT statement reads at the top of the chapter. Let's review the overall statement structure:

```
SELECT [TOP (<expression>) [PERCENT] [WITH TIES]] <column list>
[FROM <source table(s)/view(s)>]
[WHERE <restrictive condition>]
[GROUP BY <column name or expression using a column in the SELECT list>]
[HAVING <restrictive condition based on the GROUP BY results>]
[ORDER BY <column list>]
[[FOR XML {RAW|AUTO|EXPLICIT|PATH [(<element>)]}[, XMLDATA][, ELEMENTS][, BINARY
base 64]]
[OPTION (<query hint>, [, ...n])]
```

Why, if ORDER BY comes last, did we look at it before the GROUP BY? There are two reasons:

❑   ORDER BY is used far more often than GROUP BY, so I want you to have more practice with it.

❑   I want to make sure that you understand that you can mix and match all of the clauses after the FROM clause, as long as you keep them in the order that SQL Server expects them (as defined in the syntax definition).

The GROUP BY clause is used to aggregate information. Let's look at a simple query without a GROUP BY. Let's say that we want to know how many parts were ordered in a given set of orders:

```
SELECT SalesOrderID, OrderQty
FROM Sales.SalesOrderDetail
WHERE SalesOrderID IN (43660, 43670, 43672);
```

This yields a result set of:

```
SalesOrderID OrderQty
------------ --------
43660        1
43660        1
43670        1
43670        2
43670        2
43670        1
43672        6
43672        2
43672        1

(9 row(s) affected)
```

Even though we've only asked for three orders, we're seeing each individual line of detail from the orders. We can either get out our adding machine, or we can make use of the GROUP BY clause with an aggregator. In this case, we'll use SUM():

```
SELECT SalesOrderID, SUM(OrderQty)
FROM Sales.SalesOrderDetail
```

```
WHERE SalesOrderID IN (43660, 43670, 43672)
GROUP BY SalesOrderID;
```

This gets us what we were looking for:

```
SalesOrderID
------------ -----------
43660        2
43670        6
43672        9

(3 row(s) affected)
```

As you would expect, the SUM function returns totals — but totals of what? We can easily supply an *alias* for our result. Let's modify our query slightly to provide a column name for the output:

```
SELECT SalesOrderID, SUM(OrderQty) AS TotalOrderQty
FROM Sales.SalesOrderDetail
WHERE SalesOrderID IN (43660, 43670, 43672)
GROUP BY SalesOrderID;
```

This gets us the same basic output, but also supplies a header to the grouped column:

```
SalesOrderID TotalOrderQty
------------ -------------
43660        2
43670        6
43672        9

(3 row(s) affected)
```

If you're just trying to get some quick results, then there really is no need to alias the grouped column as we've done here, but many of your queries are going to be written to supply information to other elements of a larger program. The code that's utilizing your queries will need some way of referencing your grouped column; aliasing your column to some useful name can be critical in that situation. We'll examine aliasing a bit more shortly.

If we didn't supply the GROUP BY clause, the SUM would have been of all the values in all of the rows for the named column. In this case, however, we did supply a GROUP BY, and so the total provided by the SUM function is the total in each group.

> Note that when using a GROUP BY clause, all the columns in the SELECT list must either be aggregates (SUM, MIN/MAX, AVG, and so on) or columns included in the GROUP BY clause. Likewise, if you are using an aggregate in the SELECT list, your SELECT list must *only* contain aggregates, or there must be a GROUP BY clause.

We can also group based on multiple columns. To do this we just add a comma and the next column name. Let's say, for example, that we're looking for the number of orders each salesperson has taken for our first 10 customers. We can use both the SalesPersonID and CustomerID columns in our GROUP BY. (I'll explain how to use the COUNT() function shortly):

```
SELECT CustomerID, SalesPersonID, COUNT(*)
FROM Sales.SalesOrderHeader
WHERE CustomerID <= 11010
GROUP BY CustomerID, SalesPersonID
ORDER BY CustomerID, SalesPersonID;
```

This gets us counts, but the counts are pulled together based on how many orders a given salesperson took from a given customer:

```
CustomerID  SalesPersonID
----------- ------------- -----------
11000       NULL                    3
11001       NULL                    3
11002       NULL                    3
11003       NULL                    3
11004       NULL                    3
11005       NULL                    3
11006       NULL                    3
11007       NULL                    3
11008       NULL                    3
11009       NULL                    3
11010       NULL                    3

(11 row(s) affected)
```

Aggregates

When you consider that they usually get used with a GROUP BY clause, it's probably not surprising that aggregates are functions that work on groups of data. For example, in one of the previous queries, we got the sum of the OrderQty column. The sum is calculated and returned on the selected column for each group defined in the GROUP BY clause — in the case of our SUM, it was just SalesOrderID. A wide range of aggregates is available, but let's play with the most common.

> While aggregates show their power when used with a GROUP BY clause, they are not limited to grouped queries; if you include an aggregate without a GROUP BY, then the aggregate will work against the entire result set (all the rows that match the WHERE clause). The catch here is that, when not working with a GROUP BY, some aggregates can only be in the SELECT list with other aggregates — that is, they can't be paired with a column name in the SELECT list unless you have a GROUP BY. For example, unless there is a GROUP BY, AVG can be paired with SUM, but not a specific column.

AVG

This one is for computing averages. Let's try running the order quantity query we ran before, but now we'll modify it to return the average quantity per order, rather than the total for each order:

```
SELECT SalesOrderID, AVG(OrderQty)
FROM Sales.SalesOrderDetail
WHERE SalesOrderID IN (43660, 43670, 43672)
GROUP BY SalesOrderID;
```

Notice that our results changed substantially:

```
SalesOrderID
------------ -------------
43660        1
43670        1
43672        3

(3 row(s) affected)
```

You can check the math — on order number 43672 there were 3 line items totaling 9 altogether (9 / 3 = 3).

MIN/MAX

Bet you can guess these two. Yes, these grab the minimum and maximum amounts for each grouping for a selected column. Again, let's use that same query modified for the MIN function:

```
SELECT SalesOrderID, MIN(OrderQty)
FROM Sales.SalesOrderDetail
WHERE SalesOrderID IN (43660, 43670, 43672)
GROUP BY SalesOrderID;
```

Which gives the following results:

```
SalesOrderID
------------ -----------
43660        1
43670        1
43672        1

(3 row(s) affected)
```

Modify it one more time for the MAX function:

```
SELECT SalesOrderID, MAX(OrderQty)
FROM Sales.SalesOrderDetail
WHERE SalesOrderID IN (43660, 43670, 43672)
GROUP BY SalesOrderID;
```

And you come up with this:

```
SalesOrderID
------------ -----------
43660        1
43670        2
43672        6

(3 row(s) affected)
```

What if, however, we wanted both the MIN and the MAX? Simple! Just use both in your query:

```sql
SELECT SalesOrderID, MIN(OrderQty), MAX(OrderQty)
FROM Sales.SalesOrderDetail
WHERE SalesOrderID IN (43660, 43670, 43672)
GROUP BY SalesOrderID;
```

Now, this will yield an additional column and a bit of a problem:

```
SalesOrderID
------------ ----------- -----------
43660        1           1
43670        1           2
43672        1           6

(3 row(s) affected)
```

Can you spot the issue here? We've gotten back everything that we've asked for, but now that we have more than one aggregate column, we have a problem identifying which column is which. Sure, in this particular example we can be sure that the columns with the largest numbers are the columns generated by the MAX and the smallest by the MIN. The answer to which column is which is not always so apparent, so let's make use of an *alias*. An alias allows you to change the name of a column in the result set, and you can create it by using the AS keyword:

```sql
SELECT SalesOrderID, MIN(OrderQty) AS MinOrderQty, MAX(OrderQty) AS MaxOrderQty
FROM Sales.SalesOrderDetail
WHERE SalesOrderID IN (43660, 43670, 43672)
GROUP BY SalesOrderID;
```

Now our results are somewhat easier to make sense of:

```
SalesOrderID MinOrderQty MaxOrderQty
------------ ----------- -----------
43660        1           1
43670        1           2
43672        1           6

(3 row(s) affected)
```

It's worth noting that the AS keyword is actually optional. Indeed, there was a time (prior to version 6.5 of SQL Server) when it wasn't even a valid keyword. If you like, you can execute the same query as before, but remove the two AS keywords from the query — you'll see that you wind up with exactly the same results. It's also worth noting that you can alias any column (and even, as we'll see in the next chapter, table names), not just aggregates.

Let's re-run this last query, but this time we'll not use the AS keyword in some places, and we'll alias every column:

```
SELECT SalesOrderID AS "Order Number", MIN(OrderQty) MinOrderQty, MAX(OrderQty)
MaxOrderQty
FROM Sales.SalesOrderDetail
WHERE SalesOrderID IN (43660, 43670, 43672)
GROUP BY SalesOrderID;
```

Despite the AS keyword being missing in some places, we've still changed the name output for every column:

```
Order Number MinOrderQty MaxOrderQty
------------ ----------- -----------
43660        1           1
43670        1           2
43672        1           6

(3 row(s) affected)
```

I must admit that I usually don't include the AS keyword in my aliasing, but I would also admit that it's a bad habit on my part. I've been working with SQL Server since before the AS keyword was available and have, unfortunately, become set in my ways about it (I simply forget to use it). I would, however, strongly encourage you to go ahead and make use of this extra word. Why? Well, first because it reads somewhat more clearly, and second, because it's the ANSI/ISO standard way of doing things.

So then, why did I even tell you about it? Well, I got you started doing it the right way — with the AS keyword — but I want you to be aware of alternate ways of doing things, so that you aren't confused when you see something that looks a little different.

COUNT(Expression|*)

The COUNT(*) function is about counting the rows in a query. To begin with, let's go with one of the most common varieties of queries:

```
SELECT COUNT(*)
FROM HumanResources.Employee
WHERE HumanResources.Employee.BusinessEntityID = 5;
```

The record set you get back looks a little different from what you're used to from earlier queries:

```
-----------
1

(1 row(s) affected)
```

Let's look at the differences. First, as with all columns that are returned as a result of a function call, there is no default column name. If you want there to be a column name, then you need to supply an alias. Next, you'll notice that we haven't really returned much of anything. So what does this record set represent? It is the number of rows that matched the WHERE condition in the query for the table(s) in the FROM clause.

> **Keep this query in mind. This is a basic query that you can use to verify that the exact number of rows that you expect to be in a table and match your WHERE condition are indeed in there.**

Just for fun, try running the query without the WHERE clause:

```
SELECT COUNT(*)
FROM HumanResources.Employee;
```

If you haven't done any deletions or insertions into the Employee table, then you should get a record set that looks something like this:

```
-----------
290

(1 row(s) affected)
```

What is that number? It's the total number of rows in the Employee table. This is another one to keep in mind for future use.

Now, we're just getting started! If you look back at the header for this section (the COUNT section), you'll see that there are two different ways of using COUNT. We've already discussed using COUNT with the * option. Now it's time to look at it with an expression — usually a column name.

First, try running the COUNT the old way, but against a new table:

```
SELECT COUNT(*)
FROM Person.Person;
```

This is a slightly larger table, so you get a higher COUNT:

```
-----------
19972

(1 row(s) affected)
```

Now alter your query to select the count for a specific column:

```
SELECT COUNT(AdditionalContactInfo)
FROM Person.Person;
```

You'll get a result that is a bit different from the one before:

```
-----
10
Warning: Null value is eliminated by an aggregate or other SET operation.

(1 row(s) affected)
```

This new result brings with it a question: why, since the `AdditionalContactInfo` column exists for every row, is there a different COUNT for `AdditionalContactInfo` than there is for the row count in general? The answer is fairly obvious when you stop to think about it — there isn't a value, as such, for the `AdditionalContactInfo` column in every row. In short, the COUNT, when used in any form other than COUNT(*), ignores NULL values. Let's verify that NULL values are the cause of the discrepancy:

```
SELECT COUNT(*)
FROM Person.Person
WHERE AdditionalContactInfo IS NULL;
```

This should yield the following record set:

```
-----------
19962

(1 row(s) affected)
```

Now let's do the math:

10 + 19,962 = 19,972

That's 10 records with a defined value in the `AdditionalContactInfo` field and 19,962 rows where the value in the `AdditionalContactInfo` field is NULL, making a total of 19,972 rows.

> **Actually, all aggregate functions ignore NULLs except for** COUNT(*)**. Think about this for a minute — it can have a very significant impact on your results. Many users expect NULL values in numeric fields to be treated as zero when performing averages, but a NULL does not equal zero, and as such shouldn't be used as one. If you perform an AVG or other aggregate function on a column with NULLs, the NULL values will not be part of the aggregation unless you manipulate them into a non-NULL value inside the function (using** COALESCE() **or** ISNULL()**, for example). We'll explore this further in Chapter 7, but beware of this when coding in T-SQL and when designing your database.**
>
> **Why does it matter in your database design? Well, it can have a bearing on whether you decide to allow NULL values in a field or not by thinking about the way that queries are likely to be run against the database and how you want your aggregates to work.**

Before we leave the COUNT function, we had better see it in action with the GROUP BY clause.

> **For this next example, you'll need to load and execute the** BuildAndPopulateEmployee2 .sql **file included with the downloadable source code (you can get that from either the** wrox.com **or** professionalsql.com **websites).**
>
> **All references to Employees in the following examples should be aimed at the new** Employees2 **table rather than** Employees.

Let's say our boss has asked us to find out the number of employees that report to each manager. The statements that we've done thus far would either count up all the rows in the table (COUNT(*)) or all the rows in the table that didn't have null values (COUNT(ColumnName)). When we add a GROUP BY clause, these aggregators perform exactly as they did before, except that they return a count for each grouping rather than the full table. We can use this to get our number of reports:

```
SELECT ManagerID, COUNT(*)
FROM HumanResources.Employee2
GROUP BY ManagerID;
```

Notice that we are grouping only by the ManagerID — the COUNT() function is an aggregator and, therefore, does not have to be included in the GROUP BY clause.

```
ManagerID
----------- -----------
NULL        1
1           3
4           3
5           4

(4 row(s) affected)
```

Our results tell us that the manager with 1 as his/her ManagerID has 3 people reporting to him or her, and that 3 people report to the manager with ManagerID 4 as well as 4 people reporting to ManagerID 5. We are also able to tell that one Employee record had a NULL value in the ManagerID field. This employee apparently doesn't report to anyone (hmmm, president of the company I suspect?).

It's probably worth noting that we, technically speaking, could use a GROUP BY clause without any kind of aggregator, but this wouldn't make sense. Why not? Well, SQL Server is going to wind up doing work on all the rows in order to group them, but functionally speaking you would get the same result with a DISTINCT option (which we'll look at shortly), and it would operate much faster.

Now that we've seen how to operate with groups, let's move on to one of the concepts that a lot of people have problems with. Of course, after reading the next section, you'll think it's a snap.

Placing Conditions on Groups with the HAVING Clause

Up to now, all of our conditions have been against specific rows. If a given column in a row doesn't have a specific value or isn't within a range of values, then the entire row is left out. All of this happens before the groupings are really even thought about.

What if we want to place conditions on what the groups themselves look like? In other words, what if we want every row to be added to a group, but then we want to say that only after the groups are fully accumulated are we ready to apply the condition. Well, that's where the HAVING clause comes in.

The HAVING clause is used only if there is also a GROUP BY in your query. Whereas the WHERE clause is applied to each row before it even has a chance to become part of a group, the HAVING clause is applied to the aggregated value for that group.

Let's start off with a slight modification to the GROUP BY query we used at the end of the previous section — the one that tells us the number of employees assigned to each manager's EmployeeID:

```
SELECT ManagerID AS Manager, COUNT(*) AS Reports
FROM HumanResources.Employee2
GROUP BY ManagerID;
```

In the next chapter, we'll learn how to put names on the EmployeeIDs that are in the Manager column. For now though, we'll just note that there appear to be three different managers in the company. Apparently, everyone reports to these three people, except for one person who doesn't have a manager assigned — that is probably our company president (we could write a query to verify that, but we'll just trust in our assumptions for now).

We didn't put a WHERE clause in this query, so the GROUP BY was operating on every row in the table and every row is included in a grouping. To test what would happen to our COUNTs, let's add a WHERE clause:

```
SELECT ManagerID AS Manager, COUNT(*) AS Reports
FROM HumanResources.Employee2
WHERE EmployeeID != 5
GROUP BY ManagerID;
```

This yields one slight change that may be somewhat different than expected:

```
Manager      Reports
-----------  -----------
NULL         1
1            3
4            2
5            4

(4 row(s) affected)
```

No rows were eliminated from the result set, but the result for ManagerID 4 was decreased by one (what the heck does this have to do with ManagerID 5?). You see, the WHERE clause eliminated the one row where the EmployeeID was 5. As it happens, EmployeeID 5 reports to ManagerID 4, so the total for ManagerID 4 was one less (EmployeeID 5 is no longer counted for this query). ManagerID 5 was not affected, as we eliminated him or her as a report (as an EmployeeID) rather than as a manager. The key thing here is to realize that EmployeeID 5 was eliminated *before* the GROUP BY was applied.

I want to look at things a bit differently though. See if you can work out how to answer the following question. Which managers have more than three people reporting to them? You can look at the query without the WHERE clause and tell by the COUNT, but how do you tell programmatically? That is, what if we need this query to return only the managers with more than three people reporting to them? If you try to work this out with a WHERE clause, you'll find that there isn't a way to return rows based on the aggregation. The WHERE clause is already completed by the system before the aggregation is executed. That's where our HAVING clause comes in:

```
SELECT ManagerID AS Manager, COUNT(*) AS Reports
FROM HumanResources.Employee2
WHERE EmployeeID != 5
GROUP BY ManagerID
HAVING COUNT(*) > 3;
```

Try it out and you'll come up with something a little bit more like what we were after:

```
Manager      Reports
----------- -----------
5            4

(1 row(s) affected)
```

There is only one manager that has more than three employees reporting to him or her.

Outputting XML Using the FOR XML Clause

SQL Server has a number of features to natively support XML. From being able to index XML data effectively to validating XML against a schema document, SQL Server is very robust in meeting XML data storage and manipulation needs.

One of the oldest features in SQL Server's XML support arsenal is the FOR XML clause you can use with the SELECT statement. Use of this clause causes your query output to be supplied in an XML format, and a number of options are available to allow fairly specific control of exactly how that XML output is styled. I'm going to shy away from the details of this clause for now, since XML is a discussion unto itself, but we'll spend extra time with XML in Chapter 16. So for now, just trust me that it's better to learn the basics first.

Making Use of Hints Using the OPTION Clause

The OPTION clause is a way of overriding some of SQL Server's ideas of how best to run your query. Since SQL Server really does usually know what's best for your query, using the OPTION clause will more often hurt you than help you. Still, it's nice to know that it's there, just in case.

This is another one of those "I'll get there later" subjects. We talk about query hints extensively when we talk about locking later in the book, but until you understand what you're affecting with your hints, there is little basis for understanding the OPTION clause. As such, we'll defer discussion of it for now.

The DISTINCT and ALL Predicates

There's just one more major concept to get through and we'll be ready to move from the SELECT statement on to action statements. It has to do with repeated data.

Let's say, for example, that we wanted a list of the IDs for all of the products that we have sold at least 30 of in an individual sale (more than 30 at one time). We can easily get that information from the SalesOrderDetail table with the following query:

```
SELECT ProductID
FROM Sales.SalesOrderDetail
WHERE OrderQty > 30;
```

What we get back is one row matching the ProductID for every row in the SalesOrderDetail table that has an order quantity that is more than 30:

```
ProductID
-----------
709
863
863
863
863
863
863
863
715
863
...
...
869
869
867

(31 row(s) affected)
```

While this meets your needs from a technical standpoint, it doesn't really meet your needs from a reality standpoint. Look at all those duplicate rows! While we could look through and see which products sold more than 30 at a time, the number of rows returned and the number of duplicates can quickly become overwhelming. Like the problems we've discussed before, we have an answer. It comes in the form of the DISTINCT predicate on your SELECT statement.

Try re-running the query with a slight change:

```
SELECT DISTINCT ProductID
FROM Sales.SalesOrderDetail
WHERE OrderQty > 30;
```

Now you come up with a true list of the ProductIDs that sold more than 30 at one time:

```
ProductID
-----------
863
869
709
864
867
715

(6 row(s) affected)
```

As you can see, this cut down the size of your list substantially and made the contents of the list more relevant. Another side benefit of this query is that it will actually perform better than the first one. Why? Well, I go into that later in the book when I discuss performance issues further, but for now, suffice it to say that not having to return every single row means that SQL Server doesn't have to do quite as much work in order to meet the needs of this query.

As the old commercials on television go, "But wait! There's more!" We're not done with DISTINCT yet. Indeed, the next example is one that you might be able to use as a party trick to impress your programmer friends. You see, this is one that an amazing number of SQL programmers don't even realize you can do. DISTINCT can be used as more than just a predicate for a SELECT statement. It can also be used in the expression for an aggregate. What do I mean? Let's compare three queries.

First, grab a row count for the SalesOrderDetail table in AdventureWorks:

```
SELECT COUNT(*)
  FROM Sales.SalesOrderDetail;
```

If you haven't modified the SalesOrderDetail table, this should yield you around 121,317 rows.

Now run the same query using a specific column to COUNT:

```
SELECT COUNT(SalesOrderID)
  FROM Sales.SalesOrderDetail;
```

Since the SalesOrderID column is part of the key for this table, it can't contain any NULLs (more on this in the chapter in indexing). Therefore, the net count for this query is always going to be the same as the COUNT(*) — in this case, it's 121,317.

> *Key* is a term used to describe a column or combination of columns that can be used to identify a row within a table. There are actually several different kinds of keys (we'll see much more on these in Chapters 6, 8, and 9), but when the word "key" is used by itself, it is usually referring to a table's primary key. A primary key is a column (or group of columns) that is (are) effectively the unique name for that row. When you refer to a row using its primary key, you can be certain that you will get back only one row, because no two rows are allowed to have the same primary key within the same table.

Now for the fun part. Modify the query again:

```
SELECT COUNT(DISTINCT SalesOrderID)
  FROM Sales.SalesOrderDetail;
```

Now we get a substantially different result:

```
-----------
31465

(1 row(s) affected)
```

All duplicate rows were eliminated before the aggregation occurred, so you have substantially fewer rows.

Note that you can use DISTINCT *with any aggregate function, although I question whether many of the functions have any practical use for it. For example, I can't imagine why you would want an average of just the* DISTINCT *rows.*

That takes us to the ALL predicate. With one exception, it is a very rare thing indeed to see someone actually including an ALL in a statement. ALL is perhaps best understood as being the opposite of DISTINCT. Where DISTINCT is used to filter out duplicate rows, ALL says to include every row. ALL is the default for any SELECT statement, except for situations where there is a UNION. We will discuss the impact of ALL in a UNION situation in the next chapter, but for now, realize that ALL is happening any time you don't ask for a DISTINCT.

Adding Data with the INSERT Statement

By now you should pretty much have the hang of basic SELECT statements. We would be doing well to stop here, save for a pretty major problem. We wouldn't have very much data to look at if we didn't have some way of getting it into the database in the first place. That's where the INSERT statement comes in.

The full syntax for INSERT has several parts:

```
INSERT [TOP ( <expression> ) [PERCENT] ] [INTO] <tabular object>
   [(<column list>)]
   [ OUTPUT <output clause> ]
{ VALUES (<data values>) [,(<data values>)] [, …n]
   | <table source>
   | EXEC <prodecure>
   | DEFAULT VALUES
```

This is a bit wordy to worry about now, so let's simplify it a bit. The more basic syntax for an INSERT statement looks like this:

```
INSERT [INTO] <table>
   [(<column list>)]
VALUES (<data values>) [,(<data values>)] [, …n]
```

Let's look at the parts.

INSERT is the action statement. It tells SQL Server what it is that we're going to be doing with this statement; everything that comes after this keyword is merely spelling out the details of that action.

The INTO keyword is pretty much just fluff. Its sole purpose in life is to make the overall statement more readable. It is completely optional, but I highly recommend its use for the very reason that they added it to the statement: It makes things much easier to read. As we go through this section, try a few of the statements both with and without the INTO keyword. It's a little less typing if you leave it out, but it's also quite a bit stranger to read — it's up to you.

Next comes the table (technically table, view, or a common table expression, but we're just going to worry about tables for now) into which you are inserting.

Until this point, things have been pretty straightforward. Now comes the part that's a little more difficult: the column list. An explicit column list (where you specifically state the columns to receive values) is optional, but not supplying one means that you have to be extremely careful. If you don't provide an explicit column list, then each value in your INSERT statement will be assumed to match up with a column in the same ordinal position of the table in order (first value to first column, second value to second column, and so on). Additionally, a value must be supplied for every column, in order, until you reach the last column that both does not accept NULLs and has no default. (You'll see more about what I mean shortly.) The exception is an IDENTITY column, which should be skipped when supplying values (SQL Server will fill that in for you). In summary, this will be a list of one or more columns that you are going to be providing data for in the next part of the statement.

Finally, you'll supply the values to be inserted. There are two ways of doing this, but for now, we'll focus on single line inserts that use data that you explicitly provide. To supply the values, we'll start with the VALUES keyword, then follow that with a list of values separated by commas and enclosed in parentheses. The number of items in the value list must exactly match the number of columns in the column list. The data type of each value must match or be implicitly convertible to the type of the column with which it corresponds (they are taken in order).

> *On the issue of whether to specifically state a value for all columns or not, I really recommend naming every column every time, even if you just use the DEFAULT keyword or explicitly state NULL. DEFAULT will tell SQL Server to use whatever the default value is for that column (if there isn't one, you'll get an error).*

What's nice about this is the readability of code; this way it's really clear what you are doing. In addition, I find that explicitly addressing every column leads to fewer bugs.

Whew! That's confusing, so let's practice with this some.

To get started with INSERTs, UPDATEs, and DELETEs, we're going to create a couple of tables to work with. (AdventureWorks is a bit too bulky for just starting out.) To be ready to try these next few examples, you'll need to run a few statements that we haven't really discussed as yet. Try not to worry about the contents of this yet; we'll get to discussing them fully in Chapter 5.

You can either type these and execute them, or use the file called Chap3CreateExampleTables.sql included with the downloadable files for this book.

> **This next block of code is what is called a script. This particular script is made up of one batch. We will be examining batches at length in Chapter 11.**

```
/* This script creates a couple of tables for use with
** several examples in Chapter 3 of Beginning SQL Server
** 2008 Programming
*/

CREATE TABLE Stores
(
    StoreCode     char(4)       NOT NULL PRIMARY KEY,
    Name          varchar(40)   NOT NULL,
    Address       varchar(40)   NULL,
```

```
    City          varchar(20)   NOT NULL,
    State         char(2)       NOT NULL,
    Zip           char(5)       NOT NULL
);

CREATE TABLE Sales
(
    OrderNumber   varchar(20)   NOT NULL PRIMARY KEY,
    StoreCode     char(4)       NOT NULL
        FOREIGN KEY REFERENCES Stores(StoreCode),
    OrderDate     date          NOT NULL,
    Quantity      int           NOT NULL,
    Terms         varchar(12)   NOT NULL,
    TitleID       int           NOT NULL
);
```

Most of the inserts we're going to do in this chapter will be to the `Stores` table we just created, so let's review the properties for that table. To do this, expand the Tables node of whichever database was current when you ran the preceding script (probably `AdventureWorks` given the other examples we've been running) in the Object Explorer within the Management Studio. Then expand the Columns node as shown in Figure 3-3.

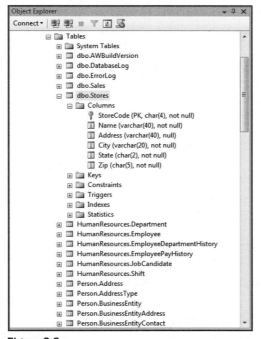

Figure 3-3

In this table, every column happens to be a `char` or `varchar`.

For your first insert, we'll eliminate the optional column list and allow SQL Server to assume we're providing something for every column:

```
INSERT INTO Stores
VALUES
    ('TEST', 'Test Store', '1234 Anywhere Street', 'Here', 'NY', '00319');
```

As stated earlier, unless we provide a different column list (we'll cover how to provide a column list shortly), all the values have to be supplied in the same order as the columns are defined in the table. After executing this query, you should see a statement that tells you that one row was affected by your query. Now, just for fun, try running the exact same query a second time. You'll get the following error:

```
Msg 2627, Level 14, State 1, Line 1
Violation of PRIMARY KEY constraint 'PK__Stores__1387E197'. Cannot insert duplicate
key in object 'dbo.Stores'.
The statement has been terminated.
```

Why did it work the first time and not the second? Because this table has a primary key that does not allow duplicate values for the `StoreCode` field. As long as we changed that one field, we could have left the rest of the columns alone and it would have taken the new row. We'll see more of primary keys in the chapters on design and constraints.

So let's see what we inserted:

```
SELECT *
FROM Stores
WHERE StoreCode = 'TEST';
```

This query yields us exactly what we inserted:

```
StoreCode Name          Address                 City                 State Zip
--------- ------------  ----------------------  -------------------  ----- -----
TEST      Test Store    1234 Anywhere Street    Here                 NY    00319

(1 row(s) affected)
```

Note that I've trimmed a few spaces off the end of each column to help it fit on a page neatly, but the true data is just as we expected it to be.

Now let's try it again with modifications for inserting into specific columns:

```
INSERT INTO Stores
    (StoreCode, Name, City, State, Zip)
VALUES
    ('TST2', 'Test Store', 'Here', 'NY', '00319');
```

Note that on the line with the data values we've changed just two things. First, we've changed the value we are inserting into the primary key column so it won't generate an error. Second, we've eliminated the value that was associated with the `Address` column, since we have omitted that column in our column list. There are a few different instances where we can skip a column in a column list and not provide any data for it in the INSERT statement. For now, we're just taking advantage of the fact that the Address column is not a required column — that is, it accepts NULLs. Since we're not providing a value for this column and since it has no default (we'll see more on defaults later on), this column will be set to NULL when we perform our INSERT. Let's verify that by rerunning our test SELECT statement with one slight modification:

```
SELECT *
FROM Stores
WHERE StoreCode = 'TST2';
```

Now we see something a little different:

```
StoreCode   Name          Address           City      State     Zip
---------   ----------    ---------------   -------   --------   ------
TST2        Test Store    NULL              Here      NY         00319

(1 row(s) affected)
```

Notice that a NULL was inserted for the column that we skipped.

Note that the columns have to be *nullable* in order to do this. What does that mean? Pretty much what it sounds like: It means that you are allowed to have NULL values for that column. Believe me, we will be discussing the nullability of columns at great length in this book, but for now, just realize that some columns allow NULLs and some don't. We can always skip providing information for columns that allow NULLs.

If, however, the column is not nullable, then one of three conditions must exist, or we will receive an error and the INSERT will be rejected:

❑   The column has been defined with a *default value*. A default is a constant value that is inserted if no other value is provided. We will learn how to define defaults in Chapter 7.

❑   The column is defined to receive some form of system-generated value. The most common of these is an IDENTITY value (covered more in the design chapter), where the system typically starts counting first at one row, increments to two for the second, and so on. These aren't really row numbers, as rows may be deleted later on and numbers can, under some conditions, get skipped, but they serve to make sure each row has its own identifier.

❑   We supply a value for the column.

Just for completeness, let's perform one more INSERT statement. This time, we'll insert a new sale into the Sales table. To view the properties of the Sales table, we can either open its Properties dialog as we did with the Stores table, or we can run a system-stored procedure called sp_help. sp_help will report information about any database object, user-defined data type, or SQL Server data type. The syntax for using sp_help is as follows:

```
EXEC sp_help <name>
```

To view the properties of the Sales table, we just have to type the following into the Query window:

```
EXEC sp_help Sales;
```

Which returns (among other things):

```
Column_name             Type         Computed    Length       Prec   Scale Nullable
----------------------  -----------  ----------- -----------  -----  ----- --------
OrderNumber             varchar      no          20                        no
StoreCode               char         no          4                         no
OrderDate               date         no          3            10     0     no
Quantity                int          no          4            10     0     no
Terms                   varchar      no          12                        no
TitleID                 int          no          4            10     0     no
```

The `Sales` table has six columns in it, but pay particular attention to the `Quantity`, `OrderDate`, and `TitleID` columns; they are of types that we haven't done `INSERT`s with up to this point.

What you need to pay attention to in this query is how to format the types as you're inserting them. We do *not* use quotes for numeric values as we have with our character data. However, the `date` data type does require quotes. (Essentially, it goes in as a string and it then gets converted to a date.)

```
INSERT INTO Sales
    (StoreCode, OrderNumber, OrderDate, Quantity, Terms, TitleID)
VALUES
    ('TEST', 'TESTORDER', '01/01/1999', 10, 'NET 30', 1234567);
```

This gets back the now familiar `(1 row(s) affected)` message. Notice, however, that I moved around the column order in my insert. The data in the VALUES portion of the insert needs to match the column list, but the column list can be in any order you choose to make it; it does not have to be in the order the columns are listed in the physical table.

> Note that while I've used the MM/DD/YYYY format that is popular in the U.S., you can use a wide variety of other formats (such as the internationally more popular YYYY-MM-DD) with equal success. The default for your server will vary depending on whether you purchase a localized copy of SQL Server or if the setting has been changed on the server.

Multirow Inserts

New with SQL Server 2008 is the ability to `INSERT` multiple rows at one time. To do this, just keep tacking on additional comma-delimited insertion values, for example:

```
INSERT INTO Sales
    (StoreCode, OrderNumber, OrderDate, Quantity, Terms, TitleID)
VALUES
    ('TST2', 'TESTORDER2', '01/01/1999', 10, 'NET 30', 1234567),
    ('TST2', 'TESTORDER3', '02/01/1999', 10, 'NET 30', 1234567);
```

This inserts both sets of values using a single statement. To check what we got, let's go ahead and look in the `Sales` table:

```
SELECT *
FROM Sales;
```

And sure enough, we get back the one row we inserted earlier along with the two rows we just inserted:

```
OrderNumber          StoreCode OrderDate  Quantity    Terms         TitleID
-------------------- --------- ---------- ----------- ------------- -----------
TESTORDER            TEST      1999-01-01 10          NET 30        1234567
TESTORDER2           TST2      1999-01-01 10          NET 30        1234567
TESTORDER3           TST2      1999-02-01 10          NET 30        1234567

(3 row(s) affected)
```

This new feature has the potential to really boost performance in situations where you are performing multiple INSERTs. *Previously, your client application would have to issue a completely separate* INSERT *statement for each row of data you wanted to* INSERT *(there were some ways around this, but they required extra thought and effort that it seems few developers were willing to put in). Using this method can eliminate many round trips to your server; just keep in mind that it also means that your application will not be backward compatible to prior versions of SQL Server.*

The INSERT INTO . . . SELECT Statement

What if we have a block of data that we want INSERTed? As we have just seen, we can perform multi-row INSERTs explicitly, but what if we want to INSERT a block of data that can be selected from another source, such as:

❑   Another table in your database

❑   A totally different database on the same server

❑   A heterogeneous query from another SQL Server or other data

❑   The same table (usually you're doing some sort of math or other adjustment in your SELECT statement, in this case)

The INSERT INTO . . . SELECT statement can INSERT data from any of these. The syntax for this statement comes from a combination of the two statements we've seen thus far — the INSERT statement and the SELECT statement. It looks something like this:

```
INSERT INTO <table name>
[<column list>]
<SELECT statement>
```

The result set created from the SELECT statement becomes the data that is added in your INSERT statement.

Let's check this out by doing something that, if you get into advanced coding, you'll find yourself doing all too often — SELECTing some data into some form of temporary table. In this case, we're going to declare a variable of type table and fill it with rows of data from our Orders table:

> **Like our early example database creation, this next block of code is what is called a script. Again, we will be examining batches at length in Chapter 11.**

```
/* This next statement is going to use code to change the "current" database
** to AdventureWorks2008. This makes certain, right in the code that we are going
** to the correct database.
*/

USE AdventureWorks2008;

/* This next statement declares our working table.
** This particular table is actually a variable we are declaring on the fly.
*/

DECLARE @MyTable Table
(
    SalesOrderID        int,
    CustomerID          char(5)
);

/* Now that we have our table variable, we're ready to populate it with data
** from our SELECT statement. Note that we could just as easily insert the
** data into a permanent table (instead of a table variable).
*/
INSERT INTO @MyTable
    SELECT SalesOrderID, CustomerID
    FROM AdventureWorks2008.Sales.SalesOrderHeader
    WHERE SalesOrderID BETWEEN 44000 AND 44010;

-- Finally, let's make sure that the data was inserted like we think
SELECT *
FROM @MyTable;
```

This should yield you results that look like this:

```
(11 row(s) affected)
SalesOrderID CustomerID
------------ ----------
44000        27918
44001        28044
44002        14572
44003        19325
44004        28061
44005        26629
44006        16744
44007        25555
44008        27678
44009        27759
44010        13680

(11 row(s) affected)
```

The first instance of (11 row(s) affected) we see is the effect of the INSERT...SELECT statement at work. Our SELECT statement returned three rows, so that's what got INSERTed into our table. We then used a straight SELECT statement to verify the INSERT.

> Note that if you try running a SELECT against @MyTable by itself (that is, outside this script), you're going to get an error. @MyTable is a declared variable and it exists only as long as our batch is running. After that, it is automatically destroyed.
>
> It's also worth noting that we could have used what's called a *temporary table*. This is similar in nature, but doesn't work in quite the same way. We will revisit temp tables and table variables in Chapters 11 through 13.

Changing What You've Got with the UPDATE Statement

The UPDATE statement, like most SQL statements, does pretty much what it sounds like it does — it updates existing data. The structure is a little bit different from a SELECT, although you'll notice definite similarities. Like the INSERT statement, it has a fairly complex set of options, but a more basic version that will meet the vast majority of your needs.

The full syntax supports the same TOP and similar predicates that were supported under SELECT and INSERT:

```
UPDATE [TOP ( <expression> ) [PERCENT] ] <tabular object>
  SET <column> = <value>[.WRITE(<expression>, <offset>, <length>)]
    [,<column> = <value>[.WRITE(<expression>, <offset>, <length>)]]
  [ OUTPUT <output clause> ]
[FROM <source table(s)>]
[WHERE <restrictive condition>]
```

Let's look at the more basic syntax:

```
UPDATE <table name>
SET <column> = <value> [,<column> = <value>]
[FROM <source table(s)>]
[WHERE <restrictive condition>]
```

An UPDATE can be created from multiple tables, but can affect only one table. What do I mean by that? Well, we can build a condition, or retrieve values from any number of different tables, but only one table at a time can be the subject of the UPDATE action. Don't sweat this one too much. We haven't looked at joining multiple tables yet (next chapter folks!), so we won't get into complex UPDATE statements here. For now, we'll look at simple updates.

Let's start by doing some updates to the data that we inserted in the INSERT statement section. Let's rerun that query to look at one row of inserted data. (Don't forget to switch back to the pubs database.):

```
SELECT *
FROM Stores
WHERE StoreCode = 'TEST';
```

Which returns the following:

```
StoreCode      Name            Address                 City     State      Zip
----------     ------------    ---------------------   -------  ---------  ----
TEST           Test Store      1234 Anywhere Street    Here     NY         00319
```

Let's update the value in the `City` column:

```
UPDATE Stores
SET City = 'There'
WHERE StoreCode = 'TEST';
```

Much like when we ran the `INSERT` statement, we don't get much back from SQL Server:

```
(1 row(s) affected)
```

Yet when we run our `SELECT` statement again, we see that the value has indeed changed:

```
StoreCode      Name            Address                 City     State      Zip
----------     ------------    ---------------------   -------  ---------  ----
TEST           Test Store      1234 Anywhere Street    There    NY         00319
```

Note that we could have changed more than one column just by adding a comma and the additional column expression. For example, the following statement would have updated both columns:

```
UPDATE Stores
SET city = 'There', state = 'NY'
WHERE StoreCode = 'TEST';
```

If we choose, we can use an expression for the `SET` clause instead of the explicit values we've used thus far. For example, we could add a suffix on all of the store names by concatenating the existing store name with a suffix:

```
UPDATE Stores
SET Name = Name + ' - ' + StoreCode;
```

After executing that `UPDATE`, run a `SELECT` statement on Stores:

```
SELECT *
FROM Stores
```

You should see the `Name` suffixed by the `StoreCode`:

```
StoreCode      Name               Address                 City     State    Zip
----------     ---------------    ---------------------   -------  ------   ----
TEST           Test Store - TEST  1234 Anywhere Street    There    NY       00319
TST2           Test Store - TST2  NULL                    Here     NY       00319
```

As you can see, a single `UPDATE` statement can be fairly powerful. Even so, this is really just the beginning. We'll see even more advanced updates in later chapters.

> While SQL Server is nice enough to let us UPDATE pretty much any column (there are a few that we can't, such as timestamps), be very careful about updating primary keys. Doing so puts you at very high risk of *orphaning* other data (data that has a reference to the data you're changing).
>
> For example, the StoreCode field in the Stores table is a primary key. If we decide to change StoreCode 10 to 35 in Stores, then any data in the Sales table that relates to that store may be orphaned and lost if the StoreCode value in all of the records relating to StoreCode 10 is not also updated to 35. As it happens, there is a constraint that references the Stores table, so SQL Server would prevent such an orphaning situation in this case (we'll investigate constraints in Chapter 7), but updating primary keys is risky at best.

The DELETE Statement

The version of the DELETE statement that we'll cover in this chapter may be one of the easiest statements of them all. Even in the more complex syntax, there's no column list, just a table name and (usually) a WHERE clause. The full version looks like this:

```
DELETE [TOP ( <expression> ) [PERCENT] ] [FROM] <tabular object>
  [ OUTPUT <output clause> ]
[FROM <table or join condition>]
[WHERE <search condition> | CURRENT OF [GLOBAL] <cursor name>]
```

The basic syntax couldn't be much easier:

```
DELETE <table name>
[WHERE <condition>]
```

The WHERE clause works just like all the WHERE clauses we've seen thus far. We don't need to provide a column list because we are deleting the entire row. (You can't delete half a row, for example.)

Because this is so easy, we'll perform only a couple of quick DELETEs that are focused on cleaning up the INSERTs that we performed earlier in the chapter. First, let's run a SELECT to make sure the first of those rows is still there:

```
SELECT *
FROM Stores
WHERE StoreCode = 'TEST';
```

If you haven't already deleted it, you should come up with a single row that matches what we added with our original INSERT statement. Now let's get rid of it:

```
DELETE Stores
WHERE StoreCode = 'TEST';
```

Note that we've run into a situation where SQL Server is refusing to DELETE this row because of referential integrity violations:

```
Msg 547, Level 16, State 0, Line 1
The DELETE statement conflicted with the REFERENCE constraint
"FK__Sales__StoreCode__1B29035F". The conflict occurred in database
"AdventureWorks", table "dbo.Sales", column 'StoreCode'.
The statement has been terminated.
```

SQL Server won't let us DELETE a row if it is referenced as part of a foreign key constraint. We'll see much more on foreign keys in Chapter 7, but for now, just keep in mind that if one row references another row (either in the same or a different table — it doesn't matter) using a foreign key, then the referencing row must be deleted before the referenced row can be deleted. One of our INSERT statements inserted a record into the Sales table that had a StoreCode of TEST — this record is referencing the record we have just attempted to DELETE.

Before we can delete the record from our Stores table, we must delete the record it is referencing in the Sales table:

```
DELETE Sales
WHERE StoreCode = 'TEST';
```

Now we can successfully rerun the first DELETE statement:

```
DELETE Stores
WHERE StoreCode_id = 'TEST';
```

You can do two quick checks to verify that the data was indeed deleted. The first happens automatically when the DELETE statement is executed; you should get a message telling you that one row was affected. The other quick check is to rerun the SELECT statement; you should get zero rows back.

For one more easy practice DELETE, we'll also kill that second row by making just a slight change:

```
DELETE Sales
WHERE StoreCode = 'TST2';
```

That's it for simple DELETEs! Like the other statements in this chapter, we'll come back to the DELETE statement when we're ready for more complex search conditions.

Summary

T-SQL is SQL Server's own brand of ANSI/ISO SQL or Structured Query Language. T-SQL is largely ANSI/ISO compliant, but it also has a number of its own extensions to the language. We'll see more of those in later chapters.

Even though, for backward compatibility, SQL Server has a number of different syntax choices that are effectively the same, wherever possible you ought to use the ANSI form. Where there are different choices available, I will usually show you all of the choices, but again, stick with the ANSI/ISO version wherever possible. This is particularly important for situations where you think your backend — or database server — might change at some point. Your ANSI code will more than likely run on the new database server; however, code that is only T-SQL definitely will not.

In this chapter, you have gained a solid taste of making use of single table statements in T-SQL, but the reality is that you often need information from more than one table. In the next chapter, we will learn how to make use of JOINs to allow us to use multiple tables.

Exercises

1. Write a query that outputs all of the columns and all of the rows from the Product table (in the Production schema) of the pubs database.

2. Modify the query in Exercise 1 so it filters down the result to just the products that have no ProductSubcategoryID. (HINT: There are 209, and you will need to be looking for NULL values.)

3. Add a new row into the ProductLocation (in the Production schema) table in the Adventure-Works database.

4. Remove the row you just added.

JOINs

Feel like a seasoned professional yet? Let me dash that feeling right away (just kidding)! While we now have the basic statements under our belt, they are only a small part of the bigger picture of the statements we will run. To put it simply, there is often not that much you can do with just one table — especially in a highly normalized database.

A *normalized* database is one where the data has been broken out from larger tables into many smaller tables for the purpose of eliminating repeating data, saving space, improving performance, and increasing data integrity. It's great stuff and vital to relational databases; however, it also means that you wind up getting your data from here, there, and everywhere.

> We will be looking into the concepts of normalization extensively in Chapter 8. For now, though, just keep in mind that the more normalized your database is, the more likely that you're going to have to join multiple tables together in order to get all the data you want.

In this chapter, I'm going to introduce you to the process of combining tables into one result set by using the various forms of the JOIN clause. These will include:

- ❑ INNER JOIN
- ❑ OUTER JOIN (both LEFT and RIGHT)
- ❑ FULL JOIN
- ❑ CROSS JOIN

We'll also learn that there is more than one syntax available to use for joins, and that one particular syntax is the right choice. In addition, we'll take a look at the UNION operator, which allows us to combine the results of two queries into one.

JOINs

When we are operating in a normalized environment, we frequently run into situations in which not all of the information that we want is in one table. In other cases, all the information we want returned is in one table, but the information we want to place conditions on is in another table. This is where the JOIN clause comes in.

A JOIN does just what it sounds like — it puts the information from two tables together into one result set. We can think of a result set as being a "virtual" table. It has both columns and rows, and the columns have data types. Indeed, in Chapter 7, we'll see how to treat a result set as if it were a table and use it for other queries.

How exactly does a JOIN put the information from two tables into a single result set? Well, that depends on how you tell it to put the data together — that's why there are four different kinds of JOINs. The thing that all JOINs have in common is that they match one record up with one or more other records to make a record that is a superset created by the combined columns of both records.

For example, let's take a record from a table we'll call Films:

FilmID	FilmName	YearMade
1	My Fair Lady	1964

Now let's follow that up with a record from a table called Actors:

FilmID	FirstName	LastName
1	Rex	Harrison

With a JOIN, we could create one record from two records found in totally separate tables:

ilmID	FilmName	YearMade	FirstName	LastName
1	My Fair Lady	1964	Rex	Harrison

This JOIN (at least apparently) joins records in a one-to-one relationship. We have one Films record joining to one Actors record.

Let's expand things just a bit and see if you can see what's happening. I've added another record to the Actors table:

FilmID	FirstName	LastName
1	Rex	Harrison
1	Audrey	Hepburn

Now let's see what happens when we join that to the very same (only one record) `Films` table:

FilmID	FilmName	YearMade	FirstName	LastName
1	My Fair Lady	1964	Rex	Harrison
1	My Fair Lady	1964	Audrey	Hepburn

As you can see, the result has changed a bit — we are no longer seeing things as being one-to-one, but rather one-to-two, or more appropriately, what we would call one-to-many. We can use that single record in the `Films` table as many times as necessary to have complete (joined) information about the matching records in the `Actors` table.

Have you noticed how they are matching up? It is, of course, by matching up the `FilmID` field from the two tables to create one record out of two.

The examples we have used here with such a limited data set would actually yield the same results no matter what kind of `JOIN` was used. Let's move on now and look at the specifics of the different `JOIN` types.

INNER JOINs

`INNER JOINs` are far and away the most common kind of `JOIN`. They match records together based on one or more common fields, as do most `JOINs`, but an `INNER JOIN` returns only the records where there are matches for whatever field(s) you have said are to be used for the `JOIN`. In our previous examples, every record was included in the result set at least once, but this situation is rarely the case in the real world.

Let's modify our tables to use an `INNER JOIN`; here's our `Films` table:

FilmID	FilmName	YearMade
1	My Fair Lady	1964
2	Unforgiven	1992

And our `Actors` table:

FilmID	FirstName	LastName
1	Rex	Harrison
1	Audrey	Hepburn
2	Clint	Eastwood
5	Humphrey	Bogart

Using an INNER JOIN, the result set would look like this:

FilmID	FilmName	YearMade	FirstName	LastName
1	My Fair Lady	1964	Rex	Harrison
1	My Fair Lady	1964	Audrey	Hepburn
2	Unforgiven	1992	Clint	Eastwood

Notice that Bogey was left out of this result set. That's because he didn't have a matching record in the Films table. If there isn't a match in both tables, then the record isn't returned. Enough theory — let's try this out in code.

The preferred code for an INNER JOIN looks something like this:

```
SELECT <select list>
FROM <first_table>
<join_type> <second_table>
        [ON <join_condition>]
```

This is the ANSI syntax, and you'll have much better luck with it on non-SQL Server database systems than you will if you use the proprietary syntax required prior to version 6.5 (and still used by many developers today). We'll take a look at the other syntax later in the chapter.

It is probably worth noting that the term "ANSI syntax" is there because the original foundations of it were created as part of an ANSI standard in the mid 1980s. That standard has since been taken over by the International Standards Organization (ISO), so you may hear it referred to based on either standards organization.

Fire up the Management Studio and take a test drive of INNER JOINs using the following code against AdventureWorks2008:

```
SELECT *
FROM Person.Person
INNER JOIN HumanResources.Employee
    ON Person.Person.BusinessEntityID = HumanResources.Employee.BusinessEntityID
```

The results of this query are too wide to print in this book, but if you run this, you should get something on the order of 290 rows back. There are several things worth noting about the results:

❑ The BusinessEntityID column appears twice, but there's nothing to say which one is from which table.

❑ All columns were returned from both tables.

❑ The first columns listed were from the first table listed.

We can figure out which `BusinessEntityID` is which just by looking at what table we selected first and matching it with the first `BusinessEntityID` column that shows up, but this is tedious at best, and at worst, prone to errors. That's one of many reasons why using the plain * operator in JOINs is ill-advised. In the case of an INNER JOIN, however, it's not really that much of a problem because we know that both `BusinessEntityID` columns, even though they came from different tables, will be exact duplicates of each other. How do we know that? Think about it — since we're doing an INNER JOIN on those two columns, they have to match or the record wouldn't have been returned! Don't get in the habit of counting on this, however. When we look at other JOIN types, we'll find that we can't depend on the JOIN values being equal.

As for all columns being returned from both tables, that is as expected. We used the * operator, which as we've learned before is going to return all columns to us. As I mentioned earlier, the use of the * operator in joins is a bad habit. It's quick and easy, but it's also dirty — it is error-prone and can result in poor performance.

As I indicated back in Chapter 3, one good principle to adopt early on is to select what you need and need what you select. What I'm getting at here is that every additional record or column that you return takes up additional network bandwidth and often additional query processing on your SQL Server. The upshot is that selecting unnecessary information hurts performance not only for the current user, but also for every other user of the system and for users of the network on which the SQL Server resides.

Select only the columns that you are going to be using and make your WHERE clause as restrictive as possible.

If you insist on using the * operator, you should use it only for the tables from which you need all the columns. That's right — the * operator can be used on a per-table basis. For example, if we wanted all of the base information for our contact, but only needed the `Employee` table to figure out their `JobTitle`, we could have changed your query to read:

```
SELECT Person.BusinessEntity.*, JobTitle
FROM Person.BusinessEntity
INNER JOIN HumanResources.Employee
ON Person.BusinessEntity.BusinessEntityID =
HumanResources.Employee.BusinessEntityID
```

If you scroll over to the right in the results of this query, you'll see that most of the Employee-related information is now gone. Indeed, we also only have one instance of the `BusinessEntityID` column. What we get in our result set contains all the columns from the `BusinessEntity` table (since we used the * qualified for just that table — your one instance of `BusinessEntityID` came from this part of the SELECT list) and the only column that had the name `JobTitle` (which happened to be from the `Employee` table). Now let's try it again, with only one slight change:

```
SELECT Person.BusinessEntity.*, BusinessEntityID
FROM Person.BusinessEntity
INNER JOIN HumanResources.Employee
        ON Person.BusinessEntity.BusinessEntityID =
HumanResources.Employee.BusinessEntityID
```

Uh, oh — this is a problem. You get an error back:

```
Msg 209, Level 16, State 1, Line 1
Ambiguous column name 'BusinessEntityID'.
```

Why did `JobTitle` work and `BusinessEntityID` not work? For just the reason SQL Server has indicated — our column name is ambiguous. While `JobTitle` exists only in the `Employee` table, `BusinessEntityID` appears in both tables. SQL Server has no way of knowing which one we want. All the instances where we have returned `BusinessEntityID` up to this point have been resolvable: that is, SQL Server could figure out which column was which. In the first query (where we used a plain * operator), we asked SQL Server to return everything — that would include *both* `BusinessEntityID` columns, so no name resolution was necessary. In our second example (where we qualified the * to be only for `BusinessEntity`), we again said nothing specifically about which `BusinessEntityID` column to use — instead, we said pull everything from the `Contact` table and `BusinessEntityID` just happened to be in that list. `JobTitle` was resolvable because there was only one `JobTitle` column, so that was the one we wanted.

When we want to refer to a column where the column name exists more than once in our `JOIN` result, we must *fully qualify* the column name. We can do this in one of two ways:

❑ Provide the name of the table that the desired column is from, followed by a period and the column name (`Table.`*`ColumnName`*)

❑ Alias the tables, and provide that alias, followed by a period and the column name (*`Alias.ColumnName`*), as shown in the previous example

The task of providing the names is straightforward enough — we've already seen how that works with the qualified * operator, but let's try our `BusinessEntityID` query again with a qualified column name:

```
SELECT Person. BusinessEntity.*, HumanResources.Employee. BusinessEntityID
FROM Person. BusinessEntity
INNER JOIN HumanResources.Employee
    ON Person. BusinessEntity. BusinessEntityID
        = HumanResources.Employee. BusinessEntityID
```

Now things are working again and the `BusinessEntityID` from the `Employee` table is added to the far right-hand side of the result set.

Aliasing the table is only slightly trickier, but can cut down on the wordiness and help the readability of your query. It works almost exactly the same as aliasing a column in the simple `SELECT`s that we did in the previous chapter — right after the name of the table, we simply state the alias we want to use to refer to that table. Note that, just as with column aliasing, we can use the `AS` keyword (but for some strange reason, this hasn't caught on as much in practice):

```
SELECT pbe.*, hre.BusinessEntityID
FROM Person.BusinessEntity pbe
INNER JOIN HumanResources.Employee hre
    ON pbe.BusinessEntityID = hre.BusinessEntityID
```

Run this code and you'll see that we receive the exact same results as in the previous query.

Be aware that using an alias is an all-or-nothing proposition. Once you decide to alias a table, you must use that alias in every part of the query. This is on a table-by-table basis, but try running some mixed code and you'll see what I mean:

```
SELECT pbe.*, HumanResources.Employee.BusinessEntityID
FROM Person.BusinessEntity pbe
INNER JOIN HumanResources.Employee hre
    ON pbe.BusinessEntityID = hre.BusinessEntityID
```

This seems like it should run fine, but it will give you an error:

```
Msg 4104, Level 16, State 1, Line 1
The multi-part identifier "HumanResources.Employee.BusinessEntityID" could not be
bound.
```

Again, you can mix and match which tables you choose to use aliasing on and which you don't, but once you make a decision for a given table, you have to be consistent in how you reference that table.

Think back to those bullet points we saw a few pages earlier; the columns from the first table listed in the JOIN were the first columns returned. Take a break for a moment and think about why that is, and what you might be able to do to control it.

SQL Server always uses a column order that is the best guess it can make at how you want the columns returned. In our first query we used one global * operator, so SQL Server didn't have much to go on. In that case, it goes on the small amount that it does have — the order of the columns as they exist physically in the table and the order of tables that you specified in your query. The nice thing is that it is extremely easy to reorder the columns — we just have to be explicit about it. The simplest way to reorder the columns would be to change which table is mentioned first, but we can actually mix and match your column order by simply explicitly stating the columns that we want (even if it is every column), and the order in which we want them.

Try It Out   A Simple JOIN

Let's try a small query to demonstrate the point:

```
SELECT pbe.BusinessEntityID, hre.JobTitle, pp.FirstName, pp.LastName
FROM Person.BusinessEntity pbe
INNER JOIN HumanResources.Employee hre
    ON pbe.BusinessEntityID = hre.BusinessEntityID
INNER JOIN Person.Person pp
  ON pbe.BusinessEntityID = pp.BusinessEntityID
WHERE hre.BusinessEntityID < 4
```

This yields a pretty simple result set:

```
BusinessEntityID  JobTitle                       FirstName   LastName
----------------  -----------------------------  ----------  ----------
1                 Chief Executive Officer        Ken         Sánchez
2                 Vice President of Engineering  Terri       Duffy
3                 Engineering Manager            Roberto     Tamburello

(3 row(s) affected)
```

How It Works

Unlike when we were nonspecific about what columns we wanted (when we just used the *), this time we were specific about what we wanted. Thus SQL Server knew exactly what to give us — the columns have come out in exactly the order that we've specified in our SELECT list. Indeed, even adding in an additional table, we were able to mix columns between all tables in the order desired.

How an INNER JOIN Is Like a WHERE Clause

In the INNER JOINs that we've done so far, we've really been looking at the concepts that will work for any JOIN type — the column ordering and aliasing is exactly the same for any JOIN. The part that makes an INNER JOIN different from other JOINs is that it is an *exclusive* JOIN — that is, it excludes all records that don't have a value in both tables (the first named, or left table, and the second named, or right table).

Our first example of this was shown in our imaginary Films and Actors tables. Bogey was left out because he didn't have a matching movie in the Films table. Let's look at a real example or two to show how this works.

While you probably haven't realized it in the previous examples, we've already been working with the exclusionary nature of the INNER JOIN. You see, the BusinessEntity table has many, many more rows than the 290 or so that we've been working with. Indeed, our BusinessEntity table has information on virtually any individual our company works with. They can be individuals associated with a particular customer or vendor, or they can be employees. Let's check this out by seeing how many rows exist in the BusinessEntity table:

```
SELECT COUNT(*)
FROM Person.BusinessEntity
```

Run this and, assuming you haven't added any new ones or deleted some, you should come up with approximately 20,777 rows; that's a lot more rows than the 290 that our Employee-related queries have been showing us!

So where did those other 20,487 rows go? As expected, they were excluded from the Employee query result set because there were no corresponding records in the Employee table. It is for this reason that an INNER JOIN is comparable to a WHERE clause. Just as the WHERE clause limits the rows returned to those that match the criteria specified, an INNER JOIN excludes rows because they have no corresponding match in the other table.

Just for a little more proof and practice, let's say we've been asked to produce a list of names associated with at least one customer and the account number of the customers they are associated with. Consider the following tables:

Person.Person	Sales.Customer
BusinessEntityID	CustomerID
PersonType	PersonID
NameStyle	StoreID
Title	TerritoryID
FirstName	AccountNumber
MiddleName	rowguid
LastName	ModifiedDate
Suffix	
EmailPromotion	
AdditionalContactInfo	
Demographics	
rowguid	
ModifiedDate	

Try coming up with this query on your own for a few minutes, then we'll dissect it a piece at a time.

The first thing to do is to figure out what data we need to return. The question calls for two different pieces of information to be returned: the person's name and the account number(s) of the customer they are associated with. The contact's name is available (in parts) from the Person.Person table. The customer's account number is available in the Sales.Customer table, so we can write the first part of our SELECT statement. For brevity's sake, we'll just worry about the first and last name of the contact:

```
SELECT LastName + ', ' + FirstName AS Name, AccountNumber
```

> *As in many development languages, the + operator can be used for concatenation of strings as well as the addition of numbers. In this case, we are just connecting the last name to the first name with a comma separator in between.*

What we need now is something to join the two tables on, and that's where we run into our first problem — there doesn't appear to be one. The tables don't seem to have anything in common on which we can base our JOIN – fortunately, looks can be deceiving.

If we were to look more closely at the definition of the Sales.Customer table, we would find that the `Customer`.`PersonID` column has a *foreign key* (an indicator that a given column is dependent on information from another column). Indeed, the `PersonID` ties back to the `BusinessEntityID` in the `Person`.`Person` table.

This is probably not a bad time to point out how I'm not really a fan of the AdventureWorks2008 database. I'll even go so far as to apologize for using it, but my publisher essentially did the writer's equivalent of holding me at gun point and forced the migration to AdventureWorks2008 as the sample for this book. The naming of these columns is one of many examples where the AdventureWorks2008 structure is almost bizarre, but we work with what we have.

The good news is that there is no requirement that the columns that we join share the same name, so we can just join the columns specifying the appropriate names for each table.

Try It Out   More Complex JOINs

Using this mismatched pair of names in your JOIN is no problem — we just keep on going with our FROM clause and JOIN keywords (don't forget to switch the database to pubs):

```
SELECT CAST(LastName + ', ' + FirstName AS varchar(35)) AS Name, AccountNumber
FROM Person.Person pp
JOIN Sales.Customer sc
  ON pp.BusinessEntityID = sc.PersonID
```

Our SELECT statement is now complete! If we execute, we get something like:

```
Name                        AccountNumber
------------------------    -------------
Robinett, David             AW00011377
Robinson, Rebecca           AW00011913
Robinson, Dorothy           AW00011952
Rockne, Carol Ann           AW00020164
Rodgers, Scott              AW00020211
Rodman, Jim                 AW00020562
...
...
He, Crystal                 AW00024634
Zheng, Crystal              AW00021127
Hu, Crystal                 AW00027980

(19119 row(s) affected)
```

Note that your sort order and, therefore, the actual names you see at the top and bottom of your results may differ from what you see here. Remember, SQL Server makes no promises about the order your results will arrive in unless you use an ORDER BY clause — since we didn't use ORDER BY, the old adage "actual results may vary" comes into play.

How It Works

If we were to do a simple SELECT * against the Person table, we would find that several contacts would be left out because, although they are considered people, they apparently aren't customers (they may be employees, vendor contacts, or perhaps just potential customers). Once again, the key to INNER JOINs is that they are exclusive.

Notice that we did not use the INNER *keyword in the query. That is because an* INNER JOIN *is the default* JOIN *type. Schools of thought vary on this, but I believe that because leaving the* INNER *keyword out has dominated the way code has been written for so long, it is almost more confusing to put it in — that's why you won't see me use it again in this book.*

OUTER JOINs

This type of JOIN is something of the exception rather than the rule. This is definitely not because they don't have their uses, but rather because:

- ❑   We, more often than not, want the kind of exclusiveness that an inner join provides.
- ❑   Many SQL writers learn inner joins and never go any further — they simply don't understand the outer variety.
- ❑   There are often other ways to accomplish the same thing.
- ❑   They are often simply forgotten about as an option.

Whereas inner joins are exclusive in nature, outer and, as we'll see later in this chapter, full joins are inclusive. It's a tragedy that people don't get to know how to make use of outer joins because they make seemingly difficult questions simple. They can also often speed performance when used instead of nested subqueries (which we will look into in Chapter 7).

Earlier in this chapter, we introduced the concept of a join having sides — a left and a right. The first named table is considered to be on the left and the second named table is considered to be on the right. With inner joins these are a passing thought at most, because both sides are always treated equally. With outer joins, however, understanding your left from your right is absolutely critical. When you look at it, it seems very simple because it is very simple, yet many query mistakes involving outer joins stem from not thinking through your left from your right.

To learn how to construct outer joins correctly, we're going to use two syntax illustrations. The first deals with the simple scenario of a two-table outer join. The second will deal with the more complex scenario of mixing outer joins with any other join.

The Simple OUTER JOIN

The first syntax situation is the easy part — most people get this part just fine:

```
SELECT <SELECT list>
FROM <the table you want to be the "LEFT" table>
<LEFT|RIGHT> [OUTER] JOIN <table you want to be the "RIGHT" table>
                    ON <join condition>
```

In the examples, you'll find that I tend to use the full syntax — that is, I include the OUTER *keyword (for example,* LEFT OUTER JOIN*). Note that the* OUTER *keyword is optional — you need only include the* LEFT *or* RIGHT *(for example,* LEFT JOIN*). In practice, I find that the* OUTER *keyword is rarely used.*

What I'm trying to get across here is that the table that comes before the JOIN keyword is considered to be the LEFT table, and the table that comes after the JOIN keyword is considered to be the RIGHT table.

OUTER JOINs are, as I've said, inclusive in nature. What specifically gets included depends on which side of the join you have emphasized. A LEFT OUTER JOIN includes all the information from the table on the left, and a RIGHT OUTER JOIN includes all the information from the table on the right. Let's put this into practice with a small query so that you can see what I mean.

Let's say we want to know what all our special offers are, the amount of each discount, and which products, if any, can have them applied. Looking over the AdventureWorks2008 database, we have a table called SpecialOffer in the Sales schema. We also have an associate table called SpecialOfferProduct that lets us know what special offers are associated with what products:

Sales.SpecialOffer	Sales.SpecialOfferProduct
SpecialOfferID	SpecialOfferID
Description	ProductID
DiscountPct	rowguid
Type	ModifiedDate
Category	
StartDate	
EndDate	
MinQty	
MaxQty	
rowguid	
ModifiedDate	

We can directly join these tables based on the SpecialOfferID. If we did this using a common INNER JOIN, it would look something like:

```
SELECT sso.SpecialOfferID, Description, DiscountPct, ProductID
FROM Sales.SpecialOffer sso
JOIN Sales.SpecialOfferProduct ssop
ON sso.SpecialOfferID = ssop.SpecialOfferID
WHERE sso.SpecialOfferID != 1
```

Note that I'm deliberately eliminating the rows with no discount (that's `SpecialOfferID 1`). This query yields 243 rows — each with an associated `ProductID`:

```
SpecialOfferID  Description                    DiscountPct     ProductID
--------------  -----------------------------  --------------  -----------
2               Volume Discount 11 to 14       0.02            707
2               Volume Discount 11 to 14       0.02            708
2               Volume Discount 11 to 14       0.02            709
2               Volume Discount 11 to 14       0.02            711
...
...

...
...
16              Mountain-500 Silver Clearance  0.40            986
16              Mountain-500 Silver Clearance  0.40            987
16              Mountain-500 Silver Clearance  0.40            988

(243 row(s) affected)
```

Think about this, though. We wanted results based on the special offers we have — not which ones were actually in use. This query only gives us special offers that have products utilizing the offer — it doesn't answer the question!

What we need is something that's going to return every special offer and the product ids where applicable.

Try It Out   Outer JOINs

In order to return every special offer and the products where applicable, we need to change only the `JOIN` type in the query:

```
SELECT sso.SpecialOfferID, Description, DiscountPct, ProductID
FROM Sales.SpecialOffer sso
LEFT OUTER JOIN Sales.SpecialOfferProduct ssop
  ON sso.SpecialOfferID = ssop.SpecialOfferID
WHERE sso.SpecialOfferID != 1
```

This yields similar results, but with one rather important difference:

```
SpecialOfferID  Description                    DiscountPct     ProductID
--------------  -----------------------------  --------------  -----------
2               Volume Discount 11 to 14       0.02            707
2               Volume Discount 11 to 14       0.02            708
2               Volume Discount 11 to 14       0.02            709
2               Volume Discount 11 to 14       0.02            711
...
...
6               Volume Discount over 60        0.20            NULL
...
...
16              Mountain-500 Silver Clearance  0.40            986
16              Mountain-500 Silver Clearance  0.40            987
```

```
16              Mountain-500 Silver Clearance  0.40          988

(244 row(s) affected)
```

If you were to perform a SELECT * against the discounts table, you'd quickly find that we have included every row from that table except for SpecialOfferID 1, which we explicitly excluded from our results.

How It Works

We are doing a LEFT JOIN, and the SpecialOffer table is on the left side of the JOIN. But what about the SpecialOfferProduct table? If we are joining and we don't have a matching record for the SpecialOfferProduct table, then what happens? Since it is not on the inclusive side of the JOIN (in this case, the LEFT side), SQL Server will fill in a NULL for any value that comes from the opposite side of the join if there is no match with the inclusive side of the JOIN. In this case, all but one of our rows have ProductIDs. What we can discern from that is that all of our SpecialOffers are associated with at least one product except one (SpecialOfferID 6).

We've answered the question then; of the 16 SpecialOffers available, only one is not being used (Volume Discount over 60).

In this case, switching to a RIGHT JOIN would yield the same thing as the INNER JOIN, as the SpecialOfferProduct table only contains rows where there is an active link between a special offer and a product. The concept is, however, exactly the same. We could, for example, switch the order that we reference the tables and then use a RIGHT JOIN.

Try It Out   RIGHT OUTER JOINs

Now, let's see what happens if we change the question to a RIGHT OUTER JOIN:

```
SELECT sso.SpecialOfferID, Description, DiscountPct, ProductID
FROM Sales.SpecialOfferProduct ssop
RIGHT OUTER JOIN Sales.SpecialOffer sso
 ON ssop.SpecialOfferID = sso.SpecialOfferID
WHERE sso.SpecialOfferID != 1
```

How It Works

If we tried the preceding query with a LEFT JOIN, we would get back just the 243 rows we got with the INNER JOIN. Run it as presented above, and we get back the unused special offer we wanted.

Finding Orphan or Non-Matching Records

We can actually use the inclusive nature of OUTER JOINs to find non-matching records in the exclusive table. What do I mean by that? Let's look at an example.

Let's change our special offer question. We want to know the store names for all the special offers that are not associated with any products. Can you come up with a query to perform this based on what we know thus far? Actually, the very last query we ran has us 90 percent of the way there. Think about it for a minute: an OUTER JOIN returns a NULL value in the ProductID column wherever there is no match. What we are looking for is pretty much the same result set we received in the previous query, except that we want to filter out any records that do have a ProductID, and we want only the special offer name. To do this, we simply change our SELECT list and add an extra condition to the WHERE clause:

```
SELECT Description
FROM Sales.SpecialOfferProduct ssop
RIGHT OUTER JOIN Sales.SpecialOffer sso
 ON ssop.SpecialOfferID = sso.SpecialOfferID
WHERE sso.SpecialOfferID != 1
   AND ssop.SpecialOfferID IS NULL
```

As expected, we have exactly the same stores that had NULL values before:

```
Description
------------------------------
Volume Discount over 60

(1 row(s) affected)
```

There is one question you might be thinking at the moment that I want to answer in anticipation, so that you're sure you understand why this will always work. The question is: "What if the discount record really has a NULL value?" Well, that's why we built a WHERE clause on the same field that was part of our JOIN. If we are joining based on the stor_id columns in both tables, then only three conditions can exist:

❑   If the SpecialOfferProduct.SpecialOfferID column has a non-NULL value, then, according to the ON operator of the JOIN clause, if a special offer record exists, then SpecialOffer.SpecialOfferID must also have the same value as SpecialOfferProduct.SpecialOfferID (look at the ON ssop .SpecialOfferID = sso.SpecialOfferID).

❑   If the SpecialOfferProduct.SpecialOfferID column has a non-NULL value, then, according to the ON operator of the JOIN clause, if a special offer record does not exist, then SpecialOffer .SpecialOfferID will be returned as NULL.

❑   If the SpecialOfferProduct.SpecialOfferID happens to have a NULL value, and SpecialOffer .SpecialOfferID also has a NULL value, there will be no join (null does not equal null), and SpecialOffer.SpecialOfferID will return NULL because there is no matching record.

A value of NULL does not join to a value of NULL. Why? Think about what we've already said about comparing NULLs — a NULL does not equal NULL. Be extra careful of this when coding. One of the more common questions I am asked is, "Why isn't this working?" in a situation where people are using an "equal to" operation on a NULL — it simply doesn't work because they are not equal. If you want to test this, try executing some simple code:

```
IF (NULL=NULL)
    PRINT 'It Does'
ELSE
    PRINT 'It Doesn''t'
```

If you execute this, you'll get the answer to whether your SQL Server thinks a NULL equals a NULL — that is, it doesn't.

Let's use this notion of being able to identify non-matching records to locate some of the missing records from one of our earlier INNER JOINs. Remember these two queries, which you ran against Adventure-Works2008?

```
SELECT pbe.BusinessEntityID, hre.JobTitle, pp.FirstName, pp.LastName
FROM Person.BusinessEntity pbe
INNER JOIN HumanResources.Employee hre
    ON pbe.BusinessEntityID = hre.BusinessEntityID
INNER JOIN Person.Person pp
 ON pbe.BusinessEntityID = pp.BusinessEntityID
WHERE hre.BusinessEntityID < 4
```

And . . .

```
SELECT COUNT(*)
FROM Person.BusinessEntity
```

The first was one of our queries where we explored the INNER JOIN. We discovered by running the second query that the first had excluded (by design) some rows. Now let's identify the excluded rows by using an OUTER JOIN.

We know from our SELECT COUNT(*) query that our first query is missing thousands of records from the BusinessEntity table. (It could conceivably be missing records from the Employee table, but we're not interested in that at the moment.) The implication is that there are records in the BusinessEntity table that do not have corresponding Employee records. This makes sense, of course, because we know that some of our persons are customers or vendor contacts. While our manager's first question was about all the employee contact information, it would be very common to ask just the opposite: "Which persons are not employees?" That question is answered with the same result obtained by asking, "Which records exist in Person that don't have corresponding records in the Employee table?" The solution has the same structure as the query to find special offers that aren't associated with any products:

```
SELECT  pp.BusinessEntityID, pp.FirstName, pp.LastName
FROM Person.Person pp
LEFT OUTER JOIN HumanResources.Employee hre
 ON pp.BusinessEntityID = hre.BusinessEntityID
WHERE hre.BusinessEntityID IS NULL
```

Just that quickly we have a list of contacts that is somewhat cleaned up to contain just customers:

```
BusinessEntityID FirstName             LastName
---------------- --------------------- --------------------------------
293              Catherine             Abel
295              Kim                   Abercrombie
2170             Kim                   Abercrombie
...

...
2088             Judy                  Zugelder
12079            Jake                  Zukowski
2089             Michael               Zwilling

(19682 row(s) affected)
```

> Note that whether you use a LEFT or a RIGHT JOIN doesn't matter as long as the correct table or group of tables is on the corresponding side of the JOIN. For example, we could have run the preceding query using a RIGHT JOIN as long as we also switched which sides of the JOIN the Person and Employee tables were on. For example, this would have yielded exactly the same results:
>
> ```
> SELECT  pp.BusinessEntityID, pp.FirstName, pp.LastName
> FROM HumanResources.Employee hre
> RIGHT OUTER JOIN Person.Person pp
>  ON pp.BusinessEntityID = hre.BusinessEntityID
> WHERE hre.BusinessEntityID IS NULL
> ```

When we take a look at even more advanced queries, we'll run into a slightly more popular way of finding records that exist in one table without there being corresponding records in another table. Allow me to preface that by saying that using JOINs is usually our best bet in terms of performance. There are exceptions to the rule that we will cover as we come across them, but in general, the use of JOINs will be best when faced with multiple options.

Dealing with More Complex OUTER JOINs

Now we're on to our second illustration and how to make use of it. This scenario is all about dealing with an OUTER JOIN mixed with some other JOIN (no matter what the variety).

It is when combining an OUTER JOIN with other JOINs that the concept of sides becomes even more critical. What's important to understand here is that everything to the "left" — or before — the JOIN in question will be treated just as if it were a single table for the purposes of inclusion or exclusion from the query. The same is true for everything to the "right" — or after — the JOIN. The frequent mistake here is to perform a LEFT OUTER JOIN early in the query and then use an INNER JOIN late in the query. The OUTER JOIN includes everything up to that point in the query, but the INNER JOIN may still create a situation where something is excluded! My guess is that you will, like most people (including me for a while), find this exceptionally confusing at first, so let's see what we mean with some examples. Because none of the databases that come along with SQL Server has any good scenarios for demonstrating this, we're going to have to create a database and sample data of our own.

If you want to follow along with the examples, the example database called Chapter4DB can be created by running Chapter4DB.sql from the downloadable source code. Simply open the file in the Management Studio query window and execute it.

> Again, in order to utilize the next several examples, you must execute the Chapter4DB.sql script included in the downloadable code for this book.

What we are going to do is to build up a query step-by-step and watch what happens. The query we are looking for will return a vendor name and the address of that vendor. The example database only has a few records in it, so let's start out by selecting all the choices from the central item of the query — the vendor. We're going to go ahead and start aliasing from the beginning, since we will want to do this in the end:

```
USE Chapter4DB

SELECT v.VendorName
FROM Vendors v
```

This yields a scant three records:

```
VendorName
---------------------------------------
Don's Database Design Shop
Dave's Data
The SQL Sequel

(3 row(s) affected)
```

These are the names of every vendor that we have at this time. Now let's add in the address information — there are two issues here. First, we want the query to return every vendor no matter what, so we'll make use of an OUTER JOIN. Next, a vendor can have more than one address and vice versa, so the database design has made use of an associate table. This means that we don't have anything to directly join the Vendors and Address tables — we must instead join both of these tables to our linking table, which is called VendorAddress. Let's start out with the logical first piece of this join:

```
SELECT v.VendorName
FROM Vendors v
LEFT OUTER JOIN VendorAddress va
          ON v.VendorID = va.VendorID
```

Because VendorAddress doesn't itself have the address information, we're not including any columns from that table in our SELECT list. VendorAddress's sole purpose in life is to be the connection point of a many-to-many relationship (one vendor can have many addresses and, as we've set it up here, an address can be the home of more than one vendor). Running this, as we expect, gives us the same results as before:

```
VendorName
---------------------------------------
Don's Database Design Shop
Dave's Data
The SQL Sequel

(3 row(s) affected)
```

Let's take a brief time-out from this particular query to check on the table against which we just joined. Try selecting all the data from the VendorAddress table:

```
SELECT *
FROM VendorAddress
```

Just two records are returned:

```
VendorID       AddressID
--------       -------------
1              1
2              3
```

(2 row(s) affected)

We know, therefore, that our OUTER JOIN is working. Since there are only two records in the VendorAddress table and three vendors are returned, we must be returning at least one row from the Vendors table that didn't have a matching record in the VendorAddress table. While we're here, we'll just verify that by briefly adding one more column back to our vendors query:

```
SELECT v.VendorName, va.VendorID
FROM Vendors v
LEFT OUTER JOIN VendorAddress va
          ON v.VendorID = va.VendorID
```

Sure enough, we wind up with a NULL in the VendorID column from the VendorAddress table:

```
VendorName                    VendorID
--------------------          --------------
Don's Database Design Shop    1
Dave's Data                   2
The SQL Sequel                NULL
```

(3 row(s) affected)

The vendor named "The SQL Sequel" would not have been returned if we were using an INNER or RIGHT JOIN. Our use of a LEFT JOIN has ensured that we get all vendors in our query result.

Now that we've tested things out a bit, let's return to our original query and then add in the second JOIN to get the actual address information. Because we don't care if we get all addresses, no special JOIN is required — at least, it doesn't appear that way at first . . .

```
SELECT v.VendorName, a.Address
FROM Vendors v
LEFT OUTER JOIN VendorAddress va
          ON v.VendorID = va.VendorID
JOIN Address a
   ON va.AddressID = a.AddressID
```

We get back the address information as expected, but there's a problem:

```
VendorName                   Address
--------------------------   ---------------
Don's Database Design Shop   1234 Anywhere
Dave's Data                  567 Main St.
```

(2 row(s) affected)

Somehow, we lost one of our vendors. That's because SQL Server is applying the rules in the order that we've stated them. We have started with an OUTER JOIN between Vendors and VendorAddress. SQL Server does just what we want for that part of the query — it returns all vendors. The issue comes when it applies the next set of instructions. We have a result set that includes all the vendors, but we now apply that result set as part of an INNER JOIN. Because an INNER JOIN is exclusive to both sides of the JOIN, only records where the result of the first JOIN has a match with the second JOIN will be included. Because only two records match up with a record in the Address table, only two records are returned in the final result set. We have two ways of addressing this:

- ❑ Add yet another OUTER JOIN
- ❑ Change the order of the JOINs

Let's try it both ways. We'll add another OUTER JOIN first:

```
SELECT v.VendorName, a.Address
FROM Vendors v
LEFT OUTER JOIN VendorAddress va
          ON v.VendorID = va.VendorID
LEFT OUTER JOIN Address a
          ON va.AddressID = a.AddressID
```

And now we get our expected result:

```
VendorName                          Address
--------------------------          ------------
Don's Database Design Shop          1234 Anywhere
Dave's Data                         567 Main St.
The SQL Sequel                      NULL

(3 row(s) affected)
```

Now do something slightly more dramatic and reorder our original query:

```
SELECT v.VendorName, a.Address
FROM VendorAddress va
JOIN Address a
   ON va.AddressID = a.AddressID
RIGHT OUTER JOIN Vendors v
          ON v.VendorID = va.VendorID
```

And we still get our desired result:

```
VendorName                          Address
--------------------------          --------------
Don's Database Design Shop          1234 Anywhere
Dave's Data                         567 Main St.
The SQL Sequel                      NULL

(3 row(s) affected)
```

The question you should be asking now is, "Which way is best?" Quite often in SQL, there are several ways of executing the query without one having any significant advantage over the other — this is *not* one of those times.

I would most definitely steer you to the second of the two solutions.

> **The rule of thumb is to get all of the** INNER JOINs **you can out of the way first; you will then find yourself using the minimum number of** OUTER JOINs **and decreasing the number of errors in your data.**

The reason has to do with navigating as quickly as possible to your data. If you keep adding OUTER JOINs not because of what's happening with the current table you're trying to add in, but because you're trying to carry through an earlier JOIN result, you are much more likely to include something you don't intend, or to make some sort of mistake in your overall logic. The second solution addresses this by using only the OUTER JOIN where necessary — just once. You can't always create a situation where the JOINs can be moved around to this extent, but you often can.

I can't stress enough how often I see errors with JOIN order. It is one of those areas that just seems to give developers fits. Time after time I get called in to look over a query that someone has spent hours verifying each section of, and it seems that at least half the time I get asked whether I know about this SQL Server "bug." The bug isn't in SQL Server — it's with the developer. If you take anything away from this section, I hope it is that JOIN order is one of the first places to look for errors when the results aren't coming up as you expect.

Seeing Both Sides with FULL JOINs

Like many things in SQL, a FULL JOIN (also known as a FULL OUTER JOIN) is basically what it sounds like — it is a matching up of data on both sides of the JOIN with everything included, no matter what side of the JOIN it is on.

FULL JOINs seem really cool when you learn them and then almost never get used. You'll find an honest politician more often than you'll find a FULL JOIN in use. Their main purpose in life is to look at the complete relationship between data without giving preference to one side or the other. You want to know about every record on both sides of the equation — with nothing left out.

A FULL JOIN is perhaps best described as what you would get if you could do a LEFT JOIN and a RIGHT JOIN in the same JOIN. You get all the records that match, based on the JOIN field(s). You also get any records that exist only on the left side, with NULLs being returned for columns from the right side. Finally, you get any records that exist only on the right side, with NULLs being returned for columns from the left side. Note that, when I say finally, I don't mean to imply that they'll be last in the query. The result order you get will (unless you use an ORDER BY clause) depend entirely on what SQL Server thinks is the least costly way to retrieve your records.

Try It Out   **FULL JOINs**

Let's just get right to it by looking back at our previous query from the section on OUTER JOINs:

```
SELECT v.VendorName, a.Address
FROM VendorAddress va
JOIN Address a
    ON va.AddressID = a.AddressID
RIGHT OUTER JOIN Vendors v
            ON v.VendorID = va.VendorID
```

What we want to do here is take it a piece at a time again and add some fields to the SELECT list that will let us see what's happening. First, we'll take the first two tables using a FULL JOIN:

```
SELECT a.Address, va.AddressID
FROM VendorAddress va
FULL JOIN Address a
      ON va.AddressID = a.AddressID
```

As it happens, a FULL JOIN on this section doesn't yield any more than a RIGHT JOIN would have:

```
Address            AddressID
--------------     -------------
1234 Anywhere      1
567 Main St.       3
999 1st St.        NULL
1212 Smith Ave     NULL
364 Westin         NULL

(5 row(s) affected)
```

But wait — there's more! Now add the second JOIN:

```
SELECT a.Address, va.AddressID, v.VendorID, v.VendorName
FROM VendorAddress va
FULL JOIN Address a
      ON va.AddressID = a.AddressID
FULL JOIN Vendors v
      ON va.VendorID = v.VendorID
```

Now we have everything:

```
Address            AddressID    VendorID    VendorName
--------------     ----------   ----------  ------------------------------
1234 Anywhere      1            1           Don's Database Design Shop
567 Main St.       3            2           Dave's Data
999 1st St.        NULL         NULL        NULL
1212 Smith Ave     NULL         NULL        NULL
364 Westin         NULL         NULL        NULL
NULL               NULL         3           The SQL Sequel

(6 row(s) affected)
```

How It Works

As you can see, we have the same two rows that we would have had with an INNER JOIN clause. Those are then followed by the three Address records that aren't matched with anything in either table. Last, but not least, we have the one record from the Vendors table that wasn't matched with anything.

Again, use a FULL JOIN when you want all records from both sides of the JOIN — matched where possible, but included even if there is no match.

CROSS JOINs

CROSS JOINs are very strange critters indeed. A CROSS JOIN differs from other JOINs in that there is no ON operator and that it joins every record on one side of the JOIN with every record on the other side of the JOIN. In short, you wind up with a Cartesian product of all the records on both sides of the JOIN. The syntax is the same as any other JOIN, except that it uses the keyword CROSS (instead of INNER, OUTER, or FULL) and that it has no ON operator. Here's a quick example:

```
SELECT v.VendorName, a.Address
FROM Vendors v
CROSS JOIN Address a
```

Think back now — we had three records in the Vendors table and five records in the Address table. If we're going to match every record in the Vendors table with every record in the Address table, then we should end up with 3 * 5 = 15 records in our CROSS JOIN:

```
VendorName                    Address
--------------------------    --------------------
Don's Database Design Shop    1234 Anywhere
Don's Database Design Shop    567 Main St.
Don's Database Design Shop    999 1st St.
Don's Database Design Shop    1212 Smith Ave
Don's Database Design Shop    364 Westin
Dave's Data                   1234 Anywhere
Dave's Data                   567 Main St.
Dave's Data                   999 1st St.
Dave's Data                   1212 Smith Ave
Dave's Data                   364 Westin
The SQL Sequel                1234 Anywhere
The SQL Sequel                567 Main St.
The SQL Sequel                999 1st St.
The SQL Sequel                1212 Smith Ave
The SQL Sequel                364 Westin

(15 row(s) affected)
```

Indeed, that's exactly what we get.

Every time I teach a SQL class, I get asked the same question about CROSS JOINs: "Why in the world would you use something like this?" I'm told there are scientific uses for it — this makes sense to me since I know there are a number of high-level mathematical functions that make use of Cartesian products. I presume that you could read a large number of samples into table structures, and then perform your CROSS JOIN to create a Cartesian product of your sample. There is, however, a much more frequently occurring use for CROSS JOINs — the creation of test data.

When you are building up a database, that database is quite often part of a larger-scale system that will need substantial testing. A recurring problem in testing of large-scale systems is the creation of large amounts of test data. By using a CROSS JOIN, you can do smaller amounts of data entry to create your test data in two or more tables, and then perform a CROSS JOIN against the tables to produce a much larger set of test data. You have a great example in the previous query — if you needed to match a group of addresses up with a group of vendors, then that simple query yields 15 records from 8. Of course, the numbers can become far more dramatic. For example, if we created a table with 50 first names and then created a table with 250 last names, we could CROSS JOIN them together to create a table with 12,500 unique name combinations. By investing in keying in 300 names, we suddenly get a set of test data with 12,500 names.

Exploring Alternative Syntax for Joins

What we're going to look at in this section is what many people still consider to be the "normal" way of coding joins. Until SQL Server 6.5, the alternative syntax we'll look at here was the only join syntax in SQL Server, and what is today called the "standard" way of coding joins wasn't even an option.

Until now, we have been using the ANSI/ISO syntax for all of our SQL statements. I highly recommend that you use the ANSI method since it has much better portability between systems and is also much more readable. It is worth noting that the old syntax is actually reasonably well supported across platforms at the current time.

The primary reason I am covering the old syntax at all is that there is absolutely no doubt that, sooner or later, you will run into it in legacy code. I don't want you staring at that code saying, "What the heck is this?"

That being said, I want to reiterate my strong recommendation that you use the ANSI syntax wherever possible. Again, it is substantially more readable and Microsoft has indicated that they may not continue to support the old syntax indefinitely. I find it very hard to believe, given the amount of legacy code out there, that Microsoft will dump the old syntax any time soon, but you never know.

Perhaps the biggest reason is that the ANSI syntax is actually more functional. Under old syntax, it was actually possible to create ambiguous query logic — where there was more than one way to interpret the query. The new syntax eliminates this problem.

Remember when I compared a JOIN to a WHERE clause earlier in this chapter? Well, there was a reason. The old syntax expresses all of the JOINs within the WHERE clause.

The old syntax supports all of the JOINs that we've done using ANSI with the exception of a FULL JOIN. If you need to perform a FULL JOIN, I'm afraid you'll have to stick with the ANSI version.

An Alternative INNER JOIN

Let's do a déjà vu thing and look back at the first `INNER JOIN` we did in this chapter:

```
USE AdventureWorks2008

SELECT *
FROM Person.Person
INNER JOIN HumanResources.Employee
    ON Person.Person.BusinessEntityID = HumanResources.Employee.BusinessEntityID
```

This got us approximately 290 rows back. Instead of using the `JOIN`, however, let's rewrite it using a `WHERE`-clause–based join syntax. It's actually quite easy — just eliminate the words `INNER JOIN`, add a comma, and replace the `ON` operator with a `WHERE` clause:

```
SELECT *
FROM Person.Person, HumanResources.Employee
WHERE Person.Person.BusinessEntityID = HumanResources.Employee.BusinessEntityID
```

It's a piece of cake and it yields us the same 290 rows we got with the other syntax.

> *This syntax is supported by virtually all major SQL systems (Oracle, DB2, MySQL, and so on) in the world today, but can create some ambiguity at what point in the query processing the restriction should be applied. It is very rare to run into such an ambiguity, but it can happen, so use the `JOIN` syntax for any new queries and edit old queries to the new syntax as you are able.*

An Alternative OUTER JOIN

> **Note that the alternative syntax for `OUTER` joins is only available if you tell SQL Server you want to run in SQL Server 2000 compatibility mode (setting the compatibility level to 80 in the `ALTER DATABASE` command).**

The alternative syntax for `OUTER JOIN`s works pretty much the same as the `INNER JOIN`, except that, because we don't have the `LEFT` or `RIGHT` keywords (and no `OUTER` or `JOIN` for that matter), we need some special operators especially built for the task. These look like this:

Alternative	ANSI
`*=`	`LEFT JOIN`
`=*`	`RIGHT JOIN`

Let's pull up the first `OUTER JOIN` we did in this chapter. It made use of the pubs database and looked something like this:

```
SELECT sso.SpecialOfferID, Description, DiscountPct, ProductID
FROM Sales.SpecialOffer sso
```

```
JOIN Sales.SpecialOfferProduct ssop
ON sso.SpecialOfferID = ssop.SpecialOfferID
WHERE sso.SpecialOfferID != 1
```

Again, we just lose the words LEFT OUTER JOIN and replace the ON operator with a WHERE clause, or, in this case, add the ON condition to the existing WHERE clause:

```
SELECT sso.SpecialOfferID, Description, DiscountPct, ProductID
FROM Sales.SpecialOffer sso,
     Sales.SpecialOfferProduct ssop
WHERE sso.SpecialOfferID *= ssop.SpecialOfferID
   AND sso.SpecialOfferID != 1
```

If you were to run this (I'd recommend against doing the change in compatibility level that would be required, but I want you to know that this kind of code is out there), we would get back the same results we did in our original OUTER JOIN query. A RIGHT JOIN would function in much the same way.

An Alternative CROSS JOIN

This is far and away the easiest of the bunch. To create a CROSS JOIN using the old syntax, you just do nothing. That is, you don't put anything in the WHERE clause of the FROM: TableA.ColumnA = TableB.ColumnA.

So, for an ultra quick example, let's take the first example from the CROSS JOIN section earlier in the chapter. The ANSI syntax looked like this:

```
USE Chapter4DB

SELECT v.VendorName, a.Address
FROM Vendors v
CROSS JOIN Address a
```

To convert it to the old syntax, we just strip out the CROSS JOIN keywords and add a comma:

```
USE Chapter4DB

SELECT v.VendorName, a.Address
FROM Vendors v, Address a
```

As with the other examples in this section, we get back the same results that we got with the ANSI syntax:

```
VendorName                     Address
-------------------------      --------------------
Don's Database Design Shop     1234 Anywhere
Don's Database Design Shop     567 Main St.
Don's Database Design Shop     999 1st St.
Don's Database Design Shop     1212 Smith Ave
Don's Database Design Shop     364 Westin
Dave's Data                    1234 Anywhere
Dave's Data                    567 Main St.
Dave's Data                    999 1st St.
```

```
Dave's Data                    1212 Smith Ave
Dave's Data                    364 Westin
The SQL Sequel                 1234 Anywhere
The SQL Sequel                 567 Main St.
The SQL Sequel                 999 1st St.
The SQL Sequel                 1212 Smith Ave
The SQL Sequel                 364 Westin

(15 row(s) affected)
```

This is supported across all versions and across most of the database management systems.

The UNION

OK, enough with all the "old syntax" versus "new syntax" stuff. Now we're into something that's the same regardless of what other join syntax you prefer — the UNION operator. UNION is a special operator we can use to cause two or more queries to generate one result set.

A UNION isn't really a JOIN, like the previous options we've been looking at — instead it's more of an appending of the data from one query right onto the end of another query (functionally, it works a little differently than this, but this is the easiest way to look at the concept). Where a JOIN combined information horizontally (adding more columns), a UNION combines data vertically (adding more rows), as illustrated in Figure 4-1.

When dealing with queries that use a UNION, there are just a few key points:

❑   All the UNIONed queries must have the same number of columns in the SELECT list. If your first query has three columns in the SELECT list, then the second (and any subsequent queries being UNIONed) must also have three columns. If the first has five, then the second must have five, too. Regardless of how many columns are in the first query, there must be the same number in the subsequent query(s).

❑   The headings returned for the combined result set will be taken only from the first of the queries. If your first query has a SELECT list that looks like SELECT Col1, Col2 AS Second, Col3 FROM..., then regardless of how your columns are named or aliased in the subsequent queries, the headings on the columns returned from the UNION will be Col1, Second, and Col3 respectively.

❑   The data types of each column in a query must be implicitly compatible with the data type in the same relative column in the other queries. Note that I'm *not* saying they have to be the same data type — they just have to be implicitly convertible (a conversion table that shows implicit versus explicit conversions can be found in Figure 1-3 of Chapter 1). If the second column in the first query were of type char(20), then it would be fine if the second column in the second query were varchar(50). However, because things are based on the first query, any rows longer than 20 would be truncated for data from the second result set.

❑   Unlike non-UNION queries, the default return option for UNIONs is DISTINCT rather than ALL. This can really be confusing to people. In your other queries, all rows were returned regardless of whether they were duplicated with another row or not, but the results of a UNION do not work that way. Unless you use the ALL keyword in your query, only one of any repeating rows will be returned.

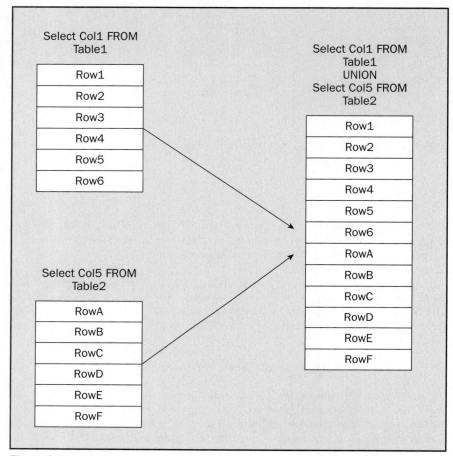

Figure 4-1

As always, let's take a look at this with an example or two.

Try It Out | UNION

First, let's look at a UNION that has some practical use to it. (It's something I could see happening in the real world — albeit not all that often.) For this example, we're going to assume that AdventureWorks is moving to a new facility and we want to send out an email to all of our customers and vendors. We want to return a list of names and email addresses to our address update. We can do this in just one query with something like this:

```
USE AdventureWorks2008

SELECT FirstName + ' ' + LastName AS Name, pe.EmailAddress
       EmailAddress
FROM Person.Person pp
JOIN Person.EmailAddress pe
  ON pp.BusinessEntityID = pe.BusinessEntityID
```

```
JOIN Sales.Customer sc
  ON pp.BusinessEntityID = sc.CustomerID

UNION

SELECT FirstName + ' ' + LastName AS Name, pe.EmailAddress
       EmailAddress
FROM Person.Person pp
JOIN Person.EmailAddress pe
  ON pp.BusinessEntityID = pe.BusinessEntityID
JOIN Purchasing.Vendor pv
  ON pp.BusinessEntityID = pv.BusinessEntityID
```

This gets back just one result set:

```
Name                   EmailAddress
-------------------    ----------------------------------------
A. Scott Wright        ascott0@adventure-works.com
Aaron Adams            aaron48@adventure-works.com
Aaron Allen            aaron55@adventure-works.com
...

...
Zachary Wilson         zachary36@adventure-works.com
Zainal Arifin          zainal0@adventure-works.com
Zheng Mu               zheng0@adventure-works.com

(10274 row(s) affected)
```

How It Works

We have our one result set from what would have been two.

SQL Server has run both queries and essentially stacked the results one on top of the other to create one combined result set. Again, notice that the headings for the returned columns all came from the SELECT list of the first of the queries.

_____

Moving on to a second example, let's take a look at how a UNION deals with duplicate rows — it's actually just the inverse of a normal query in that it assumes you want to throw out duplicates. (In your previous queries, the assumption was that you wanted to keep everything unless you used the DISTINCT keyword.) This demo has no real-world potential, but it's quick and easy to run and see how things work.

In this case, we are creating two tables from which we will select. We'll then insert three rows into each table, with one row being identical between the two tables. If our query is performing an ALL, then every row (six of them) will show up. If the query is performing a DISTINCT, then it will only return five rows (tossing out one duplicate):

```
CREATE TABLE UnionTest1
(
    idcol    int         IDENTITY,
    col2    char(3),
)
```

```
CREATE TABLE UnionTest2
(
    idcol    int         IDENTITY,
    col4     char(3),
)

INSERT INTO UnionTest1
VALUES
    ('AAA')

INSERT INTO UnionTest1
VALUES
    ('BBB')

INSERT INTO UnionTest1
VALUES
    ('CCC')

INSERT INTO UnionTest2
VALUES
    ('CCC')

INSERT INTO UnionTest2
VALUES
    ('DDD')

INSERT INTO UnionTest2
VALUES
    ('EEE')

SELECT col2
FROM UnionTest1

UNION

SELECT col4
FROM UnionTest2

PRINT 'Divider Line--------------------------'

SELECT col2
FROM UnionTest1

UNION ALL

SELECT col4
FROM UnionTest2

DROP TABLE UnionTest1
DROP TABLE UnionTest2
```

Now, look at the heart of what's returned (you'll see some one row(s) affecteds in there — just ignore them until you get to where the results of your query are visible):

```
col2
----
AAA
BBB
CCC
DDD
EEE

(5 row(s) affected)

Divider Line-------------------------
col2
----
AAA
BBB
CCC
CCC
DDD
EEE

(6 row(s) affected)
```

The first result set returned was a simple UNION statement with no additional parameters. You can see that one row was eliminated. Even though we inserted "CCC" into both tables, only one makes an appearance since the duplicate record is eliminated by default.

The second return changed things a bit. This time we used a UNION ALL and the ALL keyword ensured that we get every row back. As such, our eliminated row from the last query suddenly reappears.

Summary

In an RDBMS, the data we want is quite frequently spread across more than one table. JOINs allow us to combine the data from multiple tables in a variety of ways:

❑ Use an INNER JOIN when you want to exclude non-matching fields.

❑ Use an OUTER JOIN when you want to retrieve matches wherever possible, but also want a fully inclusive data set on one side of the JOIN.

❑ Use a FULL JOIN when you want to retrieve matches wherever possible, but also want a fully inclusive data set on both sides of the JOIN.

❑ Use a CROSS JOIN when you want a Cartesian product based on the records in two tables. This is typically used in scientific environments and when you want to create test data.

❑ Use a UNION when you want the combination of the result of a second query appended to the first query.

There are two different forms of JOIN syntax available for INNER and OUTER JOINs. I provided the legacy syntax here to help you deal with legacy code, but the newer ANSI format presented through most of this chapter is highly preferable, as it is more readable, is not prone to the ambiguities of the older syntax, and will be supported in SQL Server for the indefinite future.

Over the course of the next few chapters, we will be learning how to build our own tables and *relate* them to each other. As we do this, the concepts of what columns to join on will become even clearer.

Exercises

1. Write a query against the AdventureWorks2008 database that returns one column called Name and contains the last name of the employee with NationalIDNumber 112457891.

Creating and Altering Tables

Every time I teach the T-SQL code for creating databases, tables, keys, and constraints, I am asked the same question, "Can't you just do this in the GUI tool?" The answer is an unequivocal "Yes!" Therefore, the next question usually follows quite shortly behind, "Then why are we spending all this time learning stuff I'll never use?" The answer is just as unequivocal — you will use the regular syntax on a quasi-regular basis. The reality is you probably won't actually write the code from scratch that often, but you'll verify and edit it on the majority of all larger database projects you work on — that means that you had better know how it works.

In this chapter, we will be studying the syntax for creating your own tables. We will also take a look at how to make use of the SQL Management Studio to help us with this (after we know how to do it for ourselves).

However, before we get too deep in the actual statements that create tables and other objects, we need to digress far enough to deal with the convention for a fully qualified object name, and, to a lesser extent, object ownership.

Object Names in SQL Server

In all the queries that we've been performing so far in this book, you've seen simple naming at work. I've had you switch the active database in the Query Analyzer before running any queries and that has helped your queries to work. How? Well, SQL Server looks at only a very narrow scope when trying to identify and locate the objects you name in your queries and other statements. For example, we've been providing only the names of tables without any additional information, but there are actually four levels in the naming convention for any SQL Server table (and any other SQL Server object for that matter). A fully qualified name is as follows:

```
[ServerName.[DatabaseName.[SchemaName.]]]ObjectName
```

You must provide an object name whenever you are performing an operation on that object, but all parts of the name to the left of the object name are optional. Indeed, most of the time, they are not needed, and are therefore left off. Still, before we start creating objects, it's a good idea for us to get a solid handle on each part of the name. So let's move from the object name left.

Schema Name (aka Ownership)

If you're utilizing schemas (most older databases do not, but it appears that it will become more important in the future), you may need to indicate what schema your object is in. It is entirely possible to have two objects with the same name that reside in different schemas. If you want to access an object that is not in your default schema (set on a login-by-login basis), then you'll need to specifically state the schema name of your object. For example, let's look at what has to be one of the worst uses of schemas I've ever seen — the AdventureWorks2008 database we've already been using — and take a look at a query that gets a list of employees and what city they live in:

```
SELECT
  e.NationalIDNumber, p.FirstName,p.LastName, City
FROM
  HumanResources.Employee e
INNER JOIN
  Person.Person p on p.BusinessEntityID = e.BusinessEntityID
INNER JOIN
  Person.BusinessEntityAddress a on p.BusinessEntityID = a.BusinessEntityID
INNER JOIN
  Person.Address pa on pa.AddressID = a.AddressID
```

This example makes use of four tables spread across two schemas. If one of the two schemas involved — `HumanResources` and `Person` — happened to be our default schema, then we could have left that schema name off when naming tables in that schema. In this case, we named all schemas to be on the safe side.

> *This is another time where I have to get on the consistency soapbox. If you're going to use the schema features at all, then I highly recommend using two-part naming (schema and table name) in all of your queries. It is far too easy for a change to be made to a user's default schema or to some other alias such that your assumptions about the default are no longer valid. If you're not utilizing different schemas at all in your database design, then it's fine to leave them off (and make your code a fair amount more readable in the process), but keep in mind there may be a price to pay if later you start using schemas.*

A Little More About Schemas

The ANSI/ISO Standard for SQL has had the notion of what has been called a schema for quite some time now. SQL Server has had that same concept in place all along, but used to refer to it differently (and, indeed, had a different intent for it even if it could be used the same way). So, what you see referred to in SQL Server 2008 and other databases such as Oracle as "schema" was usually referred to as "Owner" in SQL Server 2000 and prior.

The notion of the schema used to be a sticky one. While it is still non-trivial, Microsoft has added some new twists to make the problems of schema much easier to deal with. If, however, you need to deal with backward compatibility to prior versions of SQL Server, you're going to need to either avoid the new features or use pretty much every trick they have to offer — and that means ownership (as it was known in prior versions) remains a significant hassle.

There were always some people who liked using ownership in their older designs, but I was definitely not one of them. For now, the main thing to know is that what is now "schema" is something that overlaps with an older concept called "ownership," and you may see both terms in use. Schema also becomes important in dealing with some other facets of SQL Server such as Notification Services.

Let's focus, for now, on what a schema is and how it works.

For prior releases, ownership (as it was known then) was actually a great deal like what it sounds — it was recognition, right within the fully qualified name, of who "owned" the object. Usually, this was either the person who created the object or the database owner (more commonly referred to as the dbo — I'll get to describing the dbo shortly). Things still work in a similar fashion, but the object is assigned to a schema rather than an owner. Whereas an owner related to one particular login, a schema can now be shared across multiple logins, and one login can have rights to multiple schemas.

By default, only users who are members of the sysadmin system role, or the db_owner or db_ddladmin database roles can create objects in a database.

> *The roles mentioned here are just a few of many system and database roles that are available in SQL Server 2008. Roles have a logical set of permissions granted to them according to how that role might be used. When you assign a particular role to someone, you are giving that person the ability to have all the permissions that the role has.*

Individual users can also be given the right to create certain types of database and system objects. If such individuals do indeed create an object, then, by default, that object will be assigned to whatever schema is listed as default for that login.

> **Just because a feature is there doesn't mean it should be used! Giving CREATE authority to individual users is nothing short of nightmarish. Trying to keep track of who created what, when, and for what reason becomes near impossible. In short, keep CREATE access limited to the members of the sysadmins or db_owner security roles.**

The Default Schema: dbo

Whoever creates the database is considered to be the "database owner," or dbo. Any objects that a dbo creates within that database shall be listed with a schema of dbo rather than their individual username.

For example, let's say that I am an everyday user of a database, my login name is MySchema, and I have been granted CREATE TABLE authority to a given database. If I create a table called MyTable, the owner-qualified object name would be MySchema.MyTable. Note that, because the table has a specific owner, any user other than me (remember, I'm MySchema here) of MySchema.MyTable would need to provide the two part (schema-qualified) name in order for SQL Server to resolve the table name.

Now, let's say that there is also a user with a login name of Fred. Fred is the database owner (as opposed to just any member of db_owner). If Fred creates a table called MyTable using an identical CREATE statement to that used by MySchema, the two-part table name will be dbo.MyTable. In addition, as dbo also happens to be the default owner, any user could just refer to the table as MyTable.

It's worth pointing out that members of the sysadmin role (including the sa login) always alias to the dbo. That is, no matter who actually owns the database, a member of sysadmin will always have full access as if it were the dbo, and any objects created by a member of sysadmin will, unless explicitly defined otherwise, show ownership belonging to the dbo. In contrast, objects created by members of the db_owner database role do *not* default to dbo as the default schema — they will be assigned to whatever that particular user has set as the default schema (it could be anything). Weird but true!

> *In chats I had with a few old friends at Microsoft, they seemed to be somewhat on the schema bandwagon and happy for the changes. I too am happy for the changes, but mostly because they make the use of schemas easier, not because schemas are a feature that I think everyone should rush to use.*

> *The addition of schemas adds complexity to your database no matter what you do. While they can address organizational problems in your design, those problems can usually be dealt with in other ways that produce a much more user-friendly database. In addition, schemas, while an ANSI/ISO-compliant notion, are not supported in the same way across every major RDBMS product. This means using schemas is going to have an impact on you if you're trying to write code that can support multiple platforms.*

The Database Name

The next item in the fully qualified naming convention is the database name. Sometimes you want to retrieve data from a database other than the default, or current, database. Indeed, you may actually want to JOIN data from across databases. A database-qualified name gives you that ability. For example, if you were logged in with AdventureWorks2008 as your current database, and you wanted to refer to the Orders table in the Accounting database we'll be building later in the chapter, then you could refer to it by Accounting.dbo.Orders. Since dbo is the default schema, you could also use Accounting..Orders. If a schema named MySchema owns a table named MyTable in MyDatabase, then you could refer to that table as MyDatabase.MySchema.MyTable. Remember that the current database (as determined by the USE command or in the drop-down box if you're using the SQL Server Management Studio) is always the default, so, if you want data from only the current database, then you do not need to include the database name in your fully qualified name.

Naming by Server

In addition to naming other databases on the server you're connected to, you can also "link" to another server. Linked servers give you the capability to perform a JOIN across multiple servers — even different types of servers (SQL Server, Oracle, DB2, Access — just about anything with an OLE DB provider). We'll see a bit more about linked servers later in the book, but for now, just realize that there is one more level in our naming hierarchy, that it lets you access different servers, and that it works pretty much like the database and ownership levels work.

Now, let's just add to our previous example. If we want to retrieve information from a server we have created a link with called MyServer, a database called MyDatabase, and a table called MyTable owned by MySchema, then the fully qualified name would be MyServer.MyDatabase.MySchema.MyTable.

Reviewing the Defaults

So let's look one last time at how the defaults work at each level of the naming hierarchy from right to left:

- ❑ **Object Name:** There isn't a default — you must supply an object name.

- ❑ **Ownership:** You can leave this off, in which case it will resolve first using the current user's name, and then, if the object name in question doesn't exist with the current user as owner, then it will try the dbo as the owner.

- ❑ **Database Name:** This can also be left off unless you are providing a Server Name — in which case you must provide the Database Name for SQL Servers (other server types vary depending on the specific kind of server).

- ❑ **Server Name:** You can provide the name of a linked server here, but most of the time you'll just leave this off, which will cause SQL Server to default to the server you are logged into.

If you want to skip the schema name, but still provide information regarding the database or server, then you must still provide the extra " . " for the position where the owner would be. For example, if we are logged in using the AdventureWorks2008 database on our local server, but want to refer to the Sales.Customer table in the AdventureWorks2008 database on a linked server called MyOtherServer, then we could refer to that table by using MyOtherServer.AdventureWorks2008..Customer. Since we didn't provide a specific schema name, it will assume that either the default schema for the user ID that is used to log on to the linked server or the dbo (in that order) is the schema of the object you want (in this case, Customer). Since the Customer table is not part of the dbo schema, the user would need to have a default schema of Sales or they would get an error that the object was not found. In general, I recommend explicitly naming the schema of the object you want to reference.

The CREATE Statement

In the Bible, God said, "Let there be light!" And there was light! Unfortunately, creating things isn't quite as simple for us mere mortals. We need to provide a well-defined syntax in order to create the objects in our database. To do that, we make use of the CREATE statement.

Let's look at the full structure of a CREATE statement, starting with the utmost in generality. You'll find that all the CREATE statements start out the same, and then get into the specifics. The first part of the CREATE statement will always look like:

```
CREATE <object type> <object name>
```

This will be followed by the details that vary by the nature of the object that you're creating.

CREATE DATABASE

For this part of things, we'll need to create a database called Accounting that we will also use when we start to create tables. The most basic syntax for the CREATE DATABASE statement looks like this:

```
CREATE DATABASE <database name>
```

> It's worth pointing out that, when you create a new object, no one can access it except for the person who created it, the system administrator, and the database owner (which, if the object created was a database, is the same as the person that created it). This allows you to create things and make whatever adjustments you need to make before you explicitly allow access to your object.
>
> It's also worth noting that you can use the CREATE statement only to create objects on the local server (adding in a specific server name doesn't work).

This will yield a database that looks exactly like your model database (we discussed the model database in Chapter 1). In reality, what you want is almost always different, so let's look at a fuller syntax listing:

```
CREATE DATABASE <database name>
[ON [PRIMARY]
   ([NAME = <'logical file name'>,]
    FILENAME = <'file name'>
   [, SIZE = <size in kilobytes, megabytes, gigabytes, or terabytes>]
   [, MAXSIZE = size in kilobytes, megabytes, gigabytes, or terabytes>]
   [, FILEGROWTH = <kilobytes, megabytes, gigabytes, or terabytes|percentage>])]
 [LOG ON
   ([NAME = <'logical file name'>,]
    FILENAME = <'file name'>
   [, SIZE = <size in kilobytes, megabytes, gigabytes, or terabytes>]
   [, MAXSIZE = size in kilobytes, megabytes, gigabytes, or terabytes>]
   [, FILEGROWTH = <kilobytes, megabytes, gigabytes, or terabytes|percentage>])]
[ COLLATE <collation name> ]
[ FOR ATTACH [WITH <service broker>]| FOR ATTACH_REBUILD_LOG| WITH DB_CHAINING
ON|OFF | TRUSTWORTHY ON|OFF]
[AS SNAPSHOT OF <source database name>]
[;]
```

Keep in mind that some of the preceding options are mutually exclusive (for example, if you're creating for attaching, most of the options other than file locations are invalid). There's a lot there, so let's break down the parts.

ON

ON is used in two places: to define the location of the file where the data is stored, and to define the same information for where the log is stored. You'll notice the PRIMARY keyword there — this means that what follows is the primary (or main) filegroup in which to physically store the data. You can also store data in what are called secondary filegroups — the use of which is outside the scope of this title. For now, stick with the default notion that you want everything in one file.

> SQL Server allows you to store your database in multiple files; furthermore, it allows you to collect those files into logical groupings called filegroups. The use of filegroups is a fairly advanced concept and is outside the scope of this book.

NAME

This one isn't quite what it sounds like. It is a name for the file you are defining, but only a logical name — that is, the name that SQL Server will use internally to refer to that file. You use this name when you want to resize (expand or shrink) the database and/or file.

FILENAME

This one *is* what it sounds like — the physical name on the disk of the actual operating system file in which the data and log (depending on what section you're defining) will be stored. The default here (assuming you used the simple syntax you looked at first) depends on whether you are dealing with the database itself or the log. By default, your file will be located in the `\Data` subdirectory under your main `\Program Files\Microsoft SQL Server\MSSQL10.MSSQLSERVER\MSSQL` directory (or whatever you called your main SQL Server directory if you changed it at install). If we're dealing with the physical database file, it will be named the same as your database with an `.mdf` extension. If we're dealing with the log, it will be named the same as the database file but with a suffix of `_Log` and an `.ldf` extension. You are allowed to specify other extensions if you explicitly name the files, but I strongly encourage you to stick with the defaults of `mdf` (database) and `ldf` (log file). As a side note, secondary files have a default extension of `.ndf`.

Keep in mind that, while `FILENAME` is an optional parameter, it is optional only as long as you go with the extremely simple syntax (the one that creates a new database based on the model database) that I introduced first. If you provide any of the additional information, then you must include an explicit file name — be sure to provide a full path.

SIZE

No mystery here. It is what it says — the size of the database. By default, the size is in megabytes, but you can make it kilobytes by using a KB instead of MB after the numeric value for the size, or go bigger by using GB (gigabytes) or even TB (terabytes). Keep in mind that this value must be at least as large as the model database is and must be a whole number (no decimals) or you will receive an error. If you do not supply a value for `SIZE`, then the database will initially be the same size as the model database.

MAXSIZE

This one is still pretty much what it sounds like, with only a slight twist vs. the `SIZE` parameter. SQL Server has a mechanism to allow your database to automatically allocate additional disk space (to grow) when necessary. `MAXSIZE` is the maximum size to which the database can grow. Again, the number is, by default, in megabytes, but like `SIZE`, you can use KB, GB, or TB to use different increment amounts. The slight twist is that there is no firm default. If you don't supply a value for this parameter, then there is considered to be no maximum — the practical maximum becomes when your disk drive is full.

If your database reaches the value set in the `MAXSIZE` parameter, your users will start getting errors back saying that their inserts can't be performed. If your log reaches its maximum size, you will not be able to perform any logged activity (which is most activities) in the database. Personally, I recommend setting up what is called an *alert*. You can use alerts to tell you when certain conditions exist (such as a database or log that's almost full). We'll see how to create alerts in Chapter 19.

> I recommend that you always include a value for MAXSIZE, and that you make it at least several megabytes smaller than would fill up the disk. I suggest this because a completely full disk can cause situations where you can't commit any information to permanent storage. If the log was trying to expand, the results could potentially be disastrous. In addition, even the operating system can occasionally have problems if it runs completely out of disk space.
>
> One more thing — if you decide to follow my advice on this issue, be sure to keep in mind that you may have multiple databases on the same system. If you size each of them to be able to take up the full size of the disk less a few megabytes, then you will still have the possibility of a full disk (if they all expand). There really isn't any "one right answer" for this scenario — you just need to prioritize your space according to likely usage, monitor your database sizes more closely, and set up alerts in Windows Server to notify you of low disk space situations.

FILEGROWTH

Whereas SIZE set the initial size of the database, and MAXSIZE determined just how large the database file could get, FILEGROWTH essentially determines just how fast it gets to that maximum. You provide a value that indicates by how many bytes (in KB, MB, GB, or TB) at a time you want the file to be enlarged. Alternatively, you can provide a percentage value by which you want the database file to increase. With this option, the size will go up by the stated percentage of the current database file size. Therefore, if you set a database file to start out at 1GB with a FILEGROWTH of 20 percent, then the first time it expands it will grow to 1.2GB, the second time to 1.44, and so on.

LOG ON

The LOG ON option allows you to establish that you want your log to go to a specific set of files and where exactly those files are to be located. If this option is not provided, then SQL Server will create the log in a single file and default it to a size equal to 25 percent of the data file size. In most other respects, it has the same file specification parameters as the main database file does.

> *It is highly recommended that you store your log files on a different drive than your main data files. Doing so prevents the log and main data files from competing for I/O off the disk and provides additional safety should one hard drive fail.*

COLLATE

This one has to do with the issue of sort order, case sensitivity, and sensitivity to accents. When you installed your SQL Server, you decided on a default collation, but you can override this at the database level (and, as we'll see later, also at the column level).

FOR ATTACH

You can use this option to attach an existing set of database files to the current server. The files in question must be part of a database that was, at some point, properly detached using sp_detach_db. This deprecates the older `sp_attach_db` functionality and has the advantage of access to as many as 32,000+ files — `sp_attach_db` is limited to 16.

If you use `FOR ATTACH`, you must complete the `ON PRIMARY` portion of the file location information. Other parts of the `CREATE DATABASE` parameter list can be left off as long as you are attaching the database to the same file path they were in when they were originally detached.

WITH DB CHAINING ON|OFF

Hmmm. How to address this one in a beginning kinda way . . .. Well, suffice to say this is a toughie, and is in no way a "beginning" kind of concept. With that in mind, here's the abridged version of what this relates to.

As previously mentioned, the concept of "schemas" didn't really exist in prior versions of SQL Server. Instead, we had the notion of "ownership." One of the bad things that could happen with ownership was what are called *ownership chains*. This was a situation where person A was the owner of an object, and then person B became the owner of an object that depended on person A's object. You could have person after person create objects depending on other people's objects, and there became a complex weave of permission issues based on this.

This switch is about respecting such ownership chains when they cross databases (person A's object is in DB1, and person B's object is in DB2). Turn it on, and cross database ownership chains work — turn it off, and they don't. Avoid such ownership chains as if they were the plague — they are a database equivalent to a plague, believe me!

TRUSTWORTHY

This switch is new to add an extra layer of security around access to system resources and files outside of the SQL Server context. For example, you may run a .NET assembly that touches files on your network — if so, you must identify the database that the assembly is part of as being Trustworthy.

By default this is turned off for security reasons — be certain you understand exactly what you're doing and why before you set this to on.

Building a Database

At this point, we're ready to begin building our database. Following is the statement to create it, but keep in mind that the database itself is only one of many objects that we will create on our way to a fully functional database:

```
CREATE DATABASE Accounting
ON
   (NAME = 'Accounting',
    FILENAME = 'C:\Program Files\Microsoft SQL
Server\MSSQL10.MSSQLSERVER\MSSQL\DATA\AccountingData.mdf',
    SIZE = 10,
    MAXSIZE = 50,
    FILEGROWTH = 5)
LOG ON
   (NAME = 'AccountingLog',
    FILENAME = 'C:\Program Files\Microsoft SQL
Server\MSSQL10.MSSQLSERVER\MSSQL\DATA\AccountingLog.ldf',
    SIZE = 5MB,
```

```
        MAXSIZE = 25MB,
        FILEGROWTH = 5MB);

GO
```

Now is a good time to start learning about some of the informational utilities that are available with SQL Server. We saw `sp_help` in Chapter 4, but in this case, let's try running a command called `sp_helpdb`. This one is especially tailored for database structure information, and often provides better information if we're more interested in the database itself than the objects it contains. `sp_helpdb` takes one parameter — the database name:

```
EXEC sp_helpdb 'Accounting'
```

This actually yields you two separate result sets. The first is based on the combined (data and log) information about your database:

Name	db_ size	Owner	dbid	Created	Status	Compatibility_ level
Accounting	15.00 MB	sa	9	May 28 2005	Status=ONLINE, Updateability= READ_WRITE, UserAccess= MULTI_USER, Recovery=FULL, Version=598, Collation= SQL_Latin1_ General_CP1_ CI_AS, SQLSort- Order=52, IsAutoCreate▪ Statistics, IsAutoUpdate▪ Statistics, IsFullText- Enabled	90

The actual values you receive for each of these fields may vary somewhat from mine. For example, the DBID value will vary depending on how many databases you've created and in what order you've created them. The various status messages will vary depending on what server options were in place at the time you created the database as well as any options you changed for the database along the way.

Note that the `db_size` property is the *total* of the size of the database and the size of the log.

The second provides specifics about the various files that make up your database — including their current size and growth settings:

Name	Fileid	Filename	File-group	Size	Maxsize	Growth	Usage
Accounting	1	C:\ Program Files\ Microsoft SQL Server \MSSQL10 .MSSQLSERVER \MSSQL\DATA \Accounting-Data.mdf	PRIMARY	10240 KB	51200 KB	5120 KB	data only
AccountingLog	2	C:\Program Files\ Microsoft SQL Server \MSSQL10 .MSSQLSERVER \MSSQL\DATA \Accounting-Log.ldf	NULL	5120 KB	25600 KB	5120 KB	log only

After you create tables and insert data, the database will begin to automatically grow on an as-needed basis.

CREATE TABLE

The first part of creating a table is pretty much the same as creating any object — remember that line I showed you? Well, here it is again:

```
CREATE <object type> <object name>
```

Since a table is what you want, we can be more specific:

```
CREATE TABLE Customers
```

With CREATE DATABASE, we could have stopped with just these first three keywords, and it would have built the database based on the guidelines established in the model database. With tables however, there is no model, so we need to provide some more specifics in the form of columns, data types, and special operators.

Let's look at more extended syntax:

```
CREATE TABLE [database_name.[owner].]table_name
(<column name> <data type>
[[DEFAULT <constant expression>]
    |[IDENTITY [(seed, increment) [NOT FOR REPLICATION]]]]
    [ROWGUIDCOL]
    [COLLATE <collation name>]
    [NULL|NOT NULL]
    [<column constraints>]
    |[column_name AS computed_column_expression]
    |[<table_constraint>]
    [,...n]
)
[ON {<filegroup>|DEFAULT}]
[TEXTIMAGE_ON {<filegroup>|DEFAULT}]
```

Now that's a handful — and it still has sections taken out of it for simplicity's sake! As usual, let's look at the parts, starting with the second line (we've already seen the top line).

Table and Column Names

What's in a name? Frankly — a lot. You may recall that one of my first soapbox diatribes was back in Chapter 2 and was about names. I promised then that it wouldn't be the last you heard from me on the subject, and this won't be either.

The rules for naming tables and columns are, in general, the same rules that apply to all database objects. The SQL Server documentation will refer to these as the *rules for identifiers*, and they are the same rules we observed at the end of Chapter 1. The rules are actually pretty simple; what we want to touch on here, though, are some notions about how exactly to name your objects — not specific rules governing what SQL Server will and won't accept for names, but how to go about naming your tables and columns so that they are useful and make sense.

There are a ton of different "standards" out there for naming database objects — particularly tables and columns. My rules are pretty simple:

❑ For each word in the name, capitalize the first letter and use lowercase for the remaining letters.

❑ Keep the name short, but make it long enough to be descriptive.

❑ Limit the use of abbreviations. The only acceptable use of abbreviations is when the chosen abbreviation will be recognized by everyone. Examples of abbreviations I use include "ID" to take the place of identification, "No" to take the place of number, and "Org" to take the place of organization. Keeping your names of reasonable length will require you to be more cavalier about your abbreviations sometimes, but keep in mind that, first and foremost, you want clarity in your names.

❑ When building tables based on other tables (usually called linking or associate tables), you should include the names of all parent tables in your new table name. For example, say you have a movie database where many stars can appear in many movies. If you have a `Movies` table and a `Stars` table, you may want to tie them together using a table called `MovieStars`.

❑ When you have two words in the name, do not use any separators (run the words together) — use the fact that you capitalize the first letter of each new word to figure out how to separate words.

I can't begin to tell you the battles I've had with other database people about naming issues. For example, you will find that a good many people believe that you should separate the words in your names with an underscore (_).Why don't I do it that way? Well, it's an ease of use issue. Underscores present a couple of different problems:

❑ First, many people have a difficult time typing an underscore without taking their hand away from the proper keyboard position — this leads to lots of typos.

❑ Second, in documentation it is not uncommon to run into situations where the table or column name is underlined. Underscores are, depending on the font, impossible to see when the text is underlined — this leads to confusion and more errors.

❑ Finally (and this is a nit pick), it's just more typing.

You also have the option to separate the words in the name using a regular space. If you recall my very first soapbox diatribe back in Chapter 1, you'll know that isn't really much of an option — it is extremely bad practice and creates an unbelievable number of errors. It was added to facilitate Access upsizing, and I continue to curse the person(s) who decided to put it in — I'm sure they were well-meaning, but they are now part of the cause of much grief in the database world.

This list is certainly not set in stone; rather it is just a Reader's Digest version of the rules I use when naming tables. I find that they save me a great deal of grief. I hope they'll do the same for you.

> **Consistency, consistency, consistency. Every time I teach, I always warn my class that it's a word I'm going to repeat over and over, and in no place is it more important than in naming. If you have to pick one rule to follow, then pick a rule that says that, whatever your standards are — make them just that: standard. If you decide to abbreviate for some reason, then abbreviate that word every time (the same way). Regardless of what you're doing in your naming, make it apply to the entire database consistently — consider having a standards document or style guide to make sure other developers utilize the same rules you do. This will save a ton of mistakes, and it will save your users time in terms of how long it takes for them to get to know the database.**

Data Types

There isn't much to this — the data types are as I described them in Chapter 2. You just need to provide a data type immediately following the column name — there is no default data type.

DEFAULT

We'll cover this in much more detail in our chapter on constraints, but for now, suffice to say that this is the value you want to be used for any rows that are inserted without a user-supplied value for this particular column. The default, if you use one, should immediately follow the data type.

IDENTITY

The concept of an *identity* value is very important in database design. We will cover how to use identity columns in some detail in our chapters on design. What is an identity column? Well, when you make a column an identity column, SQL Server automatically assigns a sequenced number to this column with every row you insert. The number that SQL Server starts counting from is called the *seed* value, and the amount that the value increases or decreases by with each row is called the *increment*. The default is for a seed of 1 and an increment of 1, and most designs call for it to be left that way. As an example, however, you could have a seed of 3 and an increment of 5. In this case, you would start counting from 3, and then add 5 each time for 8, 13, 18, 23, and so on.

An identity column must be numeric, and, in practice, it is almost always implemented with an `integer` or `bigint` data type.

The usage is pretty simple; you simply include the `IDENTITY` keyword right after the data type for the column. An identity option cannot be used in conjunction with a default constraint. This makes sense if you think about it — how can there be a constant default if you're counting up or down every time?

> *It's worth noting that an identity column works sequentially. That is, once you've set a seed (the starting point) and the increment, your values only go up (or down if you set the increment to a negative number). There is no automatic mechanism to go back and fill in the numbers for any rows you may have deleted. If you want to fill in blank spaces like that, you need to use SET IDENTITY_INSERT ON, which allows you to turn off (yes, turning it "on" turns it off — that is, you are turning on the ability to insert your own values, which has the effect of turning off the automatic value) the identity process for inserts from the current connection. This can, however, create havoc if you're not careful or if people are still trying to use the system as you do this, so tread carefully.*

The most common use for an identity column is to generate a new value to be used as an identifier for each row — that is, identity columns are commonly used to create a primary key for a table. Keep in mind, however, that an `IDENTITY` column and a `PRIMARY KEY` are completely separate notions — that is, just because you have an `IDENTITY` column doesn't mean that the value is unique (for example, you can reset the seed value and count back up through values you've used before). `IDENTITY` values are *usually* used as the `PRIMARY KEY` column, but they don't *have* to be used that way.

> If you've come from the Access world, you'll notice that an `IDENTITY` column is much like an `AutoNumber` column. The major difference is that you have a bit more control over it in SQL Server.

NOT FOR REPLICATION

This one is very tough to deal with at this point, so I am, at least in part, going to skip it until I come to the chapter on replication.

> **Briefly, replication is the process of automatically doing what, in a very loose sense, amounts to copying some or all of the information in your database to some other database. The other database may be on the same physical machine as the original, or it may be located remotely.**

The NOT FOR REPLICATION parameter determines whether a new identity value for the new database is assigned when the column is published to another database (via replication), or whether it keeps its existing value. There will be much more on this at a later time.

ROWGUIDCOL

This is also replication related and, in many ways, is the same in purpose to an identity column. We've already seen how using an identity column can provide you with an easy way to make sure that you have a value that is unique to each row and can, therefore, be used to identify that row. However, this can be a very error-prone solution when you are dealing with replicated or other distributed environments.

Think about it for a minute — while an identity column will keep counting upward from a set value, what's to keep the values from overlapping on different databases? Now, think about when you try to replicate the values such that all the rows that were previously in separate databases now reside in one database — uh oh! You now will have duplicate values in the column that is supposed to uniquely identify each row!

Over the years, the common solution for this was to use separate seed values for each database you were replicating to and from. For example, you may have database A that starts counting at 1, database B starts at 10,000, and database C starts at 20,000. You can now publish them all into the same database safely — for a while. As soon as database A has more than 9,999 records inserted into it, you're in big trouble.

"Sure," you say, "why not just separate the values by 100,000 or 500,000?" If you have tables with a large amount of activity, you're still just delaying the inevitable — that's where a ROWGUIDCOL comes into play.

What is a ROWGUIDCOL? Well, it's quite a bit like an identity column in that it is usually used to uniquely identify each row in a table. The difference is to what lengths the system goes to make sure that the value used is truly unique. Instead of using a numerical count, SQL Server instead uses what is known as a *Unique Identifier*. While an identity value is usually (unless you alter something) unique across time, it is not unique across space. Therefore, we can have two copies of our table running, and can have them both assigned identical identity values for what are different rows. While this is just fine to start with, it causes big problems when we try to bring the rows from both tables together as one replicated table. A unique identifier, sometimes still referred to as a *GUID*, is unique across both space and time.

> *GUIDs (or, more commonly today, UUIDs — which look the same and do a better job at performing the same task) are in widespread use in computing today. For example, if you check the registry, you'll find tons of them. A GUID is a 128-bit value — for you math types, that's 38 zeros in decimal form. If I generated a GUID every second, it would, theoretically speaking, take me millions of years to generate a duplicate given a number of that size.*

> *GUIDs are generated using a combination of information — each of which is designed to be unique in either space or time. When you combine them, you come up with a value that is guaranteed, statistically speaking, to be unique across space and time.*

There is a Windows API call to generate a GUID in normal programming, but, in addition to the ROWGUIDCOL option on a column, SQL has a special function to return a GUID — it is called the NEWID() function, and can be called at any time.

COLLATE

This works pretty much just as it did for the CREATE DATABASE command, with the primary difference being in terms of scope (here, we define at the column level rather than the database level).

NULL/NOT NULL

This one is pretty simple — it states whether the column in question accepts NULL values or not. The default, when you first install SQL Server, is to set a column to NOT NULL if you don't specify nullability. There are, however, a very large number of different settings that can affect this default, and change its behavior. For example, setting a value by using the sp_dbcmptlevel stored procedure or setting ANSI-compliance options can change this value.

> **I highly recommend explicitly stating the NULL option for every column in every table you ever build. Why? As I mentioned before, there are a large number of different settings that can affect what the system uses for a default for the nullability of a column. If you rely on these defaults, then you may find later that your scripts don't seem to work right (because you or someone else has changed a relevant setting without realizing its full effect).**

Column Constraints

We have a whole chapter coming up on constraints, so we won't spend that much time on it here. Still, it seems like a good time to review the question of what column constraints are — in short, they are restrictions and rules that you place on individual columns about the data that can be inserted into that column.

For example, if you have a column that's supposed to store the month of the year, you might define that column as being of type tinyint — but that wouldn't prevent someone from inserting the number 54 in that column. Since 54 would give us bad data (it doesn't refer to a month), we might provide a constraint that says that data in that column must be between 1 and 12. We'll see how to do this in our next chapter.

Computed Columns

You can also have a column that doesn't have any data of its own, but whose value is derived on the fly from other columns in the table. If you think about it, this may seem odd since you could just figure it out at query time, but really, this is something of a boon for many applications.

For example, let's say that we're working on an invoicing system. We want to store information on the quantity of an item we have sold, and at what price. It used to be fairly commonplace to go ahead and add columns to store this information, along with another column that stored the extended value (price times quantity). However, that leads to unnecessary wasting of disk space and maintenance hassles associated with when the totals and the base values get out of synch with each other. With a computed column, we can get around that by defining the value of our computed column to be whatever multiplying price by quantity creates.

Let's look at the specific syntax:

```
<column name> AS <computed column expression>
```

The first item is a little different; it provides a column name to go with the value. This is simply the alias that we're going to use to refer to the value that is computed, based on the expression that follows the AS keyword.

Next comes the computed column expression. The expression can be any normal expression that uses either literals or column values from the same tables. Therefore, in our example of price and quantity, we might define this column as:

```
ExtendedPrice AS Price * Quantity
```

For an example using a literal, let's say that we always charge a fixed markup on our goods that is 20 percent over our cost. We could simply keep track of cost in one column, and then use a computed column for the ListPrice column:

```
ListPrice AS Cost * 1.2
```

Pretty easy, eh? There are a few caveats and provisos though:

❑   You cannot use a subquery, and the values cannot come from a different table.

❑   In SQL Server 2000 and earlier, you could not use a computed column as any part of any key (primary, foreign, or unique) or with a default constraint. For SQL Server 2005, you can now use a computed column in constraints (you must flag the computed column as persisted if you do this, however).

❑   Special steps must be taken if you want to create indexes on computed columns. We will discuss these steps when we explore indexing in Chapter 9.

We'll look at specific examples of how to use computed columns a little later in this chapter.

Even years after they were added to the product, I'm still rather surprised that I don't hear much debate about the use of computed columns. Rules for normalization of data say that we should not have a column in our table for information that can be derived from other columns — that's exactly what a computed column is!

I'm glad the religious zealots of normalization haven't weighed into this one much, as I like computed columns as something of a compromise. By default, you aren't storing the data twice, and you don't have issues with the derived values not agreeing with the base values because they are calculated on the fly directly from the base values. However, you still get the end result you wanted. Note that, if you index the computed column, you are indeed actually storing the data (you have to for the index). This, however, has its own benefits when it comes to read performance.

This isn't the way to do everything related to derived data, but it sure is an excellent helper for many situations.

129

Table Constraints

Table constraints are quite similar to column constraints, in that they place restrictions on the data that can be inserted into the table. What makes them a little different is that they may be based on more than one column.

Again, I will be covering these in the constraints chapter, but examples of table-level constraints include PRIMARY and FOREIGN KEY constraints, as well as CHECK constraints.

> OK, so why is a CHECK constraint a table constraint? Isn't it a column constraint since it affects what you can place in a given column? The answer is that it's both. If it is based on solely one column, then it meets the rules for a column constraint. If, however (as CHECK constraints can), it is dependent on multiple columns, then you have what would be referred to as a table constraint.

ON

Remember when we were dealing with database creation, and we said we could create different filegroups? Well, the ON clause in a table definition is a way of specifically stating on which filegroup (and, therefore, physical device) you want the table located. You can place a given table on a specific physical device, or, as you will want to do in most cases, just leave the ON clause out, and it will be placed on whatever the default filegroup is (which will be the PRIMARY unless you've set it to something else). We will be looking at this usage extensively in our chapter on performance tuning.

TEXTIMAGE_ON

This one is basically the same as the ON clause we just looked at, except that it lets you move a very specific part of the table to yet a different filegroup. This clause is only valid if your table definition has text, ntext, or image column(s) in it. When you use the TEXTIMAGE_ON clause, you move only the BLOB information into the separate filegroup — the rest of the table stays either on the default filegroup or with the filegroup chosen in the ON clause.

> There can be some serious performance increases to be had by splitting your database into multiple files, and then storing those files on separate physical disks. When you do this, it means you get the I/O from both drives. Major discussion of this is outside the scope of this book, but keep this in mind as something to gather more information on should you run into I/O performance issues.

Creating a Table

All right, we've seen plenty; we're ready for some action, so let's build a few tables.

When we started this section, we looked at our standard CREATE syntax of:

```
CREATE <object type> <object name>
```

And then we moved on to a more specific start (indeed, it's the first line of our statement that will create the table) on creating a table called Customers:

```
CREATE TABLE Customers
```

Our Customers table is going to be the first table in a database we will be putting together to track our company's accounting. We'll be looking at designing a database in a couple of chapters, but we'll go ahead and get started on our database by building a couple of tables to learn our CREATE TABLE statement. We'll look at most of the concepts of table construction in this section, but we'll save a few for later on in the book. That being said, let's get started building the first of several tables.

I'm going to add in a USE <database name> line prior to my CREATE code so that I'm sure that, when I run the script, the table is created in the proper database. We'll then follow up that first line that we've already seen with a few columns.

Any script you create for regular use with a particular database should include a USE command with the name of that database. This ensures that you really are creating, altering, and dropping the objects in the database you intend. More than once have I been the victim of my own stupidity when I blindly opened up a script and executed it only to find that the wrong database was current, and any tables with the same name had been dropped (thus losing all data) and replaced by a new layout. You can also tell when other people have done this by taking a look around the master database — you'll often find several extraneous tables in that database from people running CREATE scripts that were meant to go somewhere else.

```
USE Accounting
CREATE TABLE Customers
(
    CustomerNo      int            IDENTITY  NOT NULL,
    CustomerName    varchar(30)              NOT NULL,
    Address1        varchar(30)              NOT NULL,
    Address2        varchar(30)              NOT NULL,
    City            varchar(20)              NOT NULL,
    State           char(2)                  NOT NULL,
    Zip             varchar(10)              NOT NULL,
    Contact         varchar(25)              NOT NULL,
    Phone           char(15)                 NOT NULL,
    FedIDNo         varchar(9)               NOT NULL,
    DateInSystem    smalldatetime            NOT NULL
)
```

This is a somewhat simplified table vs. what we would probably use in real life, but there's plenty of time to change it later (and we will).

Once we've built the table, we want to verify that it was indeed created, and that it has all the columns and types that we expect. To do this, we can make use of several commands, but perhaps the best is one that will seem like an old friend before you're done with this book: sp_help. The syntax is simple:

```
EXEC sp_help <object name>
```

To specify the table object that we just created, try executing the following code:

```
EXEC sp_help Customers
```

The EXEC command is used in two different ways. This rendition is used to execute a stored procedure — in this case, a system stored procedure. We'll see the second version later when we are dealing with advanced query topics and stored procedures.

> Technically speaking, you can execute a stored procedure by simply calling it (without using the EXEC keyword). The problem is that this works only if the sproc being called is the first statement of any kind in the batch. Just having sp_help Customers would have worked in the place of the previous code, but if you tried to run a SELECT statement before it — it would blow up on you. Not using EXEC leads to very unpredictable behavior and should be avoided.

Try executing the command, and you'll find that you get back several result sets one after another. The information retrieved includes separate result sets for:

- Table name, schema, type of table (system vs. user), and creation date
- Column names, data types, nullability, size, and collation
- The identity column (if one exists) including the *initial* seed and increment values
- The ROWGUIDCOL (if one exists)
- Filegroup information
- Index names (if any exist), types, and included columns
- Constraint names (if any), types, and included columns
- Foreign key (if any) names and columns
- The names of any schema-bound views (more on this in Chapter 10) that depend on the table

Now that we're certain that our table was created, let's take a look at creating yet another table — the Employees table. This time, let's talk about what we want in the table first, and then see how you do trying to code the CREATE script for yourself.

The Employees table is another fairly simple table. It should include information on:

- The employee's ID — this should be automatically generated by the system
- First name
- Optionally, middle initial
- Last name
- Title
- Social Security Number
- Salary
- The previous salary
- The amount of the last raise

❏   Date of hire

❏   Date terminated (if there is one)

❏   The employee's manager

❏   Department

Start by trying to figure out a layout for yourself.

Before we start looking at this together, let me tell you not to worry too much if your layout isn't exactly like mine. There are as many database designs as there are database designers — and that all begins with table design. We all can have different solutions to the same problem. What you want to look for is whether you have all the concepts that need to be addressed. That being said, let's take a look at one way to build this table.

We have a special column here. The EmployeeID is to be generated by the system and therefore is an excellent candidate for either an identity column or a ROWGUIDCOL. There are several reasons you might want to go one way or the other between these two, but we'll go with an identity column for a couple of reasons:

❏   It's going to be used by an average person. (Would you want to have to remember a GUID?)

❏   It incurs lower overhead.

We're now ready to start constructing our script:

```
CREATE TABLE Employees
(
   EmployeeID        int           IDENTITY  NOT NULL,
```

For this column, the NOT NULL option has essentially been chosen for us by virtue of our use of an IDENTITY column. You cannot allow NULL values in an IDENTITY column. Note that, depending on our server settings, we will, most likely, still need to include our NOT NULL option (if we leave it to the default we may get an error depending on whether the default allows NULLs).

Next up, we want to add in our name columns. I usually allow approximately 25 characters for names. Most names are far shorter than that, but I've bumped into enough that were rather lengthy (especially since hyphenated names have become so popular) that I allow for the extra room. In addition, I make use of a variable-length data type for two reasons:

❏   To recapture the space of a column that is defined somewhat longer than the actual data usually is (retrieve blank space)

❏   To simplify searches in the WHERE clause — fixed-length columns are padded with spaces, which requires extra planning when performing comparisons against fields of this type

The exception in this case is the middle initial. Since we really need to allow for only one character here, recapture of space is not an issue. Indeed, a variable-length data type would actually use more space in this case, since a varchar needs not only the space to store the data, but also a small amount of overhead space to keep track of how long the data is. In addition, ease of search is not an issue since, if we have any value in the field at all, there isn't enough room left for padded spaces.

> For the code that you write directly in T-SQL, SQL Server will automatically adjust to the padded spaces issue — that is, an 'xx' placed in a `char(5)` will be treated as being equal (if compared) to an 'xx' placed in a `varchar(5)` — this is not, however, true in your client APIs such as SqlNativeClient and ADO.NET. If you connect to a char(5) in ADO.NET, then an 'xx' will evaluate to xx with three spaces after it — if you compare it to 'xx', it will evaluate to `False`. An 'xx' placed in a varchar(5), however, will automatically have any trailing spaces trimmed, and comparing it to 'xx' in ADO.NET will evaluate to `True`.

Since a name for an employee is a critical item, we will not allow any NULL values in the first and last name columns. Middle initial is not nearly so critical (indeed, some people in the U.S. don't have a middle name at all, while my editor tells me that it's not uncommon for Brits to have several), so we will allow a NULL for that field only:

```
FirstName        varchar(25)          NOT NULL,
MiddleInitial    char(1)              NULL,
LastName         varchar(25)          NOT NULL,
```

Next up is the employee's title. We must know what they are doing if we're going to be cutting them a paycheck, so we will also make this a required field:

```
Title            varchar(25)          NOT NULL,
```

In that same paycheck vein, we must know their Social Security Number (or similar identification number outside the U.S.) in order to report for taxes. In this case, we'll use a `varchar` and allow up to 11 characters, as these identification numbers are different lengths in different countries. If you know your application is only going to require SSNs from the U.S., then you'll probably want to make it `char(11)` instead:

```
SSN              varchar(11)          NOT NULL,
```

We must know how much to pay the employees — that seems simple enough — but what comes next is a little different. When we add in the prior salary and the amount of the last raise, we get into a situation where we could use a computed column. The new salary is the sum of the previous salary and the amount of the last raise. The `Salary` amount is something that we might use quite regularly — indeed we might want an index on it to help with ranged queries, but for various reasons I don't want to do that here (we'll talk about the ramifications of indexes on computed columns in Chapter 9), so I'm going to use `LastRaise` as my computed column:

```
Salary           money                NOT NULL,
PriorSalary      money                NOT NULL,
LastRaise AS Salary - PriorSalary,
```

If we hired them, then we must know the date of hire — so that will also be required:

```
HireDate         date                 NOT NULL,
```

Note that I've chosen to use a `date` data type rather than the older standard `datetime` to save space. The `datetime` data type will store both date and time information down to fractions of a second. However, since we're primarily interested in the date of hire, not the time, the `date` will meet our needs and take up half the space.

> **Be aware that the date, time, and datetime2 data types (as opposed to the more venerable datetime and smalldatetime data types) are new with SQL Server 2008. If you need to remain backward compatible with previous versions, you'll need to stick with the datetime and smalldatetime data types.**

The date of termination is something we may not know (we'd like to think that some employees are still working for us), so we'll need to leave it nullable:

```
    TerminationDate   date                     NULL,
```

We absolutely want to know who the employee is reporting to (somebody must have hired them!) and what department they are working in:

```
    ManagerEmpID      int                      NOT NULL,
    Department        varchar(25)              NOT NULL
)
```

So, just for clarity, let's look at the entire script required to create this table:

```
USE Accounting

CREATE TABLE Employees
(
    EmployeeID        int           IDENTITY   NOT NULL,
    FirstName         varchar(25)              NOT NULL,
    MiddleInitial     char(1)                  NULL,
    LastName          varchar(25)              NOT NULL,
    Title             varchar(25)              NOT NULL,
    SSN               varchar(11)              NOT NULL,
    Salary            money                    NOT NULL,
    PriorSalary       money                    NOT NULL,
    LastRaise AS Salary - PriorSalary,
    HireDate          date                     NOT NULL,
    TerminationDate   date                     NULL,
    ManagerEmpID      int                      NOT NULL,
    Department        varchar(25)              NOT NULL
)
```

Again, I would recommend executing `sp_help` on this table to verify that the table was created as you expected.

The ALTER Statement

OK, so now we have a database and a couple of nice tables — isn't life grand? If only things always stayed the same, but they don't. Sometimes (actually, far more often than we would like), we get requests to *change* a table rather than re-create it. Likewise, we may need to change the size, file locations, or some other feature of our database. That's where our ALTER statement comes in.

Much like the CREATE statement, our ALTER statement pretty much always starts out the same:

```
ALTER <object type> <object name>
```

This is totally boring so far, but it won't stay that way. We'll see the beginnings of issues with this statement right away, and things will get really interesting (read: convoluted and confusing!) when we deal with this even further in our next chapter (when we deal with constraints).

ALTER DATABASE

Let's get right into it by taking a look at changing our database. We'll actually make a couple of changes just so we can see the effects of different things and how their syntax can vary.

Perhaps the biggest trick with the ALTER statement is to remember what you already have. With that in mind, let's take a look again at what we already have:

```
EXEC sp_helpdb Accounting
```

Notice that I didn't put the quotation marks in this time as I did when we used this stored proc earlier. That's because this system procedure, like many of them, accepts a special data type called sysname. As long as what you pass in is a name of a valid object in the system, the quotes are optional for this data type.

So, the results should be just like they were when we created the database:

Name	db_ size	Owner	dbid	Created	Status	Compati-bility_ level
Accounting	15.00 MB	sa	9	May 28 2000	Status=ONLINE, Update-ability=READ_WRITE, UserAccess=MULTI_USER, Recovery=FULL, Version=598, Collation=SQL_Latin1_ General_CP1_CI_AS, SQLSort-Order=52, IsAutoCreateStatis-tics, IsAutoUpdate-Statistics, IsFullTextEnabled	90

And . . .

Name	Fileid	Filename	File-group	Size	Maxsize	Growth	Usage
Accounting	1	c:\ Program Files\ Microsoft SQL Server\ MSSQL10 .MSSQLSERVER \MSSQL\DATA \Accounting-Data.mdf	PRI-MARY	10240 BK	51200KB	5120KB	data only
AccountingLog	2	c:\ Program Files\ Microsoft SQL Server\ MSSQL10 .MSSQLSERVER \MSSQL\DATA \Accounting-Log.ldf	NULL	5120K B	25600KB	5120KB	log only

Let's say you want to change things a bit. For example, let's say that we know that we are going to be doing a large import into our database. Currently, our database is only 15MB in size — that doesn't hold much these days. Since we have Autogrow turned on, we could just start our import, and SQL Server would automatically enlarge the database 5MB at a time. Keep in mind, however, that it's actually a fair amount of work to reallocate the size of the database. If we were inserting 100MB worth of data, then the server would have to deal with that reallocation at least 16 times (at 20MB, 25MB, 30MB, and so on). Since we know that we're going to be getting up to 100MB of data, why not just do it in one shot? To do this, we would use the ALTER DATABASE command.

The general syntax looks like this:

```
ALTER DATABASE <database name>
    ADD FILE
        ([NAME = <'logical file name'>,]
        FILENAME = <'file name'>
        [, SIZE = <size in KB, MB, GB or TB>]
        [, MAXSIZE = < size in KB, MB, GB or TB >]
        [, FILEGROWTH = <No of KB, MB, GB or TB |percentage>]) [,...n]
            [ TO FILEGROUP filegroup_name]
    [, OFFLINE ]
```

```
|ADD LOG FILE
    ([NAME = <'logical file name'>,]
     FILENAME = <'file name'>
     [, SIZE = < size in KB, MB, GB or TB >]
     [, MAXSIZE = < size in KB, MB, GB or TB >]
     [, FILEGROWTH = <No KB, MB, GB or TB |percentage>])
|REMOVE FILE <logical file name> [WITH DELETE]
|ADD FILEGROUP <filegroup name>
|REMOVE FILEGROUP <filegroup name>
|MODIFY FILE <filespec>
|MODIFY NAME = <new dbname>
|MODIFY FILEGROUP <filegroup name> {<filegroup property>|NAME =
        <new filegroup name>}
|SET <optionspec> [,...n ][WITH <termination>]
|COLLATE <collation name>
```

The reality is that you will very rarely use all that stuff — sometimes I think Microsoft just puts it there for the sole purpose of confusing the heck out of us (just kidding!).

So, after looking at all that gobbledygook, let's just worry about what we need to expand our database out to 100MB:

```
ALTER DATABASE Accounting
    MODIFY FILE
    (NAME = Accounting,
     SIZE = 100MB)
```

Note that, unlike when we created our database, we don't get any information about the allocation of space — instead, we get the rather non-verbose:

```
The command(s) completed successfully.
```

Gee — how informative . . . So, we'd better check on things for ourselves:

```
EXEC sp_helpdb Accounting
```

Name	db_ size	Owner	dbid	Created	Status	Compat-ibility_ level
Accounting	105.00 MB	Sa	9	May 28 2005	Status=ONLINE, Update-ability=READ_WRITE, UserAccess=MULTI_USER, Recovery=FULL, Version=598, Collation=SQL_Latin1_ General_CP1_CI_AS, SQLSortOrder=52, IsAutoCreate-Statis-tics, IsAutoUpdate-Statistics, IsFullText-Enabled	90

Name	Fileid	Filename	File-group	Size	Maxsize	Growth	Usage
Accounting	1	c:\ Program Files\ Microsoft SQL Server\ MSSQL10 .MSSQLSERVER \MSSQL\DATA \Accounting- Data.mdf	PRIMARY	10240 0 KB	102400 KB	5120 KB	data only
AccountingLog	2	c:\ Program Files\ Microsoft SQL Server\ MSSQL10 .MSSQLSERVER \MSSQL\DATA \Accounting- Log.ldf	NULL	5120 KB	25600 KB	5120 KB	log only

Things pretty much work the same for any of the more common database-level modifications you'll make. The permutations are, however, endless. The more complex filegroup modifications and the like are outside the scope of this book, but, if you need more information on them, I would recommend one of the more administrator-oriented books out there (and there are a ton of them).

Option and Termination Specs

SQL Server has a few options that can be set with an ALTER DATABASE statement. Among these are data-base-specific defaults for most of the SET options that are available (such as ANSI_PADDING, ARITHABORT — handy if you're dealing with indexed or partitioned views), state options (for example, single user mode or read-only), and recovery options. The effects of the various SET options are discussed where they are relevant throughout the book. This new ALTER functionality simply gives you an additional way to change the defaults for any particular database.

SQL Server also has the ability to control the implementation of some of the changes you are trying to make on your database. Many changes require that you have exclusive control over the database — something that can be hard to deal with if other users are already in the system. SQL Server gives us the ability to gracefully force other users out of the database so that we may complete our database changes. The strength of these actions ranges from waiting a number of seconds (you decide how long) before kicking other users out, all the way up to immediate termination of any option transactions (automatically rolling them back). Relatively uncontrolled (from the client's perspective) termination of transactions is not something to be taken lightly. Such an action is usually in the realm of the database administrator. As such, we will consider further discussion out of the scope of this book.

ALTER TABLE

A far, far more common need is the situation where we need to change the makeup of our table. This can range from simple things like adding a new column to more complex issues such as changing a data type.

Let's start by taking a look at the basic syntax for changing a table:

```
ALTER TABLE table_name
    {[ALTER COLUMN <column_name>
        { [<schema of new data type>].<new_data_type> [(precision [, scale])] max |
<xml schema collection>
        [COLLATE <collation_name>]
        [NULL|NOT NULL]
        |[{ADD|DROP} ROWGUIDCOL] | PERSISTED}]
    |ADD
        <column name> <data_type>
        [[DEFAULT <constant_expression>]
        |[[IDENTITY [(<seed>, <increment>) [NOT FOR REPLICATION]]]]
        [ROWGUIDCOL]
        [COLLATE <collation_name>]
            [NULL|NOT NULL]
        [<column_constraints>]
        |[<column_name> AS <computed_column_expression>]
    |ADD
        [CONSTRAINT <constraint_name>]
        {[[{PRIMARY KEY|UNIQUE}
            [CLUSTERED|NONCLUSTERED]
            {(<column_name>[ ,...n ])}]
            [WITH FILLFACTOR = <fillfactor>]
            [ON {<filegroup> | DEFAULT}]
            ]
            |FOREIGN KEY
                [(<column_name>[ ,...n])]
                REFERENCES <referenced_table> [(<referenced_column>[ ,...n])]
                [ON DELETE {CASCADE|NO ACTION}]
                [ON UPDATE {CASCADE|NO ACTION}]
                [NOT FOR REPLICATION]
            |DEFAULT <constant_expression>
                [FOR <column_name>]
            |CHECK [NOT FOR REPLICATION]
                (<search_conditions>)
        [,...n][ ,...n]
            |[WITH CHECK|WITH NOCHECK]
    | { ENABLE | DISABLE } TRIGGER
        { ALL | <trigger name> [ ,...n ] }

    |DROP
        {[CONSTRAINT] <constraint_name>
            |COLUMN <column_name>}[ ,...n]
```

```
           |{CHECK|NOCHECK} CONSTRAINT
               {ALL|<constraint_name>[ ,...n]}
           |{ENABLE|DISABLE} TRIGGER
               {ALL|<trigger_name>[ ,...n]}
        | SWITCH [ PARTITION <source partition number expression> ]
             TO [ schema_name. ] target_table
             [ PARTITION <target partition number expression> ]
    }
```

As with the CREATE TABLE command, there's quite a handful there to deal with.

So let's start an example of using this by looking back at the Employees table in the Accounting database:

```
EXEC sp_help Employees
```

For the sake of saving a few trees, I'm going to edit the results that I show here to just the part we care about — you'll actually see much more than this:

Column_name	Type	Computed	Length	Prec	Scale	Nullable
EmployeeID	int	no	4	10	0	no
FirstName	varchar	no	25			no
MiddleInitial	char	no	1			yes
LastName	varchar	no	25			no
Title	varchar	no	25			no
SSN	varchar	no	11			no
Salary	money	no	8	19	4	no
PriorSalary	money	no	8	19	4	no
LastRaise	money	yes	8	19	4	yes
HireDate	smalldatetime	no	4			no
TerminationDate	smalldatetime	no	4			yes
ManagerEmpID	int	no	4	10	0	no
Department	varchar	no	25			no

Let's say that you've decided you'd like to keep previous employer information on your employees (probably so you know who will be trying to recruit the good ones back!). That just involves adding another column, and really isn't all that tough. The syntax looks much like it did with the CREATE TABLE statement except that it has obvious alterations to it:

```
ALTER TABLE Employees
    ADD
        PreviousEmployer   varchar(30)   NULL
```

Not exactly rocket science — is it? Indeed, you could have added several additional columns at one time if you had wanted to. It would look something like this:

```
ALTER TABLE Employees
    ADD
        DateOfBirth     date       NULL,
        LastRaiseDate   date       NOT NULL
            DEFAULT '2008-01-01'
```

Notice the DEFAULT I slid in here. We haven't really looked at these yet (they are in our next chapter), but I wanted to use one here to point out a special case.

If you want to add a NOT NULL column after the fact, you have the issue of what to do with rows that already have NULL values. We have shown the solution to that here by providing a default value. The default is then used to populate the new column for any row that is already in our table.

Before we go away from this topic for now, let's take a look at what we've added:

```
EXEC sp_help Employees
```

Column_name	Type	Computed	Length	Prec	Scale	Nullable
EmployeeID	int	no	4	10	0	no
FirstName	varchar	no	25			no
MiddleInitial	char	no	1			yes
LastName	varchar	no	25			no
Title	varchar	no	25			no
SSN	varchar	no	11			no
Salary	money	no	8	19	4	no
PriorSalary	money	no	8	19	4	no
LastRaise	money	yes	8	19	4	yes

Column_name	Type	Computed	Length	Prec	Scale	Nullable
HireDate	smalldatetime	no	4			no
TerminationDate	smalldatetime	no	4			yes
ManagerEmpID	int	no	4	10	0	no
Department	varchar	no	25			no
PreviousEmployer	varchar	no	30			yes
DateOfBirth	datetime	no	8			yes
LastRaiseDate	datetime	no	8			no

As you can see, all of our columns have been added. The thing to note, however, is that they all went to the end of the column list. There is no way to add a column to a specific location in SQL Server. If you want to move a column to the middle, you need to create a completely new table (with a different name), copy the data over to the new table, DROP the existing table, and then rename the new one.

This issue of moving columns around can get very sticky indeed. Even some of the tools that are supposed to automate this often have problems with it. Why? Well, any foreign key constraints you have that reference this table must first be dropped before you are allowed to delete the current version of the table. That means that you have to drop all your foreign keys, make the changes, and then add all your foreign keys back. It doesn't end there, however; any indexes you have defined on the old table are automatically dropped when you drop the existing table — that means that you must remember to re-create your indexes as part of the build script to create your new version of the table — yuck!

*But wait! There's more! While we haven't really looked at views yet, I feel compelled to make a reference here to what happens to your views when you add a column. You should be aware that, even if your view is built using a SELECT * as its base statement, your new column will not appear in your view until you rebuild the view. Column names in views are resolved at the time the view is created for performance reasons. That means any views that have already been created when you add your columns have already resolved using the previous column list — you must either DROP and recreate the view or use an ALTER VIEW statement to rebuild it.*

The DROP Statement

Performing a DROP is the same as deleting whatever object(s) you reference in your DROP statement. It's very quick and easy, and the syntax is exactly the same for all of the major SQL Server objects (tables, views, sprocs, triggers, and so on). It goes like this:

```
DROP <object type> <object name> [, ...n]
```

Actually, this is about as simple as SQL statements get. We could drop both of our tables at the same time if we wanted:

```
USE Accounting

DROP TABLE Customers, Employees
```

And this deletes them both.

> **Be very careful with this command. There is no, "Are you sure?" kind of question that goes with this — it just assumes you know what you're doing and deletes the object(s) in question.**

The syntax is very much the same for dropping the entire database. Now let's drop the Accounting database:

```
USE master

DROP DATABASE Accounting
```

You should see the following in the Results pane:

```
Command(s) completed successfully.
```

You may run into a situation where you get an error that says that the database cannot be deleted because it is in use. If this happens, check a couple of things:

- ❑ Make sure that the database that you have as current in the Management Studio is something other than the database you're trying to drop (that is, make sure you're not using the database as you're trying to drop it).
- ❑ Ensure you don't have any other connections open (using the Management Studio or sp_who) that are showing the database you're trying to drop as the current database.

I usually solve the first one just as I did in the code example — I switch to using the master database. The second you have to check manually — I usually close other sessions down entirely just to be sure.

Using the GUI Tool

We've just spent a lot of time pounding in perfect syntax for creating a database and a couple of tables — that's enough of that for a while. Let's take a look at the graphical tool in the Management Studio that allows us to build and relate tables. From this point on, we'll not only be dealing with code, but with the tool that can generate much of that code for us.

Creating a Database Using the Management Studio

If you run the SQL Server Management Studio and expand the Databases node, you should see something like Figure 5-1.

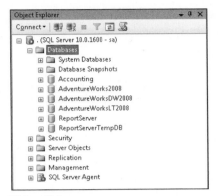

Figure 5-1

If you look closely at this screenshot, you'll see that my Accounting database is still showing even though we just dropped it in the previous example. You may or may not wind up seeing this, depending on whether you already had the Management Studio open when you dropped the database or you opened it after you dropped the database in the Query window.

Why the difference? Well, in earlier versions of SQL Server, the tools that are now the Management Studio refreshed information such as the available databases regularly. Now it updates only when it knows it has a reason to (for example, you deleted something by using the Management Studio Object Explorer instead of a Query window, or perhaps you explicitly chose to refresh). The reason for the change was performance. The old 6.5 Enterprise Manager used to be a slug performance-wise because it was constantly making round trips to "poll" the server. The newer approach performs much better, but doesn't necessarily have the most up-to-date information.

The bottom line on this is that, if you see something in the Management Studio that you don't expect to, try pressing F5 (refresh), and it should update things for you.

Now try right-clicking on the Databases node, and choose the New Database option.

This will pull up the Database Properties dialog box, and allow you to fill in the information on how you want your database created. We'll use the same choices that we did when we created the `Accounting` database at the beginning of the chapter. First comes the basic name and size info, as shown in Figure 5-2.

First, the name — this is pretty basic. We called it Accounting before, and, because we deleted the first one we created, there's no reason not to call it that again.

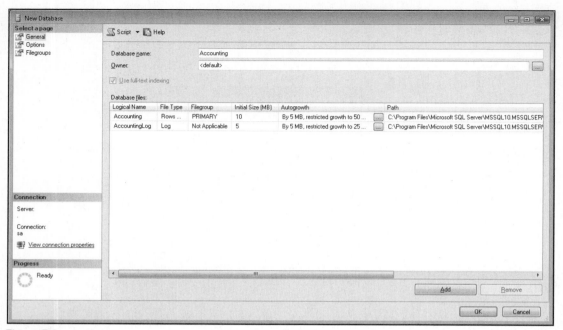

Figure 5-2

Next comes our file name, size, and growth information.

I've expanded the dialog out manually to make sure you could see everything. You may see less than what's pictured here as the default size of the dialog is not nearly enough to show it all — just grab a corner of the dialog and expand it to see the additional information.

Next let's move on to the Options tab, which contains a host of additional settings, as shown in Figure 5-3.

Perhaps the most interesting thing here, though, is the collation name. We have the choice of having each database (and, indeed, individual columns if we wish) have its own collation. For the vast majority of installs, you'll want to stick with whatever the server default was set to when the server was installed (presumably, someone had already thought this out fairly well). However, you can change it for just the current database by setting it here.

"Why," you may ask, "would I want a different collation?" Well, in the English-speaking world, a common need for specific collations would be that some applications are written expecting an "a" to be the same as an "A" — while others are expecting case sensitivity ("a" is not the same as "A"). In the old days, we would have to have separate servers set up in order to handle this. Another, non-English example would be dialect differences that are found within many countries of the world — even where they speak the same general language.

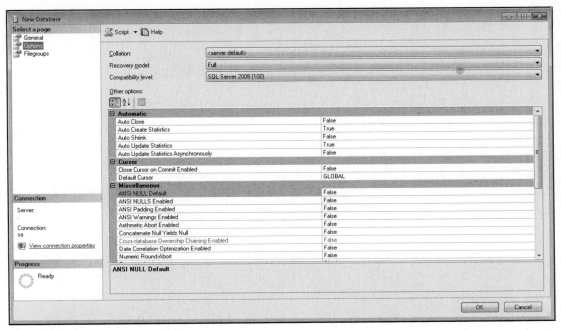

Figure 5-3

Next comes the compatibility level. This will control whether certain SQL Server 2008 syntax and keywords are supported or not. As you might expect from the name of this setting, the goal is to allow you to rollback to keywords and functional behavior that more closely matches older versions if your particular application happens to need that. For example, as you roll it back to earlier versions, some words that are keywords in later versions revert to being treated as non-keywords, and certain behaviors that have had their defaults changed in recent releases will revert to the older default.

The remaining properties will vary from install to install, but work as I described them earlier in the chapter.

OK, given that the other settings are pretty much standard fare compared with what we saw earlier in the chapter, let's go ahead and try it out. Click OK and, after a brief pause to actually create the database, you'll see it added to the tree.

Now expand the tree to show the various items underneath the Accounting node, and select the Database Diagrams node. Right-click it, and you'll get a dialog indicating that the database is missing some objects it needs to support database diagramming, as shown in Figure 5-4. Click Yes.

Note that you should only see this the first time a diagram is being created for that database. SQL Server keeps track of diagrams inside special tables that it only creates in your database if you are going to actually create a diagram that will use them.

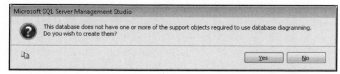

Figure 5-4

With that, you'll get an Add Table dialog, as shown in Figure 5-5. This lets us decide what tables we want to include in our diagram — we can created multiple diagrams if we wish, potentially each covering some subsection — or *submodel* — of the overall database schema. In this case, we have an empty list because we just created our database.

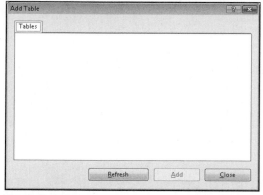

Figure 5-5

For now, just click Close (you can't add tables if there are no tables to add!), and you should get an empty diagram screen. The nice part is that you can add a table by either right-clicking and choosing the appropriate option, or by clicking on the New Table icon in the toolbar. When you choose New Table, SQL Server will ask you for the name you want to give your new table. You will then get a mildly helpful dialog box that lets you fill in your table one piece at a time — complete with labels for what you need to fill out, as shown in Figure 5-6.

Customers *		
Column Name	Data Type	Allow Nulls
CustomerNo	int	☐
CustomerName	varchar(30)	☐
Address1	varchar(50)	☐
Address2	varchar(50)	☐
City	varchar(50)	☐
State	char(2)	☐
Contact	varchar(50)	☐
Phone	char(15)	☐
FedIDNo	varchar(9)	☐
DateInSystem	smalldatetime	☐
		☐

Figure 5-6

I've gone ahead and filled in the columns as they were in our original `Customers` table, but we also need to define our first column as being an identity column. Unfortunately, we don't appear to have any way of doing that with the default grid here. To change what items we can define for our table, we need to right-click in the editing dialog, and select Table View ➪ Modify Custom.

We then get a list of items from which we can choose, shown in Figure 5-7. For now, we'll just select the extra item we need — Identity and its associated elements Seed and Increment.

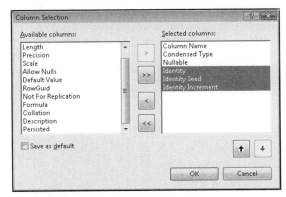

Figure 5-7

Now go back to our editing dialog and select Table View ➪ Custom to view the identity column (see Figure 5-8), and we're ready to fill in our table definition.

OK, so SQL Server can be a bit temperamental on this. If you do not check the box to make this the default, then SQL Server will change what your "custom" view looks like, but it will not make the custom view the active one — the result is that you won't see the changes you made as you exit the dialog. So, again, make sure that after changing the view, you right-click and select Table View ➪ MA Custom again. It should then look like Figure 5-8.

Customers *

Column Name	Condensed Type	Nullable	Identity	Identity Seed	Identity Increment
CustomerNo	int	No	☑	1	1
CustomerName	varchar(30)	No	☐		
Address1	varchar(50)	No	☐		
Address2	varchar(50)	No	☐		
City	varchar(50)	No	☐		
State	char(2)	No	☐		
Contact	varchar(50)	No	☐		
Phone	char(15)	No	☐		
FedIDNo	varchar(9)	No	☐		
DateInSystem	smalldatetime	No	☐		
			☐		

Figure 5-8

Once you have the table filled out, you can save the changes, and that will create your table for you.

This is really a point of personal preference, but I prefer to set the view down to just column names at this point. You can do this by clicking on the Show icon on the toolbar or, as I prefer, by right-clicking the table and choosing Table View ▷ MA Column Names. I find that this saves a lot of screen real estate and makes more room for me to work on additional tables.

Now try to add in the `Employees` table as we had it defined earlier in the chapter. The steps should be pretty much as they were for the `Customers` table, with just one little hitch — we have a computed column. To deal with the computed column, just select Modify Custom again (from the right-click menu), and add the "formula" column. Then, simply add the proper formula (in this case, Salary-PriorSalary). When you have all the columns entered, save your new table (accepting the confirmation dialog) and your diagram should have two tables in it (see Figure 5-9).

Figure 5-9

It's very important to understand that the diagramming tool that is included with SQL Server is not designed to be everything to everyone.

Presumably, since you are reading this part of this book, you are just starting out on your database journey — this tool will probably be adequate for you for a while. Eventually, you may want to take a look at some more advanced (and far more expensive) tools to help you with your database design.

Backing into the Code: The Basics of Creating Scripts with the Management Studio

One last quick introduction before we exit this chapter — we want to see the basics of having the Management Studio write our scripts for us. For now, we are going to do this as something of a quick and dirty introduction.

To generate scripts, we go into the Management Studio and right-click on the database for which we want to generate scripts. (In this case, we're going to generate scripts on our Accounting database.) On the pop-up menu, choose Script Database As ⇨ CREATE To ⇨ New Query Editor Window, as shown in Figure 5-10.

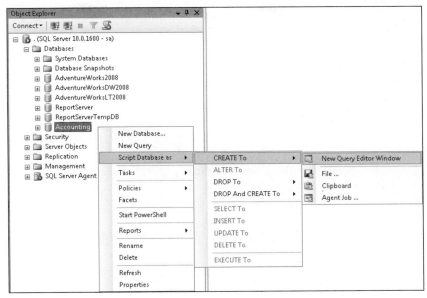

Figure 5-10

Whoa! SQL Server generates a heck of a lot more code than we saw when we created our database to begin with. Don't panic, however — all it is doing is being very explicit in scripting major database settings rather than relying on defaults as we did when we scripted it ourselves.

Note that we are not limited to scripting the database — if you want to script other objects in the database, just navigate and right-click on them much the way that you right-clicked on the Accounting database and, boom!, you've got yourself a SQL Script.

As you can see, scripting couldn't be much easier. Once you get a complex database put together, it still isn't quite as easy as it seems in this particular demonstration, but it is a lot easier than writing it all out by hand. The reality is that it really is pretty simple once you learn what the scripting options are, and we'll learn much more about those later in the book.

Summary

In this chapter, we've covered the basics of the CREATE, ALTER, and DROP statements as they relate to creating a database and tables. There are, of course, many other renditions of these that we will cover as we continue through the book. We have also taken a look at the wide variety of options that we can use in databases and tables to have full control over our data. Finally, we have begun to see the many things that we can use the Management Studio for in order to simplify our lives, and make design and scripting simpler.

At this point, you're ready to start getting into some hardcore details about how to lay out your tables, and a discussion on the concepts of normalization and more general database design. I am, however, actually going to make you wait another chapter before we get there, so that we can talk about constraints and keys somewhat before hitting the design issues.

Exercises

1. Using the Management Studio's script generator, generate SQL for both the Customers and the Employees tables.

2. Without using the Management Studio, script a database called MyDB with a starting database size of 17MB and a starting log size of 5MB — set both the log and the database to grow in 5MB increments.

3. Create a table called Foo with a single variable length character field called Col1 — limit the size of Col1 to 50 characters.

Constraints

You've heard me talk about them, but now it's time to look at them seriously — it's time to deal with constraints. We've talked a couple of times already about what constraints are, but let's review in case you decided to skip straight to this chapter.

> **A constraint is a restriction. Placed at either column or table level, a constraint ensures that your data meets certain data integrity rules.**

This goes back to the notion that I talked about back in Chapters 1 and 2, that ensuring data integrity is not the responsibility of the programs that use your database, but rather the responsibility of the database itself. If you think about it, this is really cool. Data is inserted, updated, and deleted from the database by many sources. Even in stand-alone applications (situations where only one program accesses the database), the same table may be accessed from many different places in the program. It doesn't stop there though. Your database administrator (that might mean you if you're a dual-role kind of person) may be altering data occasionally to deal with problems that arise. In more complex scenarios, you can actually run into situations where literally hundreds of different access paths exist for altering just one piece of data, let alone your entire database.

Moving the responsibility for data integrity into the database itself has been revolutionary to database management. There are still many different things that can go wrong when you are attempting to insert data into your database, but your database is now *proactive* rather than *reactive* to problems. Many problems with what programs allow into the database are now caught much earlier in the development process because, although the client program allowed the data through, the database knows to reject it. How does it do it? Primarily with constraints (data types and triggers are among the other worker bees of data integrity).

In this chapter, we'll be looking at the three different types of constraints at a high level:

- ❏ Entity constraints
- ❏ Domain constraints
- ❏ Referential integrity constraints

At a more specific level, we'll be looking at the methods of implementing each of these types of constraints, including:

- ❑ Primary key constraints
- ❑ Foreign key constraints
- ❑ Unique constraints (also known as alternate keys)
- ❑ Check constraints
- ❑ Default constraints
- ❑ Rules
- ❑ Defaults (similar to default constraints)

We'll also take a very cursory look at triggers and stored procedures (there will be much more on these later) as methods of implementing data integrity rules.

Types of Constraints

There are a number of different ways to implement constraints, but each of them falls into one of three categories — domain, entity, or referential integrity constraints, as illustrated in Figure 6-1.

Domain Constraints

Domain constraints deal with one or more columns. What we're talking about here is ensuring that a particular column or set of columns meets particular criteria. When you insert or update a row, the constraint is applied without respect to any other row in the table — it's the column's data you're interested in.

For example, if we want to confine the UnitPrice column to include only values that are greater than or equal to zero, that would be a domain constraint. Although any row that had a UnitPrice that didn't meet the constraint would be rejected, we're actually enforcing integrity to make sure that the entire column (no matter how many rows) meets the constraint. The domain is the column, and our constraint is a domain constraint.

We'll see this kind of constraint when dealing with check constraints, rules, defaults, and default constraints.

Entity Constraints

Entity constraints are all about individual rows. This form of constraint doesn't really care about a column as a whole; it's interested in a particular row, and would best be exemplified by a constraint that requires every row to have a unique value for a column or combination of columns.

"What," you say, "a unique column? Doesn't that mean it's a domain constraint?" No, it doesn't. We're not saying that a column has to meet any particular format, or that the value has to be greater or less than anything. What we're saying is that for *this* row, the same value can't already exist in some other row.

We'll see this kind of constraint when dealing with primary key and unique constraints.

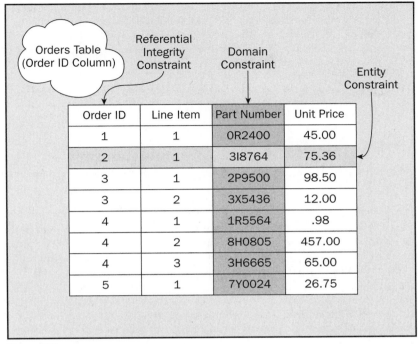

Figure 6-1

Referential Integrity Constraints

Referential integrity constraints are created when a value in one column must match the value in another column — in either the same table or, far more typically, a different table.

Let's say that we are taking orders for a product and that we accept credit cards. In order to be paid by the credit card company, we need to have some form of merchant agreement with that company. We don't want our employees to take credit cards from companies that aren't going to pay us back. That's where referential integrity comes in — it allows us to build what we would call a *domain* or *lookup table*. A domain table is a table whose sole purpose in life is to provide a limited list (often called a *domain list*) of acceptable values. In our case, we might build a table that looks something like this:

CreditCardID	CreditCard
1	VISA
2	MasterCard
3	Discover Card
4	American Express

We can then build one or more tables that *reference* the CreditCardID column of our domain table. With referential integrity, any table (such as our Orders table) that is defined as referencing our CreditCard table will have to have a column that matches up to the CreditCardID column. For each row that we insert into the referencing table, it will have to have a value that is in our domain list (it will have to have a corresponding row in the CreditCard table).

We'll see more of this as we learn about FOREIGN KEY constraints later in this chapter.

Constraint Naming

Before we get down to the nitty-gritty of constraints, we'll digress for a moment and address the issue of naming constraints.

> For each of the different types of constraints that we will be dealing with in this chapter, you can elect not to supply a name — that is, you can have SQL Server provide a name for you. Resist the temptation to do this. You'll quickly find that when SQL Server creates its own name, it isn't particularly useful.

An example of a system-generated name might be something like PK__Employees__145C0A3F. This is an SQL Server–generated name for a primary key on the Employees table of the Accounting database, which we will create later in the chapter. The "PK" is for primary key (which is the most useful naming element), the Employees is for the Employees table that it is on, and the rest is a randomly generated value to ensure uniqueness. You only get this type of naming if you create the primary key through script. If you created this table through Management Studio, it would have a name of PK_Employees.

That one isn't too bad, but you get less help on other constraints; for example, a CHECK constraint used later in the chapter might generate something like CK__Customers__22AA2996. From this, we know that it's a CHECK constraint, but we know nothing of what the nature of the CHECK is.

Since we can have multiple CHECK constraints on a table, you could wind up with all of these as names of constraints on the same table:

- ❏ CK__Customers__22AA2996
- ❏ CK__Customers__25869641
- ❏ CK__Customers__267ABA7A

Needless to say, if you needed to edit one of these constraints, it would be a pain to figure out which was which.

Personally, I either use a combination of constraint types with a phrase to indicate what it does or the name(s) of the column(s) it affects. For example, I might use CKPriceExceedsCost if I have a constraint to ensure that my users can't sell a product at a loss, or perhaps something as simple as `CKCustomerPhoneNo` on a column that ensures that phone numbers are formatted properly.

As with the naming of anything that we'll use in this book, how exactly you name things is really not all that important. What is important is that you:

❑ Be consistent.

❑ Make it something that everyone can understand.

❑ Keep it as short as you can while still meeting the preceding rules.

❑ Did I mention to be consistent?

Key Constraints

There are four different types of common keys that you may hear about in your database endeavors. These are primary keys, foreign keys, alternate keys, and inversion keys. For this chapter, we'll only take a look at the first three of these, as they provide constraints on a database.

> *An* inversion key *is basically just any index (we cover indexes in Chapter 9) that does not apply some form of constraint to the table (primary key, foreign key, unique). Inversion keys, rather than enforcing data integrity, are merely an alternative way of sorting the data.*

Keys are one of the cornerstone concepts of database design and management, so fasten your seatbelt and hold on tight. This will be one of the most important concepts you'll read about in this book, and will become absolutely critical as we move on to normalization in Chapter 8.

PRIMARY KEY Constraints

Before we define what a primary key actually is, let's digress slightly into a brief discussion of relational databases. Relational databases are constructed on the idea of being able to "relate" data. Therefore, it becomes critical in relational databases for most tables (there are exceptions, but they are very rare) to have a unique identifier for each row. A unique identifier allows you to accurately reference a record from another table in the database, thereby forming a relation between those two tables.

> *This is a wildly different concept from what we had with our old mainframe environment or the ISAM databases (dBase, FoxPro, and so on) of the '80s and early '90s. In those environments, we dealt with one record at a time. We would generally open the entire table, and go one record at a time until we found what we were looking for. If we needed data from a second table we would then open that table separately and fetch that table's data, then mix the data programmatically ourselves.*

Primary keys are the unique identifiers for each row. They must contain unique values (and hence cannot be NULL). Because of their importance in relational databases, primary keys are the most fundamental of all keys and constraints.

> **Don't confuse the primary key, which uniquely identifies each row in a table, with a GUID, which is a more generic tool, typically used to identify something (it could be anything, really) across all space and time. While a GUID can certainly be used as a primary key, they incur some overhead, and are usually not called for when we're only dealing with the contents of a table. Indeed, the only common place that a GUID becomes particularly useful in a database environment is as a primary key when dealing with replicated or other distributed data.**

A table can have a maximum of one primary key. As I mentioned earlier, it is rare to have a table in which you don't want a primary key.

When I say "rare" here, I mean very rare. A table that doesn't have a primary key severely violates the concept of relational data — it means that you can't guarantee that you can relate to a specific record. The data in your table no longer has anything that gives it distinction.

Situations where you can have multiple rows that are logically identical are actually not that uncommon, but that doesn't mean that you don't want a primary key. In these instances, you'll want to take a look at fabricating some sort of key. This approach has most often been implemented using an identity column, although using a GUID is now an appropriate alternative in some situations.

A primary key ensures uniqueness within the columns declared as being part of that primary key, and that unique value serves as an identifier for each row in that table. How do we create a primary key? Actually, there are two ways. You can create the primary key either in your CREATE TABLE command or with an ALTER TABLE command.

Much of the rest of this chapter makes use of the Accounting database you created in Chapter 5. The assumption is that the Accounting database is as it was at the end of Chapter 5 after using the Management Studio to create tables in the database.

Creating the Primary Key at Table Creation

Let's review one of our CREATE TABLE statements from the previous chapter:

```
CREATE TABLE Customers
(
    CustomerNo      int    IDENTITY    NOT NULL,
    CustomerName    varchar(30)        NOT NULL,
    Address1        varchar(30)        NOT NULL,
    Address2        varchar(30)        NOT NULL,
    City            varchar(20)        NOT NULL,
    State           char(2)            NOT NULL,
    Zip             varchar(10)        NOT NULL,
    Contact         varchar(25)        NOT NULL,
    Phone           char(15)           NOT NULL,
    FedIDNo         varchar(9)         NOT NULL,
    DateInSystem    smalldatetime      NOT NULL
);
```

This CREATE statement should seem old hat by now, but it's missing a very important piece — our PRIMARY KEY constraint. We want to identify CustomerNo as our primary key. Why CustomerNo? Well, we'll look into what makes a good primary key in the next chapter, but for now, just think about it a bit.

Do we want two customers to have the same `CustomerNo`? Definitely not. It makes perfect sense for a `CustomerNo` to be used as an identifier for a customer. Indeed, such a system has been used for years, so there's really no sense in reinventing the wheel here.

To alter our `CREATE TABLE` statement to include a `PRIMARY KEY` constraint, we just add in the constraint information right after the column(s) that we want to be part of our primary key. In this case, we would use:

```
USE Accounting;

CREATE TABLE Customers
(
    CustomerNo      int    IDENTITY    NOT NULL
        PRIMARY KEY,
    CustomerName    varchar(30)     NOT NULL,
    Address1        varchar(30)     NOT NULL,
    Address2        varchar(30)     NOT NULL,
    City            varchar(20)     NOT NULL,
    State           char(2)         NOT NULL,
    Zip             varchar(10)     NOT NULL,
    Contact         varchar(25)     NOT NULL,
    Phone           char(15)        NOT NULL,
    FedIDNo         varchar(9)      NOT NULL,
    DateInSystem    smalldatetime   NOT NULL
);
```

Since this table already exists in our Accounting database (as we left it at the end of Chapter 5), we need to also drop the table prior to running the `CREATE TABLE` script (i.e., `DROP TABLE` Customers). Notice that we altered one line (all we did was remove the comma) and added some code on a second line for that column. It was easy! Again, we just added one simple keyword (OK, so it's two words, but they operate as one) and we now have ourselves a primary key.

Creating a Primary Key on an Existing Table

Now, what if we already have a table and we want to set the primary key? That's also easy. We'll do that for our `Employees` table:

```
USE Accounting

ALTER TABLE Employees
    ADD CONSTRAINT PK_EmployeeID
    PRIMARY KEY (EmployeeID);
```

Our `ALTER` command tells SQL Server:

- ❏ That we are adding something to the table (we could also be dropping something from the table if we so chose)
- ❏ What it is that we're adding (a constraint)
- ❏ What we want to name the constraint (to allow us to address the constraint directly later)
- ❏ The type of constraint (`PRIMARY KEY`)
- ❏ The column(s) that the constraint applies to

FOREIGN KEY Constraints

Foreign keys are both a method of ensuring data integrity and a manifestation of the relationships between tables. When you add a foreign key to a table, you are creating a dependency between the table for which you define the foreign key (the *referencing* table) and the table your foreign key references (the *referenced* table). After adding a foreign key, any record you insert into the referencing table must either have a matching record in the referenced column(s) of the referenced table, or the value of the foreign key column(s) must be set to NULL. This can be a little confusing, so let's do it by example.

> *When I say that a value must be "set to NULL," I'm referring to how the actual INSERT statement looks. As we'll learn in a moment, the data may actually look slightly different once it gets in the table, depending on what options you've set in your FOREIGN KEY declaration.*

Let's create another table in our Accounting database called Orders. One thing you'll notice in this CRE-ATE script is that we're going to use both a primary key and a foreign key. A primary key, as we will see as we continue through the design, is a critical part of a table. Our foreign key is added to the script in almost exactly the same way as our primary key was, except that we must say what we are referencing. The syntax goes on the column or columns that we are placing our FOREIGN KEY constraint on, and looks something like this:

```
<column name> <data type> <nullability>
FOREIGN KEY REFERENCES <table name>(<column name>)
    [ON DELETE {CASCADE|NO ACTION|SET NULL|SET DEFAULT}]
    [ON UPDATE {CASCADE|NO ACTION|SET NULL|SET DEFAULT}]
```

Try It Out   Creating a Table with a Foreign Key

For the moment, we're going to ignore the ON clause. That leaves us, for our Orders table, with a script that looks something like this:

```
USE Accounting

CREATE TABLE Orders
(
    OrderID      int     IDENTITY    NOT NULL
        PRIMARY KEY,
    CustomerNo   int                 NOT NULL
        FOREIGN KEY REFERENCES Customers(CustomerNo),
    OrderDate    date                NOT NULL,
    EmployeeID   int                 NOT NULL
);
```

Note that the actual column being referenced must have either a PRIMARY KEY or a UNIQUE constraint defined on it (we'll discuss UNIQUE constraints later in the chapter).

> *It's also worth noting that primary and foreign keys can exist on the same column. You can see an example of this in the AdventureWorks2008 database with the SalesOrderDetail table. The primary key is composed of both the SalesOrderID and SalesOrderDetailID columns — the former is also the foreign key and references the SalesOrderHeader table. We'll actually create a table later in the chapter that has a column that is both a primary key and a foreign key.*

How It Works

Once you have successfully run the preceding code, run sp_help, and you should see your new constraint reported under the constraints section of the sp_help information. If you want to get even more to the point, you can run sp_helpconstraint. The syntax is easy:

```
EXEC sp_helpconstraint <table name>
```

Run sp_helpconstraint on our new Orders table, and you'll get information back giving you the names, criteria, and status for all the constraints on the table. At this point, our Orders table has one FOREIGN KEY constraint and one PRIMARY KEY constraint.

> When you run sp_helpconstraint on this table, the word "clustered" will appear right after the reporting of the PRIMARY KEY. This just means it has a clustered index. We will explore the meaning of this further in Chapter 9.

Our new foreign key has been referenced in the physical definition of our table, and is now an integral part of our table. As we discussed in Chapter 1, the database is in charge of its own integrity. Our foreign key enforces one constraint on our data and makes sure our database integrity remains intact.

Unlike primary keys, foreign keys are not limited to just one per table. We can have between 0 and 253 foreign keys in each table. The only limitation is that a given column can reference only one foreign key. However, you can have more than one column participate in a single foreign key. A given column that is the target of a reference by a foreign key can also be referenced by many tables.

Adding a Foreign Key to an Existing Table

Just like with primary keys, or any constraint for that matter, there are situations where we want to add our foreign key to a table that already exists. This process is similar to creating a primary key.

Try It Out   Adding a Foreign Key to an Existing Table

Let's add another foreign key to our Orders table to restrict the EmployeeID field (which is intended to have the ID of the employee who entered the order) to valid employees as defined in the Employees table. To do this, we need to be able to uniquely identify a target record in the referenced table. As I've already mentioned, you can do this by referencing either a primary key or a column with a UNIQUE constraint. In this case, we'll make use of the existing primary key that we placed on the Employees table earlier in the chapter:

```
ALTER TABLE Orders
    ADD CONSTRAINT FK_EmployeeCreatesOrder
    FOREIGN KEY (EmployeeID) REFERENCES Employees(EmployeeID);
```

Now execute sp_helpconstraint again against the Orders table, and you'll see that our new constraint has been added.

How It Works

Our latest constraint works just as the last one did — the physical table definition is aware of the rules placed on the data it is to contain. Just as it would not allow string data to be inserted into a numeric column, now it will not allow a row to be inserted into the Orders table where the referenced employee in charge of that order is not a valid EmployeeID. If someone attempts to add a row that doesn't match with an employee record, the insertion into Orders will be rejected in order to maintain the integrity of the database.

Note that while we've added two foreign keys, there is still a line down at the bottom of our sp_helpconstraint results (or under the Messages tab if you have Results in Grid selected) that says No foreign keys reference this table. This is telling us that, while we do have foreign keys in this table that reference other tables, there are no other tables out there that reference this table. If you want to see the difference, just run sp_helpconstraint on the Customers or Employees tables at this point, and you'll see that each of these tables is now referenced by our new Orders table.

Making a Table Self-Referencing

What if the column you want to refer to isn't in another table, but is actually right within the table in which you are building the reference? Can a table be both the referencing and the referenced table? You bet! Indeed, while this is far from the most common of situations, it is actually used with regularity.

Before we actually create this self-referencing constraint that references a required (non-nullable) field that's based on an identity column, it's rather critical that we get at least one row in the table prior to the foreign key being added. Why? Well, the problem stems from the fact that the identity value is chosen and filled in after the foreign key has already been checked and enforced. That means that you don't have a value yet for that first row to reference when the check happens. The only other option here is to go ahead and create the foreign key, but then disable it when adding the first row. We'll learn about disabling constraints a little later in this chapter.

OK — because this is a table that's referencing a column based on an identity column, we need to get a primer row into the table before we add our constraint:

```
INSERT INTO Employees
    (
    FirstName,
    LastName,
    Title,
    SSN,
    Salary,
    PriorSalary,
    HireDate,
    ManagerEmpID,
    Department
    )
VALUES
    (
    'Billy Bob',
    'Boson',
```

```
'Head Cook & Bottle Washer',
'123-45-6789',
100000,
80000,
'1990-01-01',
1,
'Cooking and Bottling'
);
```

Now that we have a primer row, we can add in our foreign key. In an ALTER situation, this works just the same as any other foreign key definition. We can now try this out:

```
ALTER TABLE Employees
    ADD CONSTRAINT FK_EmployeeHasManager
    FOREIGN KEY (ManagerEmpID) REFERENCES Employees(EmployeeID);
```

There is one difference with a CREATE statement. You can (but you don't have to) leave out the FOREIGN KEY phrasing and just use the REFERENCES clause. We already have our Employees table set up at this point, but if we were creating it from scratch, the script would appear as follows (pay particular attention to the foreign key on the ManagerEmpID column):

```
CREATE TABLE Employees (
    EmployeeID       int    IDENTITY    NOT NULL
        PRIMARY KEY,
    FirstName        varchar (25)       NOT NULL,
    MiddleInitial    char (1)           NULL,
    LastName         varchar (25)       NOT NULL,
    Title            varchar (25)       NOT NULL,
    SSN              varchar (11)       NOT NULL,
    Salary           money              NOT NULL,
    PriorSalary      money              NOT NULL,
    LastRaise AS Salary -PriorSalary,
    HireDate         smalldatetime      NOT NULL,
    TerminationDate  smalldatetime      NULL,
    ManagerEmpID     int                NOT NULL
        REFERENCES Employees(EmployeeID),
    Department       varchar (25)       NOT NULL
);
```

It's worth noting that, if you try to DROP the Employees table at this point (to run the second example), you're going to get an error. Why? Well, when we established the reference in our Orders table to the Employees table, the two tables became "schema-bound;" that is, the Employees table now knows that it has what is called a dependency on it. SQL Server will not let you drop a table that is referenced by another table. You have to drop the foreign key in the Orders table before SQL Server will allow you to delete the Employees table (or the Customers table for that matter).

In addition, doing the self-referencing foreign key in the constraint doesn't allow us to get our primer row in, so it's important that you do it this way only when the column the foreign key constraint is placed on allows NULLs. That way the first row can have a NULL in that column and avoid the need for a primer row.

Cascading Actions

One important difference between foreign keys and other kinds of keys is that foreign keys are *bidirectional*; that is, they not only restrict the child table to values that exist in the parent, but they also check for child rows whenever we do something to the parent (thus preventing orphans). The default behavior is for SQL Server to "restrict" the parent row from being deleted if any child rows exist. Sometimes, however, we would rather automatically delete any dependent records rather than prevent the deletion of the referenced record. The same notion applies to updates to records where we would like the dependent record to automatically reference the newly updated record. Somewhat more rare is the instance where you want to alter the referencing row to some sort of known state. For this, you have the option to set the value in the dependent row to either NULL or whatever the default value is for that column.

The process of making such automatic deletions and updates is known as *cascading*. This process, especially for deletes, can actually run through several layers of dependencies (where one record depends on another, which depends on another, and so on). So, how do we implement cascading actions in SQL Server? All we need is a modification to the syntax we use when declaring our foreign key. We just add the ON clause that we skipped at the beginning of this section.

Let's check this out by adding a new table to our Accounting database. We'll make this a table to store the individual line items in an order, and we'll call it OrderDetails:

```
CREATE TABLE OrderDetails
(
    OrderID        int            NOT NULL,
    PartNo         varchar(10)    NOT NULL,
    Description    varchar(25)    NOT NULL,
    UnitPrice      money          NOT NULL,
    Qty            int            NOT NULL,
    CONSTRAINT     PKOrderDetails
        PRIMARY KEY    (OrderID, PartNo),
    CONSTRAINT     FKOrderContainsDetails
        FOREIGN KEY    (OrderID)
            REFERENCES Orders(OrderID)
            ON UPDATE  NO ACTION
            ON DELETE  CASCADE
);
```

This time we have a whole lot going on, so let's take it apart piece by piece.

> Before we get too far into looking at the foreign key aspects of this, notice something about how the primary key was done here. Instead of placing the declaration immediately after the key, I decided to declare it as a separate constraint item. This helps facilitate the multicolumn primary key (which therefore could not be declared as a column constraint) and the clarity of the overall CREATE TABLE statement. Likewise, I could have declared the foreign key either immediately following the column or, as I did here, as a separate constraint item. I'll touch on this a little bit later in the chapter.

First, notice that our foreign key is also part of our primary key. This is not at all uncommon in child tables, and is actually almost always the case for associate tables (more on this next chapter).

Just remember that each constraint stands alone — you add, change, or delete each of them independently.

Next, look at our `foreign key` declaration:

```
FOREIGN KEY    (OrderID)
REFERENCES     Orders(OrderID)
```

We've declared our `OrderID` as being dependent on a "foreign" column. In this case, it's for a column (also called `OrderID`) in a separate table (`Orders`), but as we saw earlier in the chapter, it could just as easily have been in the same table.

> There is something of a "gotcha" when creating foreign keys that reference the same table the foreign key is being defined on. Foreign keys of this nature are not allowed to have declarative CASCADE actions. The reason for this restriction is to avoid cyclical updates or deletes; that is, situations where the first update causes another, which in turn tries to update the first. The result could be a never-ending loop.

Now, to get to the heart of our cascading issue, we need to look at our ON clauses:

```
ON UPDATE    NO ACTION
ON DELETE    CASCADE
```

We've defined two different *referential integrity actions*. As you might guess, a referential integrity action is what you want to have happen whenever the referential integrity rule you've defined is invoked. For situations where the parent record (in the `Orders` table) is updated, we've said that we do not want that update to be cascaded to our child table (`OrderDetails`). For illustration purposes, however, I've chosen a CASCADE for deletes.

Note that NO ACTION is the default, and so specifying this in our code is optional. While the "typical" way of coding this is to leave out the NO ACTION, I would encourage you to include the NO ACTION explicitly to make your intent clear.

Let's try an insert into our `OrderDetails` table:

```
INSERT INTO OrderDetails
VALUES
    (1, '4X4525', 'This is a part', 25.00, 2);
```

Unless you've been playing around with your data some, this generates an error:

```
Msg 547, Level 16, State 0, Line 1
The INSERT statement conflicted with the FOREIGN KEY constraint
"FKOrderContainsDetails". The conflict occurred in database "Accounting", table
"dbo.Orders", column 'OrderID'.
The statement has been terminated.
```

Why? Well, we haven't inserted anything into our `Orders` table yet, so how can we refer to a record in the `Orders` table if there isn't anything there?

This is going to expose you to one of the hassles of relational database work — dependency chains. A dependency chain exists when you have something that is, in turn, dependent on something else, which may yet be dependent on something else, and so on. There's really nothing you can do about this. It's just something that comes along with database work. You have to start at the top of the chain and work your way down to what you need inserted. Fortunately, the records you need are often already there, save one or two dependency levels.

OK, so in order to get our row into our `OrderDetails` table, we must also have a record already in the `Orders` table. Unfortunately, getting a row into the `Orders` table requires that we have one in the `Customers` table (remember that foreign key we built on `Orders`?). So, let's take care of it a step at a time:

```
INSERT INTO Customers -- Our Customer.
                      -- Remember that CustomerNo is
                      -- an Identity column
VALUES
    ('Billy Bob''s Shoes',
    '123 Main St.',
    ' ',
    'Vancouver',
    'WA',
    '98685',
    'Billy Bob',
    '(360) 555-1234',
    '931234567',
    GETDATE()
    );
```

Now we have a customer, so let's select against the record we just inserted to be sure:

Customer No	1
Customer Name	Billy Bob's Shoes
Address 1	123 Main Street
Address 2	
City	Vancouver
State	WA
Zip	98685
Contact	Billy Bob
Phone	(360) 555-1234
FedIDNo	931234567
DateInSystem	2000-07-1021:17:00

So we have a CustomerID of 1 (your number may be different depending on what experimentation you've done). We'll take that number and use it in our next INSERT (into Orders, finally). Let's insert an order for CustomerID 1:

```
INSERT INTO Orders
    (CustomerNo, OrderDate, EmployeeID)
VALUES
    (1, GETDATE(), 1);
```

This time, things should work fine.

> It's worth noting that the reason we don't still get an error here is that we already inserted that primer row in the Employees table; otherwise, we would have needed to get a row into that table before SQL Server would have allowed the insert into Orders (remember that Employees foreign key?).

At this point, we're ready for our insert into the OrderDetails table. Just to help with a CASCADE example we're going to be doing in a moment, we're actually going to insert not one, but two rows:

```
INSERT INTO OrderDetails
VALUES
    (1, '4X4525', 'This is a part', 25.00, 2)

INSERT INTO OrderDetails
VALUES
    (1, '0R2400', 'This is another part', 50.00, 2);
```

So, let's verify things by running a SELECT:

```
SELECT OrderID, PartNo FROM OrderDetails;
```

This gets us back to our expected two rows:

```
OrderID        PartNo
---------      ---------
1              0R2400
1              4X4525

(2 row(s) affected)
```

Now that we have our data entered, let's look at the effect a CASCADE has on the data. We'll delete a row from the Orders table, and then see what happens in OrderDetails:

```
USE Accounting

-- First, let's look at the rows in both tables
SELECT *
FROM Orders;

SELECT *
```

```
FROM OrderDetails;

-- Now, let's delete the Order record
DELETE Orders
WHERE OrderID = 1;

-- Finally, look at both sets of data again
-- and see the CASCADE effect
SELECT *
FROM Orders;

SELECT *
FROM OrderDetails;
```

This yields some interesting results:

OrderID	CustomerNo	OrderDate	EmployeeID
1	1	2000-07-13 22:18:00	1

(1 row(s) affected)

OrderID	PartNo	Description	UnitPrice	Qty
1	0R2400	This is another part	50.0000	2
1	4X4525	This is a part	25.0000	2

(2 row(s) affected)

(1 row(s) affected)

OrderID	CustomerNo	OrderDate	EmployeeID

(0 row(s) affected)

OrderID	PartNo	Description	UnitPrice	Qty

(0 row(s) affected)

Notice that even though we issued a DELETE against the Orders table only, the DELETE also cascaded to our matching records in the OrderDetails table. Records in both tables were deleted. If we had defined our table with a CASCADE update and updated a relevant record, then that, too, would have been propagated to the child table.

It's worth noting that there is no limit to the depth that a CASCADE action can reach. For example, if we had a ShipmentDetails table that referenced rows in OrderDetails with a CASCADE action, then those, too, would have been deleted just by our one DELETE in the Orders table.

This is actually one of the danger areas of cascading actions. It's very, very easy to not realize all the different things that one DELETE or UPDATE statement can do in your database. For this and other reasons, I'm not a huge fan of cascading actions. They allow people to get lazy, and that's something that's not usually a good thing when doing something like deleting data!

Those Other CASCADE Actions ...

So, those were examples of cascading updates and deletes, but what about the other two types of cascade actions I mentioned? What of SET NULL and SET DEFAULT?

These were added with SQL Server 2005, so avoid them if you want backward compatibility with SQL Server 2000, but their operation is very simple: If you perform an update that changes the parent values for a row, then the child row will be set to either NULL or whatever the default value for that column is (whichever you chose — SET NULL or SET DEFAULT). It's just that simple.

Other Things to Think About with Foreign Keys

There are some other things to think about before we're done with foreign keys. We will be coming back to this subject over and over again throughout the book, but for now, I just want to get in a couple of finer points:

❑   What makes values in foreign keys required versus optional

❑   How foreign keys are bi-directional

What Makes Values in Foreign Keys Required vs. Optional

The nature of a foreign key provides us two possible choices regarding how to fill in a column or columns that have a foreign key defined for them:

❑   Fill the column in with a value that matches the corresponding column in the referenced table.

❑   Do not fill in a value at all and leave the value NULL.

You can make the foreign key completely required (limit your users to just the first option in the preceding list) by simply defining the referencing column as NOT NULL. Since a NULL value won't be valid in the column and the foreign key requires any non-NULL value to have a match in the referenced table, you know that every row will have a match in your referenced table. In other words, the reference is required.

Allowing the referencing column to have NULLs will create the same requirement, except that the user will also have the option of supplying no value — even if there is not a match for NULL in the referenced table, the insert will still be allowed.

How Foreign Keys Are Bi-Directional

We touched on this some when we discussed CASCADE actions, but when defining foreign keys, I can't stress enough that they effectively place restrictions on *both* tables. Up to this point, we've been talking about things in terms of the referencing table; however, once the foreign key is defined, the referenced table must also live by a rule:

> By default, you cannot delete a record or update the referenced column in a referenced table if that record is referenced from the dependent table. If you want to be able to delete or update such a record, then you need to set up a CASCADE action for the delete and/or update.

Let's illustrate this "You can't delete or update a referenced record" idea.

We just defined a couple of foreign keys for the `Orders` table. One of those references the `EmployeeID` columns of the `Employees` table. Let's say, for instance, that we have an employee with an `EmployeeID` of 10 who takes many orders for us for a year or two, and then decides to quit and move on to another job. Our tendency would probably be to delete the record in the `Employees` table for that employee, but that would create a rather large problem — we would get what are called *orphaned* records in the `Orders` table. Our `Orders` table would have a large number of records that still have an `EmployeeID` of 10. If we are allowed to delete `EmployeeID` 10 from the `Employees` table, then we will no longer be able to tell which employee entered in all those orders. The value for the `EmployeeID` column of the `Orders` table will become worthless!

Now let's take this example one step further. Let's say that the employee did not quit. Instead, for some unknown reason, we wanted to change that employee's ID number. If we made the change (via an `UPDATE` statement) to the `Employees` table, but did not make the corresponding update to the `Orders` table, then we would again have orphaned records. We would have records with a value of 10 in the `EmployeeID` column of the `Orders` table with no matching employee.

Now, let's take it one more step further! Imagine that someone comes along and inserts a new record with an `EmployeeID` of 10. We now have a number of records in our `Orders` table that will be related to an employee who didn't take those orders. We would have bad data (yuck!).

Instead of allowing orphaned records, SQL Server, by default, restricts us from deleting or updating records from the referenced table (in this case, the `Employees` table) unless any dependent records have already been deleted from or updated in the referencing (in this case, `Orders`) table.

> This is actually not a bad segue into a brief discussion on or about when a `CASCADE` action makes sense and when it doesn't. Data-integrity-wise, we probably wouldn't want to allow the deletion of an employee if there are dependent rows in the `Orders` table. Not being able to trace back to the employee would degrade the value of our data. On the other hand, it may be perfectly valid (for some very strange reason) to change an employee's ID. We could `CASCADE` that update to the `Orders` table with little ill effect. Another moral to the story here is that you don't need the same `CASCADE` decision for both `UPDATE` and `DELETE` — think about each separately (and carefully).

As you can see, although the foreign key is defined on one table, it actually placed restrictions on both tables (if the foreign key is self-referenced, then both sets of restrictions are on the one table).

UNIQUE Constraints

These are relatively easy. `UNIQUE` constraints are essentially the younger sibling of primary keys in that they require a unique value throughout the named column (or combination of columns) in the table. You will often hear `UNIQUE` constraints referred to as *alternate keys*. The major differences are that they are not considered to be *the* unique identifier of a record in a table (even though you could effectively use it that way) and that you *can* have more than one `UNIQUE` constraint (remember that you can only have one primary key per table).

Once you establish a UNIQUE constraint, every value in the named columns must be unique. If you try to update or insert a row with a value that already exists in a column with a UNIQUE constraint, SQL Server will raise an error and reject the record.

> Unlike a primary key, a UNIQUE constraint does not automatically prevent you from having a NULL value. Whether NULLs are allowed or not depends on how you set the NULL option for that column in the table. Keep in mind, however, that, if you do allow NULLs, you will be able to insert only one of them (although a NULL doesn't equal another NULL, they are still considered to be duplicate from the perspective of a UNIQUE constraint).

Since there is nothing novel about this (we've pretty much already seen it with primary keys), let's get right to the code. Let's create yet another table in our Accounting database. This time, it will be our Shippers table:

```
CREATE TABLE Shippers
(
    ShipperID      int    IDENTITY    NOT NULL
        PRIMARY KEY,
    ShipperName    varchar(30)        NOT NULL,
    Address        varchar(30)        NOT NULL,
    City           varchar(25)        NOT NULL,
    State          char(2)            NOT NULL,
    Zip            varchar(10)        NOT NULL,
    PhoneNo        varchar(14)        NOT NULL
        UNIQUE
);
```

Now run sp_helpconstraint against the Shippers table, and verify that your Shippers table has been created with the proper constraints.

Creating UNIQUE Constraints on Existing Tables

Again, this works pretty much the same as with primary and foreign keys. We will go ahead and create a UNIQUE constraint on our Employees table:

```
ALTER TABLE Employees
    ADD CONSTRAINT AK_EmployeeSSN
    UNIQUE (SSN);
```

A quick run of sp_helpconstraint verifies that our constraint was created as planned, and tells us on which columns the constraint is active.

In case you're wondering, the AK I used in the constraint name here is for alternate key — much like we used PK and FK for primary and foreign keys. You will also often see a UQ or just U prefix used for UNIQUE constraint names.

CHECK Constraints

The nice thing about CHECK constraints is that they are not restricted to a particular column. They can be related to a column, but they can also be essentially table related in that they can check one column against another, as long as all the columns are within a single table and the values are for the same row being updated or inserted. They can also check that any combination of column values meets a criterion.

The constraint is defined using the same rules that you would use in a WHERE clause. Examples of the criteria for a CHECK constraint include:

Goal	SQL
Limit Month column to appropriate numbers	BETWEEN 1 AND 12
Proper SSN formatting	LIKE '[0-9][0-9][0-9]-[0-9][0-9]-[0-9][0-9][0-9][0-9]'
Limit to a specific list of Shippers	IN ('UPS', 'Fed Ex', 'USPS')
Price must be positive	UnitPrice >= 0
Referencing another column in the same row	ShipDate >= OrderDate

This really only scratches the surface, and the possibilities are virtually endless. Almost anything you could put in a WHERE clause, you can also put in your constraint. What's more, CHECK constraints are very fast performance-wise as compared to the alternatives (rules and triggers).

Still building on our Accounting database, let's add a modification to our Customers table to check for a valid date in our DateInSystem field (you can't have a date in the system that's in the future):

```
ALTER TABLE Customers
    ADD CONSTRAINT CN_CustomerDateInSystem
    CHECK
    (DateInSystem <= GETDATE ());
```

Now try to insert a record that violates the CHECK constraint; you'll get an error:

```
INSERT INTO Customers
    (CustomerName, Address1, Address2, City, State, Zip, Contact,
    Phone, FedIDNo, DateInSystem)
VALUES
    ('Customer1', 'Address1', 'Add2', 'MyCity', 'NY', '55555',
    'No Contact', '553-1212', '930984954', '12-31-2049');
Msg 547, Level 16, State 0, Line 1
```

```
The INSERT statement conflicted with the CHECK constraint
"CN_CustomerDateInSystem". The conflict occurred in database "Accounting", table
"dbo.Customers", column 'DateInSystem'.
The statement has been terminated.
```

Now if we change things to use a DateInSystem that meets the criterion used in the CHECK (anything with today's date or earlier), the INSERT works fine.

DEFAULT Constraints

This will be the first of two different types of data integrity tools that will be called something to do with "default." This is, unfortunately, very confusing, but I'll do my best to make it clear (and I think it will become so).

We'll see the other type of default when we look at rules and defaults later in the chapter.

A DEFAULT constraint, like all constraints, becomes an integral part of the table definition. It defines what to do when a new row is inserted that doesn't include data for the column on which you have defined the default constraint. You can either define it as a literal value (say, setting a default salary to zero or "UNKNOWN" for a string column) or as one of several system values such as GETDATE().

The main things to understand about a DEFAULT constraint are that:

❑ Defaults are only used in INSERT statements. They are ignored for UPDATE and DELETE statements.

❑ If any value is supplied in the INSERT, then the default is not used.

❑ If no value is supplied, the default will always be used.

Defaults are only made use of in INSERT statements. I cannot express enough how much this confuses many SQL Server beginners. Think about it this way: When you are first inserting the record, SQL Server doesn't have any kind of value for your column except what you supplied (if anything) or the default. If neither of these is supplied, then SQL Server will either insert a NULL (essentially amounting to "I don't know"), or if your column definition says NOT NULL, then SQL Server will reject the record. After that first insert, however, SQL Server already has some value for that column. If you are updating that column, then it has your new value. If the column in question isn't part of an UPDATE statement, then SQL Server just leaves what is already in the column.

If a value was provided for the column, then there is no reason to use the default. The supplied value is used.

If no value is supplied, then the default will always be used. Now this seems simple enough until you think about the circumstance where a NULL value is what you actually want to go into that column for a record. If you don't supply a value on a column that has a default defined, then the default will be used. What do you do if you really wanted it to be NULL? Say so — insert NULL as part of your INSERT statement.

> Under the heading of "One more thing," it's worth noting that there is an exception to the rule about an UPDATE command not using a default. The exception happens if you explicitly say that you want a default to be used. You do this by using the keyword DEFAULT as the value you want the column updated to.

Defining a DEFAULT Constraint in Your CREATE TABLE Statement

At the risk of sounding repetitious, this works pretty much like all the other column constraints we've dealt with thus far. You just add it to the end of the column definition.

To work an example, start by dropping the existing Shippers table that we created earlier in the chapter. This time, we'll create a simpler version of that table, including a default:

```
CREATE TABLE Shippers
(
    ShipperID       int     IDENTITY    NOT NULL
        PRIMARY KEY,
    ShipperName     varchar(30)         NOT NULL,
    DateInSystem    smalldatetime       NOT NULL
        DEFAULT GETDATE ()
);
```

After you run your CREATE script, you can again make use of sp_helpconstraint to show you what you have done. You can then test how your default works by inserting a new record:

```
INSERT INTO Shippers
    (ShipperName)
VALUES
    ('United Parcel Service');
```

Then run a SELECT statement on your Shippers table:

```
SELECT * FROM Shippers;
```

The default value has been generated for the DateInSystem column since we didn't supply a value ourselves:

```
ShipperID       ShipperName                     DateInSystem
-----------------------------------------       ---------------------------
1               United Parcel Service           2008-07-31 23:26:00

(1 row(s) affected)
```

Adding a DEFAULT Constraint to an Existing Table

While this one is still pretty much more of the same, there is a slight twist. We make use of our ALTER statement and ADD the constraint as before, but we add a FOR operator to tell SQL Server what column is the target for the DEFAULT:

```
ALTER TABLE Customers
   ADD CONSTRAINT CN_CustomerDefaultDateInSystem
      DEFAULT GETDATE() FOR DateInSystem;
```

And an extra example:

```
ALTER TABLE Customers
   ADD CONSTRAINT CN_CustomerAddress
      DEFAULT 'UNKNOWN' FOR Address1;
```

As with all constraints except for a PRIMARY KEY, we are able to add more than one per table.

> You can mix and match any and all of these constraints as you choose — just be careful not to create constraints that have mutually exclusive conditions. For example, don't have one constraint that says that col1 > col2 and another one that says that col2 > col1. SQL Server will let you do this, and you wouldn't see the issues with it until runtime.

Disabling Constraints

Sometimes we want to eliminate constraints, either just for a time or permanently. It probably doesn't take much thought to realize that SQL Server must give us some way of deleting constraints, but SQL Server also allows us to just deactivate a FOREIGN KEY or CHECK constraint while otherwise leaving it intact.

The concept of turning off a data integrity rule might seem rather ludicrous at first. I mean, why would you want to turn off the thing that makes sure you don't have bad data? First, realize that any reason for turning off a data integrity rule is going to be a temporary thing (otherwise you would be dropping it entirely). The usual reason to disable a data integrity rule is because you already have bad data. This data usually falls into two categories:

❑   Data that's already in your database when you create the constraint

❑   Data that you want to add after the constraint is already built

SQL Server allows us to turn the integrity check off long enough to deal with the bad data we want to make an exception for, and then re-enable the integrity check later — all without physically removing the data integrity check.

> You cannot disable PRIMARY KEY or UNIQUE constraints.

Ignoring Bad Data When You Create the Constraint

All this syntax has been just fine for the circumstances in which you create the constraint at the same time as you create the table. Quite often, however, data rules are established after the fact. Let's say, for instance, that you missed something when you were designing your database, and you now have some records in an `Invoicing` table that show a negative invoice amount. You might want to add a rule that won't let any more negative invoice amounts into the database, but at the same time, you want to preserve the existing records in their original state.

To add a constraint that won't apply to existing data, you make use of the `WITH NOCHECK` option when you perform the `ALTER TABLE` statement that adds your constraint. As always, let's look at an example.

The `Customers` table we created in the Accounting database has a field called `Phone`. The `Phone` field was created with a data type of `char` because we expected all of the phone numbers to be of the same length. We also set it with a length of 15 in order to ensure that we have enough room for all the formatting characters. However, we have not done anything to make sure that the records inserted into the database do indeed match the formatting criteria that we expect. To test this out, we'll insert a record in a format that is not what we're expecting, but might be a very honest mistake in terms of how someone might enter a phone number:

```
INSERT INTO Customers
    (CustomerName,
    Address1,
    Address2,
    City,
    State,
    Zip,
    Contact,
    Phone,
    FedIDNo,
    DateInSystem)
VALUES
    ('MyCust',
    '123 Anywhere',
    ' ',
    'Reno',
    'NV',
    80808,
    'Joe Bob',
    '555-1212',
    '931234567',
    GETDATE());
```

Now let's add a constraint to control the formatting of the `Phone` field:

```
ALTER TABLE Customers
    ADD CONSTRAINT CN_CustomerPhoneNo
    CHECK
    (Phone LIKE '([0-9][0-9][0-9]) [0-9][0-9][0-9]-[0-9][0-9][0-9][0-9]');
```

When we run this, we have a problem:

```
Msg 547, Level 16, State 0, Line 1
The ALTER TABLE statement conflicted with the CHECK constraint
"CN_CustomerPhoneNo". The conflict occurred in database "Accounting", table
"dbo.Customers", column 'Phone'.
```

SQL Server does not create the constraint unless the existing data meets the constraint criteria. To get around this long enough to install the constraint, either we need to correct the existing data or we must make use of the WITH NOCHECK option in our ALTER statement. To do this, we just add WITH NOCHECK to the statement as follows:

```
ALTER TABLE Customers
    WITH NOCHECK
    ADD CONSTRAINT CN_CustomerPhoneNo
    CHECK
    (Phone LIKE '([0-9][0-9][0-9]) [0-9][0-9][0-9]-[0-9][0-9][0-9][0-9]');
```

Now if we run our same INSERT statement again (remember it inserted without a problem last time), the constraint works and the data is rejected:

```
Msg 547, Level 16, State 0, Line 1
The ALTER TABLE statement conflicted with the CHECK constraint
"CN_CustomerPhoneNo". The conflict occurred in database "Accounting", table
"dbo.Customers", column 'Phone'.
```

However, if we modify our INSERT statement to adhere to our constraint and then re-execute it, the row will be inserted normally:

```
INSERT INTO Customers
    (CustomerName,
    Address1,
    Address2,
    City,
    State,
    Zip,
    Contact,
    Phone,
    FedIDNo,
    DateInSystem)
VALUES
    ('MyCust',
    '123 Anywhere',
    '',
    'Reno',
    'NV',
    80808,
    'Joe Bob',
    '(800) 555-1212',
    '931234567',
    GETDATE());
```

Try running a SELECT on the Customers table at this point. You'll see data that both does and does not adhere to our CHECK constraint criterion:

```
SELECT CustomerNo, CustomerName, Phone FROM Customers;
CustomerNo         CustomerName                    Phone
-----------        --------------------            --------------
1                  Billy Bob's Shoes               (360) 555-1234
2                  Customer1                       553-1212
3                  MyCust                          555-1212
5                  MyCust                          (800) 555-1212

(2 row(s) affected)
```

The old data is retained for back reference, but any new data is restricted to meeting the new criteria.

Temporarily Disabling an Existing Constraint

All right, so you understand why we need to be able to add new constraints that do not check old data, but why would we want to temporarily disable an existing constraint? Why would we want to let data that we know is bad be added to the database? Actually, the most common reason is basically the same reason for which we make use of the WITH NOCHECK option — old data.

Old data doesn't just come in the form of data that has already been added to your database. It may also be data that you are importing from a legacy database or some other system. Whatever the reason, the same issue still holds: You have some existing data that doesn't match up with the rules, and you need to get it into the table.

Certainly one way to do this would be to drop the constraint, add the desired data, and then add the constraint back using a WITH NOCHECK. But what a pain! Fortunately, we don't need to do that. Instead, we can run an ALTER statement with an option called NOCHECK that turns off the constraint in question. Here's the code that disables the CHECK constraint that we just added in the previous section:

```
ALTER TABLE Customers
    NOCHECK
    CONSTRAINT CN_CustomerPhoneNo;
```

Now we can run that INSERT statement again — the one we proved wouldn't work if the constraint were active:

```
INSERT INTO Customers
    (CustomerName,
    Address1,
    Address2,
    City,
    State,
    Zip,
    Contact,
    Phone,
```

```
        FedIDNo,
        DateInSystem)
VALUES
        ('MyCust',
         '123 Anywhere',
         '',
         'Reno',
         'NV',
         80808,
         'Joe Bob',
         '555-1212',
         '931234567',
         GETDATE());
```

Once again, we are able to INSERT non-conforming data to the table.

By now, you may be asking how you know whether you have the constraint turned on or not. It would be pretty tedious if you had to create a bogus record to try to insert in order to test whether your constraint is active or not. Like most (but not all) of these kinds of dilemmas, SQL Server provides a procedure to indicate the status of a constraint, and it's a procedure we've already seen, sp_helpconstraint. To execute it against our Customers table is easy:

```
EXEC sp_helpconstraint Customers;
```

The results are a little too verbose to fit into the pages of this book, but the second result set this procedure generates includes a column called status_enabled. Whatever this column says the status is can be believed. In this case, it should currently be Disabled.

When we are ready for the constraint to be active again, we simply turn it back on by issuing the same command with a CHECK in the place of the NOCHECK:

```
ALTER TABLE Customers
    CHECK
    CONSTRAINT CN_CustomerPhoneNo;
```

If you run the INSERT statement to verify that the constraint is again functional, you will see a familiar error message:

```
Msg 547, Level 16, State 0, Line 1
The INSERT statement conflicted with the CHECK constraint
"CN_CustomerDateInSystem". The conflict occurred in database "Accounting", table
"dbo.Customers", column 'DateInSystem'.
The statement has been terminated.
```

Our other option, of course, is to run sp_helpconstraint again, and check out the status_enabled column. If it shows as Enabled, then our constraint must be functional again.

Rules and Defaults — Cousins of Constraints

Rules and *defaults* have been around much longer than CHECK and DEFAULT constraints have been. They are something of an old SQL Server standby, and are definitely not without their advantages.

That being said, I'm going to digress from explaining them long enough to recommend that you look them over for backward compatibility and legacy-code familiarity only. Rules and defaults are not ANSI compliant (which creates portability issues), and they do not perform as well as constraints do. Microsoft has listed rules and defaults as there only for backward compatibility since version 7.0 — that's four versions and roughly ten years — not an encouraging thing if you're asking yourself whether this feature is going to continue to be supported in the future. I wouldn't go so far as to suggest that you start sifting through and replacing any old code that you may come across, but you should use constraints for any new code you generate.

The primary thing that sets rules and defaults apart from constraints is in their very nature; constraints are features of a table — they have no existence on their own — while rules and defaults are actual objects in and of themselves. Whereas a constraint is defined in the table definition, rules and defaults are defined independently and are then "bound" to the table after the fact.

The independent-object nature of rules and defaults gives them the ability to be reused without being redefined. Indeed, rules and defaults are not limited to being bound to just tables; they can also be bound to data types, vastly improving your ability to make highly functional user-defined data types.

Rules

A rule is incredibly similar to a CHECK constraint. The only difference beyond those I've already described is that rules are limited to working with just one column at a time. You can bind the same rule separately to multiple columns in a table, but the rule will work independently with each column and will not be aware of the other columns at all. A constraint defined as (QtyShipped <= QtyOrdered) would not work for a rule (it refers to more than one column), whereas LIKE ([0-9][0-9][0-9]) would (it applies only to whatever column the rule is bound to).

Let's define a rule so that you can see the differences firsthand:

```
CREATE RULE SalaryRule
   AS @Salary > 0;
```

Notice that what we are comparing is shown as a variable. Whatever the value is of the column being checked, that is the value that will be used in the place of @Salary. Thus, in this example, we're saying that any column our rule is bound to would have to have a value greater than zero.

If you want to go back and see what your rule looks like, you can make use of sp_helptext:

```
EXEC sp_helptext SalaryRule;
```

And it will show you your exact rule definition:

```
Text
-----------------------------------
CREATE RULE SalaryRule
       AS @Salary > 0
```

Now we've got a rule, but it isn't doing anything. If we tried to insert a record in our `Employees` table, we could still insert any value right now without any restrictions beyond data type.

To activate the rule, we need to make use of a special stored procedure called `sp_bindrule`. We want to bind our `SalaryRule` to the `Salary` column of our `Employees` table. The syntax looks like this:

```
sp_bindrule <''rule''>, <''object_name''>, [<''futureonly_flag''>]
```

The `rule` part is simple enough; that's the rule we want to bind. The `object_name` is also simple; it's the object (column or user-defined data type) to which we want to bind the rule. The only odd parameter is the `futureonly_flag`, and it applies only when the rule is bound to a user-defined data type. The default is for this to be off. However, if you set it to `True` or pass in a `1`, then the binding of the rule will apply only to new columns to which you bind the user-defined data type. Any columns that already have the data type in its old form will continue to use that form.

Since we're just binding this rule to a column, our syntax requires only the first two parameters:

```
EXEC sp_bindrule 'SalaryRule', 'Employees.Salary';
```

Take a close look at the `object_name` parameter. We have `Employees` and `Salary` separated by a "`.`" Why is that? Since the rule isn't associated with any particular table until you bind it, you need to state the table and column to which the rule will be bound. If you do not use the `tablename.column` naming structure, then SQL Server will assume that what you're naming must be a user-defined data type. If it doesn't find one, you'll get back an error message that can be a bit confusing if you hadn't intended to bind the rule to a data type:

```
Msg 15148, Level 16, State 1, Procedure sp_bindrule, Line 190
The data type or table column 'Salary' does not exist or you do not have
permission.
```

In our case, trying to insert or update an `Employees` record with a negative value violates the rule and generates an error.

If we want to remove our rule from use with this column, we make use of `sp_unbindrule`:

```
EXEC sp_unbindrule 'Employees.Salary';
```

The `futureonly_flag` parameter is usually an option, but doesn't apply to this particular example. If you use `sp_unbindrule` with the `futureonly_flag` turned on, and it is used against a user-defined data type (rather than a specific column), then the unbinding will only apply to future uses of that data type — existing columns using that data type will still make use of the rule.

Dropping Rules

If you want to completely eliminate a rule from your database, you use the same DROP syntax that we've already become familiar with for tables:

```
DROP RULE <rule name>
```

Defaults

Defaults are even more similar to their cousin — a default constraint — than a rule is to a CHECK constraint. Indeed, they work identically, with the only real differences being in the way that they are attached to a table and the default's (the object, not the constraint) support for a user-defined data type.

> The concept of defaults vs. DEFAULT constraints is wildly difficult for a lot of people to grasp. After all, they have almost the same name. If we refer to "default," then we are referring to either the object-based default (what we're talking about in this section), or a shorthand to the actual default value (that will be supplied if we don't provide an explicit value). If we refer to a "DEFAULT constraint," then we are talking about the non-object-based solution — the solution that is an integral part of the table definition.

The syntax for defining a default works much as it did for a rule:

```
CREATE DEFAULT <default name>
AS <default value>
```

Therefore, to define a default of zero for our Salary:

```
CREATE DEFAULT SalaryDefault
   AS 0;
```

Again, a default is worthless without being bound to something. To bind it, we make use of sp_bindefault, which is, other than the procedure name, identical in syntax to the sp_bindrule procedure:

```
EXEC sp_bindefault 'SalaryDefault', 'Employees.Salary';
```

To unbind the default from the table, we use sp_unbindefault:

```
EXEC sp_unbindefault 'Employees.Salary';
```

Keep in mind that the futureonly_flag also applies to this stored procedure; it is just not used here.

Dropping Defaults

If you want to completely eliminate a default from your database, you use the same DROP syntax that we've already become familiar with for tables and rules:

```
DROP DEFAULT <default name>
```

Determining Which Tables and Data Types Use a Given Rule or Default

If you ever go to delete or alter your rules or defaults, you may first want to take a look at which tables and data types are making use of them. Again, SQL Server comes to the rescue with a system-stored procedure. This one is called `sp_depends`. Its syntax looks like this:

```
EXEC sp_depends <object name>
```

`sp_depends` provides a listing of all the objects that depend on the object you've requested information about.

> Unfortunately, `sp_depends` **is not a sure bet to tell you about every object that depends on a parent object. SQL Server supports something called "deferred name resolution." Basically, deferred name resolution means that you can create objects (primary stored procedures) that depend on another object — even before the second (target of the dependency) object is created. For example, SQL Server will now allow you to create a stored procedure that refers to a table even before the said table is created. In this instance, SQL Server isn't able to list the table as having a dependency on it. Even after you add the table, it will not have any dependency listing if you use** `sp_depends`.

Triggers for Data Integrity

We've got a whole chapter coming up on triggers, but any discussion of constraints, rules, and defaults would not be complete without at least a mention of triggers.

One of the most common uses of triggers is to implement data integrity rules. Since we have that chapter coming up, I'm not going to get into it very deeply here, other than to say that triggers have a very large number of things they can do data integrity–wise that a constraint or rule could never hope to do. The downside (and you knew there had to be one) is that they incur substantial additional overhead and are, therefore, much (very much) slower in almost any circumstance. They are procedural in nature (which is where they get their power), but they also happen after everything else is done and should be used only as a relatively last resort.

Choosing What to Use

Wow. Here you are with all these choices, and now how do you figure out which is the right one to use? Some of the constraints are fairly independent (PRIMARY and FOREIGN KEYS, UNIQUE constraints) — you are using either them or nothing. The rest have some level of overlap with each other, and it can be rather confusing when deciding what to use. You've gotten some hints from me as we've been going through this chapter about what some of the strengths and weaknesses are of each of the options, but it will probably make a lot more sense if we look at them all together for a bit.

Restriction	Pros	Cons
Constraints	Fast. Can reference other columns. Happen before the command occurs. ANSI-compliant.	Must be redefined for each table. Can't reference other tables. Can't be bound to data types.
Rules, Defaults	Independent objects. Reusable. Can be bound to data types. Happen before the command occurs.	Slightly slower. Can't reference across columns. Can't reference other tables. Really meant for backward compatibility only!!!
Triggers	Ultimate flexibility. Can reference other columns and other tables. Can even use .NET to reference information that is external to your SQL Server.	Happen after the command occurs. High overhead.

The main time to use rules and defaults is if you are implementing a rather robust logical model and are making extensive use of user-defined data types. In this instance, rules and defaults can provide a lot of functionality and ease of management without much programmatic overhead. You just need to be aware that they may go away someday. Probably not soon, but someday.

Triggers should only be used when a constraint is not an option. Like constraints, they are attached to the table and must be redefined with every table you create. On the bright side, they can do most things that you are likely to want to do data integrity–wise. Indeed, they used to be the common method of enforcing foreign keys (before FOREIGN KEY constraints were added). I will cover these in some detail later in the book.

That leaves constraints, which should become your data integrity solution of choice. They are fast and not that difficult to create. Their downfall is that they can be limiting (they can't reference other tables except for a FOREIGN KEY), and they can be tedious to redefine over and over again if you have a common constraint logic.

> Regardless of what kind of integrity mechanism you're putting in place (keys, triggers, constraints, rules, defaults), the thing to remember can best be summed up in just one word — balance.
>
> Every new thing that you add to your database adds more overhead, so you need to make sure that whatever you're adding honestly has value to it before you stick it in your database. Avoid things like redundant integrity implementations (for example, I can't tell you how often I've come across a database that has both foreign keys defined for referential integrity and triggers to do the same thing). Make sure you know what constraints you have before you put the next one on, and make sure you know exactly what you hope to accomplish with it.

Summary

The different types of data integrity mechanisms described in this chapter are part of the backbone of a sound database. Perhaps the biggest power of RDBMSs is that the database can now take responsibility for data integrity rather than depending on the application. This means that even ad hoc queries are subject to the data rules and that multiple applications are all treated equally with regard to data integrity issues.

In the chapters to come, we will look at the tie between some forms of constraints and indexes, along with taking a look at the advanced data integrity rules that can be implemented using triggers. We'll also begin looking at how the choices between these different mechanisms affect our design decisions.

Adding More to Our Queries

When I first started writing about SQL Server a number of years ago, I was faced with the question of when exactly to introduce more complex queries into the knowledge mix — this book faces that question all over again. At issue is something of a "chicken or egg" thing — talk about scripting, variables, and the like first, or get to some things that a beginning user might make use of long before they do server-side scripting. This time around, the notion of more queries early won out.

Some of the concepts in this chapter are going to challenge you with a new way of thinking. You already had a taste of this just dealing with joins, but you haven't had to deal with the kind of depth that I want to challenge you with in this chapter. Even if you don't have that much procedural programming experience, the fact is that your brain has a natural tendency to break complex problems down into their smaller subparts (sub-procedures, logical steps) as opposed to solving them whole (the "set," or SQL way).

While SQL Server 2008 supports procedural language concepts now more than ever, my challenge to you is to try and see the question as a whole first. Be certain that you can't get it in a single query. Even if you can't think of a way, quite often you can break it up into several small queries and then combine them one at a time back into a larger query that does it all in one task. Try to see it as a whole and, if you can't, then go ahead and break it down, but then combine it into the whole again to the largest extent that makes sense.

This is really what's at the heart of my challenge of a new way of thinking — conceptualizing the question as a whole rather than in steps. When we program in most languages, we usually work in a linear fashion. With SQL, however, you need to think more in terms of set theory. You can liken this to math class and the notion of A union B, or A intersect B. We need to think less in terms of steps to resolve the data and more about how the data fits together.

In this chapter, we're going to be using this concept of data fit to ask what amounts to multiple questions in just one query. Essentially, we're going to look at ways of taking what seem like multiple queries and placing them into something that will execute as a complete unit. In addition, we'll also be taking a look at query performance and what you can do to get the most out of queries.

Among the topics we'll be covering in this chapter are:

❑ Nested subqueries

❑ Correlated subqueries

❑ Derived tables

❑ Making use of the EXISTS operator

❑ MERGE

❑ Optimizing query performance

We'll see how, using subqueries, we can make the seemingly impossible completely possible, and how an odd tweak here and there can make a big difference in your query performance.

What Is a Subquery?

A *subquery* is a normal T-SQL query that is nested inside another query. Subqueries are created using parentheses when you have a SELECT statement that serves as the basis for either part of the data or the condition in another query.

Subqueries are generally used to fill one of a few needs:

❑ To break a query into a series of logical steps

❑ To provide a listing to be the target of a WHERE clause together with [IN|EXISTS|ANY|ALL]

❑ To provide a lookup driven by each individual record in a parent query

Some subqueries are very easy to think of and build, but some are extremely complex — it usually depends on the complexity of the relationship between the inner (the sub) and outer (the top) queries.

It's also worth noting that most subqueries (but definitely not all) can also be written using a join. In places where you can use a join instead, the join is usually the preferable choice for a variety of reasons we will continue to explore over the remainder of the book.

I once got into a rather lengthy debate (perhaps 20 or 30 e-mails flying back and forth, with examples, reasons, and so on over a few days) with a coworker over the joins versus subqueries issue.

Traditional logic says to always use the join, and that was what I was pushing (due to experience rather than traditional logic — you've already seen several places in this book where I've pointed out how traditional thinking can be bogus). My coworker was pushing the notion that a subquery would actually cause less overhead — I decided to try it out.

What I found was essentially (as you might expect) that we were both right in certain circumstances. We will explore these circumstances fully toward the end of the chapter after you have a bit more background.

Now that we know what a subquery theoretically is, let's look at some specific types and examples of subqueries.

Building a Nested Subquery

A *nested subquery* is one that goes in only *one* direction, returning either a single value for use in the outer query, or perhaps a full list of values to be used with the IN operator. In the event you want to use an explicit = operator, then you're going to be using a query that returns a single value — that means one column from one row. If you are expecting a list back, then you'll need to use the IN operator with your outer query.

In the loosest sense, your query syntax is going to look something like one of these two syntax templates:

```
SELECT <SELECT list>
FROM <SomeTable>
WHERE <SomeColumn> = (
         SELECT <single column>
         FROM <SomeTable>
         WHERE <condition that results in only one row returned>)
```

Or:

```
SELECT <SELECT list>
FROM <SomeTable>
WHERE <SomeColumn> IN (
         SELECT <single column>
         FROM <SomeTable>
         [WHERE <condition>)]
```

Obviously, the exact syntax will vary, not only because you will be substituting the select list and exact table names, but also because you may have a multitable join in either the inner or outer queries — or both.

Nested Queries Using Single-Value SELECT Statements

Let's get down to the nitty-gritty with an explicit example. Let's say, for example, that we wanted to know the ProductIDs of every item sold on the first day any product was purchased from the system.

If you already know the first day that an order was placed in the system, then it's no problem; the query would look something like this:

```
SELECT DISTINCT sod.ProductID
FROM Sales.SalesOrderHeader soh
JOIN Sales.SalesOrderDetail sod
  ON soh.SalesOrderID = sod.SalesOrderID
WHERE OrderDate = '07/01/2001';   --This is first OrderDate in the system
```

This yields the correct results:

```
ProductID
-----------
707
708
709
...
...
776
777
778

(47 row(s) affected)
```

But let's say, just for instance, that we are regularly purging data from the system, and we still want to ask this same question as part of an automated report.

Since it's going to be automated, we can't run a query to find out what the first date in the system is and manually plug that into our query — or can we? Actually, the answer is: "Yes, we can," by putting it all into just one statement:

```
SELECT DISTINCT soh.OrderDate, sod.ProductID
FROM Sales.SalesOrderHeader soh
JOIN Sales.SalesOrderDetail sod
   ON soh.SalesOrderID = sod.SalesOrderID
WHERE OrderDate = (SELECT MIN(OrderDate) FROM Sales.SalesOrderHeader);
```

It's just that quick and easy. The inner query (`SELECT MIN...`) retrieves a single value for use in the outer query. Since we're using an equal sign, the inner query absolutely must return only one column from one single row or you will get a runtime error.

Notice that I added the order date to this new query. While it did not have to be there for the query to report the appropriate ProductID's, it does clarify what date those ProductID's are from. Under the first query, we knew what date because we had explicitly said it, but under this new query, the date is data driven, so it is often worthwhile to provide it as part of the result.

Nested Queries Using Subqueries That Return Multiple Values

Perhaps the most common of all subqueries that are implemented in the world are those that retrieve some form of domain list and use it as criteria for a query.

For this one, let's revisit a problem we looked at in Chapter 4 when we were examining outer joins. What you want is a list of all the products that have special offers.

We might write something like this:

```
SELECT ProductID, Name
FROM Production.Product
WHERE ProductID IN (
  SELECT ProductID FROM Sales.SpecialOfferProduct);
```

This returns 295 rows:

```
ProductID    Name
-----------  -------------------------------------------------
680          HL Road Frame - Black, 58
706          HL Road Frame - Red, 58
707          Sport-100 Helmet, Red
...
...
997          Road-750 Black, 44
998          Road-750 Black, 48
999          Road-750 Black, 52

(295 row(s) affected)
```

While this works just fine, queries of this type almost always fall into the category of those that can be done using an inner join rather than a nested SELECT. For example, we could get the same results as the preceding subquery by running this simple join:

```
SELECT DISTINCT pp.ProductID, Name
FROM Production.Product pp
JOIN Sales.SpecialOfferProduct ssop
 ON pp.ProductID = ssop.ProductID;
```

For performance reasons, you want to use the join method as your default solution if you don't have a specific reason for using the nested SELECT — we'll discuss this more before the chapter's done.

> *SQL Server is actually pretty smart about this kind of thing. In the lion's share of situations, SQL Server will actually resolve the nested subquery solution to the same query plan it would use on the join — indeed, if you checked the query plan for both the nested subquery and the previous join, you'd find it was the exact same plan. So, with that in mind, the truth is that most of the time, there really isn't that much difference. The problem, of course, is that I just said most of the time. When the query plans vary, the join is usually the better choice, and thus the recommendation to use that syntax by default.*

Using a Nested SELECT to Find Orphaned Records

This type of nested SELECT is nearly identical to our previous example, except that we add the NOT operator. The difference this makes when you are converting to join syntax is that you are equating to an outer join rather than an inner join.

Before we do the nested SELECT syntax, let's review one of our examples of an outer join from Chapter 4. In this query, we were trying to identify all the special offers that do not have matching products:

```
SELECT Description
FROM Sales.SpecialOfferProduct ssop
RIGHT OUTER JOIN Sales.SpecialOffer sso
 ON ssop.SpecialOfferID = sso.SpecialOfferID
WHERE sso.SpecialOfferID != 1
  AND ssop.SpecialOfferID IS NULL;
```

This returned one row:

```
Description
--------------------
Volume Discount over 60

(1 row(s) affected)
```

This is the way that, typically speaking, things should be done (or as a LEFT JOIN). I can't say, however, that it's the way that things are usually done. The join usually takes a bit more thought, so we usually wind up with the nested SELECT instead.

See if you can write this nested SELECT on your own. Once you're done, come back and take a look.

It should wind up looking like this:

```
SELECT Description
FROM Sales.SpecialOffer sso
WHERE sso.SpecialOfferID != 1
  AND sso.SpecialOfferID NOT IN
    (SELECT SpecialOfferID FROM Sales.SpecialOfferProduct);
```

This yields exactly the same record.

Correlated Subqueries

Two words for you on this section: Pay attention! This is another one of those little areas that, if you truly get it, can really set you apart from the crowd. By "get it," I don't just mean that you understand how it works, but also that you understand how important it can be.

Correlated subqueries are one of those things that make the impossible possible. What's more, they often turn several lines of code into one and create a corresponding increase in performance. The problem with them is that they require a substantially different style of thought than you're probably used to. Correlated subqueries are probably the single easiest concept in SQL to learn, understand, and then promptly forget, because the concept simply goes against the grain of how you think. If you're one of the few who choose to remember it as an option, then you will be one of the few who figure out that hard-to-figure-out problem. You'll also be someone with a far more complete tool set when it comes to squeezing every ounce of performance out of your queries.

How Correlated Subqueries Work

What makes correlated subqueries different from the nested subqueries we've been looking at is that the information travels in *two* directions rather than one. In a nested subquery, the inner query is processed only once, and that information is passed out for the outer query, which will also execute just once — essentially providing the same value or list that you would have provided if you had typed it in yourself.

With correlated subqueries, however, the inner query runs on information provided by the outer query, and vice versa. That may seem a bit confusing (that chicken or the egg thing again), but it works in a three-step process:

1. The outer query obtains a record and passes it into the inner query.
2. The inner query executes based on the passed-in value(s).
3. The inner query then passes the values from its results back to the outer query, which uses them to finish its processing.

Correlated Subqueries in the WHERE Clause

I realize that this is probably a bit confusing, so let's look at it in an example.

We'll go back to the AdventureWorks2008 database and look again at the query where we wanted to know the orders that happened on the first date that an order was placed in the system. However, this time we want to add a new twist: We want to know the SalesOrderID(s) and OrderDate of the first order in the system for each customer. That is, we want to know the first day that a customer placed an order and the IDs of those orders. Let's look at it piece by piece.

First, we want the OrderDate, SalesOrderID, and CustomerID for each of our results. All of that information can be found in the SalesOrderHeader table, so we know that our query is going to be based, at least in part, on that table.

Next, we need to know what the first date in the system was for each customer. That's where the tricky part comes in. When we did this with a nested subquery, we were only looking for the first date in the entire file — now we need a value that's by individual customer.

This wouldn't be that big a deal if we were to do it in two separate queries — we could just create a temporary table and then join back to it.

A temporary table is pretty much just what it sounds like — a table that is created for temporary use and will go away after our processing is complete. Exactly how long it will stay around is variable and is outside the scope of this chapter. We will, however, visit temporary tables a bit more as we continue through the book.

The temporary table solution might look something like this:

```
USE AdventureWorks2008;

-- Get a list of customers and the date of their first order
SELECT soh.CustomerID, MIN(soh.OrderDate) AS OrderDate
INTO #MinOrderDates
FROM Sales.SalesOrderHeader soh
GROUP BY soh.CustomerID;

-- Do something additional with that information
SELECT soh.CustomerID, soh.SalesOrderID, soh.OrderDate
FROM Sales.SalesOrderHeader soh
JOIN #MinOrderDates t
  ON soh.CustomerID = t.CustomerID
  AND soh.OrderDate = t.OrderDate
ORDER BY soh.CustomerID;

DROP TABLE #MinOrderDates;
```

We get back a little over 19,000 rows:

```
(19119 row(s) affected)
CustomerID  SalesOrderID OrderDate
----------- ------------ -----------------------
11000       43793        2001-07-22 00:00:00.000
11001       43767        2001-07-18 00:00:00.000
11002       43736        2001-07-10 00:00:00.000

...
```

```
...
30116          51106          2003-07-01 00:00:00.000
30117          43865          2001-08-01 00:00:00.000
30118          47378          2002-09-01 00:00:00.000

(19134 row(s) affected)
```

As previously stated, don't worry if your results are slightly different from those shown here — it just means you've been playing around with the AdventureWorks2008 data a little more or a little less than I have.

The fact that we are building two completely separate result sets here is emphasized by the fact that you see two different `row(s) affected` in the results. That, more often than not, has a negative impact on performance. We'll explore this further after we explore our options some more.

Sometimes using this multiple-query approach is simply the only way to get things done without using a cursor — this is not one of those times.

OK, so if we want this to run in a single query, we need to find a way to look up each individual customer. We can do this by making use of an inner query that performs a lookup based on the current `CustomerID` in the outer query. We will then need to return a value back out to the outer query so it can match things up based on the earliest order date.

It looks like this:

```
SELECT soh1.CustomerID, soh1.SalesOrderID, soh1.OrderDate
FROM Sales.SalesOrderHeader soh1
WHERE soh1.OrderDate = (SELECT Min(soh2.OrderDate)
                        FROM Sales.SalesOrderHeader soh2
                        WHERE soh2.CustomerID = soh1.CustomerID)
ORDER BY CustomerID;
```

With this, we get back the same 19,134 rows:

```
CustomerID   SalesOrderID OrderDate
-----------  ------------ -----------------------
11000        43793        2001-07-22 00:00:00.000
11001        43767        2001-07-18 00:00:00.000
11002        43736        2001-07-10 00:00:00.000

...

...
30116        51106        2003-07-01 00:00:00.000
30117        43865        2001-08-01 00:00:00.000
30118        47378        2002-09-01 00:00:00.000

(19134 row(s) affected)
```

There are a few key things to notice in this query:

❑ We see only one `row(s) affected` line — giving us a good clue that only one query plan had to be executed.

❑ The outer query (in this example) looks pretty much just like a nested subquery. The inner query, however, has an explicit reference to the outer query (notice the use of the `o1` alias).

❑ Aliases are used in both queries — even though it looks like the outer query shouldn't need one — because they are required whenever you explicitly refer to a column from the other query (inside refers to a column on the outside or vice versa).

> The latter point concerning needing aliases is a big area of confusion. The fact is that sometimes you need them and sometimes you don't. While I don't tend to use them at all in the types of nested subqueries that we looked at in the early part of this chapter, I alias everything when dealing with correlated subqueries.
>
> The hard-and-fast rule is that you must alias any table (and its related columns) that's going to be referred to by the other query. The problem is that this can quickly become very confusing. The way to be on the safe side is to alias everything — that way you're positive of which table in which query you're getting your information from.

We see that `19,134 row(s) affected` only once. That's because it affected 19,134 rows only one time. Just by observation, we can guess that this version probably runs faster than the two-query version and, in reality, it does. Again, we'll look into this a bit more shortly.

In this particular query, the outer query references only the inner query in the `WHERE` clause — it could also have requested data from the inner query to include in the select list.

Normally, it's up to us whether to use an alias or not, but with correlated subqueries they are often required. This particular query is a really great one for showing why, because the inner and outer queries are based on the same table. Since both queries are getting information from each other without aliasing, how would they know which instance of the table data that you were interested in?

Correlated Subqueries in the SELECT List

Subqueries can also be used to provide a different kind of answer in your selection results. This kind of situation is often found where the information you're after is fundamentally different from the rest of the data in your query (for example, you want an aggregation on one field, but you don't want all the baggage from that to affect the other fields returned).

To test this, let's just run a somewhat modified version of the query we used in the previous section. What we're going to say we're after here is just the account number of the customer and the first date on which that customer ordered something.

This one creates a somewhat more significant change than is probably apparent at first. We're now asking for the customer's account number, which means that we have to bring the `Customer` table into play. In addition, we no longer need to build any kind of condition in — we're asking for all customers (no restrictions), and we just want to know when each customer's first order date was.

The query actually winds up being a bit simpler than the last one, and it looks like this:

```
SELECT sc.AccountNumber,
    (SELECT Min(OrderDate)
        FROM Sales.SalesOrderHeader soh
        WHERE soh.CustomerID = sc.CustomerID)
        AS OrderDate
FROM Sales.Customer sc;
```

This returns data that looks something like this:

```
AccountNumber OrderDate
------------- ------------------------
AW00000001    NULL
AW00000002    NULL
AW00000007    NULL

...
...
AW00030102    2002-12-01 00:00:00.000
AW00030104    2002-07-01 00:00:00.000
AW00030113    2002-09-01 00:00:00.000

(19820 row(s) affected)
```

Note that there are a couple of rows that have a NULL in the Order Date column. Why do you suppose that is? The cause is, of course, because there is no record in the Orders table that matches the then current record in the Customer table (the outer query).

This brings us to a small digression to take a look at a particularly useful function for this situation — ISNULL().

Dealing with NULL Data — the ISNULL Function

There are actually a few functions specifically meant to deal with NULL data, but the one of particular use to us at this point is ISNULL(). ISNULL() accepts a variable (which we'll talk about in Chapter 11) or expression and tests it for a NULL value. If the value is indeed NULL, then the function returns some other prespecified value. If the original value is not NULL, then the original value is returned. This syntax is pretty straightforward:

```
ISNULL(<expression to test>, <replacement value if null>)
```

So, for example:

ISNULL Expression	Value Returned
ISNULL(NULL, 5)	5
ISNULL(5, 15)	5
ISNULL(MyColumnName, 0) where MyColumnName IS NULL	0
ISNULL(MyColumnName, 0) where MyColumnName = 3	3
ISNULL(MyColumnName, 0) where MyColumnName ='Fred Farmer'	Fred Farmer

Now let's see this at work in our query:

```
SELECT sc.AccountNumber,
    ISNULL(CAST((SELECT Min(OrderDate)
            FROM Sales.SalesOrderHeader soh
            WHERE soh.CustomerID = sc.CustomerID) AS varchar), 'NEVER ORDERED')
            AS OrderDate
FROM Sales.Customer sc;
```

Now, some example lines that we had problems with. We go from:

```
...
...
AW00000696    NULL
AW00000697    NULL
AW00000698    NULL
AW00011012    2003-09-17 00:00:00.000
AW00011013    2003-10-15 00:00:00.000
AW00011014    2003-09-24 00:00:00.000
...
...
```

to something a bit more useful:

```
...
...
AW00000696    NEVER ORDERED
AW00000697    NEVER ORDERED
AW00000698    NEVER ORDERED
AW00011012    Sep 17 2003 12:00AM
AW00011013    Oct 15 2003 12:00AM
AW00011014    Sep 24 2003 12:00AM
...
...
```

Notice that I also had to put the CAST() *function into play to get this to work. The reason has to do with casting and implicit conversion. Because the column* Order Date *is of type* DateTime *there is an error generated since* NEVER ORDERED *can't be converted to the* DateTime *data type. Keep* CAST() *in mind — it can help you out of little troubles like this one. This is covered further later in this chapter.*

So, at this point, we've seen correlated subqueries that provide information for both the WHERE clause and for the select list. You can mix and match these two in the same query if you wish.

Derived Tables

Sometimes you need to work with the results of a query, but you need to work with the results of that query in a way that doesn't really lend itself to the kinds of subqueries that we've discussed up to this point. An example would be where, for each row in a given table, you may have multiple results in the subquery, but you're looking for an action more complex than our IN operator provides. Essentially, what I'm talking about here are situations where you wish you could use a JOIN operator on your subquery.

It's at times like these that we turn to a somewhat lesser known construct in SQL — a *derived table*. A derived table is made up of the columns and rows of a result set from a query. (Heck, they have columns, rows, data types, and so on just like normal tables, so why not use them as such?)

Imagine for a moment that you want to get a list of account numbers and the associated territories for all accounts that ordered a particular product — say, an HL Mountain Rear Wheel. No problem! Your query might look something like this:

```
SELECT sc.AccountNumber, sst.Name
FROM Sales.SalesOrderHeader soh
JOIN Sales.SalesOrderDetail sod
  ON soh.SalesOrderID = sod.SalesOrderID
JOIN Production.Product pp
  ON sod.ProductID = pp.ProductID
JOIN Sales.Customer sc
  ON sc.CustomerID = soh.CustomerID
JOIN Sales.SalesTerritory sst
  ON sst.TerritoryID = sc.TerritoryID
WHERE pp.Name = 'HL Mountain Rear Wheel';
```

OK, so other than how many tables were required, that was easy. Now I'm going to throw you a twist — let's now say I want to know the account number and territory for all accounts that ordered not only an HL Mountain Rear Wheel, but also an HL Mountain Front Wheel. Notice that I said they have to have ordered both — now you have a problem. You're first inclination might be to write something like:

```
WHERE pp.Name = 'HL Mountain Rear Wheel'
   AND pp.Name = 'HL Mountain Front Wheel'
```

But that's not going to work at all — each row is for a single product, so how can it have both HL Mountain Rear Wheel and HL Mountain Front Wheel as the name at the same time? Nope — that's not going to get it at all (indeed, while it will run, you'll never get any rows back).

What we really need here is to join the results of a query to find buyers of HL Mountain Rear Wheel with the results of a query to find buyers of HL Mountain Front Wheel. How do we join results, however? Well, as you might expect given the title of this section, through the use of derived tables.

To create our derived table, we need two things:

❑ To enclose our query that generates the result set in parentheses

❑ To alias the results of the query, so it can be referenced as a table

So, the syntax looks something like this:

```
SELECT <select list>
FROM (<query that returns a regular resultset>) AS <alias name>
JOIN <some other base or derived table>
```

So let's take this now and apply it to our requirements. Again, what we want are the account numbers and territories of all the companies that have ordered both HL Mountain Rear Wheel and HL Mountain Front Wheel. So our query should look something like this:

```
SELECT DISTINCT sc.AccountNumber, sst.Name
FROM Sales.Customer AS sc
JOIN Sales.SalesTerritory sst
  ON sc.TerritoryID = sst.TerritoryID
JOIN
   (SELECT CustomerID
  FROM Sales.SalesOrderHeader soh
  JOIN Sales.SalesOrderDetail sod
        ON soh.SalesOrderID = sod.SalesOrderID
  JOIN Production.Product pp
        ON sod.ProductID = pp.ProductID
  WHERE pp.Name = 'HL Mountain Rear Wheel') AS dt1
   ON sc.CustomerID = dt1.CustomerID
JOIN
   (SELECT CustomerID
  FROM Sales.SalesOrderHeader soh
  JOIN Sales.SalesOrderDetail sod
        ON soh.SalesOrderID = sod.SalesOrderID
  JOIN Production.Product pp
        ON sod.ProductID = pp.ProductID
  WHERE Name = 'HL Mountain Front Wheel') AS dt2
   ON sc.CustomerID = dt2.CustomerID;
```

We wind up with 58 accounts:

```
AccountNumber  Name
-------------  ---------------------------
AW00029484     Southeast
AW00029490     Northwest
AW00029499     Canada

...

...
AW00030108     Canada
AW00030113     United Kingdom
AW00030118     Central

(58 row(s) affected)
```

If you want to check things out on this, just run the queries for the two derived tables separately and compare the results.

For this particular query, I needed to use the DISTINCT *keyword. If I didn't, then I would have potentially received multiple rows for each customer — for example, AW00029771 has ordered the HL Mountain Rear Wheel twice, so I would have gotten one record for each. I only asked which customers had ordered both, not how many had they ordered.*

As you can see, we were able to take a seemingly impossible query and make it both possible and even reasonably well performing.

Keep in mind that derived tables aren't the solutions for everything. For example, if the result set is going to be fairly large and you're going to have lots of joined records, then you may want to look at using a temporary table and building an index on it (derived tables have no indexes). Every situation is different, but now you have one more weapon in your arsenal.

The EXISTS Operator

I call EXISTS an operator, but Books Online calls it a keyword. That's probably because it defies description in some senses. It's an operator much like the IN keyword is, but it also looks at things just a bit differently.

When you use EXISTS, you don't really return data — instead, you return a simple TRUE/FALSE regarding the existence of data that meets the criteria established in the query that the EXISTS statement is operating against.

Let's go right to an example, so you can see how this gets applied. What we're going to query here is a list of persons who are employees:

```
SELECT BusinessEntityID, LastName + ', ' + FirstName AS Name
FROM Person.Person pp
WHERE EXISTS
   (SELECT BusinessEntityID
          FROM HumanResources.Employee hre
          WHERE hre.BusinessEntityID = pp.BusinessEntityID);
```

As we might expect, this gets us a relatively small subset of our Person table — 290 of them:

```
BusinessEntityID Name
---------------- ----------------------------------------------------------
263              Trenary, Jean
78               D'sa, Reuben
242              Poe, Deborah
...
...
95               Scardelis, Jim
215              Harrington, Mark
112              Evans, John

(290 row(s) affected)
```

We could have easily done this same thing with a join:

```
SELECT pp.BusinessEntityID, LastName + ', ' + FirstName AS Name
FROM Person.Person pp
JOIN HumanResources.Employee hre
  ON pp.BusinessEntityID = hre.BusinessEntityID;
```

This join-based syntax, for example, would have yielded exactly the same results (subject to possible sort differences). So why, then, would we need this new syntax? Performance — plain and simple.

When you use the EXISTS keyword, SQL Server doesn't have to perform a full row-by-row join. Instead, it can look through the records until it finds the first match and stop right there. As soon as there is a single match, the EXISTS is true, so there is no need to go further.

Let's take a brief look at things the other way around — that is, what if our query wanted the persons who were *not* employees? Under the join method that we looked at in Chapter 4, we would have had to make some significant changes in the way we went about getting our answers. First, we would have to use an outer join. Then we would perform a comparison to see whether any of the Employee records were NULL.

It would look something like this:

```
SELECT pp.BusinessEntityID, LastName + ', ' + FirstName AS Name
FROM Person.Person pp
LEFT JOIN HumanResources.Employee hre
  ON pp.BusinessEntityID = hre.BusinessEntityID
WHERE hre.BusinessEntityID IS NULL;
```

Which returns 19,682 rows:

```
BusinessEntity  ID Name
--------------  ---------------------------------------------------------------
293             Abel, Catherine
295             Abercrombie, Kim
2170            Abercrombie, Kim
...

...
2088            Zugelder, Judy
12079           Zukowski, Jake
2089            Zwilling, Michael

(19682 row(s) affected)
```

To do the same change over when we're using EXISTS, we add only one word to the original EXIST query — NOT:

```
SELECT BusinessEntityID, LastName + ', ' + FirstName AS Name
FROM Person.Person pp
WHERE NOT EXISTS
    (SELECT BusinessEntityID
            FROM HumanResources.Employee hre
            WHERE hre.BusinessEntityID = pp.BusinessEntityID);
```

And we get back those exact same 19,682 rows.

The performance difference here is, in most cases, even more marked than with the inner join. SQL Server just applies a little reverse logic versus the straight EXISTS statement. In the case of the NOT we're now using, SQL can still stop looking as soon as it finds one matching record — the only difference is that it knows to return FALSE for that lookup rather than TRUE. Performance-wise, everything else about the query is the same.

Using EXISTS in Other Ways

One common use of EXISTS is to check for the existence of a table before running a CREATE statement. You may want to drop an existing table, or you just may way to change to an ALTER statement or some other statement that adjusts the existing table if there is one. One of the most common ways you'll see this done will look something like this:

```
IF EXISTS
   (SELECT *
    FROM sys.objects
    WHERE OBJECT_NAME(object_id) = 'foo'
      AND SCHEMA_NAME(schema_id) = 'dbo'
      AND OBJECTPROPERTY(object_id, 'IsUserTable') = 1)
BEGIN
   DROP TABLE dbo.foo;
   PRINT 'Table foo has been dropped';
END
GO


CREATE TABLE dbo.foo
(
   Column1 int IDENTITY(1,1) NOT NULL,
   Column2 varchar(50)NULL
);
```

Since EXISTS returns nothing but TRUE or FALSE, that means it works as an excellent conditional expression. The preceding example will run the DROP TABLE code only if the table exists; otherwise, it skips over that part and moves right into the CREATE statement. This avoids one of two errors showing up when you run the script. First, that it can't run the CREATE statement (which would probably create other problems if you were running this in a script where other tables were depending on this being done first) because the object already exists. Second, that it couldn't DROP the table (this pretty much just creates a message that might be confusing to a customer who installs your product) because it didn't exist. You're covered for both.

As an example of this, let's write our own CREATE script for something that's often skipped in the automation effort — the database. But creation of the database is often left as part of some cryptic directions that say something like "create a database called 'xxxx'." The fun part is when the people who are actually installing it (who often don't know what they're doing) start including the quotes, or create a database that is too small, or a host of other possible and very simple errors to make. This is the point where I hope you have a good tech support department.

Instead, we'll just build a little script to create the database object that could go with AdventureWorks2008. For safety's sake, we'll call it AdventureWorksCreate. We'll also keep the statement to a minimum because we're interested in the EXISTS rather than the CREATE command:

```
USE MASTER;
GO
```

```
IF NOT EXISTS
  (SELECT 'True'
   FROM sys.databases
   WHERE name = 'AdventureWorksCreate')
BEGIN
   CREATE DATABASE AdventureWorksCreate;
END
ELSE
BEGIN
   PRINT 'Database already exists. Skipping CREATE DATABASE Statement';
END
GO
```

The first time you run this, there won't be any database called AdventureWorksCreate (unless by sheer coincidence you created something called that before we got to this point), so you'll get a response that looks like this:

```
Command(s) completed successfully.
```

This was unhelpful in terms of telling you what exactly was done, but at least you know it thinks it did what you asked.

Now run the script a second time and you'll see a change:

```
Database already exists. Skipping CREATE DATABASE Statement
```

So, without much fanfare or fuss, we've added a rather small script that will make things much more usable for the installers of your product. That may be an end user who bought your off-the-shelf product, or it may be you — in which case it's even better that it's fully scripted.

The long and the short of it is that EXISTS is a very handy keyword indeed. It can make some queries run much faster, and it can also simplify some queries and scripts.

A word of caution here — this is another one of those places where it's easy to get trapped in "traditional thinking." While EXISTS blows other options away in a large percentage of queries where EXISTS is a valid construct, that's not always the case. For example, the query used as a derived table example can also be written with a couple of EXISTS operators (one for each product), but the derived table happens to run more than twice as fast. That's definitely the exception, not the rule — EXISTS will normally smoke a derived table for performance. Just remember that rules are sometimes made to be broken.

Mixing Data Types: CAST and CONVERT

You'll see both CAST and CONVERT used frequently. Indeed, we've touched briefly on both of these already in this chapter. Considering how often we'll use these two functions, this seems like a good time to look a little closer at what they can do for you.

Both CAST and CONVERT perform data-type conversions for you. In most respects, they both do the same thing, with the exception that CONVERT also does some date-formatting conversions that CAST doesn't offer.

So, the question probably quickly rises in your mind, "Hey, if CONVERT *does everything that* CAST *does, and* CONVERT *also does date conversions, why would I ever use* CAST*?" I have a simple answer for that — ANSI/ISO compliance.* CAST *is ANSI/ISO-compliant, but* CONVERT *isn't — it's that simple.*

Let's take a look for the syntax for each.

```
CAST (expression AS data_type)
```

```
CONVERT(data_type, expression[, style])
```

With a little flip-flop on which goes first and the addition of the formatting option on CONVERT (with the style argument), they have basically the same syntax.

CAST and CONVERT can deal with a wide variety of data-type conversions that you'll need to do when SQL Server won't do it implicitly for you. For example, converting a number to a string is a very common need. To illustrate:

```
SELECT 'The Customer has an Order numbered ' + SalesOrderID
FROM Sales.SalesOrderHeader
WHERE CustomerID = 29825;
```

will yield an error:

```
Msg 245, Level 16, State 1, Line 1
Conversion failed when converting the varchar value 'The Customer has an Order
numbered ' to data type int.
```

But change the code to convert the number first:

```
SELECT 'The Customer has an Order numbered ' + CAST(SalesOrderID AS varchar)
FROM Sales.SalesOrderHeader
WHERE CustomerID = 29825;
```

And you get a much different result:

```
-----------------------------------------------------------------
The Customer has an Order numbered 43659
The Customer has an Order numbered 44305
The Customer has an Order numbered 45061
The Customer has an Order numbered 45779
The Customer has an Order numbered 46604
The Customer has an Order numbered 47693
The Customer has an Order numbered 48730
The Customer has an Order numbered 49822
The Customer has an Order numbered 51081
The Customer has an Order numbered 55234
The Customer has an Order numbered 61173
The Customer has an Order numbered 67260

(12 row(s) affected)
```

The conversions can actually get a little less intuitive also. For example, what if you wanted to convert a timestamp column into a regular number? A timestamp is just a binary number, so the conversion isn't any really big deal:

```
CREATE TABLE ConvertTest
(
    ColID    int    IDENTITY,
    ColTS    timestamp
);
GO

INSERT INTO ConvertTest
    DEFAULT VALUES;

SELECT ColTS AS Uncoverted, CAST(ColTS AS int) AS Converted
FROM ConvertTest;
```

This yields something like (your exact numbers will vary):

```
(1 row(s) affected)
Uncoverted              Converted
-----------------       -------------
0x00000000000000C9      201

(1 row(s) affected)
```

We can also convert dates:

```
SELECT OrderDate, CAST(OrderDate AS varchar) AS Converted
FROM Sales.SalesOrderHeader
WHERE SalesOrderID = 43663;
```

This yields something similar to (your exact format may change depending on system date configuration):

```
OrderDate               Converted
---------------------   -----------------------------
2001-07-01 00:00:00.000 Jul  1 2001 12:00AM

(1 row(s) affected)
```

Notice that CAST can still do date conversion; you just don't have any control over the formatting as you do with CONVERT. For example:

```
SELECT OrderDate, CONVERT(varchar(12), OrderDate, 111) AS Converted
FROM Sales.SalesOrderHeader
WHERE SalesOrderID = 43663;
```

This yields:

```
OrderDate               Converted
---------------------   ------------
2001-07-01 00:00:00.000 2001/07/01

(1 row(s) affected)
```

Which is quite a bit different from what CAST did. Indeed, you could have converted to any one of 34 two-digit- or four-digit-year formats.

```
SELECT OrderDate, CONVERT(varchar(12), OrderDate, 5) AS Converted
FROM Sales.SalesOrderHeader
WHERE SalesOrderID = 43663;
```

This returns:

```
OrderDate                Converted
----------------------   ------------
2001-07-01 00:00:00.000  01-07-01

(1 row(s) affected)
```

All you need is to supply a code at the end of the CONVERT function (111 in the preceding example gave us the Japan standard, with a four-digit year, and 5 the Italian standard, with a two-digit year) that tells which format you want. Anything in the 100s is a four-digit year; anything less than 100, with a few exceptions, is a two-digit year. The available formats can be found in Books Online under the topic of CONVERT or CASE.

> *Keep in mind that you can set a* split point *that SQL Server will use to determine whether a two-digit year should have a 20 added on the front or a 19. The default breaking point is 49/50 — a two-digit year of 49 or less will be converted using a 20 on the front. Anything higher will use a 19. These can be changed in the database server configuration (administrative issues are discussed in Chapter 19).*

The MERGE Command

The MERGE command is new with SQL Server 2008 and provides a somewhat different way of thinking about DML statements. With MERGE, we have the prospect of combining multiple DML action statements (INSERT, UPDATE, DELETE) into one overall action, improving performance (they can share many of the same physical operations) and simplifying transactions. MERGE makes use of a special USING clause that winds up working somewhat like a CTE. The result set in the USING clause can then be used to conditionally apply your INSERT, UPDATE, and DELETE statements. The basic syntax looks something like this:

```
MERGE [ TOP ( <expression> ) [ PERCENT ] ]
  [ INTO ] <target table> [ WITH ( <hint> ) ] [ [ AS ] <alias> ]
  USING <source query>
    ON <condition for join with target>
  [ WHEN MATCHED [ AND <clause search condition> ]
      THEN <merge matched> ]
  [ WHEN NOT MATCHED [ BY TARGET ] [ AND <clause search condition> ]
      THEN <merge not matched> ]
  [ WHEN NOT MATCHED BY SOURCE [ AND <clause search condition> ]
      THEN <merge matched> ]
  [ <output clause> ]
  [ OPTION ( <query hint> [ ,...n ] ) ];
```

Let's use the example of receiving a shipment for inventory. We'll assume that we're keeping a special roll up table of our sales for reporting purposes. We want to run a daily query that will add any new sales to our monthly rollup. On the first night of the month, this is pretty much a no-brainer, as, since there are no other roll up records for the month, any sales for the day are just rolled up and inserted. On the second day, however, we have a different scenario: We need to roll up and insert new records as we did the first day, but we only need to update existing records (for products that have already sold that month).

Let's take a look at how MERGE can manage both actions in one step. Before we get going on this, however, we need to create our roll up table:

```
USE AdventureWorks2008

CREATE TABLE Sales.MonthlyRollup
(
   Year       smallint    NOT NULL,
   Month      tinyint     NOT NULL,
   ProductID int          NOT NULL
     FOREIGN KEY
       REFERENCES Production.Product(ProductID),
   QtySold    int         NOT NULL,
   CONSTRAINT PKYearMonthProductID
     PRIMARY KEY
       (Year, Month, ProductID)
);
```

This is a pretty simple example of a monthly roll up table making it very easy to get sales totals by product for a given year and month. To make use of this, however, we need to regularly populate it with rolled up values from our detail table. To do this, we'll use MERGE.

First, we need to start by establishing a result set that will figure out from what rows we need to be sourcing data for our roll up. For purposes of this example, we'll focus on August of 2003 and start with our query for the first day of the month:

```
SELECT soh.OrderDate, sod.ProductID, SUM(sod.OrderQty) AS QtySold
FROM Sales.SalesOrderHeader soh
JOIN Sales.SalesOrderDetail sod
  ON soh.SalesOrderID = sod.SalesOrderID
WHERE soh.OrderDate >= '2003-08-01'
  AND soh.OrderDate < '2003-08-02'
GROUP BY soh.OrderDate, sod.ProductID;
```

This gets us the total sales, by ProductID, for every date in our range (our range just happens to be limited to one day).

There is a bit of a trap built into how we've done this up to this point. I've set the GROUP BY to use the OrderDate, but OrderDate is a datetime data type as opposed to just a date data type. If our orders were to start coming in with actual times on them, it would mess with our assumption of the orders all grouping nicely into one date. If this were a production environment, we would want to cast the Order-Date to a date data type or use DATEPART to assure that the grouping was by day rather than by time.

With this, we're ready to build our merge:

```
MERGE Sales.MonthlyRollup AS smr
USING
(
```

```
    SELECT soh.OrderDate, sod.ProductID, SUM(sod.OrderQty) AS QtySold
    FROM Sales.SalesOrderHeader soh
    JOIN Sales.SalesOrderDetail sod
      ON soh.SalesOrderID = sod.SalesOrderID
    WHERE soh.OrderDate >= '2003-08-01' AND soh.OrderDate < '2003-08-02'
    GROUP BY soh.OrderDate, sod.ProductID
) AS s
ON (s.ProductID = smr.ProductID)
WHEN MATCHED THEN
  UPDATE SET smr.QtySold = smr.QtySold + s.QtySold
WHEN NOT MATCHED THEN
  INSERT (Year, Month, ProductID, QtySold)
  VALUES (DATEPART(yy, s.OrderDate),
          DATEPART(m, s.OrderDate),
          s.ProductID,
          s.QtySold);
```

Note that the semicolon is required at the end of the MERGE statement. While the semicolon remains optional on most SQL Statements for backward-compatibility reasons, you'll find it working its way into more and more statements as a required delimiter of the end of the statement. This is particularly true for multipart statements such as MERGE.

When you run this, you should get 192 rows affected, assuming you haven't been altering the data in AdventureWorks2008. Now, since our Sales.MonthlyRollup table was empty, there wouldn't have been any matches, so all rows were inserted. We can verify that by querying our Sales.MonthlyRollup table:

```
SELECT *
FROM Sales.MonthlyRollup;
```

This gets us back the expected 192 rows:

```
Year    Month ProductID   QtySold
------  ----- ----------- -----------
2003    8     707         242
2003    8     708         281
2003    8     711         302
...
...
2003    8     997         43
2003    8     998         138
2003    8     999         103

(192 row(s) affected)
```

Every row that was in the basic SELECT that powered our MERGE wound up being inserted into our table. Let's move on, however, to the second day of the month:

```
MERGE Sales.MonthlyRollup AS smr
USING
(
  SELECT soh.OrderDate, sod.ProductID, SUM(sod.OrderQty) AS QtySold
  FROM Sales.SalesOrderHeader soh
  JOIN Sales.SalesOrderDetail sod
    ON soh.SalesOrderID = sod.SalesOrderID
  WHERE soh.OrderDate >= '2003-08-02' AND soh.OrderDate < '2003-08-03'
```

```
    GROUP BY soh.OrderDate, sod.ProductID
) AS s
ON (s.ProductID = smr.ProductID)
WHEN MATCHED THEN
    UPDATE SET smr.QtySold = smr.QtySold + s.QtySold
WHEN NOT MATCHED THEN
    INSERT (Year, Month, ProductID, QtySold)
    VALUES (DATEPART(yy, s.OrderDate),
            DATEPART(m, s.OrderDate),
            s.ProductID,
            s.QtySold);
```

We update the date we're running this for (simulating running it on the second day of the month), and running it should get us 38 rows:

```
(38 row(s) affected)
```

But something is different this time — we already had rows in the table that our new batch of sales may have matched up with. We know we affected 38 rows, but *how* did we affect them? Rerun the SELECT on our table:

```
SELECT *
FROM Sales.MonthlyRollup;
```

And instead of 230 rows (the 192 plus the 38), we only get 194 rows. Indeed, 36 of our 38 rows were repeat sales and were therefore treated as updates, rather than insertions. Two rows (ProductIDs 882 and 928) were sales of products that had not been previously sold in that month and thus needed to be inserted as new rows — one pass over the data, but the equivalent of two statements ran.

We could perform similar actions that decide to delete rows based on matched or not matched conditions.

A Brief Look at BY TARGET versus BY SOURCE

In the examples above, we've largely ignored the issue of which is the table to be matched when determining the action to be performed. The default is BY TARGET, and thus all of our examples (which haven't used the BY keyword at all) have been analyzed on whether there is or isn't a match in the target table (the table named immediately after the MERGE keyword). The comparison, from a matching perspective, is similar to an outer join. As a join is analyzed, there can be a match on the source side, the target side, or both. If you have specified BY TARGET (or not used the BY keyword at all since matching by target is the default), the action (insert, update, or delete) is applied only if the target side of the join has a match. Likewise, if you have specified BY SOURCE, then the merge action is only applied if the source side of the join has a match.

Most of the time, you can map a particular merge action to a specific match scenario:

- ❑   NOT MATCHED [BY TARGET]: This typically maps to a scenario where you are going to be inserting rows into a table based on data you found in the source.

- ❑   MATCHED [BY TARGET]: This implies that the row already exists in the target, and thus it is likely you will be performing an update action on the target table row.

- ❑   NOT MATCHED BY SOURCE: This is typically utilized to deal with rows that are missing (and likely deleted) from the source table, and you will usually be deleting the row in the target under this scenario (though you may also just update the row to set an inactive flag or similar marker).

There are other possible mixes, but these easily cover the bulk of things that most any SQL developer will see.

The Output Clause

The MERGE command also provides us the option of outputting what amounts to a SELECT statement with the details of what actions were actually performed by the MERGE. The OUTPUT keyword is essentially a substitute for SELECT, but brings along several special operators to allow us to match up to the merged data. These include:

❑ $action: Returns INSERTED, UPDATED, or DELETED, as appropriate, to indicate the action taken for that particular row

❑   inserted: A reference to an internal working table that contains a reference to any data inserted for a given row, note that this includes the current values for data that has been updated.

❑   deleted: A reference to an internal working table that contains a reference to any data deleted from a given row, note that this includes the previous values for data that has been updated.

We will visit the inserted *and* deleted *tables in much more detail when we explore triggers in Chapter 15.*

Let's try these out by resetting our MonthlyRollup table, and executing our MERGE statements again with the OUTPUT clause included. Start by truncating the MonthlyRollup table to clear out our previous work:

```
USE AdventureWorks2008
TRUNCATE TABLE Sales.MonthlyRollup;
```

This clears all data out of our table and resets everything about the table to a state as though it had just been created using the CREATE command. We're now ready to execute our first MERGE statement again, but this time we'll include the OUTPUT clause:

```
MERGE Sales.MonthlyRollup AS smr
USING
(
  SELECT soh.OrderDate, sod.ProductID, SUM(sod.OrderQty) AS QtySold
  FROM Sales.SalesOrderHeader soh
  JOIN Sales.SalesOrderDetail sod
    ON soh.SalesOrderID = sod.SalesOrderID
  WHERE soh.OrderDate >= '2003-08-01' AND soh.OrderDate < '2003-08-02'
  GROUP BY soh.OrderDate, sod.ProductID
) AS s
ON (s.ProductID = smr.ProductID)
WHEN MATCHED THEN
  UPDATE SET smr.QtySold = smr.QtySold + s.QtySold
WHEN NOT MATCHED THEN
  INSERT (Year, Month, ProductID, QtySold)
  VALUES (DATEPART(yy, s.OrderDate),
          DATEPART(m, s.OrderDate),
          s.ProductID,
          s.QtySold)
```

```
OUTPUT $action,
       inserted.Year,
       inserted.Month,
       inserted.ProductID,
       inserted.QtySold,
       deleted.Year,
       deleted.Month,
       deleted.ProductID,
       deleted.QtySold;
```

This, of course, performs exactly the same action it did the first time we ran it (inserting 192 rows), but this time we get a result set back that provides information about the action taken:

$action	Year	Month	ProductID	QtySold	Year	Month	ProductID	QtySold
INSERT	2003	8	707	242	NULL	NULL	NULL	NULL
INSERT	2003	8	708	281	NULL	NULL	NULL	NULL
INSERT	2003	8	711	302	NULL	NULL	NULL	NULL
...								
...								
INSERT	2003	8	997	43	NULL	NULL	NULL	NULL
INSERT	2003	8	998	138	NULL	NULL	NULL	NULL
INSERT	2003	8	999	103	NULL	NULL	NULL	NULL

```
(192 row(s) affected)
```

Notice that, since we only had inserted rows in this particular query, all of the data from the deleted table is null. Things change quickly though when we run the second MERGE statement (with the same OUTPUT clause added):

```
MERGE Sales.MonthlyRollup AS smr
USING
(
  SELECT soh.OrderDate, sod.ProductID, SUM(sod.OrderQty) AS QtySold
  FROM Sales.SalesOrderHeader soh
  JOIN Sales.SalesOrderDetail sod
    ON soh.SalesOrderID = sod.SalesOrderID
  WHERE soh.OrderDate >= '2003-08-02' AND soh.OrderDate < '2003-08-03'
  GROUP BY soh.OrderDate, sod.ProductID
) AS s
ON (s.ProductID = smr.ProductID)
WHEN MATCHED THEN
  UPDATE SET smr.QtySold = smr.QtySold + s.QtySold
WHEN NOT MATCHED THEN
  INSERT (Year, Month, ProductID, QtySold)
  VALUES (DATEPART(yy, s.OrderDate),
          DATEPART(m, s.OrderDate),
          s.ProductID,
          s.QtySold)
OUTPUT $action,
       inserted.Year,
       inserted.Month,
       inserted.ProductID,
       inserted.QtySold,
```

```
            deleted.Year,
            deleted.Month,
            deleted.ProductID,
            deleted.QtySold;
```

This time we see more than one action and, in the case of UPDATED results, we have data for both the inserted (the new values) and deleted (the old values) tables:

```
$action     Year    Month ProductID    QtySold       Year    Month ProductID    QtySold
----------  ------  ----- -----------  -----------   ------  ----- -----------  -----------
INSERT      2003    8     928          2             NULL    NULL  NULL         NULL
INSERT      2003    8     882          1             NULL    NULL  NULL         NULL
UPDATE      2003    8     707          249           2003    8     707          242

...
...
UPDATE      2003    8     963          32            2003    8     963          31
UPDATE      2003    8     970          54            2003    8     970          53
UPDATE      2003    8     998          139           2003    8     998          138

(38 row(s) affected)
```

Performance Considerations

We've already touched on some of the macro-level "what's the best thing to do" stuff as we've gone through the chapter, but, like most things in life, it's not as easy as all that. What I want to do here is provide something of a quick reference for performance issues for your queries. I'll try to steer you toward the right kind of query for the right kind of situation.

> Yes, it's time again folks for one of my now famous soapbox diatribes. At issue this time is the concept of blanket use of blanket rules.
>
> What we're going to be talking about in this section is the way that things *usually* work. The word "usually" is extremely operative here. There are very few rules in SQL that will be true 100 percent of the time. In a world full of exceptions, SQL has to be at the pinnacle of that — exceptions are a dime a dozen when you try to describe the performance world in SQL Server.
>
> In short, you need to gauge just how important the performance of a given query is. If performance is critical, then don't take these rules too seriously — instead, use them as a starting point, and then TEST, TEST, TEST!!!

JOINs versus Subqueries versus ?

This is that area I mentioned earlier in the chapter that I had a heated debate with a coworker over. And, as you might expect when two people have such conviction in their points of view, both of us were correct up to a point (and, it follows, wrong up to a point).

The long-standing, traditional viewpoint about subqueries has always been that you are much better off using joins instead if you can. This is absolutely correct — sometimes. In reality, it depends on a large number of factors. The following is a table that discusses some of the issues that the performance balance will depend on and which side of the equation they favor.

Situation	Favors
The value returned from a subquery is going to be the same for every row in the outer query.	Pre-query. Declaring a variable and then selecting the needed value into that variable will allow the would-be subquery to be executed just once, rather than once for every record in the outer table.
Both tables are relatively small (say 10,000 records or less).	Subqueries. I don't know the exact reasons, but I've run several tests on this and it held up pretty much every time. I suspect that the issue is the lower overhead of a lookup versus a join.
The match, after considering all criteria, is going to return only one value.	Subqueries. Again, there is much less overhead in going and finding just one record and substituting it than having to join the entire table.
The match, after considering all criteria, is going to return relatively few values and there is no index on the lookup column.	Subqueries. A single lookup or even a few lookups will usually take less overhead than a hash join.
The lookup table is relatively small, but the base table is large.	Nested subqueries if applicable; joins if versus a correlated subquery. With subqueries the lookup will happen only once and is relatively low overhead. With correlated subqueries, however, you will be cycling the lookup many times — in this case, the join would be a better choice.
Correlated subquery vs. join	JOIN. Internally, a correlated subquery is going to create a nested-loop situation. This can create quite a bit of overhead. It is substantially faster than cursors in most instances, but slower than other options that might be available.
Derived tables vs. whatever	Derived tables typically carry a fair amount of overhead to them, so proceed with caution. The thing to remember is that they are run (derived, if you will) once, and then they are in memory, so most of the overhead is in the initial creation and the lack of indexes (in larger result sets). They can be fast or slow — it just depends. Think before coding on these.
EXISTS vs. whatever	EXISTS. It does not have to deal with multiple lookups for the same match. Once it finds one match for that particular row, it is free to move on to the next lookup — this can seriously cut down on overhead.

These are just the highlights. The possibilities of different mixes and additional situations are positively endless.

> I can't stress enough how important it is when in doubt — heck, even when you're not in doubt but performance is everything — to make reasonable tests of competing solutions to a problem. Most of the time the blanket rules will be fine, but not always. By performing reasonable tests, you can be certain you've made the right choice.

Summary

The query options you learned back in Chapters 3 and 4 cover perhaps 80 percent or more of the query situations that you run into, but it's that other 20 percent that can kill you. Sometimes the issue is whether you can even find a query that will give you the answers you need. Sometimes it's that you have a particular query or sproc that has unacceptable performance. Whatever the case, you'll run across plenty of situations where simple queries and joins just won't fit the bill. You need something more and, hopefully, the options covered in this chapter have given you a little extra ammunition to deal with those tough situations.

Exercises

1. Write a query that returns the hire dates of all AdventureWorks2008 employees in MM/DD/YY format.

2. Write separate queries using a JOIN, a subquery, and then an EXISTS, to list all Adventure-Works2008 persons who have not placed an order.

3. Show the most recent 5 orders that were purchased from account numbers that have spent more than $70,000 with AdventureWorks.

Being Normal: Normalization and Other Basic Design Issues

I can imagine you as being somewhat perplexed about the how and why of some of the tables we've constructed thus far. With the exception of a chapter or two, this book has tended to have an *online transaction-processing*, or *OLTP*, flair to the examples. Don't get me wrong; I will point out, from time to time, some of the differences between OLTP and its more analysis-oriented cousin *Online Analytical Processing (OLAP)*. My point is that you will, in most of the examples, be seeing a table design that is optimized for the most common kind of database — OLTP. As such, the table examples will typically have a database layout that is, for the most part, *normalized* to what is called the third normal form.

So what is "normal form"? We'll be taking a very solid look at that in this chapter, but, for the moment, let's just say that it means your data has been broken out into a logical, non-repetitive format that can easily be reassembled into the whole. In addition to normalization (which is the process of putting your database into normal form), we'll also be examining the characteristics of OLTP and OLAP databases. And, as if we didn't have enough between those two topics, we'll also be looking at many examples of how the constraints we've already seen are implemented in the overall solution.

This is probably going to be one of the toughest chapters in the book to grasp because of a paradox in what to learn first. Some of the concepts used in this chapter refer to things we'll be covering later — such as triggers and stored procedures. On the other hand, it is difficult to relate those topics without understanding their role in database design.

I strongly recommend reading this chapter through, and then coming back to it again after you've read several of the subsequent chapters.

Tables

This is going to seem beyond basic, but let's briefly review what exactly a table is. We're obviously not talking about the kind that sits in your kitchen, but, rather, the central object of any database.

A table is a collection of instances of data that have the same general *attributes*. These instances of data are organized into *rows* and *columns* of data. A table should represent a "real-world" collection of data (often referred to as an *entity*), and will have *relationships* with information in other tables. A drawing of the various entities (tables) and relationships (how they work together) is usually referred to as an Entity-Relationship Diagram — or *ER Diagram*. Sometimes the term "ER Diagram" will even be shortened further down to *ERD*.

By connecting two or more tables through their various relationships, you are able to temporarily create other tables as needed from the combination of the data in both tables (you've already seen this to some degree in Chapters 4 and 5). A collection of related entities are then grouped together into a database.

Keeping Your Data "Normal"

Normalization is something of the cornerstone model of modern OLTP database design. Normalization first originated along with the concept of relational databases. Both came from the work of E. F. Codd (IBM) in 1969. Codd put forth the notion that a database "consists of a series of unordered tables that can be manipulated using non-procedural operations that return tables."

Several things are key about this:

❑ Order must be unimportant.

❑ The tables would be able to "relate" to each other in a non-procedural way (indeed, Codd called tables "relations").

❑ That, by relating these base tables, you would be able to create a virtual table to meet a new need.

Normalization was a natural offshoot of the design of a database of "relations."

The concept of normalization has to be one of most over-referenced and yet misunderstood concepts in programming. Everyone thinks they understand it, and many do in at least its academic form. Unfortunately, it also tends to be one of those things that many database designers wear like a cross — it is somehow their symbol that they are "real" database architects. What it really is, however, is a symbol that they know what the normal forms are — and that's all. Normalization is really just one piece of a larger database design picture. Sometimes you need to normalize your data — then again, sometimes you need to deliberately de-normalize your data. Even within the normalization process, there are often many ways to achieve what is technically a normalized database.

My point in this latest soapbox diatribe is that normalization is a theory, and that's all it is. Once you choose whether to implement a normalized strategy or not, what you have is a database — hopefully the best one you could possibly design. Don't get stuck on what the books (including this one) say you're supposed to do — do what's right for the situation that you're in. As the author of this book, all I can do is relate concepts to you — I can't implement them for you, and neither can any other author (at least not with the written word). You need to pick and choose between these concepts in order to achieve the best fit and the best solution. Now, excuse me while I put that soapbox away, and we'll get on to talking about the normal forms and what they purportedly do for us.

Let's start off by saying that there are six normal forms. For those of you who have dealt with databases and normalization some before, that number may come as a surprise. You are very likely to hear that a fully normalized database is one that is normalized to the third normal form — doesn't it then follow that there must be only three normal forms? Perhaps it will make those same people who thought there were only three normal forms feel better that in this book we're only going to be looking to any extent at the three forms you've heard about, as they are the only three that are put to any regular use in the real world. I will, however, take a brief (very brief) skim over the other three forms just for posterity.

We've already looked at how to create a primary key and some of the reasons for using one in our tables — if we want to be able to act on just one row, then we need to be able to uniquely identify that row. The concepts of normalization are highly dependent on issues surrounding the definition of the primary key and what columns are dependent on it. One phrase you might hear frequently in normalization is:

The key, the whole key, and nothing but the key.

The somewhat fun addition to this is:

The key, the whole key, and nothing but the key, so help me Codd!

This is a super-brief summarization of what normalization is about out to the third normal form. When you can say that all your columns are dependent only on the whole key and nothing more or less, then you are at the third normal form.

Let's take a look at the various normal forms and what each does for us.

Before the Beginning

You actually need to begin by getting a few things in place even before you try to get your data into first normal form. You have to have a thing or two in place before you can even consider the table to be a true entity in the relational database sense of the word:

❑ The table should describe one and only one entity. (No trying to shortcut and combine things!)

❑ All rows must be unique, and there must be a primary key.

❑ The column and row order must not matter.

The place to start, then, is by identifying the right entities to have. Some of these will be fairly obvious, others will not. Many of them will be exposed and refined as you go through the normalization process. At the very least, go through and identify all the obvious entities.

If you're familiar with object-oriented programming, then you can liken the most logical top-level entities to objects in an object model.

Let's think about a hyper-simple model — our sales model again. To begin with, we're not going to worry about the different variations possible, or even what columns we're going to have — instead, we're just going to worry about identifying the basic entities of our system.

First, think about the most basic process. What we want to do is create an entity for each atomic unit that we want to be able to maintain data on in the process. Our process then, looks like this: a customer calls or comes in and talks to an employee who takes an order.

A first pass on this might have one entity: Orders.

> *As you become more experienced at normalization, your first pass at something like this is probably going to yield you quite a few more entities right from the beginning. For now though, we'll just take this one and see how the normalization process shows us the others that we need.*

Assuming you've got your concepts down of what you want your entities to be, the next place to go is to figure out your beginning columns and, from there, a primary key. Remember that a primary key provides a unique identifier for each row.

We can peruse our list of columns and come up with *key candidates*. Your list of key candidates should include any column that can potentially be used to uniquely identify each row in your entity. There is, otherwise, no hard and fast rule on what column has to be the primary key (this is one of many reasons you'll see such wide variation in how people design databases that are meant to contain the same basic information). In some cases, you will not be able to find even one candidate key, and you will need to make one up (remember `Identity` and `rowguid()` columns?).

We already created an `Orders` table in the previous chapter, but for example purposes let's take a look at a very common implementation of an `Orders` table in the old flat file design:

Orders
OrderNo
CustomerNo
CustomerName
CustomerAddress
CustomerCity
CustomerState
CustomerZip
OrderDate
ItemsOrdered
Total

Since this is an `Orders` table, and logically, an order number is meant to be one to an order, I'm going go with `OrderNo` as my primary key.

OK, so now we have a basic entity. Nothing about this entity cares about the ordering of columns (tables are, by convention, usually organized as having the primary key as the first column(s), but, technically speaking, it doesn't have to be that way). Nothing in the basic makeup of this table cares about the ordering of the rows. The table, at least superficially, describes just one entity. In short, we're ready to begin our normalization process (actually, we sort of already have).

The First Normal Form

The first normal form (*1NF*) is all about eliminating repeating groups of data and guaranteeing *atomicity* (the data is self-contained and independent). At a high level, it works by creating a primary key (which we already have), then moving any repeating data groups into new tables, creating new keys for those tables, and so on. In addition, we break out any columns that combine data into separate rows for each piece of data.

In the more traditional flat file designs, repeating data was commonplace — as was having multiple pieces of information in a column. This was rather problematic in a number of ways:

❑ At that time, disk storage was extremely expensive. Storing data multiple times means wasted space. Data storage has become substantially less expensive, so this isn't as big an issue as it once was.

❑ Repetitive data means more data to be moved, and larger I/O counts. This means that performance is hindered as large blocks of data must be moved through the data bus and or network. This, even with today's much faster technology, can have a substantial negative impact on performance.

❑ The data between rows of what should have been repeating data often did not agree, creating something of a data paradox and a general lack of data integrity.

❑ If you wanted to query information out of a column that has combined data, then you had to first come up with a way to parse the data in that column (this was extremely slow).

Now, there are a lot of columns in our table, and I probably could have easily tossed in a few more. Still, the nice thing about it is that I could query everything out of one place when I wanted to know about orders.

Just to explore what this means, however, let's take a look at what some data in this table might look like. Note that I'm going to cut out a few columns here just to help things fit on a page, but I think you'll still be able to see the point:

Order No	Order Date	Customer No	Customer Name	Customer Address	ItemsOrdered
100	1/1/99	54545	ACME Co	1234 1st St.	1A4536, Flange, 7lbs, $75;4-OR2400, Injector, .5lbs, $108;4-OR2403, Injector, .5lbs, $116;1-4I5436, Head, 63lbs, $750
101	1/1/99	12000	Sneed Corp.	555 Main Ave.	1-3X9567, Pump, 5lbs, $62.50
102	1/1/99	66651	ZZZ & Co.	4242 SW 2nd	7-8G9200; Fan, 3lbs, $84;1-8G5437, Fan, 3lbs, $15;1-3H6250, Control, 5lbs, $32
103	1/2/99	54545	ACME Co	1234 1st St.	40-8G9200, Fan, 3lbs, $480;1-2P5523, Housing, 1lb, $165;1-3X9567, Pump, 5lbs, $42

We have a number of issues to deal with in this table if we're going to normalize it. While we have a functional primary key (yes, these existed long before relational systems), we have problems with both of the main areas of the first normal form:

❑   I have repeating groups of data (customer information). I need to break that out into a different table.

❑   The `ItemsOrdered` column does not contain data that is atomic in nature.

We can start by moving several columns out of the table:

OrderNo (PK)	OrderDate	CustomerNo	ItemsOrdered
100	1/1/1999	54545	1A4536, Flange, 7lbs, $75;4-OR2400, Injector, .5lbs, $108;4-OR2403, Injector, .5lbs, $116;1-4I5436, Head, 63lbs, $750
101	1/1/1999	12000	1-3X9567, Pump, 5lbs, $62.50
102	1/1/1999	66651	7-8G9200; Fan, 3lbs, $84;1-8G5437, Fan, 3lbs, $15;1-3H6250, Control, 5lbs, $32
103	1/2/1999	54545	40-8G9200, Fan, 3lbs, $480;1-2P5523, Housing, 1lbs, $165;1-3X9567, Pump, 5lbs, $42

And putting them into their own table:

CustomerNo (PK)	CustomerName	CustomerAddress
54545	ACME Co	1234 1st St.
12000	Sneed Corp.	555 Main Ave.
66651	ZZZ & Co.	4242 SW 2nd

There are several things to notice about the old and new tables:

❑   We must have a primary key for our new table to ensure that each row is unique. For our Customers table, there are two candidate keys — CustomerNo and CustomerName. CustomerNo was actually created just to serve this purpose and seems the logical choice — after all, it's entirely conceivable that you could have more than one customer with the same name. (For example, there have to be hundreds of companies named ACME in the U.S.)

❑   Although we've moved the data out of the Orders table, we still need to maintain a reference to the data in the new Customers table. This is why you still see the CustomerNo (the primary key) column in the Orders table. Later on, when we build our references, we'll create a foreign key constraint to force all orders to have valid customer numbers.

❑ We were able to eliminate an instance of the information for ACME Co. That's part of the purpose of moving data that appears in repetitive groups — to just store it once. This both saves us space and prevents conflicting values.

❑ We moved only repeating *groups* of data. We still see the same order date several times, but it doesn't really fit into a group — it's just a relatively random piece of data that has no relevance outside of this table.

So, we've dealt with our repeating data; next, we're ready to move onto the second violation of first normal form — atomicity. If you take a look at the `ItemsOrdered` column, you'll see that there are actually several different pieces of data there:

❑ Anywhere from one to many individual part numbers

❑ Quantity weight information on each of those parts

Part number, weight, and price are each atomic pieces of data if kept to themselves, but combined into one lump grouping you no longer have atomicity.

> *Believe it or not, things were sometimes really done this way. At first glance, it seemed the easy thing to do — paper invoices often had just one big block area for writing up what the customer wanted, and computer-based systems were often just as close to a clone of paper as someone could make it.*

We'll go ahead and break things up — and, while we're at it, we'll add in a new piece of information in the form of a unit price, as shown in Figure 8-1. The problem is that, once we break up this information, our primary key no longer uniquely identifies our rows — our rows are still unique, but the primary key is now inadequate.

Order No (PK)	Order Date	Customer No	Part No	Description	Qty	Unit Price	Total Price	Wt.
100	1/1/1999	54545	1A4536	Flange	5	15	75	6
100	1/1/1999	54545	0R2400	Injector	4	27	108	.5
100	1/1/1999	54545	0R2403	Injector	4	29	116	.5
100	1/1/1999	54545	4I5436	Head	1	750	750	3
101	1/1/1999	12000	3X9567	Pump	1	62.50	62.50	5
102	1/1/1999	66651	8G9200	Fan	7	12	84	3
102	1/1/1999	66651	8G5437	Fan	1	15	15	3
102	1/1/1999	66651	3H6250	Control	1	32	32	5
103	1/2/1999	54545	8G9200	Fan	40	12	480	3
103	1/2/1999	54545	2P5523	Housing	1	165	165	1
103	1/2/1999	54545	3X9567	Pump	1	42	42	5

Figure 8-1

For now, we'll address this by adding a line item number to our table, as shown in Figure 8-2, so we can, again, uniquely identify our rows.

Order No (PK)	Line Item (PK)	Order Date	Customer No	Part No	Description	Qty	Unit Price	Total Price	Wt.
100	1	1/1/1999	54545	1A4536	Flange	5	15	75	6
100	2	1/1/1999	54545	0R2400	Injector	4	27	108	.5
100	3	1/1/1999	54545	0R2403	Injector	4	29	116	.5
100	4	1/1/1999	54545	4I5436	Head	1	750	750	3
101	1	1/1/1999	12000	3X9567	Pump	1	62.50	62.50	5
102	1	1/1/1999	66651	8G9200	Fan	7	12	84	3
102	2	1/1/1999	66651	8G5437	Fan	1	15	15	3
102	3	1/1/1999	66651	3H6250	Control	1	32	32	5
103	1	1/2/1999	54545	8G9200	Fan	40	12	480	3
103	2	1/2/1999	54545	2P5523	Housing	1	165	165	1
103	3	1/2/1999	54545	3X9567	Pump	1	42	42	5

Figure 8-2

> Rather than create another column as we did here, we also could have taken the approach of making `PartNo` part of our primary key. The fallout from this would have been that we could not have had the same part number appear twice in the same order. We'll briefly discuss keys based on more than one column — or composite keys — in our next chapter.

At this point, we meet our criteria for first normal form. We have no repeating groups of data, and all columns are atomic. We do have issues with data having to be repeated within a column (because it's the same for all rows for that primary key), but we'll deal with that shortly.

The Second Normal Form

The next phase in normalization is to go to the second normal form (*2NF*). Second normal form further reduces the incidence of repeated data (not necessarily groups).

Second normal form has two rules to it:

❑ The table must meet the rules for first normal form. (Normalization is a building block kind of process — you can't stack the third block on if you don't have the first two there already.)

❑ Each column must depend on the *whole* key.

Our example has a problem — actually, it has a couple of them — in this area. Let's look at the first normal form version of our `Orders` table again (Figure 8-2) — is every column dependent on the whole key? Are there any that need only part of the key?

The answers are no and yes respectively. There are two columns that only depend only on the `OrderNo` column — not the LineItem column. The columns in question are `OrderDate` and `CustomerNo`; both are the same for the entire order regardless of how many line items there are. Dealing with these requires that we introduce yet another table. At this point, we run across the concept of a *header* vs. a *detail* table for the first time.

Sometimes what is, in practice, one entity still needs to be broken out into two tables and, thus, two entities. The header is something of the parent table of the two tables in the relationship. It contains information that needs to be stored only once while the detail table stores the information that may exist in multiple instances. The header usually keeps the name of the original table, and the detail table usually has a name that starts with the header table name and adds on something to indicate that it is a detail table (for example, OrderDetails). For every one header record, you usually have at least one detail record and may have many, many more. This is one example of a kind of relationship (a one-to-many relationship) that you look at in the next major section.

So let's take care of this by splitting our table again. We'll actually start with the detail table since it's keeping the bulk of the columns. From this point forward, we'll call this table OrderDetails:

OrderNo (PK)	LineItem (PK)	PartNo	Description	Qty	Unit Price	Total Price	Wt
100	1	1A4536	Flange	5	15	75	6
100	2	OR2400	Injector	4	27	108	.5
100	3	OR2403	Injector	4	29	116	.5
100	4	4I5436	Head	1	750	750	3
101	1	3X9567	Pump	1	62.50	62.50	5
102	1	8G9200	Fan	7	12	84	3
102	2	8G5437	Fan	1	15	15	3
102	3	3H6250	Control	1	32	32	5
103	1	8G9200	Fan	40	12	480	3
103	2	2P5523	Housing	1	165	165	1
103	3	3X9567	Pump	1	42	42	5

Then we move on to what, although you could consider it to be the new table of the two, will serve as the header table and thus keep the Orders name:

OrderNo (PK)	OrderDate	CustomerNo
100	1/1/1999	54545
101	1/1/1999	12000
102	1/1/1999	66651
103	1/2/1999	54545

So, now you have second normal form. All of our columns depend on the entire key. I'm sure you won't be surprised to hear that we still have a problem or two though — we'll deal with them next.

The Third Normal Form

This is the relative end of the line. There are technically levels of normalization beyond this, but none that get much attention outside of academic circles. We'll look at those extremely briefly next, but first we need to finish the business at hand.

I mentioned at the end of our discussion of the second normal form that we still had problems — we still haven't reached the third normal form (*3NF*). The third normal form deals with the issue of having all the columns in our table not just be dependent on something — but dependent on the right thing. The third normal form has just three rules to it:

❑   The table must be in 2NF (I told you this was a building block thing).

❑   No column can have any dependency on any other non-key column.

❑   You cannot have derived data.

We already know that we're in the second normal form, so let's look at the other two rules.

First, do we have any columns that have dependencies other than the primary key? Yes! Actually, there are a couple of columns that are dependent on the PartNo as much as, if not more than, the primary key of this table. Weight and Description are both entirely dependent on the PartNo column — we again need to split into another table.

> *Your first tendency here might be to also lump* UnitPrice *into this category, and you would be partially right. The* Products *table that we will create here can and should have a* UnitPrice *column in it — but it will be of a slightly different nature. Indeed, perhaps it would be better named* ListPrice, *as it is the cost we have set in general for that product. The difference for the* UnitPrice *in the* OrderDetails *table is twofold. First, we may offer discounts that would change the price at time of sale. This means that the price in the* OrderDetails *record may be different than the planned price that you will keep in the* Products *table. Second, the price we plan to charge will change over time with factors such as inflation, but changes in future prices will not change what we have charged on our actual orders of the past. In other words, price is one of those odd circumstances where there are really two flavors of it — one dependent on the* PartNo, *and one dependent on the primary key for the* OrderDetails *table (in other words* OrderID *and* LineItem).*

First, we need to create a new table (we'll call it Products) to hold our part information. This new table will hold the information that we had in OrderDetails that was more dependent on PartNo than on OrderID or LineItem:

PartNo (PK)	Description	Wt
1A4536	Flange	6
OR2400	Injector	.5
OR2403	Injector	.5

PartNo (PK)	Description	Wt
4I5436	Head	3
3X9567	Pump	5
8G9200	Fan	3
8G5437	Fan	3
3H6250	Control	5
8G9200	Fan	3
2P5523	Housing	1
3X9567	Pump	5

You can then chop all but the foreign key out of the OrderDetails table:

OrderNo (PK)	LineItem (PK)	PartNo	Qty	Unit Price	Total Price
100	1	1A4536	5	15	75
100	2	OR2400	4	27	108
100	3	OR2403	4	29	116
100	4	4I5436	1	750	750
101	1	3X9567	1	62.50	62.50
102	1	8G9200	7	12	84
102	2	8G5437	1	15	15
102	3	3H6250	1	32	32
103	1	8G9200	40	12	480
103	2	2P5523	1	165	165
103	3	3X9567	1	42	42

That takes care of problem number 1 (cross-column dependency), but doesn't deal with derived data. We have a column called TotalPrice that contains data that can actually be derived from multiplying Qty by UnitPrice. This is a no-no in normalization.

Derived data is one of the places that you'll see me "de-normalize" data most often. Why? Speed! A query that reads `WHERE TotalPrice > $100` runs faster than one that reads `WHERE Qty * UnitPrice > 50` — particularly if we are able to index our computed `TotalPrice`.

On the other side of this, however, I do sometimes take more of a hybrid approach by utilizing a computed column and letting SQL Server keep a sum of the other two columns for us (you may recall us using this idea for our the `PreviousSalary` example in the `Employees` table of the Accounting database in Chapter 5). If this is a very important column from a performance perspective (you're running lots of columns that filter based on the values in this column), then you may want to add an index to your new computed column. The significance of this is that the index "materializes" the computed data. What does that mean? Well, it means that even SQL Server doesn't have to calculate the computed column on the fly — instead, it calculates it once when the row is stored in the index, and, thereafter, uses the precalculated column. It can be very fast indeed, and we'll examine it further in Chapter 9. That said, there is a trade off (if there wasn't, everyone would do it this way all the time, right?) — space. You're storing data that doesn't need to be stored, and if you do that to every possible piece of derived data, then it can really add up. More space means more data to read, and that can mean things actually get *slower*. The point here is to weigh your options, and make a balanced choice.

So, to reach the third normal form, we just need to drop off the `TotalPrice` column and compute it when needed.

Other Normal Forms

There are a few other forms out there that are considered, at least by academics, to be part of the normalization model. These include:

❑   **Boyce-Codd** (considered really just to be a variation on third normal form): This one tries to address situations where you have multiple overlapping candidate keys. This can only happen if:

   a.   All the candidate keys are composite keys (that is, it takes more than one column to make up the key).

   b.   There is more than one candidate key.

   c.   The candidate keys each have at least one column that is in common with another candidate key.

   This is typically a situation where any number of solutions works, and almost never gets logically thought of outside the academic community.

❑   **Fourth Normal Form:** This one tries to deal with issues surrounding multi-valued dependence. This is the situation where, for an individual row, no column depends on a column other than the primary key and depends on the whole primary key (meeting third normal form). However, there can be rather odd situations where one column in the primary key can depend separately on other columns in the primary key. These are rare, and don't usually cause any real problem. As such, they are largely ignored in the database world, and we will not address them here.

❏ **Fifth Normal Form:** This deals with non-loss and loss decompositions. Essentially, there are certain situations where you can decompose a relationship such that you cannot logically recompose it into its original form. Again, these are rare, largely academic, and we won't deal with them any further here.

This is, of course, just a really quick look at these — and that's deliberate on my part. The main reason you need to know these in the real world is either to impress your friends (or prove to them you're a "know it all") and to not sound like an idiot when some database guru comes to town and starts talking about them. However you choose to use it, I do recommend against attempting to use it to get dates . . . .

Relationships

Well, I've always heard from women that men immediately leave the room if you even mention the word "relationship." With that in mind, I hope that I didn't just lose about half my readers.

I am, of course, kidding — but not by as much as you might think. Experts say the key to successful relationships is that you know the role of both parties and that everyone understands the boundaries and rules of the relationship that they are in. I can be talking about database relationships with that statement every bit as much as people relationships.

There are three different kinds of major relationships:

❏ One-to-one

❏ One-to-many

❏ Many-to-many

Each of these has some variations depending on whether one side of the relationship is nullable or not. For example, instead of a one-to-one relationship, you might have a zero or one-to-one relationship.

One-to-One

This is exactly what it says it is. A one-to-one relationship is one where the fact that you have a record in one table means that you have exactly one matching record in another table.

To illustrate a one-to-one relationship, let's look at a slight variation of a piece of our earlier example. Imagine that you have customers — just as we did in our earlier example. This time, however, we're going to imagine that we are a subsidiary of a much larger company. Our parent company wants to be able to track all of its customers, and to be able to tell the collective total of each customer's purchases — regardless of which subsidiary(s) the customer made purchases with.

Even if all the subsidiaries run out of one server at the main headquarters, there's a very good chance that the various subsidiaries would be running with their own databases. One way to track all customer information, which would facilitate combining it later, would be to create a master customer database owned by the parent company. The subsidiaries would then maintain their own customer table, but do so with a one-to-one relationship to the parent company's customer table. Any customer record created in the parent company would imply that you needed to have one in the subsidiaries also. Any creation of a customer record in a subsidiary would require that one also be created in the parent company's copy.

A second example — one that used to apply frequently to SQL Server prior to version 7.0 — is when you have too much information to fit in one row. Remember that the maximum row size for SQL Server is 8060 bytes of non-BLOB data. That's a lot harder to fill than version 6.5's 1962 bytes, but you can still have situations that require you to store a very large number of columns or even fewer very wide columns. One way to get around this problem was to actually create two different tables and split our rows between the tables. We could then impose a one-to-one relationship. The combination of the matching rows in the two tables then meets our larger row size requirement.

> **SQL Server has no inherent method of enforcing a true one-to-one relationship. You can say that table A requires a matching record in table B, but when you then add that table B must have a matching record in table A, you create a paradox — which table gets the record first? If you need to enforce this kind of relationship in SQL Server, the best you can do is force all inserts to be done via a stored procedure. The stored procedure can have the logic to insert into both tables or neither table. Neither foreign key constraints nor triggers can handle this circular relationship.**

Zero or One-to-One

SQL Server can handle the instance of zero or one-to-one relationships. This is essentially the same as a one-to-one, with the difference that one side of the relationship has the option of either having a record or not.

Going back to our parent company vs. subsidiary example, you might prefer to create a relationship where the parent company needs to have a matching record for each subsidiary's records, but the subsidiary doesn't need the information from the parent. You could, for example, have subsidiaries that have very different customers (such as a railroad and a construction company). The parent company wants to know about *all* the customers regardless of what business they came from, but your construction company probably doesn't care about your railroad customers. In such a case, you would have *zero or one* construction customers to *one* parent company customer record.

Zero or one-to-one relationships can be enforced in SQL Server through:

❑ A combination of a unique or primary key with a foreign key constraint. A foreign key constraint can enforce that *at least* one record must exist in the "one" (or parent company in our example) table, but it can't ensure that *only* one exists (there could be more than one). Using a primary key or unique constraint would ensure that one was indeed the limit.

❑ Triggers. Note that triggers would be required in both tables.

> **The reason SQL Server can handle a zero or one-to-one, but not a one-to-one relationship is due to the "which goes first" problem. In a true one-to-one relationship, you can't insert into either table because the record in the other table isn't there yet — it's a paradox. However, with a zero or one-to-one, you can insert into the required table first (the "one"), and the optional table (the zero or one), if desired, second. This same problem will hold true for the "one-to-one or many" and the "one to zero, one, or many" relationships also.**

One-to-One or Many

This is one form of your run-of-the-mill, average, everyday foreign key kind of relationship. Usually, this is found in some form of header/detail relationship. A great example of this would be our Orders situation, as shown in Figure 8-3. OrderDetails (the one or many side of the relationship) doesn't make much sense without an Orders header to belong to (does it do you much good to have an order for a part if you don't know who the order is for?). Likewise, it doesn't make much sense to have an order if there wasn't anything actually ordered (for example, "Gee, look, ACME company ordered absolutely nothing yesterday.").

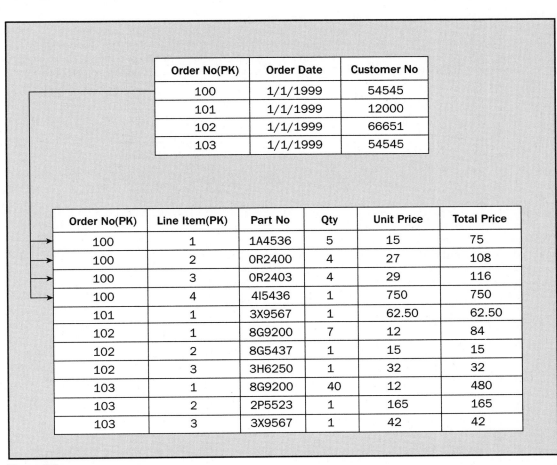

Order No(PK)	Order Date	Customer No
100	1/1/1999	54545
101	1/1/1999	12000
102	1/1/1999	66651
103	1/1/1999	54545

Order No(PK)	Line Item(PK)	Part No	Qty	Unit Price	Total Price
100	1	1A4536	5	15	75
100	2	0R2400	4	27	108
100	3	0R2403	4	29	116
100	4	4I5436	1	750	750
101	1	3X9567	1	62.50	62.50
102	1	8G9200	7	12	84
102	2	8G5437	1	15	15
102	3	3H6250	1	32	32
103	1	8G9200	40	12	480
103	2	2P5523	1	165	165
103	3	3X9567	1	42	42

Figure 8-3

This one, however, gives us the same basic problem that we had with one-to-one relationships. It's still that chicken or egg thing — which came first? Again, in SQL Server, the only way to implement this fully is by restricting all data to be inserted or deleted via stored procedures.

One-to-Zero, One, or Many

This is the other, and perhaps even more common, form of the run-of-the-mill, average, everyday, foreign key relationship. The only real difference in implementation here is that the referencing field (the one in the table that has the foreign key constraint) is allowed to be null; that is, the fact that you have a record in the "one" table, doesn't necessarily mean that you have any instances of matching records in the referencing table.

Imagine for a moment the scenario where we track what shipper is used for orders that are shipped, but where we also have a will call counter for customer pickup. If there is a shipper, then we want to limit it to our approved list of shippers, but it's still quite possible that there won't be any shipper at all, as illustrated in Figure 8-4.

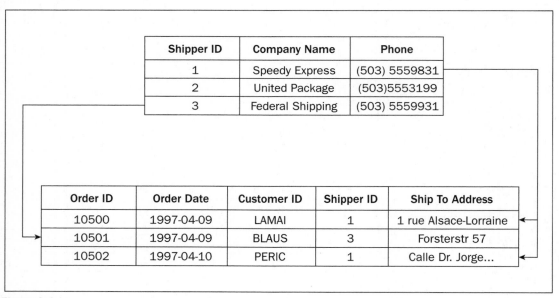

Figure 8-4

A virtually identical example can be found in the AdventureWorks2008 database in the relationship between `Purchasing.PurchaseOrderHeader` and `Purchasing.ShipMethod`, with the only real difference being that this is a list of companies shipping *to* us rather than *from* us.

> This kind of relationship usually sets up what is called a domain relationship. A domain is a limited list of values that the dependent table must choose from — nothing outside the domain list is considered a valid option. The table that holds the rows that make up the domain list is commonly referred to as a domain or lookup table. Nearly all databases you create are going to have at least one, and probably many, domain tables in them. Our Shippers table is a domain table — the purpose of having it isn't just to store the information on the name and phone number of the shipper, but also to limit the list of possible shippers in the Orders table.

In SQL Server, we can enforce this kind of relationship through two methods:

❑ **FOREIGN KEY constraint:** You simply declare a FOREIGN KEY constraint on the table that serves as the "many" side of the relationship, and reference the table and column that is to be the "one" side of the relationship (you'll be guaranteed only one in the referenced table since you must have a PRIMARY KEY or UNIQUE constraint on the column(s) referenced by a foreign key).

❑ **Triggers:** Actually, for all the early versions of SQL Server, this was the only option for true referential integrity. You actually need to add two triggers — one for each side of the relationship. Add a trigger to the table that is the "many" side of the relationship and check that any row inserted or changed in that table has a match in the table it depends on (the "one" side of the relationship). Then, you add a delete trigger and an update trigger to the other table — this trigger checks records that are being deleted (or changed) from the referenced table to make sure that it isn't going to *orphan* (make it so it doesn't have a reference).

We've previously discussed the performance ramifications of the choices between the two in Chapter 6. Using a FOREIGN KEY constraint is generally faster — particularly when there is a violation. That being said, triggers may still be the better option in situations where you're going to have a trigger executing anyway (or some other special constraint need).

Many-to-Many

In this type of relationship, both sides of the relationship may have several records — not just one — that match. An example of this would be the relationship of products to orders. A given order may have many different products in the order. Likewise, any given product may be ordered many times. We still may, however, want to relate the tables in question — for example, to ensure that an order is for a product that we know about (it's in our Products table).

SQL Server has no way of physically establishing a direct many-to-many relationship, so we cheat by having an intermediate table to organize the relationship. Some tables create our many-to-many relationships almost by accident as a normal part of the normalization process — others are created entirely from scratch for the sole purpose of establishing this kind of relationship. This latter "middleman" kind of table is often called either a *linking table*, an *associate table*, or sometimes a *merge table*.

First, let's look at a many-to-many relationship that is created in the normal course of normalization. An example of this can be found in the Accounting database's OrderDetails table (we created the Accounting database in Chapters 5 and 6), which creates a many-to-many relationship between our Orders and Products tables, shown in Figure 8-5.

Order No (PK)	Order Date	Customer No
100	1/1/1999	54545
101	1/1/1999	12000
102	1/1/1999	66651
103	1/1/1999	54545

Order No (PK)	Line Item (PK)	Part No	Qty	Unit Price	Total Price
100	1	1A4536	5	15	75
100	2	0R2400	4	27	108
100	3	0R2403	4	29	116
100	4	4I5436	1	750	750
101	1	3X9567	1	62.50	62.50
102	1	8G9200	7	12	84
102	2	8G5437	1	15	15
102	3	3H6250	1	32	32
103	1	8G9200	40	12	480
103	2	2P5523	1	165	165
103	3	3X9567	1	42	42

Part No (PK)	Description	wt
1A4536	Flange	6
0R2400	Injector	.5
0R2403	Injector	.5
4I5436	Head	3
3X9567	Pump	5
8G9200	Fan	3
8G5437	Fan	3
3H6250	Control	5
2P5523	Housing	1

Figure 8-5

By using the join syntax that we learned back in Chapter 4, we can relate one product to the many orders that it's been part of, or we can go the other way and relate an order to all the products on that order.

Let's move on now to our second example — one where we create an associate table from scratch just so we can have a many-to-many relationship. We'll take the example of a user and a group of rights that a user can have on the system.

We might start with a `Permissions` table that looks something like this:

PermissionID	Description
1	Read
2	Insert
3	Update
4	Delete

Then we add a `Users` table:

UserID	Full Name	Password	Active
JohnD	John Doe	Jfz9..nm3	1
SamS	Sam Spade	klk93)md	1

Now comes the problem — how do we define what users have which permissions? Our first inclination might be to just add a column called `Permissions` to our `Users` table:

UserID	Full Name	Password	Permissions	Active
JohnD	John Doe	Jfz9..nm3	1	1
SamS	Sam Spade	klk93)md	3	1

This seems fine for only a split second, and then a question begs to be answered — what about when our users have permission to do more than one thing?

In the older, flat file days, you might have just combined all the permissions into the one cell, like:

UserID	Full Name	Password	Permissions	Active
JohnD	John Doe	Jfz9..nm3	1,2,3	1
SamS	Sam Spade	klk93)md	1,2,3,43	1

This violates our first normal form, which said that the values in any column must be atomic. In addition, this would be very slow because you would have to procedurally parse out each individual value within the cell.

What we really have between these two tables, Users and Permissions, is a many-to-many relationship — we just need a way to establish that relationship within the database. We do this by adding an associate table, as shown in Figure 8-6. Again, this is a table that, in most cases, doesn't add any new data to our database other than establishing the association between rows in two other tables.

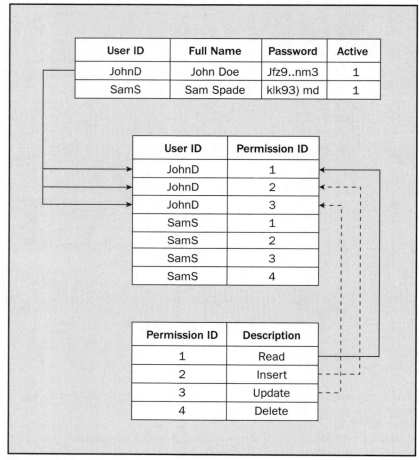

Figure 8-6

With the addition of our new table (we'll call it UserPermissions), we can now mix and match permissions to our users.

Note that, for either example, the implementation of referential integrity is the same — each of the base tables (the tables that hold the underlying data and have the many-to-many relationship) has a one-to-many relationship with the associate table. This can be done via either a trigger or a FOREIGN KEY constraint.

Diagramming

Entity Relationship Diagrams (ERDs) are an important tool in good database design. Small databases can usually be easily created from a few scripts and implemented directly without drawing things out at all. The larger your database gets, however, the faster it becomes very problematic to just do things "in your head." ERDs solve a ton of problems because they allow you to quickly visualize and understand both the entities and their relationships.

Fortunately, SQL Server includes a *very* basic diagramming tool that you can use as a starting point for building rudimentary ERDs.

Before the first time I wrote this topic, I debated for a long while about how I wanted to handle this. On one hand, serious ER diagramming is usually done with an application that is specifically designed to be an ER diagramming tool. These tools almost always support at least one of a couple of industry standard diagramming methods. Even some of the more mass-market diagramming tools — such as Visio — support a couple of ERD methodologies. SQL Server has an ERD tool built in, and therein lies the problem. The tools that are included with SQL Server 2008 are a variation on a toolset and diagramming methodology that Microsoft has used in a number of tools for many years now. The problem is that they do not compete with any ERD standard that I've seen anywhere else. As I've done every time I've written on this topic, I've decided to stick with what I know you have — the built-in tools. I do, however, encourage you to examine the commercially available ERD tools out there to see the rich things that they offer to simplify your database design efforts.

You can open up SQL Server's built-in tools by navigating to the Diagrams node of the database you want to build a diagram for (expand your server first, then the database). Some of what we are going to see you'll find familiar — some of the dialogs are the same as we saw in Chapter 5 when we were creating tables.

The SQL Server diagramming tools don't give you all that many options, so you'll find that you'll get to know them fairly quickly. Indeed, if you're familiar with the relationship editor in Access, then much of the SQL Server tools will seem very familiar.

Try It Out   Diagramming

Let's start by creating our first diagram. You can create your new diagram by right-clicking the Diagrams node underneath the AdventureWorks2008 database and choosing the New Database Diagram option.

As we saw back in Chapter 5, you may (if it's the first time you've tried to create a diagram) see a dialog come up warning you that some of the objects needed to support diagramming aren't in the database and asking if you want to create them — choose Yes.

SQL Server starts us out with the same Add Table dialog (see Figure 8-7) we saw in Chapter 5 — the only thing different is the tables listed.

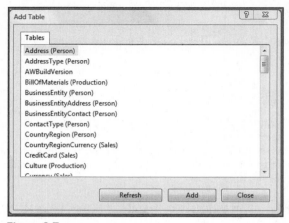

Figure 8-7

Select all of the tables (remember to hold down the Ctrl key to select more than one table) as shown in Figure 8-8.

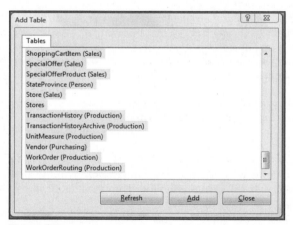

Figure 8-8

And then click Add and, after a brief pause while SQL Server draws all the tables you selected, click the Close button. SQL Server has added our tables to the diagram, but, depending on your screen resolution, they are probably very difficult to see due to the zoom on the diagram. To pull more of the tables into view, change the zoom setting in the toolbar. Finding the right balance between being able to see many tables at once versus making them so small you can't read them is a bit of a hassle, but you should be able to adjust to something that meets your particular taste — for now, I've set mine at 75 percent so I can squeeze in more of the tables at once (fitting all tables in is not that realistic with a database of any real size table count wise) as shown in Figure 8-9.

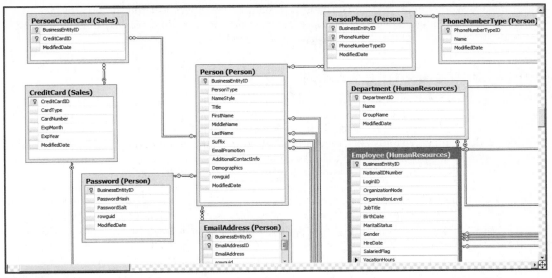

Figure 8-9

How It Works

You'll notice right away that there is a lot more than what we saw with our first look at the diagram tools back in Chapter 5. SQL Server enumerates through each table we have said we want added and analyzed to determine what other objects are associated with those tables. The various other items you see beyond the table itself are some of the many other objects that tie into tables — primary keys and foreign keys.

So, having gotten a start, let's use this diagram as a launching point for explaining how the diagramming tool works and building a few tables here and there.

Tables

Each table has its own window you can move around. The primary key is shown with the little symbol of a key in the column to the left of the name like the one next to the `CustomerID` in Figure 8-10.

Figure 8-10

Just like in Chapter 5, this is the default view for the table — you can select from several others that allow you to edit the very makeup of the table. To check out your options for views of a table, just right-click the table that you're interested in. The default is column names only, but you should also take an interest in the choice of Custom as we did in Chapter 5; this or Standard is what you would use when you want to edit the table from right within the diagram (very nice!).

Adding and Deleting Tables

You can add a new table to the diagram in one of two ways.

If you have a table that already exists in the database (but not in the diagram), but now you want to add it to your diagram, you simply click the Add Table button on the diagramming window's toolbar. You'll be presented with a list of all the tables in the database — just choose the one that you want to add, and it will appear along with any relationships it has to other tables in the diagram.

If you want to add a completely new table, click on New Table on the diagramming window's toolbar or right-click in the diagram and choose New Table; you'll be asked for a name for the new table, and the table will be added to the diagram in Column Properties view. Simply edit the properties to have the column names, data types, and so on that you want, and you have a new table in the database.

> Let me take a moment to point out a couple of gotchas in this process.
>
> First, don't forget to add a primary key to your table. SQL Server does not automatically do this, nor does it even prompt you (as Access does). This is a somewhat less than intuitive process. To add a primary key, you must select the columns that you want to have in the key. Then right-click and choose Set Primary Key.
>
> Next, be aware that your new table is not actually added to the database until you choose to save — this is also true of any edits that you make along the way.

Try It Out   Adding Tables from Within the Diagram

Let's go ahead and add a table to our database just to learn how it works.

Start by clicking on the New Table button in the diagramming window's toolbar. When prompted for a name, choose a name of CustomerNotes (see Figure 8-11). You should then get a new window table using the Standard view:

Notice that I've added several columns to my table along with a primary key (remember, select the columns you want to be the primary key, and then right-click and choose Set Primary Key). Before you click to save this, let's try something out — open up the Management Studio, and try to run a query against your new table:

```
USE AdventureWorks 2008;

SELECT * FROM CustomerNotes;
```

Back comes an error message:

```
Msg 208, Level 16, State 1, Line 1
Invalid object name 'CustomerNotes'.
```

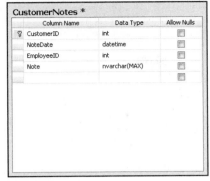

Figure 8-11

That's because our table exists only as an edited item on the diagram — it won't be added until we actually save our changes.

> If you look at the `CustomerNotes` table in the diagram window at this point, you should see a * to the right of the name — that's there to tell you that there are unsaved changes in that table.

Now, switch back to the Management Studio. There are two save options:

❏ **Save:** This saves the changes to both the diagram and to the database (this is the little disk icon on the toolbar).

❏ **Generate Change Script:** This saves the changes to a script so it can be run at a later time. (This is found in the Table Designer menu or as an icon on the Table Designer toolbar.

> The Table Designer toolbar contains several smart icons that provide quick access to many frequently used table design features. Unfortunately, it does not come up by default in the designer under the RTM version of SQL Server 2008. You can add it by right-clicking open space in the toolbar and selecting the Table Designer toolbar.

Go ahead and just choose Save, and you'll be prompted for the name of your diagram and confirmation (after all, you're about to alter your database — there's no "undo" for this).

Confirm the changes, and try running that query again against your `CustomerNotes` table. You should not receive an error this time because the table has now been created. (You won't get any rows back, but the query should still run.)

How It Works

When we create a diagram, SQL Server creates script behind the scenes that looks basically just as our scripts did back in Chapter 6 when we were scripting our own changes. However, these scripts are not actually generated and run until we choose to save the diagram.

OK, we've got our `CustomerNotes` table into the database, but now we notice a problem — the way our primary key is declared, we can only have only one note per customer. More than likely, we are going to keep taking more and more notes on the customer over time. That means that we need to change our primary key, and leaves us with a couple of options depending on our requirements:

❑ **Make the date part of our primary key:** This is problematic from two standpoints. First, we're tracking which employee took the note — what if two different employees wanted to add notes at the same time? We could, of course, potentially address this by also adding `EmployeeID` to the primary key. Second, what's to say that even the same employee wouldn't want to enter two completely separate notes on the same day (OK, so, since this is a datetime field, they could do it as long as they didn't get two rows inserted at the same millisecond — but just play along with me here)? Oops, now even having the `EmployeeID` in the key doesn't help us.

❑ **Add another column to help with the key structure:** We could either do this by adding a counter column for each note per customer. As yet another alternative, we could just add an identity column to ensure uniqueness — it means that our primary key doesn't really relate to anything, but that isn't always a big deal (though it does mean that we have one more index that has to be maintained) and it does allow us to have a relatively unlimited number of notes per customer.

I'm going to take the approach of adding a column I'll call "Sequence" to the table. By convention (it's not a requirement and not everyone does it this way), primary keys are normally the first columns in your table. If we were going to be doing this by script ourselves, we'd probably just issue an `ALTER TABLE` statement and `ADD` the column — this would stick our new column down at the end of our column list. If we wanted to fix that, we'd have to copy all the data out to a holding table, drop any relationships to or from the old table, drop the old table, `CREATE` a new table that has the columns and column order we want, then re-establish the relationships and copy the data back in (a long and tedious process). With the diagramming tools, however, SQL Server takes care of all that for us.

To insert a new row in the middle of everything, I just right-click on the row that is to immediately follow the row I want to insert and select Insert Column. The tool is nice enough to bump everything down for me to create space just like Figure 8-12.

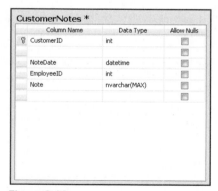

Figure 8-12

I can then add in my new column, and reset the Primary Key as shown in Figure 8-13 (select both rows, right-click and choose Set Primary Key).

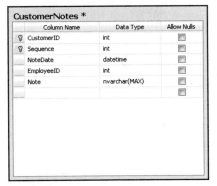

Figure 8-13

Now just save, and you have a table with the desired column order. Just to verify this, try using sp_help:

```
EXEC sp_help CustomerNotes;
```

You'll see that we have the column order we expect:

```
....
CustomerID
Sequence
NoteDate
EmployeeID
Note
....
```

> **Depending on your specific option settings, you may run into an error here when you save the CustomerNotes table. At issue is a safety feature that is new with SQL Server 2008, and is meant to prevent you from accidentally overwriting tables while in the designer. If you get an error referencing an option called "Prevent saving changes that require table re-creation," you can find that in the Options dialog under the Tools menu — you'll need to navigate to the Designers ➤ Table and Database Designers item in this dialog, and then deselect the "Prevent saving changes that require table re-creation" option. Your table should then save without further difficulty.**

Making things like column order changes happens to be one area where the built-in tools positively excel. I've used a couple of other ERD tools, and they all offered the promise of synchronizing a change in column order between the database and the diagram — the success has been pretty hit and miss. (In other words, be very careful about doing it around live data.)

Also, under the heading of one more thing — use the scripting option rather than the live connection to the database to make changes like this if you're operating against live data. That way you can fully test the script against test databases before risking your real data. Be sure to also fully back up your database before making this kind of change.

Editing Table Properties and Objects That Belong to the Table

Beyond the basic attributes that we've looked at thus far, we can also edit many other facets of our table. How to get at these to edit or add to them happens in two different ways:

❑ **Properties:** These are edited in a window that pops up and docks, by default, on the right-hand side of the Management Studio inside the diagramming window. To bring up the properties window, click the Properties Window icon on the toolbar in the Management Studio.

❑ **Objects that belong to the table, such as Indexes, Constraints, and Relationships:** These are edited in their own dialog, which you can access by right-clicking on the table in the diagram and choosing the item that you want to set.

These are important facets of our diagram-based editing, so let's look at some of the major players.

Properties Window

Figure 8-14 shows the Properties window for our `CustomerNotes` table.

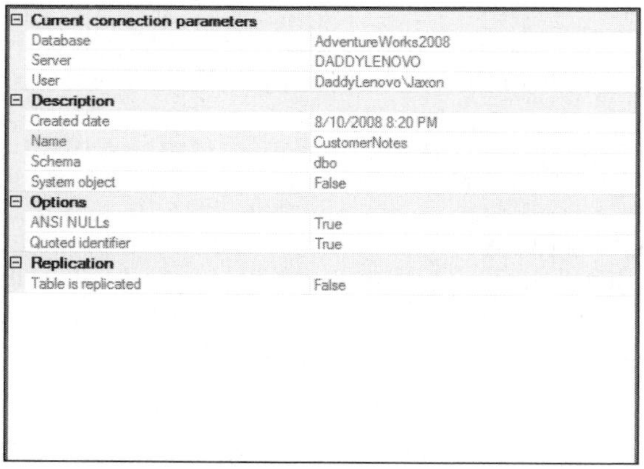

Current connection parameters	
Database	AdventureWorks2008
Server	DADDYLENOVO
User	DaddyLenovo\Jaxon
Description	
Created date	8/10/2008 8:20 PM
Name	CustomerNotes
Schema	dbo
System object	False
Options	
ANSI NULLs	True
Quoted identifier	True
Replication	
Table is replicated	False

Figure 8-14

You can use this properties window to set several key table properties — most notably what schema the table belongs to as well as whether the table has an `Identity` column.

Relationships

You get to this dialog by right-clicking the table heading and choosing Relationships or by selecting the Relationships icon on the Table Designer toolbar. Much like it sounds, this dialog allows us to edit the nature of the relationships between tables. As you can see from Figure 8-15, the relationships for the `CustomerNotes` table doesn't yet have anything in it.

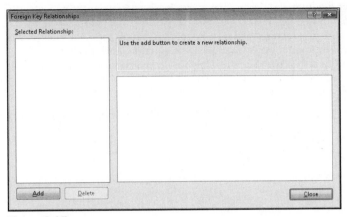

Figure 8-15

For now, just realize that we can edit just about anything to do with relationships here. We could, for example, create a relationship to another table just by clicking Add and filling out the various boxes. Again, we'll look into this further in a page or two.

Indexes/Keys

A lot of this dialog may be something of a mystery to you at this point — we haven't gotten to our chapter on indexing yet, so some of the terms may seem a bit strange. Still, let's take a look at what we get in Figure 8-16 (again, either right-click the table heading and choose Indexes/Keys..., or choose the Manage Indexes and Keys icon from the Table Designer toolbar).

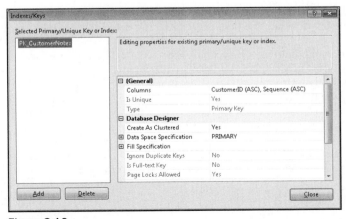

Figure 8-16

From here, you can, as I'm sure you can imagine, create, edit, and delete indexes. You can also establish which filegroup you want the index to be stored on (in most instances, you'll just want to leave this alone). We'll look further into indexes in our next chapter.

Check Constraints

Moving on to the next menu option (or icon if you're using the toolbar to get to these dialogs that we'll examine here), we can manage check constraints as shown in Figure 8-17.

Again, this one is pretty much grayed out. Why? Well, there aren't any constraints of any kind other than a primary key defined for our `CustomerNotes` table, and that primary key is dealt with on the Index/Keys tab. This particular dialog is for check constraints only — if you want to see this tab in full action, then you need to click Add and add a constraint.

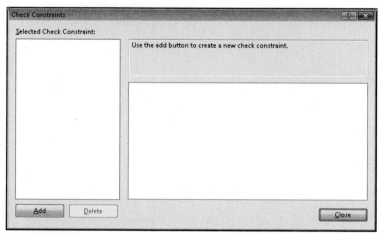

Figure 8-17

Relationships

Well, we've seen what the diagramming tool offers us relative to tables, so, as promised, next up on our list to review is the relationship line (and the underlying details of that relationship).

Looking at a relationship line, the side with the key is the side that is the "one" side of a relationship. The side that has the infinity symbol represents your "many" side. The tools have no relationship line available to specifically represent relationships where zero is possible (it still uses the same line). In addition, the only relationships that actually show in the diagram are ones that are declared using foreign key constraints. Any relationship that is enforced via triggers — regardless of the type of relationship — will not cause a relationship line to appear.

Looking at our AdventureWorks2008 diagram again, and try right-clicking the `SalesOrderHeader` table and selecting Relationships. This brings up a more populated version of the Relationship dialog we looked at in the previous section — the Relationships dialog for the `SalesOrderHeader` table is shown in Figure 8-18.

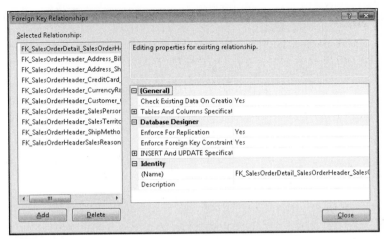

Figure 8-18

From here, we can edit the nature of our relationship, including such things as cascading actions, whether the foreign key is enabled or disabled (for example, if we want to deliberately add data in that violates the relationship), and even the name of the relationship.

Database designers seem to vary widely in their opinion regarding names for relationships. Some don't care what they are named, but I prefer to use a verb phrase to describe my relationships — for example, in our Customers/Orders relationship, I would probably name it CustomerHasOrders or something of that ilk. It's nothing critical — most of the time you won't even use it — but I find that it can be really helpful when I'm looking at a long object list or a particularly complex ER Diagram where the lines may run across the page past several unrelated entities.

Adding Relationships in the Diagramming Tool

Just drag and drop — it's that easy. The only trick is making sure that you start and end your drag in the places you meant to. If in doubt, select the column(s) you're interested in before starting your drag.

Try It Out   **Adding a Relationship**

Let's add a relationship between our new `CustomerNotes` table (we created it in the last section) and the `Customers` table — after all, if it's a customer note we probably want to make sure that we are taking notes on a valid customer. To do this, click and hold in the gray area to the left of the `CustomerID` column in the `Customers` table, then drag your mouse until it is pointing at the `CustomerID` column in the `CustomerNotes` table. A dialog box should pop up to confirm the column mapping between the related tables (see Figure 8-19).

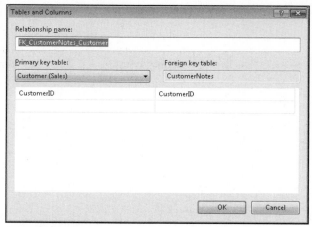

Figure 8-19

If you did your drag and drop right, the names of the columns on both sides of the relationship should come up right to start with, but if they came up with something other than you expected, don't worry too much about — just click the combo box for the table you want to change columns for and select the new column, changing the name of the relationship from the default of FK_CustomerNotes_Customers to FKCustomerHasNotes. As soon as you click OK, you will be taken to the more standard relationship dialog so you can set any other settings you may want to adjust before you save the new relationship to the table. Go ahead and change the DELETE and UPDATE CASCADE actions to CASCADE — ensuring that if the related customer record ever gets updated or deleted, the notes for that customer will also get updated or deleted as necessary. You can see what this looks like in Figure 8-20.

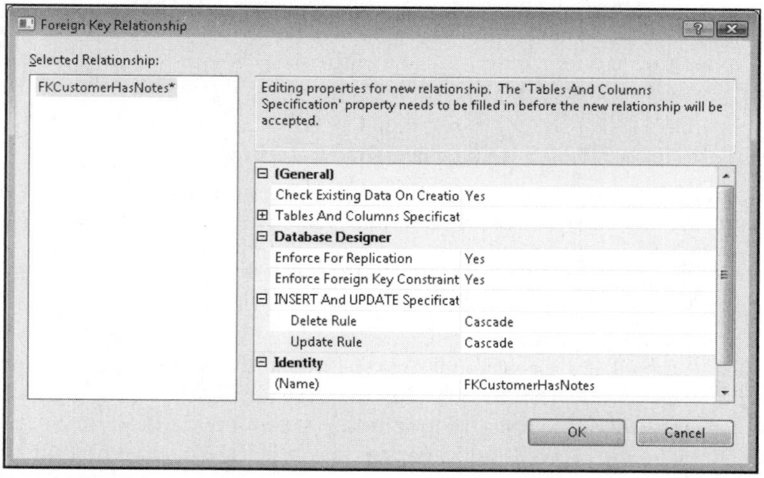

Figure 8-20

With this done, you can click OK and see the new relationship line in your diagram.

How It Works

Much like when we added the table in the previous section, SQL Server is constructing SQL behind the scenes to make the changes you need. So far, it has added the relationship to the diagram only — if you hover over that relationship, you even see a tooltip with the relationship's name and nature, as shown in Figure 8-21.

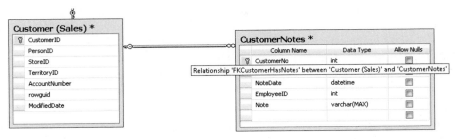

Figure 8-21

Notice the asterisk on both tables!!! The changes we have made have only been added to the change list that you've made to the diagram — they will not be added to the physical database until you choose to save the diagram!

There is an instance where the way the line is displayed will change — when we "disable" the foreign key. We saw how to disable constraints in our last chapter, and we can do it in the Relationship dialog by changing the Enforce Foreign Key Constraint drop-down setting to No. When you do that, your line will change to let you know that the constraint has been disabled. It will now look something like Figure 8-22.

Figure 8-22

If you see one of these, you're first question should be "Why is that disabled?" Maybe it was intentional, but you'll want to be sure.

De-Normalization

I'm going to keep this relatively short since this tends to get into fairly advanced concepts, but remember not to get carried away with the normalization of your data.

As I stated early in this chapter, normalization is one of those things that database designers sometimes wear like a cross. It's somehow turned into a religion for them, and they begin normalizing data for the sake of normalization rather than for good things it does to their database. Here are a couple of things to think about in this regard:

❑ If declaring a computed column or storing some derived data is going to allow you to run a report more effectively, then by all means put it in. Just remember to take into account the benefit vs. the risk. (For example, what if your "summary" data gets out of synch with the data it can be derived from? How will you determine that it happened, and how will you fix it if it does happen?)

❑ Sometimes, by including just one (or more) de-normalized column in a table, you can eliminate or significantly cut down the number of joins necessary to retrieve information. Watch for these scenarios — they actually come up reasonably frequently. I've dealt with situations where adding one column to one commonly used base table cut a nine-table join down to just three, and cut the query time by about 90 percent in the process.

❑ If you are keeping historical data — data that will largely go unchanged and is just used for reporting — then the integrity issue becomes a much smaller consideration. Once the data is written to a read-only area and verified, you can be reasonably certain that you won't have "out of sync" problems, which are one of the major problems that data normalization addresses. At that point, it may be much nicer (and faster) to just "flatten" (de-normalize) the data out into a few tables, and speed things up.

❑ The fewer tables that have to be joined, the happier your users who do their own reports are going to be. The user base out there continues to get more and more savvy with the tools they are using. Increasingly, users are coming to their DBA and asking for direct access to the database to be able to do their own custom reporting. For these users, a highly normalized database can look like a maze and become virtually useless. De-normalizing your data can make life much easier for these users.

All that said, if in doubt, normalize things. There is a reason why that is the way relational systems are typically designed. When you err on the side of normalizing, you are erring on the side of better data integrity, and on the side of better performance in a transactional environment.

Beyond Normalization

In this section, we're going to look into a basic set of "beyond normalization" rules of the road in design. Very few of these are hard and fast kind of rules — they are just things to think about. The most important thing to understand here is that, while normalization is a big thing in database design, it is not the only thing.

Keep It Simple

I run into people on a regular basis who have some really slick ways to do things differently than it's ever been done before. Some of the time, I wind up seeing some ideas that are incredibly cool and incredibly useful. Other times I see ideas that are incredibly cool, but not very useful. As often as not though, I see ideas that are neither — they may be new, but that doesn't make them good.

Before I step too hard on your creative juices here, let me clarify what I'm trying to get across — don't accept the "because we've always done it that way" approach to things, but also recognize that the tried and true probably continues to be tried for a reason — it usually works.

SQL Server 2008 continues to bring all new ways to overdo it in terms of making things too complex. Complex data rules and even complex data types are available through powerful and flexible new additions to the product (code driven functions and data types). Try to avoid instilling more complexity in your database than you really need to. A minimalist approach usually (but not always) yields something that is not only easier to edit, but also runs a lot faster.

Choosing Data Types

In keeping with the minimalist idea, choose what you need, but only what you need.

For example, if you're trying to store months (as the number, 1-12) — those can be done in a single byte by using a `tinyint`. Why then, do I regularly come across databases where a field that's only going to store a month is declared as an `int` (which is 4 bytes)? Don't use an `nchar` or `nvarchar` if you're never going to do anything that requires Unicode — these data types take up two bytes for every one as compared to their non-Unicode cousins.

> There is a tendency to think about this as being a space issue. When I bring this up in person, I sometimes hear the argument, "Ah, disk space is cheap these days!" Well, beyond the notion that a name-brand SCSI hard drive still costs more than I care to throw away on laziness, there's also a network bandwidth issue. If you're passing an extra 100 bytes down the wire for every row, and you pass a 100 record result, then that's about 10K worth of extra data you just clogged your network with. Still not convinced? Now, say that you have just 100 users performing 50 transactions per hour — that's over 50MB of wasted network bandwidth per hour.
>
> The bottom line is, most things that happen with your database will happen repetitively — that means that small mistakes snowball and can become rather large.

Err on the Side of Storing Things

There was an old movie called *The Man Who Knew Too Much* — Hitchcock I believe — that man wasn't keeping data.

Every time that you're building a database, you're going to come across the question of, "Are we going to need that information later?" Here's my two-bit advice on that — if in doubt, keep it. You see, most of the time you can't get back the data that has already come and gone.

I guarantee that at least once (and probably many, many more times than that), a customer (remember, customers are basically anyone who needs something from you — there is such a thing as an internal customer, not just the ones in Accounts Receivable) will come to you and say something like, "Can you give me a report on how much we paid each non-incorporated company last year?"

OK, so are you storing information on whether your vendor is a corporation or not? You had better be if you are subject to U.S. tax law (1099 reporting). So you turn around and say that you can handle that, and the customer replies, "Great! Can you print that out along with their address as of the end of the year?"

Oops — I'm betting that you don't have past addresses, or at the very least, aren't storing the date that the address changed. In short, you never know what a user of your system is going to ask for — try and make sure you have it. Just keep in mind that you don't want to be moving unnecessary amounts of data up and down your network wire (see my comments on choosing a data type). If you're storing the data just for posterity, then make sure you don't put it in any of your application's SELECT statements if it isn't needed (actually, this should be your policy regardless of why you're storing the data).

> If you think that there may be legal ramifications either way (both in keeping it and in getting rid of it), consult your attorney. Sometimes you're legally obligated to keep data a certain amount of time; other times it's best to get rid of information as soon as legally possible.

Drawing Up a Quick Example

Let's walk quickly through a process of designing the invoicing database that we've already started with during our section on normalization. For the most part, we're going to just be applying the diagramming tools to what we've already designed, but we'll also toss in a few new issues to show how they affect our design.

Creating the Database

Unlike a lot of the third-party diagramming tools out there, the SQL Server diagramming tools will not create the database for you — you have to already have it created in order to get as far as having the diagram available to work with.

We're not going to be playing with any data to speak of, so just create a small database called Invoice. I'll go ahead and use the dialog in the Management Studio for the sake of this example.

After right-clicking on the Databases node of my server and selecting New Database, I enter information in for a database called Invoice that is set up as 3MB in size.

Since we've already had a chapter on creating databases (and for the sake of brevity), I'm just going to accept the defaults on all the other options, as shown in Figure 8-23.

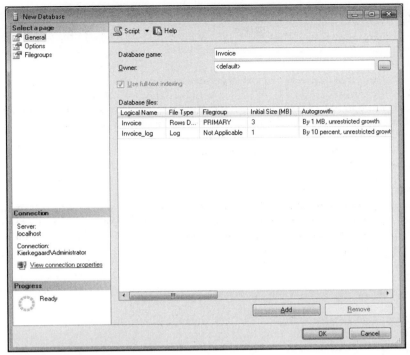

Figure 8-23

Adding the Diagram and Our Initial Tables

As we did when creating our AdventureWorks2008 diagram, expand the node for our database (it should have been added underneath the Databases node, but you may need to right click the databases node and choose "Refresh") and accept the dialog asking if you want to add the objects needed to support diagramming. Then right-click on the Diagrams node and select New Database Diagram. The Add Table dialog pops up, but since there are no user tables in our database, we'll just want to click Close so we wind up with a clean sheet.

Now we're ready to start adding new tables. You can either click the New Table icon on the toolbar, or right-click anywhere in the diagram and select New Table. Let's start off by adding in the Orders table, as shown in Figure 8-24.

	Column Name	Condensed Type	Nullable	Default Value	Identity
🔑	OrderID	int	No		✓
	OrderDate	date	No	SYSDATETIME()	☐
	CustomerNo	int	No		☐
					☐

Orders *

Figure 8-24

> Note that I've changed from the default view — which doesn't have Default Value and Identity as part of it — over to the "custom" view. I also had to choose to Modify Custom and select the Default Value and Identity columns to be added to my custom view.

Let's stop long enough to look at a couple of the decisions that we made here. While we had addressed the issue of normalization, we hadn't addressed any of the other basics yet. First up of those was the question of data types.

Because `OrderID` is the primary key for the table, we need to be sure that we allow enough room for our values to be unique as we insert more and more data. If this was a table we weren't going to be making very many inserts into, we might choose a smaller data type, but since it is our `Orders` table (and we hope to be entering lots of orders), we'll push the size up a bit. In addition, numeric order numbers seem suitable (make sure you ask your customers about issues like this) and facilitate the use of an automatic numbering mechanism in the form of an identity column. If you need more than 2 billion or so order numbers (in which case, I may want some stock in your company), you can take a look at the larger `BigInt` data type. (Suffice to say that I'm certain you won't have too many orders for that data type to hold — just keep in mind the extra space used, although that's often trivial in the larger schema of how much space the database as a whole is using.)

With `OrderDate`, we've gone with the new `Date` data type. You may want to utilize one of the `DateTime` data types instead if you want the time of day on your order in addition to just the date. Date is more compact and meets the need for our simple invoicing database. Be careful in your `DateTime` data type choices though; you'll find that some of them work easier in some languages than others do. For example, Visual Basic prior to .NET threw fits when you played around with `smalldatetime` fields, and could even be temperamental with the then standard `DateTime`. You could get around the problems, but it was a pain. Even with .NET, you're generally going to want to use the newer `DateTime2` data type instead of `DateTime`, as it has a more direct crossover to the `DateTime` data type in .NET.

Our customer has told us (and we've seen in the earlier sample data), that `CustomerNo` is five digits, all numeric. This is one of those areas where you start saying to your customer, "Are you sure you're never going to be using alpha characters in there?" Assuming the answer is yes, we can go with an integer since it is:

❏ Faster on lookups.

❏ Smaller in size — 4 bytes will cover a 5-digit number easily, but it takes 5 bytes minimum (6 if you're using variable-length fields) to handle 5 characters.

   Note that we're kind of cheating on this one — realistically, the customer number for this table is really being defined by the relationship we're going to be building with the `Customers` *table. Since that's the last table we'll see in this example, we're going ahead and filling in the blanks for this field now.*

After data types, we also had to decide on the size of the column — this was a no-brainer for this particular table since all the data types have fixed sizes.

Next on the hit list is whether the rows can be null or not. In this case, we're sure that we want all this information and that it should be available at the time we enter the order, so we won't allow nulls.

I've touched on this before, but you just about have to drag me kicking and screaming in order to get me to allow nulls in my databases. There are situations where you just can't avoid it — "undefined" values are legitimate. I'll still often fill text fields with actual text saying "Value Unknown" or something like that.

The reason I do this is because nullable fields promote errors in much the same way that undeclared variables do. Whenever you run across null values in the table you wind up asking yourself, "Gee, did I mean for that to be there, or did I forget to write a value into the table for that row?" — that is, do I have a bug in my program?

The next issue we faced was default values. We couldn't have a default for OrderID because we're making it an identity column (the two are mutually exclusive). For OrderDate, however, a default made some level of sense. If an OrderDate isn't provided, then we're going to assume that the order date is today. Last, but not least, is the CustomerNo — which customer would we default to? Nope — can't do that here.

Next up was the issue of an identity column. OrderID is an ideal candidate for an identity column — the value has no meaning other than keeping the rows unique. Using a counter such as an identity field gives us a nice, presentable, and orderly way to maintain that unique value. We don't have any reason to change the identity seed and increment, so we won't. We'll leave it starting at one and incrementing by one.

Now we're ready to move on to our next table — the OrderDetails table as defined in Figure 8-25.

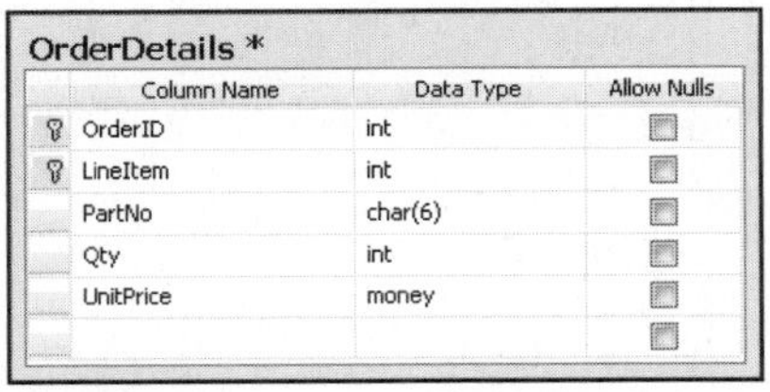

Figure 8-25

For this table, the OrderID column is going to have a foreign key to it, so our data type is decided for us — it must be of the same type and size as the field it's referencing, so it's going to be an int.

The LineItem is going to start over again with each row, so we probably could have gotten as little as a tinyint here. We're going to go with an int on this one just for safety's sake. (I've had people exceed limits that have been set on this sort of thing before.)

PartNo is, for this table, actually going to be defined by the fact that it needs to match up with the PartNo in the Products table. It's going to be using a char(6) in that table (we'll come to it shortly), so that's what we'll make it here.

Qty is guesswork. The question is, what's the largest order you can take as far as quantity for one line-item goes? Since we don't know what we're selling, we can't really make a guess on a maximum quantity (for example, if we were selling barrels of oil, it might be bought literally millions of barrels at a time). We're also using an int here, but we would have needed a data type that accepted decimals if we were selling things like gallons of fuel or things by weight, so be sure to consider your needs carefully.

`UnitPrice` is relatively easy: As this field is going to hold a monetary value, its data type hints at `money`. Be careful with this though. How many decimal places do you really need? U.S. developers are going to tend toward thinking they only need two (several currencies often trade in more decimal places), but what about commodity items? For example, gasoline is generally sold in fractions of a cent. The `money` data type handles 4 decimal places, which meets most currency needs.

Moving along, we're again (no surprise here) considering all data fields to be required. No, we're not allowing nulls anywhere.

No defaults seem to make sense for this table, so we're skipping that part also.

Identity? The temptation might be to mark `OrderID` as an identity column again. Don't do that! Remember that `OrderID` is a value that we're going to match to a column in another table. That table will already have a value (as it happens, set by identity, but it didn't necessarily have to be that way), so setting our column to identity would cause a collision. We would be told that we can't do our insert because we're trying to set an identity value. All the other columns either get their data from another table or require user input of the data. `IsRowGuid` does not apply again.

That takes us to our `Products` and `Customers` tables, as shown in Figures 8-26 and 8-27 respectively.

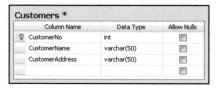

Products *

	Column Name	Data Type	Allow Nulls
🔑	PartNo	char(6)	☐
	Description	varchar(15)	☐
	Weight	tinyint	☐
			☐

Figure 8-26

Customers *

	Column Name	Data Type	Allow Nulls
🔑	CustomerNo	int	☐
	CustomerName	varchar(50)	☐
	CustomerAddress	varchar(50)	☐
			☐

Figure 8-27

Let's hit the highlights on the choices here and move on.

`PartNo` has been defined by the data that we saw when we were looking at normalization. It's a numeric, followed by an alpha, followed by four numerics. That's six characters, and it seems to be fixed. We would want to hold the customer to the cross about the notion that the size of the part number can't get any larger but, assuming that's OK, we'll go with a `char(6)` here. That's because a `char` takes up slightly less overhead than a `varchar`, and we know that the length is going to always remain the same (this means that there's no benefit from the variable size).

Let me reiterate the importance of being sure that your customers are really considering their future needs. The PartNo column using a simple 6-character field is an example of where you might want to be very suspicious. Part numbers are one of those things that people develop new philosophies on almost as often as my teenage daughter develops new taste in clothes. Today's inventory manager will swear that's all they ever intend to use and will be sincere in it, but tomorrow there's a new inventory manager or perhaps your organization merges with another organization that uses a 10-digit numeric part number. Expanding the field isn't that bad of a conversion, but any kind of conversion carries risks, so you want to get it right the first time.

`Description` is one of those guessing games. Sometimes a field like this is going to be driven by your user interface requirements (don't make it wider than can be displayed on the screen), other times you're just going to be truly guessing at what is "enough" space. Here you use a variable-length `char` over a regular `char` for two reasons:

❑   To save a little space

❑   So we don't have to deal with trailing spaces (look at the `char` vs. `varchar` data types back in Chapter 1 if you have questions on this)

We haven't used an `nchar` or `nvarchar` because this is a simple invoicing system for a U.S. business, and we're not concerned about localization issues. If you're dealing with a multilingual scenario, you'll want to pay much more attention to the Unicode data types. You'll also want to consider them if you're storing inherently international information such as URLs, which can easily have kanji and similar characters in them.

`Weight` is similar to `Description` in that it is going to be somewhat of a guess. We've chosen a `tinyint` here because our products will not be over 255 pounds. Note that we are also preventing ourselves from keeping decimal places in our weight (integers only). As we discussed back under `PartNo`, make sure you consider your needs carefully — conservative can be great, but being over-conservative can cause a great deal of work later.

We described the `CustomerNo` field back when we were doing the `Orders` table.

`CustomerName` and `CustomerAddress` are pretty much the same situation as `Description` — the question is, how much is enough? But we need to be sure that we don't give too much.

As before, all fields are required (there will be no nulls in either table) and no defaults are called for. Identity columns also do not seem to fit the bill here as both the customer number and part number have special formats that do not lend themselves to the automatic numbering system that an identity provides.

Adding the Relationships

OK, to make the diagram less complicated, I've gone through all four of my tables and changed the view on them down to just `Column Names`. You can do this, too, by simply right-clicking on the table and selecting the Column Names menu choice.

You should get a diagram that looks similar to Figure 8-28.

Figure 8-28

You may not have the exact same positions for your table, but the contents should be the same. We're now ready to start adding relationships, but we probably ought to stop and think about what kind of relationships we need.

All the relationships that we'll draw with the relationship lines in our SQL Server diagram tool are going to be one-to-zero, one, or many relationships. SQL Server doesn't really know how to do any other kind of relationship implicitly. As we discussed earlier in the chapter, you can add things such as unique constraints and triggers to augment what SQL Server will do naturally with relations, but, assuming you don't do any of that, you're going to wind up with a one-to-zero, one, or many relationship.

> *The bright side is that this is by far the most common kind of relationship out there. In short, don't sweat it that SQL Server doesn't cover every base here. The standard foreign key constraint (which is essentially what your reference line represents) fits the bill for most things that you need to do, and the rest can usually be simulated via some other means.*

We're going to start with the central table in our system — the Orders table. First, we'll look at any relationships that it may need. In this case, we have one — it needs to reference the Customers table. This is going to be a one-to-many relationship with Customers as the parent (the one) and Orders as the child (the many) table.

To build the relationship (and a foreign key constraint to serve as the foundation for that relationship), we're going to simply click and hold in the leftmost column of the Customers table (in the gray area) right where the CustomerNo column is. We'll then drag to the same position (the gray area) next to the CustomerNo column in the Orders table and let go of the mouse button. SQL Server promptly pops up with the first of two dialogs to confirm the configuration of this relationship. The first, shown in Figure 8-29, confirms which columns actually relate.

> *As I pointed out earlier in the chapter, don't sweat it if the names that come up don't match with what you intended — just use the combo boxes to change them back so both sides have CustomerNo in them. Note also that the names don't have to be the same — keeping them the same just helps ease confusion in situations where they really are the same.*

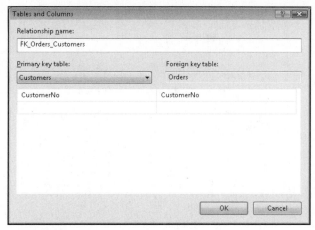

Figure 8-29

Click OK for this dialog, and then also click OK to accept the defaults of the Foreign Key Relationship dialog. As soon as we click OK on the second dialog, we have our first relationship in our new database, as in Figure 8-30.

Figure 8-30

Now we'll just do the same thing for our other two relationships. We need to establish a one-to-many relationship from Orders to OrderDetails (there will be one order header for one or more order details) based on OrderID. Also, we need a similar relationship going from Products to OrderDetails (there will be one Products record for many OrderDetails records) based on ProductID as shown in Figure 8-31.

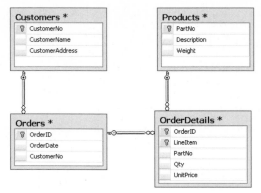

Figure 8-31

Adding Some Constraints

As we were going through the building of our tables and relationships, I mentioned a requirement that we still haven't addressed. This requirement needs a constraint to enforce it: the part number is formatted as 9A9999 where "9" indicates a numeric digit 0–9 and "A" indicates an alpha (non-numeric) character.

Let's add that requirement now by right-clicking the `Products` table and selecting Check Constraints to bring up the dialog shown in Figure 8-32.

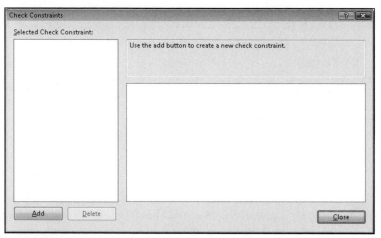

Figure 8-32

It is at this point that we are ready to click Add and define our constraint. To restrict part numbers entered to the format we've established, we're going to need to make use of the LIKE operator:

```
(PartNo LIKE '[0-9][A-Z][0-9][0-9][0-9][0-9]')
```

This will essentially evaluate each character that the user is trying to enter in the `PartNo` column of our table. The first character will have to be 0 through 9 , the second A through Z (an alpha), and the next four will again have to be numeric digits (the 0 through 9 thing again). We just enter this into the text box labeled Expression. In addition, we're going to change the default name for our constraint from `CK_Products` to `CKPartNo`, as shown in Figure 8-33.

That didn't take us too long — and we now have our first database that we designed!!!

This was, of course, a relatively simple model — but we've now done the things that make up perhaps 90 percent or more of the actual data architecture.

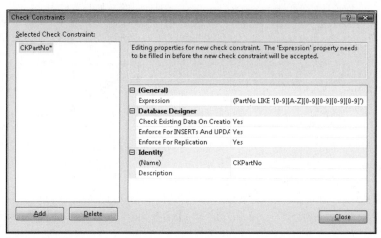

Figure 8-33

Summary

Database design is a huge concept, and one that has many excellent books dedicated to it as their sole subject. It is essentially impossible to get across every database design notion in just a chapter or two.

In this chapter, I have, however, gotten you off to a solid start. We've seen that data is considered normalized when we take it out to the third normal form. At that level, repetitive information has been eliminated and our data is entirely dependent on our key — in short, the data is dependent on: "The key, the whole key, and nothing but the key." We've seen that normalization is, however, not always the right answer — strategic de-normalization of our data can simplify the database for users and speed reporting performance. Finally, we've looked at some non-normalization related concepts in our database design, plus how to make use of the built-in diagramming tools to design our database.

In our next chapter, we will be taking a very close look at how SQL Server stores information and how to make the best use of indexes.

Exercises

1. Normalize the following data into the third normal form:

Patient	SSN	Physician	Hospital	Treatment	AdmitDate	ReleaseDate
Sam Spade	555-55-5555	Albert Schweitzer	Mayo Clinic	Lobotomy	10/01/2005	11/07/2005
Sally Nally	333-33-3333	Albert Schweitzer	NULL	Cortizone Injection	10/10/2005	10/10/2005
Peter Piper	222-22-2222	Mo Betta	Mustard Clinic	Pickle Extraction	11/07/2005	11/07/2005
Nicki Doohickey	123-45-6789	Sheila Sheeze	Mustard Clinic	Cortizone Injection	11/07/2005	11/07/2005

SQL Server Storage and Index Structures

Indexes are a critical part of your database planning and system maintenance. They provide SQL Server (and any other database system for that matter) with additional ways to look up data and take shortcuts to that data's physical location. Adding the right index can cut huge percentages of time off your query executions. Unfortunately, too many poorly planned indexes can actually increase the time it takes for your query to run. Indeed, indexes tend to be one of the most misunderstood objects that SQL Server offers, and therefore, they also tend to be one of the most mismanaged.

We will be studying indexes rather closely in this chapter from both a developer's and an administrator's point of view, but in order to understand indexes, you also need to understand how data is stored in SQL Server. For that reason, we will also take a look at SQL Server's data-storage mechanism.

SQL Server Storage

Data in SQL Server can be thought of as existing in something of a hierarchy of structures. The hierarchy is pretty simple. Some of the objects within the hierarchy are things that you will deal with directly, and will therefore understand easily. A few others exist under the covers, and while they can be directly addressed in some cases, they usually are not. Let's take a look at them one by one.

The Database

OK — this one is easy. I can just hear people out there saying, "Duh! I knew that." Yes, you probably did, but I point it out as a unique entity here because it is the highest level of storage (for a given server). This is also the highest level at which a *lock* can be established, although you cannot explicitly create a database-level lock.

> *A lock is something of a hold and a place marker that is used by the system. As you do development using SQL Server — or any other database for that matter — you will find that understanding and managing locks is absolutely critical to your system.*

We will be looking into locking extensively in Chapter 14, but we will see the lockability of objects within SQL Server discussed in passing as we look at storage.

The Extent

An *extent* is the basic unit of storage used to allocate space for tables and indexes. It is made up of eight contiguous 64KB data *pages*.

The concept of allocating space based on extents, rather than actual space used, can be somewhat difficult to understand for people used to operating system storage principles. The important points about an extent include:

❑ Once an extent is full, the next record will take up not just the size of the record, but the size of a whole new extent. Many people who are new to SQL Server get tripped up in their space estimations in part due to the allocation of an extent at a time rather than a record at a time.

❑ By pre-allocating this space, SQL Server saves the time of allocating new space with each record.

It may seem like a waste that a whole extent is taken up just because one too many rows were added to fit on the currently allocated extent(s), but the amount of space wasted this way is typically not that much. Still, it can add up — particularly in a highly fragmented environment — so it's definitely something you should keep in mind.

The good news in taking up all this space is that SQL Server skips some of the allocation-time overhead. Instead of worrying about allocation issues every time it writes a row, SQL Server deals with additional space allocation only when a new extent is needed.

Don't confuse the space that an extent is taking up with the space that a database takes up. Whatever space is allocated to the database is what you'll see disappear from your disk drive's available-space number. An extent is merely how things are, in turn, allocated within the total space reserved by the database.

The Page

Much like an extent is a unit of allocation within the database, a *page* is the unit of allocation within a specific extent. There are eight pages to every extent.

A page is the last level you reach before you are at the actual data row. Whereas the number of pages per extent is fixed, the number of rows per page is not — that depends entirely on the size of the row, which can vary. You can think of a page as being something of a container for both table- and index-row data. A row is, in general, not allowed to be split between pages.

There are a number of different *page types*. For purposes of this book, the types we care about are:

❑ **Data** — *Data pages* are pretty self-explanatory. They are the actual data in your table, with the exception of any BLOB data that is not defined with the text-in-row option, `varchar(max)` or `varbinary(max)`.

❑ **Index** — *Index pages* are also pretty straightforward: They hold both the non-leaf and leaf level pages (we'll examine what these are later in the chapter) of a non-clustered index, as well as the non-leaf level pages of a clustered index. These index types will become much clearer as we continue through this chapter.

Page Splits

When a page becomes full, it splits. This means more than just a new page being allocated — it also means that approximately half the data from the existing page is moved to the new page.

The exception to this process is when a clustered index is in use. If there is a clustered index and the next inserted row would be physically located as the last record in the table, then a new page is created, and the new row is added to the new page without relocating any of the existing data. We will see much more on page splits as we investigate indexes.

Rows

You have heard much about "row level locking," so it shouldn't be a surprise to hear this term. Rows can be up to 8KB.

In addition to the limit of 8,060 characters, there is also a maximum of 1,024 standard (non-sparse) columns. In practice, you'll find it very unusual to run into a situation where you run out of columns before you run into the 8,060 character limit. 1,024 gives you an average column width of just under 8 bytes. For most uses, you'll easily exceed that average (and therefore exceed the 8,060 characters before the 1,024 columns). The exception to this tends to be in measurement and statistical information — where you have a large number of different things that you are storing numeric samples of. Still, even those applications will find it a rare day when they bump into the 1,024-column-count limit. When you do, you can explore the notion of sparse columns, so let's look at that.

Sparse Columns

Sparse columns, in terms of a special data structure, is new with SQL Server 2008. These are meant to deal with the recurring scenario where you have columns that you essentially just need "sometimes." That is, they are going to be null a high percentage of the time. There are many scenarios where, if you bump into a few of these kinds of columns, you tend to bump into a ton of them. Using sparse columns, you can increase the total number of allowed columns in a single table to 30,000.

Internally, the data from columns marked as being sparsely populated is embedded within a single column — allowing a way to break the former limitation of 1,024 columns without major architectural changes.

`Image`, `text`, `ntext`, `geography`, `geometry`, `timestamp`, and all user-defined data types are prohibited from being marked as a sparse column.

> While sparse columns are handled natively by newer versions of the SQL Native Client, other forms of data access will have varying behavior when accessing sparse columns. The sparse property of a column will be transparent when selecting a column by name, but when selecting it using a "*" in the select list, different client access methods will vary between supplying the sparse columns as a unified XML column vs. not showing those columns at all. You'll want to upgrade your client libraries as soon as reasonably possible.

Sparse columns largely fall under the heading of "advanced topic," but I do want you to know they are there and can be a viable solution for particular scenarios.

Understanding Indexes

Webster's dictionary defines an index as:

A list (as of bibliographical information or citations to a body of literature) arranged usually in alphabetical order of some specified datum (as author, subject, or keyword).

I'll take a simpler approach in the context of databases and say it's a way of potentially getting to data a heck of a lot quicker. Still, the Webster's definition isn't too bad — even for our specific purposes.

Perhaps the key thing to point out in the Webster's definition is the word "usually" that's in there. The definition of "alphabetical order" changes depending on a number of rules. For example, in SQL Server, we have a number of different collation options available to us. Among these options are:

❑ **Binary** — Sorts by the numeric representation of the character (for example, in ASCII, a space is represented by the number 32, the letter "D" is 68, and the letter "d" is 100). Because everything is numeric, this is the fastest option. Unfortunately, it's not at all the way in which people think, and can also really wreak havoc with comparisons in your WHERE clause.

❑ **Dictionary order** — This sorts things just as you would expect to see in a dictionary, with a twist. You can set a number of different additional options to determine sensitivity to case, accent, and character set.

It's fairly easy to understand that if we tell SQL Server to pay attention to case, then "A" is not going to be equal to "a." Likewise, if we tell it to be case insensitive, then "A" will be equal to "a." Things get a bit more confusing when you add accent sensitivity. SQL Server pays attention to diacritical marks, and therefore "a" is different from "á," which is different from "à." Where many people get even more confused is in how collation order affects not only the equality of data, but also the sort order (and, therefore, the way it is stored in indexes).

By way of example, let's look at the equality of a couple of collation options in the following table, and what they do to our sort order and equality information:

Collation Order	Comparison Values	Index Storage Order
Dictionary order, case insensitive, accent insensitive (the default)	A = a = à = á = â = Ä = ä = Å = å	a, A, à, â, á, Ä, ä, Å, åt
Dictionary order, case insensitive, accent insensitive, uppercase preference	A = a = à = á = â = Ä = ä = Å = å	A, a, à, â, á, Ä, ä, Å, å
Dictionary order, case sensitive	A ≠ a, Ä ≠ ä, Å ≠ å, a ≠ à ≠ á ≠ â ≠ ä ≠ å, A ≠ Ä ≠ Å	A, a, à, á, â, Ä, ä, Å, å

The point here is that what happens in your indexes depends on the collation information you have established for your data. Collation can be set at the database and column level, so you have a fairly fine granularity in your level of control. If you're going to assume that your server is case insensitive, then you need to be sure that the documentation for your system deals with this, or you had better plan on a lot of tech support calls — particularly if you're selling outside of the United States. Imagine you're an independent software vendor (ISV) and you sell your product to a customer who installs it on an existing server (which is going to seem like an entirely reasonable thing to the customer), but that existing server happens to be an older server that's set up as case sensitive. You're going to get a support call from one very unhappy customer.

> **Once the collation order has been set, changing it is very difficult (but possible), so be certain of the collation order you want before you set it.**

B-Trees

The concept of a *Balanced Tree*, or *B-Tree*, is certainly not one that was created with SQL Server. Indeed, B-Trees are used in a very large number of indexing systems, both in and out of the database world.

A B-Tree simply attempts to provide a consistent and relatively low-cost method of finding your way to a particular piece of information. The *Balanced* in the name is pretty much self-descriptive. A B-Tree is, with the odd exception, self-balancing, meaning that every time the tree branches, approximately half the data is on one side, and half is on the other side. The *Tree* in the name is also probably pretty obvious at this point (hint: tree, branch — see a trend here?). It's there because, when you draw the structure, then turn it upside down, it has the general form of a tree.

A B-Tree starts at the *root node* (another stab at the tree analogy there, but not the last). This root node can, if there is a small amount of data, point directly to the actual location of the data. In such a case, you would end up with a structure that looked something like Figure 9-1.

So, we start at the root and look through the records until we find the last page that starts with a value less than what we're looking for. We then obtain a pointer to that node and look through it until we find the row that we want.

In most situations though, there is too much data to reference from the root node, so the root node points at intermediate nodes — or what are called *non-leaf level nodes*. Non-leaf level nodes are nodes that are somewhere in between the root and the node that tells you where the data is physically stored. Non-leaf level nodes can then point to other non-leaf level nodes, or to *leaf level nodes* (last tree analogy reference — I promise). Leaf level nodes are the nodes where you obtain the real reference to the actual physical data. Much like the leaf is the end of the line for navigating the tree, the node we get to at the leaf level is the end of the line for our index. From there, we can go straight to the actual data node that has our data on it.

As you can see in Figure 9-2, we start with the root node just as before, then move to the node that starts with the highest value that is equal to or less than what we're looking for and is also in the next level down. We then repeat the process: Look for the node that has the highest starting value at or below the value for which we're looking. We keep doing this, level by level down the tree, until we get to the leaf level — from there we know the physical location of the data and can quickly navigate to it.

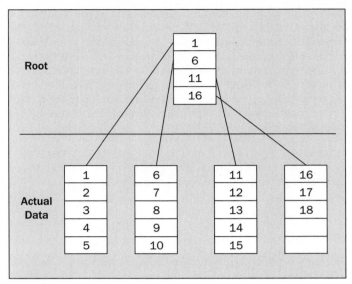

Figure 9-1

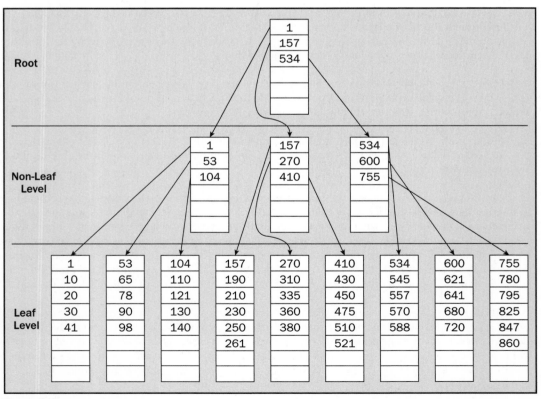

Figure 9-2

Page Splits — A First Look

All of this works quite nicely on the read side of the equation — it's the insert that gets a little tricky. Recall that the *B* in B-Tree stands for *balanced*. You may also recall that I mentioned that a B-Tree is balanced because about half the data is on either side every time you run into a branch in the tree. B-Trees are sometimes referred to as *self-balancing* because the way new data is added to the tree generally prevents them from becoming lopsided.

When data is added to the tree, a node will eventually become full and will need to split. Because in SQL Server, a node equates to a page, this is called a *page split*, illustrated in Figure 9-3.

> *When a page split occurs, data is automatically moved around to keep things balanced. The first half of the data is left on the old page, and the rest of the data is added to a new page — thus you have about a 50-50 split, and your tree remains balanced.*

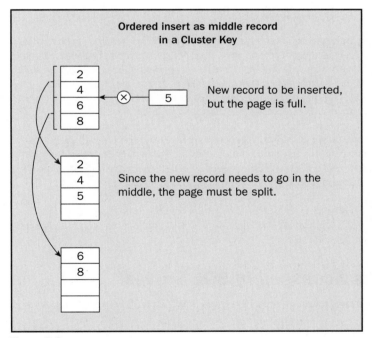

Figure 9-3

If you think about this splitting process a bit, you'll realize that it adds a substantial amount of overhead at the time of the split. Instead of inserting just one page, you are:

❑   Creating a new page

❑   Migrating rows from the existing page to the new page

❑   Adding your new row to one of the pages

❑   Adding another entry in the parent node

But the overhead doesn't stop there. Since we're in a tree arrangement, you have the possibility for something of a cascading action. When you create the new page (because of the split), you need to make another entry in the parent node. This entry in the parent node also has the potential to cause a page split at that level, and the process starts all over again. Indeed, this possibility extends all the way up to and can even affect the root node.

If the root node splits, then you actually end up creating two additional pages. Because there can be only one root node, the page that was formerly the root node is split into two pages and becomes a new intermediate level of the tree. An entirely new root node is then created, and will have two entries (one to the old root node, one to the split page).

Needless to say, page splits can have a very negative impact on system performance and are characterized by behavior where your process on the server seems to just pause for a few seconds (while the pages are being split and rewritten).

We will talk about page-split prevention before we're done with this chapter.

> *While page splits at the leaf level are a common fact of life, page splits at intermediate nodes happen far less frequently. As your table grows, every layer of the index will experience page splits, but because the intermediate nodes have only one entry for several entries on the next lower node, the number of page splits gets less and less frequent as you move further up the tree. Still, for a split to occur above the leaf level, there must have already been a split at the next lowest level — this means that page splits up the tree are cumulative (and expensive performance-wise) in nature.*

SQL Server has a number of different types of indexes (which we will discuss shortly), but they all make use of this B-Tree approach in some way or another. Indeed, they are all very similar in structure, thanks to the flexible nature of a B-Tree. Still, we shall see that there are indeed some significant differences, and these can have an impact on the performance of our system.

> *For an SQL Server index, the nodes of the tree come in the form of pages, but you can actually apply this concept of a root node, the non-leaf level, the leaf level, and the tree structure to more than just SQL Server or even just databases.*

How Data Is Accessed in SQL Server

In the broadest sense, there are only two ways in which SQL Server retrieves the data you request:

- ❏   Using a table scan
- ❏   Using an index

Which method SQL Server uses to run your particular query will depend on what indexes are available, what columns you are asking about, what kind of joins you are doing, and the size of your tables.

Use of Table Scans

A *table scan* is a pretty straightforward process. When a table scan is performed, SQL Server starts at the physical beginning of the table, looking through every row in the table. As it finds rows that match the criteria of your query, it includes them in the result set.

You may hear lots of bad things about table scans, and in general, they will be true. However, table scans can actually be the fastest method of access in some instances. Typically, this is the case when retrieving data from rather small tables. The exact size where this becomes the case will vary widely according to the width of your table and the specific nature of the query.

See if you can spot why the use of EXISTS *in the* WHERE *clause of your queries has so much to offer performance-wise when it fits the problem. When you use the* EXISTS *operator, SQL Server stops as soon as it finds one record that matches the criteria. If you had a million-record table and it found a matching record on the third record, then use of the* EXISTS *option would have saved you the reading of 999,997 records!* NOT EXISTS *works in much the same way.*

Use of Indexes

When SQL Server decides to use an index, the process actually works somewhat similarly to a table scan, but with a few shortcuts.

During the query optimization process, the optimizer takes a look at all the available indexes and chooses the best one (this is primarily based on the information you specify in your joins and WHERE clause, combined with statistical information SQL Server keeps on index makeup). Once that index is chosen, SQL Server navigates the tree structure to the point of data that matches your criteria and again extracts only the records it needs. The difference is that since the data is sorted, the query engine knows when it has reached the end of the current range it is looking for. It can then end the query, or move on to the next range of data as necessary.

If you ponder the query topics we've studied thus far (Chapter 7 specifically), you may notice some striking resemblances to how the EXISTS option works. The EXISTS keyword allowed a query to quit running the instant that it found a match. The performance gains using an index are similar or better than EXISTS since the process of searching for data can work in a similar fashion; that is, the server can use the sort of the index to know when there is nothing left that's relevant and can stop things right there. Even better, however, is that by using an index, we don't have to limit ourselves to Boolean situations (does the piece of data I was after exist — yes or no?). We can apply this same notion to both the beginning and end of a range. We are able to gather ranges of data with essentially the same benefits that using an index gives to finding data. What's more, we can do a very fast lookup (called a SEEK) of our data rather than hunting through the entire table.

Don't get the impression from my comparing what indexes do to what the EXISTS *operator does that indexes replace the* EXISTS *operator altogether (or vice versa). The two are not mutually exclusive; they can be used together, and often are. I mention them here together only because they have the similarity of being able to tell when their work is done, and quit before getting to the physical end of the table.*

Index Types and Index Navigation

Although there are nominally two types of base index structures in SQL Server (*clustered* and *non-clustered*), there are actually, internally speaking, three different types:

❑ Clustered indexes

❑ Non-clustered indexes, which comprise:

    ❑ Non-clustered indexes on a heap

    ❑ Non-clustered indexes on a clustered index

The way the physical data is stored varies between clustered and non-clustered indexes. The way SQL Server traverses the B-Tree to get to the end data varies between all three index types.

All SQL Server indexes have leaf level and non-leaf level pages. As we mentioned when we discussed B-Trees, the leaf level is the level that holds the "key" to identifying the record, and the non-leaf level pages are guides to the leaf level.

The indexes are built over either a clustered table (if the table has a clustered index) or what is called a heap (what's used for a table without a clustered index).

Clustered Tables

A *clustered table* is any table that has a clustered index on it. Clustered indexes are discussed in detail shortly, but what they mean to the table is that the data is physically stored in a designated order. Individual rows are uniquely identified through the use of the *cluster key* — the columns that define the clustered index.

> *This should bring to mind the question, "What if the clustered index is not unique?" That is, how can a clustered index be used to uniquely identify a row if the index is not a unique index? The answer lies under the covers: SQL Server forces any clustered indexes to be unique — even if you don't define them that way. Fortunately, it does this in a way that doesn't change how you use the index. You can still insert duplicate rows if you wish, but SQL Server will add a suffix to the key internally to ensure that the row has a unique identifier.*

Heaps

A *heap* is any table that does not have a clustered index on it. In this case, a unique identifier, or row ID (RID), is created based on a combination of the extent, pages, and row offset (places from the top of the page) for that row. A RID is only necessary if there is no cluster key available (no clustered index).

Clustered Indexes

A *clustered index* is unique for any given table — you can only have one per table. You don't have to have a clustered index, but you'll find it to be one of the most commonly chosen types for a variety of reasons that will become apparent as we look at our index types.

What makes a clustered index special is that the leaf level of a clustered index is the actual data — that is, the data is re-sorted to be stored in the same physical order of the index sort criteria state. This means that once you get to the leaf level of the index, you're done; you're at the data. Any new record is inserted according to its correct physical order in the clustered index. How new pages are created changes depending on where the record needs to be inserted.

In the case of a new record that needs to be inserted into the middle of the index structure, a normal page split occurs. The last half of the records from the old page are moved to the new page, and the new record is inserted into the new or old page as appropriate.

In the case of a new record that is logically at the end of the index structure, a new page is created, but only the new record is added to the new page, as shown in Figure 9-4.

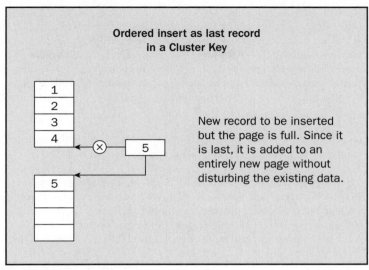

Figure 9-4

Navigating the Tree

As I've indicated previously, even the indexes in SQL Server are stored in a B-Tree. Theoretically, a B-Tree always has half of the remaining information in each possible direction as the tree branches. Let's take a look at a visualization of what a B-Tree looks like for a clustered index (Figure 9-5).

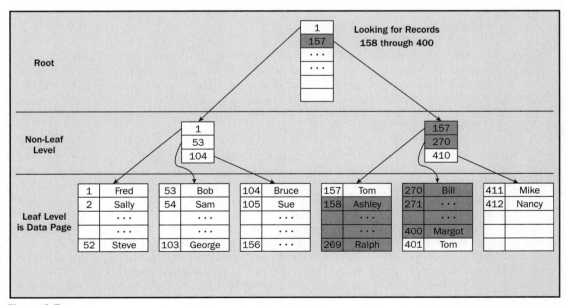

Figure 9-5

As you can see, it looks essentially identical to the more generic B-Trees we discussed earlier in the chapter. In this case, we're doing a range search (something clustered indexes are particularly good at) for numbers 158–400. All we have to do is navigate to the first record and include all remaining records on that page. We know we need the rest of that page because the information from the node one level up lets us know that we'll also need data from a few other pages. Because this is an ordered list, we can be sure it's continuous — that means if the next page has records that should be included, then the rest of this page must be included. We can just start spewing out data from those pages without having to do any verification.

We start off by navigating to the root node. SQL Server is able to locate the root node based on an entry that you can see in the system metadata view called sys.indexes.

By looking through the page that serves as the root node, we can figure out what the next page we need to examine is (the second page on the second level as we have it drawn here). We then continue the process. With each step we take down the tree, we are getting to smaller and smaller subsets of data. Eventually, we will get to the leaf level of the index. In the case of our clustered index, getting to the leaf level of the index means that we are also at our desired row(s) and our desired data.

> I can't stress enough the importance of this distinction: With a clustered index, when you've fully navigated the index, you've fully navigated to your data. How much of a performance difference this can make will really show its head as we look at non-clustered indexes — particularly when the non-clustered index is built over a clustered index.

Non-Clustered Indexes on a Heap

Non-clustered indexes on a heap work very similarly to clustered indexes in most ways. They do, however, have a few notable differences:

The leaf level is not the data — instead, it is the level at which you are able to obtain a pointer to that data. This pointer comes in the form of a row identifier or RID, which, as we described earlier in the chapter, is made up of the extent, page, and row offset for the particular row being pointed to by the index. Even though the leaf level is not the actual data (instead, it has the RID), we only have one more step than with a clustered index. Because the RID has the full information on the location of the row, we can go directly to the data.

Don't, however, misunderstand this "one more step" to mean that there's only a small amount of overhead difference and that non-clustered indexes on a heap will run close to as fast as a clustered index. With a clustered index, the data is physically in the order of the index. That means, for a range of data, when you find the row that has the beginning of your data on it, there's a good chance that the other rows are on that page with it (that is, you're already physically almost to the next record since they are stored together). With a heap, the data is not linked together in any way other than through the index. From a physical standpoint, there is absolutely no sorting of any kind. This means that from a physical read standpoint, your system may have to retrieve records from all over the file. Indeed, it's quite possible (possibly even probable) that you will wind up fetching data from the same page several separate times. SQL Server has no way of knowing it will have to come back to that physical location because there was no link between the data. With the clustered index, it knows that's the physical sort, and can therefore grab it all in just one visit to the page.

Just to be fair to the non-clustered index on a heap here vs. the clustered index, the odds are extremely high that any page that was already read once will still be in the memory cache and, as such, will be retrieved extremely quickly. Still, it does add some additional logical operations to retrieve the data.

Figure 9-6 shows the same search we performed on the clustered index, only with a non-clustered index on a heap this time.

Through most of the index navigation, things work exactly as they did before. We start out at the same root node, and we traverse the tree dealing with more and more focused pages until we get to the leaf level of our index. This is where we run into the difference. With a clustered index, we could have stopped right here, but with a non-clustered index, we have more work to do. If the non-clustered index is on a heap, then we have just one more level to go. We take the Row ID from the leaf level page and navigate to it. It is not until this point that we are at our actual data.

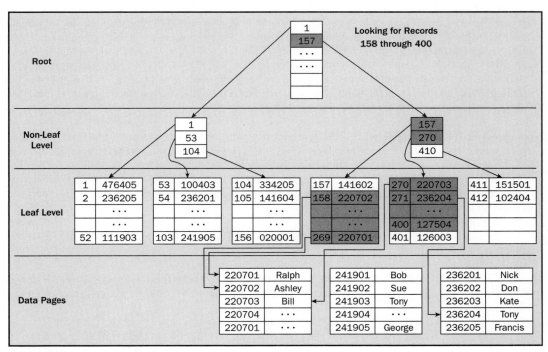

Figure 9-6

Non-Clustered Indexes on a Clustered Table

With *non-clustered indexes on a clustered table*, the similarities continue — but so do the differences. Just as with non-clustered indexes on a heap, the non-leaf level of the index looks pretty much as it did for a clustered index. The difference does not come until we get to the leaf level.

At the leaf level, we have a rather sharp difference from what we've seen with the other two index structures: We have yet another index to look over. With clustered indexes, when we got to the leaf level, we found the actual data. With non-clustered indexes on a heap, we didn't find the actual data, but did find an identifier that let us go right to the data (we were just one step away). With non-clustered indexes on a clustered table, we find the cluster key. That is, we find enough information to go and make use of the clustered index.

We end up with something that looks like Figure 9-7.

What we end up with is two entirely different kinds of lookups.

In the example from our diagram, we start off with a ranged search. We do one single lookup in our index and are able to look through the non-clustered index to find a continuous range of data that meets our criterion (LIKE 'T%'). This kind of lookup, where we can go right to a particular spot in the index, is called a *seek*.

The second kind of lookup then starts — the lookup using the clustered index. This second lookup is very fast; the problem lies in the fact that it must happen multiple times. You see, SQL Server retrieved a list from the first index lookup (a list of all the names that start with "T"), but that list doesn't logically match up with the cluster key in any continuous fashion. Each record needs to be looked up individually, as shown in Figure 9-8.

Needless to say, this multiple-lookup situation introduces more overhead than if we had just been able to use the clustered index from the beginning. The first index search — the one through our non-clustered index — requires very few logical reads.

For example, if I have a table with 1,000 bytes per row and I do a lookup similar to the one in our drawing (say, something that would return five or six rows); it would only take something to the order of 8–10 logical reads to get the information from the non-clustered index. However, that only gets me as far as being ready to look up the rows in the clustered index. Those lookups would cost approximately 3–4 logical reads *each*, or 15–24 additional reads. That probably doesn't seem like that big a deal at first, but look at it this way:

 Logical reads went from 3 minimum to 24 maximum — that's an 800 percent increase in the amount of work that had to be done.

Now expand this thought out to something where the range of values from the non-clustered index wasn't just five or six rows, but five or six thousand, or five or six *hundred* thousand rows — that's going to be a huge impact.

> *Don't let the extra overhead vs. a clustered index scare you — the point isn't meant to scare you away from using indexes, but rather to point out that a non-clustered index is generally not going to be as efficient as a clustered index from a read perspective (it can, in some instances, actually be a better choice at insertion time). An index of any kind is usually (there are exceptions) the fastest way to do a lookup. We'll explain what index to use and why later in the chapter.*

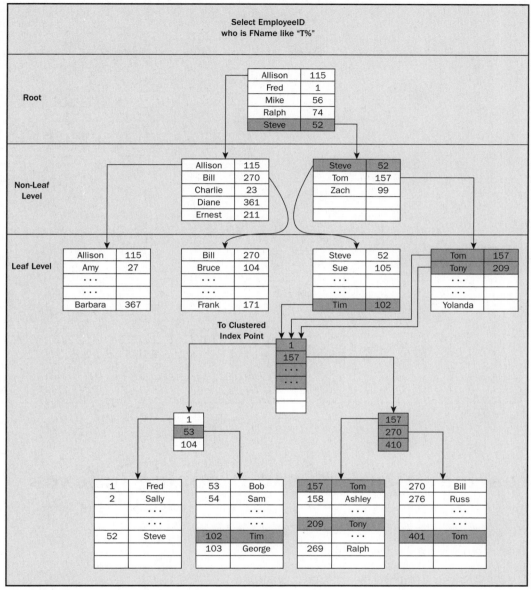

Figure 9-7

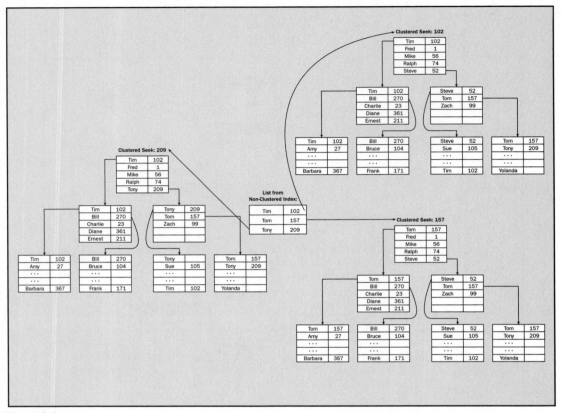

Figure 9-8

Creating, Altering, and Dropping Indexes

These work much as they do on other objects such as tables. Let's take a look at each, starting with the CREATE.

Indexes can be created in two ways:

❑ Through an explicit CREATE INDEX command

❑ As an implied object when a constraint is created

Each of these has its own quirks about what it can and can't do, so let's look at each of them individually.

The CREATE INDEX Statement

The CREATE INDEX statement does exactly what it sounds like — it creates an index on the specified table or view based on the stated columns.

The syntax to create an index is somewhat drawn out and introduces several items that we haven't really talked about up to this point:

```
CREATE [UNIQUE] [CLUSTERED|NONCLUSTERED]
INDEX <index name> ON <table or view name>(<column name> [ASC|DESC] [,...n])
INCLUDE (<column name> [, ...n])
[WITH
[PAD_INDEX = { ON | OFF }]
[[,] FILLFACTOR = <fillfactor>]
[[,] IGNORE_DUP_KEY  = { ON | OFF }]
[[,] DROP_EXISTING = { ON | OFF }]
[[,] STATISTICS_NORECOMPUTE = { ON | OFF }]
[[,] SORT_IN_TEMPDB = { ON | OFF }]
[[,] ONLINE = { ON | OFF }]
[[,] ALLOW_ROW_LOCKS = { ON | OFF }
[[,] ALLOW_PAGE_LOCKS = { ON | OFF }
[[,] MAXDOP = <maximum degree of parallelism>
]
[ON {<filegroup> | <partition scheme name> | DEFAULT }]
```

There is legacy syntax available for many of these options, and so you may see that syntax put into use to support prior versions of SQL Server. That syntax is, however, considered deprecated and will be removed at some point. I highly recommend that you stay with the newer syntax where possible.

> **There is a similar but sufficiently different syntax for creating XML indexes. That will be handled separately at the end of this section.**

Loosely speaking, this statement follows the same CREATE <object type> <object name> syntax that we've seen plenty of already (and will see even more of). The primary hitch in things is that we have a few intervening parameters that we haven't seen elsewhere.

Just as we'll see with views in our next chapter, we do have to add an extra clause onto our CREATE statement to deal with the fact that an index isn't really a stand-alone kind of object. It has to go together with a table or view, and we need to state the table that our column(s) are ON.

After the ON <table or view name>(<column name>) clause, everything is optional. You can mix and match these options. Many of them are seldom used, but some (such as FILLFACTOR) can have a significant impact on system performance and behavior, so let's look at them one by one.

ASC/DESC

These two allow you to choose between an ascending and a descending sort order for your index. The default is ASC, which is, as you might guess, ascending order.

A question that might come to mind is why ascending vs. descending matters — SQL Server can just look at an index backwards if it needs the reverse sort order. Life is not, however, always quite so simple. Looking at the index in reverse order works just fine if you're dealing with only one column, or if your sort is always the same for all columns, but what if you needed to mix sort orders within an index? That is, what if you need one column to be sorted ascending, but the other descending? Since the indexed columns are stored together, reversing the way you look at the index for one column would also reverse the order for the additional columns. If you explicitly state that one column is ascending and the other is descending, then you invert the second column right within the physical data — there is suddenly no reason to change the way that you access your data.

As a quick example, imagine a reporting scenario where you want to order your employee list by the hire date, beginning with the most recent (a descending order), but you also want to order by their last name (an ascending order). Before indexes were available, SQL Server would have to do two operations — one for the first column and one for the second. Having control over the physical sort order of our data provides flexibility in the way we can combine columns.

INCLUDE

This one is supported with SQL Server 2005 and later. Its purpose is to provide better support for what are called *covered queries*.

When you INCLUDE columns as opposed to placing them in the ON list, SQL Server only adds them at the leaf level of the index. Because each row at the leaf level of an index corresponds to a data row, what you're doing is essentially including more of the raw *data* in the leaf level of your index. If you think about this, you can probably make the guess that INCLUDE really applies only to non-clustered indexes (clustered indexes already *are* the data at the leaf level, so there would be no point).

Why does this matter? Well, as we'll discuss further as the book goes on, SQL Server stops working as soon as it has what it actually needs. So if while traversing the index it can find all the data that it needs without continuing to the actual data row, then it won't bother going to the data row (what would be the point?). By including a particular column in the index, you may "cover" a query that utilizes that particular index at the leaf level and save the I/O associated with using that index pointer to go to the data page.

> *Careful not to abuse this one! When you include columns, you are enlarging the size of the leaf level of your index pages. That means fewer rows will fit per page, and therefore, more I/O may be required to see the same number of rows. The result may be that your effort to speed up one query may slow down others. To quote an old film from the eighties, "Balance, Danielson — balance!" Think about the effects on all parts of your system, not just the particular query you're working on that moment.*

WITH

WITH is an easy one; it just tells SQL Server that you will indeed be supplying one or more of the options that follow.

PAD_INDEX

In the syntax list, this one comes first — but that will seem odd when you understand what PAD_INDEX does. In short, it determines just how full the non-leaf level pages of your index are going to be (as a percentage) when the index is first created. You don't state a percentage on PAD_INDEX because it will use whatever percentage you specify in the FILLFACTOR option that follows. Setting PAD_INDEX = ON would be meaningless without a FILLFACTOR (which is why it seems odd that it comes first).

FILLFACTOR

When SQL Server first creates an index, the pages are, by default, filled as full as they can be, minus two records. You can set the FILLFACTOR to be any value between 1 and 100. This number will determine how full your pages are as a percentage, once index construction is completed. Keep in mind, however, that as your pages split, your data will still be distributed 50-50 between the two pages — you cannot control the fill percentage on an ongoing basis other than regularly rebuilding the indexes (something you should do).

We use a FILLFACTOR when we need to adjust the page densities. Think about things this way:

❑   If it's an OLTP system, you want the FILLFACTOR to be low.

❑   If it's an OLAP or other very stable (in terms of changes — very few additions and deletions) system, you want the FILLFACTOR to be as high as possible.

❑   If you have something that has a medium transaction rate and a lot of report-type queries against it, then you probably want something in the middle (not too low, not too high).

If you don't provide a value, then SQL Server will fill your pages to two rows short of full, with a minimum of one row per page (for example, if your row is 8,000 characters wide, you can fit only one row per page, so leaving things two rows short wouldn't work).

IGNORE_DUP_KEY

The IGNORE_DUP_KEY option is a way of doing little more than circumventing the system. In short, it causes a unique constraint to have a slightly different action from that which it would otherwise have.

Normally, a unique constraint, or unique index, does not allow any duplicates of any kind — if a transaction tried to create a duplicate based on a column that is defined as unique, then that transaction would be rolled back and rejected. After you set the IGNORE_DUP_KEY option, however, you'll get mixed behavior. You will still receive an error message, but the error will only be of a warning level. The record is still not inserted.

This last line — the record is still not inserted — is a critical concept from an IGNORE_DUP_KEY standpoint. A rollback isn't issued for the transaction (the error is a warning error rather than a critical error), but the duplicate row will have been rejected.

Why would you do this? Well, it's a way of storing unique values without disturbing a transaction that tries to insert a duplicate. For whatever process is inserting the would-be duplicate, it may not matter at all that it's a duplicate row (no logical error from it). Instead, that process may have an attitude that's more along the lines of, "Well, as long as I know there's one row like that in there, I'm happy — I don't care whether it's the specific row that I tried to insert or not."

DROP_EXISTING

If you specify the DROP_EXISTING option, any existing index with the name in question will be dropped prior to construction of the new index. This option is much more efficient than simply dropping and re-creating an existing index when you use it with a clustered index. If you rebuild an exact match of the existing index, SQL Server knows that it need not touch the non-clustered indexes, while an explicit drop and create would involve rebuilding all non-clustered indexes twice in order to accommodate the different row locations. If you change the structure of the index using DROP_EXISTING, the NCIs are rebuilt only once instead of twice. Furthermore, you cannot simply drop and re-create an index created by a constraint, for example, to implement a certain fillfactor. DROP_EXISTING is a workaround to this.

STATISTICS_NORECOMPUTE

By default, SQL Server attempts to automate the process of updating the statistics on your tables and indexes. By selecting the STATISTICS_NORECOMPUTE option, you are saying that you will take responsibility for the updating of the statistics. In order to turn this option off, you need to run the UPDATE STATISTICS command, but not use the NORECOMPUTE option.

I strongly recommend against using this option. Why? Well, the statistics on your index are what the query optimizer uses to figure out just how helpful your index is going to be for a given query. The statistics on an index are changing constantly as the data in your table goes up and down in volume and as the specific values in a column change. When you combine these two facts, you should be able to see that not updating your statistics means that the query optimizer is going to be running your queries based on out-of-date information. Leaving the automatic statistics feature on means that the statistics will be updated regularly (just how often depends on the nature and frequency of your updates to the table). Conversely, turning automatic statistics off means that you will either be out of date, or you will need to set up a schedule to manually run the UPDATE STATISTICS command.

SORT_IN_TEMPDB

Using this option makes sense only when tempdb is stored on a physically separate drive from the database that is to contain the new index. This is largely an administrative function, so I'm not going to linger on this topic for more than a brief overview of what it is and why it only makes sense when tempdb is on a separate physical device.

When SQL Server builds an index, it has to perform multiple reads to take care of the various index construction steps:

1. Read through all the data, constructing a leaf row corresponding to each row of actual data. Just like the actual data and final index, these go into pages for interim storage. These intermediate pages are not the final index pages, but rather a holding place to temporarily store things every time the sort buffers fill up.

2. A separate run is made through these intermediate pages to merge them into the final leaf pages of the index.

3. Non-leaf pages are built as the leaf pages are being populated.

If the SORT_IN_TEMPDB option is not used, then the intermediate pages are written out to the same physical files that the database is stored in. This means that the reads of the actual data have to compete with the writes of the build process. The two cause the disk heads to move to different places (read vs. write). The result is that the disk heads are constantly moving back and forth — this takes time.

If, on the other hand, SORT_IN_TEMPDB is used, then the intermediate pages will be written to tempdb rather than the database's own file. If they are on separate physical drives, this means that there is no competition between the read and write operations of the index build. Keep in mind, however, that this works only if `tempdb` is on a separate physical drive from your database file; otherwise, the change is only in name, and the competition for I/O is still a factor.

If you're going to use `SORT_IN_TEMPDB`, *make sure that there is enough space in* `tempdb` *for large files.*

ONLINE

Setting this to `ON` forces the table to remain available for general access, and does not create any locks that block users from the index and/or table. By default, the full index operation will grab the locks (eventually a table lock) needed for full and efficient access to the table. The side effect, however, is that your users are blocked out. (Yeah, it's a paradox; you're likely building an index to make the database more usable, but you essentially make the table unusable while you do it.)

Now, you're probably thinking something like: "Oh, that sounds like a good idea — I'll do that every time so my users are unaffected." Poor thinking. Keep in mind that any index construction like that is probably a very I/O-intensive operation, so it is affecting your users one way or the other. Now, add that there is a lot of additional overhead required in the index build for it to make sure that it doesn't step on the toes of any of your users. If you let SQL Server have free reign over the table while it's building the index, then the index will be built much faster, and the overall time that the build is affecting your system will be much smaller.

`ONLINE` index operations are supported only in the Enterprise Edition of SQL Server. You can execute the index command with the `ONLINE` directive in other editions, but it will be ignored, so don't be surprised if you use `ONLINE` and find your users still being blocked out by the index operation if you're using a lesser edition of SQL Server.

ALLOW ROW/PAGE LOCKS

This is a longer term directive than `ONLINE` and is a very, very advanced topic. For purposes of this book and taking into consideration how much we've introduced so far on locking, let's stick with a pretty simple explanation.

Through much of the book thus far, we have repeatedly used the term "lock." As explained early on, this is something of a placeholder to avoid conflicts in data integrity. The `ALLOW` settings we're looking at here determine whether this index will allow row or page locks or not. This falls under the heading of *extreme* performance tweak.

MAXDOP

This is overriding the system setting for the maximum degree of parallelism for purposes of building this index. Parallelism is not something I talk about elsewhere in this book, so we'll give you a mini-dose of it here.

In short, the degree of parallelism is how many processes are put to use for one database operation (in this case, the construction of an index). There is a system setting called the max degree of parallelism that allows you to set a limit on how many processors per operation. The `MAXDOP` option in the index creation options allows you to set the degree of parallelism to be either higher or lower than the base system setting, as you deem appropriate.

ON

SQL Server gives you the option of storing your indexes separately from the data by using the ON option. This can be nice from a couple of perspectives:

❑   The space that is required for the indexes can be spread across other drives.

❑   The I/O for index operations does not burden the physical data retrieval.

There's more to this, but this is hitting the area of *highly* advanced stuff. It is very data and use dependent, and so we'll consider it out of the scope of this book.

Creating XML Indexes

XML indexes were first added in SQL Server 2005. The indexing of something as unstructured as XML has been a problem that many have tried to solve, but few have done with any real success, so count your lucky stars that you have this fine tool available if you're storing XML data. Let's get to what XML indexes are about.

This is another of those "chicken or egg?" things, in that we haven't really looked at XML at all in this book thus far. Still, I consider this more of an index topic than an XML topic. Indeed, the XML create syntax supports all the same options we saw in the previous look at the CREATE statement, with the exception of IGNORE_DUP_KEY and ONLINE. So, for a bit of hyper-fast background:

Unlike the relational data that we've been looking at thus far, XML tends to be relatively unstructured. It utilizes tags to identify data, and can be associated with what's called a schema to provide type and validation information to that XML-based data. The unstructured nature of XML requires the notion of "navigating" or "path" information to find a data "node" in an XML document. Now indexes, on the other hand, try and provide very specific structure and order to data — this poses something of a conflict.

You can create indexes on columns in SQL Server that are of XML type. The primary requirements of doing this are:

❑   The table containing the XML you want to index *must* have a clustered index on it.

❑   A "primary" XML index must exist on the XML data column before you can create "secondary" indexes (more on this in a moment).

❑   XML indexes can be created only on columns of XML type (and an XML index is the only kind of index you can create on columns of that type).

❑   The XML column must be part of a base table — you cannot create the index on a view.

The Primary XML Index

The first index you create on an XML index must be declared as a "primary" index. When you create a primary index, SQL Server creates a new clustered index that combines the clustered index of the base table together with data from whatever XML node you specify.

Secondary XML Indexes

Nothing special here — much as non-clustered indexes point to the cluster key of the clustered index, secondary XML indexes point at primary XML indexes. Once you create a primary XML index, you can create up to 248 more XML indexes on that XML column.

Implied Indexes Created with Constraints

I guess I call this one "index by accident." It's not that the index shouldn't be there — it has to be there if you want the constraint that created the index. It's just that I've seen an awful lot of situations where the only indexes on the system were those created in this fashion. Usually, this implies that the administrators and/or designers of the system are virtually oblivious to the concept of indexes.

However, you'll also find yet another bizarre twist on this one — the situation where the administrator or designer knows how to create indexes, but doesn't really know how to tell what indexes are already on the system and what they are doing. This kind of situation is typified by duplicate indexes. As long as they have different names, SQL Server will be more than happy to create them for you.

Implied indexes are created when one of two constraints is added to a table:

❑   A PRIMARY KEY
❑   A UNIQUE constraint (aka, an *alternate key*)

We've seen plenty of the CREATE syntax up to this point, so I won't belabor it; however, it should be noted that all the options except for {CLUSTERED|NONCLUSTERED} and FILLFACTOR are not allowed when creating an index as an implied index to a constraint.

Creating Indexes on Sparse and Geospatial Columns

These are definitely beyond the scope of a beginning book, but sparse columns and data with a geospatial data type can both have special indexes created on them. Again, keep this in mind if you have application for these special-needs types of columns.

Choosing Wisely: Deciding What Index Goes Where and When

By now, you're probably thinking to yourself, "Gee, I'm always going to create clustered indexes!" There are plenty of good reasons to think that way. Just keep in mind that there are also some reasons not to.

Choosing what indexes to include and what not to can be a tough process, and in case that wasn't enough, you have to make some decisions about what type you want them to be. The latter decision is made simultaneously easier and harder by the fact that you can only have one clustered index. It means that you have to choose wisely to get the most out of it.

Selectivity

Indexes, particularly non-clustered indexes, are primarily beneficial in situations where there is a reasonably high level of *selectivity* within the index. By selectivity, I'm referring to the percentage of values in the column that are unique. The higher the percentage of unique values within a column, the higher the selectivity is said to be, and the greater the benefit of indexing.

If you think back to our sections on non-clustered indexes — particularly the section on non-clustered indexes versus a clustered index — you will recall that the lookup in the non-clustered index is really only the beginning. You still need to make another loop through the clustered index in order to find the real data. Even with the non-clustered index on a heap, you still end up with multiple physically separate reads to perform.

If one lookup in your non-clustered index is going to generate multiple additional lookups in a clustered index, then you are probably better off with the table scan. The exponential effect that's possible here is actually quite amazing. Consider that the looping process created by the non-clustered index is not worth it if you don't have somewhere in the area of 90–95 percent uniqueness in the indexed column.

Clustered indexes are substantially less affected by this because, once you're at the start of your range of data — unique or not — you're there. There are no additional index pages to read. Still, more than likely, your clustered index has other things for which it could be put to greater use.

> *One other exception to the rule of selectivity has to do with foreign keys. If your table has a column that is a* foreign key, *then in all likelihood, you're going to benefit from having an index on that column. Why* foreign keys *and not other columns? Well, foreign keys are frequently the target of joins with the table they reference. Indexes, regardless of selectivity, can be very instrumental in join performance because they allow what is called a* merge join. *A merge join obtains a row from each table and compares them to see if they match the join criteria (what you're joining on). Since there are indexes on the related columns in both tables, the* seek *for both rows is very fast.*

> *The point here is that selectivity is not everything, but it is a big issue to consider. If the column in question is not in a foreign key situation, then it is almost certainly the second only to the, "How often will this be used?" question in terms of issues you need to consider.*

Watching Costs: When Less Is More

Remember that while indexes speed up performance when reading data, they are actually very costly when modifying data. Indexes are not maintained by magic. Every time that you make a modification to your data, any indexes related to that data also need to be updated.

When you insert a new row, a new entry must be made into every index on your table. Remember, too, that when you update a row, it is handled as a delete and insert — again, your indexes have to be updated. But wait! There's more! (Feeling like a late-night infomercial here.) When you delete records, again, you must update all the indexes, too — not just the data. For every index that you create, you are creating one more block of entries that have to be updated.

Notice, by the way, that I said entries plural — not just one. Remember that a B-Tree has multiple levels to it. Every time that you make a modification to the leaf level, there is a chance that a page split will occur, and that one or more non-leaf level page must also be modified to have the reference to the proper leaf page.

Sometimes — quite often actually — not creating that extra index is the thing to do. Sometimes, the best thing to do is choose your indexes based on the transactions that are critical to your system and use the table in question. Does the code for the transaction have a WHERE clause in it? What column(s) does it use? Is there a sorting required?

Choosing That Clustered Index

Remember that you can have only one, so you need to choose it wisely.

By default, your primary key is created with a clustered index. This is often the best place to have it, but not always (indeed, it can seriously hurt you in some situations), and if you leave things this way, you won't be able to use a clustered index anywhere else. The point here is don't just accept the default. Think about it when you are defining your primary key — do you really want it to be a clustered index?

If you decide that you indeed want to change things, that is, you don't want to declare things as being clustered, just add the NONCLUSTERED keyword when you create your table. For example:

```
CREATE TABLE MyTableKeyExample
(
    Column1    int IDENTITY
       PRIMARY KEY NONCLUSTERED,
    Column2    int
)
```

Once the index is created, the only way to change it is to drop and rebuild it, so you want to get it set correctly up front.

Keep in mind that if you change which column(s) your clustered index is on, SQL Server will need to do a complete resorting of your entire table (remember, for a clustered index, the table sort order and the index order are the same). Now, consider a table you have that is 5,000 characters wide and has a million rows in it — that is an awful lot of data that has to be reordered. Several questions should come to mind from this:

❑ How long will it take? It could be a long time, and there really isn't a good way to estimate that time.

❑ Do I have enough space? Figure that in order to do a resort on a clustered index, you will, on average, need an *additional* 1.2 times (the working space plus the new index) the amount of space your table is already taking up. This can turn out to be a very significant amount of space if you're dealing with a large table — make sure you have the room to do it in. All this activity will, by the way, happen in the database itself, so this will also be affected by how you have your maximum size and growth options set for your database.

❑ Should I use the SORT_IN_TEMPDB option? If tempdb is on a separate physical array from your main database and it has enough room, then the answer is probably yes.

The Pros

Clustered indexes are best for queries when the column(s) in question will frequently be the subject of a ranged query. This kind of query is typified by use of the BETWEEN statement or the < or > symbols. Queries that use a GROUP BY and make use of the MAX, MIN, and COUNT aggregators are also great examples of queries that use ranges and love clustered indexes. Clustering works well here because the search can go straight to a particular point in the physical data, keep reading until it gets to the end of the range, and then stop. It is extremely efficient.

Clusters can also be excellent when you want your data sorted (using ORDER BY) based on the cluster key.

The Cons

There are two situations in which you don't want to create that clustered index. The first is fairly obvious — when there's a better place to use it. I know I'm sounding repetitive here, but don't use a clustered index on a column just because it seems like the thing to do (primary keys are the common culprit here). Be sure that you don't have another column that it's better suited to first.

Perhaps the much bigger no-no use for clustered indexes, however, is when you are going to be doing a lot of inserts in a non-sequential order. Remember that concept of page splits? Well, here's where it can come back and haunt you big time.

Imagine this scenario: You are creating an accounting system. You would like to make use of the concept of a transaction number for your primary key in your transaction files, but you would also like those transaction numbers to be somewhat indicative of what kind of transaction it is (it really helps troubleshooting for your accountants). So you come up with something of a scheme — you'll place a prefix on all the transactions indicating what sub-system they come out of. They will look something like this:

```
ARXXXXXX            Accounts Receivable Transactions
GLXXXXXX            General Ledger Transactions
APXXXXXX            Accounts Payable Transactions
```

where XXXXXX will be a sequential numeric value.

This seems like a great idea, so you implement it, leaving the default of the clustered index going on the primary key.

At first glance, everything about this setup looks fine. You're going to have unique values, and the accountants will love the fact that they can infer where something came from based on the transaction number. The clustered index seems to make sense since they will often be querying for ranges of transaction IDs.

Ah, if only it were that simple. Think about your inserts for a bit. With a clustered index, we originally had a nice mechanism to avoid much of the overhead of page splits. When a new record was inserted that was to go after the last record in the table, then even if there was a page split, only that record would go to the new page — SQL Server wouldn't try and move around any of the old data. Now we've messed things up though.

New records inserted from the General Ledger will wind up going on the end of the file just fine (GL is last alphabetically, and the numbers will be sequential). The AR and AP transactions have a major problem though — they are going to be doing non-sequential inserts. When AP000025 gets inserted and there isn't room on the page, SQL Server is going to see AR000001 in the table and know that it's not a sequential insert. Half the records from the old page will be copied to a new page before AP000025 is inserted.

The overhead of this can be staggering. Remember that we're dealing with a clustered index, and that the clustered index is the data. The data is in index order. This means that when you move the index to a new page, you are also moving the data. Now imagine that you're running this accounting system in a typical OLTP environment (you don't get much more OLTP-like than an accounting system) with a bunch of data-entry people keying in vendor invoices or customer orders as fast as they can. You're going to have page splits occurring constantly, and every time you do, you're going to see a brief hesitation for users of that table while the system moves data around.

Fortunately, there are a couple of ways to avoid this scenario:

❑ Choose a cluster key that is going to be sequential in its inserting. You can either create an identity column for this, or you may have another column that logically is sequential to any transaction entered regardless of the system.

❑ Choose not to use a clustered index on this table. This is often the best option in a situation like this, since an insert into a non-clustered index on a heap is usually faster than one on a cluster key.

Even as I've told you to lean toward sequential cluster keys to avoid page splits, you also have to realize that there's a cost there. Among the downsides of sequential cluster keys are concurrency (two or more people trying to get to the same object at the same time). It's all about balancing out what you want, what you're doing, and what it's going to cost you elsewhere.

This is perhaps one of the best examples of why I have gone into so much depth about how things work. You need to think through how things are actually going to get done before you have a good feel for what the right index to use (or not to use) is.

Column Order Matters

Just because an index has two columns, it doesn't mean that the index is useful for any query that refers to either column.

An index is only considered for use if the first column listed in the index is used in the query. The bright side is that there doesn't have to be an exact one-for-one match to every column — just the first. Naturally, the more columns that match (in order), the better, but only the first creates a definite do-not-use situation.

Think about things this way. Imagine that you are using a phone book. Everything is indexed by last name and then first name — does this sorting do you any real good if all you know is that the person you want to call is named Fred? On the other hand, if all you know is that his last name is Blake, the index will still serve to narrow the field for you.

One of the more common mistakes that I see in index construction is the belief that one index that includes all the columns is going to be helpful for all situations. Indeed, what you're really doing is storing all the data a second time. The index will totally be ignored if the first column of the index isn't mentioned in the JOIN, ORDER BY, or WHERE clauses of the query.

ALTER INDEX

The ALTER INDEX command is somewhat deceptive in what it does. Up until now, ALTER commands have always been about changing the definition of your object. You ALTER tables to add or disable constraints and columns, for example. ALTER INDEX is different — it is all about maintenance and zero about structure. If you need to change the makeup of your index, you still need either to DROP and CREATE it or to CREATE and use the index with the DROP_EXISTING=ON option.

As you saw earlier in the chapter, SQL Server gives you an option for controlling just how full your leaf level pages are and, if you choose, another option to deal with non-leaf level pages. Unfortunately, these are proactive options. They are applied once, and then you need to reapply them as necessary by rebuilding your indexes and reapplying the options.

In the upcoming section on maintenance, we'll look more at the wheres and whys of utilizing this command, but for now, take it on faith that you'll use maintenance commands like ALTER INDEX as part of your regular maintenance routine.

The ALTER INDEX syntax looks like this:

```
ALTER INDEX { <name of index> | ALL }
    ON <table or view name>
    { REBUILD
        [ [ WITH (
          [ PAD_INDEX  = { ON | OFF } ]
        | [[,] FILLFACTOR = <fillfactor>
        | [[,] SORT_IN_TEMPDB = { ON | OFF } ]
        | [[,] IGNORE_DUP_KEY = { ON | OFF } ]
        | [[,] STATISTICS_NORECOMPUTE = { ON | OFF } ]
        | [[,] ONLINE = { ON | OFF } ]
        | [[,] ALLOW_ROW_LOCKS = { ON | OFF } ]
        | [[,] ALLOW_PAGE_LOCKS = { ON | OFF } ]
        | [[,] MAXDOP = <max degree of parallelism>
                ) ]
          | [ PARTITION = <partition number>
                [ WITH ( <partition rebuild index option>
                       [ ,...n ] ) ] ] ]
    | DISABLE
    | REORGANIZE
        [ PARTITION = <partition number> ]
        [ WITH ( LOB_COMPACTION = { ON | OFF } ) ]
    | SET ([ ALLOW_ROW_LOCKS= { ON | OFF } ]
          | [[,] ALLOW_PAGE_LOCKS = { ON | OFF } ]
          | [[,] IGNORE_DUP_KEY = { ON | OFF } ]
          | [[,] STATISTICS_NORECOMPUTE = { ON | OFF } ]
          )
    } [ ; ]
```

Several of the options are common to the CREATE INDEX command, so I will skip redefining those particular ones here. Beyond that, a fair amount of the ALTER-specific options are fairly detailed and relate to dealing with things like fragmentation (we'll get to fragmentation and maintenance shortly) or are more administrator oriented and usually used on an ad hoc basis to deal with very specific problems. The core elements here should, however, be part of your regular maintenance planning.

We'll start by looking at a couple of top parameters and then look at the options that are part of your larger maintenance-planning needs.

Index Name

We can name a specific index if you want to maintain one specific index, or use ALL to indicate that you want to perform this maintenance on every index associated with the named table.

Table or View Name

Pretty much just what it sounds like — the name of the specific object (table or view) that you want to perform the maintenance on. Note that it needs to be one specific table (you can feed it a list and say "do all of these please!").

REBUILD

This is the "industrial-strength" approach to fixing an index. If you run ALTER INDEX with this option, the old index is completely thrown away and a new one reconstructed from scratch. The result is a truly optimized index, where every page in both the leaf and non-leaf levels of the index has been reconstructed as you have defined it (either with defaults or using switches to change things like the fillfactor). If the index in question is a clustered index, then the physical data is also reorganized.

By default, the pages will be reconstituted to be full, minus two records. Just as with the CREATE TABLE syntax, you can set the FILLFACTOR to be any value between 0 and 100. This number will be the percent that your pages are full once the database reorganization is complete. Remember, though, that as your pages split, your data will still be distributed 50-50 between the two pages — you cannot control the fill percentage on an ongoing basis unless you regularly rebuild the indexes.

> *Careful on this one. As soon as you kick off a* rebuild, *the index you are working on is essentially gone until the* rebuild *is complete. Any queries that rely on that index may become exceptionally slow (potentially by orders of magnitude). This is the sort of thing you want to test on an offline system first to have an idea how long it's going to take, and then schedule to run in off hours (preferably with someone monitoring it to be sure it's back online when peak hours come along).*

This one can have major side effects while it runs, and thus it falls squarely in the domain of the database administrator in my not so humble opinion.

DISABLE

This one does what it says, only in somewhat drastic fashion. It would be nice if all this command did was take your index offline until you decided further what you wanted to do, but instead, it essentially marks the index as unusable. Once an index has been disabled, it must be rebuilt (not reorganized, but rebuilt) before it will be active again.

This is one you're very, very rarely going to do yourself (you would more likely just drop the index). It is far more likely to happen during an SQL Server upgrade or some other oddball situation.

> Yet another BE CAREFUL! warning on this one. If you disable the clustered index
> for your table, it has the effect of disabling the table. The data will remain, but will
> be inaccessible by all indexes (since they all depend on the clustered index) until
> you rebuild the clustered index.

REORGANIZE

BINGO!, from the developer perspective. With REORGANIZE, you hit much more of a happy medium in
life. When you reorganize your index, you get a slightly less complete optimization than you get with a
full rebuild, but one that occurs online (users can still utilize the index).

This should, if you're paying attention, bring about the question, "What exactly do you mean by '*slightly
less complete*'?" Well, REORGANIZE works only on the leaf level of your index — non-leaf levels of the
index go untouched. This means that you're not quite getting a full optimization, but for the lion's share
of indexes, that is not where your real cost of fragmentation is (though it can happen, and your mileage
may vary).

Given its much lower impact on users, this is usually the tool you'll want to use as part of your regular
maintenance plan. We'll look into this a bit more later when talking fragmentation.

Dropping Indexes

If you're constantly reanalyzing the situation and adding indexes, don't forget to drop indexes, too.
Remember the overhead on inserts. It doesn't make much sense to look at the indexes that you need
and not also think about which indexes you do not need. Always ask yourself: "Can I get rid of any of
these?"

The syntax to drop an index is pretty much the same as that used to drop a table. The only hitch is that
you need to qualify the index name with the table or view it is attached to:

```
DROP INDEX <table or view name>.<index name>
```

And it's gone.

Take a Hint from the Query Plan

New with SQL Server 2008 is an indexing hint right within the query-plan information that will tell you
about any indexes that the query optimizer thought would have helped, but that didn't exist.

Use the Database Engine Tuning Advisor

It is my hope that you'll learn enough about indexes not to need the Database Engine Tuning Advisor all
that much, but it still can be quite handy. It works by taking a workload file, which you generate using
the SQL Server Profiler (discussed in *Professional SQL Server 2008 Programming*), and looking over that
information for what indexes and/or partitions will work best on your system.

The Database Engine Tuning Advisor is found on the Tools menu of the SQL Server Management Studio. It can also be reached as a separate program item from the Windows Start menu. Like most any tuning tool, I don't recommend using this tool as the sole way to decide what indexes to build, but it can be quite handy at making some suggestions that you may not have thought of.

Maintaining Your Indexes

As developers, we often tend to forget about our product after it goes out the door. For many kinds of software, that's something you can get away with just fine — you ship it, then you move on to the next product or next release. However, with database-driven projects, it's virtually impossible to get away with. You need to take responsibility for the product well beyond the delivery date.

Please don't take me to mean that you have to go serve a stint in the tech support department — I'm actually talking about something even more important: *maintenance planning*.

There are really two issues to be dealt with in terms of the maintenance of indexes:

❑ Page splits
❑ Fragmentation

Both are related to page density, and while the symptoms are substantially different, the troubleshooting tool is the same, as is the cure.

Fragmentation

We've already talked about page splits quite a bit, but we haven't really touched on *fragmentation*. I'm not talking about the fragmentation that you may have heard of with your O/S files and the defrag tool you use, because that won't help with database fragmentation.

Fragmentation happens when your database grows, pages split, and then data is eventually deleted. While the B-Tree mechanism is really not that bad at keeping things balanced from a growth point of view, it doesn't really have a whole lot to offer as you delete data. Eventually, you may get down to a situation where you have one record on this page, a few records on that page — a situation where many of your data pages are holding only a small fraction of the amount of data that they could hold.

The first problem with this is probably the first you would think about — wasted space. Remember that SQL Server allocates an extent of space at a time. If only one page has one record on it, then that extent is still allocated.

The second problem is the one that is more likely to cause you grief: Records that are spread out all over the place cause additional overhead in data retrieval. Instead of just loading up one page and grabbing the 10 rows it requires, SQL Server may have to load 10 separate pages to get that same information. It isn't just reading the row that causes effort — SQL Server has to read that page in first. More pages = more work on reads.

That being said, database fragmentation does have its good side — OLTP systems positively love fragmentation. Any guesses as to why? Page splits. Pages that don't have much data in them can have data inserted with little or no risk of page splits.

So, high fragmentation equates to poor read performance, but it also equates to excellent insert performance. As you might expect, this also means that OLAP systems really don't like fragmentation.

Identifying Fragmentation vs. Likelihood of Page Splits

SQL Server provides a special metadata function called sys.dm_db_index_physical_stats that is particularly useful in helping us identify just how full the pages and extents in our database are. We can then use that information to make some decisions about what we want to do to maintain our database.

sys.dm_db_index_physical_stats is what is called a *table valued function* (we'll learn more about these in Chapter 13). In short, this means that while it's a function, you can use it much as you would a table, which means that you can actually stick WHERE conditions on it and other similar constructs. The syntax for the function itself is pretty simple:

```
sys.dm_db_index_physical_stats (
    { <database id> | NULL | 0 | DEFAULT }
    , { <object id> | NULL | 0 | DEFAULT }
    , { <index id> | NULL | 0 | -1 | DEFAULT }
    , { <partition no> | NULL | 0 | DEFAULT }
    , { <mode> | NULL | DEFAULT }
)
```

Note that it is demanding the rather non-intuitive ids as input values rather than the logical names that you might be more used to. Fortunately, SQL Server gives us a number of functions that work on returning the proper id for a given object on the server or in the database.

As an example of how to use this, let's get the all information index information from the Sales .SalesOrderDetail table. Since we've said we want all the indexes in the table, we just need the id for the table — not any individual indexes. Since the function is table valued, we need to write a query to return the results from the function. For example:

```
DECLARE @db_id SMALLINT;
DECLARE @object_id INT;
SET @db_id = DB_ID(N'AdventureWorks2008');
SET @object_id = OBJECT_ID(N'AdventureWorks2008.Sales.SalesOrderDetail');
SELECT database_id, object_id, index_id, index_depth, avg_fragmentation_in_percent,
page_count
FROM sys.dm_db_index_physical_stats(@db_id,@object_id,NULL,NULL,NULL);
```

The output is far more self-describing that the previous tools were in this area:

```
database_id object_id   index_id   index_depth avg_fragmentation_in_percent page_count
----------- ----------- ---------- ----------- ---------------------------- ----------
8           610101214   1          3           0.565885206143896            1237
8           610101214   2          3           1.70731707317073             410
8           610101214   3          2           6.14035087719298             228

(3 row(s) affected)
```

The function also has a veritable sea of other information available, so feel free to explore further, but let's walk through the columns that are most interesting in terms of fragmentation.

A number of fields tell you things like what kind of index structure it is (clustered vs. non-clustered), number of fragmented pages, and other things of interest. There are also several columns that reside firmly at the advanced level of advanced SQL Server, so don't be too stressed if you don't understand every column this function offers.

Stat	What It Means
database id	The SQL Server internal identifier for the database you want to run the function against. NULL results in information being returned on all databases. Keep in mind that by choosing the NULL option, all subsequent parameters must also be set to NULL. 0 and DEFAULT all are functionally equivalent to NULL for this parameter.
object id	The SQL Server internal identifier for the table you want to run the function against. NULL results in information being returned on all tables. Keep in mind that by choosing the NULL option, all subsequent parameters must also be set to NULL. 0 and DEFAULT all are functionally equivalent to NULL for this parameter.
index id	The internal identifier for the index you want to run the function against. NULL results in information being returned on all indexes. Note that if the table is clustered, the clustered index will always be numbered 1, and if the table is a heap, then the heap will be index 0. Non-clustered indexes will be numbers 2 or higher. By choosing the NULL option, partition_no must also be set to NULL. -1 and DEFAULT all are functionally equivalent to NULL for this parameter.
partition no	This is a bit beyond the scope of this book, but tables and indexes can be partitioned into separate physical storage units. Use this parameter to identify a specific partition you want fragmentation information on. NULL results in information being returned on all partitions. 1 and DEFAULT all are functionally equivalent to NULL for this parameter.
Mode	Mode defines the level of scan used to generate the statistics returned. Choices include DEFAULT, NULL, LIMITED, SAMPLED, or DETAILED. DEFAULT and NULL are functionally equivalent to LIMITED.

Continued

Stat	What It Means
Logical Scan Fragmentation	The percentage of pages that are out of order as checked by scanning the leaf pages of an index. Only relevant to scans related to a clustered table. An out-of-order page is one for which the next page indicated in the index allocation map (IAM) is different from that pointed to by the next page pointer in the leaf page.
Extent Scan Fragmentation	This one is telling whether an extent is not physically located next to the extent that it should be logically located next to. This just means that the leaf pages of your index are not physically in order (though they still can be logically), and it shows what percentage of the extents this problem pertains to.

Now, the question is how do we use this information once we have it? The answer is, of course, that it depends.

Using the output from our fragmentation query, we have a decent idea of whether our database is full, fragmented, or somewhere in between (the latter is, most likely, what we want to see). If we're running an OLAP system, then having full pages would be great — fragmentation would bring on depression. For an OLTP system, we would want much the opposite (although only to a point).

So, how do we take care of the problem? To answer that, we need to look into the concept of index rebuilding and fillfactors.

ALTER INDEX and FILLFACTOR

As we saw earlier in the chapter, SQL Server gives us an option for controlling just how full our leaf level pages are and, if we choose, another option to deal with non-leaf level pages. Unfortunately, these are proactive options. They are applied once, and then you need to reapply them as necessary by rebuilding or reorganizing your indexes to reapply the options.

To rebuild indexes, we can either drop them and create them again (if you do, using the DROP_EXISTING option usually is a good idea), or make use of the ALTER INDEX command with the REBUILD option. Keep in mind, however, what was said previously about rebuilding indexes — unless you have the ONLINE option available, rebuilding indexes takes the index (and possibly the entire table) totally offline until the rebuild is complete. In general, reorganizing is going to be a better option.

A reorg affects only the leaf level of the index (where most of the issue is likely to be anyway) and keeps the index online while the reorg is taking place. Reorganizing your indexes restructures all the leaf level information in those indexes, and reestablishes a base percentage that your pages are full. If the index in question is a clustered index, then the physical data is also reorganized. Unfortunately, REORGANIZE does not allow for the change of several index settings, such as FILLFACTOR.

If the index has not had a specific fillfactor specified, the pages will be reconstituted to be full, minus two records. Just as with the CREATE TABLE syntax, you can set the FILLFACTOR to be any value between 1 and 100 as long as you are doing a full rebuild (as opposed to just a reorg). This number will be the percent that your pages are full once the database reorganization is complete. Remember, though, that as your pages split, your data will still be distributed 50-50 between the two pages — you cannot control the fill percentage on an ongoing basis other than by regularly rebuilding the indexes.

We use a FILLFACTOR when we need to adjust the page densities. As already discussed, lower page densities (and therefore lower FILLFACTORs) are ideal for OLTP systems where there are a lot of insertions; this helps prevent page splits. Higher page densities are desirable with OLAP systems (fewer pages to read, but no real risk of page splitting due to few to no inserts).

If we wanted to rebuild the index that serves as the primary key for the Sales.SalesOrderDetail table we were looking at earlier with a fill factor of 65, we would issue an ALTER INDEX command as follows:

```
ALTER INDEX PK_SalesOrderDetail_SalesOrderID_SalesOrderDetailID
  ON Sales.SalesOrderDetail
    REBUILD WITH (FILLFACTOR = 100)
```

This would be a good time to digress and revisit the idea of your object names. Notice how long this name is. The more characters, the more chance for typos. Balance that against the need for the name to be meaningful. For this particular query, my own naming conventions would probably have dropped the inclusion of the table name (when referring to an index, you usually already know what table you're talking about) and eliminated the underscores to wind up with something like PKSalesOrderIDSalesOrderDetailID. The name implies the nature of the index (it's supporting a primary key) and the columns involved. Be careful, however, with using the column name idea. On the rare occasion you wind up with several columns in your index, it can make for an unruly index name.

We can then re-run the sys.dm_db_index_physical_stats to see the effect:

database_id	object_id	index_id	index_depth	avg_fragmentation_in_percent	page_count
8	610101214	1	3	0.0810372771474878	1234
8	610101214	2	3	1.70731707317073	410
8	610101214	3	2	6.14035087719298	228

```
(3 row(s) affected)
```

The big one to notice here is the change in avg_fragmentation_in_percent. Assuming we're looking for high page densities (higher read performance), then we want the number as low as possible. The number didn't quite reach 0 percent because SQL Server has to deal with page and row sizing, but it gets as close as it can.

Several things to note about ALTER TABLE REINDEX/REORG and FILLFACTOR:

❑ If a FILLFACTOR isn't provided, then the ALTER TABLE will use whatever setting was used to build the index previously. If one has never been specified, then the FILLFACTOR will make the page full (which is too full for most situations).

❑ If a FILLFACTOR is provided, then that value becomes the default FILLFACTOR for that index.

❑ While a REORGANIZE is done live and a REBUILD can be (if you have the licensing required to enable that feature), I strongly recommend against it. It locks resources and can cause a host of problems. At the very least, look at doing it at non-peak hours.

Summary

Indexes are sort of a cornerstone topic in SQL Server or any other database environment, and are not something to be taken lightly. They can drive your performance successes, but they can also drive your performance failures.

Top-level things to think about with indexes:

❑ Clustered indexes are usually faster than non-clustered indexes (one could come very close to saying always, but there are exceptions).

❑ Only place non-clustered indexes on columns where you are going to get a high level of selectivity (that is, 95 percent or more of the rows are unique).

❑ All Data Manipulation Language (DML: INSERT, UPDATE, DELETE, SELECT) statements can benefit from indexes, but inserts, deletes, and updates (remember, they use a delete and insert approach) are slowed by indexes. The lookup part of a query is helped by the index, but anything that modifies data will have extra work to do (to maintain the index in addition to the actual data).

❑ Indexes take up space.

❑ Indexes are used only if the first column in the index is relevant to your query.

❑ Indexes can hurt as much as they help — know why you're building the index, and don't build indexes you don't need.

❑ Indexes can provide structured data performance to your unstructured XML data, but keep in mind that like other indexes, there is overhead involved.

When you're thinking about indexes, ask yourself these questions:

Question	Response
Are there a lot of inserts or modifications to this table?	If yes, keep indexes to a minimum. This kind of table usually has modifications done through single-record lookups of the primary key, and usually, this is the only index you want on the table. If the inserts are non-sequential, think about using something other than a clustered index.
Is this a reporting table? That is, not many inserts, but reports run lots of different ways?	More indexes are fine. Target the clustered index to frequently used information that is likely to be extracted in ranges. OLAP installations will often have many times the number of indexes seen in an OLTP environment.
Is there a high level of selectivity on the data?	If yes, and it is frequently the target of a WHERE clause, then add that index.
Have I dropped the indexes I no longer need?	If not, why not?
Do I have a maintenance strategy established?	If not, why not?

Exercises

1. Name at least two ways of determining what indexes can be found on the `HumanResources`
    `.Employee` table in the AdventureWorks2008 database.

2. Create a non-clustered index on the `ModifiedDate` column of the `Production.ProductModel`
    table in the AdventureWorks2008 database.

3. Delete the index you created in Exercise 2.

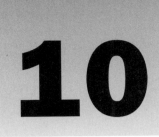

Views

Up to this point, we've been dealing with base objects — objects that have some level of substance of their own. In this chapter, we're going to go virtual (well, mostly anyway), and take a look at views.

Views have a tendency to be used either too much, or not enough — rarely just right. When we're done with this chapter, you should be able to use views to:

❑ Reduce apparent database complexity for end users

❑ Prevent sensitive columns from being selected, while still affording access to other important data

❑ Add additional indexing to your database to speed query performance — even when you're not using the view the index is based on

A view is, at its core, really nothing more than a stored query. What's great is that you can mix and match your data from base tables (or other views) to create what will, in most respects, function just like another base table. You can create a simple query that selects from only one table and leaves some columns out, or you can create a complex query that joins several tables and makes them appear as one.

Simple Views

The syntax for a view, in its most basic form, is a combination of a couple of things we've already seen in the book — the basic CREATE statement that we saw back in Chapter 5, plus a SELECT statement like we've used over and over again:

```
CREATE VIEW <view name>
AS
<SELECT statement>
```

The preceding syntax just represents the minimum, of course, but it's still all we need in a large percentage of the situations. The more extended syntax looks like this:

```
CREATE VIEW [<schema name>].<view name> [(<column name list>)]
[WITH [ENCRYPTION] [[,] SCHEMABINDING] [[,] VIEW_METADATA]]
AS
<SELECT statement>
[WITH CHECK OPTION][;]
```

We'll be looking at each piece of this individually, but, for now, let's go ahead and dive right in with an extremely simple view.

Try It Out   **Creating a Simple View**

We'll call this one our customer phone list, and create it as CustomerPhoneList_vw in the Accounting database that we created back in Chapter 5:

```
USE Accounting;
GO

CREATE VIEW CustomerPhoneList_vw
AS
    SELECT CustomerName, Contact, Phone
    FROM Customers;
```

Notice that when you execute the CREATE statement in the Management Studio, it works just like all the other CREATE statements we've done — it doesn't return any rows. It just lets us know that the view has been created:

```
Command(s) completed successfully.
```

Now switch to using the grid view (if you're not already there) to make it easy to see more than one result set. Then run a SELECT statement against your view — using it just as you would for a table — and another against the Customers table directly:

```
SELECT * FROM CustomerPhoneList_vw;

SELECT * FROM Customers;
```

How It Works

What you get back looks almost identical to the previous result set — indeed, in the columns that they have in common, the two result sets *are* identical. To clarify how SQL Server is looking at your query on the view, let's break it down logically a bit. The SELECT statement in your view is defined as:

```
SELECT CustomerName, Contact, Phone
FROM Customers;
```

So when you run:

```
SELECT * FROM CustomerPhoneList_vw;
```

you are essentially saying to SQL Server: "Give me all of the rows and columns you get when you run the statement SELECT CustomerName, Contact, Phone FROM Customers."

We've created something of a pass-through situation — that is, our view hasn't really changed anything, but rather just "passed through" a filtered version of the data it was accessing. What's nice about that is that we have reduced the complexity for the end user. In this day and age, where we have so many tools to make life easier for the user, this may not seem like all that big of a deal — but to the user, it is.

> Be aware that, by default, there is nothing special done for a view. The view runs just as if it were a query run from the command line — there is no pre-optimization of any kind. This means that you are adding one more layer of overhead between the request for data and the data being delivered, and thus, that a view is never going to run as fast as if you had just run the underlying SELECT statement directly. That said, views exist for a reason — be it security or simplification for the user — balance your need against the overhead as would seem to fit your particular situation.

Let's go with another view that illustrates what we can do in terms of hiding sensitive data. For this example, let's go back to our Employees table in our Accounting database (we'll create a special version of the now familiar Accounting database a little later in the chapter). Take a look at the table layout:

Employees
EmployeeID
FirstName
MiddleInitial
LastName
Title
SSN
Salary
HireDate
TerminationDate
ManagerEmpID
Department

Federal law in the U.S. protects some of this information — we must limit access to a "need to know" basis. Other columns, however, are free for anyone to see. What if we want to expose the unrestricted columns to a group of people, but don't want them to be able to see the general table structure or data? One solution would be to keep a separate table that includes only the columns that we need:

Employees
EmployeeID
FirstName
MiddleInitial
LastName
Title
HireDate
TerminationDate
ManagerEmpID
Department

While on the surface this would meet our needs, it is extremely problematic:

❑ We use disk space twice.

❑ We have a synchronization problem if one table gets updated and the other doesn't.

❑ We have double I/O operations (you have to read and write the data in two places instead of one) whenever we need to insert, update, or delete rows.

Views provide an easy and relatively elegant solution to this problem. When we use a view, the data is stored only once (in the underlying table or tables) — eliminating all of the problems just described. Instead of building our completely separate table, we can just build a view that will function in a nearly identical fashion.

To make sure we know the state of our Accounting database, let's create a special version of it for use in the next example or two. To do this, load the CChapter10AccountingDBCreate.sql file (supplied with the source code) into the Management Studio and run it. Then add the following view to the AccountingChapter10 database:

```
USE AccountingChapter10;
GO

CREATE VIEW Employees_vw
AS
SELECT    EmployeeID,
          FirstName,
          MiddleInitial,
          LastName,
          Title,
```

```
          HireDate,
          TerminationDate,
          ManagerEmpID,
          Department
   FROM Employees;
```

We are now ready to let everyone have access — directly or indirectly — to the data in the Employees table. Users who have the "need to know" can now be directed to the Employees table, but we continue to deny access to other users. Instead, the users who do not have that "need to know" can have access to our Employees_vw view. If they want to make use of it, they do it just the same as they would against a table:

```
SELECT *
FROM Employees_vw;
```

> This actually gets into one of the sticky areas of naming conventions. Because I've been using the _vw suffix, it's pretty easy to see that this is a view and not a table. Sometimes, you'd like to make things a little more hidden than that, so you might want to deliberately leave the _vw off. Doing so means that you have to use a different name (Employees is already the name of the base table), but you'd be surprised how many users won't know that there's a difference between a view and a table if you do it this way.

Views as Filters

This will probably be one of the shortest sections in the book. Why? Well, it doesn't get much simpler than this.

You've already seen how to create a simple view — you just use an easy SELECT statement. How do we filter the results of our queries? With a WHERE clause. Views use a WHERE in exactly the same way.

Let's take our Employees_vw view from the last section, and beef it up a bit by making it a list of only current employees. To do this, only two changes need to be made.

First, we have to filter out employees who no longer work for the company. Would a current employee have a termination date? Probably not, so, if we limit our results to rows with a NULL TerminationDate, then we've got what we're after.

The second change illustrates another simple point about views working just like queries — the column(s) contained in the WHERE clause do not need to be included in the SELECT list. In this case, it doesn't make any sense to include the termination date in the result set as we're talking about current employees.

Try It Out   Using a View to Filter Data

With these two things in mind, let's create a new view by changing our old view around just a little bit:

```
CREATE VIEW CurrentEmployees_vw
AS
SELECT    EmployeeID,
          FirstName,
          MiddleInitial,
          LastName,
          Title,
          HireDate,
          ManagerEmpID,
          Department
FROM Employees
WHERE TerminationDate IS NULL;
```

In addition to the name change and the WHERE clause we've added, note that we've also eliminated the TerminationDate column from the SELECT list.

Let's test how this works a little bit by running a straight SELECT statement against our Employees table and limiting our SELECT list to the things that we care about:

```
SELECT    EmployeeID,
          FirstName,
          LastName,
          TerminationDate
FROM Employees;
```

This returns a few columns from all the rows in the entire table:

```
EmployeeID          FirstName          LastName          TerminationDate
-----------         --------------     ------------      ------------------------
1                   Joe                Dokey             NULL
2                   Peter              Principle         NULL
3                   Steve              Smith             1997-01-31
4                   Howard             Kilroy            NULL
5                   Mary               Contrary          1998-06-15
6                   Billy              Bob               NULL

(6 row(s) affected)
```

Now let's check out our view:

```
SELECT    EmployeeID,
          FirstName,
          LastName
FROM CurrentEmployees_vw;
```

Our result set has become a bit smaller:

```
EmployeeID          FirstName       LastName
-------------       ----------      ----------------
1                   Joe             Dokey
2                   Peter           Principle
4                   Howard          Kilroy
6                   Billy           Bob

(4 row(s) affected)
```

A few people are missing versus our first select — just the way we wanted it.

How It Works

As we've discussed before, the view really is just a SELECT statement that's been hidden from the user so that they can ignore what the SELECT statement says, and instead just consider the results it produces just as if it were a table — you can liken this to the derived tables we discussed back in Chapter 7. Because our data was filtered down before we referenced the view by name, our query doesn't even need to consider that data (the view has done that for us).

More Complex Views

Even though I use the term "complex" here — don't let that scare you. The toughest thing in views is still, for the most part, simpler than most other things in SQL.

What we're doing with more complex views is really just adding joins, summarization, and perhaps some column renaming.

Perhaps one of the most common uses of views is to flatten data — that is, the removal of complexity that we outlined at the beginning of the chapter. Imagine that we are providing a view for management to make it easier to check on sales information. No offense to managers who are reading this book, but managers who write their own complex queries are still a rather rare breed — even in the information age.

For an example, let's briefly go back to using the AdventureWorks2008 database. Our manager would like to be able to do simple queries that will tell him or her what orders have been placed for what parts and which account number was used to place the order. So, we create a view that they can perform very simple queries on — remember that we are creating this one in AdventureWorks2008:

```
USE AdventureWorks2008
GO

CREATE VIEW CustomerOrders_vw
AS
SELECT sc.AccountNumber,
```

```
            soh.SalesOrderID,
            soh.OrderDate,
            sod.ProductID,
            pp.Name,
            sod.OrderQty,
            sod.UnitPrice,
            sod.UnitPriceDiscount * sod.UnitPrice * sod.OrderQty AS TotalDiscount,
            sod.LineTotal
FROM    Sales.Customer AS sc
INNER JOIN Sales.SalesOrderHeader AS soh
        ON sc.CustomerID = soh.CustomerID
INNER JOIN Sales.SalesOrderDetail AS sod
        ON soh.SalesOrderID = sod.SalesOrderID
INNER JOIN Production.Product AS pp
        ON sod.ProductID = pp.ProductID;
```

Now do a SELECT:

```
SELECT *
FROM CustomerOrders_vw;
```

You wind up with a bunch of rows — over 121,000 — but you also wind up with information that is far simpler for the average manager to comprehend and sort out. What's more, with not that much training, the manager (or whoever the user might be) can get right to the heart of what they are looking for:

```
SELECT AccountNumber, LineTotal
FROM CustomerOrders_vw
WHERE OrderDate = '01/07/2002';
```

The user didn't need to know how to do a four-table join — that was hidden in the view. Instead, they only need limited skill (and limited imagination for that matter) in order to get the job done.

```
AccountNumber LineTotal
------------- --------------------------------------
AW00014937    3578.270000
AW00018710    3578.270000
AW00025713    699.098200
AW00020558    699.098200

(4 row(s) affected)
```

However, we could make our query even more targeted. Let's say that we only want our view to return yesterday's sales. We'll make only slight changes to our query:

```
USE AdventureWorks2008
GO
```

```
CREATE VIEW YesterdaysOrders_vw
AS
SELECT sc.AccountNumber,
       soh.SalesOrderID,
```

```
            soh.OrderDate,
            sod.ProductID,
            pp.Name,
            sod.OrderQty,
            sod.UnitPrice,
            sod.UnitPriceDiscount * sod.UnitPrice * sod.OrderQty AS TotalDiscount,
            sod.LineTotal
FROM    Sales.Customer AS sc
INNER JOIN   Sales.SalesOrderHeader AS soh
        ON sc.CustomerID = soh.CustomerID
INNER JOIN   Sales.SalesOrderDetail AS sod
        ON soh.SalesOrderID = sod.SalesOrderID
INNER JOIN Production.Product AS pp
        ON sod.ProductID = pp.ProductID
WHERE CAST(soh.OrderDate AS Date) =
        CAST(DATEADD(day,-1,GETDATE()) AS Date);
```

All the dates in the AdventureWorks2008 database are old enough that this view wouldn't return any data, so let's modify a few existing rows to test it:

```
USE AdventureWorks2008

UPDATE Sales.SalesOrderHeader
SET OrderDate = CAST(DATEADD(day,-1,GETDATE()) AS Date),
    DueDate = CAST(DATEADD(day,11,GETDATE()) AS Date),
    ShipDate = CAST(DATEADD(day,6,GETDATE()) AS Date)
WHERE Sales.SalesOrderID BETWEEN 43659 AND 43662;
```

The core of this is a relatively simple update statement that is resetting the dates on a few orders to be relative to yesterday (the day before whatever day you run that update statement). The GETDATE() function is, just as you would expect, getting your current date. We'll discuss some of the other pieces in a bit. For now, I'll ask that you just take this one largely on faith, and trust that you'll need to run this to have a value in AdventureWorks2008 that will come up for our view. You should see a result from the Management Studio that looks something like this:

```
(31,465 row(s) affected)
```

Be aware that the message will appear on the Messages *tab only if you are using the Management Studio's* Results In Grid *mode. It should show up in your Results table if you're in text mode.*

The OrderID might vary, but the rest should hold pretty true.

Now let's run a query against your view and see what we get:

```
SELECT AccountNumber, SalesOrderID, OrderDate FROM YesterdaysOrders_vw;
```

You can see that our four orders do show up. Indeed, since each has several line items, you should wind up with a total of 121,317 rows:

```
AccountNumber SalesOrderID OrderDate
------------- ------------ -----------------------
AW00000676    43659        2007-09-30 00:00:00.000
```

```
AW00000676    43659        2007-09-30 00:00:00.000
AW00000676    43659        2007-09-30 00:00:00.000
AW00000676    43659        2007-09-30 00:00:00.000
...
...
AW00000227    43662        2007-09-30 00:00:00.000
AW00000227    43662        2007-09-30 00:00:00.000

(51 row(s) affected)
```

The DATEADD and CAST Functions

The join, while larger than most of the ones we've done this far, is still pretty straightforward. We keep adding tables, joining a column in each new table to a matching column in the tables that we've already named. As always, note that the columns do not have to have the same name — they just have to have data that relates to one another.

Since this was a relatively complex join, let's take a look at what we are doing in the query that supports this view.

The WHERE clause is where things get interesting:

```
WHERE CAST(soh.OrderDate AS Date) =
      CAST(DATEADD(day,-1,GETDATE()) AS Date)
```

It's a single comparison, but we used several functions to come up with our result.

It would be very tempting to just compare the OrderDate in the SalesOrderHeader table to GETDATE() (today's date) minus one day — the subtraction operation is what the DATEADD function is all about. DATEADD can add (you subtract by using negative numbers) any amount of time you want to deal with. You just tell it what date you want to operate on, and what unit of time you want to add to it (days, weeks, years, minutes, and so on). On the surface, you should just be able to grab today's date with GETDATE() and then use DATEADD to subtract one day. The problem is that GETDATE() returns the datetime data type and therefore includes the current time of day, so we would get back only rows from the previous day that happened at the same time of day down to 3.3333 milliseconds (the level of precision for a datetime field) — not a likely match. So we took things one more step and used the CAST function to cast the dates on both sides of the equation to a data type that does not support time-of-day-less before comparison. Therefore, the view will show any sale that happened any time on the previous date.

> Note that this code would not have worked on SQL Server 2005 and earlier installations, as the Date data type is new with SQL Server 2008. In older versions of SQL Server, we would use the CONVERT function to change the date to a varchar formatted without the time, and then perform the comparison.

Using a View to Change Data — Before INSTEAD OF Triggers

As we've said before, a view works *mostly* like a table does from an in-use perspective (obviously, creating them works quite a bit differently). Now we're going to come across some differences, however.

It's surprising to many, but you can run INSERT, UPDATE, and DELETE statements against a view successfully. There are several things, however, that you need to keep in mind when changing data through a view:

❑ If the view contains a join, you won't, in most cases, be able to INSERT or DELETE data unless you make use of an INSTEAD OF trigger. An UPDATE can, in some cases (as long as you are only updating columns that are sourced from a single table), work without INSTEAD OF triggers, but it requires some planning, or you'll bump into problems very quickly.

❑ If your view references only a single table, then you can INSERT data using a view without the use of an INSTEAD OF trigger provided all the required fields in the table are exposed in the view or have defaults. Even for single table views, if there is a column not represented in the view that does not have a default value, then you must use an INSTEAD OF trigger if you want to allow an INSERT.

❑ You can, to a limited extent, restrict what is and isn't inserted or updated in a view.

Now — I've already mentioned INSTEAD OF triggers several times. The problem here is the complexity of INSTEAD OF triggers and that we haven't discussed triggers to any significant extent yet. As is often the case in SQL Server items, we have something of the old chicken vs. egg thing going ("Which came first?"). I need to discuss INSTEAD OF triggers because of their relevance to views, but we're also not ready to talk about INSTEAD OF triggers unless we understand both of the objects (tables and views) that they can be created against.

The way we are going to handle things for this chapter is to address views the way they used to be — before there was such a thing as INSTEAD OF triggers. While we won't deal with the specifics of INSTEAD OF triggers in this chapter, we'll make sure we understand when they must be used. We'll then come back and address these issues more fully when we look briefly at INSTEAD OF triggers in Chapter 15.

> *Having said that, I will provide this bit of context — An* INSTEAD OF *trigger is a special kind of trigger that essentially runs "instead" of whatever statement caused the trigger to fire. The result is that it can see what your statement would have done, and then make decisions right in the trigger about how to resolve any conflicts or other issues that might have come up. It's very powerful, but also fairly complex stuff, which is why we defer it for now.*

Dealing with Changes in Views with Joined Data

If the view has more than one table, then using a view to modify data is, in many cases, out — sort of anyway — unless you use an INSTEAD OF trigger (more on this in a moment). Since it creates some ambiguities in the key arrangements, Microsoft locks you out by default when there are multiple tables. To resolve this, you can use an INSTEAD OF trigger to examine the altered data and explicitly tell SQL Server what you want to do with it.

Required Fields Must Appear in the View or Have Default Value

By default, if you are using a view to insert data (there must be a single table SELECT in the underlying query or at least you must limit the insert to affect just one table and have all required columns represented), then you must be able to supply some value for all required fields (fields that don't allow NULLs). Note that by "supply some value" I don't mean that it has to be in the SELECT list — a default covers the bill rather nicely. Just be aware that any columns that do not have defaults and do not accept

NULL values will need to appear in the view in order for INSERTs to be allowed through the view. The only way to get around this is — you guessed it — with an INSTEAD OF trigger.

Limit What's Inserted into Views — WITH CHECK OPTION

The WITH CHECK OPTION is one of those obscure features in SQL Server. The rules are simple — in order to update or insert data using the view, the resulting row must qualify to appear in the view results. Restated, the inserted or updated row must meet any WHERE criterion that's used in the SELECT statement that underlies your view.

Try It Out   **WITH CHECK OPTION**

To illustrate the WITH CHECK OPTION, let's continue working with the AdventureWorks2008 database, and create a view to show only Portland, Oregon area addresses. We have only limited fields to work with in our Address table, so we're going to have to make use of the PostalCode in order to figure out where the area address is. We've been provided enough information to allow us to filter based on PostalCodes that start with 970, 971, and 972 for the Portland side of the border, and 98660 to 98699 for the Vancouver, Washington side, so we apply it in a view:

```
CREATE VIEW PortlandAreaAddresses_vw
AS
SELECT AddressID,
       AddressLine1,
       City,
       StateProvinceID,
       PostalCode,
       ModifiedDate
FROM Person.Address
WHERE PostalCode LIKE '970%'
   OR PostalCode LIKE '971%'
   OR PostalCode LIKE '972%'
   OR PostalCode LIKE '986[6-9]%'
WITH CHECK OPTION;
```

Run a SELECT * against this view, and you return about 792 rows:

```
AddressID  AddressLine1          City        StProvID PostalCode ModifiedDate
---------- --------------------- ----------- -------- ---------- ------------
22         636 Vine Hill Way     Portland    58       97205      2001-06-24
312        1286 Cincerto Circle  Lake Oswego 58       97034      2002-01-23
322        1 Mt. Dell Drive      Portland    58       97205      2002-01-24
...
...
29792      5186 Oeffler Ln.      Beaverton   58       97005      2003-03-20
29822      2613 West I St.       Beaverton   58       97005      2003-12-25
29856      1132 Plymouth Dr.     Lake Oswego 58       97034      2004-04-07

(792 row(s) affected)
```

Now try to update one of the rows using the view — set the `PostalCode` to anything other than a value starting with 97 or 98:

```
UPDATE PortlandAreaAddresses_vw
SET PostalCode = '33333'   -- it was 97205
WHERE AddressID = 22;
```

SQL Server promptly tells you that you are a scoundrel and that you should be burned at the stake for your actions — well, not really, but it does make its point:

```
Msg 550, Level 16, State 1, Line 1
The attempted insert or update failed because the target view either specifies WITH
CHECK OPTION or spans a view that specifies WITH CHECK OPTION and one or more rows
resulting from the operation did not qualify under the CHECK OPTION constraint.
The statement has been terminated.
```

How It Works

Our `WHERE` clause filters things in the view to show only postal codes that start with 970, 971, 972, or 9866-9869, and the `WITH CHECK OPTION` says any `INSERT` or `UPDATE` statements must meet that `WHERE` clause criteria (which a (33333) postal code doesn't).

Since our update wouldn't meet the `WHERE` clause criteria, it is thrown out; however, if we were to update the row right in the base table:

```
UPDATE Person.Address
SET PostalCode = '33333'   -- it was 97205
WHERE AddressID = 22;
```

SQL Server is a lot friendlier:

```
(1 row(s) affected)
```

The restriction applies only to the view — not to the underlying table. This can actually be quite handy in a rare circumstance or two. Imagine a situation where you want to allow some users to insert or update data in a table, but only when the updated or inserted data meets certain criteria. We could easily deal with this restriction by adding a `CHECK` constraint to our underlying table — but this might not always be an ideal solution.

Imagine now that we've added a second requirement — we still want other users to be able to `INSERT` data into the table without meeting these criteria. Uh oh, the `CHECK` constraint will not discriminate between users. By using a view together with a `WITH CHECK OPTION`, we can point the restricted users to the view, and let the unrestricted users make use of the base table or a view that has no such restriction.

Note that this works on an `INSERT`, too. Run an `INSERT` that violates the `WHERE` clause and you'll see your old friend, the "terminator" error, exactly as we did with the `UPDATE`.

Editing Views with T-SQL

The main thing to remember when you edit views with T-SQL is that you are completely replacing the existing view. The only differences between using the ALTER VIEW statement and the CREATE VIEW statement are:

- ❑ ALTER VIEW expects to find an existing view, whereas CREATE doesn't.
- ❑ ALTER VIEW retains any permissions that have been established for the view.
- ❑ ALTER VIEW retains any dependency information.

The second of these is the biggie. If you perform a DROP, and then use a CREATE, you have *almost* the same effect as using an ALTER VIEW statement. The problem is that you need to entirely re-establish your permissions on who can and can't use the view.

Dropping Views

It doesn't get much easier than this:

```
DROP VIEW <view name>, [<view name>,[ ...n]]
```

And it's gone.

Creating and Editing Views in the Management Studio

For people who really don't know what they are doing, this has to be a rather cool feature in the Management Studio. Building views is a snap, and you really don't have to know all that much about queries in order to get it done.

To take a look at this, fire up the Management Studio, open up the AdventureWorks2008 database sub-node of the Databases node and right-click Views. Select New View, and up comes the dialog shown in Figure 10-1.

This dialog makes it easy for us to choose which tables we're going to be including data from. The Address table is selected in Figure 10-1, but we're going to be working with not only a different table — but *four* other tables.

This should beg the question: "How do I select more than one table?" Easy — just hold down your Ctrl key while selecting all the tables you want. For now, start by clicking on the Customer table, and then press and hold your Ctrl key while you also select the SalesOrderHeader, SalesOrderDetail, and Product tables. You should wind up with all of them highlighted. Now click Add, and SQL Server will add several tables to our view (indeed, on most systems, you should be able to see them being added to the view editor that we're about to take a look at).

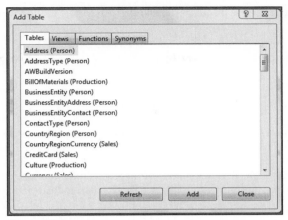

Figure 10-1

Before we close the Add Table dialog, take a moment to notice the Views, Functions, and Synonym tabs along the top of this dialog. Because views can reference these objects directly, the dialog gives you a way of adding them directly.

For now, however, just click Add and check out the view editor that is brought up, as in Figure 10-2.

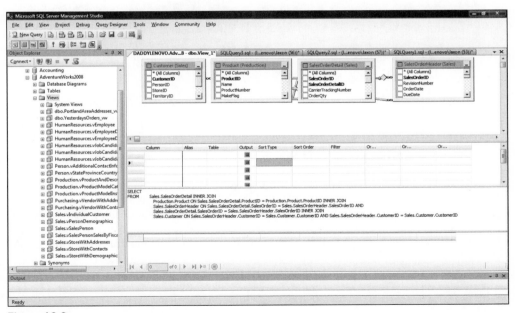

Figure 10-2

There are four panes to the View Builder — each of which can be independently turned on or off:

- ❑ The Diagram pane
- ❑ The Criteria pane
- ❑ The SQL pane
- ❑ The Results pane

For those of you who have worked with Access at all, the Diagram pane works much as it does in Access queries. You can add and remove tables, and even define relationships. Each of those added tables, checked columns, and defined relationships will automatically be reflected in the SQL pane in the form of the SQL required to match the diagram. To identify each of the icons on the toolbar, just hover your mouse pointer over them for a moment or two, and you will get a ToolTip that indicates the purpose of each button.

> You can add tables either by right-clicking in the Diagram pane (the top one in Figure 10-2) and choosing Add Table or by clicking on the Add Table toolbar button (the one with an arrow pointing right in the very top left of the icon).

Now select some columns, as shown in Figure 10-3.

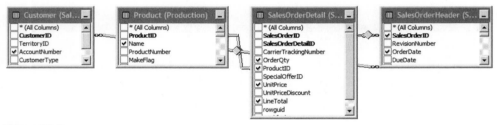

Figure 10-3

Note that I am just showing the diagram pane here to save space. If you have the Grid pane up while you check the above, then you would see each column appear in the Grid pane as you select it. With the SQL pane up, you will also see it appear in the SQL code.

In case you haven't recognized it yet, we're building the same view that we built as our first complex view (`CustomerOrders_vw`). The only thing that's tricky at all is the computed column (`TotalDiscount`). To do that one, either we have to manually type the equation into the SQL pane, or we can type it into the Column column in the Grid pane along with its alias (see Figure 10-4).

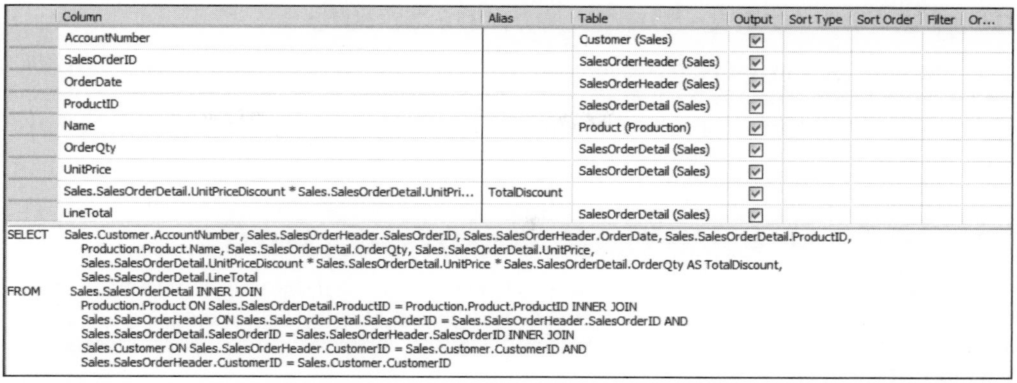

Column	Alias	Table	Output	Sort Type	Sort Order	Filter	Or...
AccountNumber		Customer (Sales)	☑				
SalesOrderID		SalesOrderHeader (Sales)	☑				
OrderDate		SalesOrderHeader (Sales)	☑				
ProductID		SalesOrderDetail (Sales)	☑				
Name		Product (Production)	☑				
OrderQty		SalesOrderDetail (Sales)	☑				
UnitPrice		SalesOrderDetail (Sales)	☑				
Sales.SalesOrderDetail.UnitPriceDiscount * Sales.SalesOrderDetail.UnitPri...	TotalDiscount		☑				
LineTotal		SalesOrderDetail (Sales)	☑				

```
SELECT   Sales.Customer.AccountNumber, Sales.SalesOrderHeader.SalesOrderID, Sales.SalesOrderHeader.OrderDate, Sales.SalesOrderDetail.ProductID,
         Production.Product.Name, Sales.SalesOrderDetail.OrderQty, Sales.SalesOrderDetail.UnitPrice,
         Sales.SalesOrderDetail.UnitPriceDiscount * Sales.SalesOrderDetail.UnitPrice * Sales.SalesOrderDetail.OrderQty AS TotalDiscount,
         Sales.SalesOrderDetail.LineTotal
FROM     Sales.SalesOrderDetail INNER JOIN
         Production.Product ON Sales.SalesOrderDetail.ProductID = Production.Product.ProductID INNER JOIN
         Sales.SalesOrderHeader ON Sales.SalesOrderDetail.SalesOrderID = Sales.SalesOrderHeader.SalesOrderID AND
         Sales.SalesOrderDetail.SalesOrderID = Sales.SalesOrderHeader.SalesOrderID INNER JOIN
         Sales.Customer ON Sales.SalesOrderHeader.CustomerID = Sales.Customer.CustomerID AND
         Sales.SalesOrderHeader.CustomerID = Sales.Customer.CustomerID
```

Figure 10-4

When all is said and done, the View Builder gives us the following SQL code:

```
SELECT   Sales.Customer.AccountNumber,
         Sales.SalesOrderHeader.SalesOrderID,
         Sales.SalesOrderHeader.OrderDate,
         Sales.SalesOrderDetail.ProductID,
         Production.Product.Name,
         Sales.SalesOrderDetail.OrderQty,
         Sales.SalesOrderDetail.UnitPrice,
         Sales.SalesOrderDetail.UnitPriceDiscount *
            Sales.SalesOrderDetail.UnitPrice *
            Sales.SalesOrderDetail.OrderQty AS TotalDiscount,
         Sales.SalesOrderDetail.LineTotal
FROM     Sales.SalesOrderDetail
INNER JOIN Production.Product
  ON Sales.SalesOrderDetail.ProductID = Production.Product.ProductID
INNER JOIN Sales.SalesOrderHeader
  ON Sales.SalesOrderDetail.SalesOrderID = Sales.SalesOrderHeader.SalesOrderID
  AND Sales.SalesOrderDetail.SalesOrderID = Sales.SalesOrderHeader.SalesOrderID
INNER JOIN Sales.Customer
  ON Sales.SalesOrderHeader.CustomerID = Sales.Customer.CustomerID
  AND Sales.SalesOrderHeader.CustomerID = Sales.Customer.CustomerID
```

While it's not formatted the same, if you look it over, you'll find that it's basically the same code we wrote by hand!

> If you've been struggling with learning your T-SQL query syntax, you can use this tool to play around with the syntax of a query. Just drag and drop some tables into the Diagram pane, select the column you want from each table, and, for the most part, SQL Server will build you a query — you can then use the syntax from the View Builder to learn how to build it yourself next time.

Now go ahead and save it (the disk icon in the toolbar is how I do it) as `CustomerOrders2_vw` and close the View Builder.

Editing Views in the Management Studio

Modifying your view in the Management Studio is as easy as creating it was. The only real difference is that you need to navigate to your specific view and right-click it — then choose Modify, and you'll be greeted with the same friendly query designer that we used with our query when it was created.

Auditing: Displaying Existing Code

What do you do when you have a view, but you're not sure what it does? The first option should be easy at this point — just go into the Management Studio like you're going to edit the view. Go to the Views sub-node, select the view you want to edit, right-click, and choose Modify View. You'll see the code behind the view complete with color-coding.

Unfortunately, we don't always have the option of having the Management Studio around to hold our hand through this stuff (we may be using a lighter weight tool of some sort. The bright side is that we have two reliable ways of getting at the actual view definition:

❑   `sp_helptext`

❑   The `sys.modules metadata` function

Using `sp_helptext` is highly preferable, as when new releases come out, it will automatically be updated for changes to the system tables.

> *There is, arguably, a third option: directly accessing the syscomments system table. Microsoft has been warning for a couple of releases now about not using system tables directly. As of this writing, syscomments is still there, but the results that come out of it when you run a query have some bogus information in them. They may work fine for you, but, given that Microsoft has been recommending against using syscomments for a while now, it probably makes sense to move on to the more "approved" methods.*

Let's run `sp_helptext` against one of the views we created in our AdventureWorks2008 database earlier in the chapter — YesterdaysOrders_vw:

```
EXEC sp_helptext YesterdaysOrders_vw;
```

SQL Server obliges us with the code for the view:

```
Text
--------------------------------------------------------------------
CREATE VIEW YesterdaysOrders_vw
AS
SELECT    sc.AccountNumber,
          soh.SalesOrderID,
          soh.OrderDate,
          sod.ProductID,
          pp.Name,
          sod.OrderQty,
          sod.UnitPrice,
          sod.UnitPriceDiscount * sod.UnitPrice * sod.OrderQty AS TotalDiscount,
          sod.LineTotal
```

```
FROM      Sales.Customer AS sc
INNER JOIN   Sales.SalesOrderHeader AS soh
      ON sc.CustomerID = soh.CustomerID
INNER JOIN   Sales.SalesOrderDetail AS sod
      ON soh.SalesOrderID = sod.SalesOrderID
INNER JOIN Production.Product AS pp
      ON sod.ProductID = pp.ProductID
WHERE CAST(soh.OrderDate AS Date) =
      CAST(DATEADD(day,-1,GETDATE()) AS Date)
```

Now let's try it the other way — using the `sys.sql_modules` metadata function. The only major hassle with using this function is that all the objects are coded in object IDs.

> Object IDs are SQL Server's internal way of keeping track of things. They are integer values rather than the names that you're used to for your objects. In general, they are outside the scope of this book, but it is good to realize they are there, as you will find them used by scripts you may copy from other people or just bump into them later in your SQL endeavors.

Fortunately, you can get around this by using the `OBJECT_ID()` function:

```
SELECT *
FROM sys.sql_modules
WHERE object_id = OBJECT_ID('dbo.YesterdaysOrders_vw');
```

Again, you get the same block of code (indeed, all `sp_helptext` does is run what amounts to this same query).

> Note that, by default, the Results in Text option in the Query window limits the results from any individual column to just 256 characters, so running the previous `sys.sql_modules` query may get you a truncated version of the text for the view. If you look at it in grid mode, the limit is 64k, so everything comes through. You can change the maximum number of characters per column by going to Tools ⇨ Options ⇨ Query Results ⇨ SQL Server ⇨ Results to Text and changing the appropriate setting.

Protecting Code: Encrypting Views

If you're building any kind of commercial software product, odds are that you're interested in protecting your source code. Views are the first place we see the opportunity to do just that.

All you have to do to encrypt your view is use the `WITH ENCRYPTION` option. This one has a couple of tricks to it if you're used to the `WITH CHECK OPTION` clause:

❑ `WITH ENCRYPTION` goes after the name of the view, but *before* the `AS` keyword

❑ `WITH ENCRYPTION` does not use the `OPTION` keyword

In addition, remember that if you use an ALTER VIEW statement, you are entirely replacing the existing view except for access rights. This means that the encryption is also replaced. If you want the altered view to be encrypted, then you must use the WITH ENCRYPTION clause in the ALTER VIEW statement.

Let's do an ALTER VIEW on our CustomerOrders_vw view that we created in AdventureWorks2008. If you haven't yet created the CustomerOrders_vw view, then just change the ALTER to CREATE:

```
ALTER VIEW CustomerOrders_vw
WITH ENCRYPTION
AS
SELECT     sc.AccountNumber,
           soh.SalesOrderID,
           soh.OrderDate,
           sod.ProductID,
           pp.Name,
           sod.OrderQty,
           sod.UnitPrice,
           sod.UnitPriceDiscount * sod.UnitPrice * sod.OrderQty AS TotalDiscount,
           sod.LineTotal
FROM       Sales.Customer AS sc
INNER JOIN    Sales.SalesOrderHeader AS soh
       ON sc.CustomerID = soh.CustomerID
INNER JOIN    Sales.SalesOrderDetail AS sod
       ON soh.SalesOrderID = sod.SalesOrderID
INNER JOIN Production.Product AS pp
       ON sod.ProductID = pp.ProductID;
```

Now do an sp_helptext on your CustomerOrders_vw:

```
EXEC sp_helptext CustomerOrders_vw
```

SQL Server promptly tells us that it can't do what we're asking:

```
The text for object 'CustomerOrders_vw' is encrypted.
```

The heck you say, and promptly go to the sys.sql_modules metadata function:

```
SELECT *
FROM sys.sql_modules
WHERE object_id = OBJECT_ID('dbo.CustomerOrders_vw');
```

But that doesn't get you very far either — SQL Server recognizes that the table was encrypted and will give you a NULL result.

In short — your code is safe and sound. Even if you pull it up in other viewers (such as the Management Studio, which actually won't even give you the Modify option on an encrypted table), you'll find it useless.

> Make sure you store your source code somewhere before using the WITH ENCRYPTION option. Once it's been encrypted, there is no way to get it back. If you haven't stored your code away somewhere and you need to change it, then you may find yourself re-writing it from scratch.

About Schema Binding

Schema binding essentially takes the things that your view is dependent upon (tables or other views), and "binds" them to that view. The significance of this is that no one can make alterations to those objects (CREATE, ALTER) unless they drop the schema-bound view first.

Why would you want to do this? Well, there are a few reasons why this can come in handy:

❑   It prevents your view from becoming "orphaned" by alterations in underlying objects. Imagine, for a moment, that someone performs a DROP or makes some other change (even deleting a column could cause your view grief), but doesn't pay attention to your view. Oops. If the view is schema bound, then this is prevented from happening.

❑   To allow indexed views: If you want an index on your view, you *must* create it using the SCHEMABINDING option. (We'll look at indexed views just a few paragraphs from now.)

❑   If you are going to create a schema-bound user-defined function (and there are instances where your function *must* be schema bound) that references your view, then your view must also be schema bound.

Keep these in mind as you are building your views.

Making Your View Look Like a Table with VIEW_METADATA

This option has the effect of making your view look very much like an actual table to DB-LIB, ODBC, and OLE-DB clients. Without this option, the metadata passed back to the client API is that of the base table(s) that your view relies on.

Providing this metadata information is required to allow for any client-side cursors (cursors your client application manages) to be updatable. Note that, if you want to support such cursors, you're also going to need to use an INSTEAD OF trigger.

Indexed (Materialized) Views

When a view is referred to, the logic in the query that makes up the view is essentially incorporated into the calling query. Unfortunately, this means that the calling query just gets that much more complex. The extra overhead of figuring out the impact of the view (and what data it represents) on the fly can actually get very high. What's more, you're often including additional joins into your query in the form of the tables that are joined in the view. Indexed views give us a way of taking care of some of this impact before the query is ever run.

An indexed view is essentially a view that has had a set of unique values "materialized" into the form of a clustered index. The advantage of this is that it provides a very quick lookup in terms of pulling the information behind a view together. After the first index (which must be a clustered index against a unique set of values), SQL Server can also build additional indexes on the view using the cluster key from the first index as a reference point. That said, nothing comes for free — there are some restrictions about when you can and can't build indexes on views (I hope you're ready for this one — it's an awfully long list!):

❑   The view must use the SCHEMABINDING option.

❑   If it references any user-defined functions (more on these later), then these must also be schema bound.

❑   The view must not reference any other views — just tables and UDFs.

❑   All tables and UDFs referenced in the view must utilize a two-part (not even three-part and four-part names are allowed) naming convention (for example dbo.Customers, BillyBob .SomeUDF) and must also have the same owner as the view.

❑   The view must be in the same database as all objects referenced by the view.

❑   The ANSI_NULLS and QUOTED_IDENTIFIER options must have been turned on (using the SET command) at the time the view and all underlying tables were created.

❑   Any functions referenced by the view must be deterministic.

To create an example indexed view, let's start by making a few alterations to the CustomerOrders_vw object that we created earlier in the chapter:

```
ALTER VIEW CustomerOrders_vw
WITH SCHEMABINDING
AS
SELECT    sc.AccountNumber,
          soh.SalesOrderID,
          soh.OrderDate,
          sod.ProductID,
          pp.Name,
          sod.OrderQty,
          sod.UnitPrice,
          sod.UnitPriceDiscount * sod.UnitPrice * sod.OrderQty AS TotalDiscount,
          sod.LineTotal
FROM      Sales.Customer AS sc
INNER JOIN    Sales.SalesOrderHeader AS soh
      ON sc.CustomerID = soh.CustomerID
INNER JOIN    Sales.SalesOrderDetail AS sod
      ON soh.SalesOrderID = sod.SalesOrderID
INNER JOIN Production.Product AS pp
      ON sod.ProductID = pp.ProductID;
```

The big thing to notice here is that we had to make our view use the SCHEMABINDING option. This is really just the beginning though — we don't have an indexed view as yet. Instead, what we have is a view that *can* be indexed. Before we actually build the index, let's get a baseline of how queries against our view would currently be executed. Take a simple SELECT against the view:

```
SELECT * FROM CustomerOrders_vw;
```

Seems simple enough, but remember that there are four tables underlying this view. If we choose to display the estimated execution plan (one of the icons on the toolbar) as shown in Figure 10-5, we see a somewhat complex set of steps to execute our query.

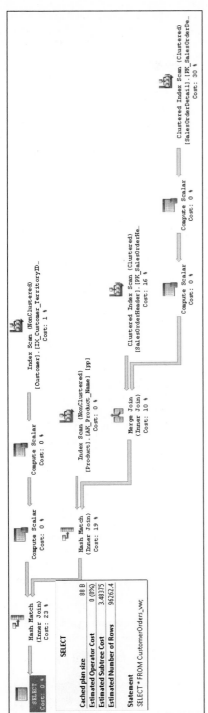

SELECT
Cost: 0 %

Hash Match
(Inner Join)
Cost: 23 %

SELECT

Cached plan size	88 B
Estimated Operator Cost	0 (0%)
Estimated Subtree Cost	3.48375
Estimated Number of Rows	9626.2.4

Statement
SELECT * FROM CustomerOrders_vw;

Compute Scalar
Cost: 0 %

Hash Match
(Inner Join)
Cost: 19 %

Compute Scalar
Cost: 0 %

Index Scan (NonClustered)
[Customer].[IX_Customer_TerritoryID...
Cost: 1 %

Index Scan (NonClustered)
[Product].[AK_Product_Name] [pp]
Cost: 0 %

Merge Join
(Inner Join)
Cost: 10 %

Clustered Index Scan (Clustered)
[SalesOrderHeader].[PK_SalesOrderHe...
Cost: 16 %

Compute Scalar
Cost: 0 %

Compute Scalar
Cost: 0 %

Clustered Index Scan (Clustered)
[SalesOrderDetail].[PK_SalesOrderDe...
Cost: 30 %

Figure 10-5

You can get the yellow popup by hovering your mouse over the top-left node of the execution plan. This is the top node of the execution plan, and looking at the Estimated Subtree Cost on this node shows us the estimated coast for the entire query (for me, it is 3.49114). Now that we've seen how complex the query is and seen the estimated cost, we're ready to move on to creating the index.

When we create the index, the first index created on the view must be both clustered and unique:

```
CREATE UNIQUE CLUSTERED INDEX ivCustomerOrders
ON CustomerOrders_vw(AccountNumber, SalesOrderID, ProductID);
```

Once this command has executed, we have a clustered index on our view (Figure 10-6), and we're ready to again check out our Estimated Execution Plan for our basic SELECT.

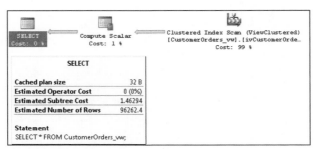

Figure 10-6

Notice that this is a substantially more simplistic query. The estimated cost of execution has also dropped by over 50%. Does this mean our index is a good idea? Well, simply put — no. It means it *might* be. Much like any index, you need to keep in mind the maintenance cost of the index. How much is maintaining this index going to slow down INSERT, UPDATE, and DELETE statements against the underlying tables? Basically, it's a balancing act, and each database and each index is a separate decision. That said, indexed views can be a powerful tool to have in your arsenal, so weigh them carefully!

Summary

Views tend to be either the most over- or most under-used tools in most of the databases I've seen. Some people like to use them to abstract seemingly everything (often forgetting that they are adding another layer to the process when they do this). Others just seem to forget that views are even an option. Personally, like most things, I think you should use a view when it's the right tool to use — not before, not after. Things to remember with views include:

❑   Stay away from building views based on views — instead, adapt the appropriate query information from the first view into your new view.

❑   Remember that a view using the WITH CHECK OPTION provides some flexibility that can't be duplicated with a normal CHECK constraint.

❑ Encrypt views when you don't want others to be able to see your source code — either for commercial products or general security reasons, but also remember to keep a copy of your unencrypted code; it can't be retrieved after you've encrypted it.

❑ Using an ALTER VIEW completely replaces the existing view other than permissions. This means you must include the WITH ENCRYPTION and WITH CHECK OPTION clauses in the ALTER statement if you want encryption and restrictions to be in effect in the altered view.

❑ Use sp_helptext to display the supporting code for a view — avoid using the system tables.

❑ Minimize the user of views for production queries — they add additional overhead and hurt performance.

Common uses for views include:

❑ Filtering rows

❑ Protecting sensitive data

❑ Reducing database complexity

❑ Abstracting multiple physical databases into one logical database

In our next chapter, we'll take a look at batches and scripting. Batches and scripting will lead us right into stored procedures — the closest thing that SQL Server has to its own programs.

Exercises

1. Add a view called HumanResources.Managers in the AdventureWorks2008 database that shows only employees that supervise other employees.

2. Change the view you just created to be encrypted.

3. Build an index against your new view based on the ManagerID and EmployeeID columns.

Writing Scripts and Batches

Whether you've realized it or not, you've already been writing SQL *scripts*. Every CREATE statement that you write, every ALTER, every SELECT is all (if you're running a single statement) or part (multiple statements) of a script. It's hard to get excited, however, over a script with one line in it — could you imagine Hamlet's "To be, or not to be ..." if it had never had the lines that follow — you wouldn't have any context for what he was talking about.

SQL scripts are much the same way. Things get quite a bit more interesting when you string several commands together into a longer script — a full play or at least an act to finish our Shakespeare analogy. Now imagine that we add a richer set of language elements from .NET to the equation — now we're ready to write an epic!

Scripts generally have a unified goal. That is, all the commands that are in a script are usually building up to one overall purpose. Examples include scripts to build a database (these might be used for a system installation), scripts for system maintenance (backups, Database Consistency Checker utilities (DBCCs), index defragmentation, and more) — scripts for anything where several commands are usually run together.

We will be looking into scripts during this chapter and adding in the notion of *batches* — which control how SQL Server groups your commands together. In addition, we will take a look at *sqlcmd* — the command-line utility, and how it relates to scripts.

> *sqlcmd was first added in SQL Server 2005. For backward compatibility only, SQL Server continues to support osql.exe (the previous tool that did command line work). You may also see references to isql.exe (do not confuse this with isqlw.exe), which served this same function in earlier releases. isql.exe is no longer supported.*

Script Basics

A script technically isn't a script until you store it in a file where it can be pulled up and reused. SQL scripts are stored as text files. The SQL Server Management Studio provides many tools to help you with your script writing. The basic query window is color coded to help you not only recognize keywords, but also understand their nature. In addition, you have Intellisense, a step debugger, code templates, the object browser, and more.

Scripts are usually treated as a unit. That is, you are normally executing the entire script or nothing at all. They can make use of both system functions and local variables. As an example, let's look at a script that would insert order records in the Accounting database that we created back in Chapter 5:

```
USE Accounting;
DECLARE @Ident int;

INSERT INTO Orders
(CustomerNo,OrderDate, EmployeeID)
VALUES
(1, GETDATE(), 1);
SELECT @Ident = @@IDENTITY;
INSERT INTO OrderDetails
(OrderID, PartNo, Description, UnitPrice, Qty)
VALUES
(@Ident, '2R2416', 'Cylinder Head', 1300, 2);
SELECT 'The OrderID of the INSERTed row is ' + CONVERT(varchar(8),@Ident);
```

If you didn't keep your populated version of the Accounting database, a script to re-create it in a state usable for this chapter can be downloaded from the Wrox support Website (`wrox.com`*) or my personal support site at* `www.professionalsql.com`*.*

We have six distinct commands working here, covering a range of different things that we might do in a script. We're using both system functions and local variables, the USE statement, INSERT statements, and both assignment and regular versions of the SELECT statement. They are all working in unison to accomplish one task — to insert complete orders into the database.

The USE Statement

The USE statement sets the current database. This affects any place where we are making use of default values for the database portion of our fully qualified object name. In this particular example, we have not indicated what database the tables in our INSERT or SELECT statements are from, but, since we've included a USE statement prior to our INSERT and SELECT statements, they will use that database (in this case, Accounting). Without our USE statement, we would be at the mercy of whoever executes the script to make certain that the correct database was current when the script was executed.

> Don't take this as meaning that you should always include a USE statement in your script — it depends on what the purpose of the script is. If your intent is to have a general-purpose script, then leaving out the USE statement might actually be helpful.
>
> Usually, if you are naming database-specific tables in your script (that is, non-system tables), then you want to use the USE command. I also find it very helpful if the script is meant to modify a specific database — as I've said in prior chapters, I can't tell you how many times I've accidentally created a large number of tables in the master database that were intended for a user database.

Next we have a DECLARE statement to declares a variable. We've seen DECLARE statements used in a few scripts used earlier in the book, but let's visit them a bit more formally.

Declaring Variables

The DECLARE statement has a pretty simple syntax:

```
DECLARE @<variable name> <variable type>[= <value>][,
  @<variable name> <variable type>[= <value>][,
  @<variable name> <variable type>[= <value>]]]
```

You can declare just one variable at a time, or several. It's common to see people reuse the DECLARE statement with each variable they declare, rather than use the comma-separated method. It's up to you, but no matter which method you choose, you must initialize the variable (using the "=" syntax) or the value of your variable will be NULL until you explicitly set it to some other value.

In this case, we've declared a local variable called @ident as an integer. I've chosen not to initialize it as the whole purpose of this variable is to accept a value from another source. Technically, we could have gotten away without declaring this variable — instead, we could have chosen to just use @@IDENTITY directly. @@IDENTITY is a system function. It is always available, and supplies the last identity value that was assigned in the current connection. As with most system functions, you should make a habit of explicitly moving the value in @@IDENTITY to a local variable. That way, you're sure that it won't get changed accidentally. There was no danger of that in this case, but, as always, be consistent.

> I like to move a value I'm taking from a system function into my own variable. That way I can safely use the value and know that it's being changed only when I change it. With the system function itself, you sometimes can't be certain when it's going to change because most system functions are not set by you, but by the system. That creates a situation where it would be very easy to have the system change a value at a time you weren't expecting it, and wind up with the most dreaded of all computer terms: unpredictable results.

Setting the Value in Your Variables

Well, we now know how to declare our variables, but the question that follows is, "How do we change their values?" There are two ways to set the value in a variable. You can use a SELECT statement or a SET statement. Functionally, they work almost the same, except that a SELECT statement has the power to have the source value come from a column within the SELECT statement.

So why have two ways of doing this? Actually, I still don't know. After publishing four books that ask this very question, I figured someone would e-mail me and give me a good answer — they didn't. Suffice to say that SET is now part of the ANSI/ISO standard, and that's why it's been put in there. However, I can't find anything wrong with the same functionality in SELECT — even ANSI/ISO seems to think that it's OK. I'm sure there's a purpose in the redundancy, but what it is I can't tell you. That said, there are some differences in the way they are used in practice.

Setting Variables Using SET

SET is usually used for setting variables in the fashion that you would see in more procedural languages. Examples of typical uses would be:

```
SET @TotalCost = 10
SET @TotalCost = @UnitCost * 1.1
```

Notice that these are all straight assignments that use either explicit values or another variable. With a SET, you cannot assign a value to a variable from a query — you have to separate the query from the SET. For example:

```
USE AdventureWorks2008;

DECLARE @Test money;
SET @Test = MAX(UnitPrice) FROM [Order Details];
SELECT @Test;
```

causes an error, but:

```
USE AdventureWorks2008;

DECLARE @Test money;
SET @Test = (SELECT MAX(UnitPrice) FROM Sales.SalesOrderDetail);
SELECT @Test;
```

works just fine.

> *Although this latter syntax works, by convention, code is never implemented this way. Again, I don't know for sure why it's "just not done that way," but I suspect that it has to do with readability — you want a SELECT statement to be related to retrieving table data, and a SET to be about simple variable assignments.*

Setting Variables Using SELECT

SELECT is usually used to assign variable values when the source of the information you're storing in the variable is from a query. For example, our last illustration would be typically done using a SELECT:

```
USE AdventureWorks2008;

DECLARE @Test money;
SELECT @Test = MAX(UnitPrice) FROM Sales.SalesOrderDetail;
SELECT @Test;
```

Notice that this is a little cleaner (it takes less verbiage to do the same thing).

So again, the convention on when to use which goes like this:

❑ Use SET when you are performing a simple assignment of a variable — where your value is already known in the form of an explicit value or some other variable.

❑ Use SELECT when you are basing the assignment of your variable on a query.

I'm not going to pick any bones about the fact that you'll see me violate this last convention in many places in this book. Using SET *for variable assignment first appeared in version 7.0, and I must admit that nearly a decade after that release, I still haven't completely adapted yet. Nonetheless, this seems to be something that's really being pushed by Microsoft and the SQL Server community, so I strongly recommend that you start out on the right foot and adhere to the convention.*

Reviewing System Functions

There are over 30 parameterless system functions available. The older ones in the mix start with an @@ sign — a throwback to when they were commonly referred to as "Global Variables." Thankfully that name has gone away in favor of the more accurate "system functions," and the majority of all system functions now come without the @@ prefix. Some of the ones you should be most concerned with are in the table that follows:

Variable	Purpose	Comments
@@DATEFIRST	Returns what is currently set as the first day of the week (say, Sunday vs. Monday).	Is a system-wide setting — if someone changes the setting, you may not get the result you expect.
@@ERROR	Returns the error number of the last T-SQL statement executed on the current connection. Returns 0 if no error.	Is reset with each new statement. If you need the value preserved, move it to a local variable immediately after the execution of the statement for which you want to preserve the error code.
@@IDENTITY	Returns the last identity value inserted as a result of the last INSERT or SELECT INTO statement.	Is set to NULL if no identity value was generated. This is true even if the lack of an identity value was due to a failure of the statement to run. If multiple inserts are performed by just one statement, then only the last identity value is returned.
IDENT_CURRENT()	Returns the last identity value inserted for a specified table regardless of session or scope.	Nice in the sense that it doesn't get overwritten if you're inserting into multiple tables, but can give you a value other than what you were expecting if other connections are inserting into the specific table.
@@OPTIONS	Returns information about options that have been set using the SET command.	Since you get only one value back, but can have many options set, SQL Server uses binary flags to indicate what values are set. To test whether the option you are interested is set, you must use the option value together with a bitwise operator.

Continued

Variable	Purpose	Comments
@@REMSERVER	Used only in stored procedures. Returns the value of the server that called the stored procedure.	Handy when you want the sproc to behave differently depending on the remote server (often a geographic location) from which it was called. Still, in this era of .NET, I would question whether anything needing this variable might have been better written using other functionality found in .NET.
@@ROWCOUNT	One of the most used system functions. Returns the number of rows affected by the last statement.	Commonly used in non runtime error checking. For example, if you try to DELETE a row using a WHERE clause, and no rows are affected, then that would imply that something unexpected happened. You can then raise an error manually.
SCOPE_IDENTITY	Similar to @@IDENTITY, but returns the last identity inserted within the current session and scope.	Very useful for avoiding issues where a trigger or nested stored procedure has performed additional inserts that have overwritten your expected identity value.
@@SERVERNAME	Returns the name of the local server that the script is running from.	Can be changed by using sp_addserver and then restarting SQL Server, but rarely required.
@@TRANCOUNT	Returns the number of active transactions — essentially the transaction nesting level — for the current connection.	A ROLLBACK TRAN statement decrements @@TRANCOUNT to 0 unless you are using save points. BEGIN TRAN increments @@TRANCOUNT by 1, COMMIT TRAN decrements @@TRANCOUNT by 1.
@@VERSION	Returns the current version of SQL Server as well as the date, processor, and O/S architecture.	Unfortunately, this doesn't return the information into any kind of structured field arrangement, so you have to parse it if you want to use it to test for specific information. Also be sure to check out the xp_msver extended stored procedure.

Don't worry if you don't recognize some of the terms in a few of these. They will become clear in due time, and you will have this table or Appendix A to look back on for reference at a later date. The thing to remember is that there are sources you can go to in order to find out a whole host of information about the current state of your system and your activities.

Using @@IDENTITY

`@@IDENTITY` is one of the most important of all the system functions. An identity column is one where we don't supply a value, and SQL Server inserts a numbered value automatically.

In our example case, we obtain the value of `@@IDENTITY` right after performing an insert into the `Orders` table. The issue is that we don't supply the key value for that table — it's automatically created as we do the insert. Now we want to insert a record into the `OrderDetails` table, but we need to know the value of the primary key in the associated record in the `Orders` table (remember, there is a foreign key constraint on the `OrderDetails` table that references the `Orders` table). Because SQL Server generated that value instead of us supplying it, we need to have a way to retrieve that value for use in our dependent inserts later on in the script. `@@IDENTITY` gives us that automatically generated value because it was the last statement run.

In this example, we could have easily gotten away with not moving `@@IDENTITY` to a local variable — we could have just referenced it explicitly in our next `INSERT` query. I make a habit of always moving it to a local variable, however, to avoid errors on the occasions when I do need to keep a copy. An example of this kind of situation would be if we had yet another `INSERT` that was dependent on the identity value from the `INSERT` into the `Orders` table. If I hadn't moved it into a local variable, then it would be lost when I did the next `INSERT`, because it would have been overwritten with the value from the `OrderDetails` table, which, since `OrderDetails` has no identity column, means that `@@IDENTITY` would have been set to `NULL`. Moving the value of `@@IDENTITY` to a local variable also let me keep the value around for the statement where I printed out the value for later reference.

Let's create a couple of tables to try this out:

```
CREATE TABLE TestIdent
(
   IDCol    int    IDENTITY
   PRIMARY KEY
);

CREATE TABLE TestChild1
(
   IDcol    int
   PRIMARY KEY
   FOREIGN KEY
   REFERENCES TestIdent(IDCol)
);

CREATE TABLE TestChild2
(
   IDcol    int
   PRIMARY KEY
   FOREIGN KEY
   REFERENCES TestIdent(IDCol)
);
```

What we have here is a parent table — it has an identity column for a primary key (as it happens, that's the only column it has). We also have two child tables. They each are the subject of an identifying relationship — that is, they each take at least part (in this case all) of their primary key by placing a foreign key on another table (the parent). So what we have is a situation where the two child tables need to get their key from the parent. Therefore, we need to insert a record into the parent first, and then retrieve the identity value generated so we can make use of it in the other tables.

Try It Out   **Using @@IDENTITY**

Now that we have some tables to work with, we're ready to try a little test script:

```
/*******************************************
** This script illustrates how the identity
** value gets lost as soon as another INSERT
** happens
******************************************* */

DECLARE @Ident   int;  -- This will be a holding variable
/* We'll use it to show how we can
** move values from system functions
** into a safe place.
*/
INSERT INTO TestIdent
  DEFAULT VALUES;
SET @Ident = @@IDENTITY;
PRINT 'The value we got originally from @@IDENTITY was ' +
CONVERT(varchar(2),@Ident);
PRINT 'The value currently in @@IDENTITY is ' + CONVERT(varchar(2),@@IDENTITY);

/* On this first INSERT using @@IDENTITY, we're going to get lucky.
** We'll get a proper value because there is nothing between our
** original INSERT and this one. You'll see that on the INSERT that
** will follow after this one, we won't be so lucky anymore. */
INSERT INTO TestChild1
VALUES
  (@@IDENTITY);

PRINT 'The value we got originally from @@IDENTITY was ' +
CONVERT(varchar(2),@Ident);
IF (SELECT @@IDENTITY) IS NULL
  PRINT 'The value currently in @@IDENTITY is NULL';
ELSE
  PRINT 'The value currently in @@IDENTITY is ' + CONVERT(varchar(2),@@IDENTITY);
-- The next line is just a spacer for our print out
PRINT '';
/* The next line is going to blow up because the one column in
** the table is the primary key, and primary keys can't be set
** to NULL. @@IDENTITY will be NULL because we just issued an
** INSERT statement a few lines ago, and the table we did the
** INSERT into doesn't have an identity field. Perhaps the biggest
** thing to note here is when @@IDENTITY changed - right after
** the next INSERT statement. */
INSERT INTO TestChild2
VALUES
  (@@IDENTITY);
```

How It Works

What we're doing in this script is seeing what happens if we depend on @@IDENTITY directly rather than moving the value to a safe place. When we execute the preceding script, everything's going to work just fine until the final INSERT. That final statement is trying to make use of @@IDENTITY directly, but the preceding INSERT statement has already changed the value in @@IDENTITY. Because that statement is on a table with no identity column, the value in @@IDENTITY is set to NULL. Because we can't have a NULL value in our primary key, the last INSERT fails:

```
(1 row(s) affected)
The value we got originally from @@IDENTITY was 1
The value currently in @@IDENTITY is 1

(1 row(s) affected)
The value we got originally from @@IDENTITY was 1
The value currently in @@IDENTITY is NULL

Msg 515, Level 16, State 2, Line 41
Cannot insert the value NULL into column 'IDcol', table
'Accounting.dbo.TestChild2'; column does not allow nulls. INSERT fails.
The statement has been terminated.
```

If we make just one little change (to save the original @@IDENTITY value):

```
/******************************************
** This script illustrates how the identity
** value gets lost as soon as another INSERT
** happens
****************************************** */

DECLARE @Ident    int;  -- This will be a holding variable

/* We'll use it to show how we can
** move values from system functions
** into a safe place.
*/
INSERT INTO TestIdent
  DEFAULT VALUES;
SET @Ident = @@IDENTITY;
PRINT 'The value we got originally from @@IDENTITY was ' +
CONVERT(varchar(2),@Ident);
PRINT 'The value currently in @@IDENTITY is ' + CONVERT(varchar(2),@@IDENTITY);

/* On this first INSERT using @@IDENTITY, we're going to get lucky.
** We'll get a proper value because there is nothing between our
** original INSERT and this one. You'll see that on the INSERT that
** will follow after this one, we won't be so lucky anymore. */
INSERT INTO TestChild1
VALUES
  (@@IDENTITY);

PRINT 'The value we got originally from @@IDENTITY was ' +
CONVERT(varchar(2),@Ident);
IF (SELECT @@IDENTITY) IS NULL
  PRINT 'The value currently in @@IDENTITY is NULL';
```

```
ELSE
   PRINT 'The value currently in @@IDENTITY is ' + CONVERT(varchar(2),@@IDENTITY);
-- The next line is just a spacer for our print out
PRINT '';
/* This time all will go fine because we are using the value that
** we have placed in safekeeping instead of @@IDENTITY directly.*/
INSERT INTO TestChild2
VALUES
   (@Ident);
```

This time everything runs just fine:

```
(1 row(s) affected)
The value we got originally from @@IDENTITY was 1
The value currently in @@IDENTITY is 1
(1 row(s) affected)
The value we got originally from @@IDENTITY was 1
The value currently in @@IDENTITY is NULL
(1 row(s) affected)
```

> In this example, it was fairly easy to tell that there was a problem because of the attempt at inserting a NULL into the primary key. Now, imagine a far less pretty scenario — one where the second table did have an identity column. You could easily wind up inserting bogus data into your table and not even knowing about it — at least not until you already had a very serious data integrity problem on your hands!

Using @@ROWCOUNT

In the many queries that we ran up to this point, it's always been pretty easy to tell how many rows a statement affected — the Query window tells us. For example, if we run:

```
USE AdventureWorks2008
SELECT * FROM Person.Person;
```

then we see all the rows in Person, but we also see a count on the number of rows affected by our query (in this case, it's all the rows in the table):

```
(19972 row(s) affected)
```

But what if we need to *programmatically* know how many rows were affected? Much like @@IDENITY, @@ROWCOUNT is an invaluable tool in the fight to know what's going on as your script runs — but this time the value is how many rows were affected rather than our identity value.

Let's examine this just a bit further with an example:

```
USE AdventureWorks2008;
GO
```

```
DECLARE @RowCount int;   --Notice the single @ sign
SELECT * FROM Person.Person;
SELECT @RowCount = @@ROWCOUNT;
```

This again shows us all the rows, but notice the new line that we got back:

```
The value of @@ROWCOUNT was 19972
```

We'll take a look at ways this might be useful when we look at stored procedures later in the book. For now, just realize that this provides us with a way to learn something about what a statement did, and it's not limited to use SELECT statements — UPDATE, INSERT, and DELETE also set this value.

> If you look through the example, you might notice that, much as I did with @@IDENTITY, I chose to move the value off to a holding variable. @@ROWCOUNT will be reset with a new value the very next statement, so, if you're going to be doing multiple activities with the @@ROWCOUNT value, you should move it into a safe keeping area.

Batches

A *batch* is a grouping of T-SQL statements into one logical unit. All of the statements within a batch are combined into one execution plan, so all statements are parsed together and must pass a validation of the syntax or none of the statements will execute. Note, however, that this does not prevent runtime errors from happening. In the event of a runtime error, any statement that has been executed prior to the runtime error will still be in effect. To summarize, if a statement fails at parse-time, then nothing runs. If a statement fails at runtime, then all statements until the statement that generated the error have already run.

All the scripts we have run up to this point are made up of one batch each. Even the script we've been analyzing so far this in chapter makes up just one batch. To separate a script into multiple batches, we make use of the GO statement. The GO statement:

❑   Must be on its own line (nothing other than a comment can be on the same line); there is an exception to this discussed shortly, but think of a GO as needing to be on a line to itself.

❑   Causes all statements since the beginning of the script or the last GO statement (whichever is closer) to be compiled into one execution plan and sent to the server independently of any other batches.

❑   Is not a T-SQL command, but, rather, a command recognized by the various SQL Server command utilities (sqlcmd and the Query window in the Management Studio).

A Line to Itself

The GO command should stand alone on its own line. Technically, you can start a new batch on the same line after the GO command, but you'll find this puts a serious damper on readability. T-SQL statements cannot precede the GO statement, or the GO statement will often be misinterpreted and cause either a parsing error or some other unexpected result. For example, if I use a GO statement after a WHERE clause:

```
SELECT * FROM Person.Person WHERE ContactID = 1 GO
```

the parser becomes somewhat confused:

```
Msg 102, Level 15, State 1, Line 1
Incorrect syntax near 'GO'.
```

Each Batch Is Sent to the Server Separately

Because each batch is processed independently, an error in one batch does not prevent another batch from running. To illustrate, take a look at some code:

```
USE AdventureWorks2008;

DECLARE @MyVarchar varchar(50);   --This DECLARE only lasts for this batch!

SELECT @MyVarchar = 'Honey, I''m home...';

PRINT 'Done with first Batch...';

GO


PRINT @MyVarchar;   --This generates an error since @MyVarchar
                    --isn't declared in this batch
PRINT 'Done with second Batch';

GO


PRINT 'Done with third batch';   -- Notice that this still gets executed
                                 -- even after the error

GO
```

If there were any dependencies between these batches, then either everything would fail — or, at the very least, everything after the point of error would fail — but it doesn't. Look at the results if you run the previous script:

```
Done with first Batch...
Msg 137, Level 15, State 2, Line 2
Must declare the scalar variable "@MyVarchar".
Done with third batch
```

Again, each batch is completely autonomous in terms of runtime issues. Keep in mind, however, that you can build in dependencies in the sense that one batch may try to perform work that depends on the first batch being complete — we'll see some of this in the next section when I talk about what can and can't span batches.

GO Is Not a T-SQL Command

Thinking that GO is a T-SQL command is a common mistake. GO is a command that is only recognized by the editing tools (Management Studio, sqlcmd). If you use a third-party tool, then it may or may not support the GO command, but most that claim SQL Server support will.

When the editing tool encounters a GO statement, it sees it as a flag to terminate that batch, package it up, and send it as a single unit to the server — *without* including the GO. That's right, the server itself has absolutely no idea what GO is supposed to mean.

If you try to execute a GO command in a pass-through query using ODBC, OLE DB, ADO, ADO.NET, SqlNativeClient, or any other access method, you'll get an error message back from the server. The GO is merely an indicator to the tool that it is time to end the current batch, and time, if appropriate, to start a new one.

Errors in Batches

Errors in batches fall into two categories:

❏   Syntax errors

❏   Runtime errors

If the query parser finds a *syntax error*, processing of that batch is cancelled immediately. Since syntax checking happens before the batch is compiled or executed, a failure during the syntax check means none of the batch will be executed — regardless of the position of the syntax error within the batch.

Runtime errors work quite a bit differently. Any statement that has already executed before the runtime error was encountered is already done, so anything that statement did will remain intact unless it is part of an uncommitted transaction. (Transactions are covered in Chapter 14, but the relevance here is that they imply an all or nothing situation.) What happens beyond the point of the runtime error depends on the nature of the error. Generally speaking, runtime errors terminate execution of the batch from the point where the error occurred to the end of the batch. Some runtime errors, such as a referential-integrity violation, will only prevent the offending statement from executing — all other statements in the batch will still be executed. This later scenario is why error checking is so important — we will cover error checking in full in our chapter on stored procedures (Chapter 12).

When to Use Batches

Batches have several purposes, but they all have one thing in common — they are used when something has to happen either before or separately from everything else in your script.

Statements That Require Their Own Batch

There are several commands that absolutely must be part of their own batch. These include:

❏   CREATE DEFAULT

❏   CREATE PROCEDURE

❏   CREATE RULE

❏   CREATE TRIGGER

❏   CREATE VIEW

If you want to combine any of these statements with other statements in a single script, then you will need to break them up into their own batch by using a GO statement.

> Note that, if you DROP an object, you may want to place the DROP in its own batch or at least with a batch of other DROP statements. Why? Well, if you're going to later create an object with the same name, the CREATE will fail during the parsing of your batch unless the DROP has already happened. That means you need to run the DROP in a separate and prior batch so it will be complete when the batch with the CREATE statement executes.

Using Batches to Establish Precedence

Perhaps the most likely scenario for using batches is when precedence is required — that is, you need one task to be completely done before the next task starts. Most of the time, SQL Server deals with this kind of situation just fine — the first statement in the script is the first executed, and the second statement in the script can rely on the server being in the proper state when the second statement runs. There are times, however, when SQL Server can't resolve this kind of issue.

Let's take the example of creating a database together with some tables:

```
USE master;

CREATE DATABASE Test;

CREATE TABLE TestTable
(
    col1    int,
    col2    int
);
```

Execute this and, at first, it appears that everything has gone well:

```
Command(s) completed successfully.
```

However, things are not as they seem — check out the INFORMATION_SCHEMA in the Test database:

```
USE Test;

SELECT TABLE_CATALOG
FROM INFORMATION_SCHEMA.TABLES
WHERE TABLE_NAME = 'TestTable';
```

And you'll notice something is missing:

```
TABLE_CATALOG
--------------------
AdventureWorks2008
(1 row(s) affected)
```

Hey! Why was the table created in the wrong database? The answer lies in what database was current when we ran the CREATE TABLE statement. In my case, it happened to be the master database, so that's where my table was created.

Note that you may have been somewhere other than the master database when you ran this, so you may get a different result. That's kind of the point though — you could be in pretty much any database. That's why making use of the USE statement is so important.

When you think about it, this seems like an easy thing to fix — just make use of the USE statement, but before we test our new theory, we have to get rid of the old (OK, not that old) database:

```
USE MASTER;
DROP DATABASE Test;
```

We can then run our newly modified script:

```
CREATE DATABASE Test;
```

```
USE Test;
```

```
CREATE TABLE TestTable
(
    col1    int,
    col2    int
);
```

Unfortunately, this has its own problems:

```
Msg 911, Level 16, State 1, Line 3
Database 'Test' does not exist. Make sure that the name is entered correctly.
```

The parser tries to validate your code and finds that you are referencing a database with your USE command that doesn't exist. Ahh, now we see the need for our batches. We need the CREATE DATABASE statement to be completed before we try to use the new database:

```
CREATE DATABASE Test;
GO
```

```
USE Test;
CREATE TABLE TestTable
(
    col1    int,
    col2    int
);
```

Now things work a lot better. Our immediate results look the same:

```
Command(s) completed successfully.
```

But when we run our INFORMATION_SCHEMA query, things are confirmed:

```
TABLE_CATALOG
-------------------
Test
(1 row(s) affected)
```

Let's move on to another example that shows an even more explicit need for precedence.

When you use an ALTER TABLE statement that significantly changes the type of a column or adds columns, you cannot make use of those changes until the batch that makes the changes has completed.

If we add a column to our `TestTable` table in our Test database and then try to reference that column without ending the first batch:

```
USE Test;

ALTER TABLE TestTable
  ADD col3 int;
INSERT INTO TestTable
  (col1, col2, col3)
VALUES
  (1,1,1);
```

we get an error message — SQL Server cannot resolve the new column name, and therefore complains:

```
Msg 207, Level 16, State 1, Line 6
Invalid column name 'col3'.
```

Add one simple GO statement after the ADD col3 int, however, and everything is working fine:

```
(1 row(s) affected)
```

sqlcmd

sqlcmd is a utility that allows you to run scripts from a command prompt in a Windows command box. This can be very nice for executing conversion or maintenance scripts, as well as a quick and dirty way to capture a text file.

sqlcmd replaces the older osql. osql is still included with SQL Server for backward compatibility only. An even older command-line utility — isql — is no longer supported.

The syntax for running sqlcmd from the command line includes a large number of different switches, and looks like this:

```
sqlcmd
[ { { -U <login id> [ -P <password> ] } | -E } ]
[ -z <new password> ] [ -Z <new password> and exit]
[-S <server name> [ \<instance name> ] ] [ -H <workstation name> ] [ -d <db name> ]
[ -l <login time out> ] [ -t <query time out> ] [ -h <header spacing> ]
[ -s <col separator> ] [ -w <col width> ] [ -a <packet size> ]
[ -e ] [ -I ]
[ -c <cmd end> ] [ -L [ c ] ] [ -q "<query>" ] [ -Q "<query>" ]
[ -m <error level> ] [ -V ] [ -W ] [ -u ] [ -r [ 0 | 1 ] ]
[ -i <input file> ] [ -o <output file> ]
[ -f <codepage> | i:<input codepage> [ <, o: <output codepage> ]
[ -k [ 1 | 2 ] ]
[ -y <display width> ] [-Y <display width> ]
[ -p [ 1 ] ] [ -R ] [ -b ] [ -v var="<value>" ] [ -A ] [ -X [ 1 ] ] [ -x ]
[ -? ]
]
```

The single biggest thing to keep in mind with these flags is that many of them (but, oddly enough, not all of them) are case sensitive. For example, both -Q and -q will execute queries, but the first will exit sqlcmd when the query is complete, and the second won't.

So, let's try a quick query direct from the command line. Again, remember that this is meant to be run from the Windows command prompt (don't use the Management Console):

```
SQLCMD -Usa -Pmypass -Q "SELECT * FROM AdventureWorks2008.Production.Location"
```

The –P is the flag that indicates the password. If your server is configured with something other than a blank password (and it should be!), then you'll need to provide that password immediately following the –P with no space in between. If you are using Windows authentication instead of SQL Server authentication, then substitute a –E and nothing else in the place of both the –U and –P parameters (remove both, but replace with just one –E).

If you run this from a command prompt, you should get something like:

```
C:\>SQLCMD -E -Q "SELECT * FROM AdventureWorks2008.Production.Location"
LocationID Name                                              CostRate      Avail
ability ModifiedDate
---------- -------------------------------------------------- ------------ -----
------- ----------------------
         1 Tool Crib                                              0.0000
    .00 1998-06-01 00:00:00.000
         2 Sheet Metal Racks                                      0.0000
    .00 1998-06-01 00:00:00.000
         3 Paint Shop                                             0.0000
    .00 1998-06-01 00:00:00.000
         4 Paint Storage                                          0.0000
    .00 1998-06-01 00:00:00.000
         5 Metal Storage                                          0.0000
    .00 1998-06-01 00:00:00.000
         6 Miscellaneous Storage                                  0.0000
    .00 1998-06-01 00:00:00.000
         7 Finished Goods Storage                                 0.0000
    .00 1998-06-01 00:00:00.000
        10 Frame Forming                                         22.5000
  96.00 1998-06-01 00:00:00.000
        20 Frame Welding                                         25.0000
 108.00 1998-06-01 00:00:00.000
        30 Debur and Polish                                      14.5000
 120.00 1998-06-01 00:00:00.000
        40 Paint                                                 15.7500
 120.00 1998-06-01 00:00:00.000
        45 Specialized Paint                                     18.0000
  80.00 1998-06-01 00:00:00.000
        50 Subassembly                                           12.2500
 120.00 1998-06-01 00:00:00.000
        60 Final Assembly                                        12.2500
 120.00 1998-06-01 00:00:00.000

(14 rows affected)

C:\>
```

Now, let's create a quick text file to see how it works when including a file. At the command prompt, type the following:

```
C:\>copy con testsql.sql
```

This should take you down to a blank line (with no prompt of any kind), where you can enter in this:

```
SELECT * FROM AdventureWorks2008.Production.Location
```

Then press F6 and Return (this ends the creation of our text file). You should get back a message like:

```
1 file(s) copied.
```

Now let's retry our earlier query using a script file this time. The command line at the prompt has only a slight change to it:

```
C:\>sqlcmd -Usa -Pmypass -i testsql.sql
```

This should get us exactly the same results as we had when we ran the query using -Q. The major difference is, of course, that we took the command from a file. The file could have had hundreds — if not thousands — of different commands in it.

Try It Out   Generating a Text File with sqlcmd

As a final example of sqlcmd, let's utilize it to generate a text file that we might import into another application for analysis (Excel for example).

Back in Chapter 10, we created a view that listed yesterday's orders for us. First, we're going to take the core query of that view, and stick it into a text file:

```
C:\copy con YesterdaysOrders.sql
```

This should again take you down to a blank line (with no prompt of any kind), where you can enter this:

```
USE AdventureWorks2008

SELECT    sc.AccountNumber,
          soh.SalesOrderID,
          soh.OrderDate,
          sod.ProductID,
          pp.Name,
          sod.OrderQty,
          sod.UnitPrice,
          sod.UnitPriceDiscount * sod.UnitPrice * sod.OrderQty AS TotalDiscount,
          sod.LineTotal
FROM      Sales.Customer AS sc
INNER JOIN    Sales.SalesOrderHeader AS soh
      ON sc.CustomerID = soh.CustomerID
INNER JOIN    Sales.SalesOrderDetail AS sod
      ON soh.SalesOrderID = sod.SalesOrderID
INNER JOIN Production.Product AS pp
      ON sod.ProductID = pp.ProductID
WHERE CAST(soh.OrderDate AS Date) =
      CAST(DATEADD(day,-1,GETDATE()) AS Date)
```

Again press F6 and press Enter to tell Windows to save the file for you.

We now have our text file source for our query, and are nearly ready to have sqlcmd help us generate our output. First, however, is that we need there to be some data from yesterday (none of the sample data is going to have data from yesterday unless you just ran the UPDATE statement we used in Chapter 10 to change to orders to yesterday's date. Just to be sure of which update I'm talking about here, I mean the one shown in the views chapter. So, with this in mind, let's run that statement one more time (you can do this through the Query window if you like):

```
USE AdventureWorks2008

UPDATE Sales.SalesOrderHeader
SET OrderDate = CAST(DATEADD(day,-1,GETDATE()) AS Date),
    DueDate = CAST(DATEADD(day,11,GETDATE()) AS Date),
    ShipDate = CAST(DATEADD(day,6,GETDATE()) AS Date)
WHERE SalesOrderID < 43663;
```

OK, so we have at least one row that is an order with yesterday's date now. So we're most of the way ready to go; however, we've said we want our results to a text file, so we'll need to add some extra parameters to our sqlcmd command line this time to tell SQL Server where to put the output:

```
C:\>sqlcmd -UMyLogin -PMyPass -iYesterdaysOrders.sql -oYesterdaysOrders.txt
```

There won't be anything special or any fanfare when sqlcmd is done running this — you'll simply get your Windows drive prompt again (C:\ most likely), but check out what is in our YesterdaysOrders.txt file now:

```
C:\>TYPE YesterdaysOrders.txt
```

This gives us our one row:

```
C:\>TYPE YesterdaysOrders.txt
Changed database context to 'AdventureWorks2008'.
AccountNumber SalesOrderID OrderDate                ProductID    Name
                                        OrderQty UnitPrice          TotalDiscount
        LineTotal
------------- ------------ ------------------------ ----------- -----------------
-------------------------------- -------- -------------------- -----------------
------ ------------------------------------
AW00000676              43659 2007-10-06 00:00:00.000            776 Mountain-100 Blac
k, 42                           1        2024.9940
0.0000                          2024.994000
AW00000676              43659 2007-10-06 00:00:00.000            777 Mountain-100 Blac
k, 44                           3        2024.9940
0.0000                          6074.982000
AW00000676              43659 2007-10-06 00:00:00.000            778 Mountain-100 Blac
k, 48                           1        2024.9940
0.0000                          2024.994000
...
...
AW00000227              43662 2007-10-06 00:00:00.000            738 LL Road Frame - B
lack, 52                        1        178.5808
0.0000                          178.580800
AW00000227              43662 2007-10-06 00:00:00.000            766 Road-650 Black, 6
0                               3        419.4589
0.0000                          1258.376700
```

```
AW00000227                43662 2007-10-06 00:00:00.000          755 Road-450 Red, 60
                                           1                874.7940
0.0000                               874.794000

(51 rows affected)
C:\>
```

How It Works

We started out by bundling the SQL commands we would need into a single script — first, the USE command, and then the actual SELECT statement.

We then executed our statement using sqlcmd. The –U and –P commands provided the login username and password information just as they did earlier in the chapter. The –i parameter told sqlcmd that we had an input file, and we included that file name *immediately* following the –i parameter. Finally, we included the –o parameter to tell sqlcmd that we wanted the output written to a file (we, of course, then provided a file name — YesterdaysOrders.txt). Don't get confused by the two files both named YesterdaysOrders — they are separate files with the .sql and .txt files separating what their particular use is for.

There is a wide variety of different parameters for sqlcmd, but the most important are the login, the password, and the one that says what you want to do (straight query or input file). You can mix and match many of these parameters to obtain fairly complex behavior from this seemingly simple command-line tool.

Dynamic SQL: Generating Your Code On the Fly with the EXEC Command

OK, so all this saving stuff away in scripts is all fine and dandy, but what if you don't know what code you need to execute until runtime?

As a side note, notice that we are done with sqlcmd for now — the following examples should be run utilizing the Management Console.

SQL Server allows us, with a few gotchas, to build our SQL statement on-the-fly using string manipulation. The need to do this usually stems from not being able to know the details about something until runtime. The syntax looks like this:

```
EXEC ({<string variable>|'<literal command string>'})
```

Or:

```
EXECUTE ({<string variable>|'<literal command string>'})
```

As with executing a stored proc, whether you use the EXEC or EXECUTE makes no difference.

Let's build an example in the AdventureWorks2008 database by creating a dummy table to grab dynamic information out of:

```
USE AdventureWorks2008;
GO

--Create The Table. We'll pull info from here for our dynamic SQL
CREATE TABLE DynamicSQLExample
(
    TableID       int   IDENTITY   NOT NULL
        CONSTRAINT PKDynamicSQLExample
                   PRIMARY KEY,
    SchemaName   varchar(128)    NOT NULL,
    TableName    varchar(128)    NOT NULL
);
GO

/* Populate the table. In this case, We're grabbing every user
** table object in this database                               */
INSERT INTO DynamicSQLExample
SELECT s.name AS SchemaName, t.name AS TableName
    FROM sys.schemas s
    JOIN sys.tables t
      ON s.schema_id = t.schema_id;
```

This should get us a response something like:

```
(73 row(s) affected)
```

To quote the old advertising disclaimer: "Actual results may vary." It's going to depend on which examples you've already followed along with in the book, which ones you haven't, and for which ones you took the initiative and did a DROP on once you were done with them. In any case, don't sweat it too much.

OK, so what we now have is a list of all the tables in our current database. Now let's say that we wanted to select some data from one of the tables, but we wanted to identify the table only at runtime by using its ID. For example, I'll pull out all the data for the table with an ID of 1:

```
DECLARE @SchemaName     varchar(128);
DECLARE @TableName      varchar(128);

-- Grab the table name that goes with our ID
SELECT @SchemaName = SchemaName, @TableName = TableName
    FROM DynamicSQLExample
    WHERE TableID = 25;

-- Finally, pass that value into the EXEC statement
EXEC ('SELECT * FROM ' + @SchemaName + '.' + @TableName);
```

If your table names went into the `DynamicSQLExample` table the way mine did, then a `TableID` of 25 should equate to the `Production.UnitMeasure` table. If so, you should wind up with something like this (the rightmost columns have been snipped for brevity):

```
UnitMeasureCode Name                    ModifiedDate
--------------- --------------------    -----------------------
BOX             Boxes                   1998-06-01 00:00:00.000
BTL             Bottle                  1998-06-01 00:00:00.000
C               Celsius                 1998-06-01 00:00:00.000
...
...
PC              Piece                   1998-06-01 00:00:00.000
PCT             Percentage              1998-06-01 00:00:00.000
PT              Pint, US liquid         1998-06-01 00:00:00.000

(38 row(s) affected)
```

The Gotchas of EXEC

Like most things that are of interest, using EXEC is not without its little trials and tribulations. Among the gotchas of EXEC are:

❑   It runs under a separate scope than the code that calls it — that is, the calling code can't reference variables inside the EXEC statement, and the EXEC can't reference variables in the calling code after they are resolved into the string for the EXEC statement. If you need to pass values between your dynamic SQL and the routine that calls it, consider using sp_executesql.

❑   By default, it runs under the same security context as the current user — not that of the calling object (an object generally runs under the context of the object's owner, not the current user).

❑   It runs under the same connection and transaction context as the calling object (we'll discuss this further in Chapter 14).

❑   Concatenation that requires a function call must be performed on the EXEC string prior to actually calling the EXEC statement — you can't do the concatenation of function in the same statement as the EXEC call.

❑   EXEC cannot be used inside a user-defined function.

Each of these can be a little difficult to grasp, so let's look at each individually.

The Scope of EXEC

Determining variable scope with the EXEC statement is something less than intuitive. The actual statement line that calls the EXEC statement has the same scope as the rest of the batch or procedure that the EXEC statement is running in, but the code that is performed as a result of the EXEC statement is considered to be in its own batch. As is so often the case, this is best shown with an example:

```
USE AdventureWorks2008;
/* First, we'll declare to variables. One for stuff we're putting into
** the EXEC, and one that we think will get something back out (it won't)
*/
```

```
DECLARE @InVar    varchar(50);
DECLARE @OutVar   varchar(50);

-- Set up our string to feed into the EXEC command
SET @InVar = 'SELECT @OutVar = FirstName FROM Person.Contact WHERE ContactID = 1';
-- Now run it
EXEC (@Invar);
-- Now, just to show there's no difference, run the select without using a in variable
EXEC ('SELECT @OutVar = FirstName FROM Person.Contac WHERE ContactID = 1');
-- @OutVar will still be NULL because we haven't been able to put anything in it
SELECT @OutVar;
```

Now, look at the output from this:

```
Msg 137, Level 15, State 1, Line 1
Must declare the scalar variable "@OutVar".
Msg 137, Level 15, State 1, Line 1
Must declare the scalar variable "@OutVar".


--------------------------------------------------

NULL

(1 row(s) affected)
```

SQL Server wastes no time in telling us that we are scoundrels and clearly don't know what we're doing. Why do we get a `Must Declare` error message when we have already declared @OutVar? Because we've declared it in the outer scope — not within the EXEC itself.

Let's look at what happens if we run things a little differently:

```
USE AdventureWorks2008;
-- This time, we only need one variable. It does need to be longer though.
DECLARE @InVar varchar(200);
/* Set up our string to feed into the EXEC command. This time we're going
** to feed it several statements at a time. They will all execute as one
** batch.
*/
SET @InVar = 'DECLARE @OutVar varchar(50);
SELECT @OutVar = FirstName FROM Person.Person WHERE BusinessEntityID  = 1;
SELECT ''The Value Is '' + @OutVar';
-- Now run it
EXEC (@Invar);
```

This time we get back results closer to what we expect:

```
--------------------------------------------------------------

The Value Is Ken
```

Notice the way that I'm using two quote marks right next to each other to indicate that I really want a quote mark rather than to terminate my string.

So, what we've seen here is that we have two different scopes operating, and nary the two shall meet. There is, unfortunately, no way to pass information between the inside and outside scopes without using an external mechanism such as a temporary table or a special stored procedure called sp_executesql.

If you decide to use a temp table to communicate between scopes, just remember that any temporary table created within the scope of your EXEC statement will only live for the life of that EXEC statement.

> This behavior of a temp table only lasting the life of your EXEC procedure will show up again when we are dealing with triggers and sprocs.

A Small Exception to the Rule

There is one thing that happens inside the scope of the EXEC that can be seen after the EXEC is done — system functions — so, things like @@ROWCOUNT can still be used. Again, let's look at a quick example:

```
USE AdventureWorks2008;

EXEC('SELECT * FROM Production.UnitMeasure');

SELECT 'The Rowcount is ' + CAST(@@ROWCOUNT as varchar);
```

This yields (after the result set):

```
The Rowcount is 38
```

Security Contexts and EXEC

This is a tough one to cover at this point because we haven't covered the issues yet with stored procedures and security. Still, the discussion of the EXEC command belonged here rather than in the sprocs chapter, so here we are (this is the only part of this discussion that gets wrapped up in sprocs, so bear with me).

When you give someone the right to run a stored procedure, you imply that they also gain the right to perform the actions called for within the sproc. For example, let's say we had a stored procedure that lists all the employees hired within the last year. Someone who has rights to execute the sproc can do so (and get results back) even if they do not have rights to the Employees table directly. This is really handy for reasons we will explore later in our sprocs chapter.

Developers usually assume that this same implied right is valid for an EXEC statement also — it isn't. Any reference made inside an EXEC statement will, by default, be run under the security context of the current user. So, let's say I have the right to run a procedure called spNewEmployees, but I do not have rights to the Employees table. If spNewEmployees gets the values by running a simple SELECT statement, then everything is fine. If, however, spNewEmployees uses an EXEC statement to execute that SELECT statement, the EXEC statement will fail because I don't have the rights to perform a SELECT on the Employees table.

Since we don't have that much information on sprocs yet, I'm going to bypass further discussion of this for now, but we will come back to it when we discuss sprocs later on.

Use of Functions in Concatenation and EXEC

This one is actually more of a nuisance than anything else because there is a reasonably easy workaround. Simply put, you can't run a function against your EXEC string in the argument for an EXEC. For example:

```
USE AdventureWorks2008;
```

```
-- This won't work
DECLARE @NumberOfLetters int = 15;
EXEC('SELECT LEFT(Name,' + CAST(@NumberOfLetters AS varchar) + ') AS ShortName
FROM Production.Product');
GO
-- But this does
DECLARE @NumberOfLetters AS int = 15;
DECLARE @str AS varchar(255);
SET @str = 'SELECT LEFT(Name,' + CAST(@NumberOfLetters AS varchar) + ') AS ShortName
FROM Production.Product';
EXEC(@str);
```

The first instance gets an error message because the CAST function needs to be fully resolved prior to the EXEC line:

```
Msg 102, Level 15, State 1, Line 9
Incorrect syntax near 'CAST'.
```

But the second line works just fine because it is already a complete string:

```
ShortName
---------------
Adjustable Race
All-Purpose Bik
AWC Logo Cap
...
...
Women's Tights,
Women's Tights,
Women's Tights,
```

EXEC and UDFs

This is a tough one to touch on because we haven't gotten to user-defined functions as yet, but suffice to say that you are not allowed to use EXEC to run dynamic SQL within a UDF — period. (EXEC to run a sproc is, however, legal in a few cases.)

Control-of-Flow Statements

Control-of-flow statements are a veritable must for any programming language these days. I can't imagine having to write my code where I couldn't change what commands to run depending on a condition. T-SQL offers most of the classic choices for control of flow situations, including:

- ❑   IF ... ELSE
- ❑   GOTO
- ❑   WHILE
- ❑   WAITFOR
- ❑   TRY/CATCH

We also have the CASE statement (aka SELECT CASE, DO CASE, and SWITCH/BREAK in other languages), but it doesn't have quite the level of control-of-flow capabilities that you've come to expect from other languages.

The IF ... ELSE Statement

IF ... ELSE statements work much as they do in any language, although I equate them closest to C in the way they are implemented. The basic syntax is:

```
IF <Boolean Expression>
    <SQL statement> | BEGIN <code series> END
[ELSE
    <SQL statement> | BEGIN <code series> END]
```

The expression can be pretty much any expression that evaluates to a Boolean.

This brings us back to one of the most common traps that I see SQL programmers fall into — improper user of NULLs. I can't tell you how often I have debugged stored procedures only to find a statement like:

IF @myvar = NULL

This will, of course, never be true on most systems (see below), and will wind up bypassing all their NULL values. Instead, it needs to read:

IF @myvar IS NULL

The exception to this is dependent on whether you have set the ANSI_NULLS option ON or OFF. The default is that this is ON, in which case you'll see the behavior just described. You can change this behavior by setting ANSI_NULLS to OFF. I strongly recommend against this since it violates the ANSI standard. (It's also just plain wrong.)

Note that only the very next statement after the IF will be considered to be conditional (as per the IF). You can include multiple statements as part of your control-of-flow block using BEGIN...END, but we'll discuss that one a little later in the chapter.

To show off a simple version of this, let's run an example that's very common to build scripts. Imagine for a moment that we want to CREATE a table if it's not there, but to leave it alone if it already exists. We could make use of the EXISTS operator. (You may recall my complaint that the Books Online calls EXISTS a keyword when I consider it an operator.)

```
-- We'll run a SELECT looking for our table to start with to prove it's not there
SELECT 'Found Table ' + s.name + '.' + t.name
    FROM sys.schemas s
    JOIN sys.tables t
        ON s.schema_id = t.schema_id
    WHERE s.name = 'dbo'
      AND t.name = 'OurIFTest';
```

```
-- Now we're run our conditional CREATE statement
IF NOT EXISTS (
    SELECT s.name AS SchemaName, t.name AS TableName
        FROM sys.schemas s
        JOIN sys.tables t
            ON s.schema_id = t.schema_id
        WHERE s.name = 'dbo'
          AND t.name = 'OurIFTest'
                )
    CREATE TABLE OurIFTest(
        Col1    int         PRIMARY KEY
        );

-- And now look again to prove that it's been created.
SELECT 'Found Table ' + s.name + '.' + t.name
    FROM sys.schemas s
    JOIN sys.tables t
        ON s.schema_id = t.schema_id
    WHERE s.name = 'dbo'
      AND t.name = 'OurIFTest';
```

The meat of this is in the middle — notice that our CREATE TABLE statement runs only if no matching table already exists. The first check we did on it (right at the beginning of the script) found the table didn't exist, so we know that the IF is going to be true and our CREATE TABLE will execute.

```
------------------------------------------------------------------------

(0 row(s) affected)


------------------------------------------------------------------Found
Table dbo.OurIFTest

(1 row(s) affected)
```

The ELSE Clause

Now this thing about being able to run statements conditionally is just great, but it doesn't really deal with all the scenarios we might want to deal with. Quite often — indeed, most of the time — when we deal with an IF condition, we have specific statements we want to execute not just for the true condition, but also a separate set of statements that we want to run if the condition is false — or the ELSE condition.

> You will run into situations where a Boolean cannot be evaluated — that is, the result is unknown (for example, if you are comparing to a NULL). Any expression that returns a result that would be considered as an unknown result will be treated as FALSE.

The ELSE statement works pretty much as it does in any other language. The exact syntax may vary slightly, but the nuts and bolts are still the same; the statements in the ELSE clause are executed if the statements in the IF clause are not.

To expand our earlier example just a bit, let's actually print a warning message out if we do not create our table:

```
-- Now we're run our conditional CREATE statement
IF NOT EXISTS (
    SELECT s.name AS SchemaName, t.name AS TableName
        FROM sys.schemas s
        JOIN sys.tables t
            ON s.schema_id = t.schema_id
        WHERE s.name = 'dbo'
          AND t.name = 'OurIFTest'
                )
    CREATE TABLE OurIFTest(
        Col1    int         PRIMARY KEY
        );
ELSE
        PRINT 'WARNING: Skipping CREATE as table already exists';
```

If you have already run the preceding example, then the table will already exist, and running this second example should get you the warning message:

```
WARNING: Skipping CREATE as table already exists
```

Grouping Code into Blocks

Sometimes you need to treat a group of statements as though they were all one statement (if you execute one, then you execute them all — otherwise, you don't execute any of them). For instance, the IF statement will, by default, consider only the very next statement after the IF to be part of the conditional code. What if you want the condition to require several statements to run? Life would be pretty miserable if you had to create a separate IF statement for each line of code you wanted to run if the condition holds.

Thankfully, like most any language with an IF statement, SQL Server gives us a way to group code into blocks that are considered to all belong together. The block is started when you issue a BEGIN statement and continues until you issue an END statement. It works like this:

```
IF <Expression>
BEGIN    --First block of code starts here -- executes only if
         --expression is TRUE
    Statement that executes if expression is TRUE
    Additional statements
    ...
    ...
    Still going with statements from TRUE expression
    IF <Expression>    --Only executes if this block is active
        BEGIN
            Statement that executes if both outside and inside
                expressions are TRUE
            Additional statements
            ...
            ...
            Still statements from both TRUE expressions
        END
```

```
        Out of the condition from inner condition, but still
          part of first block
    END    --First block of code ends here
    ELSE
    BEGIN
       Statement that executes if expression is FALSE
       Additional statements
       ...
       ...
       Still going with statements from FALSE expression
    END
```

Notice our ability to nest blocks of code. In each case, the inner blocks are considered to be part of the outer block of code. I have never heard of there being a limit to how many levels deep you can nest your BEGIN...END blocks, but I would suggest that you minimize them. There are definitely practical limits to how deep you can keep them readable — even if you are particularly careful about the formatting of your code.

Just to put this notion into play, let's make yet another modification to table creation. This time, we're going to provide an informational message regardless of whether the table was created or not.

```sql
-- This time we're adding a check to see if the table DOES already exist
-- We'll remove it if it does so that the rest of our example can test the
-- IF condition. Just remove this first IF EXISTS block if you want to test
-- the ELSE condition below again.
IF EXISTS (
    SELECT s.name AS SchemaName, t.name AS TableName
      FROM sys.schemas s
      JOIN sys.tables t
          ON s.schema_id = t.schema_id
     WHERE s.name = 'dbo'
       AND t.name = 'OurIFTest'
            )
    DROP TABLE OurIFTest;

-- Now we're run our conditional CREATE statement
IF NOT EXISTS (
    SELECT s.name AS SchemaName, t.name AS TableName
      FROM sys.schemas s
      JOIN sys.tables t
          ON s.schema_id = t.schema_id
     WHERE s.name = 'dbo'
          AND t.name = 'OurIFTest'
            )
    BEGIN
        PRINT 'Table dbo.OurIFTest not found.';
        PRINT 'CREATING: Table dbo.OurIFTest';
        CREATE TABLE OurIFTest(
            Col1    int    PRIMARY KEY
            );
    END
ELSE
        PRINT 'WARNING: Skipping CREATE as table already exists';
```

Now, I've mixed all sorts of uses of the IF statement there. I have the most basic IF statement — with no BEGIN...END or ELSE. In my other IF statement, the IF portion uses a BEGIN...END block, but the ELSE does not.

I did this one this way just to illustrate how you can mix them. That said, I recommend you go back to my old axiom of "be consistent." It can be really hard to deal with what statement is being controlled by what IF...ELSE condition if you are mixing the way you group things. In practice, if I'm using BEGIN...END on any statement within a given IF, then I use them for every block of code in that IF statement even if there is only one statement for that particular condition.

The CASE Statement

The CASE statement is, in some ways, the equivalent of one of several different statements depending on the language from which you're coming. Statements in procedural programming languages that work in a similar way to CASE include:

❑   Switch: C, C#, C++, Java, php, Perl, Delphi

❑   Select Case: Visual Basic

❑   Do Case: Xbase

❑   Evaluate: COBOL

I'm sure there are others — these are just from the languages that I've worked with in some form or another over the years. The big drawback in using a CASE statement in T-SQL is that it is, in many ways, more of a substitution operator than a control-of-flow statement.

There is more than one way to write a CASE statement — with an input expression or a Boolean expression. The first option is to use an input expression that will be compared with the value used in each WHEN clause. The SQL Server documentation refers to this as a *simple CASE*:

```
CASE <input expression>
WHEN <when expression> THEN <result expression>
[...n]
[ELSE <result expression>]
END
```

Option number two is to provide an expression with each WHEN clause that will evaluate to TRUE/FALSE. The docs refer to this as a *searched CASE*:

```
CASE
WHEN <Boolean expression> THEN <result expression>
[...n]
[ELSE <result expression>]
END
```

Perhaps what's nicest about CASE is that you can use it "inline" with (that is, as an integral part of) a SELECT statement. This can actually be quite powerful.

A Simple CASE

A simple CASE takes an expression that equates to a Boolean result. Let's get right to an example:

```
Use AdventureWorks2008;
GO

SELECT TOP 10 SalesOrderID,
            SalesOrderID % 10 AS 'Last Digit',
            Position = CASE SalesOrderID % 10
                        WHEN 1 THEN 'First'
                        WHEN 2 THEN 'Second'
                        WHEN 3 THEN 'Third'
                        WHEN 4 THEN 'Fourth'
                        ELSE 'Something Else'
                    END
FROM Sales.SalesOrderHeader;
```

For those of you who aren't familiar with it, the % operator is for a *modulus*. A modulus works in a similar manner to the divide by (/), but it gives you only the remainder — therefore, 16 % 4 = 0 (4 goes into 16 evenly), but 16 % 5 = 1 (16 divided by 5 has a remainder of 1). In the example, since we're dividing by 10, using the modulus is giving us the last digit of the number we're evaluating.

Let's see what we got with this:

```
SalesOrderID Last Digit  Position
------------ ----------- ---------------
43793        3           Third
51522        2           Second
57418        8           Something Else
43767        7           Something Else
51493        3           Third
72773        3           Third
43736        6           Something Else
51238        8           Something Else
53237        7           Something Else
43701        1           First
(10 row(s) affected)
```

Notice that whenever there is a matching value in the list, the THEN clause is invoked. Since we have an ELSE clause, any value that doesn't match one of the previous values will be assigned whatever we've put in our ELSE. If we had left the ELSE out, then any such value would be given a NULL.

Let's go with one more example that expands on what we can use as an expression. This time, we'll use another column from our query:

```
USE AdventureWorks2008;
GO

SELECT TOP 10 SalesOrderID % 10 AS 'OrderLastDigit',
    ProductID % 10 AS 'ProductLastDigit',
    "How Close?" = CASE SalesOrderID % 10
        WHEN ProductID % 1 THEN 'Exact Match!'
        WHEN ProductID % 1 - 1 THEN 'Within 1'
        WHEN ProductID % 1 + 1 THEN 'Within 1'
```

```
            ELSE 'More Than One Apart'
    END
FROM Sales.SalesOrderDetail
ORDER BY SalesOrderID DESC;
```

Notice that we've used equations at every step of the way on this one, yet it still works. . . .

```
OrderLastDigit ProductLastDigit How Close?
-------------- ---------------- -------------------
3              2                More Than One Apart
3              9                More Than One Apart
3              8                More Than One Apart
2              2                More Than One Apart
2              8                More Than One Apart
1              7                Within 1
1              0                Within 1
1              1                Within 1
0              2                Exact Match!
0              4                Exact Match!
(10 row(s) affected)
```

As long as the expression evaluates to a specific value that is of compatible type to the input expression, it can be analyzed, and the proper THEN clause applied.

A Searched CASE

This one works pretty much the same as a simple CASE, with only two slight twists:

❑   There is no input expression (remember that's the part between the CASE and the first WHEN).

❑   The WHEN expression must evaluate to a Boolean value (whereas in the simple CASE examples we've just looked at, we used values such as 1, 3, and ProductID + 1).

Perhaps what I find the coolest about this kind of CASE is that we can completely change around what is forming the basis of our expression — mixing and matching column expressions, depending on our different possible situations.

As usual, I find the best way to get across how this works is via an example:

```
SELECT TOP 10 SalesOrderID % 10 AS 'OrderLastDigit',
    ProductID % 10 AS 'ProductLastDigit',
    "How Close?" = CASE
        WHEN (SalesOrderID % 10) < 3 THEN 'Ends With Less Than Three'
        WHEN ProductID = 6 THEN 'ProductID is 6'
        WHEN ABS(SalesOrderID % 10 - ProductID) <= 1 THEN 'Within 1'
        ELSE 'More Than One Apart'
    END
FROM Sales.SalesOrderDetail
ORDER BY SalesOrderID DESC;
```

This is substantially different from our simple CASE examples, but it still works:

```
OrderLastDigit ProductLastDigit How Close?
-------------- ---------------- -------------------------
3              2                More Than One Apart
3              9                More Than One Apart
```

```
3              8              More Than One Apart
2              2              Ends With Less Than Three
2              8              Ends With Less Than Three
1              7              Ends With Less Than Three
1              0              Ends With Less Than Three
1              1              Ends With Less Than Three
0              2              Ends With Less Than Three
0              4              Ends With Less Than Three
(10 row(s) affected)
```

There are a few of things to pay particular attention to in how SQL Server evaluated things:

❑ Even when two conditions evaluate to TRUE, only the first condition is used. For example, the second-to-last row meets both the first (the last digit is smaller than 3) and third (the last digit is within 1 of the ProductID) conditions. For many languages, including Visual Basic, this kind of statement always works this way. If you're from the C world (or one of many similar languages), however, you'll need to remember this when you are coding; no "break" statement is required — it always terminates after one condition is met.

❑ You can mix and match what fields you're using in your condition expressions. In this case, we used SalesOrderID, ProductID, and both together.

❑ You can perform pretty much any expression as long as, in the end, it evaluates to a Boolean result.

Let's try this out with a slightly more complex example. In this example, we're not going to do the mix-and-match thing — instead, we'll stick with just the one column we're looking at (we could change columns being tested — but, most of the time, we won't need to). Instead, we're going to deal with a more real-life scenario that I helped solve for a rather large e-commerce site.

The scenario is this: Marketing people really like nice clean prices. They hate it when you apply a 10 percent markup over cost, and start putting out prices like $10.13, or $23.19. Instead, they like slick prices that end in numbers like 49, 75, 95, or 99. In our scenario, we're supposed to create a possible new price list for analysis, and they want it to meet certain criteria.

If the new price ends with less than 50 cents (such as our previous $10.13 example), then marketing would like the price to be bumped up to the same dollar amount but ending in 49 cents ($10.49 for our example). Prices ending with 50 cents to 75 cents should be changed to end in 75 cents, and prices ending with more than 75 cents should be changed to end with 95 cents. Let's take a look at some examples of what they want:

If the New Price Would Be	Then It Should Become
$10.13	$10.49
$17.57	$17.75
$27.75	$27.75
$79.99	$79.95

Technically speaking, we could do this with nested `IF...ELSE` statements, but:

❑ It would be much harder to read — especially if the rules were more complex.

❑ We would have to implement the code using a cursor (*bad!*) and examine each row one at a time.

In short — *yuck*!

A `CASE` statement is going to make this process relatively easy. What's more, we're going to be able to place our condition inline to our query and use it as part of a set operation — this almost always means that we're going to get much better performance than we would with a cursor.

Our marketing department has decided they would like to see what things would look like if we increased prices by 10 percent, so we'll plug a 10 percent markup into a `CASE` statement, and, together with a little extra analysis, we'll get the numbers we're looking for:

```
USE AdventureWorks2008;
GO

/* I'm setting up some holding variables here. This way, if we get asked
** to run the query again with a slightly different value, we'll only have
** to change it in one place.
*/
DECLARE @Markup     money;
DECLARE @Multiplier money;

SELECT @Markup = .10;              -- Change the markup here
SELECT @Multiplier = @Markup + 1; -- We want the end price, not the amount
                                  -- of the increase, so add 1


/* Now execute things for our results. Note that we're limiting things
** to the top 10 items for brevity -- in reality, we either wouldn't do this
** at all, or we would have a more complex WHERE clause to limit the
** increase to a particular set of products
*/
SELECT TOP 10 ProductID, Name, ListPrice,
   ListPrice * @Multiplier AS "Marked Up Price", "New Price" =
   CASE WHEN FLOOR(ListPrice * @Multiplier + .24)
            > FLOOR(ListPrice * @Multiplier)
                  THEN FLOOR(ListPrice * @Multiplier) + .95
        WHEN FLOOR(ListPrice * @Multiplier + .5) >
            FLOOR(ListPrice * @Multiplier)
                  THEN FLOOR(ListPrice * @Multiplier) + .75
        ELSE FLOOR(ListPrice * @Multiplier) + .49
   END
FROM Production.Product
WHERE ProductID % 10 = 0  -- this is just to help the example
ORDER BY ProductID DESC;
```

The `FLOOR` function you see here is a pretty simple one — it takes the value supplied and rounds down to the nearest integer.

Now, I don't know about you, but I get very suspicious when I hear the word "analysis" come out of someone's lips — particularly if that person is in a marketing or sales role. Don't get me wrong — those people are doing their jobs just like I am. The thing is, once they ask a question one way, they usually want to ask the same question another way. That being the case, I went ahead and set this up as a script — now all we need to do when they decide they want to try it with 15 percent is make a change to the initialization value of @Markup. Let's see what we got this time with that 10 percent markup though:

```
ProductID Name                              ListPrice   Marked Up Price  New Price
--------- -------------------------------   ----------  ---------------  ----------
990       Mountain-500 Black, 42            539.99      593.989          593.9500
980       Mountain-400-W Silver, 38         769.49      846.439          846.4900
970       Touring-2000 Blue, 46             1214.85     1336.335         1336.4900
960       Touring-3000 Blue, 62             742.35      816.585          816.7500
950       ML Crankset                       256.49      282.139          282.4900
940       HL Road Pedal                     80.99       89.089           89.4900
930       HL Mountain Tire                  35.00       38.50            38.7500
920       LL Mountain Frame - Silver, 52    264.05      290.455          290.4900
910       HL Mountain Seat/Saddle           52.64       57.904           57.9500
900       LL Touring Frame - Yellow, 50     333.42      366.762          366.9500

(10 row(s) affected)
```

Look these over for a bit, and you'll see that the results match what we were expecting. What's more, we didn't have to build a cursor to do it.

Looping with the WHILE Statement

The WHILE statement works much as it does in other languages to which you have probably been exposed. Essentially, a condition is tested each time you come to the top of the loop. If the condition is still TRUE, then the loop executes again — if not, you exit.

The syntax looks like this:

```
WHILE <Boolean expression>
      <sql statement> |
[BEGIN
      <statement block>
      [BREAK]
      <sql statement> | <statement block>
      [CONTINUE]
END]
```

While you can just execute one statement (much as you do with an IF statement), you'll almost never see a WHILE that isn't followed by a BEGIN. . . END with a full statement block.

The BREAK statement is a way of exiting the loop without waiting for the bottom of the loop to come and the expression to be re-evaluated.

I'm sure I won't be the last to tell you this, but using a BREAK is generally thought of as something of bad form in the classical sense. I tend to sit on the fence on this one. I avoid using them if reasonably possible. Most of the time, I can indeed avoid them just by moving a statement or two around while still coming up with the same results. The advantage of this is usually more readable code. It is simply easier to handle a looping structure (or any structure for that matter) if you have a single point of entry and a single exit. Using a BREAK violates this notion.

All that being said, sometimes you can actually make things worse by reformatting the code to avoid a BREAK. In addition, I've seen people write much slower code for the sake of not using a BREAK statement — bad idea.

The CONTINUE statement is something of the complete opposite of a BREAK statement. In short, it tells the WHILE loop to go back to the beginning. Regardless of where you are in the loop, you immediately go back to the top and re-evaluate the expression (exiting if the expression is no longer TRUE).

We'll go ahead and do something of a short example here just to get our feet wet. As I mentioned before, WHILE loops tend to be rare in non-cursor situations, so forgive me if this example seems lame.

What we're going to do is create something of a monitoring process using our WHILE loop and a WAIT-FOR command (we'll look at the specifics of WAITFOR in our next section). We're going to be automatically updating our statistics once per day:

```
WHILE 1 = 1
BEGIN
    WAITFOR TIME '01:00';
    EXEC sp_updatestats;
    RAISERROR('Statistics Updated for Database', 1, 1) WITH LOG;
END
```

This would update the statistics for every table in our database every night at 1 AM and write a log entry of that fact to both the SQL Server log and the Windows application log. If you want check to see if this works, leave this running all night and then check your logs in the morning.

Note that an infinite loop like this isn't the way that you would normally want to schedule a task. If you want something to run every day, set up a job using the Management Studio. In addition to not keeping a connection open all the time (which the preceding example would do), you also get the capability to make follow up actions dependent on the success or failure of your script. Also, you can e-mail or net-send messages regarding the completion status.

The WAITFOR Statement

There are often things that you either don't want to or simply can't have happen right this moment, but you also don't want to have to hang around waiting for the right time to execute something.

No problem — use the WAITFOR statement and have SQL Server wait for you. The syntax is incredibly simple:

```
WAITFOR
    DELAY <'time'> | TIME <'time'>
```

The `WAITFOR` statement does exactly what it says it does — that is, it waits for whatever you specify as the argument to occur. You can specify either an explicit time of day for something to happen, or you can specify an amount of time to wait before doing something.

The DELAY Parameter

The `DELAY` parameter choice specifies an amount of time to wait. You cannot specify a number of days — just time in hours, minutes, and seconds. The maximum allowed delay is 24 hours. So, for example:

```
WAITFOR DELAY '01:00';
```

would run any code prior to the `WAITFOR`, then reach the `WAITFOR` statement, and stop for one hour, after which execution of the code would continue with whatever the next statement was.

The TIME Parameter

The `TIME` parameter choice specifies to wait until a specific time of day. Again, we cannot specify any kind of date — just the time of day using a 24-hour clock. Once more, this gives us a one-day time limit for the maximum amount of delay. For example:

```
WAITFOR TIME '01:00';
```

would run any code prior to the `WAITFOR`, then reach the `WAITFOR` statement, and stop until 1 AM, after which execution of the code would continue with whatever the next statement was after the `WAITFOR`.

TRY/CATCH Blocks

In days of yore (meaning anything before SQL Server 2005), our error-handling options were pretty limited. We could check for error conditions, but we had to do so proactively. Indeed, in some cases we could have errors that would cause us to leave our procedure or script without an opportunity to trap it at all (this can still happen, but we have options that really cut down the instances where it does). We're going to save a more full discussion of error handling for our stored procedures discussion in Chapter 12, but we'll touch on the fundamentals of the new `TRY/CATCH` blocks here.

A `TRY/CATCH` block in SQL Server works remarkably similarly to those used in any C-derived language (C, C++, C#, Delphi, and a host of others). The syntax looks like this:

```
BEGIN TRY
    { <sql statement(s)> }
END TRY
BEGIN CATCH
    { <sql statement(s)> }
END CATCH [ ; ]
```

In short, SQL Server will "try" to run anything within the `BEGIN...END` that goes with your `TRY` block. If, and only if, you have an error condition that has an error level of 11–19 occurs, then SQL Server will exit the TRY block immediately and begin with the first line in your CATCH block. Since there are more possible error levels than just 11–19, take a look at what we have there:

Error Level	Nature
1–10	Informational only. This would include things like context changes such as settings being adjusted or NULL values found while calculating aggregates. These will not trigger a CATCH block, so if you need to test for this level of error, you'll need to do so manually by checking @@ERROR.
11–19	Relatively severe errors, but ones that can be handled by your code (foreign key violations, as an example). Some of these can be severe enough that you are unlikely to want to continue processing (such as a memory exceeded error), but at least you can trap them and exit gracefully.
20–25	Very severe. These are generally system-level errors. Your server-side code will never know this kind of error happened, as the script and connection will be terminated immediately.

Keep these in mind — if you need to handle errors outside the 11–19 level range, then you'll need to make other plans.

Now, to test this out, we'll make some alterations to our CREATE script that we built back when we were looking at IF...ELSE statements. You may recall that part of the reason for our original test to see whether the table already existed was to avoid creating an error condition that might have caused our script to fail. That kind of test is the way things have been done historically (and there really wasn't much in the way of other options). With the advent of TRY/CATCH blocks, we could just try the CREATE and then handle the error if one were given:

```
BEGIN TRY
    -- Try and create our table
    CREATE TABLE OurIFTest(
        Col1    int         PRIMARY KEY
        );
END TRY
BEGIN CATCH
    -- Uh oh, something went wrong, see if it's something
    -- we know what to do with
    DECLARE @ErrorNo    int,
            @Severity    tinyint,
            @State       smallint,
            @LineNo       int,
            @Message     nvarchar(4000);
    SELECT
        @ErrorNo = ERROR_NUMBER(),
        @Severity = ERROR_SEVERITY(),
        @State = ERROR_STATE(),
        @LineNo = ERROR_LINE (),
        @Message = ERROR_MESSAGE();
```

```
     IF @ErrorNo = 2714 -- Object exists error, we knew this might happen
        PRINT 'WARNING: Skipping CREATE as table already exists';
     ELSE -- hmm, we don't recognize it, so report it and bail
        RAISERROR(@Message, 16, 1 );
END CATCH
```

Notice I used some special functions to retrieve the error condition, so let's take a look at those.

Also note that I moved them into variables that were controlled by me so they would not be lost.

Function	Returns
ERROR_NUMBER()	The actual error number. If this is a system error, there will be an entry in the sysmessages table (use sys.messages to look it up) that matches to that error and contains some of the information you'll get from the other error-related functions.
ERROR_SEVERITY()	This equates to what is sometimes called "error level" in other parts of this book and Books Online. My apologies for the inconsistency — I'm guilty of perpetuating something that Microsoft started doing a version or two ago.
ERROR_STATE()	I use this as something of a place mark. This will always be 1 for system errors. When I discuss error handling in more depth in the next chapter, you'll see how to raise your own errors. At that point, you can use state to indicate things like at what point in your stored procedure, function, or trigger the error occurred (this helps with situations where a given error can be handled in any one of many places).
ERROR_PROCEDURE()	We did not use this in the preceding example, as it is only relevant to stored procedures, functions, and triggers. This supplies the name of the procedure that caused the error — very handy if your procedures are nested at all, as the procedure that causes the error may not be the one to actually handle that error.
ERROR_LINE()	Just what it says — the line number of the error.
ERROR_MESSAGE()	The text that goes with the message. For system messages, this is the same as what you'll see if you select the message from the sys.messages function. For user-defined errors, it will be the text supplied to the RAISERROR function.

In our example, I utilized a known error id that SQL Server raises if we attempt to create an object that already exists. You can see all system error messages by selecting them from the sys.messages table function.

Beginning with SQL Server 2005, the sys.messages *output got so lengthy that it's hard to find what you're looking for by just scanning it. My solution is less than elegant but is rather effective — I just artificially create the error I'm looking for and see what error number it gives me (simple solutions for simple minds like mine!).*

I simply execute the code I want to execute (in this case, the CREATE statement) and handle the error if there is one — there really isn't much more to it than that.

We will look at error handling in a far more thorough fashion our next chapter. In the meantime, you can use TRY/CATCH to give basic error handling to your scripts.

Summary

Understanding scripts and batches is the cornerstone to an understanding of programming with SQL Server. The concepts of scripts and batches lay the foundation for a variety of functions from scripting complete database builds to programming stored procedures and triggers.

Local variables have scope for only one batch. Even if you have declared the variable within the same overall script, you will still get an error message if you don't re-declare it (and start over with assigning values) before referencing it in a new batch.

There are many system functions available. We provided a listing of some of the most useful system functions, but there are many more. Try checking out the Books Online or Appendix A at the back of this book for some of the more obscure ones. System functions do not need to be declared, and are always available. Some are scoped to the entire server, while others return values specific to the current connection.

You can use batches to create precedence between different parts of your scripts. The first batch starts at the beginning of the script, and ends at the end of the script or the first GO statement — whichever comes first. The next batch (if there is another) starts on the line after the first one ends and continues to the end of the script or the next GO statement — again, whichever comes first. The process continues to the end of the script. The first batch from the top of the script is executed first; the second is executed second, and so on. All commands within each batch must pass validation in the query parser, or none of that batch will be executed; however, any other batches will be parsed separately and will still be executed (if they pass the parser).

We saw how we can create and execute SQL dynamically. This can afford us the opportunity to deal with scenarios that aren't always 100 percent predictable or situations where something we need to construct our statement is actually itself a piece of data.

Finally, we took a look at the control of flow constructs that SQL Server offers. By mixing these constructs, we are able to conditionally execute code, create loops, or provide for a form of string substitution.

In the next couple of chapters, we will take the notions of scripting and batches to the next level, and apply them to stored procedures, user-defined functions, and triggers — the closest things that SQL Server has to actual programs.

Exercises

1. Write a simple script that creates two integer variables (one called Var1 and one called Var2), places the values 2 and 4 in them respectively, and then outputs the value of the two variables added together.

2. Create a variable called MinOrder and populate it with the smallest line item amount after discount for AdventureWorks2008 CustomerID 1 (Careful: we're dealing with currency here, so don't just assume you're going to use an int.) Output the final value of MinOrder.

3. Use sqlcmd to output the results of the query SELECT COUNT(*) FROM Customers to the console window.

Stored Procedures

Ah, the good stuff. If you're a programmer coming from a procedural language, then this is probably the part you've been waiting for. It's time to get down to the main variety of code of SQL Server, but before we get going too far down that road, I need to prepare you for what lies ahead. There's probably a lot less than you're expecting and, at the very same time, a whole lot more. The good news is that, with SQL Server 2008, you have .NET support — giving us a veritable "oo la la!" of possibilities.

You see, a *stored procedure*, sometimes referred to as a *sproc* (which I usually say as one word, but I've sometimes heard pronounced as "ess-proc"), is really just something of a script — or more correctly speaking, a *batch* — that is stored in the database rather than in a separate file. Now this comparison is not an exact one by any means — sprocs have things, such as input parameters, output parameters, and return values, that a script doesn't really have, but the comparison is not that far off either.

For now, SQL Server's only "programming" language continues to be T-SQL, and that leaves us miles short of the kind of procedural horsepower that you expect when you think of a true programming language. However, T-SQL blows C, C++, Visual Basic, Java, Delphi, or whatever away when it comes to what T-SQL is supposed to do — work on data definition, manipulation, and access. But T-SQL's horsepower stops right about there — at data access and management. In short, it has an adequate amount of power to get most simple things done, but it's not always the place to do it.

For this chapter, we're not going to worry all that much about T-SQL's shortcomings — instead, we'll focus on how to get the most out of T-SQL, and even toss in a smattering of what .NET can add to the picture. We'll take a look at parameters, return values, control of flow, looping structures, both basic and advanced error trapping, and more. In short, this is a big chapter that deals with many subjects. All of the major subject areas are broken up into their own sections, so you can take them one step at a time, but let's start right out with the basics of getting a sproc created.

Creating the Sproc: Basic Syntax

Creating a sproc works pretty much the same as creating any other object in a database, except that it uses the AS keyword that you first saw when we took a look at views. The basic syntax looks like this:

```
CREATE PROCEDURE|PROC <sproc name>
    [<parameter name> [schema.]<data type> [VARYING] [= <default value>] [OUT [PUT]]
[READONLY]
    [,<parameter name> [schema.]<data type> [VARYING] [= <default value>] [OUT[PUT]]
[READONLY]
[,  ...
    ...
        ]]
[WITH
    RECOMPILE| ENCRYPTION | [EXECUTE AS { CALLER|SELF|OWNER|<'user name'>}]
[FOR REPLICATION]
AS
    <code> | EXTERNAL NAME <assembly name>.<assembly class>.<method>
```

As you can see, we still have our basic CREATE <Object Type> <Object Name> syntax that is the backbone of every CREATE statement. The only oddity here is the choice between PROCEDURE and PROC. Either option works just fine, but as always, I recommend that you be consistent regarding which one you choose (personally, I like the saved keystrokes of PROC). The name of your sproc must follow the rules for naming as outlined in Chapter 1.

After the name comes a list of parameters. Parameterization is optional, and we'll defer that discussion until a little later in the chapter.

Last, but not least, comes your actual code following the AS keyword.

An Example of a Basic Sproc

Perhaps the best example of basic sproc syntax is to get down to the most basic of sprocs — a sproc that returns all the columns in all the rows on a table — in short, everything to do with a table's data.

I would hope that by now you have the query that would return all the contents of a table down cold (Hint: SELECT * FROM...). If not, then I would suggest a return to the chapter on basic query syntax. In order to create a sproc that performs this basic query — we'll do this one against the Employee table (in the HumanResources schema) — we just add the query in the code area of the sproc syntax:

```
USE AdventureWorks2008

GO
CREATE PROC spEmployee
AS
    SELECT * FROM HumanResources.Employee;
```

Not too rough, eh? If you're wondering why I put the GO keyword in before the CREATE syntax (if we were just running a simple SELECT statement, we wouldn't need it), it's because most non-table CREATE statements cannot share a batch with any other code. Indeed, even with a CREATE TABLE statement, leaving out the GO can become rather dicey. In this case, having the USE command together with our CREATE PROC statement would have been a no-no and would have generated an error.

Now that we have our sproc created, let's execute it to see what we get:

```
EXEC spEmployee;
```

We get exactly what we would have gotten if we had run the SELECT statement that's embedded in the sproc:

```
BusinessEntityID NationalIDNumber LoginID
---------------- ---------------- ------------------------------------------------------------
1                295847284        adventure-works\ken0           ---
2                245797967        adventure-works\terri0                     ---
3                509647174        adventure-works\roberto0                   ---
...
288              954276278        adventure-works\rachel0                    ---
289              668991357        adventure-works\jae0           ---
290              134219713        adventure-works\ranjit0                    ---
(290 row(s) affected)
```

Note that I've trimmed several columns from the right-hand side of the result set (we can only fit so much in the width of a book!) — you'll get additional columns for things like JobTitle, BirthDate, *and so on).*

You've just written your first sproc. It was easy, of course, and frankly, for most situations, sproc writing isn't nearly as difficult as most database people would like to have you think (job preservation), but there are lots of possibilities, and we've only seen the beginning.

Changing Stored Procedures with ALTER

I'm going to admit something here — I cut and pasted almost all the text you're about to read in this and the next section ("Dropping Sprocs") from the chapter on views. What I'm pointing out by telling you this is that they work almost identically from the standpoint of what an ALTER statement does.

The main thing to remember when you edit sprocs with T-SQL is that you are completely replacing the existing sproc. The only differences between using the ALTER PROC statement and the CREATE PROC statement are:

❑   ALTER PROC expects to find an existing sproc, where CREATE doesn't.

❑   ALTER PROC retains any permissions (also often referred to as *rights*) that have been established for the sproc. It keeps the same object ID within system objects and allows the dependencies to be kept. For example, if procedure A calls procedure B and you drop and recreate procedure B, you no longer see the dependency between the two. If you use ALTER, it is all still there.

❑   ALTER PROC retains any dependency information on other objects that may call the sproc being altered.

The latter of these three is the biggie.

> If you perform a DROP and then use a CREATE, you have almost the same effect as using an ALTER PROC statement with one rather big difference — if you DROP and CREATE, then you will need to entirely reestablish your permissions on who can and can't use the sproc.

Dropping Sprocs

It doesn't get much easier than this:

```
DROP PROC|PROCEDURE <sproc name>[;]
```

And it's gone.

Parameterization

A stored procedure gives you some (or in the case of .NET, a *lot* of) procedural capability and also gives you a performance boost (more on that later), but it wouldn't be much help in most circumstances if it couldn't accept some data to tell it what to do. For example, it doesn't do much good to have a spDeleteVendor stored procedure if we can't tell it what vendor we want to delete, so we use an *input parameter*. Likewise, we often want to get information back out of the sproc — not just one or more recordsets of table data, but also information that is more direct. An example here might be where we update several records in a table and we'd like to know just how many we updated. Often, this isn't easily handed back in recordset form, so we make use of an *output parameter*.

From outside the sproc, parameters can be passed in either by position or by reference. From the inside, it doesn't matter which way they come in — they are declared the same either way.

Declaring Parameters

Declaring a parameter requires two to four of these pieces of information:

❑ The name
❑ The data type
❑ The default value
❑ The direction

The syntax is:

```
@parameter_name [AS] datatype [= default|NULL] [VARYING] [OUTPUT|OUT]
```

The name has a pretty simple set of rules to it. First, it must start with the @ sign (just like variables do). Other than that, the rules for naming are pretty much the same as the rules for naming described in Chapter 1, except that they cannot have embedded spaces.

The data type, much like the name, must be declared just as you would for a variable — with a valid SQL Server built-in or user-defined data type.

One special thing in declaring the data type is to remember that, when declaring a parameter of type CURSOR, *you must also use the* VARYING *and* OUTPUT *options. The use of this type of parameter is pretty unusual and well outside the scope of this book, but keep it in mind in case you see it in books online or other documentation and wonder what that's all about.*

Note also that OUTPUT *can be abbreviated to* OUT.

The default is the first place we start to see any real divergence from variables. Where variables are always initialized to a NULL value, parameters are not. Indeed, if you don't supply a default value, then the parameter is assumed to be required, and a beginning value must be supplied when the sproc is called.

So, for example, let's try a slightly different version of our previous sproc. This time, we'll be supplying name information from the Person.Person table and accepting a filter for the last name:

```
USE AdventureWorks2008;

GO

CREATE PROC spEmployeeByName
    @LastName  nvarchar(50)
AS

SELECT p.LastName, p.FirstName, e.JobTitle, e.HireDate
FROM Person.Person p
JOIN HumanResources.Employee e
    ON p. BusinessEntityID = e.BusinessEntityID
WHERE p.LastName LIKE @LastName + '%';
```

Try this sproc supplying the required default:

```
EXEC spEmployeeByName 'Dobney';
```

And you get a very short list back (indeed, just one employee):

```
LastName      FirstName    JobTitle                        HireDate
------------  -----------  ------------------------------  ----------
Dobney        JoLynn       Production Supervisor - WC60    1998-01-26
```

> **Be careful using wildcard matches, such as the LIKE statement used in the preceding code. This particular example would likely perform OK because the wildcard is at the end. Keep in mind that wildcards used at the beginning of a search effectively eliminate the opportunity for SQL Server to use an index since any starting character is potentially a match.**

Now check what happens if we don't supply the default:

```
EXEC spEmployeeByName;
```

SQL Server wastes no time in informing us of the error of our ways:

```
Msg 201, Level 16, State 4, Procedure spEmployeeByName, Line 0
Procedure or Function 'spEmployeeByName' expects parameter '@LastName', which was
not supplied.
```

Because no default was provided, the parameter is assumed to be required.

Supplying Default Values

To make a parameter optional, you have to supply a default value. To do this, you just add an = together with the value you want to use for a default after the data type, but before the comma. Once you've done this, the users of your sproc can decide to supply no value for that parameter, or they can provide their own value.

So, for example, if we wanted to allow the parameter in our previous example to be optional, we would just modify the parameter declaration to include a default:

```
USE AdventureWorks2008;
```

```
DROP PROC spEmployeeByName; -- Get rid of the previous version
GO
CREATE PROC spEmployeeByName
@LastName nvarchar(50) = NULL
AS
IF @LastName IS NOT NULL
    SELECT p.LastName, p.FirstName, e.JobTitle, e.HireDate
    FROM Person.Person p
    JOIN HumanResources.Employee e
        ON p.BusinessEntityID = e.BusinessEntityID
    WHERE p.LastName LIKE @LastName + '%';
ELSE
    SELECT p.LastName, p.FirstName, e.JobTitle, e.HireDate
    FROM Person.Person p
    JOIN HumanResources.Employee e
        ON p.BusinessEntityID = e.BusinessEntityID;
```

Notice how I have made use of the control of flow constructs we learned in the previous chapter on scripting to decide which is the better query to run. The differences are subtle, with only the addition of a WHERE clause really differentiating the choices.

Given our new default, we can now run the sproc without a parameter:

```
EXEC spEmployeeByName;
```

And, as expected, we get a more full result set:

```
LastName       FirstName    JobTitle                         HireDate
-----------    ----------   ----------------------------     ----------
Sánchez        Ken          Chief Executive Officer          1999-02-15
Duffy          Terri        Vice President of Engineering     1998-03-03
Tamburello     Roberto      Engineering Manager              1997-12-12
...
...
Valdez         Rachel       Sales Representative             2003-07-01
Pak            Jae          Sales Representative             2002-07-01
Vakey Chudu    Ranjit        Sales Representative              2002-07-01

(290 row(s) affected)
```

If we were to run this with the same parameter (Dobney) as before, we would still wind up with the same results as we did before — the only change is that we've now allowed the parameter to be optional and handled the situation where the parameter was not supplied.

Creating Output Parameters

Sometimes you want to pass non-recordset information out to whatever called your sproc. One example of this would create a modified version of our last two sprocs.

Perhaps one of the most common uses for this is with sprocs that do inserts into tables with identity values. Often the code calling the sproc wants to know what the identity value was when the process is complete.

To show this off, we'll utilize a stored procedure that is already in the AdventureWorks2008 database — uspLogError. It looks like this:

```
-- uspLogError logs error information in the ErrorLog table about the
-- error that caused execution to jump to the CATCH block of a
-- TRY...CATCH construct. This should be executed from within the scope
-- of a CATCH block otherwise it will return without inserting error
-- information.
CREATE PROCEDURE [dbo].[uspLogError]
    @ErrorLogID [int] = 0 OUTPUT -- contains the ErrorLogID of the row inserted
AS                               -- by uspLogError in the ErrorLog table
BEGIN
    SET NOCOUNT ON;

    -- Output parameter value of 0 indicates that error
    -- information was not logged
    SET @ErrorLogID = 0;

    BEGIN TRY
        -- Return if there is no error information to log
        IF ERROR_NUMBER() IS NULL
            RETURN;

        -- Return if inside an uncommittable transaction.
        -- Data insertion/modification is not allowed when
        -- a transaction is in an uncommittable state.
        IF XACT_STATE() = -1
        BEGIN
            PRINT 'Cannot log error since the current transaction is in an
uncommittable state. '
                + 'Rollback the transaction before executing uspLogError in order
to successfully log error information.';
            RETURN;
        END

        INSERT [dbo].[ErrorLog]
            (
            [UserName],
            [ErrorNumber],
            [ErrorSeverity],
            [ErrorState],
```

```
                [ErrorProcedure],
                [ErrorLine],
                [ErrorMessage]
                )
        VALUES
                (
                CONVERT(sysname, CURRENT_USER),
                ERROR_NUMBER(),
                ERROR_SEVERITY(),
                ERROR_STATE(),
                ERROR_PROCEDURE(),
                ERROR_LINE(),
                ERROR_MESSAGE()
                );

        -- Pass back the ErrorLogID of the row inserted
        SET @ErrorLogID = @@IDENTITY;
    END TRY
    BEGIN CATCH
        PRINT 'An error occurred in stored procedure uspLogError: ';
        EXECUTE [dbo].[uspPrintError];
        RETURN -1;
    END CATCH
END;
```

Note the sections that I've highlighted here — these are the core to our output parameter. The first declares the parameter as being an output parameter. The second makes the insert that utilizes the identity value, and, finally, the SET statement captures the identity value. When the procedure exists, the value in @ErrorLogID is passed to the calling script.

Let's utilize our TRY/CATCH example from the tail end of the last chapter, but this time we'll make the call to uspLogError:

```
USE AdventureWorks2008;

BEGIN TRY
-- Try and create our table
CREATE TABLE OurIFTest(
    Col1    int     PRIMARY KEY
    )
END TRY
BEGIN CATCH
    -- Uh oh, something went wrong, see if it's something
    -- we know what to do with
    DECLARE @MyOutputParameter int;

    IF ERROR_NUMBER() = 2714 -- Object exists error, we knew this might happen
    BEGIN
        PRINT 'WARNING: Skipping CREATE as table already exists';
        EXEC dbo.uspLogError @ErrorLogID = @MyOutputParameter OUTPUT;
        PRINT 'A error was logged. The Log ID for our error was '
                + CAST(@MyOutputParameter AS varchar);
    END
```

```
    ELSE     -- hmm, we don't recognize it, so report it and bail
        RAISERROR('something not good happened this time around', 16, 1 );
END CATCH
```

If you run this in a database that does not already have the `OurIFTest` table, then you will get a simple:

```
Command(s) completed successfully.
```

But run it where the `OurIFTest` table already exists (for example, run it twice if you haven't run the `CREATE` code before) and you get something to indicate the error:

```
WARNING: Skipping CREATE as table already exists
A error was logged. The Log ID for our error was 3
```

Note that the actual error number you see will depend on whether the ErrorLog table has already had other errors inserted in it before you ran this test.

Now run a little select against the error log table:

```
SELECT *
FROM ErrorLog
WHERE ErrorLogID = 3; -- change this value to whatever your
                      -- results said it was logged as
```

And you can see that the error was indeed properly logged:

```
ErrorLogID  UserName    ErrorMessage
----------- ----------- -------------------------------------------------
3           dbo         There is already an object named 'OurIFTest' ...

(1 row(s) affected)
```

There are several things that you should take note of between the sproc itself and the usage of it by the calling script:

❑ The `OUTPUT` keyword was required for the output parameter in the sproc declaration.

❑ You must use the `OUTPUT` keyword when you call the sproc, much as you did when you declared the sproc. This gives SQL Server advance warning about the special handling that parameter will require. Be aware, however, that forgetting to include the `OUTPUT` keyword won't create a runtime error (you won't get any messages about it), but the value for the output parameter won't be moved into your variable (you'll just wind up with what was already there — most likely a `NULL` value). This means that you'll have what I consider to be the most dreaded of all computer terms — unpredictable results.

❑ The variable you assign the output result to does *not* have to have the same name as the internal parameter in the sproc. For example, in our previous sproc, the internal parameter in the error logging sproc was called `@ErrorLogID`, but the variable the value was passed to was called `@MyOutputParameter`.

❑ The `EXEC` (or `EXECUTE`) keyword was required since the call to the sproc wasn't the first thing in the batch (you can leave off the `EXEC` if the sproc call is the first thing in a batch) — personally, I recommend that you train yourself to use it regardless.

Confirming Success or Failure with Return Values

You'll see return values used in a couple of different ways. The first is to actually return data, such as an identity value or the number of rows that the sproc affected. Consider this an evil practice from the dark ages. Instead, move on to the way that return values should be used and what they are really there for — determining the execution status of your sproc.

If it sounds like I have an opinion on how return values should be used, it's because I most definitely do. I was actually originally taught to use return values as a "trick" to get around having to use output parameters — in effect, as a shortcut. Happily, I overcame this training. The problem is that, like most shortcuts, you're cutting something out and, in this case, what you're cutting out is rather important.

Using return values as a means of returning data back to your calling routine clouds the meaning of the return code when you need to send back honest-to-goodness error codes. In short — don't go there!

Return values are all about indicating success or failure of the sproc, and even the extent or nature of that success or failure. For the C-style programmers among you, this should be a fairly easy strategy to relate to — it is a common practice to use a function's return value as a success code, with any non-zero value indicating some sort of problem. If you stick with the default return codes in SQL Server, you'll find that the same rules hold true.

How to Use RETURN

Actually, your program will receive a return value whether you supply one or not. By default, SQL Server automatically returns a value of zero when your procedure is complete.

To pass a return value back from our sproc to the calling code, we simply use the RETURN statement:

```
RETURN [<integer value to return>]
```

> **Note that the return value must be an integer.**

Perhaps the biggest thing to understand about the RETURN statement is that it unconditionally exits from your sproc. That is, no matter where you are in your sproc, not one single more line of code will execute after you have issued a RETURN statement.

By unconditionally, I don't mean that a RETURN statement is executed regardless of where it is in code. On the contrary, you can have many RETURN statements in your sproc, and they will only be executed when the normal conditional structure of your code issues the command. Once that happens, however, there is no turning back.

Let's illustrate this idea of how a RETURN statement affects things by writing a very simple test sproc:

```
USE AdventureWorks2008;
GO
```

```
CREATE PROC spTestReturns
AS
    DECLARE @MyMessage          varchar(50);
    DECLARE @MyOtherMessage     varchar(50);

    SELECT @MyMessage = 'Hi, it''s that line before the RETURN';
    PRINT @MyMessage;
    RETURN;
    SELECT @MyOtherMessage = 'Sorry, but we won''t get this far';
    PRINT @MyOtherMessage;
RETURN;
```

Note that I didn't choose to initialize the two message variables in the declaration this time. Why? Well, in this case, I believe it makes for substantiallly more readable code if I keep the initialization on it's own line — this is going to be true with most any string variable where the initial value is more than a few characters long.

OK, now we have a sproc, but we need a small script to test out a couple of things for us. What we want to see is:

❑   What gets printed out

❑   What value the RETURN statement returns

To capture the value of a RETURN statement, we need to assign it to a variable during our EXEC statement. For example, the following code would assign whatever the return value is to @ReturnVal:

```
EXEC @ReturnVal = spMySproc;
```

Now let's put this into a more useful script to test out our sproc:

```
DECLARE @Return int;

EXEC @Return = spTestReturns;
SELECT @Return;
```

Short but sweet — when we run it, we see that the RETURN statement did indeed terminate the code before anything else could run:

```
Hi, it's that line before the RETURN


-----------
0
(1 row(s) affected)
```

We also got back the return value for our sproc, which was zero. Notice that the value was zero even though we didn't specify a specific return value. That's because the default is always zero.

Think about this for a minute — if the return value is zero by default, then that means that the default return is also, in effect, "No Errors." This has some serious dangers to it. The key point here is to make sure that you always explicitly define your return values — that way, you are reasonably certain to be returning the value you intended, rather than something by accident.

Now, just for grins, let's alter that sproc to verify that we can send whatever integer value we want back as the return value:

```
USE AdventureWorks2008;
GO

ALTER PROC spTestReturns
AS
    DECLARE @MyMessage        varchar(50);
    DECLARE @MyOtherMessage   varchar(50);

    SELECT @MyMessage = 'Hi, it''s that line before the RETURN';
    PRINT @MyMessage
    RETURN 100;
    SELECT @MyOtherMessage = 'Sorry, but we won''t get this far';
    PRINT @MyOtherMessage;
RETURN;
```

Now rerun your test script and you'll get the same result save for that change in return value:

```
Hi, it's that line before the RETURN

-----------
100
(1 row(s) affected)
```

More On Dealing with Errors

Sure. We don't need this section. I mean, our code never has errors, and we never run into problems, right? OK, well, now that we've had our moment of fantasy for today, let's get down to reality. Things go wrong — it's just the way that life works in the wonderful world of software engineering. Fortunately, we can do something about it. Unfortunately, you're probably not going to be happy with the tools you have. Fortunately again, there are ways to make the most out of what you have, and ways to hide many of the inadequacies of error handling in the SQL world.

OK, so we got a taste of error handling at the end of the previous chapter when we looked at TRY/CATCH blocks. Indeed, those are the way to perform traditional error handling when you only need to support SQL Server 2005 and newer. There is, however, a lot more to think about in SQL Server errors and error handling than just TRY/CATCH. So let's take a bit deeper look at things. . . .

Three common error types can happen in SQL Server:

❑   Errors that create runtime errors and stop your code from proceeding further.

❑   Errors that SQL Server knows about, but that don't create runtime errors such that your code stops running (these can also be referred to as *inline* errors).

❑   Errors that are more logical in nature and to which SQL Server is essentially oblivious.

Now, here things get a bit sticky and versions become important, so hang with me as we go down a very much winding road. . . .

As I write this, most SQL Server texts for 2008 are not out, but I'll go ahead and venture the same guess that I made in the 2005 version of this book — that is, most beginning books will not discuss much in the way of prior versions. Indeed, I've generally avoided discussion of how things were done in prior versions as it just adds more complexity. That said, I'm going to touch on prior versions in this section. Why? Well, most database developers will work with code that predates SQL Server 2005 (when TRY/CATCH was first introduced). Well, there was no formal error handler in SQL Server 2000 and earlier.

With this is mind, I'm going to give you a slimmed-down version of how error handling used to be — if for no other reason than to help you grasp the "why they did it that way" in older code you may come across. If you're certain that you're going to be a "SQL Server 2005 code or newer only" kinda DBA, then, by all means, feel free to skip this.

One thing remains common between the old and new error handling models — higher-level runtime errors.

It is possible to generate errors that will cause SQL Server to terminate the script immediately. This was true prior to TRY/CATCH, and it remains true even in the TRY/CATCH era. Errors that have enough severity to generate a runtime error are problematic from the SQL Server side of the equation. TRY/CATCH logic is a bit more flexible for some errors than what we had prior to SQL Server 2005, but we still have times where our sproc doesn't even know that something bad happened because the sproc in question terminated immediately and without notice (at least not to the sproc itself) on the error. On the bright side, all the current data access object models pass through the message on such errors, so you know about them in your client application and can do something about them there.

The Way We Were ...

In SQL Server 2000 and earlier, there was no formal error handler. You did not have an option that said, "If any error happens, go run this code over in this other spot." Instead, we had to monitor for error conditions within our code and then decide what to do at the point we detected the error (possibly well after the actual error occurred).

Handling Inline Errors

Inline errors are those pesky little things where SQL Server keeps running as such, but hasn't, for some reason, succeeded in doing what you wanted it to do. For example, try to insert a record into the Person .BusinessEntityContact table that doesn't have a corresponding record in the BusinessEntity or Person table:

```
USE AdventureWorks2008;
GO

INSERT INTO Person.BusinessEntityContact
        (BusinessEntityID
        ,PersonID
        ,ContactTypeID)
    VALUES
        (0,0,1);
```

SQL Server won't perform this insert for you because there is a FOREIGN KEY constraint on both BusinessEntityID and PersonID that references other tables. Since there is not a matching record in both tables, the record we are trying to insert into Person.BusinessEntityContact violates both of those foreign key constraints and is rejected:

```
Msg 547, Level 16, State 0, Line 1
The INSERT statement conflicted with the FOREIGN KEY constraint
"FK_BusinessEntityContact_Person_PersonID". The conflict occurred in database
"AdventureWorks2008", table "Person.Person", column 'BusinessEntityID'.
The statement has been terminated.
```

Pay attention to that error 547 up there — that's something of which we can make use.

It's worth noting that just the first foreign-key violation shows up in the error SQL Server provided. This is because SQL Server got to that error, saw it, and knew there was no point in going further. If we fixed the first error, then the second would be detected and we would again error out.

Making Use of @@ERROR

We already talked some about this bad boy when we were looking at scripting, but it's time to get a lot friendlier with this particular system function.

To review, @@ERROR contains the error number of the last T-SQL statement executed. If the value is zero, then no error occurred. This is somewhat similar to the ERROR_NUMBER() function we saw in the last chapter when we first discussed TRY/CATCH blocks. While ERROR_NUMBER() is only valid within a CATCH block (and remains the same regardless of where you are within that CATCH block), @@ERROR receives a new value with each statement you execute.

> The caveat with @@ERROR is that it is reset with each new statement. This means that if you want to defer analyzing the value, or you want to use it more than once, you need to move the value into some other holding bin — a local variable that you have declared for this purpose.

Play with this just a bit using the INSERT example from before:

```
USE AdventureWorks2008;
GO

DECLARE    @Error    int;

-- Bogus INSERT - there is no PersonID or BusinessEntityID of 0. Either of
-- these could cause the error we see when running this statement.
INSERT INTO Person.BusinessEntityContact
        (BusinessEntityID
        ,PersonID
        ,ContactTypeID)
    VALUES
        (0,0,1);

-- Move our error code into safekeeping. Note that, after this statement,
-- @@Error will be reset to whatever error number applies to this statement
```

```
SELECT @Error = @@ERROR;

-- Print out a blank separator line
PRINT '';

-- The value of our holding variable is just what we would expect
PRINT 'The Value of @Error is ' + CONVERT(varchar, @Error);

-- The value of @@ERROR has been reset - it's back to zero
-- since our last statement (the PRINT) didn't have an error.
PRINT 'The Value of @@ERROR is ' + CONVERT(varchar, @@ERROR);
```

Now execute your script and you can examine how @@ERROR is affected:

```
Msg 547, Level 16, State 0, Line 4
The INSERT statement conflicted with the FOREIGN KEY constraint
"FK_BusinessEntityContact_Person_PersonID". The conflict occurred in database
"AdventureWorks2008", table "Person.Person", column 'BusinessEntityID'.

The statement has been terminated.

The Value of @Error is 547
The Value of @@ERROR is 0
```

This illustrates pretty quickly the issue of saving the value from @@ERROR. The first error statement is only informational in nature. SQL Server has thrown that error, but hasn't stopped the code from executing. Indeed, the only part of that message that your sproc has access to is the error number. That error number resides in @@ERROR for just that next T-SQL statement; after that, it's gone.

> Notice that @Error and @@ERROR are two separate and distinct variables and can be referred to separately. This isn't just because of the case difference. (Depending on how you have your server configured, case sensitivity can affect your variable names.) It's because of the difference in scope. The @ or @@ is part of the name, so the number of @ symbols on the front makes each one separate and distinct from the other.

Using @@ERROR in a Sproc

OK, so let's start with an assumption here: If you're using @@ERROR, then the likelihood is that you are not using TRY/CATCH blocks. If you have not made this choice for backward compatibility reasons, I'm going to bop you upside the head and suggest you reconsider — TRY/CATCH is the much cleaner and all-around better way.

> TRY/CATCH will handle varieties of errors that in previous versions would have ended your script execution.

That said, TRY/CATCH is out of the equation if backward compatibility with SQL Server 2000 or prior is what you need, so let's take a quick look.

What we're going to do is look at two short procedures. Both are based on things we have already done in scripting or in earlier stored-procedure examples, but we want to take a look at how inline error checking works when it works, and how it doesn't when it doesn't (in particular, when inline does not work, but TRY/CATCH would).

Let's start with the referential integrity example we did earlier in this chapter:

```
USE AdventureWorks2008;
GO

INSERT INTO Person.BusinessEntityContact
        (BusinessEntityID
        ,PersonID
        ,ContactTypeID)
    VALUES(0,0,1);
```

You may recall this got us a simple 547 error. This is one of those that are trappable. We could trap this in a simple script, but let's do it as a sproc since procedural stuff is supposedly what we're working on here.

```
USE AdventureWorks2008
GO

CREATE PROC spInsertValidatedBusinessEntityContact
    @BusinessEntityID int,
    @PersonID int,
    @ContactTypeID int
AS
BEGIN

    DECLARE @Error int;

    INSERT INTO Person.BusinessEntityContact
            (BusinessEntityID
            ,PersonID
            ,ContactTypeID)
    VALUES
        (@BusinessEntityID, @PersonID, @ContactTypeID);

    SET @Error = @@ERROR;

    IF @Error = 0
        PRINT 'New Record Inserted';
    ELSE
    BEGIN
        IF @Error = 547 -- Foreign Key violation. Tell them about it.
            PRINT 'At least one provided parameter was not found. Correct and retry';
        ELSE -- something unknown
            PRINT 'Unknown error occurred. Please contact your system admin';
    END
END
```

Now try executing this with values that work:

```
EXEC spInsertValidatedBusinessEntityContact 1, 1, 11;
```

Our insert happens correctly, so no error condition is detected (because there isn't one).

```
(1 row(s) affected)
New Record Inserted
```

Now, try something that should blow up:

```
EXEC spInsertValidatedBusinessEntityContact 0, 1, 11;
```

And you see not only the actual SQL Server message, but the message from our error trap (note that there is no way of squelching the SQL Server message).

```
Msg 547, Level 16, State 0, Procedure spInsertValidatedBusinessEntityContact, Line
11
The INSERT statement conflicted with the FOREIGN KEY constraint
"FK_BusinessEntityContact_Person_PersonID". The conflict occurred in database
"AdventureWorks2008", table "Person.Person", column 'BusinessEntityID'.
The statement has been terminated.

At least one provided parameter was not found. Correct and retry
```

As you can see, we were able to detect our error without a TRY/CATCH block.

Now, let's move on to an example of why TRY/CATCH is better — a situation where a TRY/CATCH works fine, but where inline error checking fails. To show this one off, all we need to do is use our example for TRY/CATCH that we used in the scripting chapter. It looked like this:

```
BEGIN TRY
    -- Try and create our table
    CREATE TABLE OurIFTest(
        Col1      int          PRIMARY KEY
        )
END TRY
BEGIN CATCH
    -- Uh oh, something went wrong, see if it's something
    -- we know what to do with
    DECLARE @ErrorNo    int,
            @Severity   tinyint,
            @State      smallint,
            @LineNo     int,
            @Message    nvarchar(4000);

    SELECT
        @ErrorNo = ERROR_NUMBER(),
        @Severity = ERROR_SEVERITY(),
        @State = ERROR_STATE(),
        @LineNo = ERROR_LINE (),
        @Message = ERROR_MESSAGE();

    IF @ErrorNo = 2714 -- Object exists error, we knew this might happen
        PRINT 'WARNING: Skipping CREATE as table already exists';
    ELSE -- hmm, we don't recognize it, so report it and bail
        RAISERROR(@Message, 16, 1 );
END CATCH
```

It worked just fine. But if we try to do this using inline error checking, we have a problem:

```
CREATE TABLE OurIFTest(
    Col1    int         PRIMARY KEY
    );
IF @@ERROR != 0
    PRINT 'Problems!';
ELSE
    PRINT 'Everything went OK!';
```

Run this (you'll need to run it twice to generate the error if the table isn't already there) and we quickly find out that, without the TRY block, SQL Server aborts the script entirely on the particular error we're generating here:

```
Msg 2714, Level 16, State 6, Line 2
There is already an object named 'OurIFTest' in the database.
```

Notice that our PRINT statements never got a chance to execute — SQL Server had already terminated processing. With TRY/CATCH we were able to trap and handle this error, but using inline error checking, our attempts to trap an error like this fail.

Handling Errors Before They Happen

Sometimes you have errors that SQL Server doesn't really have an effective way to even know about, let alone tell you about. Other times we want to prevent the errors before they happen. These we need to check for and handle ourselves.

To try this out, let's make a new version of an existing sproc in AdventureWorks2008 called HumanResources .uspUpdateEmployeeHireInfo — we'll call ours HumanResources.uspUpdateEmployeeHireInfo2. In this, let's address some business rules that are logical in nature, but not necessarily implemented in the database (or, in this case, even possible to handle with constraints). Let's start by taking a look at the existing sproc:

```
CREATE PROCEDURE HumanResources.uspUpdateEmployeeHireInfo2
    @BusinessEntityID int,
    @JobTitle nvarchar(50),
    @HireDate datetime,
    @RateChangeDate datetime,
    @Rate money,
    @PayFrequency tinyint,
    @CurrentFlag dbo.Flag
WITH EXECUTE AS CALLER
AS
BEGIN
    SET NOCOUNT ON;

    BEGIN TRY
        BEGIN TRANSACTION;

        UPDATE HumanResources.Employee
        SET JobTitle = @JobTitle,
```

```
            HireDate = @HireDate,
            CurrentFlag = @CurrentFlag
    WHERE BusinessEntityID = @BusinessEntityID;

    INSERT INTO HumanResources.EmployeePayHistory
        (BusinessEntityID,
         RateChangeDate,
         Rate,
         PayFrequency)
    VALUES (@BusinessEntityID, @RateChangeDate, @Rate, @PayFrequency);

    COMMIT TRANSACTION;
END TRY
BEGIN CATCH
    -- Rollback any active or uncommittable transactions before
    -- inserting information in the ErrorLog
    IF @@TRANCOUNT > 0
    BEGIN
        ROLLBACK TRANSACTION;
    END

    EXECUTE dbo.uspLogError;
END CATCH;
END;
```

What's going on in this sproc is pretty straightforward: There are two statements (one to update the existing employee record and one to handle the additional history record) plus a very generic error handler. What we're going to do is add some new code to this sproc to recognize some errors that might occur and provide return values that will notify the client of more specific error information. We're not going to take the time to trap every potential error here, but we will catch some basics just to show how things might work. (Feel free to explore further on your own.)

The error handler in this sproc is very generic and doesn't really do anything that is specific to this particular sproc, so let's start by considering some of the errors that might occur in this sproc, for example:

❑ **An Employee Whose BusinessEntityID doesn't already exist:** The UPDATE statement in the sproc will actually run just fine (no errors) without a valid BusinessEntityID. It will just fail to find a match and wind up affecting zero rows; the error here is logical in nature, and SQL Server will see no problem with it at all. We should detect the error ourselves and trap it at this point before the sproc continues (since there is a foreign key between EmployeePayHistory and Employee, SQL Server will wind up raising an error on the INSERT statement when it can't find a matching BusinessEntityID).

❑ **Two updates affecting the same BusinessEntityID at the same RateChangeDate:** Again, the UPDATE statement will have no issues with such an update, but the INSERT statement will (the primary key for EmployeePayHistory is the composite of BusinessEntityID and RateChangeDate).

Let's address each of these in a new version of the sproc.

First, let's lay some groundwork. While SQL Server doesn't really have the concept of a constant, I'm going to use some variables as though they are constants. By doing so, I'm going to get away from just returning numbers and, instead, return a variable name that will make my code more readable by indicating the nature of the error I'm returning.

```
...
...
SET NOCOUNT ON;

-- Set up "constants" for error codes
DECLARE @BUSINESS_ENTITY_ID_NOT_FOUND int,
        @DUPLICATE_RATE_CHANGE int

SET     @BUSINESS_ENTITY_ID_NOT_FOUND = -1000
SET     @DUPLICATE_RATE_CHANGE = -2000

BEGIN TRY
...
...
```

You may be curious as to why I'm using negative values here for my errors. While there is no real standard on such things, I tend to use positive values for return codes that are informational in nature (perhaps there are multiple possible successful outcomes and I want to indicate which successful outcome occurred) and negative values for errors. You can find your own path on such things; just make sure you follow the cardinal rule — be consistent! Also, I am deliberately not using the initialization syntax that became available in SQL Server 2008 (I would change the declare to DECLARE @BUSINESS_ENTITY_ ID_NOT_FOUND int = -1000). This is purely for backward compatibility reasons, so adjust accordingly.

Next, we can test how many rows were affected by the UPDATE to HumanResources.Employee and utilize that to detect a BusinessEntityID Not Found error:

```
...
...
UPDATE HumanResources.Employee
SET JobTitle = @JobTitle,
    HireDate = @HireDate,
    CurrentFlag = @CurrentFlag
WHERE BusinessEntityID = @BusinessEntityID;

IF @@ROWCOUNT > 0
-- things happened as expected
   INSERT INTO HumanResources.EmployeePayHistory
       (BusinessEntityID,
        RateChangeDate,
        Rate,
        PayFrequency)
   VALUES (@BusinessEntityID, @RateChangeDate, @Rate, @PayFrequency);
ELSE
-- ruh roh, the update didn't happen, so skip the insert,
-- set the return value and exit
BEGIN
  PRINT 'BusinessEntityID Not Found';
  ROLLBACK TRAN;
  RETURN @BUSINESS_ENTITY_ID_NOT_FOUND;
END
    ...
    ...
```

Note the removal of the `HireDate` *column from the* `UPDATE`.

As we discussed earlier, the `RETURN` will immediately exit the sproc supplying the return value provided (in this case, –1000 — the amount matching our variable). Our client application can now test the return value and match it against a known list of possible errors.

That moves us on to our second potential error. We have a couple of ways we can handle this. We could pre-query the `EmployeePayHistory` table to see if it already has a matching row, and then avoid the `INSERT` entirely. Alternatively, we can just allow SQL Server to detect the error and just beef up the error handler to address that known possibility. In this case, I'm going to opt for the latter. It is almost always better to treat the rule and handle the exception. We would like to think that this particular error is going to be very infrequent, so we'll largely assume it isn't going to happen and address it when it does. With this in mind, we only need to make some alterations to our error handler:

```
...
...
BEGIN CATCH
        -- Rollback any active or uncommittable transactions before
        -- inserting information in the ErrorLog
        IF @@TRANCOUNT > 0
        BEGIN
            ROLLBACK TRANSACTION;
        END

        EXECUTE dbo.uspLogError;

        IF ERROR_NUMBER() = 2627    -- Primary Key violation
        BEGIN
            PRINT 'Duplicate Rate Change Found';
            RETURN @DUPLICATE_RATE_CHANGE;
        END
END CATCH;
...
...
```

OK, so with all these changes in place, let's take a look at our new overall sproc. While this is a new sproc, I'm highlighting only those lines that change versus the original we cloned it from:

```
CREATE PROCEDURE HumanResources.uspEmployeeHireInfo2</codeScreen>
    @BusinessEntityID [int],
    @JobTitle [nvarchar](50),
    @HireDate [datetime],
    @RateChangeDate [datetime],
    @Rate [money],
    @PayFrequency [tinyint],
    @CurrentFlag [dbo].[Flag]
WITH EXECUTE AS CALLER
AS
BEGIN
    SET NOCOUNT ON;
```

```sql
        -- Set up "constants" for error codes
    DECLARE @BUSINESS_ENTITY_ID_NOT_FOUND int = -1000,
            @DUPLICATE_RATE_CHANGE        int = -2000;

BEGIN TRY
    BEGIN TRANSACTION;

    UPDATE HumanResources.Employee
    SET JobTitle = @JobTitle,
        HireDate = @HireDate,
        CurrentFlag = @CurrentFlag
    WHERE BusinessEntityID = @BusinessEntityID;

    IF @@ROWCOUNT > 0
    -- things happened as expected
      INSERT INTO HumanResources.EmployeePayHistory
         (BusinessEntityID,
          RateChangeDate
          Rate,
          PayFrequency)
      VALUES
         (@BusinessEntityID,
          @RateChangeDate,
          @Rate,
          @PayFrequency);
    ELSE
    -- ruh roh, the update didn't happen, so skip the insert,
    -- set the return value and exit
    BEGIN
      PRINT 'BusinessEntityID Not Found';
      ROLLBACK TRAN;
      RETURN @BUSINESS_ENTITY_ID_NOT_FOUND;
    END

        COMMIT TRANSACTION;
END TRY
BEGIN CATCH
    -- Rollback any active or uncommittable transactions before
    -- inserting information in the ErrorLog
    IF @@TRANCOUNT > 0
    BEGIN
        ROLLBACK TRANSACTION;
    END

    EXECUTE dbo.uspLogError;

    IF ERROR_NUMBER() = 2627    -- Primary Key violation
    BEGIN
        PRINT 'Duplicate Rate Change Found';
        RETURN @DUPLICATE_RATE_CHANGE;
    END
END CATCH;
END;
```

Go ahead and run this once:

```
DECLARE @Return int;

EXEC @Return = HumanResources.uspEmployeeHireInfo2
    @BusinessEntityID = 1,
    @JobTitle = 'His New Title',
    @HireDate = '1996-07-01',
    @RateChangeDate = '2008-07-31',
    @Rate = 15,
    @PayFrequency = 1,
    @CurrentFlag = 1;

SELECT @Return;
```

And everything seems to run fine, but execute it a second time and we get some different results:

```
Duplicate Rate Change Found

-----------
-2000

(1 row(s) affected)
```

We tried to insert a second row with the same pay history, but SQL Server wouldn't allow that. We've used PRINT to supply informative output in case the statement is being executed without the Query window, and we're outputting a specific return value that the client can match against a value in a resource list.

Now, let's try the same basic test, but use an invalid BusinessEntityID:

```
DECLARE @Return int;

EXEC @Return = HumanResources.uspEmployeeHireInfo2
    @BusinessEntityID = 99999,
    @JobTitle = 'My Invalid Employee',;
    @HireDate = '2008-07-31',
    @RateChangeDate = '2008-07-31',
    @Rate = 15,
    @PayFrequency = 1,
    @CurrentFlag = 1;

SELECT @Return;
```

We get a similar error message and return code, but each is slightly different to allow for the specific error detected:

```
BusinessEntityID Not Found

-----------
-1000

(1 row(s) affected)
```

Note that this wasn't a SQL Server error — as far as SQL Server's concerned, everything about life is just fine. What's nice, though, is that, were we using a client program (say one you wrote in C#, VB.NET, C++, or some other language), we would, as with our duplicate insert pay history item, be able to track the −1000 against a known constant and send a very specific message to the end user.

Manually Raising Errors

Sometimes you have errors that SQL Server doesn't really know about, but you wish it did. For example, perhaps in the previous example you don't want to return −1000. Instead, you'd like to be able to create a runtime error at the client end that the client would then use to invoke an error handler and act accordingly. To do this, you use the RAISERROR command in T-SQL. The syntax is pretty straightforward:

```
RAISERROR (<message ID | message string | variable>, <severity>, <state>
[, <argument>
[,<...n>]] )
[WITH option[,...n]]
```

Let's take a look at what these mean.

Message ID/Message String

The message ID or message string you provide determines which message is sent to the client.

Using a message ID creates a manually raised error with the ID that you specified and the message that is associated with that ID as found in the sys.messages system view in the master database.

> *If you want to see what your SQL Server has as predefined messages, you can always perform a* SELECT * FROM master.sys.messages. *This includes any messages you've manually added to your system using the* sp_addmessage *stored procedure or through the SQL Server Management Studio.*

You can also just supply a message string in the form of ad hoc text without creating a more permanent message in the system:

```
RAISERROR ('Hi there, I''m an error', 1, 1);
```

This raises a rather simple error message:

```
Hi there, I'm an error
Msg 50000, Level 1, State 1
```

Notice that the assigned message number, even though you didn't supply one, is 50000. This is the default error value for any ad hoc error. It can be overridden using the WITH SETERROR option.

Severity

We got a quick overview of this when looking at TRY/CATCH in the chapter on scripting. For those of you already familiar with Windows servers, severity should be an old friend. *Severity* is an indication of just how bad things really are based on this error. For SQL Server, however, what severity codes mean can get a little bizarre. They can range from informational (severities 1–18), to system level (19–25), and even catastrophic (20–25). If you raise an error of severity 19 or higher (system level), the `WITH LOG` option must also be specified; 20 and higher automatically terminates the users' connections. (Kind of fun if you're feeling particularly ornery, but they *hate* that!)

So, let's get back to what I meant by bizarre. SQL Server actually varies its behavior into more ranges than Windows does, or even than the Books Online will tell you about. Errors fall into six major groupings:

1–10	Purely informational, but will return the specific error code in the message information
11–16	If you do not have a `TRY`/`CATCH` block set up, then these terminate execution of the procedure and raise an error at the client. The state is shown to be whatever value you set it to. If you have a `TRY`/`CATCH` block defined, then that handler will be called rather than raising an error at the client.
17	Usually, only SQL Server should use this severity. Basically, it indicates that SQL Server has run out of resources — for example, `tempdb` was full — and can't complete the request. Again, a `TRY`/`CATCH` block will get this before the client does.
18–19	Both of these are severe errors and imply that the underlying cause requires system administrator attention. With 19, the `WITH LOG` option is required, and the event will show up in the Windows Event Log. These are the final levels at which you can trap the error with a `TRY`/`CATCH` block — after this, it will go straight to the client.
20–25	Your world has just caved in, as has the user's connection. Essentially, this is a fatal error. The connection is terminated. As with 19, you must use the `WITH LOG` option and a message will, if applicable, show up in the Event Log.

State

State is an ad hoc value. It's something that recognizes that exactly the same error may occur at multiple places within your code. The notion is that this gives you an opportunity to send something of a place marker for where exactly the error occurred.

State values can be between 1 and 127. If you are troubleshooting an error with Microsoft tech support, they apparently have some arcane knowledge that hasn't been shared with you about what some of these mean. I'm told that if you make a tech-support call to Microsoft, they are likely to ask about and make use of this state information.

Error Arguments

Some predefined errors accept arguments. These allow you to make the error somewhat more dynamic by changing to the specific nature of the error. You can also format your error messages to accept arguments.

When you want to use dynamic information in what is otherwise a static error message, you need to format the fixed portion of your message so that it leaves room for the parameterized section of the message. You do so by using placeholders. If you're coming from the C or C++ world, then you'll recognize the parameter placeholders immediately; they are similar to the `printf` command arguments. If you're not from the C world, these may seem a little odd to you. All the placeholders start with the % sign and are then coded for the kind of information you'll be passing to them, as shown in the following table.

Placeholder Type Indicator	Type of Value
D	Signed integer; Books Online indicates that it is an acceptable choice, but I've had problems getting it to work as expected
O	Unsigned octal
P	Pointer
S	String
U	Unsigned integer
X or x	Unsigned hexadecimal

In addition, there is the option to prefix any of these placeholder indicators with some additional flag and width information:

Flag	What It Does
– (dash or minus sign)	Left-justify; only makes a difference when you supply a fixed width
+ (plus sign)	Indicates the positive or negative nature if the parameter is a signed numeric type
0	Tells SQL Server to pad the left side of a numeric value with zeros until it reaches the width specified in the width option
# (pound sign)	Applies only to octal and hex values; tells SQL Server to use the appropriate prefix (0 or 0x) depending on whether it is octal or hex
' '	Pads the left of a numeric value with spaces if positive

Last, but not least, you can also set the width, precision, and long/short status of a parameter:

❑ **Width** — Set by simply supplying an integer value for the amount of space you want to hold for the parameterized value. You can also specify a *, in which case SQL Server will automatically determine the width according to the value you've set for precision.

❑ **Precision** — Determines the maximum number of digits output for numeric data.

❑ **Long/Short** — Set by using an h (short) or I (long) when the type of the parameter is an integer, octal, or hex value.

Let's use this in a simple example:

```
RAISERROR ('This is a sample parameterized %s, along with a zero
padding and a sign%+010d',1,1, 'string', 12121);
```

If you execute this, you get back something that looks a little different from what's in the quotation marks:

```
This is a sample parameterized string, along with a zero
padding and a sign+000012121
Msg 50000, Level 1, State 1
```

The extra values supplied were inserted, in order, into your placeholders, with the final value being reformatted as specified.

WITH <option>

Currently, you can mix and match three options when you raise an error:

❑   LOG

❑   SETERROR

❑   NOWAIT

WITH LOG

This tells SQL Server to log the error to the SQL Server error log and the Windows Application Log. This option is required with severity levels that are 19 or higher.

WITH SETERROR

By default, a RAISERROR command doesn't set @@ERROR with the value of the error you generated. Instead, @@ERROR reflects the success or failure of your actual RAISERROR command. SETERROR overrides this and sets the value of @@ERROR to be equal to your error ID.

WITH NOWAIT

Immediately notifies the client of the error.

Adding Your Own Custom Error Messages

We can make use of a special system stored procedure to add messages to the system. The sproc is called sp_addmessage, and the syntax looks like this:

```
sp_addmessage [@msgnum =] <msg id>,
[@severity =] <severity>,
[@msgtext =] <'msg'>
[, [@lang =] <'language'>]
[, [@with_log =] [TRUE|FALSE]]
[, [@replace =] 'replace']
```

All the parameters mean pretty much the same thing that they did with RAISERROR, except for the addition of the language and replace parameters and a slight difference with the WITH LOG option.

@lang

This specifies the language to which this message applies. What's cool here is that you can specify a separate version of your message for any language supported in syslanguages.

@with_log

This works just the same as it does in RAISERROR in that, if set to TRUE, the message will be automatically logged to both the SQL Server error log and the NT application log when raised (the latter only when running under NT). The only trick here is that you indicate that you want this message to be logged by setting this parameter to TRUE rather than using the WITH LOG option.

> Be careful of this one in the Books Online. Depending on how you read it, it would be easy to interpret it as saying that you should set @with_log to a string constant of 'WITH_LOG', when you should set it to TRUE. Perhaps even more confusing is that the REPLACE option looks much the same, and it must be set to the string constant rather than TRUE.

@replace

If you are editing an existing message rather than creating a new one, then you must set the @replace parameter to 'REPLACE'. If you leave this off, you'll get an error if the message already exists.

> Creating a set list of additional messages for use by your applications can greatly enhance reuse, but more importantly, it can significantly improve readability of your application. Imagine if every one of your database applications made use of a constant list of custom error codes. You could then easily establish a constants file (a resource or include library, for example) that had a listing of the appropriate errors; you could even create an include library that had a generic handling of some or all of the errors. In short, if you're going to be building multiple SQL Server apps in the same environment, consider using a set list of errors that is common to all your applications. Keep in mind, however, that many system administrators do not like application-specific changes to affect the master database (which is where your custom error message is written), so if you are not in control of your own server, make sure that custom error messages will be allowed on the server before writing code that depends on them.

Using sp_addmessage

As has already been indicated, sp_addmessage creates messages in much the same way as we create ad hoc messages using RAISERROR.

As an example, let's assume that AdventureWorks2008 was implementing a rule that said that orders couldn't be entered if they were more than seven days old. Knowing this rule, we could add our own custom message that tells the user about issues with their order date:

```
sp_addmessage
    @msgnum = 60000,
    @severity = 10,
    @msgtext = '%s is not a valid Order date.
Order date must be within 7 days of current date.';
```

Execute the sproc and it confirms the addition of the new message: `Command(s) completed successfully`.

> *No matter what database you're working with when you run* `sp_addmessage`, *the actual message is added to the master database and can be viewed at any time by looking at the* `sys.messages` *system view. The significance of this is that, if you migrate your database to a new server, the messages will need to be added again to that new server (the old ones will still be in the master database of the old server). As such, I strongly recommend keeping all your custom messages stored in a script somewhere so they can easily be added into a new system.*

Removing an Existing Custom Message

To get rid of the custom message use:

```
sp_dropmessage <message number>
```

What a Sproc Offers

Now that we've spent some time looking at how to build a sproc, we probably ought to ask the question as to why to use them. Some of the reasons are pretty basic; others may not come to mind right away if you're new to the RDBMS world. The primary benefits of sprocs include:

❑   Making processes that require procedural action callable

❑   Security

❑   Performance

Creating Callable Processes

As I've already indicated, a sproc is something of a script that is stored in the database. The nice thing is that, because it is a database object, we can call to it — you don't have to manually load it from a file before executing it.

Sprocs can call to other sprocs (called *nesting*). For SQL Server 2008, you can nest up to 32 levels deep. This gives you the capability of reusing separate sprocs much as you would make use of a subroutine in a classic procedural language. The syntax for calling one sproc from another sproc is exactly the same as it is calling the sproc from a script.

Using Sprocs for Security

Many people don't realize the full use of sprocs as a tool for security. Much like views, we can create a sproc that returns a recordset without having to give the user authority to the underlying table. Granting someone the right to execute a sproc implies that they can perform any action within the sproc, provided that the action is taken within the context of the sproc. That is, if we grant someone authority to execute a sproc that returns all the records in the Customers table, but not access to the actual Customers table, then the user will still be able to get data out of the Customers table, provided they do it by using the sproc (trying to access the table directly won't work).

What can be really handy here is that we can give someone access to modify data through the sproc, but then only give them read access to the underlying table. They will be able to modify data in the table provided that they do it through your sproc (which will likely be enforcing some business rules). They can then hook directly up to your SQL Server using Excel, Access, or whatever to build their own custom reports with no risk of "accidentally" modifying the data.

> Setting users up to directly link to a production database via Access or Excel has to be one of the most incredibly powerful and yet stupid things you can do to your system. While you are empowering your users, you are also digging your own grave in terms of the resources they will use and long-running queries they will execute (naturally, they will be oblivious to the havoc this causes your system).
>
> If you really must give users direct access, then consider using replication or backup and restores to create a completely separate copy of the database (or just the tables they need access to) for them to use. This will help insure you against record locks, queries that bog down the system, and a whole host of other problems.

Sprocs and Performance

Generally speaking, sprocs can do a lot to help the performance of your system. Keep in mind, however, that like most things in life, there are no guarantees — indeed, some processes can be created in sprocs that will substantially slow the process if the sproc hasn't been designed intelligently.

Where does that performance come from? Well, when we create a sproc, the process works something like what you see in Figure 12-1.

We start by running our CREATE PROC procedure. This parses the query to make sure that the code should actually run. The one difference versus running the script directly is that the CREATE PROC command can make use of what's called *deferred name resolution*. Deferred name resolution ignores the fact that you may have some objects that don't exist yet. This gives you the chance to create these objects later.

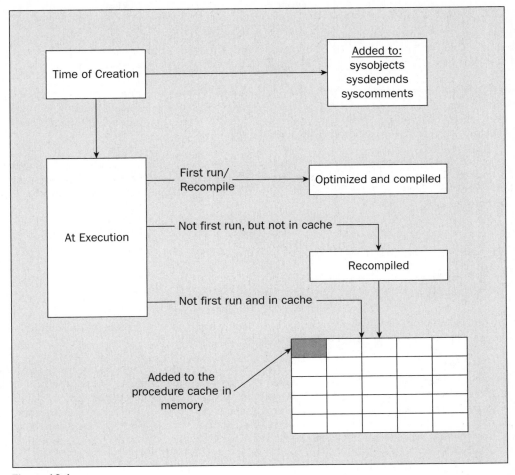

Figure 12-1

After the sproc has been created, it sits in wait for the first time that it is executed. At that time, the sproc is optimized and a query plan is compiled and cached on the system. Subsequent times that we run our sproc will, unless we specify otherwise using the WITH RECOMPILE option, generally use that cached query plan rather than creating a new one. (There are situations where the sproc will be recompiled, but that is beyond the scope of this book.) This means that whenever the sproc is used it can skip much of the optimization and compilation process. Exactly how much time this saves varies depending on the complexity of the batch, the size of the tables involved in the batch, and the number of indexes on each table. Usually, the amount of time saved is seemingly small — say, perhaps 1 second or less for most scenarios — yet that difference can really add up in terms of percentage (1 second is still 100 percent faster than 2 seconds). The difference can become even more extreme when we need to make several calls or when we are in a looping situation.

When a Good Sproc Goes Bad

Perhaps one of the most important things to recognize on the downside of sprocs is that, unless you manually interfere (using the WITH RECOMPILE option), they are optimized based on either the first time that they run or when the statistics have been updated on the table(s) involved in any queries.

That "optimize once, use many times" strategy is what saves the sproc time, but it's a double-edged sword. If our query is dynamic in nature (the query is built up as it goes using the EXEC command), then the sproc may be optimized for the way things ran the first time, only to find that things never run that way again — in short, it may be using the wrong plan!

It's not just dynamic queries in sprocs that can cause this scenario either. Imagine a web page that lets us mix and match several criteria for a search. For example, let's say that we wanted to add a sproc to the AdventureWorks2008 database that would support a web page that allows users to search for an order based on:

- ❑   Customer name
- ❑   Sales Order ID
- ❑   Product ID
- ❑   Order date

The user is allowed to supply any mix of the information, with each new piece of information supplied making the search a little more restricted and theoretically faster.

The approach we would probably take to this would be to have more than one query and to select the right query to run depending on what was supplied by the user. The first time that we execute our sproc, it is going to run through a few IF...ELSE statements and pick the right query to run. Unfortunately, it's just the right query for that particular time we ran the sproc (and an unknown percentage of the other times). Any time after that first time the sproc selects a different query to run, it will still be using the query plan based on the first time the sproc ran. In short, the query performance is really going to suffer.

Using the WITH RECOMPILE Option

We can choose to use the security and compartmentalization of code benefits of a sproc, but still ignore the precompiled code side of things. This lets us get around this issue of not using the right query plan, because we're certain that a new plan was created just for this run. To do this, we make use of the WITH RECOMPILE option, which can be included in two different ways.

First, we can include the WITH RECOMPILE at runtime. We simply include it with our execution script:

```
EXEC spMySproc '1/1/2004'
   WITH RECOMPILE
```

This tells SQL Server to throw away the existing execution plan and create a new one — but just this once. That is, just for this time that we've executed the sproc using the WITH RECOMPILE option.

We can also choose to make things more permanent by including the WITH RECOMPILE option right within the sproc. If we do things this way, we add the WITH RECOMPILE option immediately before our AS statement in our CREATE PROC or ALTER PROC statements.

If we create our sproc with this option, then the sproc will be recompiled each time that it runs, regardless of other options chosen at runtime.

Extended Stored Procedures (XPs)

The advent of .NET in SQL Server has really changed the area of Extended Stored Procedures. These used to be the bread and butter of the hard-core code scenarios — when you hit those times where basic T-SQL and the other features of SQL Server just wouldn't give you what you needed.

With the availability of .NET to deal with things like O/S file access and other external communication or complex formulas, the day of the XP would seem to be waning. XPs still have their place in the world for few reasons:

❏   Times where performance is so critical that you want the code running genuinely in process to SQL Server (this is truly a *radical* approach in the .NET era)

❏   Situations where your administrators will not allow .NET code to execute for security reasons (though allowing XPs, but not .NET, is somewhat silly if you ask me …)

For purposes of this book, I'll merely say that SQL Server does allow for the idea of externally written code that runs as a .DLL in process with SQL Server. XPs are created using C or C++.

A Brief Look at Recursion

Recursion is one of those things that isn't used very often in programming. Still, it's also one of those things for which, when you need it, there never seems to be anything else that will quite do the trick. As a "just in case," a brief review of what recursion is seems in order.

The brief version is that *recursion* is the situation where a piece of code calls itself. The dangers here should be fairly self-evident — if it calls itself once, then what's to keep it from calling itself over and over again? The answer to that is *you*. That is, *you* need to make sure that if your code is going to be called recursively, you provide a *recursion check* to make sure you bail out when it's appropriate.

I'd love to say that the example I'm going to use is all neat and original — but it isn't. Indeed, for an example, I'm going to use the classic recursion example that's used with about every textbook recursion discussion I've ever seen — please accept my apologies now. It's just that it's an example that can be understood by just about anyone, so here we go.

So what is that classic example? Factorials. For those who have had a while since math class (or their last recursion discussion), a factorial is the value you get when you take a number and multiply it successively by that number less one, then the next value less one, and so on, until you get to one. For example, the factorial of 5 is 120 — that's 5*4*3*2*1.

So, let's look at an implementation of such a recursive sproc:

```
CREATE PROC spFactorial
@ValueIn int,
```

```
@ValueOut int OUTPUT
AS
DECLARE @InWorking int;
DECLARE @OutWorking int;
IF @ValueIn != 1
BEGIN
      SELECT @InWorking = @ValueIn - 1;

      EXEC spFactorial @InWorking, @OutWorking OUTPUT;

      SELECT @ValueOut = @ValueIn * @OutWorking;
END
ELSE
BEGIN
      SELECT @ValueOut = 1;
END
RETURN;
GO
```

So, what we're doing is accepting a value in (that's the value we want a factorial of) and providing a value back out (the factorial value we've computed). The surprising part is that our sproc does not, in one step, do everything it needs to calculate the factorial. Instead, it just takes one number's worth of the factorial and then turns around and calls itself. The second call will deal with just one number's worth and then again call itself. This can go on and on up to a limit of 32 levels of recursion. Once SQL Server gets 32 levels deep, it will raise an error and end processing.

> Note that any calls into .NET assemblies count as an extra level in your recursion count, but anything you do within those assemblies does *not* count against the recursion limit. While .NET functionality in SQL Server is beyond the scope of this book, keep in mind that it is a potential way around nesting level issues.

Let's try out our recursive sproc with a little script:

```
DECLARE @WorkingOut int;
DECLARE @WorkingIn int;
SELECT @WorkingIn = 5;
EXEC spFactorial @WorkingIn, @WorkingOut OUTPUT;

PRINT CAST(@WorkingIn AS varchar) + ' factorial is ' + CAST(@WorkingOut AS varchar);
```

This gets us the expected result of 120:

```
5 factorial is 120
```

You can try different values for @WorkingIn and things should work just fine with two rather significant hitches:

❑   Arithmetic overflow when our factorial grows too large for the int (or even bigint) data type

❑   The 32-level recursion limit

You can test the arithmetic overflow easily by putting any large number in — anything bigger than about 13 will work for this example.

Testing the 32-level recursion limit takes a little bit more modification to our sproc. This time, we'll determine the *triangular* of the number. This is very similar to finding the factorial, except that we use addition rather than multiplication. Therefore, 5 triangular is just 15 (5+4+3+2+1). Let's create a new sproc to test this one out — it will look just like the factorial sproc with only a few small changes:

```
CREATE PROC spTriangular
@ValueIn int,
@ValueOut int OUTPUT
AS
DECLARE @InWorking int;
DECLARE @OutWorking int;
IF @ValueIn != 1
BEGIN
        SELECT @InWorking = @ValueIn - 1;

        EXEC spTriangular @InWorking, @OutWorking OUTPUT;

        SELECT @ValueOut = @ValueIn + @OutWorking;
END
ELSE
BEGIN
        SELECT @ValueOut = 1;
END
RETURN;
GO
```

As you can see, there weren't that many changes to be made. Similarly, we only need to change our sproc call and the PRINT text for our test script:

```
DECLARE @WorkingOut int;
DECLARE @WorkingIn int;
SELECT @WorkingIn = 5;
EXEC spTriangular @WorkingIn, @WorkingOut OUTPUT;

PRINT CAST(@WorkingIn AS varchar) + ' Triangular is ' + CAST(@WorkingOut AS
varchar);
```

Running this with an @ValueIn of 5 gets our expected 15:

```
5 Triangular is 15
```

However, if you try to run it with an @ValueIn of more than 32, you get an error:

```
Msg 217, Level 16, State 1, Procedure spTriangular, Line 10
Maximum stored procedure, function, trigger, or view nesting level exceeded (limit 32).
```

I'd love to say there's some great workaround to this, but, unless you can somehow segment your recursive calls (run it 32 levels deep, then come all the way back out of the call stack, then run down it again), you're pretty much out of luck. Just keep in mind that most recursive functions can be rewritten to be a more standard looping construct — which doesn't have any hard limit. Be sure you can't use a loop before you force yourself into recursion.

Debugging

Long ago and far away (SQL Server 2000), the Management Studio had real live debugging tools. They were a little clunky, in the sense that they really only worked around stored procedures (there wasn't a way to debug just a script, and debugging triggers required you to create a sproc that would fire the trigger), but, with some work-arounds here and there, we had the long-sought-after debugger. SQL Server 2005 came along and removed all debugging functionalityfrom the Management Studio (it was in the product, but you had to use the Visual Studio installation that is part of the Business Intelligence Development Studio in order to get at it — not very handy in any case, but nonexistent if you didn't install BIDS for some reason). I'm happy to say that debugging is back in the Management Studio, and it's better than ever!

Starting the Debugger

Unlike previous versions, the debugger in SQL Server 2008 is pretty easy to find. Much of using the debugger works as it does in VB or C# — probably like most modern debuggers, for that matter. Simply choose the Debug menu (available when a query window is active). You can then choose from options to get things started: Start Debugging (Alt+F5) or Step Into (F11).

Let's do a little bit of setup to show the debugger in action, both in a standard script and in a stored procedure scenario. To do this, we'll use the script we were just working with in the previous section (to exercise the spTriangular stored procedure we also created earlier in the chapter). The script looked like this:

```
DECLARE @WorkingOut int;
DECLARE @WorkingIn int = 5;

EXEC spTriangular @WorkingIn, @WorkingOut OUTPUT;

PRINT CAST(@WorkingIn AS varchar) + ' Triangular is '
    + CAST(@WorkingOut AS varchar);`
```

With this script as the active query window, let's start a debugging run with the Step Into option (choose it from the Debug menu or simply press F11).

Parts of the Debugger

Several things are worth noticing when the Debugger window first comes up:

❑ The yellow arrow on the left (Shown in Figure 12-2) indicates the *current execution line* — this is the next line of code that will be executed if we do a "go" or we start stepping through the code.

❑ There are icons at the top (see Figure 12-3) to indicate our different options, including:

❑ **Continue:** This will run to the end of the sproc or the next breakpoint (including a watch condition).

❑ **Step Into:** This executes the next line of code and stops prior to running the following line of code, regardless of what procedure or function that code is in. If the line of code being executed is calling a sproc or function, then Step Into has the effect of calling that sproc or function, adding it to the call stack, changing the locals window to represent the newly nested sproc rather than the parent, and then stopping at the first line of code in the nested sproc.

❑ **Step Over:** This executes every line of code required to take us to the next statement that is at the same level in the call stack. If you are not calling another sproc or a UDF, then this command will act just like a Step Into. If, however, you are calling another sproc or a UDF, then a Step Over will take you to the statement immediately following where that sproc or UDF returned its value.

❑ **Step Out:** This executes every line of code up to the next line of code at the next highest point in the call stack. That is, we will keep running until we reach the same level as whatever code called the level we are currently at.

❑ **Stop Debugging:** Again, this does what it says — it stops execution immediately. The debugging window does remain open, however.

❑ **Toggle Breakpoints and Remove All Breakpoints:** In addition, you can set breakpoints by clicking in the left margin of the code window. Breakpoints are points that you set to tell SQL Server to "stop here!" when the code is running in debug mode. This is handy in big sprocs or functions where you don't want to have to deal with every line — you just want it to run up to a point and stop every time it gets there.

```
DECLARE @WorkingOut int
DECLARE @WorkingIn int = 5

EXEC spTriangular @WorkingIn, @WorkingOut OUTPUT

PRINT CAST(@WorkingIn AS varchar) + ' Triangular is '
    + CAST(@WorkingOut AS varchar)
```

Figure 12-2

Figure 12-3

In addition, there is a choice that brings up the Breakpoints window, which is a list of all breakpoints that are currently set (again, handy in larger blocks of code). There are also a few of what we'll call "status" windows; let's go through a few of the more important of these.

The Locals Window

As I indicated back at the beginning of the book, I'm pretty much assuming that you have experience with some procedural language out there. As such, the Locals window (shown in Figure 12-4 as it matches with the current statement shown in Figure 12-3) probably isn't all that new of a concept to you. Simply put it shows you the current value of all the variables that are currently in scope. The list of variables in the Locals window may change (as may their values) as you step into nested sprocs and back out again. Remember — these are only those variables that are in scope as of the next statement to run.

In Figure 12-4, we're at the start of our first run through this sproc, so the value for the @ValueIn parameter has been set, but all other variables and parameters are not yet set and thus are effectively null.

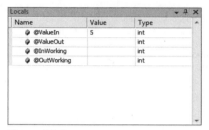

Figure 12-4

Three pieces of information are provided for each variable or parameter:

❑ The name

❑ The current value

❑ The data type

However, perhaps the best part to the Locals window is that you can edit the values in each variable. That means it's a lot easier to change things on the fly to test certain behaviors in your sproc.

The Watch Window

Here you can set up variables that you want to keep track of regardless of where you currently are in the call stack. You can either manually type in the name of the variable you want to watch, or you can select that variable in code, right click, and then select Add Watch. In Figure 12-5, I've added a watch for @ValueOut, but, since we haven't addressed that variable in code, you can see that no value has been set for it as yet.

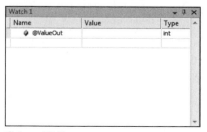

Figure 12-5

The Call Stack Window

The Call Stack window provides a listing of all the sprocs and functions that are currently active in the process that you are running. The handy thing here is that you can see how far in you are when you are running in a nested situation, and you can change between the nesting levels to verify what current variable values are at each level.

In Figure 12-6, I've stepped into the code for spTriangular such that we're down to it processing the working value of 3. If you're following along, you can just watch the @ValueIn variable in your Locals window and see how it changes as we step in. Our call stack now has several instances of spTriangular running as we've stepped into it (One for 5, one for 4, and now one for 3), as well as providing information on what statement is next in the current scope.

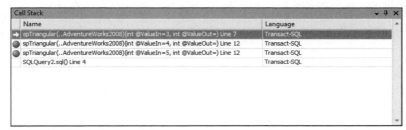

Figure 12-6

The Output Window

Much as it sounds, the Output window is the spot where SQL Server prints any output. This includes result sets as well as the return value when your sproc has completed running, but also provides debug information from the process we're debugging. Some example output from the middle of a debug run is shown in Figure 12-7.

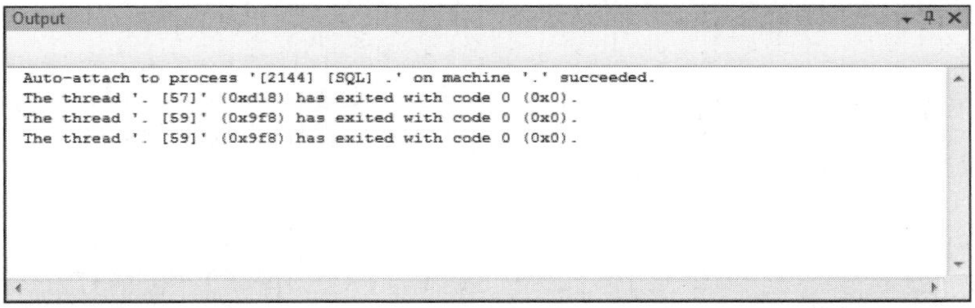

Figure 12-7

The Command Window

The Command window is probably going to be beyond common use as it is in SQL Server 2008. In short, it allows you something of a command line mode to access debugger commands and other objects. It is, however, cryptic at best and, as of this writing, relatively undocumented. Examples of commands you could issue would be something like:

```
>Debug.StepInto
```

There are a whole host of commands available to Intellisense, but you'll find that most of these are not actually available when debugging.

Using the Debugger Once It's Started

Now that we have the preliminaries out of the way and the debugger window up, we're ready to start walking through our code. If you were walking through some of the descriptions before, stop the debugger and restart it so we're in the same place.

The first executable line of our sproc is a bit deceptive — it is the DELCARE statement for @WorkingIn. Normally variable declarations are not considered executable, but, in this case, we are initializing the variable as part of the declaration, so the initialization code is seen by the debugger. You should notice that none of our variables has yet been set (the initialization code will be next to run, but has not actually executed yet). Step forward (using the menu choice, the tool tip, or simply press F11) and you should see (via the Locals window) @WorkingIn get initialized to our value of 5 — @WorkingOut is not initialized as part of the declaration.

Use the Step Into key one more time. We enter into our first execution of the spTriangular stored procedure and land at the first executable line in the sproc — our IF statement.

Since the value of @ValueIn is indeed not equal to 1, we step into the BEGIN...END block specified by our IF statement. Specifically, we move to our SELECT statement that initializes the @InWorking parameter for this particular execution of the procedure. As we'll see later, if the value of @ValueIn had indeed been one, we would have immediately dropped down to our ELSE statement.

Again, step forward one line by pressing F11, or using the Step Into icon or menu choice, until just *before* you enter the next instance of spTriangular.

Pay particular attention to the value of @InWorking in the Locals window. Notice that it changed to the correct value (@ValueIn is currently 5, so 5–1 is 4) as set by our SELECT statement. Also notice that our Call Stack window has only the current instance of our sproc in it (plus the current statement) — since we haven't stepped down into our nested versions of the sproc yet, we only see one instance.

Now go ahead and step into our next statement. Since this is the execution of a sproc, we're going to see a number of different things change in the debugger. Notice that it *appears* that our arrow that indicates the current statement jumped back up to the IF statement. Why? Well, this is a new instance of what is otherwise the same sproc. We can tell this based on our Call Stack window — notice that it now has two instances of our sproc listed. The one at the top (with the yellow arrow) is the current instance, and the one with the red breakpoint dot is a parent instance that is now waiting for something further up in the call stack. Notice also that the @ValueIn parameter has the value of 4 – that is the value we passed in from the outer instance of the sproc.

If you want to see the value of variables in the scope of the outer instance of the sproc, just double-click on that instance's line in the Call Stack window (the one with the green arrow) and you'll see several things changed in our debugging windows.

There are two things to notice here. First, the values of our variables have changed back to those in the scope of the outer (and currently selected) instance of the sproc. Second, the icon for our current execution line is different. This new green arrow is meant to show that this is the current line in this instance of the sproc, but it is not the current line in the overall call stack.

Go back to the current instance by clicking on the top item in the Call Stack window. Then step in three more times. This should bring you to the top line (the IF statement) in our third instance of the sproc. Notice that our call stack has become three deep and that the values of our variables and parameters in the Locals window have changed again. Last, but not least, notice that this time our @ValueIn parameter has a value of 3. Repeat this process until the @ValueIn parameter has a value of 1.

Step into the code one more time and you'll see a slight change in behavior. This time, since the value in @ValueIn is equal to 1, we move into the BEGIN...END block defined with our ELSE statement.

Since we've reached the bottom, we're ready to start going back up the call stack. Use Step Into through the last line of our procedure and you'll find that our call stack is back to only four levels. Also, notice that our output parameter (@OutWorking) has been appropriately set.

This time, let's do something different and do a Step Out (Shift+F11). If you're not paying attention, it will look like absolutely nothing has changed.

> **In this case, to use the old cliché, looks are deceiving. Again, notice the change in the Call Stack window and in the values in the Locals window — we stepped out of what was then the current instance of the sproc and moved up a level in the Call Stack. If we now keep stepping into the code (F11), then our sproc has finished running and we'll see the final version of our status windows and their respective finishing values. A big word of caution here! If you want to be able to see the truly final values (such as an output parameter being set), make sure that you use the Step Into option to execute the last line of code.**
>
> *If you use an option that executes several lines at once, such as a Go or Step Out, all you will get is the output window without any final variable information.*
>
> **A work-around is to place a break point on the last point at which you expect to perform a RETURN in the outermost instance of your sproc. That way, you can run in whatever debug mode you want, but still have execution halt in the end so you can inspect your final variables.**

So, you should now be able to see how the Debugger can be very handy indeed.

.NET Assemblies

Because of just how wide open a topic assemblies are, as well as their potential to add exceptional complexity to your database, these are largely considered out of scope for this title, save for one thing — letting you know they are there.

.NET assemblies can be associated with your system and utilized to provide the power behind truly complex operations. You could, just as an example, use a .NET assembly in a user-defined function to provide data from an external data source (perhaps one that has to be called on the fly, such as a new feed or stock quote), even though the structure and complex communications required would have ruled out such a function in prior versions.

Without going into too much detail on them for now, let's look at the syntax for adding an assembly to your database:

```
CREATE ASSEMBLY  <assembly name> AUTHORIZATION <owner name> FROM <path to assembly>
WITH PERMISSION_SET = [SAFE | EXTERNAL_ACCESS | UNSAFE]
```

The CREATE ASSEMBLY part of things works as pretty much all our CREATE statements have — it indicates the type of object being created and the object name.

Then comes the AUTHORIZATION — this allows you to set a context that the assembly is always to run under. That is, if it has tables it needs to access, how you set the user or rolename in AUTHORIZATION will determine whether it can access those tables or not.

After that, we go to the FROM clause. This is essentially the path to your assembly, along with the manifest for that assembly.

Finally, we have WITH PERMISSION_SET. This has three options:

- ❑ **SAFE:** This one is, at the risk of sounding obvious, well . . . safe. It restricts the assembly from accessing anything that is external to SQL Server. Things like files or the network are not available to the assembly.

- ❑ **EXTERNAL_ACCESS:** This allows external access, such as to files or the network, but requires that the assembly still run as managed code.

- ❑ **UNSAFE:** This one is, at the risk of again sounding obvious, unsafe. It allows your assembly not only to access external system objects, but also to run unmanaged code.

I cannot stress enough the risks you are taking when running .NET assemblies in *anything* other than SAFE mode. Even in EXTERNAL_ACCESS mode you are allowing the users of your system to access your network, files, or other external resources in what is essentially an aliased mode — that is, they may be able to get at things that you would rather they not get at, and they will be aliased on your network to whatever your SQL Server login is while they are making those accesses. Be very, very careful with this stuff.

.NET assemblies will be discussed extensively in *Professional SQL Server 2008 Programming*.

Summary

Wow! That's a lot to have to take in for one chapter. Still, this is among the most important chapters in the book in terms of being able to function as a developer in SQL Server.

Sprocs are the backbone of code in SQL Server. We can create reusable code and get improved performance and flexibility at the same time. We can use a variety of programming constructs that you might be familiar with from other languages, but sprocs aren't meant for everything.

Pros to sprocs include:

❑   Usually better performance

❑   Possible use as a security insulation layer (control how a database is accessed and updated)

❑   Reusable code

❑   Compartmentalization of code (can encapsulate business logic)

❑   Flexible execution depending on dynamics established at runtime

Cons to sprocs include:

❑   Not portable across platforms (Oracle, for example, has a completely different kind of implementation of sprocs)

❑   May get locked into the wrong execution plan in some circumstances (actually hurting performance)

Sprocs are not the solution to everything, but they are still the cornerstones of SQL Server programming. In the next chapter, we'll take a look at the sprocs' very closely related cousin — the UDF.

User-Defined Functions

Well, here we are already at one of my favorite topics. Long after their introduction, user-defined functions — or UDFs — remain one of the more underutilized and misunderstood objects in SQL Server. In short, these were awesome when Microsoft first introduced them in SQL Server 2000, and the addition of .NET functionality back in SQL Server 2005 just added all that much more to them. One of the best things about UDFs from your point of view is, provided you've done the book in order, you already know most of what you need to write them. They are actually very, very similar to stored procedures — they just have certain behaviors and capabilities about them that set them apart and make them *the* answer in many situations.

In this chapter, we're not only going to introduce what UDFs are, but we're also going to take a look at the different types of UDFs, how they vary from stored procedures (often called sprocs), and, of course, what kinds of situations we might want to use them in. Finally, we'll take a quick look at how you can use .NET to expand on their power.

What a UDF Is

A user-defined function is, much like a sproc, an ordered set of T-SQL statements that are pre-optimized and compiled and can be called to work as a single unit. The primary difference between them is how results are returned. Because of things that need to happen in order to support these different kinds of returned values, UDFs have a few more limitations to them than sprocs do.

> OK, so I've said what a UDF is, so I suspect I ought to take a moment to say what it is not. A UDF is definitely NOT a replacement for a sproc — they are just a different option that offers us yet one more form of code flexibility.

With a sproc, you can pass parameters in and also get values in parameters passed back out. You can return a value, but that value is really intended to indicate success or failure rather than return data. You can also return result sets, but you can't really use those result sets in a query without first inserting them into some kind of table (usually a temporary table) to work with them further.

Even using a table valued output parameter, you still need to make at least one additional step before using the results in a query.

With a UDF, however, you can pass parameters *in*, but not out. Instead, the concept of output parameters has been replaced with a much more robust return value. As with system functions, you can return a scalar value — what's particularly nice, however, is that this value is not limited to just the integer data type as it would be for a sproc. Instead, you can return most SQL Server data types (more on this in the next section).

As they like to say in late-night television commercials: "But wait! There's more!" The "more" is that you are actually not just limited to returning scalar values — you can also return tables. This is wildly powerful, and we'll look into this fully later in the chapter.

So, to summarize, we have two types of UDFs:

❑   Those that return a scalar value

❑   Those that return a table

Let's take a look at the general syntax for creating a UDF:

```
CREATE FUNCTION [<schema name>.]<function name>
    ( [ <@parameter name> [AS] [<schema name>.]<data type> [ = <default value>
[READONLY]]
       [ ,...n ] ] )
RETURNS {<scalar type>|TABLE [(<table definition>)]}
    [ WITH [ENCRYPTION]|[SCHEMABINDING]|
[ RETURNS NULL ON NULL INPUT | CALLED ON NULL INPUT ] | [EXECUTE AS {
CALLER|SELF|OWNER|<'user name'>} ]
]
[AS] { EXTERNAL NAME <external method> |
BEGIN
    [<function statements>]
    {RETURN <type as defined in RETURNS clause>|RETURN (<SELECT statement>)}
END }[;]
```

This is kind of a tough one to explain because parts of the optional syntax are dependent on the choices you make elsewhere in your CREATE statement. The big issues here are whether you are returning a scalar data type or a table and whether you're doing a T-SQL-based function or doing something utilizing the CLR and .NET. Let's look at each type individually.

UDFs Returning a Scalar Value

This type of UDF is probably the most like what you might expect a function to be. Much like most of SQL Server's own built-in functions, they will return a scalar value to the calling script or procedure; functions such as GETDATE() or USER() return scalar values.

As I indicated earlier, one of the truly great things about a UDF is that you are not limited to an integer for a return value — instead, it can be of any valid SQL Server data type (including user-defined data types!), except for BLOBs, cursors, and timestamps. Even if you wanted to return an integer, a UDF should look very attractive to you for two different reasons:

❑ Unlike sprocs, the whole purpose of the return value is to serve as a meaningful piece of data — for sprocs, a return value is meant as an indication of success or failure and, in the event of failure, to provide some specific information about the nature of that failure.

❑ You can perform functions inline to your queries (for instance, include it as part of your SELECT statement) — you can't do that with a sproc.

So, that said, let's create a simple UDF to get our feet wet on the whole idea of how we might utilize them differently from a sproc. I'm not kidding when I say this is a simple one from a code point of view, but I think you'll see how it illustrates my sprocs versus UDFs point.

One of the most common function-like requirements I see is a desire to see if an entry in a datetime field occurred on a specific day. The usual problem here is that your datetime field has specific time-of-day information that prevents it from easily being compared with just the date. Indeed, we've already seen this problem in some of our comparisons in previous chapters.

Let's go back to our Accounting database that we created in Chapter 5. Imagine for a moment that we want to know all the orders that came in today. Let's start by adding a few orders in with today's date. We'll just pick customer and employee IDs we know already exist in their respective tables (if you don't have any records there, you'll need to insert a couple of dummy rows to reference). I'm also going to create a small loop to add in several rows:

```
USE Accounting;

DECLARE @Counter   int = 1;

WHILE @Counter <= 10
BEGIN
    INSERT INTO Orders
        VALUES (1, DATEADD(mi,@Counter,GETDATE()), 1);
    SET @Counter = @Counter + 1;
END
```

So, this gets us 10 rows inserted, with each row being inserted with today's date, but one minute apart from each other.

OK, if you're running this just before midnight, some of the rows may dribble over into the next day, so be careful — but it will work fine for everyone except the night owls.

So, now we're ready to run a simple query to see what orders we have today. We might try something like:

```
SELECT *
FROM Orders
WHERE OrderDate = GETDATE();
```

Unfortunately, this query will not get us anything back at all. This is because GETDATE() gets the current time down to the millisecond — not just the day. This means that any query based on GETDATE() is very unlikely to return us any data — even if it happened on the same day (it would have had to have happened within in the same minute for a smalldatetime, within a millisecond for a full datetime field, and potentially down to as close as 100 milliseconds for datetime2).

The typical solution is to convert the date to a string and back in order to truncate the time information, and then perform the comparison.

It might look something like:

```
SELECT *
FROM Orders
WHERE CONVERT(varchar(12), OrderDate, 101) = CONVERT(varchar(12), GETDATE(), 101)
```

It is certainly worth noting that you could also do this by simply casting the value of @Date to the date data type. I've chosen to use CONVERT here just to show a more backward-compatible way of truncating dates (SQL Server 2005 and earlier did not support the date data type).

This time, we will get back every row with today's date in the OrderDate column, regardless of what time of day the order was taken. Unfortunately, this isn't exactly the most readable code. Imagine you had a large series of dates you needed to perform such comparisons against — it can get very ugly indeed.

So now let's look at doing the same thing with a simple user-defined function. First, we'll need to create the actual function. This is done with the new CREATE FUNCTION command, and it's formatted much like a sproc. For example, we might code this function like this:

```
CREATE FUNCTION dbo.DayOnly(@Date date)
RETURNS date
AS
BEGIN
    RETURN @Date;
END
```

where the date returned from GETDATE() is passed in as the parameter and the task of converting the date is included in the function body and the truncated date is returned.

Note that the preceding version is a SQL Server 2008 compatible version, relying on the coercion into the parameter's date data type to truncate the time. If you wanted to do a truncation like this in SQL Server 2005 (as we did with the query-based example), you would need to use the CONVERT function as we did before. For example:

```
CREATE FUNCTION dbo.DayOnly(@Date datetime)
RETURNS varchar(12)
AS
BEGIN
    RETURN CONVERT(varchar(12), @Date, 101);
END
```

To see this function in action, let's re-format our query slightly:

```
SELECT *
FROM Orders
WHERE dbo.DayOnly(OrderDate) = dbo.DayOnly(GETDATE());
```

We get back the same set as with the stand-alone query. Even for a simple query like this one, the new code is quite a bit more readable. The call works pretty much as it would from most languages that support functions. There is, however, one hitch — the schema is required. SQL Server will, for some reason, not resolve scalar value functions the way it does with other objects.

As you might expect, there is a lot more to UDFs than just readability. You can embed queries in them and use them as an encapsulation method for subqueries. Almost anything you can do procedurally that returns a discrete value could also be encapsulated in a UDF and used inline with your queries.

Let's take a look at a very simple subquery example. The subquery version looks like this:

```
USE AdventureWorks2008;

SELECT Name,
       ListPrice,
       (SELECT AVG(ListPrice) FROM Production.Product) AS Average,
       ListPrice - (SELECT AVG(ListPrice) FROM Production.Product)
         AS Difference
FROM Production.Product
WHERE ProductSubCategoryID = 1; -- The Mountain Bikes Sub-cat
```

This gets us back a pretty simple set of data:

```
Name                          ListPrice    Average          Difference
----------------------------- ------------ ---------------- --------------
Mountain-100 Silver, 38       3399.99      438.6662         2961.3238
Mountain-100 Silver, 42       3399.99      438.6662         2961.3238
Mountain-100 Silver, 44       3399.99      438.6662         2961.3238
Mountain-100 Silver, 48       3399.99      438.6662         2961.3238
Mountain-100 Black, 38        3374.99      438.6662         2936.3238
Mountain-100 Black, 42        3374.99      438.6662         2936.3238

...

...
Mountain-500 Silver, 52       564.99       438.6662         126.3238
Mountain-500 Black, 40        539.99       438.6662         101.3238
Mountain-500 Black, 42        539.99       438.6662         101.3238
Mountain-500 Black, 44        539.99       438.6662         101.3238
Mountain-500 Black, 48        539.99       438.6662         101.3238
Mountain-500 Black, 52        539.99       438.6662         101.3238

(32 row(s) affected)
```

Let's try it again, only this time we'll encapsulate both the average and the difference into two functions. The first encapsulates the task of calculating the average and the second does the subtraction.

```
CREATE FUNCTION dbo.AveragePrice()
RETURNS money
WITH SCHEMABINDING
AS
BEGIN
    RETURN (SELECT AVG(ListPrice) FROM Production.Product);
END
GO
```

```
CREATE FUNCTION dbo.PriceDifference(@Price money)
RETURNS money
AS
BEGIN
   RETURN @Price - dbo.AveragePrice();
END
```

Notice that it's completely legal to embed one UDF in another one.

Note that the WITH SCHEMABINDING *option works for functions just the way that it did for views — if a function is built using schema-binding, then any object that function depends on cannot be altered or dropped without first removing the schema-bound function. In this case, schema-binding wasn't really necessary, but I wanted to point out its usage and also prepare this example for something we're going to do with it a little later in the chapter.*

Now let's run our query using the new functions instead of the old subquery model:

```
USE AdventureWorks2008

SELECT Name,
       ListPrice,
       dbo.AveragePrice() AS Average,
       dbo.PriceDifference(ListPrice) AS Difference
FROM Production.Product
WHERE ProductSubCategoryID = 1; -- The Mountain Bikes Sub-cat
```

This yields us the same results we had with our subquery.

Note that, beyond the readability issue, we also get the added benefit of reuse out of this. For a little example like this, it probably doesn't seem like a big deal, but as your functions become more complex, it can be quite a time saver.

UDFs That Return a Table

User-defined functions in SQL Server are not limited to just returning scalar values. They can return something far more interesting — tables. Now, while the possible impacts of this are sinking in on you, I'll go ahead and add that the table that is returned is, for the most part, usable much as any other table is. You can perform a JOIN against it and even apply WHERE conditions against the results. It's *very* cool stuff indeed.

To make the change to using a table as a return value is not hard at all — a table is just like any other SQL Server data type as far as a UDF is concerned. To illustrate this, we'll build a relatively simple one to start:

```
USE AdventureWorks2008
GO

CREATE FUNCTION dbo.fnContactList()
RETURNS TABLE
```

```
AS
RETURN (SELECT BusinessEntityID,
            LastName + ', ' + FirstName AS Name
        FROM Person.Person);
GO
```

This function returns a table of selected records and does a little formatting — joining the last and first names, and separating them with a comma.

At this point, we're ready to use our function just as we would use a table:

```
SELECT *
FROM dbo.fnContactList();
```

Now, let's add a bit more fun into things. What we did with this table up to this point could have been done just as easily — more easily, in fact — with a view. But what if we wanted to parameterize a view? What if, for example, we wanted to accept last-name input to filter our results (without having to manually put in our own WHERE clause)? It might look something like this:

```
--CREATE our view
CREATE VIEW vFullContactName
AS
SELECT p.BusinessEntityID,
            LastName + ', ' + FirstName AS Name,
            ea.EmailAddress
        FROM Person.Person as p
        LEFT OUTER JOIN Person.EmailAddress ea
            ON ea.BusinessEntityID = p.BusinessEntityID;
GO
```

This would yield us what was asked for, with a twist. We can't parameterize things right in the view itself, so we're going to have to include a WHERE clause in our query:

```
SELECT *
FROM vFullContactName
WHERE Name LIKE 'Ad%';
```

This should get you results that look something like this:

```
BusinessEntityID Name                                    EmailAddress
---------------- ------------------------------------    -----------------------------------
67               Adams, Jay                              jay0@adventure-works.com
301              Adams, Frances                          frances0@adventure-works.com
305              Adams, Carla                            carla0@adventure-works.com

...

...
16901            Adams, Adam                             adam46@adventure-works.com
16902            Adams, Eric                             eric57@adventure-works.com
16910            Adams, Jackson                          jackson47@adventure-works.com

(87 row(s) affected)
```

To simplify things a bit, we'll encapsulate everything in a function instead:

```
USE AdventureWorks2008;
GO


CREATE FUNCTION dbo.fnContactSearch(@LastName nvarchar(50))
RETURNS TABLE
AS
RETURN (SELECT p.BusinessEntityID,
            LastName + ', ' + FirstName AS Name,
            ea.EmailAddress
        FROM Person.Person as p
        LEFT OUTER JOIN Person.EmailAddress ea
          ON ea.BusinessEntityID = p.BusinessEntityID
        WHERE LastName Like @LastName + '%');
GO
```

Now we're set up pretty well — to execute it, we just call the function and provide the parameter:

```
SELECT *
FROM fnContactSearch('Ad');
```

And we get back the same result set — no WHERE clause, no filtering the SELECT list, and, as our friends down under would say, no worries; we can use this over and over again without having to use the old cut-and-paste trick. Note, also, that while you could have achieved similar results with a sproc and an EXEC command, you couldn't directly join the results of the sproc to another table.

Well, all this would probably be exciting enough, but sometimes we need more than just a single SELECT statement. Sometimes, we want more than just a parameterized view. Indeed, much as we saw with some of our scalar functions, we may need to execute multiple statements in order to achieve the results that we want. User-defined functions support this notion just fine. Indeed, they can return tables that are created using multiple statements — the only big difference when using multiple statements is that you must both name and define the metadata (much as you would for a temporary table) for what you'll be returning.

To illustrate this example, we'll discuss a very common problem in the relational database world — hierarchical data.

Imagine for a moment that you are working in the human resources department. You have an Employee table, and it has a unary relationship (a foreign key that relates to another column in the same table) that relates employees to their bosses through the ManagerID column — that is, the way you know who is someone's boss, is by relating the ManagerID column back to another EmployeeID. A very common need in a scenario like this is to be able to create a reporting tree — that is, a list of all of the people who exist below a given manager in an organization chart.

Historically, relational databases had a major weakness in dealing with hierarchical data. Numerous articles, white papers, and books have been written on this subject. Fortunately for us, SQL Server 2008 introduces a new methodology for dealing with hierarchical data. The newly introduced features are the hierarchyID data type and a collection of built-in functions to help deal with tree type data structures in your relational database. These new features are somewhat advanced and take quite a bit of effort to master, so I am going to defer drilling into these topics. We're going to consider them to be out of the scope of this book — see the Advanced Data Structures chapter in Professional level title for more information on the new `HierarchyID` data type.

> *If you would like to see examples of the new hierarchical functionality that is part of SQL Server 2008, check out the* `OrganizationNode` *and* `OrganizationLevel` *columns of the* `HumanResources.Employee` *table in AdventureWorks2008.*

To continue our discussion of hierarchical data, we are going to handle hierarchies the way we've been forced to for ages — call it the "old school method." Since AdventureWorks2008 doesn't have an a good example of this older (and still far more prevalent) way of doing hierarchical data, we'll create our own version of the `Employee` table (we'll call it `Employee2`) that implements this "old school method" of addressing hierarchies. If you ran the `BuildAndPopulateEmployee2.sql` file back in Chapter 3, then you already have this new version of `Employee`. If you didn't, go ahead and execute it now (again, it is available on the `wrox.com` or `professionalsql.com` websites).

The table created by this script is represented in Figure 13-1.

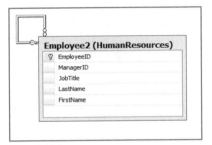

Figure 13-1

Assuming you've executed the script and have the `Employee2` table, let's see if we can retrieve a list of reports for Karla Huntington.

At first glance, this seems pretty easy. If we wanted to know all the people who report to Karla, we might write a query that would join the `Employee` table back to itself — something like:

```
USE AdventureWorks2008;

SELECT
        TheReport.EmployeeID,
        TheReport.JobTitle,
        TheReport.LastName,
        TheReport.FirstName
FROM
        HumanResources.Employee2 as TheBoss
JOIN HumanResources.Employee2 AS TheReport
        ON TheBoss.EmployeeID = TheReport.ManagerID
WHERE TheBoss.LastName = 'Huntington' AND TheBoss.FirstName = 'Karla';
```

Again, at first glance, this might appear to give us what we want:

```
EmployeeID  JobTitle                       LastName              FirstName
----------- ------------------------------ --------------------- --------------------
5           VP of Engineering              Olsen                 Ken
6           VP of Professional Services    Cross                 Gary
7           VP of Security                 Lebowski              Jeff
(3 row(s) affected)
```

But, in reality, we have a bit of a problem here. At issue is that we want all of the people in Karla's reporting chain — not just those who report to Karla directly, but those who report to people who report to Karla, and so on. You see that if you look at all the records in our newly created Employee2 table, you'll find a number of employees who report to Ken Olsen, but they don't appear in the results of this query.

OK, so some of the quicker or more experienced among you may now be saying something like, "Hey, no problem! I'll just join back to the Employee2 *table one more time and get the next level of reports!" You could probably make this work for such a small data set, or for any situation where the number of levels of your hierarchy is fixed — but what if the number of hierarchy levels isn't fixed? What if people are reporting to Robert Cheechov, and still others report to people under Robert Cheechov — it could go on virtually forever. Now what? Glad you asked. . . .*

What we really need is a function that will return all the levels of the hierarchy below whatever EmployeeID (and, therefore, ManagerID) we provide — we need a tree. To do this, we have a classic example of the need for *recursion*. A block of code is said to recurse any time it calls itself. We saw an example of this in the previous chapter with our spTriangular stored procedure. Let's think about this scenario for a moment:

1. We need to figure out all the people who report to the manager that we want.

2. For each person in Step 1, we need to know who reports to him or her.

3. Repeat Step 2 until there are no more subordinates.

This is recursion all the way. What this means is that we're going to need several statements to make our function work: some statements to figure out the current level and at least one more to call the same function again to get the next lowest level.

Keep in mind that UDFs are going to have the same recursion limits that sprocs had — that is, you can only go to 32 levels of recursion, so, if you have a chance of running into this limit, you'll want to get creative in your code to avoid errors.

Let's put it together. Notice the couple of changes in the declaration of our function. This time, we need to associate a name with the return value (in this case, @Reports) — this is required any time you're using multiple statements to generate your result. Also, we have to define the table that we will be returning — this allows SQL Server to validate whatever we try to insert into that table before it is returned to the calling routine.

```
CREATE FUNCTION dbo.fnGetReports
       (@EmployeeID AS int)
       RETURNS @Reports TABLE
```

```
          (
          EmployeeID    int         NOT NULL,
          ManagerID   int          NULL
          )
AS
BEGIN

/* Since we'll need to call this function recursively - that is once for each
** reporting employee (to make sure that they don't have reports of their
** own), we need a holding variable to keep track of which employee we're
** currently working on. */
DECLARE @Employee AS int;

/* This inserts the current employee into our working table. The significance
** here is that we need the first record as something of a primer due to the
** recursive nature of the function - this is how we get it. */
INSERT INTO @Reports
    SELECT EmployeeID, ManagerID
    FROM HumanResources.Employee2
    WHERE EmployeeID = @EmployeeID;

/* Now we also need a primer for the recursive calls we're getting ready to
** start making to this function. This would probably be better done with a
** cursor, but we haven't gotten to that chapter yet, so.... */
SELECT @Employee = MIN(EmployeeID)
FROM HumanResources.Employee2
WHERE ManagerID = @EmployeeID;

/* This next part would probably be better done with a cursor but we haven't
** gotten to that chapter yet, so we'll fake it. Notice the recursive call
** to our function! */
WHILE @Employee IS NOT NULL
    BEGIN
        INSERT INTO @Reports
            SELECT *
            FROM fnGetReports(@Employee);

            SELECT @Employee = MIN(EmployeeID)
            FROM HumanResources.Employee2
            WHERE EmployeeID > @Employee
                AND ManagerID = @EmployeeID;
    END

RETURN;

END
GO
```

I've written this one to provide just minimal information about the employee and his or her manager —
I can join back to the Employee2 table, if need be, to fetch additional information. I also took a little bit
of liberty with the requirements on this one and added in the selected manager to the results. This was
done primarily to support the recursion scenario and also to provide something of a base result for our

result set. Speaking of which, let's look at our results — Karla is `EmployeeID` 4; to do this, we'll feed that into our function:

```
SELECT * FROM fnGetReports(4);
```

This gets us not only the original one person who reported to Karla Huntington, but also those who report to Ken Olsen (who reports to Ms. Huntington) and Ms. Huntington herself (remember, I added her in as something of a starting point).

```
EmployeeID  ManagerID
----------- -----------
4           1
5           4
8           5
9           5
10          5
11          5
6           4
7           4

(8 row(s) affected)
```

Now, let's go the final step here and join this back to actual data. We'll use it much as we did our original query looking for the reports of Karla Huntington:

```
DECLARE @EmployeeID int;

SELECT @EmployeeID = EmployeeID
FROM HumanResources.Employee2 e
WHERE LastName = 'Huntington'
AND FirstName = 'Karla';

SELECT e.EmployeeID, e.LastName, e.FirstName, m.LastName AS ReportsTo
FROM HumanResources.Employee2 AS e
JOIN dbo.fnGetReports(@EmployeeID) AS r
  ON e.EmployeeID = r.EmployeeID
JOIN HumanResources.Employee2 AS m
  ON m.EmployeeID = r.ManagerID;
```

This gets us back all seven employees who are under Ms. Huntington:

```
EmployeeID  LastName         FirstName         ReportsTo
----------- ---------------- ----------------- ---------------
4           Huntington       Karla             Smith
5           Olsen            Ken               Huntington
8           Gutierrez        Ron               Olsen
9           Bray             Marky             Olsen
10          Cheechov         Robert            Olsen
11          Gale             Sue               Olsen
6           Cross            Gary              Huntington
7           Lebowski         Jeff              Huntington

(8 row(s) affected)
```

So, as you can see, we can actually have very complex code build our table results for us, but it's still a table that results and, as such, it can be used just like any other table.

Understanding Determinism

Any coverage of UDFs would be incomplete without discussing determinism. If SQL Server is going to build an index over something, it has to be able to deterministically define (define with certainty) what the item being indexed is. Why does this matter to functions? Well, because we can have functions that feed data to things that will be indexed (computed column or indexed view).

User-defined functions can be either deterministic or non-deterministic. The determinism is not defined by any kind of parameter, but rather by what the function is doing. If, given a specific set of valid inputs, the function will return exactly the same value every time, then the function is said to be deterministic. An example of a built-in function that is deterministic is SUM(). The sum of 3, 5, and 10 is always going to be 18 — *every* time the function is called with those values as inputs. The value of GETDATE(), however, is non-deterministic — it changes pretty much every time you call it.

To be considered deterministic, a function has to meet four criteria:

❑ The function must be schema-bound. This means that any objects that the function depends on will have a dependency recorded and no changes to those objects will be allowed without first dropping the dependent function.

❑ All other functions referred to in your function, regardless of whether they are user- or system-defined, must also be deterministic.

❑ The function cannot reference tables that are defined outside the function itself. (Use of table variables is fine. Temporary tables are fine as long they are defined inside the scope of the function.)

❑ The function cannot use an extended stored procedure.

The importance of determinism shows up if you want to build an index on a view or computed column. Indexes on views or computed columns are only allowed if the result of the view or computed column can be reliably determined. This means that, if the view or computed column refers to a non-deterministic function, no index will be allowed on that view or column. This situation isn't necessarily the end of the world, but you will want to think about whether a function is deterministic or not before creating indexes against views or columns that use that function.

So, this should beget the question: "How do I figure out whether my function is deterministic or not?" Well, beyond checking the rules we've already described, you can also have SQL Server tell you whether your function is deterministic or not — it's stored in the IsDeterministic property of the object. To check this out, you can make use of the OBJECTPROPERTY function. For example, we could check out the determinism of our DayOnly function that we used earlier in the chapter:

```
USE Accounting;

SELECT OBJECTPROPERTY(OBJECT_ID('DayOnly'), 'IsDeterministic');
```

It may come as a surprise to you (or maybe not) that the response is that this function is *not* deterministic:

```
-----------
0
(1 row(s) affected)
```

Look back through the list of requirements for a deterministic function and see if you can figure out why this one doesn't meet the grade.

When I was working on this example, I got one of those not so nice little reminders about how it's the little things that get you. You see, I was certain this function should be deterministic, and, of course, it wasn't. After too many nights writing until the morning hours, I completely missed the obvious — SCHEMABINDING.

Fortunately, we can fix the only problem this one has. All we need to do is add the WITH SCHEMABINDING option to our function, and we'll see better results:

```
ALTER FUNCTION dbo.DayOnly(@Date date)
RETURNS date
WITH SCHEMABINDING
AS
BEGIN
    RETURN @Date;
END
```

Now, we just rerun our OBJECTPROPERTY query:

```
-----------
1
(1 row(s) affected)
```

And voilà — a deterministic function!

We can compare this, however, with our AveragePrice function that we built in the AdventureWorks2008 database. It looked something like this:

```
CREATE FUNCTION dbo.AveragePrice()
RETURNS money
WITH SCHEMABINDING
AS
BEGIN
    RETURN (SELECT AVG(ListPrice) FROM Production.Product);
END
GO

CREATE FUNCTION dbo.PriceDifference(@Price money)
RETURNS money
AS
BEGIN
    RETURN @Price - dbo.AveragePrice();
END
```

In this function we used schema-binding right from the beginning, so let's look at our OBJECTPROPERTY:

```
USE AdventureWorks2008;

SELECT OBJECTPROPERTY(OBJECT_ID('AveragePrice'), 'IsDeterministic');
```

Despite being schema-bound, this one still comes back as being non-deterministic. That's because this function references a table that isn't local to the function (a temporary table or table variable created inside the function).

Under the heading of "one more thing," it's also worth noting that the `PriceDifference` function we created at the same time as `AveragePrice` is also non-deterministic. For one thing, we didn't make it schema-bound, but, more important, it references `AveragePrice` — if you reference a non-deterministic function, then the function you're creating is non-deterministic by association.

Debugging User-Defined Functions

This actually works just the same as the sproc example we saw in Chapter 12.

Simply set up a script that calls your function, and begin stepping through the script (using the toolbar icon, or pressing F11). You can then step right into your UDF.

.NET in a Database World

As we discussed in Chapter 12, the ability to use .NET assemblies in our stored procedures and functions was added to SQL Server back in SQL Server 2005. Much as it does with sprocs, this has enormous implications for functions.

Considering most who read this title will be beginners, it's hard to fully relate the impact that .NET has in our database world. The reality is that you won't use it all that often, and yet, when you do, the effects can be profound. Need to implement a complex formula for a special function? No problem. Need to access external data sources such as credit card authorization companies and such things? No problem. Need to access other complex data sources? No problem. In short, things we used to have to either skip or perform extremely complex development to achieve (in some cases, it was all smoke and mirrors before) suddenly become relatively straightforward.

What does this mean in terms of functions? Well, I already gave the example of implementing a complex formula in a function. But now imagine something like external tabular data — let's say representing a `.csv` or some other data in a tabular fashion — very doable with a .NET assembly created as a function in SQL Server.

.NET assemblies in SQL Server remain, however, something of an advanced concept, and one I'll defer to the Professional series title for SQL Server 2008. That said, it's important to understand that the option is available and consider it as something worth researching in that "Wow, I have no idea how we're going to do this!" situation.

Summary

What we added in this chapter was, in many ways, not new at all. Indeed, much of what goes into user-defined functions is the same set of statements, variables, and general coding practices that we have already seen in scripting and stored procedures. However, UDFs still provide us a wonderful new area of functionality that was not previously available in SQL Server. We can now encapsulate a wider range of code, and even use this encapsulated functionality inline with our queries. What's more, we can now also provide parameterized views and dynamically created tables.

User-defined functions are, in many ways, the most exciting of all the new functionality added to SQL Server. In pondering their uses, I have already come to realize that I'm only scratching the surface of their potential. Over the life of this next release, I suspect that developers will implement UDFs in ways I have yet to dream of — let's hope you'll be one of those developers!

Exercise

1. Reimplement the `spTriangular` function from Chapter 12 as a function instead of a stored procedure.

Transactions and Locks

This is one of those chapters that, when you go back to work, makes you sound like you've had your Wheaties today. Nothing we're going to cover in this chapter is wildly difficult, yet transactions and locks tend to be two of the most misunderstood areas in the database world. As such, this beginning (or at least I think it's a basic) concept is going to make you start to look like a real pro.

In this chapter, we're going to:

- ❏ Demystify transactions
- ❏ Examine how the SQL Server log and checkpoints work
- ❏ Unlock your understanding of locks

We'll learn why these topics are so closely tied to each other and how to minimize problems with each.

Transactions

Transactions are all about *atomicity*. Atomicity is the concept that something should act as a unit. From our database standpoint, it's about the smallest grouping of one or more statements that should be considered to be *all or nothing*.

Often, when dealing with data, we want to make sure that if one thing happens, another thing happens, or that neither of them does. Indeed, this can be carried out to the degree where 20 things (or more) all have to happen together or nothing happens. Let's look at a classic example.

Imagine that you are a banker. Sally comes in and wants to transfer $1,000 from checking to savings. You are, of course, happy to oblige, so you process her request.

Behind the scenes, something like this is happening:

```
UPDATE checking
    SET Balance = Balance - 1000
    WHERE Account = 'Sally'
UPDATE savings
    SET Balance = Balance + 1000
    WHERE Account = 'Sally'
```

This is a hyper-simplification of what's going on, but it captures the main thrust of things: You need to issue two different statements — one for each account.

Now what if the first statement executes and the second one doesn't? Sally would be out a thousand dollars! That might, for a short time, seem OK from your perspective (heck, you just made a thousand bucks!), but not for long. By that afternoon you'd have a steady stream of customers leaving your bank — it's hard to stay in the bank business with no depositors.

What you need is a way to be certain that if the first statement executes, the second statement executes. There really isn't a way that we can be certain of that — all sorts of things can go wrong, from hardware failures to simple things, such as violations of data integrity rules. Fortunately, however, there is a way to do something that serves the same overall purpose — we can essentially forget that the first statement ever happened. We can enforce at least the notion that if one thing didn't happen, then nothing did — at least within the scope of our *transaction*.

In order to capture this notion of a transaction, however, we need to be able to define very definite boundaries. A transaction has to have very definitive beginning and end points. Actually, every SELECT, INSERT, UPDATE, and DELETE statement you issue in SQL Server is part of an implicit transaction. Even if you issue only one statement, that one statement is considered to be a transaction — everything about the statement will be executed, or none of it will. Indeed, by default, that is the length of a transaction — one statement.

But what if we need to have more than one statement be all or nothing, as in our preceding bank example? In such a case, we need a way of marking the beginning and end of a transaction, as well as the success or failure of that transaction. To that end, there are several T-SQL statements that we can use to mark these points in a transaction. We can:

❑   **BEGIN a transaction:** Set the starting point.

❑   **COMMIT a transaction:** Make the transaction a permanent, irreversible part of the database.

❑   **ROLLBACK a transaction:** Say essentially that we want to forget that it ever happened.

❑   **SAVE a transaction:** Establish a specific marker to allow us to do only a partial rollback.

Let's look over all of these individually before we put them together into our first transaction.

BEGIN TRAN

The beginning of the transaction is probably one of the easiest concepts to understand in the transaction process. Its sole purpose in life is to denote the point that is the beginning of a unit. If, for some reason, we are unable or do not want to commit the transaction, this is the point to which all database activity will be rolled back. That is, everything beyond this point that is not eventually committed will effectively be forgotten, as far as the database is concerned.

The syntax is:

```
BEGIN TRAN[SACTION] [<transaction name>|<@transaction variable>]
  [ WITH MARK [ <'description'> ]]
```

I won't dwell on the WITH MARK option here, as it is a topic having to do with very advanced point in time transaction work, which tends to be more administrator oriented and is well outside of the scope of this book.

COMMIT TRAN

The committing of a transaction is the end of a completed transaction. At the point that you issue the COMMIT TRAN, the transaction is considered *durable*. That is, the effect of the transaction is now permanent and will last even if you have a system failure (as long as you have a backup or the database files haven't been physically destroyed). The only way to undo whatever the transaction accomplished is to issue a new transaction that, functionally speaking, is a reverse of your first transaction.

The syntax for a COMMIT looks pretty similar to a BEGIN:

```
COMMIT TRAN[SACTION] [<transaction name>|<@transaction variable>]
```

ROLLBACK TRAN

Whenever I think of a ROLLBACK, I think of the old movie *The Princess Bride*. If you've ever seen the film (if you haven't, I highly recommend it), you'll know that the character Vizzini (considered a genius in the film) always says, "If anything goes wrong, go back to the beginning."

That is some mighty good advice. A ROLLBACK does just what Vizzini suggests — it goes back to the beginning. In this case, it's your transaction that goes back to the beginning. Anything that happened since the associated BEGIN statement is effectively forgotten. The only exception to going back to the beginning is through the use of what are called *save points*, which we'll describe shortly.

The syntax for a ROLLBACK again looks pretty much the same as a BEGIN or COMMIT, with the exception of allowance for a save point.

```
ROLLBACK TRAN[SACTION] [<transaction name>|<save point name>|
    <@transaction variable>|<@savepoint variable>]
```

SAVE TRAN

To save a transaction is essentially to create something of a bookmark. You establish a name for your bookmark (you can have more than one). After this bookmark is established, you can reference it in a rollback. What's nice about this is that you can roll back to the exact spot in the code that you want to just by naming a save point to which you want to roll back.

The syntax is simple enough:

```
SAVE TRAN[SACTION] [<save point name>| <@savepoint variable>]
```

The thing to remember about save points is that they are cleared on ROLLBACK — that is, even if you save five save points, once you perform one ROLLBACK they are all gone. You can start setting new save points again and rolling back to those, but whatever save points you had when the ROLLBACK was issued are gone.

SAVE TRAN can get extremely confusing and I can't recommend it for the beginning user, but keep it in mind as being there.

How the SQL Server Log Works

You definitely must have the concept of transactions down before you try to figure out how SQL Server tracks what's what in your database. You see, what you *think* of as your database is only rarely a complete version of all the data. Except for rare moments when it happens that everything has been written to disk, the data in your database is made up of not only the data in the physical database file(s), but also any transactions that have been committed to the *log* since the last checkpoint.

In the normal operation of your database, most activities that you perform are logged to the *transaction log*, rather than written directly to the database. A *checkpoint* is a periodic operation that forces all dirty pages for the database currently in use to be written to disk. Dirty pages are log or data pages that have been modified after they were read into the cache, but the modifications have not yet been written to disk. Without a checkpoint the log would fill up and/or use all the available disk space. The process works something like the diagram in Figure 14-1.

> *Don't mistake all this as meaning that you have to do something special to get your data out of the cache. SQL Server handles all of this for you. This information is only provided here to facilitate your understanding of how the log works and, from there, the steps required to handle a transaction. Whether something is in cache or not can make a big difference to performance, so understanding when things are logged and when things go in and out of the cache can be a big deal when you are seeking maximum performance.*

Note that the need to read data into a cache that is already full is not the only reason that a checkpoint would be issued. Checkpoints can be issued under the following circumstances:

❑   By a manual statement (using the CHECKPOINT command)

❑   At normal shutdown of the server (unless the WITH NOWAIT option is used)

❑   When you change any database option (for example, single user only, dbo only, and so on)

❑   When the Simple Recovery option is used and the log becomes 70 percent full

❑   When the amount of data in the log since the last checkpoint (often called the *active* portion of the log) exceeds the size that the server could recover in the amount of time specified in the *recovery interval* option

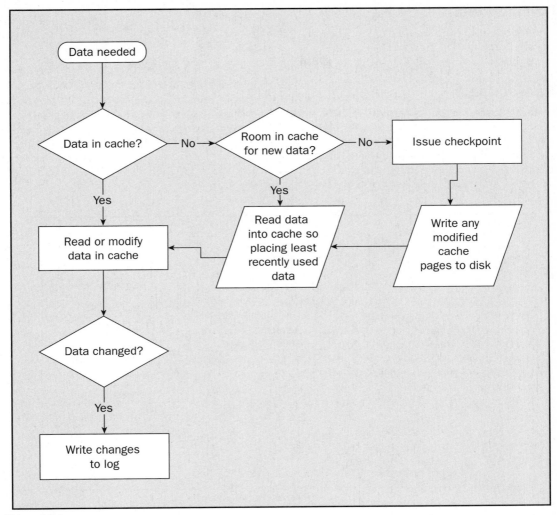

Figure 14-1

Failure and Recovery

A *recovery* happens every time that SQL Server starts. SQL Server takes the database file, then applies (by writing them out to the physical database file) any committed changes that are in the log since the last checkpoint. Any changes in the log that do not have a corresponding commit are rolled back — that is, they are essentially forgotten.

Let's take a look at how this works depending on how transactions have occurred in your database. Imagine five transactions that span the log as pictured in Figure 14-2.

Let's look at what would happen to these transactions one by one.

Transaction 1

Absolutely nothing would happen. The transaction has already been through a checkpoint and has been fully committed to the database. There is no need to do anything at recovery, because any data that is read into the data cache would already reflect the committed transaction.

Transaction 2

Even though the transaction existed at the time that a checkpoint was issued, the transaction had not been committed (the transaction was still going). Without that commitment, the transaction does not actually participate in the checkpoint. This transaction would, therefore, be *rolled forward*. This is just a fancy way of saying that we would need to read all the related pages back into cache, then use the information in the log to rerun all the statements that we ran in this transaction. When that's finished, the transaction should look exactly as it did before the system failed.

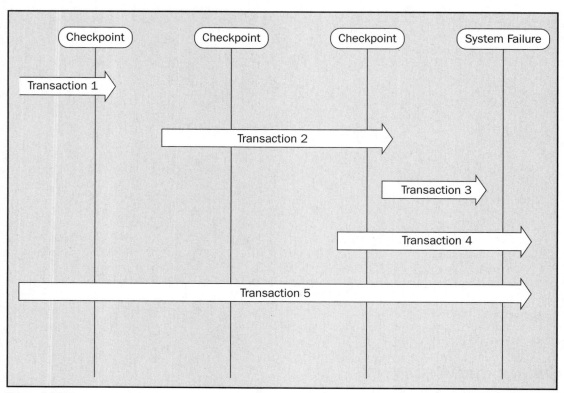

Figure 14-2

Transaction 3

It may not look the part, but this transaction is exactly the same as Transaction 2 from the standpoint of what needs to be done. Again, because Transaction 3 wasn't finished at the time of the last checkpoint, it did not participate in that checkpoint — just like Transaction 2 didn't. The only difference is that Transaction 3 didn't even exist at that time, but from a recovery standpoint that makes no difference — it's where the commit is issued that makes all the difference.

Transaction 4

This transaction wasn't completed at the time of system failure and must therefore be rolled back. In effect, it never happened from a row-data perspective. The user would have to reenter any data, and any process would need to start from the beginning.

Transaction 5

This one is no different from Transaction 4. It appears to be different because the transaction has been running longer, but that makes no difference. The transaction was not committed at the time of system failure and must therefore be rolled back.

Implicit Transactions

Primarily for compatibility with other major RDBMS systems, such as Oracle or DB2, SQL Server supports (it is off by default, but can be turned on if you choose) the notion of what is called an *implicit transaction*. Implicit transactions do not require a BEGIN TRAN statement — instead, they are automatically started with your first statement. They then continue until you issue a COMMIT TRAN or ROLLBACK TRAN statement. The next transaction then begins with your next statement.

> *Implicit transactions are dangerous territory and are well outside the scope of this book. Suffice to say that I highly recommend that you leave this option off unless you have a very specific reason to turn it on (such as compatibility with code written in another system).*

Locks and Concurrency

Concurrency is a major issue for any database system. It addresses the notion of two or more users each trying to interact with the same object at the same time. The nature of that interaction may be different for each user (updating, deleting, reading, inserting), and the ideal way to handle the competition for control of the object changes depending on just what all the users in question are doing and just how important their actions are. The more users — more specifically, the more transactions — that you can run with reasonable success at the same time, the higher your concurrency is said to be.

In the OLTP environment, concurrency is usually the first thing we deal with in data and it is the focus of most of the database notions put forward in this book. (OLAP is usually something of an afterthought — it shouldn't necessarily be that way, but it is.) Dealing with the issue of concurrency can be critical to the performance of your system. At the foundation of dealing with concurrency in databases is a process called *locking*.

Locks are a mechanism for preventing a process from performing an action on an object that conflicts with something already being done to that object. That is, you can't do some things to an object if someone else got there first. What you can and cannot do depends on what the other user is doing. Locks are also a means of describing what is being done, so the system knows if the second process action is compatible with the first process or not. For example, 1, 2, 10, 100, 1,000, or whatever number of user connections the system can handle, are usually all able to share the same piece of data at the same time as long as they all want the record on a read-only basis. Think of it as being like a crystal shop: Lots of people can be in looking at things — even the same thing — as long as they don't go to move it, buy it, or otherwise change it. If more than one person does that at the same time, you're liable to wind up with broken crystal. That's why the shopkeeper usually keeps a close eye on things and will usually decide who gets to handle things first.

433

The SQL Server *lock manager* is that shopkeeper. When you come into the SQL Server store, the lock manager asks what your intent is — what it is you're going to be doing. If you say "just looking," and no one else already there is doing anything other than just looking, then the lock manager will let you in. If you want to buy (update or delete) something, then the lock manager will check to see if anyone's already there. If so, you must wait, and everyone who comes in behind you will also wait. When you are let in to buy, no one else will be let in until you are done.

By doing things this way, SQL Server is able to help us avoid a mix of different problems that can be created by concurrency issues. We will examine the possible concurrency problems and how to set a *transaction isolation level* that will prevent each, but for now, let's move on to what can and cannot be locked, and what kinds of locks are available.

What Problems Can Be Prevented by Locks

Locks can address four major problems:

❑ Dirty reads

❑ Non-repeatable reads

❑ Phantoms

❑ Lost updates

Each of these presents a separate set of problems and can be handled by a mix of solutions that usually includes proper setting of the transaction isolation level. Just to help make things useful as you look back at this chapter later, I'm going to include information on which transaction isolation level is appropriate for each of these problems. We'll take a complete look at isolation levels shortly, but for now, let's first make sure that we understand what each of these problems is all about.

Dirty Reads

Dirty reads occur when a transaction reads a record that is part of another transaction that isn't complete yet. If the first transaction completes normally, then it's unlikely there's a problem. But what if the transaction were rolled back? You would have information from a transaction that never happened from the database's perspective!

Let's look at it in an example series of steps:

Transaction 1 Command	Transaction 2 Command	Logical Database Value	Uncommitted Database Value	What Transaction 2 Shows
BEGIN TRAN		3		
UPDATE col = 5	BEGIN TRAN	3	5	
SELECT anything	SELECT @var = col	3	5	5
ROLLBACK	UPDATE anything SET whatever = @var	3		5

Oops — problem!!!

Transaction 2 has now made use of a value that isn't valid! If you try to go back and audit to find where this number came from, you'll wind up with no trace and an extremely large headache.

Fortunately, this scenario can't happen if you're using the SQL Server default for the transaction isolation level (called READ COMMITTED, which will be explained later in the section, "Setting the Isolation Level").

Non-Repeatable Reads

It's really easy to get this one mixed up with a dirty read. Don't worry about that — it's only terminology. Just get the concept.

A *non-repeatable read* is caused when you read the record twice in a transaction and a separate transaction alters the data in the interim. For this one, let's go back to our bank example. Remember that we don't want the value of the account to go below 0 dollars:

Transaction 1	Transaction 2	@Var	What Transaction 1 *Thinks* Is in the Table	Value in Table
BEGIN TRAN		NULL		125
SELECT @Var = value FROM table	BEGIN TRAN	125	125	125
	UPDATE value, SET value = value – 50			75
IF @Var >=100	END TRAN	125	125	75
UPDATE value, SET value = value – 100		125	125 (waiting for lock to clear)	75
(Finish, wait for lock to clear, then continue)		125	75	Either: -25 (If there isn't a CHECK constraint enforcing > 0) Or: Error 547 (If there is a CHECK)

Again, we have a problem. Transaction 1 has pre-scanned (which can be a good practice in some instances — remember that section, "Handling Errors Before They Happen," in Chapter 12?) to make sure that the value is valid and that the transaction can go through (there's enough money in the account). The problem is that before the UPDATE was made, Transaction 2 beat Transaction 1 to the punch. If there isn't any CHECK constraint on the table to prevent the negative value, then it would indeed be set to –25, even though it logically appeared that we prevented this through the use of our IF statement.

We can prevent this problem in only two ways:

❑   Create a CHECK constraint and monitor for the 547 Error.

❑   Set our isolation level to be REPEATABLE READ or SERIALIZABLE.

The CHECK constraint seems fairly obvious. The thing to realize here is that you are taking something of a reactive rather than a proactive approach with this method. Nonetheless, in most situations we have a potential for non-repeatable reads, so this would be my preferred choice in most circumstances.

We'll be taking a full look at isolation levels shortly, but for now, suffice it to say that there's a good chance that setting it to REPEATABLE READ or SERIALIZABLE is going to cause you as many headaches as it solves (or more). Still, it's an option.

Phantoms

No, we're not talking the *of the Opera* kind here — what we're talking about are records that appear mysteriously, as if unaffected by an UPDATE or DELETE statement that you've issued. This can happen quite legitimately in the normal course of operating your system and doesn't require any kind of elaborate scenario to illustrate. Here's a classic example of how this happens.

Let's say you are running a fast food restaurant. If you're running a typical establishment of that kind, you probably have a fair number of employees working at the minimum wage as defined by the government. The government has just decided to raise the minimum wage from $6.50 to $7.50 per hour, and you want to run an UPDATE on the EmployeePayHistory table to move anyone making less than $7.50 per hour up to the new minimum wage. "No problem," you say, and you issue the rather simple statement:

```
UPDATE HumanResources.EmployeePayHistory
SET HourlyRate = 7.50
WHERE HourlyRate < 7.50;

ALTER TABLE Employees
    ADD ckWage CHECK (HourlyRate >= CONSTRAINT 7.50);
GO
```

That was a breeze, right? *Wrong*! Just for illustration, we're going to say that you get an error message back:

```
Msg 547, Level 16, State 1, Line 1
ALTER TABLE statement conflicted with COLUMN CHECK constraint 'ckWage'. The
conflict occurred in database 'AdventureWorks2008', table 'EmployeePayHistory',
column 'Rate'.
```

So you run a quick SELECT statement checking for values below $7.50, and sure enough you find one. The question is likely to come rather quickly, "How did that get there? I just did the UPDATE that should have fixed that!" You did run the statement, and it ran just fine — you just got a *phantom*.

The instances of phantom reads are rare and require just the right circumstances to happen. In short, someone performed an INSERT statement at the very same time your UPDATE was running. Since it was an entirely new row, it didn't have a lock on it and it proceeded just fine.

The only cure for this is setting your transaction isolation level to SERIALIZABLE, in which case any updates to the table must not fall within your WHERE clause or they will be locked out.

Lost Updates

Lost updates happen when one update is successfully written to the database, but is accidentally over-written by another transaction. I can just hear you right about now, "Yikes! How could that happen?"

Lost updates can happen when two transactions read an entire record, then one writes updated information back to the record and the other writes updated information back to the record. Let's look at an example.

Let's say that you are a credit analyst for your company. You get a call that customer X has reached their credit limit and would like an extension, so you pull up their customer information to take a look. You see that they have a credit limit of $5,000 and that they appear to always pay on time.

While you're looking, Sally, another person in your credit department, pulls up customer X's record to enter a change in the address. The record she pulls up also shows the credit limit of $5,000.

At this point, you decide to go ahead and raise customer X's credit limit to $7,500, and press Enter. The database now shows $7,500 as the credit limit for customer X.

Sally now completes her update to the address, but she's using the same edit screen that you are — that is, she updates the entire record. Remember what her screen showed as the credit limit? $5,000. Oops, the database now shows customer X with a credit limit of $5,000 again. Your update has been lost!

The solution to this depends on your code somehow recognizing that another connection has updated your record between when you read the data and when you went to update it. How this recognition happens varies depending on what access method you're using.

Lockable Resources

There are six *lockable resources* for SQL Server, and they form a hierarchy. The higher level the lock, the less *granularity* it has (that is, you're choosing a higher and higher number of objects to be locked a cas-cading type of action just because the object that contains them has been locked). These include, in ascending order of granularity:

❑ **Database:** The entire database is locked. This happens usually during database schema changes.

❑ **Table:** The entire table is locked. This includes all the data-related objects associated with that table, including the actual data rows (every one of them) and all the keys in all the indexes associated with the table in question.

❑ **Extent:** The entire extent is locked. Remember than an extent is made up of eight pages, so an extent lock means that the lock has control of the extent, the eight data or index pages in that extent, and all the rows of data in those eight pages.

❑ **Page:** All the data or index keys on that page are locked.

❑ **Key:** There is a lock on a particular key or series of keys in an index. Other keys in the same index page may be unaffected.

❑ **Row or Row Identifier (RID):** Although the lock is technically placed on the row identifier (an internal SQL Server construct), it essentially locks the entire row.

Lock Escalation and Lock Effects on Performance

Escalation is all about recognizing that maintaining a finer level of granularity (say, a row lock instead of a page lock) makes a lot of sense when the number of items being locked is small. However, as we get more and more items locked, the overhead associated with maintaining those locks actually hinders performance. It can cause the lock to be in place longer (thus creating contention issues — the longer the lock is in place, the more likely that someone will want that particular record). When you think about this for a bit, you'll realize there's probably a balancing act to be done somewhere, and that's exactly what the lock manager uses escalation to do.

When the number of locks being maintained reaches a certain threshold, the lock is escalated to the next highest level and the lower-level locks do not have to be so tightly managed (freeing resources and helping speed over contention).

Note that the escalation is based on the number of locks rather than the number of users. The importance here is that you can single-handedly lock a table by performing a mass update — a row lock can graduate to a page lock, which then escalates to a table lock. That means that you could potentially be locking every other user out of the table. If your query makes use of multiple tables, it's actually quite possible to wind up locking everyone out of all of those tables.

> *While you certainly would prefer not to lock all the other users out of your object, there are times when you still need to perform updates that are going to have that effect. There is very little you can do about escalation other than to keep your queries as targeted as possible. Recognize that escalations will happen, so make sure you've thought about what the possible ramifications of your query are.*

Lock Modes

Beyond considering just what resource level you're locking, you also should consider what lock mode your query is going to acquire. Just as there are a variety of resources to lock, there are also a variety of *lock modes*.

Some modes are exclusive of each other (which means they don't work together). Some modes do nothing more than essentially modify other modes. Whether modes can work together is based on whether they are *compatible* (we'll take a closer look at compatibility between locks later in this chapter).

Just as we did with lockable resources, let's take a look at lock modes one by one.

Shared Locks

This is the most basic type of lock there is. A *shared lock* is used when you need only to read the data — that is, you won't be changing anything. A shared lock wants to be your friend, as it is compatible with other shared locks. That doesn't mean that it still won't cause you grief — while a shared lock doesn't mind any other kind of lock, there are other locks that don't like shared locks.

Shared locks tell other locks that you're out there. It's the old, "Look at me! Ain't I special?" thing. They don't serve much of a purpose, yet they can't really be ignored. However, one thing that shared locks do is prevent users from performing dirty reads.

Exclusive Locks

Exclusive locks are just what they sound like. Exclusive locks are not compatible with any other lock. They cannot be achieved if any other lock exists, nor will they allow a new lock of any form to be created on the resource while the exclusive lock is still active. This prevents two people from updating, deleting, or whatever at the same time.

Update Locks

Update locks are something of a hybrid between shared locks and exclusive locks. An update lock is a special kind of placeholder. Think about it — in order to do an update, you need to validate your WHERE clause (assuming there is one) to figure out just what rows you're going to be updating. That means that you only need a shared lock, until you actually go to make the physical update. At the time of the physical update, you'll need an exclusive lock.

Update locks indicate that you have a shared lock that's going to become an exclusive lock after you've done your initial scan of the data to figure out what exactly needs to be updated. This acknowledges the fact that there are two distinct stages to an update:

1. The stage where you are figuring out what meets the WHERE clause criteria (what's going to be updated). This is the part of an update query that has an update lock.

2. The stage where, if you actually decide to perform the update, the lock is upgraded to an exclusive lock. Otherwise, the lock is converted to a shared lock.

What's nice about this is that it forms a barrier against one variety of *deadlock*. A deadlock is not a type of lock in itself, but rather a situation where a paradox has been formed. A deadlock arises if one lock can't do what it needs to do in order to clear because another lock is holding that resource — the problem is that the opposite resource is itself stuck waiting for the lock to clear on the first transaction.

Without update locks, these deadlocks would crop up all the time. Two update queries would be running in shared mode. Query A completes its query and is ready for the physical update. It wants to escalate to an exclusive lock, but it can't because Query B is finishing its query. Query B then finishes the query, except that it needs to do the physical update. In order to do that, Query B must escalate to an exclusive lock, but it can't because Query A is still waiting. This creates an impasse.

Instead, an update lock prevents any other update locks from being established. The instant that the second transaction attempts to achieve an update lock, they will be put into a wait status for whatever the lock timeout is — the lock will not be granted. If the first lock clears before the lock timeout is reached, then the lock will be granted to the new requester and that process can continue. If not, an error will be generated.

Update locks are compatible only with shared locks and intent shared locks.

Intent Locks

An *intent lock* is a true placeholder and is meant to deal with the issue of object hierarchies. Imagine a situation where you have a lock established on a row, but someone wants to establish a lock on a page or extent, or modify a table. You wouldn't want another transaction to go around yours by going higher up the hierarchy, would you?

Without intent locks, the higher-level objects wouldn't even know that you had the lock at the lower level. Intent locks improve performance, as SQL Server needs to examine intent locks only at the table level (not check every row or page lock on the table) to determine if a transaction can safely lock the entire table. Intent locks come in three different varieties:

❏ **Intent shared lock:** A shared lock has been, or is going to be, established at some lower point in the hierarchy. For example, a page is about to have a page-level shared lock established on it. This type of lock applies only to tables and pages.

❏ **Intent exclusive lock:** This is the same as intent shared, but with an exclusive lock about to be placed on the lower-level item.

❏ **Shared with intent exclusive lock:** A shared lock has been, or is about to be, established lower down the object hierarchy, but the intent is to modify data, so it will become an intent exclusive at some point.

Schema Locks

These come in two flavors:

❏ **Schema modification lock (Sch-M):** A schema change is being made to the object. No queries or other CREATE, ALTER, or DROP statements can be run against this object for the duration of the Sch-M lock.

❏ **Schema stability lock (Sch-S):** This is very similar to a shared lock; this lock's sole purpose is to prevent a Sch-M, since there are already locks for other queries (or CREATE, ALTER, or DROP statements) active on the object. This is compatible with all other lock types.

Bulk Update Locks

A *bulk update lock* (*BU*) is really just a variant of a table lock with one little (but significant) difference. Bulk update locks will allow parallel loading of data — that is, the table is locked from any other *normal* activity (T-SQL statements), but multiple BULK INSERT or bcp operations can be performed at the same time.

Lock Compatibility

The table that follows shows the compatibility of the resource lock modes (listed in increasing lock strength). Existing locks are shown by the columns, requested locks by the rows:

	IS	S	U	IX	SIX	X
Intent Shared (IS)	YES	YES	YES	YES	YES	NO
Shared (S)	YES	YES	YES	NO	NO	NO
Update (U)	YES	YES	NO	NO	NO	NO
Intent Exclusive (IX)	YES	NO	NO	YES	NO	NO
Shared with Intent Exclusive (SIX)	YES	NO	NO	NO	NO	NO
Exclusive (X)	NO	NO	NO	NO	NO	NO

Also:

- ❑ The Sch-S is compatible with all lock modes except the Sch-M.
- ❑ The Sch-M is incompatible with all lock modes.
- ❑ The BU is compatible only with schema stability and other bulk update locks.

Specifying a Specific Lock Type — Optimizer Hints

Sometimes you want to have more control over the way the locking goes, either in your query or perhaps in your entire transaction. You can do this by making use of what are called *optimizer hints*.

Optimizer hints are ways of explicitly telling SQL Server to escalate a lock to a specific level. They are included right after the name of the table (in your SQL Statement) that they are to affect.

Optimizer hints are seriously on the advanced side of things. They are often abused by people who are experienced SQL Server developers, and they are not to be trifled with.

Think of it this way — Microsoft has invested literally millions of dollars in such things as their query optimizer and knowing what locks to utilize in what situations. Query hints are meant to adjust for the little things the optimizer may not know about, but in the vast majority of cases you are *not* going to know more than their optimizer team did. Shy away from these until the later stages of your SQL Server learning process (and I promise, I'll cover them well in the *Professional* version of this book).

Determining Locks Using the Management Studio

Perhaps the nicest way of all to take a look at your locks is using the Management Studio. The Management Studio will show you locks in two different sorts — by *process ID* or by *object* — utilizing the Activity Monitor.

To make use of the Management Studio's lock display, just navigate to the *<Server>* ➪ Activity Monitor node of the Management Studio, where *<Server>* is the top level node for the server you want to monitor activity on. SQL Server should come up with a new window that looks something like Figure 14-3.

Just expand the node that you're interested in (the Overview section is expanded by default — I've manually expanded the Processes section) and you can scroll around to find a large number of metrics — including whatever locks are currently active on the system.

Perhaps the coolest feature of the Activity Monitor is that when you right-click on a specific process in the Process window, you get the option of easily starting a SQL Profiler trace against that particular process. This can be very handy when you are troubleshooting a variety of situations.

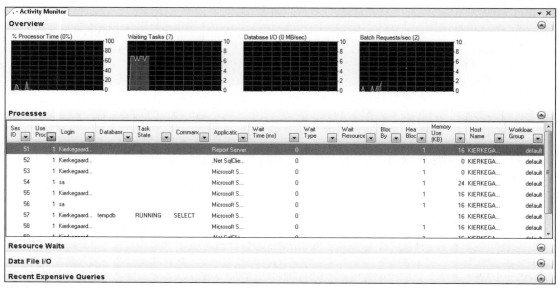

Figure 14-3

Setting the Isolation Level

We've seen that several different kinds of problems can be prevented by different locking strategies. We've also seen what kinds of locks are available and how they have an impact on the availability of resources. Now it's time to take a closer look at how these process management pieces work together to ensure overall data integrity — to make certain that you can get the results you expect.

The first thing to understand about the relationship between transactions and locks is that they are inextricably linked with each other. By default, any lock that is data modification related will, once created, be held for the duration of the transaction. If you have a long transaction, this means that your locks may be preventing other processes from accessing the objects you have a lock on for a rather long time. It probably goes without saying that this can be rather problematic.

However, that's only the default. In fact, there are actually five different *isolation levels* that you can set:

❑   READ COMMITTED (the default)

❑   READ UNCOMMITTED

❑   REPEATABLE READ

❑   SERIALIZABLE

❑   SNAPSHOT

The syntax for switching between them is pretty straightforward:

```
SET TRANSACTION ISOLATION LEVEL <READ COMMITTED|READ UNCOMMITTED
    |REPEATABLE READ|SERIALIZABLE|SNAPSHOT>
```

The change in isolation level will affect only the current connection, so you don't need to worry about adversely affecting other users (or them affecting you).

Let's start by looking at the default situation (READ COMMITTED) a little more closely.

READ COMMITTED

With READ COMMITTED, any shared locks you create will be automatically released as soon as the statement that created them is complete. That is, if you start a transaction, run several statements, run a SELECT statement, and then run several more statements, the locks associated with the SELECT statement are freed as soon as the SELECT statement is complete — SQL Server doesn't wait for the end of the transaction.

Action queries (UPDATE, DELETE, and INSERT) are a little different. If your transaction performs a query that modifies data, then those locks will be held for the duration of the transaction (in case you need to roll back).

By keeping this level of default with READ COMMITTED, you can be sure that you have enough data integrity to prevent dirty reads. However, non-repeatable reads and phantoms can still occur.

READ UNCOMMITTED

READ UNCOMMITTED is the most dangerous of all isolation level choices, but also has the highest performance in terms of speed.

Setting the isolation level to READ UNCOMMITTED tells SQL Server not to set any locks and not to honor any locks. With this isolation level, it is possible to experience any of the various concurrency issues we discussed earlier in the chapter (most notably a dirty read).

Why would one ever want to risk a dirty read? When I watch the newsgroups on Usenet, I see the question come up on a regular basis. It's surprising to a fair number of people, but there are actually good reasons to have this isolation level, and they almost always have to do with reporting.

In an OLTP environment, locks are both your protector and your enemy. They prevent data integrity problems, but they also often prevent or block you from getting at the data you want. It is extremely commonplace to see a situation where the management wants to run reports regularly, but the data entry people are often prevented from or delayed in entering data because of locks held by the manager's reports.

By using READ UNCOMMITTED, you can often get around this problem — at least for reports where the numbers don't have to be exact. For example, let's say that a sales manager wants to know just how much has been done in sales so far today. Indeed, we'll say he's a micro-manager and asks this same question (in the form of rerunning the report) several times a day.

If the report happened to be a long-running one, then there's a high chance that his running it would damage the productivity of other users due to locking considerations. What's nice about this report, though, is that it is a truly nebulous report — the exact values are probably meaningless. The manager is really just looking for ballpark numbers.

By having an isolation level of READ UNCOMMITTED, we do not set any locks, so we don't block any other transactions. Our numbers will be somewhat suspect (because of the risk of dirty reads), but we don't need exact numbers anyway and we know that the numbers are still going to be close, even on the off chance that a dirty read is rolled back.

You can get the same effect as READ UNCOMMITTED by adding the NOLOCK optimizer hint in your query. The advantage to setting the isolation level is that you don't have to use a hint for every table in your query or use it in multiple queries. The advantage to using the NOLOCK optimizer hint is that you don't need to remember to set the isolation level back to the default for the connection. (With READ UNCOMMITTED you do.)

REPEATABLE READ

The REPEATABLE READ escalates your isolation level somewhat and provides an extra level of concurrency protection by preventing not only dirty reads (the default already does that), but also preventing non-repeatable reads.

That prevention of non-repeatable reads is a big upside, but holding even shared locks until the end of the transaction can block users' access to objects, and therefore hurt productivity. Personally, I prefer to use other data integrity options (such as a CHECK constraint together with error handling) rather than this choice, but it remains an available option.

The equivalent optimizer hint for the REPEATABLE READ isolation level is REPEATABLEREAD (these are the same, only no space).

SERIALIZABLE

SERIALIZABLE is something of the fortress of isolation levels. It prevents all forms of concurrency issues except for a lost update. Even phantoms are prevented.

When you set your isolation to SERIALIZABLE, you're saying that any UPDATE, DELETE, or INSERT to the table or tables used by your transaction must not meet the WHERE clause of any statement in that transaction. Essentially, if the user was going to do something that your transaction would be interested in, then it must wait until your transaction has been completed.

The SERIALIZABLE isolation level can also be simulated by using the SERIALIZABLE or HOLDLOCK optimizer hint in your query. Again, like the READ UNCOMMITTED and NOLOCK debate, the option of not having to set it every time versus not having to remember to change the isolation level back is the big issue.

Going with an isolation level of SERIALIZABLE would, on the surface, appear to be the way you want to do everything. Indeed, it does provide your database with the highest level of what is called consistency — that is, the update process works the same for multiple users as it would if all your users did one transaction at a time (processed things serially).

As with most things in life, however, there is a trade-off. Consistency and concurrency can, in a practical sense, be thought of as polar opposites. Making things SERIALIZABLE *can prevent other users from getting to the objects they need — that equates to lower concurrency. The reverse is also true — increasing concurrency (by going to a* REPEATABLE READ, *for example) reduces the consistency of your database.*

*My personal recommendation on this is to stick with the default (*READ COMMITTED*) unless you have a specific reason not to.*

SNAPSHOT

SNAPSHOT is the newest of the isolation levels (it was added in SQL Server 2005) and most closely resembles a combination of the READ COMMITTED and READ UNCOMMITTED. It's important to note that SNAPSHOT is not available by default — instead it becomes available only if a special option, ALLOW_SNAPSHOT_ISOLATION, has been activated for the database.

Much like READ UNCOMMITTED, SNAPSHOT does not create any locks, nor does it generally honor them. The primary difference between the two is that they recognize changes taking place in the database at different times. Any change in the database, regardless of when or if it is committed, is seen by queries running the READ UNCOMMITTED isolation level. With SNAPSHOT only changes that were committed prior to the start of the SNAPSHOT transaction are seen. From the start of the SNAPSHOT transaction, all data is viewed exactly as it was committed at the start of the transaction.

There are two special things to note relating to SNAPSHOT. *First, a special database option has to be turned on before you can even use the* SNAPSHOT *isolation level, and that option must be on for every database included in your transaction (keep this in mind in case your queries span databases). Next, while* SNAPSHOT *does not generally pay attention to or set locks, there is one special instance where it will. If there is a database recovery rollback in progress when the* SNAPSHOT *takes place, then the* SNAPSHOT *transaction will set a special lock in place to serve as something of a placeholder and then wait for the rollback to complete. As soon as the rollback is complete, the lock is removed and the* SNAPSHOT *will move forward normally.*

Dealing with Deadlocks (aka "a 1205")

OK, so now you've seen locks, and you've also seen transactions. Now that you've got both, we can move on to the rather pesky problem of dealing with *deadlocks*.

As we've already mentioned, a deadlock is not a type of lock in itself, but rather a situation where a paradox has been formed by other locks. Like it or not, you'll bump into these on a regular basis (particularly when you're just starting out), and you'll be greeted with an error number *1205*. So prolific is this particular problem that you'll hear many a database developer refer to them simply by the number.

Deadlocks are caused when one lock can't do what it needs to do in order to clear, because a second lock is holding that resource, and vice versa. When this happens, somebody has to win the battle, so SQL Server chooses a deadlock *victim*. The deadlock victim's transaction is then rolled back and is notified that this happened through the 1205 error. The other transaction can continue normally (indeed, it will be entirely unaware that there was a problem, other than seeing an increased execution time).

How SQL Server Figures Out There's a Deadlock

Every five seconds SQL Server checks all the current transactions for what locks they are waiting on, but haven't yet been granted. As it does this, it essentially makes a note that the request exists. It will then recheck the status of all open lock requests again and, if one of the previous requests has still not been granted, it will recursively check all open transactions for a circular chain of lock requests. If it finds such a chain, then one or more deadlock victims will be chosen.

How Deadlock Victims Are Chosen

By default, a deadlock victim is chosen based on the cost of the transactions involved. The transaction that costs the least to rollback will be chosen (in other words, SQL Server has to do the least number of things to undo it). You can, to some degree, override this by using the DEADLOCK_PRIORITY SET option available in SQL Server; this is, however, generally both ill advised and out of the scope of this book.

Avoiding Deadlocks

Deadlocks can't be avoided 100 percent of the time in complex systems, but you can almost always totally eliminate them from a practical standpoint — that is, make them so rare that they have little relevance to your system.

To cut down or eliminate deadlocks, follow these simple (OK, usually simple) rules:

- ❏   Use your objects in the same order.
- ❏   Keep your transactions as short as possible and in one batch.
- ❏   Use the lowest transaction isolation level necessary.
- ❏   Do not allow open-ended interruptions (user interactions, batch separations) within the same transaction.
- ❏   In controlled environments, use bound connections.

Nearly every time I run across deadlocking problems, at least one (usually more) of these rules has been violated. Let's look at each one individually.

Use Objects in the Same Order

This is the most common problem area within the few rules that I consider to be basic. What's great about using this rule is that it almost never costs you anything to speak of — it's more a way of thinking. You decide early in your design process how you want to access your database objects — including order — and it becomes a habit in every query, procedure, or trigger that you write for that project.

Think about it for a minute — if our problem is that our two connections each have what the other wants, then it implies that we're dealing with the problem too late in the game. Let's look at a simple example.

Consider that we have two tables: Suppliers and Products. Now say that we have two processes that make use of both of these tables. Process 1 accepts inventory entries, updates Products with the new amount of products on hand, and then updates Suppliers with the total amount of products that we've purchased. Process 2 records sales; it updates the total amount of products sold in the `Suppliers` table, then decreases the inventory quantity in `Products`.

If we run these two processes at the same time, we're begging for trouble. Process 1 will grab an exclusive lock on the `Products` table. Process 2 will grab an exclusive lock on the `Suppliers` table. Process 1 then attempts to grab a lock on the `Suppliers` table, but it will be forced to wait for Process 2 to clear its existing lock. In the meantime, Process 2 tries to create a lock on the `Products` table, but it will have to wait for Process 1 to clear its existing lock. We now have a paradox — both processes are waiting on each other. SQL Server will have to pick a deadlock victim.

Now let's rearrange that scenario, with Process 2 changed to first decrease the inventory quantity in `Products`, then update the total amount of products sold in the `Suppliers` table. This is a functional equivalent to the first way we organized the processes, and it will cost us nothing to perform it this new way. The impact though, will be stunning — no more deadlocks (at least not between these two processes)! Let's walk through what will now happen.

When we run these two processes at the same time, Process 1 will grab an exclusive lock on the `Products` table (so far, it's the same). Process 2 will then also try to grab a lock on the `Products` table, but will be forced to wait for Process 1 to finish (notice that we haven't done anything with `Suppliers` yet). Process 1 finishes with the `Products` table, but doesn't release the lock because the transaction isn't complete yet. Process 2 is still waiting for the lock on `Products` to clear. Process 1 now moves on to grab a lock on the `Suppliers` table. Process 2 continues to wait for the lock to clear on `Products`. Process 1 finishes and commits or rolls back the transaction as required, but frees all locks in either case. Process 2 now is able to obtain its lock on the `Products` table and moves through the rest of its transaction without further incident.

Just swapping the order in which these two queries are run has eliminated a potential deadlock problem. Keep things in the same order wherever possible and you, too, will experience far less in the way of deadlocks.

Keeping Transactions as Short as Possible

This is another of the basics. Again, it should become just an instinct — something you don't really think about, something you just do.

This is one that never has to cost you anything really. Put what you need to put in the transaction and keep everything else out — it's just that simple. Why this works isn't rocket science — the longer the transaction is open and the more it touches (within the transaction), the higher the likelihood that you're going to run into some other process that wants one or more of the objects that you're using (reducing concurrency). If you keep your transaction short, you minimize the number of objects that can potentially cause a deadlock, plus you cut down on the time that you have your lock on them. It's as simple as that.

Keeping transactions in one batch minimizes network roundtrips during a transaction, reducing possible delays in completing the transaction and releasing locks.

Use the Lowest Transaction Isolation Level Possible

This one is considerably less basic and requires some serious thought. As such, it isn't surprising just how often it isn't thought of at all. Consider it Rob's axiom — that which requires thought is likely not to be thought of. Be different: Think about it.

We have several different transaction isolation levels available. The default is READ COMMITTED. Using a lower isolation level holds shared locks for a shorter duration than using a higher isolation level does, thereby reducing locking contention.

No Open-Ended Transactions

This is probably the most commonsense of all the recommendations here, but it's one that's often violated because of past practices.

One of the ways we used to prevent lost updates (mainframe days here, folks!) was just to grab the lock and hold it until we were done with it. I can't tell you how problematic this was (can you say *yuck*?).

Imagine this scenario (it's a real-life example): Someone in your service department likes to use update screens (exclusive locks) instead of display screens (shared locks) to look at data. He goes on to look at a work order. Now his buddy calls and asks if he's ready for lunch. "Sure!" comes the reply, and the service clerk heads off to a rather long lunch (one to two hours). Everyone who is interested in this record is now locked out of it for the duration of this clerk's lunch.

Wait — it gets worse. In the days of the mainframe, you used to see the concept of queuing far more often (it actually can be quite efficient). Now someone submits a print job (which is queued) for this work order. It sits in the queue waiting for the record lock to clear. Since it's a queue environment, every print job your company has for work orders now piles up behind that first print job (which is going to wait for that person's lunch before clearing).

This is a rather extreme example, but I'm hoping that it clearly illustrates the point. Don't ever create locks that will still be open when you begin some form of open-ended process. Usually we're talking user interaction (like our lunch lover), but it could be any process that has an open-ended wait to it.

Summary

Transactions and locks are both cornerstones of how SQL Server works and, therefore, maximizing your development of solutions in SQL Server.

By using transactions, you can make sure that everything you need to have happen as a unit happens, or none of it does. SQL Server's use of locks ensures that we avoid the pitfalls of concurrency to the maximum extent possible (you'll never avoid them entirely, but it's amazing how close you can come with a little — OK, a lot — of planning). By using the two together, you are able to pass what the database industry calls the *ACID* test. If a transaction is ACID, then it has:

❑ **Atomicity:** The transaction is all or nothing.

❑ **Consistency:** All constraints and other data integrity rules have been adhered to, and all related objects (data pages, index pages) have been updated completely.

❑ **Isolation:** Each transaction is completely isolated from any other transaction. The actions of one transaction cannot be interfered with by the actions of a separate transaction.

❑ **Durability:** After a transaction is completed, its effects are permanently in place in the system. The data is *safe,* in the sense that things such as a power outage or other non-disk system failure will not lead to data that is only half written.

In short, by using transactions and locks, you can minimize deadlocks, ensure data integrity, and improve the overall efficiency of your system.

In our next chapter, we'll be looking at triggers. Indeed, we'll see that, for many of the likely uses of triggers, the concepts of transactions and rollbacks will be at the very center of the trigger.

Triggers

Ah, triggers. Triggers are cool, triggers are neat, and triggers are our friends. At the very same time, triggers are evil, triggers are ugly, and triggers are our enemy. In short, I am often asked, "Should I use triggers?" The answer is, like most things in SQL, it depends. There's little that's black and white in the wonderful world of SQL Server — triggers are definitely a very plain shade of gray.

From a beginner's point of view (and by this chapter in this book, I hope you're a lot less of a beginner — but still . . .), you really want to be *certain* you know what you're doing before you go the triggers route, so sit back, listen, learn, and decide for yourself whether they are right for you.

In this chapter, we'll try to look at triggers in all of their colors — from black all the way to white and a whole lot in between. The main issues we'll be dealing with include:

- ❑   What is a trigger?
- ❑   Using triggers for more flexible referential integrity
- ❑   Using triggers to create flexible data integrity rules
- ❑   Using INSTEAD OF triggers to create more flexible updatable views
- ❑   Other common uses for triggers
- ❑   Controlling the firing order of triggers
- ❑   Performance considerations

By the time we're done, you should have an idea of just how complex the decision about when and where not to use triggers is. You'll also have an inkling of just how powerful and flexible they can be.

Most of all, if I've done my job well, you won't be a trigger extremist (which *so* many SQL Server people I meet are) with the distorted notion that triggers are evil and should never be used. Neither will you side with at the other end of the spectrum, who think that triggers are the solution to all the world's problems. The right answer in this respect is that triggers can do a lot for you, but they can also cause a lot of problems. The trick is to use them when they are the right things to use, and not to use them when they aren't.

Some common uses of triggers include:

❑ Enforcing referential integrity: Although I recommend using Declarative Referential Integrity (DRI) whenever possible, there are many things that DRI won't do (for example, referential integrity across databases or even servers, many complex types of relationships, and so on).

❑ Creating audit trails, which means writing out records that keep track of not just the most current data, but also the actual change history for each record. This may become less popular with the new change-data tracking that SQL Server 2008 adds, but triggers are the way it has been done historically.

❑ Cresting functionality similar to a CHECK constraint, but which works across tables, databases, or even servers.

❑ Substituting your own statements in the place of a user's action statement (usually used to enable inserts in complex views).

In addition, you have the new, but likely much more rare case (like I said, they are new, so only time will tell for sure), Data Definition Language (DDL) trigger, which is about monitoring changes in the structure of your table.

And these are just a few. So, with no further ado, let's look at exactly what a trigger is.

What Is a Trigger?

A trigger is a special kind of stored procedure that responds to specific events. There are two kinds of triggers: Data Definition Language (DDL) triggers and Data Manipulation Language (DML) triggers.

DDL triggers fire in response to someone changing the structure of your database in some way (CREATE, ALTER, DROP, and similar statements). These are critical to some installations (particularly high-security installations), but are pretty narrow in use. In general, you will only need to look into using these where you need extreme auditing of changes/history of your database structure. Their use is a fairly advanced concept and, as such, I'm covering them here as mostly a "be aware these exist" thing, and we'll move on to the meatier version of triggers.

DML triggers are pieces of code that you attach to a particular table or view. Unlike sprocs, where you need to explicitly invoke the code, the code in triggers is automatically run whenever the event(s) you attached the trigger to occur in the table. Indeed, you *can't* explicitly invoke triggers — the only way to do this is by performing the required action in the table that they are assigned to.

Beyond not being able to explicitly invoke a trigger, you'll find two other things that exist for sprocs but are missing from triggers: parameters and return codes.

While triggers take no parameters, they do have a mechanism for figuring out what records they are supposed to act on (we'll investigate this further later in the chapter). And, while you can use the RETURN *keyword, you cannot return a specific return code (because you didn't explicitly call the trigger, what would you return a return code to?).*

What events can you attach triggers to? The three action query types you use in SQL. So, there are three types of triggers, plus hybrids that come from mixing and matching the events and timing that fire them:

- ❏   INSERT triggers
- ❏   DELETE triggers
- ❏   UPDATE triggers
- ❏   A mix and match of any of the above

It's worth noting that there are times when a trigger will not fire, even though it seems that the action you are performing falls into one of the preceding categories. At issue is whether the operation you are doing is in a logged activity or not. For example, a DELETE *statement is a normal, logged activity that would fire any delete trigger, but a* TRUNCATE TABLE, *which has the effect of deleting rows, just deallocates the space used by the table — there is no individual deletion of rows logged, and no trigger is fired. Bulk operations will not, by default, fire triggers (you can explicitly tell the bulk operation to fire the triggers).*

The syntax for creating triggers looks an awful lot like all of our other CREATE syntax examples, except, as with a table, it has to be attached to a table — a trigger can't stand on its own.

Let's take a look:

```
CREATE TRIGGER <trigger name>
    ON [<schema name>.]<table or view name>
    [WITH ENCRYPTION | EXECUTE AS <CALLER | SELF | <user> >]
    {{{FOR|AFTER} <[DELETE] [,] [INSERT] [,] [UPDATE]>} |INSTEAD OF}
    [WITH APPEND]
    [NOT FOR REPLICATION]
AS
    < <sql statements> | EXTERNAL NAME <assembly method specifier> >
```

As you can see, the all too familiar CREATE <object type> <object name> is still there, as well as the execution stuff we've seen in many other objects — we've just added the ON clause to indicate the table to which this trigger is going to be attached, as well as when and under what conditions it fires.

ON

This part just names the object you are creating the trigger against. Keep in mind that, if the type of the trigger is an AFTER trigger (if it uses FOR or AFTER to declare the trigger), then the target of the ON clause must be a table — AFTER triggers are not supported for views.

WITH ENCRYPTION

This works just as it does for views and sprocs. If you add this option, you can be certain that no one will be able to view your code (not even you!). This is particularly useful if you are going to be building software for commercial distribution, or if you are concerned about security and don't want your users to be able to see what data you're modifying or accessing. Obviously, you should keep a copy of the code required to create the trigger somewhere else, in case you want to re-create it sometime later.

As with views and sprocs, the thing to remember when using the WITH ENCRYPTION option is that you must reapply it every time you use ALTER on your trigger. If you make use of an ALTER TRIGGER statement and do not include the WITH ENCRYPTION option, then the trigger will no longer be encrypted.

The FOR|AFTER vs. the INSTEAD OF Clause

In addition to deciding what kind of queries will fire your trigger (INSERT, UPDATE, and/or DELETE), you also have some choice as to when the trigger fires. While the FOR (alternatively, you can use the keyword AFTER if you choose) trigger is the one that has been around a long time and that people generally think of, you also have the ability to run what is called an INSTEAD OF trigger. Which of these two you use will affect whether you enter your trigger before the data has been modified or after. In either case, you will be in your trigger before any changes are truly committed to the database.

Confusing? Probably. Let's try it a different way with a diagram that shows where each choice fires (see Figure 15-1).

The thing to note here is that, regardless of which choice you make, SQL Server will put together two working tables — one holding a copy of the records that were inserted (and, incidentally, called Inserted) and one holding a copy of any records that were deleted (called Deleted). We'll look into the uses of these working tables a little later. For now realize that, with INSTEAD OF triggers, the creation of these working tables will happen *before* any constraints are checked, with FOR triggers, these tables will be created after constraints are checked. The key to INSTEAD OF triggers is that you can actually run your own code in the place of whatever the user requested. This means we can clean up ambiguous INSERT problems in views. It also means that we can take action to clean up constraint violations before the constraint is even checked.

> *As positively glorious as this sounds, this is actually pretty complex stuff. It means that you need to anticipate every possibility. In addition, it means that you are effectively adding a preprocess (a process that runs before the main code) to every query that changes data in any way for this table (this is not a good thing performance wise). Cool as they sound, INSTEAD OF triggers fall in the category of fairly advanced stuff and are well outside the scope of this book.*

Triggers using the FOR and AFTER declaration behave identically to each other. The big difference between them and INSTEAD OF triggers is that they build their working tables *after* any constraints have been checked.

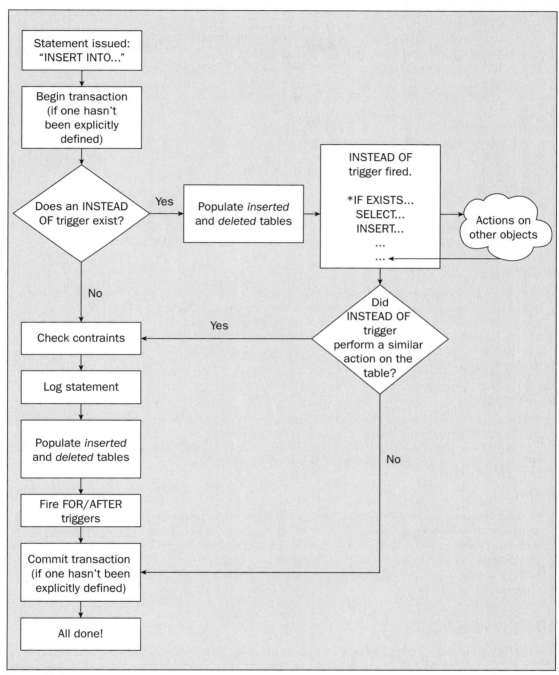

Figure 15-1

FOR|AFTER

The FOR (or, alternatively, you can use AFTER) clause indicates under what type of action(s) you want this trigger to fire. You can have the trigger fire whenever there is an INSERT, UPDATE, or DELETE, or any mix of the three. So, for example, your FOR clause could look something like:

```
FOR INSERT, DELETE
```

... or:

```
FOR UPDATE, INSERT
```

... or:

```
FOR DELETE
```

As stated in the section about the ON clause, triggers declared using the FOR or AFTER clause can be attached only to tables — no views are allowed (see INSTEAD OF triggers for those).

INSERT Trigger

The code for any trigger that you mark as being FOR INSERT will be executed anytime that someone inserts a new row into your table. For each row that is inserted, SQL Server will create a copy of that new row and insert it in a special table that exists only within the scope of your trigger. That table is called Inserted, and we'll see much more of it over the course of this chapter. The big thing to understand is that the Inserted table lives only as long as your trigger does. Think of it as not existing before your trigger starts or after your trigger completes.

DELETE Trigger

This works much the same as an INSERT trigger does, save that the Inserted table will be empty (after all, you deleted rather than inserted, so there are no records for the Inserted table). Instead, a copy of each record that was deleted is inserted into another table called Deleted. That table, like the Inserted table, is limited in scope to just the life of your trigger.

UPDATE Trigger

More of the same, save for a twist. The code in a trigger declared as being FOR UPDATE will be fired whenever an existing record in your table is changed. The twist is that there's no such table as UPDATED. Instead, SQL Server treats each row as if the existing record had been deleted and a totally new record was inserted. As you can probably guess from that, a trigger declared as FOR UPDATE contains not one but two special tables called Inserted and Deleted. The two tables have exactly the same number of rows, of course.

WITH APPEND

WITH APPEND is something of an oddball and, in all honesty, you're pretty unlikely to use it; nonetheless, we'll touch on it briefly. WITH APPEND applies only when you are running in 6.5 compatibility mode (which can be set using sp_dbcmptlevel) — something that should be exceedingly rare at this point (it's been out of date for nearly a decade now).

SQL Server 6.5 and prior did not allow multiple triggers of the same type on any single table. For example, if you had already declared a trigger called `trgCheck` to enforce data integrity on updates and inserts, then you couldn't create a separate trigger for cascading updates. Once one update (or insert, or delete) trigger was created, that was it — you couldn't create another trigger for the same type of action. WITH APPEND gets around this problem by explicitly telling SQL Server that we want to add this new trigger even though we already have a trigger of that type on the table — both will be fired when the appropriate trigger action (INSERT, UPDATE, DELETE) occurs. It's a way of having a bit of both worlds.

NOT FOR REPLICATION

Adding this option slightly alters the rules for when the trigger is fired. With this option in place, the trigger will not be fired whenever a replication-related task modifies your table. Usually a trigger is fired (to do the housekeeping, cascading, and so on) when the original table is modified and there is often no point in doing it again.

AS

Exactly as it was with sprocs, this is the meat of the matter. The AS keyword tells SQL Server that your code is about to start. From this point forward, we're into the scripted portion of your trigger.

Using Triggers for Data Integrity Rules

Although they shouldn't be your first option, triggers can also perform the same functionality as a CHECK constraint or even a DEFAULT. The answer to the question "Should I use triggers vs. CHECK constraints?" is the rather definitive: "It depends." If a CHECK can do the job, then it's probably the preferable choice. There are times, however, when a CHECK constraint just won't do the job, or when something inherent in the CHECK process makes it less desirable than a trigger. Examples of where you would want to use a trigger over a CHECK include:

❑   Your business rule needs to reference data in a separate table.

❑   Your business rule needs to check the *delta* (difference between before and after) of an UPDATE.

❑   You require a customized error message.

A summary table of when to use what type of data integrity mechanism is provided at the end of Chapter 6.

This really just scratches the surface of things. Since triggers are highly flexible, deciding when to use them really just comes down to balancing your need to get something special done with the overhead triggers incur and other approaches you might take to address your need.

Dealing with Requirements Sourced from Other Tables

CHECK constraints are great — fast and efficient — but they don't do everything you'd like them to. Perhaps the biggest shortcoming shows up when you need to verify data across tables.

To illustrate this, let's take a look at the `Sales.SalesOrderDetail` and `Sales.SpecialOfferProduct` tables in the AdventureWorks2008 database. The relationship looks like Figure 15-2.

Figure 15-2

So under normal DRI, you can be certain that no `SalesOrderDetail` item can be entered into the `SalesOrderDetail` table unless there is a matching `ProductID` in the `SpecialOfferProduct` table (even if the special offer record is "no discount"). We are, however, looking for something more than just the norm here.

Our Inventory department has been complaining that our Customer Support people keep placing orders for products that are marked discontinued. They would like to have such orders rejected before they get into the system.

We can't deal with this using a `CHECK` constraint, because the place where we know about the discontinued status (the `Product` table) is a separate table from where we are placing the restriction (the `SalesOrderDetail` table). Don't sweat it though — you can tell the Inventory department, "No problem!" You just need to use a trigger:

```
CREATE TRIGGER Sales.SalesOrderDetailNotDiscontinued
    ON Sales.SalesOrderDetail
    FOR INSERT, UPDATE
AS
    IF EXISTS
        (
        SELECT 'True'
        FROM Inserted i
        JOIN Production.Product p
            ON i.ProductID = p.ProductID
        WHERE p.DiscontinuedDate IS NOT NULL
        )
    BEGIN
        RAISERROR('Order Item is discontinued. Transaction Failed.',16,1)
        ROLLBACK TRAN
    END
```

Let's go ahead and test out our handiwork. First, we need a record or two that will fail when it hits our trigger. Unfortunately, AdventureWorks2008 has apparently never discontinued a product before — we'll just have to change that...

```
UPDATE Production.Product
SET DiscontinuedDate = '01-01-2008'
WHERE ProductID = 680
```

Now, knowing that we have a discontinued product, let's go ahead and add an order detail item that violates the constraint. Note that I've chosen an existing order (43659) to tack this item onto:

```
INSERT INTO Sales.SalesOrderDetail
VALUES
(43659, '4911-403C-98', 1, 680, 1, 1431.50,0.00, NEWID(), GETDATE())
```

This gets the rejection that we expect:

```
Msg 50000, Level 16, State 1, Procedure SalesOrderDetailNotDiscontinued, Line 14
Order Item is discontinued. Transaction Failed.
Msg 3609, Level 16, State 1, Line 1
The transaction ended in the trigger. The batch has been aborted.
```

Remember that we could, if desired, also create a custom error message to raise, instead of the ad hoc message that we used with the RAISERROR command.

If you're working along with these, but trying to keep your AdventureWorks2008 database close to its original state, don't forget to return ProductID 680 back to its null discontinued date.

Using Triggers to Check the Delta of an Update

Sometimes, you're not interested as much in what the value was or is, as you are in how much it changed. While there isn't any one column or table that gives you that information, you can calculate it by making use of the Inserted and Deleted tables in your trigger.

To check this out, let's take a look at the Production.ProductInventory table. ProductInventory has a column called Quantity. Recently, there has been a rush on several products, and Adventure-Works2008 has been selling out of several things. Since AdventureWorks2008 needs more than just a few customers to stay in business in the long run, it has decided to institute a rationing system on their products. The Inventory department has requested that we prevent orders from being placed that try to sell more than half of the units in stock for any particular product.

To implement this, we make use of both the Inserted and Deleted tables:

```
CREATE TRIGGER Production.ProductIsRationed
    ON Production.ProductInventory
    FOR UPDATE
AS
```

```
IF EXISTS
    (
    SELECT 'True'
    FROM Inserted i
    JOIN Deleted d
        ON i.ProductID = d.ProductID
       AND i.LocationID = d.LocationID
    WHERE (d.Quantity - i.Quantity) > d.Quantity / 2
       AND d.Quantity - i.Quantity > 0
    )
BEGIN
    RAISERROR('Cannot reduce stock by more than 50%% at once.',16,1)
    ROLLBACK TRAN
END
```

Before we test this, let's analyze what we're doing here.

First, we're making use of an `IF EXISTS` just as we have throughout this chapter. We want to do the rollback only if something exists that meets the evil, mean, and nasty criteria that we'll be testing for.

Then we join the `Inserted` and `Deleted` tables together — this is what gives us the chance to compare the two.

Our `WHERE` clause is the point where things might become a bit confusing. The first line of it is pretty straightforward. It implements the nominal statement of our business requirement; updates to the `Quantity` column that are more than half the units we previously had on hand will meet the `EXISTS` criterion and cause the conditional code to run (rejecting the transaction).

The next line, though, is not quite so straightforward. As with all things in programming, we need to think beyond the nominal statement of the problem, and think about other ramifications. The requirement really applies only to reductions in orders — we certainly don't want to restrict how many units are put *in* stock — so we make sure that we worry only about updates where the number in stock after the update is less than before the update. The > 0 requirement also addresses the scenario where there was only one item in stock. In such a scenario, we want to go ahead and sell that last one, but 1-1 is greater than ½, and the trigger would have rejected it without our > 0 addition.

If both of these conditions have been met (over 50 percent and a reduction, rather than addition, to the inventory), then we raise the error. Notice the use of two % signs, rather than one, in `RAISERROR`. Remember that a % works as a placeholder for a parameter, so one % by itself won't show up when your error message comes out. By putting two in a row (%%), we let SQL Server know that we really did want to print out a percent sign.

OK — let's check how it works. We'll just pick a record and try to do an update that reduces the stock by more than 50 percent:

```
UPDATE Production.ProductInventory
SET Quantity = 1  -- Was 408 if you want to set it back
WHERE ProductID = 1
  AND LocationID = 1
```

I just picked out "Adjustable Race" as our victim, but you could have chosen any `ProductID`, as long as you set the value to less than 50 percent of its previous value. If you do, you'll get the expected error:

```
Msg 50000, Level 16, State 1, Procedure ProductIsRationed, Line 16
Cannot reduce stock by more than 50% at once.
Msg 3609, Level 16, State 1, Line 1
The transaction ended in the trigger. The batch has been aborted.
```

Note that we could have also implemented this in the `SalesOrderDetail` table by referencing the actual order quantity against the current `Quantity` amount, but we would have run into several problems:

❑ **Updates that change:** Is the process that's creating the `SalesOrderDetail` record updating `ProductInventory` before or after the `SalesOrderDetail` record? That makes a difference in how we make use of the `Quantity` value in the `ProductInventory` table to calculate the effect of the transaction.

❑ **The inventory external to the `SalesOrderDetails` table updates would not be affected:** They could still reduce the inventory by more than half (this may actually be a good thing in many circumstances, but it's something that has to be thought about).

Using Triggers for Custom Error Messages

We've already touched on this in some of our other examples, but remember that triggers can be handy for when you want control over the error message or number that gets passed out to your user or client application.

With a CHECK constraint for example, you're just going to get the standard 547 error along with its rather nondescript explanation. As often as not, this is less than helpful in terms of the user really figuring out what went wrong — indeed, your client application often doesn't have enough information to make an intelligent and helpful response on behalf of the user.

In short, sometimes you create triggers when there is already something that would give you the data integrity that you want, but won't give you enough information to handle it.

> It's worth noting that the need for custom error messages in SQL Server should be relatively rare, although passing custom error codes is often useful. Why not pass the custom error message? Well, one would think that you probably have an application layer on top of it, and it is likely going to want to put more context on the error anyway, so the SQL-Server-specific text may not be all that useful. Using a special error code may, however, be very useful to your application in terms of determining what exactly happened and applying the correct client-side error handling code.

Other Common Uses for Triggers

In addition to the straight data integrity uses, triggers have a number of other uses. Indeed, the possibilities are fairly limitless, but here are a few common examples:

❑ Updating summary information

❑ Feeding de-normalized tables for reporting

❑ Setting condition flags

As you can see, the possibilities are pretty far reaching — it's really all about your particular situation and the needs of your particular system.

Other Trigger Issues

You have most of it now but if you're thinking you are finished with triggers, then think again. As I indicated early in the chapter, triggers create an awful lot to think about. The sections that follow attempt to point out some of the biggest issues you need to consider, plus provide some information on additional trigger features and possibilities.

Triggers Can Be Nested

A nested trigger is one that did not fire directly as a result of a statement that you issued, but rather because of a statement that was issued by another trigger.

This can actually set off quite a chain of events, with one trigger causing another trigger to fire which, in turn, causes yet another trigger to fire, and so on. Just how deep the triggers can fire depends on:

❑ Whether nested triggers are turned on for your system (This is a system-wide, not database-level option; it is set using the Management Studio or sp_configure, and defaults to on.)

❑ Whether there is a limit of nesting to 32 levels deep.

❑ Whether a trigger has already been fired. A trigger can, by default, be fired only once per trigger transaction. Once fired, it will ignore any other calls as a result of activity that is part of the same trigger action. Once you move on to an entirely new statement (even within the same overall transaction), the process can start all over again.

In most circumstances, you actually want your triggers to nest (thus the default), but you need to think about what's going to happen if you get into a circle of triggers firing triggers. If it comes back around to the same table twice, then the trigger will not fire the second time, and something you think is important may not happen; for example, a data integrity violation may get through. It's also worth noting that, if you do a ROLLBACK anywhere in the nesting chain, the entire chain is rolled back. In other words, the entire nested trigger chain behaves as a transaction.

Triggers Can Be Recursive

What is a recursive trigger? A trigger is said to be recursive when something the trigger does eventually causes that same trigger to be fired. It may be directly (by an action query done to the table on which the trigger is set) or indirectly (through the nesting process).

Recursive triggers are rare. Indeed, by default, recursive triggers are turned off. This is, however, a way of dealing with the situation just described where you are nesting triggers and you want the update to happen the second time around. Recursion, unlike nesting, is a database-level option and can be set using the sp_dboption system sproc.

The danger in recursive triggers is that you'll get into some form of unintended loop. As such, you'll need to make sure that you get some form of recursion check in place to stop the process if necessary.

Triggers Don't Prevent Architectural Changes

This is a classic good news/bad news story.

Using triggers is positively great in terms of making it easy to make architecture changes. Indeed, I often use triggers for referential integrity early in the development cycle (when I'm more likely to be making lots of changes to the design of the database), and then change to DRI late in the cycle when I'm close to production.

When you want to drop a table and re-create it using DRI, you must first drop all the constraints before dropping the table. This can create quite a maze in terms of dropping multiple constraints, making your changes, and then adding the constraints again. It can be quite a wild ride trying to make sure that everything drops that is supposed to so that your changed scripts will run. Then it's just as wild a ride to make sure that you've got everything back on that needs to be. Triggers take care of all this because they don't care that anything has changed until they actually run. There's the rub, though — when they run. You see, it means that you may change architecture and break several triggers without even realizing that you've done it. It won't be until the first time that those triggers try to address the object(s) in question that you find the error of your ways. By that time, you may find together exactly what you did and why.

Both sides have their hassles — just keep the hassles in mind no matter which method you're employing.

Triggers Can Be Turned Off Without Being Removed

Sometimes, just like with CHECK constraints, you want to turn off the integrity feature so you can perform some valid action that will violate the constraint. (Importation of data is probably the most common of these.)

Another common reason for doing this is when you are performing some sort of bulk insert (importation again), but you are already 100 percent certain the data is valid. In this case, you may want to turn off the triggers to eliminate their overhead and speed up the insert process.

You can turn a trigger off and on by using an ALTER TABLE statement. The syntax looks like this:

```
ALTER TABLE <table name>
    <ENABLE|DISABLE> TRIGGER <ALL|<trigger name>>
```

As you might expect, my biggest words of caution in this area are, don't forget to re-enable your triggers!

One last thing. If you're turning them off to do some form of mass importation of data, I highly recommend that you kick out all your users and go either to single-user mode, dbo-only mode, or both. This will ensure that no one sneaks in behind you while you have the triggers turned off.

Trigger Firing Order

In long ago releases of SQL Server (7.0 and prior), we had no control over firing order. Indeed, you may recall me discussing how there was only one of any particular kind of trigger (INSERT, UPDATE, DELETE) prior to 7.0, so firing order was something of a moot point. Later releases of SQL Server provide a limited amount of control over which triggers go in what order. For any given table (not views, since firing order can be specified only for AFTER triggers and views accept only INSTEAD OF triggers), you can elect to have one (and only one) trigger fired first. Likewise, you may elect to have one (and only one) trigger fired last. All other triggers are considered to have no preference on firing order — that is, there is no guarantee what order triggers with a firing order of NONE will fire in, other than that they will fire after the FIRST trigger (if there is one) is complete and before the LAST trigger (again, if there is one) begins (see Figure 15-3).

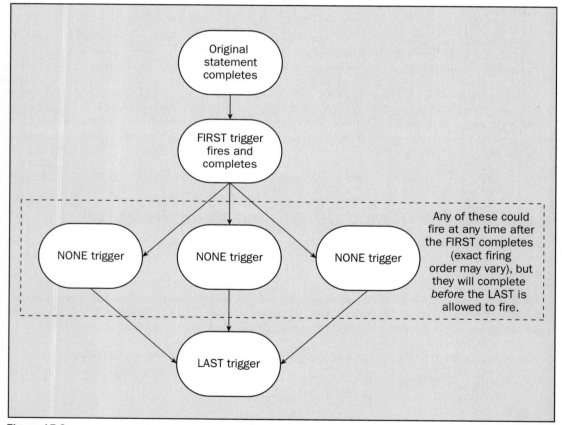

Figure 15-3

The creation of a trigger that is to be FIRST or LAST works just the same as any other trigger. You state the firing order preference after the trigger has already been created using a special system stored procedure, sp_settriggerorder.

The syntax of sp_settriggerorder looks like this:

```
sp_settriggerorder[@triggername =] '<trigger name>',
    [@order =] '{FIRST|LAST|NONE}',
    [@stmttype =] '{INSERT|UPDATE|DELETE}'
    [, [@namespace =] {'DATABASE' | 'SERVER' | NULL} ]
```

There can be only one trigger that is considered to be FIRST for any particular action (INSERT, UPDATE, or DELETE). Likewise, there can be only one LAST trigger for any particular action. Any number of triggers can be considered to be NONE — that is, the number of triggers that don't have a particular firing order is unlimited.

So, the question should be, why do I care what order they fire in? Well, often you won't care at all. At other times, it can be important logic-wise or just a good performance idea. Let's consider what I mean in a bit more detail.

Controlling Firing Order for Logic Reasons

Why would you *need* to have one trigger fire before another? The most common reason would be that the first trigger lays some sort of foundation for, or otherwise validates, what will come afterwards. Separate triggers also allow one part of the code to be disabled (remember that NO CHECK thing we did a few sections ago?) while other parts of the code continue to function. The downside is that, if you go ahead and separate your code into separate triggers, you lose the logical stepping order that the code had when it was in one trigger.

By having at least a simple level of control over firing order, we have something of the best of both worlds — we can logically separate our triggers, but still maintain the necessary order of precedence on what piece of code runs first or last.

Controlling Firing Order for Performance Reasons

On the performance front, a FIRST trigger is the only one that really has any big thing going for it. If you have multiple triggers, but only one of them is likely to generate a rollback (for example, it may be enforcing a complex data integrity rule that a constraint can't handle), you would want to consider making such a trigger a FIRST trigger. This ensures that your most likely cause of a rollback is already considered before you invest any more activity in your transaction. The more you do before the rollback is detected, the more that will have to be rolled back. Get the highest probability of a rollback happening determined before performing additional activity.

INSTEAD OF Triggers

INSTEAD OF triggers were added in SQL Server 2000 and remain one of the more complex features of SQL Server. While it is well outside the scope of a "beginning" concept, I'm still a big believer in even the beginner learning about what things are *available*, and so we'll touch on what these are about here.

Essentially, an INSTEAD OF trigger is a block of code we can use as an interceptor for anything that anyone tries to do to our table or view. We can either go ahead and do whatever the user requests or, if we choose, we can go so far as doing something that is entirely different.

Like regular triggers, INSTEAD OF triggers come in three different flavors: INSERT, UPDATE, and DELETE. In each case, the most common use is the same — resolving ambiguity about which table(s) are to receive the actual changes when you're dealing with a view based on multiple tables.

Performance Considerations

I've seen what appear almost like holy wars happen over the pros and cons, evil and good, and light and dark of triggers. The worst of it tends to come from purists — people who love the theory, and that's all they want to deal with, or people that have figured out how flexible triggers are and want to use them for seemingly everything.

My two-bits worth on this is, as I stated early in the chapter, use them when they are the right things to use. If that sounds sort of noncommittal and ambiguous — good! Programming is rarely black and white, and databases are almost never that way. I will, however, point out some facts for you to think about.

Triggers Are Reactive Rather Than Proactive

What I mean here is that triggers happen after the fact. By the time that your trigger fires, the entire query has run and your transaction has been logged (but not committed and only to the point of the statement that fired your trigger). This means that if the trigger needs to roll things back, it has to undo what is potentially a ton of work that's already been done. *Slow!* Keep this knowledge in balance though. How big an impact this adds up to depends strongly on how big your query is.

So what, you say. Well, compare this to the notion of constraints, which are proactive — that is, they happen before your statement is really executed. That means they detect things that will fail and prevent them from happening earlier in the process. This will usually mean that they will run at least slightly faster — much faster on more complex queries. Note that this extra speed really shows itself to any significant extent only when a rollback occurs.

What's the end analysis here? Well, if you're dealing with very few rollbacks, and/or the complexity and execution time of the statements affected are low, then there probably isn't much of a difference between triggers and constraints. There's some, but probably not much. If, however, the number of rollbacks is unpredictable or you know it's going to be high, you'll want to stick with constraints if you can (and frankly, I suggest sticking with constraints unless you have a very specific reason not to).

Triggers Don't Have Concurrency Issues with the Process That Fires Them

You may have noticed throughout this chapter that we often make use of the ROLLBACK statement, even though we don't issue a BEGIN TRAN. That's because a trigger is always implicitly part of the same transaction as the statement that caused the trigger to fire.

If the firing statement was not part of an explicit transaction (one where there was a BEGIN TRAN), then it would still be part of its own one-statement transaction. In either case, a ROLLBACK TRAN issued inside the trigger will still roll back the entire transaction.

Another upshot of this part-of-the-same-transaction business is that triggers inherit the locks already open on the transaction they are part of. This means that we don't have to do anything special to make sure that we don't bump into the locks created by the other statements in the transaction. We have free access within the scope of the transaction, and we see the database based on the modifications already placed by previous statements within the transaction.

Using IF UPDATE() and COLUMNS_UPDATED

In an UPDATE trigger, we can often limit the amount of code that actually executes within the trigger by checking to see whether the column(s) we are interested in are the ones that have been changed. To do this, we make use of the UPDATE() or COLUMNS_UPDATED() functions. Let's look at each.

The UPDATE() Function

The UPDATE() function has relevance only within the scope of a trigger. Its sole purpose in life is to provide a boolean response (true/false) to whether a particular column has been updated or not. You can use this function to decide whether a particular block of code needs to run or not — for example, if that code is relevant only when a particular column is updated.

Let's run a quick example of this by modifying one of our earlier triggers.

```
ALTER TRIGGER Production.ProductIsRationed
    ON Production.ProductInventory
    FOR UPDATE
AS
    IF UPDATE(Quantity)
    BEGIN
        IF EXISTS
          (
          SELECT 'True'
          FROM Inserted i
          JOIN Deleted d
            ON i.ProductID = d.ProductID
          AND i.LocationID = d.LocationID
          WHERE (d.Quantity - i.Quantity) > d.Quantity / 2
            AND d.Quantity > 0
          )
        BEGIN
          RAISERROR('Cannot reduce stock by more than 50%% at once.',16,1)
          ROLLBACK TRAN
        END
    END
```

With this change, we will now limit the rest of the code to run only when the Quantity column (the one we care about) has been changed. The user can change the value of any other column and we don't care. This means that we'll be executing fewer lines of code and, therefore, this trigger will perform slightly better than our previous version.

The COLUMNS_UPDATED() Function

This one works somewhat differently from UPDATE(), but has the same general purpose. What COLUMNS_ UPDATED() gives us is the ability to check multiple columns at one time. In order to do this, the function uses a bitmask that relates individual bits in one or more bytes of varbinary data to individual columns in the table. It ends up looking something like Figure 15-4.

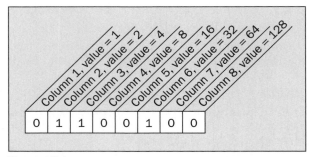

Figure 15-4

In this case, our single byte of data is telling us that the second, third, and sixth columns were updated — the rest were not.

In the event that there are more than eight columns, SQL Server just adds another byte on the right-hand side and keeps counting (see Figure 15-5).

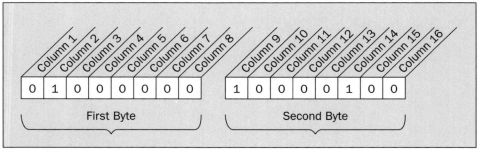

Figure 15-5

This time the second, ninth, and fourteenth columns were updated.

I can hear you out there: "Gee, that's nice — but how do I make any use of this?" Well, to answer that, we have to get into the world of boolean algebra.

Making use of this information means that you need to add up the binary value of all the bytes, considering the leftmost digit to be the least significant. So, if you want your comparison to take into account 2,

5, and 7, then you need to add the binary value of each bit: 2 + 16 + 64. Then you need to compare the sum of the binary values of your columns to the bitmask by using bitwise operators:

- ❏ | Represents bitwise OR
- ❏ & Represents bitwise AND
- ❏ ^ Represents bitwise Exclusive OR

As I read back over what I've just written, I realize that it is correct, but about as clear as mud, so let's look a little closer at what I mean with a couple of examples.

Imagine that we updated a table that contained five columns. If we updated the first, third, and fifth columns, the bitmask used by COLUMNS_UPDATED would contain 10101000, from 1 + 4 + 16 = 21. We could use:

- ❏ COLUMNS_UPDATED() > 0 to find out if any column was updated
- ❏ COLUMNS_UPDATED() ^ 21 = 0 to find out if *all* of the columns specified (in this case 1, 3, and 5) were updated and nothing else was
- ❏ COLUMNS_UPDATED() & 21 = 21 to find out if all of the columns specified were updated, but the state of other columns doesn't matter
- ❏ COLUMNS_UPDATED | 21 != 21 to find out if any column *other* than those we're interested in was updated

Understand that this is tough stuff — boolean math is not exactly the easiest of concepts to grasp for most people, so check things carefully and TEST, TEST, TEST!

Keep It Short and Sweet

I feel like I'm stating the obvious here, but it's for a good reason.

I can't tell you how often I see bloated, stupid code in sprocs and triggers. I don't know whether it's that people get in a hurry, or if they just think that the medium they are using is fast anyway, so it won't matter.

Remember that a trigger is part of the same transaction as the statement in which it is called. This means the statement is not complete until your trigger is complete. Think about it — if you write long-running code in your trigger, this means that every piece of code that you create that causes that trigger to fire will, in turn, be long running. This can really cause heartache when you are trying to figure out why your code is taking so long to run. You write what appears to be a very efficient sproc, but it performs terribly. You may spend weeks and yet never figure out that your sproc is fine — it just fires a trigger that isn't.

Don't Forget Triggers When Choosing Indexes

Another common mistake. You look through all your sprocs and views figuring out what the best mix of indexes is — and totally forget that you have significant code running in your triggers.

This is the same notion as the "Short and Sweet" section — long-running queries make for long-running statements which, in turn, lead to long-running everything. Don't forget your triggers when you optimize!

Try Not to Roll Back Within Triggers

This one's hard since rollbacks are so often a major part of what you want to accomplish with your triggers.

Just remember that AFTER triggers (which are far and away the most common type of trigger) happen after most of the work is already done — that means a rollback is expensive. This is where DRI picks up almost all of its performance advantage. If you are using many ROLLBACK TRAN statements in your triggers, then make sure that you preprocess looking for errors before you execute the statement that fires the trigger. Because SQL Server can't be proactive in this situation, you need to be proactive for it. Test for errors beforehand rather than waiting for the rollback.

Dropping Triggers

Dropping triggers works only slightly differently than it has worked for almost everything else thus far. The only real trick is that, like tables, trigger names are scoped at the schema level. This means that you can have two objects with a trigger of the same name, as long as the object the trigger is placed against it in a different schema than the other trigger of the same name. Restated, the trigger is named in terms of the schema it's in, rather than the object it is associated with — odd when you realize it is subsidiary to the table or view it is attached to. The syntax looks like:

```
DROP TRIGGER [<schema>.]<trigger name>
```

Other than the schema issue, dropping triggers is pretty much the same as any other drop.

Debugging Triggers

Most everything to do with the debugger works the same for triggers as it does for anything else. The only real trick is a result of the fact that you can't directly call triggers in the way you can scripts or stored procedures.

Fortunately, most developer types are reasonably intelligent people, so, if you think about it, you probably can anticipate how we can get around starting the debugger for triggers — we just need to debug a statement that causes a trigger to fire.

> *In releases prior to SQL Server 2008, direct debugging of scripts wasn't available in 2005 and earlier. This meant you needed to create a stored procedure that would cause a trigger to be debugged if you wanted to debug that trigger — happily, this is no longer the case.*

Since we reviewed the basics of debugging fairly thoroughly in Chapter 12, let's cut right to the proverbial chase and look at debugging triggers in action. All we need to do to show this off is run a bit of code that exercises the trigger we most recently worked with in this chapter. We can then step into that script, so we can watch the debugger run through it line by line:

```
BEGIN TRAN
   -- This one should work
   UPDATE Production.ProductInventory
   SET Quantity = 400   -- Was 408 if you want to set it back
   WHERE ProductID = 1
      AND LocationID = 1

   -- This one shouldn't
   UPDATE Production.ProductInventory
   SET Quantity = 1   -- Was 408 if you want to set it back
   WHERE ProductID = 1
      AND LocationID = 1
IF @@TRANCOUNT > 0
   ROLLBACK TRAN
```

With this script up in the Query Window in Management Studio, we can just press F11 to step into the script (or set a breakpoint and then use any of the several options that start the debugger). We start, of course, at the BEGIN TRAN statement. Continue to step into (F11) until you execute the first UPDATE statement, and note that you wind up in the trigger. Figure 15-6 shows the call stack as you enter the trigger for the first time.

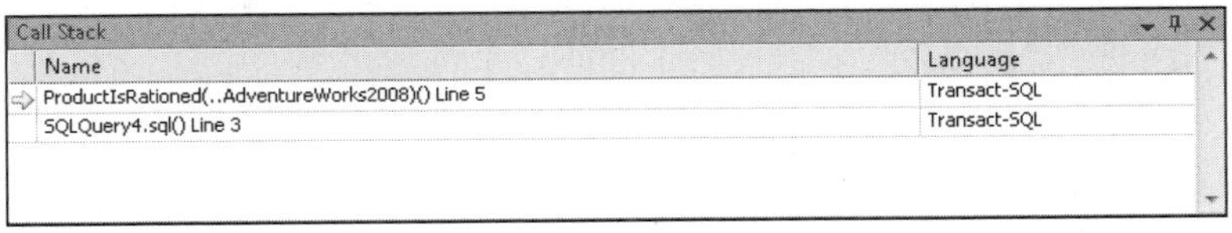

Figure 15-6

Now, go ahead and step out of the first UPDATE, and into the second UPDATE. Since the first UPDATE statement didn't match the violation test in the trigger, you exited almost immediately, but this second time you should see, as you step through, that the code that aborts the transaction fires.

In short, we were able to utilize a single script that, in this case, had two statements meant to test the two possible code paths in our trigger. Obviously, you would need more complex scripting to handle the possible code paths for more complex triggers, but, beyond that, the debugging needs are pretty much as they are for testing any other code in T-SQL.

Summary

Triggers are an extremely powerful tool that can add tremendous flexibility to both your data integrity and the overall operation of your system. That being said, they are not something to take lightly. Triggers can greatly enhance the performance of your system if you use them for proper summarization of data, but they can also be the bane of your existence. They can be very difficult to debug (even now that we have the debugger), and a poorly written trigger affects not only the trigger itself, but any statement that causes that trigger to fire.

Before you get too frustrated with triggers — or before you get too bored with the couple of trigger templates that fill about 90 percent of your trigger needs — keep in mind that there are a large number of tools out there that will auto-generate triggers for you that meet certain requirements.

16

A Brief XML Primer

So, here we are — most of our structural stuff is done at this point, and we're ready to start moving on to the peripheral stuff. That is, we're ready to start looking at things that are outside of what one usually actively thinks of when working with relational database systems. It's not that some of the items we still have to cover aren't things that you would normally expect out of a relational database system — it's just that we don't really *need* these in order to have a functional SQL Server. Indeed, there are so many things included in SQL Server now, that it's difficult to squeeze everything into one book.

This chapter will start by presenting some background for what has become an increasingly integral part of SQL Server — XML. We will then move on to looking at some of the many features SQL Server has to support XML. The catch here is that XML is really entirely its own animal — it's a completely different kind of thing than the relational system we've been working with up to this point. Why then does SQL Server include so much functionality to support it? The short answer is that XML is probably the most important thing to happen to data since the advent of data warehousing.

XML has actually been around for years now, but, while the talk was big, its actual usage was not what it could have been. Since the late '90s, XML has gone into wider and wider use as a generic way to make data feeds and reasonable-sized data documents available. XML provides a means to make data self-describing — that is, you can define type and validation information that can go along with the XML document so that no matter who the consumer is (even if they don't know anything about how to connect to SQL Server), they can understand what the rules for that data are.

XML is often not a very good place to *store* data, but it is a positively spectacular way of making data *useful* — as such, the ways of utilizing XML will likely continue to grow, and grow, and grow.

So, with all that said, in this chapter we'll look at:

❑ What XML is

❑ What other technologies are closely tied to XML

I mentioned a bit ago that XML is usually not a good way to store data, but there are exceptions. One way that XML is being utilized for data storage is for archival purposes. XML compresses very well, and it is in a very open kind of format that will be well understood for many years to come — if not forever. Compare that to, say, just taking a SQL Server 2008 backup. A decade from now when you need to restore some old data to review archival information, you may very well not have a SQL Server installation that can handle such an old backup file, but odds are very strong indeed that you'll have something around that can both decompress (assuming you used a mainstream compression library such as ZIP) and read your data. Very handy for such "deep" archives.

XML Basics

There are tons and tons of books out there on XML (for example, Wrox's *Professional XML*, by Evjen et al). Given how full this book already is, my first inclination was to shy away from adding too much information about XML itself, and assume that you already knew something about XML. I have, however, come to realize that even all these years after XML hit the mainstream, I continue to know an awful lot of database people who think that XML "is just some Web technology," and, therefore, have spent zero time on it — they couldn't be more wrong.

XML is first and foremost an *information* technology. It is *not* a Web-specific technology at all. Instead, it just tends to be thought of that way (usually by people who don't understand XML) for several reasons — such as:

❑ XML is a *markup* language, and looks a heck of a lot like HTML to the untrained eye.

❑ XML is often easily *transformed* into HTML. As such, it has become a popular way to keep the information part of a page, with a final transformation into HTML only on request — a separate transformation can take place based on criteria (such as what browser is asking for the information).

❑ One of the first widely used products to support XML was Microsoft's Internet Explorer.

❑ The Internet is quite often used as a way to exchange information, and that's something that XML is ideally suited for.

Like HTML, XML is a text-based markup language. Indeed, they are both derived from the same original language, called SGML. SGML has been around for much longer than the Internet (at least what we think of as the Internet today), and is most often used in the printing industry or in government related documentation. Simply put, the "S" in SGML doesn't stand for simple (for the curious, SGML stands for "standard generalized markup language") — SGML is anything but intuitive and is actually a downright pain to learn. (I can only read about 35 percent of SGML documents that I've seen. I have, however, been able to achieve a full 100 percent nausea rate when reading any SGML.) XML, on the other hand, tends to be reasonably easy to decipher.

So, this might have you asking the question: "Great — where can I get a listing of XML tags?" Well, you can't — at least, not in the sense that you're thinking when you ask the question. XML has very few tags that are actually part of the language. Instead, it provides ways of defining your own tags and utilizing tags defined by others (such as the industry groups I mentioned earlier in the chapter). XML is largely about flexibility — which includes the ability for you to set your own rules for your XML through the use of either an XML schema document or the older Document Type Definition (DTD).

An XML document has very few rules placed on it just because it happens to be XML. The biggie is that it must be what is called *well formed*. We'll look into what well formed means shortly. Now, just because an XML document meets the criteria of being well formed doesn't mean that it would be classified as being valid. Valid XML must not only be well formed, but must also live up to any restrictions placed on the XML document by XML schemas or DTDs that document references. We will briefly examine DTDs and XML schemas later on in this chapter.

XML can also be transformed. The short rendition of what this means is that it is relatively easy for you to turn XML into a completely different XML representation or even a non-XML format. One of the most common uses for this is to transform XML into HTML for rendering on the Web. The need for this transformation presents us with our first mini-opportunity to compare and contrast HTML with XML. In the simplest terms, XML is about information, and HTML is about presentation.

The information stored in XML is denoted through the use of what are called elements and attributes. *Elements* are usually created through the use of an opening and a closing tag (there's an exception, but we'll see that later) and are identified with a case-sensitive name (no spaces allowed). *Attributes* are items that further describe elements and are embedded in the element's start tag. Attribute values must be in matched single or double quotes.

Parts of an XML Document

Well, a few of the names have already flown by, but it makes sense, before we get too deep into things, to stop and create something of a glossary of terms that we're going to be utilizing while talking about XML documents.

What we're really going to be doing here is providing a listing of all the major parts of an XML document that you will run into, as shown in Figure 16-1. Many of the parts of the document are optional, though a few are not. In some cases, having one thing means that you have to have another. In other cases, the parts of the document are relatively independent of each other.

We will take things in something of a hierarchical approach (things that belong "inside" of something will be listed after whatever they belong inside of), and where it makes sense, in the order you'll come across them in a given XML document.

The Document

The document encompasses everything from the very first character to the last. When we refer to an XML document, we are referring to both the structure and the content of that particular XML document.

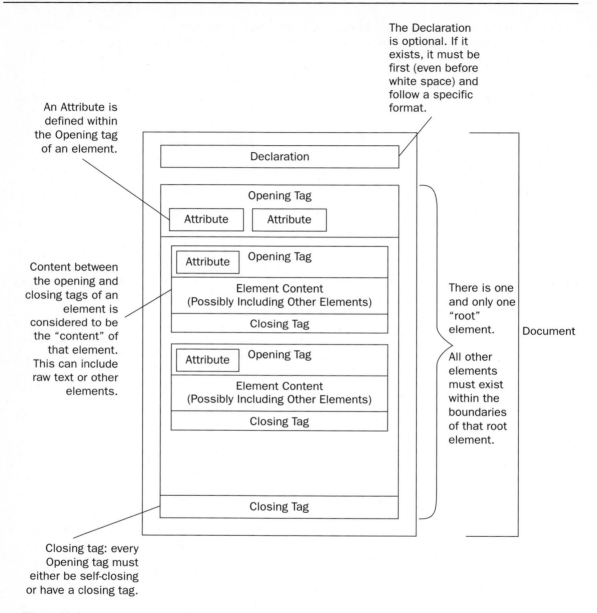

The Declaration is optional. If it exists, it must be first (even before white space) and follow a specific format.

An Attribute is defined within the Opening tag of an element.

Content between the opening and closing tags of an element is considered to be the "content" of that element. This can include raw text or other elements.

There is one and only one "root" element.

All other elements must exist within the boundaries of that root element.

Document

Closing tag: every Opening tag must either be self-closing or have a closing tag.

Figure 16-1

Declaration

The *declaration* is technically optional, but, as a practical matter, should always be included. If it exists, it must be the very first thing in the document. *Nothing* can be before the declaration, not even white space (spaces, carriage returns, tabs, whatever) — nothing.

The declaration is made with a special tag that begins with a question mark (which indicates that this tag is a preprocessor directive) and the xml moniker:

```
<?xml version="1.0"?>
```

The declaration has one required attribute (something that further describes the element) — the *version*. In the preceding example, we've declared that this is an XML document and also that it is to comply with version 1.0 (as of this writing, there is also a version 1.1, though you'll want to stick with 1.0 wherever possible) of the XML specification.

The declaration can optionally have one additional attribute — this one is called encoding, and it describes the nature of the character set this XML document utilizes. XML can handle a few different character sets, most notably UTF-16 and UTF-8. UTF-16 is essentially the Unicode specification, which is a 16-bit encoding specification that allows for most characters in use in the world today. The default encoding method is UTF-8, which is backward compatible to the older ASCII specification. A full declaration would look like this:

```
<?xml version='1.0' encoding='UTF-8'?>
```

Elements that start with the letters xml *are strictly forbidden by the specification — instead, they are reserved for future expansion of the language.*

Elements

Elements serve as a piece of glue to hold together descriptive information about something — it honestly could be anything. Elements define a clear start and end point for your descriptive information. Usually, elements exist in matched pairs of tags known as an opening tag and a closing tag. Optionally, however, the opening tag can be *self-closing* — essentially defining what is known as an *empty element*.

The structure for an XML element looks pretty much as HTML tags do. An opening tag will begin with an opening angle bracket (<), contain a name and possibly some attributes, and then a closing angle bracket (>):

```
<ATagForANormalElement >
```

The exception to the rule is if the element is self-closing, in which case the closing angle bracket of the opening tag is preceded with a forward slash (/):

```
<AselfClosingElement/>
```

Closing tags will look exactly like the opening tag (case sensitive), but start with a slash (/) before the name of the element it's closing:

```
<ATagForANormalElement >       <== Opening Tag
Some data or whatever can go in here.
We're still going strong with our data.
</ATagForANormalElement >      <== Closing Tag
```

Elements can also contain attributes (which we'll look at shortly) as part of the opening (but not the clos-ing) tag for the element. Finally, elements can contain other elements, but, if they do, the inner element must be closed before closing the outer element:

```
<OuterElement>
   <InnerElement>
   </InnerElement>
</OuterElement>
```

We will come back to elements shortly when we look at what it means to be well formed.

Nodes

When you map out the hierarchies that naturally form in an XML document, they wind up taking on the familiar tree model that you see in just about any hierarchical relationship, illustrated in Figure 16-2. Each intersection point in the tree is referred to as a *node*.

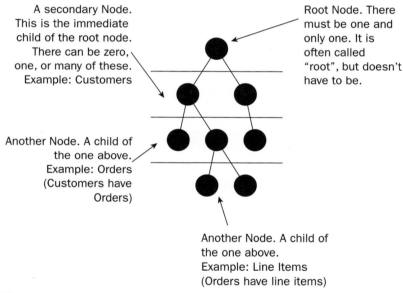

A secondary Node. This is the immediate child of the root node. There can be zero, one, or many of these. Example: Customers

Root Node. There must be one and only one. It is often called "root", but doesn't have to be.

Another Node. A child of the one above. Example: Orders (Customers have Orders)

Another Node. A child of the one above. Example: Line Items (Orders have line items)

Figure 16-2

The contents of an XML document can be navigated based on node levels and the values in the attrib-utes and elements of particular nodes.

The "Root" Node

Perhaps one of the most common points of confusion in XML documents is over what is called the *root node*. Every XML document must have exactly one (no more, no less) root node. The root node is an ele-ment that contains any other elements in the document (if there are any). You can think of the root node as being the unification point that ties all the nodes below it together and gives them structure within the scope of any particular XML document. So, what's all the confusion about? Well, it usually falls into two camps: Those that don't know they need to have a singular root node (which you now know), and those who don't understand how root nodes are named (which you will understand in a moment).

Because the general statement is usually "You must have a root node," people usually interpret that to mean that they must have a node that is called `root`. Indeed, you'll occasionally find XML documents that do have a root node named `Root` (or `root` or `ROOT`). The reality, however, is that root nodes follow the exact same naming scheme as any other element with only one exception — the name must be unique throughout the document. That is, no other element in the entire document can have the same name as the root.

> **The existence of a root node is a key difference between an XML document and an XML fragment. Often, when extracting things from SQL Server, you'll be extracting little pieces of XML that belong to a large whole. We refer to these as XML fragments. Because an XML fragment is not supposed to be the whole document, we don't expect these to have a root node.**

Attributes

Attributes exist only within the context of an element. They are implemented as a way of further describing an element, and are placed within the boundaries of the opening tag for the element:

```
<SomeElement MyFirstAttribute="Hi There" MySecondAttribute="25">
     Optionally, some other XML
</SomeElement>
```

Regardless of the data type of the information in the value for the attribute, the value must be enclosed in either single or double quotes.

> *By default, XML documents have no concept of data type. We will investigate ways of describing the rules of individual document applications later in this chapter. At that time, we'll see that there are some ways of ensuring data type — it's just that you set the rules for it; XML does not do that by itself.*

No Defects — Being Well Formed

The part of the rules that define how XML must look — that is, what elements are okay, how they are defined, what parts they have — is about whether an XML document is well formed or not.

Actually, all SGML-based languages have something of the concept of being well formed. Heck, even HTML has something of the concept of being well formed — it's just that it has been largely lost in the fact that HTML is naturally more forgiving and that browsers ignore many errors.

If you're used to HTML at all, then you've seen some pretty sloppy stuff as far as a tag-based language goes. XML has much stricter rules about what is and isn't OK. The short rendition looks like this:

❑   Every XML document *must* have a unique "root" node.

❑   Every tag must have a matching (case sensitive) closing tag unless the opening tag is self-closing.

❑   Tags cannot straddle other tags.

❑   You can't use restricted characters for anything other than what they indicate to the XML parser. If you need to represent any of these special characters, then you need to use an escape sequence (which will be translated back to the character you requested).

It's worth noting that HTML documents are more consistently "well formed" than in years past. Around the time that XML came out, a specification for XHTML was also developed — that is, HTML that is also valid XML. Many developers today try and make their HTML meet XHTML standards with the result being, at the least, much more well formed HTML.

The following is an example of a document that is well formed:

```
<?xml version="1.0" encoding="UTF-8"?>

<ThisCouldBeCalledAnything>
  <AnElement>
    <AnotherElement AnAttribute="Some Value">
      <AselfClosingElement AnAttributeThatNeedsASpecialCharacter="Fred&quot;s
flicks"/>
    </AnotherElement>
  </AnElement>
</ThisCouldBeCalledAnything>
```

Notice that we didn't need to have a closing tag at all for the declaration. That's because the declaration is a preprocessor directive — not an element. Essentially, it is telling the XML parser some things it needs to know before the parser can get down to the real business of dealing with our XML.

So, this has been an extremely abbreviated version of what's required for your XML document to be considered to be well formed, but it pretty much covers the basics for the limited scope of our XML coverage in this book.

Understanding these concepts is going to be absolutely vital to your survival (well, comprehension at least) in the rest of the chapter. The example that is covered next should reinforce things for you, but, if after looking at the XML example, you find you're still confused, then read the preceding text again or check out Professional XML or some other XML book. Your sanity depends on knowing this stuff before you move on to the styling and schema issues at the end of the chapter.

An XML Example

OK — if there's one continuing theme throughout this book, it's got to be that I don't like explaining things without tossing out an example or two. As I've said earlier, this isn't an XML book, so I'm not going to get carried away with my examples here, but let's at least take a look at what we're talking about.

Throughout the remainder of this chapter, you're going to find that life is an awful lot easier if you have some sort of XML editing tool (Microsoft offers a free one called XML Notepad. I've tended toward a product called XMLSpy, which was one of the earliest full function XML editors). Because XML is text based, you can easily open and edit XML documents in Notepad — the problem is that you're not going to get any error checking. How are you going to know that your document is well formed? Sure, you can look it over if it's just a few lines, but get to a complete document or a style sheet document (we will discuss transformations later in the chapter), and life will quickly become very difficult.

As a side note, you can perform a rather quick and dirty check to see whether your XML is well formed or not by opening the document in Microsoft's Internet Explorer — it will complain to you if the document is not well formed.

For this example, we're going to look at an XML representation of what some of our AdventureWorks2008 data might look like. In this case, I'm going to take a look at some order information. We're going to start with just a few things and grow from there.

First, we know that we need a root node for any XML document that we're going to have. The root node can be called anything we want, as long as it is unique within our document. A common way of dealing with this is to call the root `root`. Another common example would be to call it something representative of what the particular XML document is all about.

For our purposes, we'll start off with something hyper-simple, and just use `root`:

```
<root>
</root>
```

Just that quickly we've created our first well-formed XML document. Notice that it didn't include the `<?xml>` tag that we saw in the earlier illustration. We could have put that in, but it's actually an optional item. The only restriction related to it is that, if you include it, it must be first. For best practice reasons as well as clearness, we'll go ahead and add it:

```
<?xml version="1.0" encoding="UTF-8"?>
<root>
</root>
```

Actually, by the rules of XML, any tag starting with `<?xml>` is considered to be a reserved tag — that is, you shouldn't name your tags that, as they are reserved for current or future use of the W3C as XML goes into future versions.

So, moving on, we have our first well-formed XML document. Unfortunately, this document is about as plain as it can get — it doesn't really tell us anything. Well, for our example, we're working on describing order information, so we might want to start putting in some information that is descriptive of an order. Let's start with a `SalesOrderHeader` tag:

```
<?xml version="1.0" encoding="UTF-8"?>
<root>
   <SalesOrderHeader/>
</root>
```

OK — so this is getting monotonous — isn't it? We now know that we have one order in our XML document, but we still don't know anything about it. Let's expand on it some by adding a few attributes:

```
<?xml version="1.0" encoding="UTF-8"?>
<root>
   <SalesOrderHeader CustomerID="510" SalesOrderID="43663"
OrderDate="2001-07-01T00:00:00" />
</root>
```

Well, it doesn't really take a rocket scientist to be able to discern the basics about our order at this point:

❑ The customer's ID number is 510.

❑ The order ID number was 43663.

❑ The order was placed on July 1, 2001.

Basically, as we have things, it equates to a row in the `SalesOrderHeader` table in AdventureWorks2008 in SQL Server. If the customer had several orders, it might look something like:

```xml
<?xml version="1.0" encoding="UTF-8"?>
<root>
 <SalesOrderHeader CustomerID="510" SalesOrderID="43663"
OrderDate="2001-07-01T00:00:00"/>
 <SalesOrderHeader CustomerID="510" SalesOrderID="44281"
OrderDate="2001-10-01T00:00:00"/>
 <SalesOrderHeader CustomerID="510" SalesOrderID="45040"
OrderDate="2002-01-01T00:00:00"/>
 <SalesOrderHeader CustomerID="510" SalesOrderID="46606"
OrderDate="2002-07-01T00:00:00"/>
 <SalesOrderHeader CustomerID="510" SalesOrderID="47661"
OrderDate="2002-10-01T00:00:00"/>
 <SalesOrderHeader CustomerID="510" SalesOrderID="49824"
OrderDate="2003-04-01T00:00:00"/>
 <SalesOrderHeader CustomerID="510" SalesOrderID="55285"
OrderDate="2003-10-01T00:00:00"/>
 <SalesOrderHeader CustomerID="510" SalesOrderID="61178"
OrderDate="2004-01-01T00:00:00"/>
 </root>
```

While this is a perfectly legal — and even well formed — example of XML, it doesn't really represent the hierarchy of the data as we might wish. We might, for example, wish to build our XML a little differently, and represent the notion that customers are usually considered to be higher in the hierarchical chain (they are the "parent" to orders if you will). We could represent this by changing the way we express customers. Instead of an attribute, we could make it an element in its own right — including having its own attributes — and nest that particular customer's orders inside the customer element:

```xml
<?xml version="1.0" encoding="UTF-8"?>
<root>
<Customer CustomerID="510" AccountNumber="AW00000510">
 <SalesOrderHeader SalesOrderID="43663" OrderDate="2001-07-01T00:00:00"/>
 <SalesOrderHeader SalesOrderID="44281" OrderDate="2001-10-01T00:00:00"/>
 <SalesOrderHeader SalesOrderID="45040" OrderDate="2002-01-01T00:00:00"/>
 <SalesOrderHeader SalesOrderID="46606" OrderDate="2002-07-01T00:00:00"/>
 <SalesOrderHeader SalesOrderID="47661" OrderDate="2002-10-01T00:00:00"/>
 <SalesOrderHeader SalesOrderID="49824" OrderDate="2003-04-01T00:00:00"/>
 <SalesOrderHeader SalesOrderID="55285" OrderDate="2003-10-01T00:00:00"/>
 <SalesOrderHeader SalesOrderID="61178" OrderDate="2004-01-01T00:00:00"/>
</Customer>
</root>
```

If we have more than one customer, that's not a problem — we just add another customer node:

```xml
<?xml version="1.0" encoding="UTF-8"?>
<root>
<Customer CustomerID="510" AccountNumber="AW00000510">
 <SalesOrderHeader SalesOrderID="43663" OrderDate="2001-07-01T00:00:00"/>
 <SalesOrderHeader SalesOrderID="44281" OrderDate="2001-10-01T00:00:00"/>
 <SalesOrderHeader SalesOrderID="45040" OrderDate="2002-01-01T00:00:00"/>
 <SalesOrderHeader SalesOrderID="46606" OrderDate="2002-07-01T00:00:00"/>
 <SalesOrderHeader SalesOrderID="47661" OrderDate="2002-10-01T00:00:00"/>
 <SalesOrderHeader SalesOrderID="49824" OrderDate="2003-04-01T00:00:00"/>
 <SalesOrderHeader SalesOrderID="55285" OrderDate="2003-10-01T00:00:00"/>
 <SalesOrderHeader SalesOrderID="61178" OrderDate="2004-01-01T00:00:00"/>
 </Customer>
<Customer CustomerID="512" AccountNumber="AW00000512">
 <SalesOrderHeader SalesOrderID="46996" OrderDate="2002-08-01T00:00:00"/>
 <SalesOrderHeader SalesOrderID="48018" OrderDate="2002-11-01T00:00:00"/>
 <SalesOrderHeader SalesOrderID="49090" OrderDate="2003-02-01T00:00:00"/>
 <SalesOrderHeader SalesOrderID="50231" OrderDate="2003-05-01T00:00:00"/>
 </Customer>
 </root>
```

Indeed, this can go to unlimited levels of hierarchy (subject, of course, to whatever your parser can handle). We could, for example, add a level for individual line items in the order.

Determining Elements vs. Attributes

The first thing to understand here is that there is no hard and fast rule for determining what should be an element vs. an attribute. An attribute describes the properties of the element that it is an attribute of. Child elements — or child "nodes" — of an element do much the same thing. So how, then, do we decide which should be which? Why are attributes even necessary? Well, like most things in life, it's something of a balancing act.

Attributes make a lot of sense in situations where the value is a one-to-one relationship with, and is inherently part of, the element. In AdventureWorks2008, for example, we have only one customer number per customer ID — this is ideal for an attribute. As we are transforming our relational data to XML, the columns of a table will often make good attributes to an element directly related to individual rows of a table.

Elements tend to make more sense if there is more of a one-to-many relationship between the element and what's describing it. In our example earlier in the chapter, there are many sales orders for each customer. Technically speaking, we could have had each order be an attribute of a customer element, but then we would have needed to repeat much of the customer element information over and over again. Similarly, if our AdventureWorks2008 database allowed for the notion of customers having aliases (multiple account numbers — similar to how they have multiple contacts), then we may have wanted to have an AccountNumber element under the customer and have its attribute describe individual instances of names.

Whichever way you go here, stick to one rule I've emphasized many times throughout the book — be consistent. Once something of a given nature is defined as being an attribute in one place, lean toward keeping it an attribute in other places unless its nature is somehow different in the new place you're using it. One more time: Be consistent.

Namespaces

With all this freedom to create your own tags, to mix and match data from other sources, and just otherwise do your own thing, there are bound to be a few collisions here and there about what things are going to use what names in which places. For example, an element with a name of "letter" might have entirely different structure, rules, and meaning to an application built for libraries (for whom a letter is probably a document written from one person to another person) than it would to another application, say one describing fonts (which might describe the association between a character set and a series of glyphs).

To take this example a little further, the nature of XML is such that industry organizations around the world are slowly agreeing on naming and structure conventions to describe various types of information in their industry. Library organizations may have agreed on element formats describing books, plays, movies, letters, essays, and so on. At the same time, the operating systems and/or graphics industries may have agreed on element formats describing pictures, fonts, and document layouts.

Now, imagine that we, the poor hapless developers that we are, have been asked to write an application that needs to render library content. Obviously, library content makes frequent use of things like fonts — so, when you refer to something called "letter" in your XML, are you referring to something to do with the font or is it a letter from a person to another person (say, from Thomas Jefferson to George Washington)? We have a conflict, and we need a way to resolve it.

That's where namespaces come in. *Namespaces* describe a domain of elements and attributes and what their structure is. The structure that supports letters in libraries would be described in a libraries namespace. Likewise, the graphics industry would likely have their own namespace(s) that would describe letters as they relate to that industry. The information for a namespace is stored in a reference document, and can be found using a Uniform Resource Identifier (URI) — a special name, not dissimilar from a URL — that will eventually resolve to our reference document.

When we build our XML documents that refer to both library and graphics constructs, then we simply reference the namespaces for those industries. In addition, we qualify elements and attributes whose nature we want the namespace to describe. By qualifying our names using namespaces, we make sure that, even if a document has elements that are structurally different but have the same name, we can refer to the parts of our document with complete confidence that we are not referring to the wrong kind of element or attribute.

To reference a namespace to the entire document, we simply add the reference as a special attribute (called `xmlns`) to our root. The reference will provide both a local name (how we want to refer to the namespace) and the URI that will eventually resolve to our reference document. We can also add namespace references (again, using `xmlns`) to other nodes in the document if we want to apply only that particular namespace within the scope of the node we assign the namespace, too.

What follows is an example of an XML document (technically, this is what we call a schema) that we will be utilizing later in the chapter. Notice several things about it as relates to namespaces:

The document references three namespaces — one each for XDR (this happens to be an XDR document), a Microsoft data type namespace (this one builds a list about the number and nature of different data types), and, last, but not least, a special SQL namespace used for working with SQL Server XML integration.

Some attributes (including one in the root) are qualified with namespace information (see the `sql:relation` attribute, for example).

```
<?xml version="1.0" encoding="UTF-8"?>
<Schema xmlns="urn:schemas-microsoft-com:xml-data"
            xmlns:dt="urn:schemas-microsoft-com:data types"
            xmlns:sql="urn:schemas-microsoft-com:xml-sql"
            sql:xsl='../Customers.xsl'>
<ElementType name="Root" content="empty"  />
<ElementType name="Customers" sql:relation="Customers">
        <AttributeType name="CustomerID"/>
        <AttributeType name="CompanyName"/>
        <AttributeType name="Address"/>
        <AttributeType name="City"/>
        <AttributeType name="Region"/>
        <AttributeType name="PostalCode"/>
        <attribute type="CustomerID" sql:field="CustomerID"/>
        <attribute type="CompanyName" sql:field="CompanyName"/>
        <attribute type="Address" sql:field="Address"/>
        <attribute type="City" sql:field="City"/>
        <attribute type="Region" sql:field="Region"/>
        <attribute type="PostalCode" sql:field="PostalCode"/>
</ElementType>
</Schema>
```

The `sql` data type references a couple of special attributes. We do not have to worry about whether the Microsoft data types namespace also has a field or relation data type because we are fully qualifying our attribute names. Even if the data types namespace does have an attribute called `field`, our XML parser will still know to treat this element by the rules of the `sql` namespace.

Element Content

Another notion of XML and elements that deserves mention (which is close to all it will get here) is the concept of element content.

Elements can contain data beyond the attribute level and nested elements. While nested elements are certainly one form of element content (one element contains the other), XML also allows for row text information to be contained in an element. For example, we could have an XML document that looked something like the following:

```
<?xml version="1.0" encoding="UTF-8"?>
<root>
  <Customer CustomerID="ALFKI" CompanyName="Alfreds Futterkiste">
   <Note Date="1997-08-25T00:00:00">
   The customer called in today and placed another order. Says they really like our
work and would like it if we would consider establishing a location closer to their
base of operations.
   </Note>
   <Note Date="1997-08-26T00:00:00">
   Followed up with the customer on new location. Customer agrees to guarantee us
$5,000 per month in business to help support a new office.
   </Note>
  </Customer>
</root>
```

The contents of the Note elements, such as "The customer called ... " are neither an element nor an attribute, yet they are valid XML data.

Be aware that such data exists in XML, but SQL Server will not output data in this format using any of the automatic styling methods. The row/column approach of RDBMS systems lends itself far better to elements and attributes. To output data such as our notes, you would need to use some of the methods that allow for more explicit output formats of your XML (and these can be non-intuitive at best) or perform a transformation on the output after you select it. We will look at transformations as the last item in this chapter.

Being Valid vs. Being Well Formed — Schemas and DTDs

Just because an XML document is well formed does not mean that it is *valid XML*. Now, while that is sinking in on you I'll tell you that *no* XML is considered "valid" unless it has been validated against some form of specification document. Currently, there are only two recognized types of specification documents — a Document Type Definition, or DTD, and an XML schema.

The basic premise behind both varieties of validation documents is much the same. While XML as a language defines the most basic rules that a XML document must comply with, DTDs and XML schemas seek to define what the rules are for a particular *class* of XML document. The two approaches are implemented somewhat differently and each offers distinct advantages over the other:

❑ **DTDs:** This is the old tried and true. DTDs are utilized in SGML (XML is an SGML application — you can think of SGML being a superset of XML, but incredibly painful to learn), and have the advantage of being a very well-known and accepted way of doing things. There are tons of DTDs already out there that are just waiting for you to utilize them.

The downside (you knew there had to be one — right?) is that the "old" is operative in my "old tried and true" statement. Not that being old is a bad thing, but in this case, DTDs are definitely not up to speed with what else has happened in document technology. DTDs do not really allow for such seemingly rudimentary things as restricting data types. You'll find that DTDs — at least in terms of being used with XML — are largely being treated as deprecated at this point in favor of XML schemas.

❑ **XML schemas:** XML schemas have the distinct advantage of being strongly typed. What's cool about them is that you can effectively establish your own complex data types — types that are made up based on combinations of one or more other data types (including other complex data types) or require specialized pattern matching (for example, a Social Security number is just a number, but it has special formatting that you could easily enforce via an XML schema). XML schemas also have the advantage, as their name suggests, of being an XML document themselves. This means that a lot of the skills in writing your XML documents also apply to writing schemas (though there's still plenty to learn) and that schemas can, themselves, be self-describing — right down to validating themselves against yet another schema.

What SQL Server Brings to the Party

So, now we have all the basics of what XML *is* down. What we need is to understand the relevance in SQL Server.

XML functionality was a relatively late addition to SQL Server. Indeed, it first appeared as a downloadable add-on to SQL Server 7.0. What's more, a significant part of the functionality was originally more an addition to Internet Information Server (IIS) than to SQL Server.

With SQL Server 2000, the XML side of things moved to what Microsoft called a "Web Release" model, and was updated several times. With SQL Server 2005, XML finished moving into the core product. While most of the old functionality remains supported, SQL Server continues to add more core features that makes XML an integral part of things rather than the afterthought that XML sometimes seemed to be in early releases.

What functionality? Well, in SQL Server 2008 XML comes to the forefront in several places:

❑   Support for multiple methods of selecting data out of normal columns and receiving them in XML format

❑   Support for storing XML data natively within SQL Server using the XML data type

❑   Support for querying data that is stored in its original XML format using XQuery (a special query language for XML) and other methods

❑   Support for enforcing data integrity in the data being stored in XML format using XML schemas

❑   Support for indexing XML data

❑   Support for hierarchical data — granting special support for the tree-like structures that are so common in XML data

And this is just the mainstream stuff.

The support for each of these often makes use of several functional areas of XML support, so let's look at XML support one piece at a time.

Defining a Column as Being of XML Type

We've already seen the most basic definition of an XML column. For example, if we examined the most basic definition of the `Production.ProductModel` table in the AdventureWorks2008 database, it would look something like this:

```
CREATE TABLE Production.ProductModel
(
    ProductModelID      int                 IDENTITY(1,1) PRIMARY KEY NOT NULL,
    Name                dbo.Name            NOT NULL,
    CatalogDescription  xml                 NULL,
    Instructions        xml                 NULL,
    rowguid             uniqueidentifier    ROWGUIDCOL NOT NULL,
    ModifiedDate        datetime            NOT NULL
        CONSTRAINT DF_ProductModel_ModifiedDate  DEFAULT (GETDATE()),
);
```

So, let's ask ourselves what we have here in terms of our two XML columns.

1.   We have defined them as XML, so we will have our XML data type methods available to us (more on those coming up soon).

2. We have allowed NULLs but could have just as easily chosen NOT NULL as a constraint. Note, however, that the NOT NULL would be enforced on whether the row had any data for that column, not whether that data was valid.

3. Our XML is considered "non-typed XML." That is, since we have not associated any schema with it, SQL Server doesn't really know anything about how this XML is supposed to behave to be considered "valid."

The first of these is implied in any column that is defined with the data type XML rather than just plain text. We will see much more about this in our next XML data type section.

The second goes with any data type in SQL Server — we can specify whether we allow NULL data or not for that column.

So, the real meat in terms of changes we can make at definition time has to do with whether we specify our XML column as being typed or non-typed XML. The non-typed definition we used in the preceding example means that SQL Server knows very little about any XML stored in the column and, therefore, can do little to police its validity. If we set the column up as being typed XML, then we are providing much more definition about what is considered "valid" for any XML that goes in our column.

The AdventureWorks2008 database already has schema collections that match the validation we want to place on our two XML columns, so let's look at how we would change our CREATE statement to adjust to typed XML:

```
CREATE TABLE Production.ProductModel
(
    ProductModelID      int IDENTITY(1,1) PRIMARY KEY NOT NULL,
    Name                dbo.Name NOT NULL,
    CatalogDescription  xml
        (CONTENT [Production].[ProductDescriptionSchemaCollection]) NULL,
    Instructions        xml
        (CONTENT [Production].[ManuInstructionsSchemaCollection]) NULL,
    rowguid             uniqueidentifier ROWGUIDCOL NOT NULL,
    ModifiedDate        datetime NOT NULL
        CONSTRAINT DF_ProductModel_ModifiedDate  DEFAULT (GETDATE())
);
```

This represents the way it is defined in the actual AdventureWorks2008 sample. In order to insert a record into the Production.ProductModel table, you must either leave the CatalogDescription and Instructions fields blank or supply XML that is valid when tested against their respective schemas.

XML Schema Collections

XML schema collections are really nothing more than named persistence of one or more schema documents into the database. The name amounts to a handle to your set of schemas. By referring to that collection, you are indicating that the XML typed column or variable must be valid when matched against all of the schemas in that collection.

We can view existing schema collections. To do this, we utilize the built-in XML_SCHEMA_NAMESPACE() function. The syntax looks like this:

```
XML_SCHEMA_NAMESPACE( <SQL Server schema> , <xml schema collection> , [<namespace>] )
```

This is just a little confusing, so let's touch on these parameters just a bit:

Parameter	Description
`SQL Server schema`	This is your relational database schema (not to be confused with the XML schema). For example, for the table `Production.ProductModel`, `Production` is the relational schema. For `Sales.SalesOrderHeader`, `Sales` is the relational schema.
`xml schema collection`	The name used when the XML schema collection was created. In your `CREATE` table example previously, you referred to the `ProductDescriptionSchemaCollection` and `ManuInstructionSSchemaCollection` XML schema collections.
`namespace`	Optional name for a specific namespace within the XML schema collection. Remember that XML schema collections can contain multiple schema documents — this would return anything that fell within the specified namespace.

So, to use this for the `Production.ManuInstructionsSchemaCollection` schema collection, we would make a query like this:

```
SELECT XML_SCHEMA_NAMESPACE('Production','ManuInstructionsSchemaCollection');
```

This spews forth a ton of unformatted XML:

```
<xsd:schema xmlns:xsd="http://www.w3.org/2001/XMLSchema"
xmlns:t="http://schemas.microsoft.com/sqlserver/2004/07/adventure-works/ProductMode
lManuInstructions"
targetNamespace="http://schemas.microsoft.com/sqlserver/2004/07/adventure-works/Pro
ductModelManuInstructions" elementFormDefault="qualified"><xsd:element
name="root"><xsd:complexType mixed="true"><xsd:complexContent
mixed="true"><xsd:restriction base="xsd:anyType"><xsd:sequence><xsd:element
name="Location" maxOccurs="unbounded"><xsd:complexType
mixed="true"><xsd:complexContent mixed="true"><xsd:restriction
base="xsd:anyType"><xsd:sequence><xsd:element name="step" type="t:StepType"
maxOccurs="unbounded" /></xsd:sequence><xsd:attribute name="LocationID"
type="xsd:integer" use="required" /><xsd:attribute name="SetupHours"
type="xsd:decimal" /><xsd:attribute name="MachineHours" type="xsd:decimal"
/><xsd:attribute name="LaborHours" type="xsd:decimal" /><xsd:attribute
name="LotSize" type="xsd:decimal"
/></xsd:restriction></xsd:complexContent></xsd:complexType></xsd:element></xsd:sequ
ence></xsd:restriction></xsd:complexContent></xsd:complexType></xsd:element><xsd:
complexType name="StepType" mixed="true"><xsd:complexContent
mixed="true"><xsd:restriction base="xsd:anyType"><xsd:choice minOccurs="0"
maxOccurs="unbounded"><xsd:element name="tool" type="xsd:string" /><xsd:element
name="material" type="xsd:string" /><xsd:element name="blueprint" type="xsd:string"
/><xsd:element name="specs" type="xsd:string" /><xsd:element name="diag"
type="xsd:string"
/></xsd:choice></xsd:restriction></xsd:complexContent></xsd:complexType></xsd:schema>
```

SQL Server strips out any whitespace between tags, so if you create a schema collection with all sorts of pretty indentations for readability, SQL Server will remove them for the sake of efficient storage.

> Again, note that the default number of characters returned for text results in Management Studio is only 256 characters. If you're using text view, you will want to go Tools ⇨ Options ⇨ Query Results ⇨ SQL Server ⇨ Results to Text and change the maximum number of characters displayed.

Creating, Altering, and Dropping XML Schema Collections

The CREATE, ALTER, and DROP notions for XML schema collections work in a manner that is *mostly* consistent with how other such statements have worked thus far in SQL Server. We'll run through them here, but pay particular attention to the ALTER statement, as it is the one that has a few quirks we haven't seen in other ALTER statements we've worked with.

CREATE XML SCHEMA COLLECTION

Again, the CREATE is your typical CREATE <object type> <object name> syntax that we've seen throughout the book, and uses the AS keyword we've seen with stored procedures, views, and other less structured objects:

```
CREATE XML SCHEMA COLLECTION [<SQL Server schema>.] <collection name>
    AS { <schema text> | <variable containing the schema text> }
```

So if, for example, we wanted to create an XML schema collection that is similar to the Production .ManuInstructionsSchemaCollection collection in AdventureWorks2008, we might execute something like the following:

```
CREATE XML SCHEMA COLLECTION ProductDescriptionSchemaCollectionSummaryRequired
  AS
    '<xsd:schema targetNamespace="http://schemas.microsoft.com/sqlserver/2004/07/
adventure-works/ProductModelWarrAndMain"

xmlns="http://schemas.microsoft.com/sqlserver/2004/07/adventure-works/ProductModelW
arrAndMain"
        elementFormDefault="qualified"
        xmlns:xsd="http://www.w3.org/2001/XMLSchema" >
        <xsd:element name="Warranty"  >
            <xsd:complexType>
                <xsd:sequence>
                    <xsd:element name="WarrantyPeriod" type="xsd:string"  />
                    <xsd:element name="Description" type="xsd:string"  />
                </xsd:sequence>
            </xsd:complexType>
        </xsd:element>
    </xsd:schema>
```

```
    <xs:schema targetNamespace="http://schemas.microsoft.com/sqlserver/2004/07/
adventure-works/ProductModelDescription"
        xmlns="http://schemas.microsoft.com/sqlserver/2004/07/adventure-works/
ProductModelDescription"
        elementFormDefault="qualified"
        xmlns:mstns="http://tempuri.org/XMLSchema.xsd"
        xmlns:xs="http://www.w3.org/2001/XMLSchema"
        xmlns:wm="http://schemas.microsoft.com/sqlserver/2004/07/adventure-works/
ProductModelWarrAndMain" >
        <xs:import namespace="http://schemas.microsoft.com/sqlserver/2004/07/
adventure-works/ProductModelWarrAndMain" />
        <xs:element name="ProductDescription" type="ProductDescription" />
            <xs:complexType name="ProductDescription">
                <xs:sequence>
                    <xs:element name="Summary" type="Summary" minOccurs="1" />
                </xs:sequence>
                <xs:attribute name="ProductModelID" type="xs:string" />
                <xs:attribute name="ProductModelName" type="xs:string" />
            </xs:complexType>
            <xs:complexType name="Summary" mixed="true" >
                <xs:sequence>
                    <xs:any processContents="skip" namespace="http://www.w3.org/
1999/xhtml" minOccurs="0" maxOccurs="unbounded" />
                </xs:sequence>
            </xs:complexType>
    </xs:schema>';
```

Note that the URL portion of the namespace declaration must be entered on a single line. It is shown here word wrapped onto multiple lines because there is a limit to the number of characters we can show per line in print. Make sure you include the entire URL on a single line.

This one happens to be just like the `Production.ManuInstructionsSchemaCollection` schema collection, but I've altered the schema to require the summary element rather than having it optional. Since the basic structure is the same, I utilized the same namespaces.

ALTER XML SCHEMA COLLECTION

This one is just slightly different from other ALTER statements in the sense that it is limited to just adding new pieces to the collection. The syntax looks like this:

```
ALTER XML SCHEMA COLLECTION [<SQL Server schema>.] <collection name>
    ADD { <schema text> | <variable containing the schema text> }
```

I would not be at all surprised if the functionality of this is boosted a bit in a later service pack, but, in the meantime, let me stress that this is a tool for adding to your schema collection rather than changing or removing what's there.

DROP XML SCHEMA COLLECTION

This is one of those classic "does what it says" things and works just like any other DROP:

```
DROP XML SCHEMA COLLECTION  [<SQL Server schema>.] <collection name>
```

So, to get rid of our `ProductDescriptionSchemaCollectionSummaryRequired` schema collection we created earlier, we could execute:

```
DROP XML SCHEMA COLLECTION ProductDescriptionSchemaCollectionSummaryRequired;
```

And it's gone.

XML Data Type Methods

The XML data type carries several intrinsic methods with it. These methods are unique to the XML data type, and no other current data type has anything that is at all similar. The syntax within these methods varies a bit because they are based on different, but mostly industry-standard, XML access methods. The basic syntax for calling the method is standardized though:

```
<instance of xml data type>.<method>
```

There are a total of five methods available:

❑ `.query`: An implementation of the industry-standard XQuery language. This allows you to access your XML by running XQuery-formatted queries. XQuery allows for the prospect that you may be returning multiple pieces of data rather than a discrete value.

❑ `.value`: This one allows you to access a discrete value within a specific element or attribute.

❑ `.modify`: This is Microsoft's own extension to XQuery. Whereas XQuery is limited to requesting data (no modification language), the `modify` method extends XQuery to allow for data modification.

❑ `.nodes`: Used to break up XML data into individual, more relational-style rows.

❑ `.exist`: Much like the `IF EXISTS` clause we use extensively in standard SQL, the `exist()` XML data type method tests to see whether a specific kind of data exists. In the case of `exist()`, the test is to see whether a particular node or attribute has an entry in the instance of XML you're testing.

.query (SQL Server's Implementation of XQuery)

`.query` is an implementation of the industry standard XQuery language. The result works much like a SQL query, except that the results are for matching XML data nodes rather than relational rows and columns.

`.query` requires a parameter that is a valid XQuery to be run against your instance of XML data. For example, if we wanted the steps out of the product documentation for ProductID 66, we could run the following:

```
SELECT ProductModelID, Instructions.query('declare namespace PI="http://
schemas.microsoft.com/sqlserver/2004/07/adventure-works/ProductModelManuInstructions";
    /PI:root/PI:Location/PI:step') AS Steps
FROM Production.ProductModel
WHERE ProductModelID = 66;
```

Note that the URL portion of the namespace declaration must be entered on a single line. They are shown here word wrapped onto multiple lines because there is a limit to the number of characters we can show per line in print. Make sure you include the entire URL on a single line.

The result is rather verbose, so I've truncated the right side of it, but you can see that we've trimmed things down such that we're getting only those nodes at the step level or lower in the XML hierarchy:

```
ProductModelID Steps
-------------- ---------------------------------------------------
66             <PI:step xmlns:PI="http://schemas.microsoft.com/sqlser...
                      Put the <PI:material>Seat post Lug (Product N...
               </PI:step><PI:step xmlns:PI="http://schemas.micro...
                      Insert the <PI:material>Pinch Bolt (Product N...
               </PI:step><PI:step xmlns:PI="http://schemas.micro...
                      Attach the <PI:material>LL Seat (Product Numb...
               </PI:step><PI:step xmlns:PI="http://schemas.micro...
                      Inspect per specification <PI:specs>FI-620</P...
               </PI:step>

(1 row(s) affected)
```

It's also worth pointing out that all the XML still came in one column in one row per data row in the database.

> It bears repeating that .query cannot modify data; it is a read-only operation.

Notice, by the way, my need to declare the namespace in this. Since a namespace is declared as part of the referenced schema collection, you can see how it really expands and virtually destroys the readability of our query. We can fix that by using the WITH XMLNAMESPACES() declaration:

```
WITH XMLNAMESPACES ('http://schemas.microsoft.com/sqlserver/2004/07/
adventure-works/ProductModelManuInstructions' AS PI)

SELECT ProductModelID, Instructions.query('/PI:root/PI:Location/PI:step') AS Steps
FROM Production.ProductModel
WHERE ProductModelID = 66;
```

Note that the URL portion of the namespace declaration must be entered on a single line. They are shown here word wrapped onto multiple lines because there is a limit to the number of characters we can show per line in print. Make sure you include the entire URL on a single line.

Gives you a somewhat more readable query, but yields the same result set.

You may find it interesting to navigate to the actual URL of the ProductManualInstructions. After a brief introductory HTML page, it will point you at the actual schema document used by the query.

.value

The .value method is all about querying discrete data. It uses a special XML path language called XPath to locate a specific node and extract a scalar value. The syntax looks like this:

```
<instance of xml data type>.value (<XPath location>, <non-xml SQL Server Type>)
```

The trick here is to make certain that the XPath specified really will return a discrete value.

If, for example, we wanted to know the value of the LaborHours attribute in the first Location element for ProductModelID 66, we might write something like:

```
WITH XMLNAMESPACES ('http://schemas.microsoft.com/sqlserver/2004/07/
adventure-works/ProductModelManuInstructions' AS PI)

SELECT ProductModelID,
    Instructions.value('(/PI:root/PI:Location/@LaborHours)[1]',
                       'decimal (5,2)') AS Location
FROM Production.ProductModel
WHERE ProductModelID = 66;
```

Note that the URL portion of the namespace declaration must be entered on a single line. They are shown here word wrapped onto multiple lines because there is a limit to the number of characters we can show per line in print. Make sure you include the entire URL on a single line.

Check the results:

```
ProductModelID Location
-------------- -------------------------------------
66             1.50

(1 row(s) affected)
```

Note that SQL Server has extracted just the specified attribute value (in this case, the LaborHours attribute of the Location node) as a discrete piece of data. The data type of the returned values must be castable into a non-XML type in SQL Server, and must return a scalar value — that is, you cannot have multiple rows.

.modify

Ah, here things get just a little interesting.

XQuery, left in its standard W3C form, is a read-only kind of thing — that is, it is great for selecting data but offers no equivalents to INSERT, UPDATE, or DELETE. Bummer deal! Well, Microsoft is apparently having none of that and has done its own extension to XQuery to provide data manipulation for XQuery. This extension to XQuery is called XML Data Manipulation Language, or XML DML. XML DML adds three new commands to XQuery:

❑ insert
❑ delete
❑ replace value of

> Note that these new commands, like all XML keywords, are case sensitive.

Each of these does what it implies, with replace value of taking the place of SQL's UPDATE statement.

If, for example, we wanted to increase the original 1.5 labor hours in our `.value` example, we might write something like:

```
WITH XMLNAMESPACES ('http://schemas.microsoft.com/sqlserver/2004/07/
adventure-works/ProductModelManuInstructions' AS PI)

UPDATE Production.ProductModel
SET Instructions.modify('replace value of (/PI:root/PI:Location/@LaborHours)[1]
with 1.75')
WHERE ProductModelID = 66;
```

Note that the URL portion of the namespace declaration must be entered on a single line. They are shown here word wrapped onto multiple lines because there is a limit to the number of characters we can show per line in print. Make sure you include the entire URL on a single line.

Now if we re-run our `.value` command:

```
WITH XMLNAMESPACES
('http://schemas.microsoft.com/sqlserver/2004/07/adventure-works/ProductModelManuIn
structions' AS PI)

SELECT ProductModelID, Instructions.value('(/PI:root/PI:Location/@LaborHours)[1]',
'decimal (5,2)') AS Location
FROM Production.ProductModel
WHERE ProductModelID = 66;
```

Note that the URL portion of the namespace declaration must be entered on a single line. They are shown here word wrapped onto multiple lines because there is a limit to the number of characters we can show per line in print. Make sure you include the entire URL on a single line.

We get a new value:

```
ProductModelID Location
-------------- ---------------------------------------
66             1.75

(1 row(s) affected)
```

Note the way that this is essentially an UPDATE *within an* UPDATE. *We are modifying the SQL Server row, so we must use an* UPDATE *statement to tell SQL Server that our row of relational data (which just happens to have XML within it) is to be updated. We must also use the* `replace value of` *keyword to specify the XML portion of the update.*

.nodes

`.nodes` is used to take blocks of XML and separate what would have, were it stored in a relational form, been multiple rows of data. Taking one XML document and breaking it into individual parts in this way is referred to as *shredding* the document.

What we are doing with `.nodes` is essentially breaking the instances of XML data into their own table (with as many rows as there are instances of data meeting that XQuery criteria). As you might expect, this means we need to treat `.nodes` results as a table rather than as a column. The primary difference between .nodes and a typical table is that we must *cross apply* our .nodes results back to the specific table that we are sourcing our XML data from. So, .nodes really involves more syntax than just ".nodes" — think of it somewhat like a join, but using the special CROSS APPLY keyword in the place of the JOIN and .nodes instead of the ON clause. It looks like this:

```
SELECT <column list>
FROM <source table>
CROSS APPLY <column name>.nodes(<XQuery>) AS <table alias for your .nodes results>
```

This is fairly confusing stuff, so let's look back at our .value example earlier. We see a query that looked for a specific entry and, therefore, got back exactly one result:

```
WITH XMLNAMESPACES
('http://schemas.microsoft.com/sqlserver/2004/07/adventure-works/ProductModelManuIn
structions' AS PI)

SELECT ProductModelID,
    Instructions.value('(/PI:root/PI:Location/@LaborHours)[1]',
                    'decimal (5,2)') AS Location
FROM Production.ProductModel
WHERE ProductModelID = 66;
```

Note that the URL portion of the namespace declaration must be entered on a single line. They are shown here word wrapped onto multiple lines because there is a limit to the number of characters we can show per line in print. Make sure you include the entire URL on a single line.

.value expects a scalar result, so we needed to make certain our XQuery would return just that single value per individual row of XML. .nodes tells SQL Server to use XQuery to map to a specific location and treat each entry found in that XQuery as an individual row instead of a discrete value.

```
WITH XMLNAMESPACES
('http://schemas.microsoft.com/sqlserver/2004/07/adventure-works/
ProductModelManuInstructions' AS PI)

SELECT pm.ProductModelID,
    pmi.Location.value('./@LocationID', 'int') AS LocationID,
    pmi.Location.value('./@LaborHours', 'decimal(5,2)') AS LaborHours
FROM Production.ProductModel pm
CROSS APPLY pm.Instructions.nodes('/PI:root/PI:Location') AS pmi(Location);
```

Note that the URL portion of the namespace declaration must be entered on a single line. They are shown here word wrapped onto multiple lines because there is a limit to the number of characters we can show per line in print. Make sure you include the entire URL on a single line.

Notice that through the use of our .nodes method, we are essentially turning one table (ProductModel) into two tables (the source table and the .nodes results from the Instructions column within the ProductModel table). Take a look at the results:

```
ProductModelID LocationID  LaborHours
-------------- ----------- ------------------------------------
7              10          2.50
7              20          1.75
```

7	30	1.00
7	45	0.50
7	50	3.00
7	60	4.00
10	10	2.00
10	20	1.50
10	30	1.00
10	4	1.50
10	50	3.00
10	60	4.00
43	50	3.00
44	50	3.00
47	10	1.00
47	20	1.00
47	50	3.50
48	10	1.00
48	20	1.00
48	50	3.50
53	50	0.50
66	50	1.75
67	50	1.00

```
(23 row(s) affected)
```

As you can see, we are getting back multiple rows for many of what were originally a single row in the `ProductModel` table. For example, `ProductModelID` 7 had six different instances of the `Location` element, so we received six rows instead of just the single row that existed in the `ProductModel` table.

While this is, perhaps, the most complex of the various XML data type methods, the power that it gives you to transform XML data for relational use is virtually limitless.

.exist

`.exist` works something like the `EXISTS` statement in SQL. It accepts an expression (in this case, an XQuery expression rather than a SQL expression) and will return a Boolean indication of whether the expression was true or not. (`NULL` is also a possible outcome.)

If, in our `.modify` example, we had wanted to show rows that contain steps that had spec elements, we could have used `.exist`:

```
WITH XMLNAMESPACES ('http://schemas.microsoft.com/sqlserver/2004/07/
adventure-works/ProductModelManuInstructions' AS PI)

SELECT ProductModelID, Instructions
FROM Production.ProductModel
WHERE Instructions.exist('/PI:root/PI:Location/PI:step/PI:specs') = 1
```

Pay particular attention to the point at which the test condition is being applied!

For example, the code would show us rows where at least one step had a spec element in it — it does not necessarily require that every step have the spec element. If we wanted every element to be tested, we would either need to pull the elements out as individual rows (using `.nodes`) or place the test condition in the XQuery.

Note that the URL portion of the namespace declaration must be entered on a single line. They are shown here word wrapped onto multiple lines because there is a limit to the number of characters we can show per line in print. Make sure you include the entire URL on a single line.

Enforcing Constraints Beyond the Schema Collection

We are, of course, used to the concept of constraints by now. We've dealt with them extensively in this book. Well, if our relational database needs constraints, it follows that our XML data does too. Indeed, we've already implemented much of the idea of constraints in XML through the use of schema collections. But what if we want to enforce requirements that go beyond the base schema?

Surprisingly, you cannot apply XML data type methods within a constraint declaration. How do you get around this problem? Well, wrap the tests up in a user-defined function (UDF), and then utilize that function in your constraint.

I have to admit I'm somewhat surprised that the methods are not usable within the CONSTRAINT *declaration, but things like functions are. All I can say is "go figure. . . ." I'll just quietly hope they fix this in a future release, as it seems a significant oversight on something that shouldn't have been all that difficult (yeah, I know — easy for me to say since they have to write that code, not me!).*

Retrieving Relational Data in XML Format

Retrieving relational data is the area that SQL Server already had largely figured out even in the older releases. We had a couple of different options, and we had still more options within those options — between them all, things have been pretty flexible for quite some time. Let's take a look . . . .

The FOR XML Clause

This clause is at the root of many of the different integration models available. It is essentially just an option added onto the end of the existing T-SQL SELECT statement, but serves as the primary method for taking data stored in normal relational format and outputting it as XML.

Let's look at the SELECT statement syntax from Chapter 3:

```
SELECT [TOP (<expression>) [PERCENT] [WITH TIES]] <column list>
[FROM <source table(s)/view(s)>]
[WHERE <restrictive condition>]
[GROUP BY <column name or expression using a column in the SELECT list>]
[HAVING <restrictive condition based on the GROUP BY results>]
[ORDER BY <column list>]
[[FOR XML {RAW|AUTO|EXPLICIT|PATH [(<element>)]}
   [, XMLDATA | XMLSCHEMA [(<target namespace>)]]
   [, ELEMENTS [XSINIL | ABSENT]][, BINARY base 64][ROOT('<root definition>')]]]
[OPTION (<query hint>, [, ...n])]
```

Most of this should seem pretty trivial by now — after all, we've been using this syntax throughout a lot of hard chapters by this time — but it's time to focus in on that FOR XML line . . . .

FOR XML provides three different initial options for how you want your XML formatted in the results:

❑   RAW: This sends each row of data in your result set back as a single data element, with the element name of "row" and with each column listed as an attribute of the "row" element. Even if you join multiple tables, RAW outputs the results with the same number of elements as you would have rows in a standard SQL query.

❑   AUTO: This option labels each element with the table name or alias that represents the source of the data. If there is data output from more than one table in the query, the data from each table is split into separate, nested elements. If AUTO is used, then an additional option, ELEMENTS, is also supported if you would like column data presented as elements rather than as attributes.

❑   EXPLICIT: This one is certainly the most complex to format your query with, but the end result is that you have a high degree of control of what the XML looks like in the end. With this option, you impose something of a hierarchy for the data that's being returned, and then format your query such that each piece of data belongs to a specific hierarchy level (and gets assigned a tag accordingly) as desired. This choice has largely been supplanted by the PATH option, and is here primarily for backward compatibility.

❑   PATH: This was added to try and provide the level of flexibility of EXPLICIT in a more usable format — this is generally going to be what you want to use when you need a high degree of control of the format of the output.

   Note that none of these options provide the required root element. If you want the XML document to be considered to be well formed, then you will need to wrap the results with proper opening and closing tags for your root element or have SQL Server do it for you (using the ROOT option described later). While this is in some ways a hassle, it is also a benefit — it means that you can build more complex XML by stringing multiple XML queries together and wrapping the different results into one XML file.

In addition to the four major formatting options, there are other optional parameters that further modify the output that SQL Server provides in an XML query:

❑   XMLDATA/XMLSCHEMA: These tell SQL Server that you would like to prepend one of two forms of an XML schema to the results. XMLDATA works under the older XDR format, which was common before the W3C finalized the spec for XML schema documents. You'll want to use XMLSCHEMA here unless you have a very specific reason for using the older XDR format, as the XMLDATA option is provided only for backward compatibility and does not support newer data types added in SQL Server 2005 and 2008.

❑   ELEMENTS: This option is available only when you are using the AUTO formatting option. It tells SQL Server that you want the columns in your data returned as nested elements rather than as attributes.

❑   BINARY BASE64: This tells SQL Server to encode any binary columns (binary, varbinary, image) in base64 format. This option is implied (SQL Server will use it even if you don't state it) if you are also using the AUTO option. It is required when using EXPLICIT and RAW queries.

❑   TYPE: Tells SQL Server to return the results reporting the XML data type instead of the default Unicode character type.

❑   ROOT: This option will have SQL Server add the root node for you so you don't have to. You can either supply a name for your root or use the default (root).

Let's explore all these options in a little more detail.

RAW

This is something of the "no fuss, no muss" option. The idea here is to just get it done — no fanfare, no special formatting at all — just the absolute minimum to translate a row of relational data into an element of XML data. The element is named "row" (creative, huh?), and each column in the Select list is added as an attribute using whatever name the column would have appeared with, if you had been running a more traditional SELECT statement.

One downside to the way in which attributes are named is that you need to make certain that every column has a name. Normally, SQL Server will just show no column heading if you perform an aggregation or other calculated column and don't provide an alias — when doing XML queries, everything MUST have a name, so don't forget to alias calculated columns.

So, let's start things out with something relatively simple. Imagine that our manager has asked us to provide a query that lists a few customers' orders — say CustomerIDs 1 and 2. After cruising through just the first five or so chapters of the book, you would probably say "No problem!" and supply something like:

```sql
USE AdventureWorks2008;

SELECT Sales.Customer.CustomerID,
  Sales.Customer.AccountNumber,
  Sales.SalesOrderHeader.SalesOrderID,
  CAST(Sales.SalesOrderHeader.OrderDate AS date) AS OrderDate
FROM Sales.Customer
JOIN Sales.SalesOrderHeader
  ON Sales.Customer.CustomerID = Sales.SalesOrderHeader.CustomerID
WHERE Sales.Customer.CustomerID = 29890 OR Sales.Customer.CustomerID = 30067;
```

So, you go hand your boss the results:

```
CustomerID   AccountNumber  SalesOrderID  OrderDate
-----------  -------------  ------------  ----------
29890        AW00029890     43671         2008-08-16
29890        AW00029890     45049         2008-08-16
29890        AW00029890     45790         2008-08-16
29890        AW00029890     46619         2008-08-16
29890        AW00029890     47672         2008-08-16
29890        AW00029890     48732         2008-08-16
29890        AW00029890     49866         2008-08-16
29890        AW00029890     61187         2008-08-16
30067        AW00030067     43672         2008-08-16
30067        AW00030067     44294         2008-08-16
30067        AW00030067     45052         2008-08-16
30067        AW00030067     45792         2008-08-16
30067        AW00030067     46622         2008-08-16
30067        AW00030067     47673         2008-08-16
30067        AW00030067     48768         2008-08-16
30067        AW00030067     49860         2008-08-16
30067        AW00030067     51100         2008-08-16
30067        AW00030067     55287         2008-08-16
30067        AW00030067     61222         2008-08-16
30067        AW00030067     67272         2008-08-16
(20 row(s) affected)
```

Easy, right? Well, now the boss comes back and says, "Great — now I'll just have Billy Bob write something to turn this into XML — too bad that will probably take a day or two." This is your cue to step in and say, "Oh, why didn't you say so?" and simply add three key words:

```
USE AdventureWorks2008;

SELECT Sales.Customer.CustomerID,
   Sales.Customer.AccountNumber,
   Sales.SalesOrderHeader.SalesOrderID,
   CAST(Sales.SalesOrderHeader.OrderDate AS date) AS OrderDate
FROM Sales.Customer
JOIN Sales.SalesOrderHeader
   ON Sales.Customer.CustomerID = Sales.SalesOrderHeader.CustomerID
WHERE Sales.Customer.CustomerID = 29890 OR Sales.Customer.CustomerID = 30067
FOR XML RAW;
```

You have just made the boss very happy. The output is a one-to-one match versus what we would have seen in the result set had we run just a standard SQL query:

```
<row CustomerID="1" AccountNumber="AW00000001" SalesOrderID="43860" OrderDate="Aug
1 2001" />
<row CustomerID="1" AccountNumber="AW00000001" SalesOrderID="44501" OrderDate="Nov
1 2001" />
<row CustomerID="1" AccountNumber="AW00000001" SalesOrderID="45283" OrderDate="Feb
1 2002" />
<row CustomerID="1" AccountNumber="AW00000001" SalesOrderID="46042" OrderDate="May
1 2002" />
<row CustomerID="2" AccountNumber="AW00000002" SalesOrderID="46976" OrderDate="Aug
1 2002" />
<row CustomerID="2" AccountNumber="AW00000002" SalesOrderID="47997" OrderDate="Nov
1 2002" />
<row CustomerID="2" AccountNumber="AW00000002" SalesOrderID="49054" OrderDate="Feb
1 2003" />
<row CustomerID="2" AccountNumber="AW00000002" SalesOrderID="50216" OrderDate="May
1 2003" />
<row CustomerID="2" AccountNumber="AW00000002" SalesOrderID="51728" OrderDate="Aug
1 2003" />
<row CustomerID="2" AccountNumber="AW00000002" SalesOrderID="57044" OrderDate="Nov
1 2003" />
<row CustomerID="2" AccountNumber="AW00000002" SalesOrderID="63198" OrderDate="Feb
1 2004" />
<row CustomerID="2" AccountNumber="AW00000002" SalesOrderID="69488" OrderDate="May
1 2004" />
```

Be aware that Management Studio will truncate any column where the length exceeds the number set in the Options menu in the Results to Text tab (maximum is 8192). This issue exists in the results window (grid or text) and if you output directly to a file. This is an issue with the tool — not SQL Server itself. If you use another method to retrieve results (ADO for example), you shouldn't encounter an issue with this.

We have one element in XML for each row of data our query produced. All column information, regardless of what table was the source of the data, is represented as an attribute of the "row" element. The downside of this is that we haven't represented the true hierarchical nature of our data — orders are only placed by customers. The upside, however, is that the XML DOM — if that's the model you're using — is going to be much less deep and, hence, will have a slightly smaller footprint in memory and perform better, depending on what you're doing.

AUTO

AUTO takes a somewhat different approach to our data than RAW does. AUTO tries to format things a little better for us — naming elements based on the table (or the table alias if you use one). In addition, AUTO recognizes the notion that our data probably has some underlying hierarchical notion to it that is supposed to be represented in the XML.

Let's go back to our customer orders example from the last section. This time, we'll make use of the AUTO option, so we can see the difference versus the rather plain output we got with RAW. We'll also make extensive use of aliasing to make our elements have more realistic names:

```
USE AdventureWorks2008;
```

```
SELECT Customer.CustomerID,
  Customer.AccountNumber,
  [Order].SalesOrderID,
  CAST([Order].OrderDate AS date) AS OrderDate
FROM Sales.Customer Customer
JOIN Sales.SalesOrderHeader [Order]
  ON Customer.CustomerID = [Order].CustomerID
WHERE Customer.CustomerID = 29890 OR Customer.CustomerID = 30067
FOR XML AUTO;
```

The first apparent difference is that the element name has changed to the name or alias of the table that is the source of the data. Notice also that I was able to output XML that included the SQL Server keyword Order by delimiting it in square brackets. Another even more significant difference appears when we look at the XML more thoroughly (I have again cleaned up the output a bit for clarity):

```
<Customer CustomerID="1" AccountNumber="AW00000001">
 <Order SalesOrderID="43860" OrderDate="Aug  1 2001" />
 <Order SalesOrderID="44501" OrderDate="Nov  1 2001" />
 <Order SalesOrderID="45283" OrderDate="Feb  1 2002" />
 <Order SalesOrderID="46042" OrderDate="May  1 2002" />
</Customer>
<Customer CustomerID="2" AccountNumber="AW00000002">
 <Order SalesOrderID="46976" OrderDate="Aug  1 2002" />
 <Order SalesOrderID="47997" OrderDate="Nov  1 2002" />
 <Order SalesOrderID="49054" OrderDate="Feb  1 2003" />
 <Order SalesOrderID="50216" OrderDate="May  1 2003" />
 <Order SalesOrderID="51728" OrderDate="Aug  1 2003" />
 <Order SalesOrderID="57044" OrderDate="Nov  1 2003" />
 <Order SalesOrderID="63198" OrderDate="Feb  1 2004" />
 <Order SalesOrderID="69488" OrderDate="May  1 2004" />
</Customer>
```

Data that is sourced from our second table (as determined by the SELECT list) is nested inside the data sourced from the first table. In this case, our Order elements are nested inside our Customer elements. If a column from the Order table were listed first in our select list, then Customer would be nested inside Order.

Pay attention to this business of the ordering of your SELECT list. Think about the primary question your XML query is meant to solve. Arrange your SELECT list such that the style that it produces is fitting for the goal of your XML. Sure, you could always re-style it into the different form — but why do that if SQL Server could have just produced it for you that way in the first place?

The downside to using AUTO is that the resulting XML data model ends up being slightly more complex. The upside is that the data is more explicitly broken up into a hierarchical model. This makes life easier when the elements are more significant breaking points — such as where you have a doubly sorted report (for example, Order sorted within Customer).

EXPLICIT

The word "explicit" is an interesting choice for this option — it loosely describes the kind of language you're likely to use while trying to create your query. The EXPLICIT option takes much more effort to prepare, but it also rewards that effort with very fine granularity of control over what's an element and what's an attribute, as well as what elements are nested in what other elements. EXPLICIT enables you to define each level of the hierarchy and how each level is going to look. In order to define the hierarchy, you create what is internally called the *universal table*. The universal table is, in many respects, just like any other result set you might produce in SQL Server. It is usually produced by making use of UNION statements to piece it together one level at a time, but you could, for example, build much of the data in a UDF and then make a SELECT against that to produce the final XML. The big difference between the universal table and a more traditional result set is that you must provide sufficient metadata right within your result set such that SQL Server can then transform that result set into an XML document in the schema you desire.

What do I mean by "sufficient metadata"? Well, to give you an idea of just how complex this can be, let's look at a real universal table:

Tag	Parent	Customer!1!CustomerID	Customer!1!CompanyName	Order!2!OrderID	Order!2!OrderDate
1	NULL	ALFKI	Alfreds Futterkiste	NULL	NULL
2	1	ALFKI	Alfreds Futterkiste	10643	1997-08-25 00:00:00.000
2	1	ALFKI	Alfreds Futterkiste	10692	1997-10-03 00:00:00.000
2	1	ALFKI	Alfreds Futterkiste	10702	1997-10-13 00:00:00.000
2	1	ALFKI	Alfreds Futterkiste	10835	1998-01-15 00:00:00.000
2	1	ALFKI	Alfreds Futterkiste	10952	1998-03-16 00:00:00.000
2	1	ALFKI	Alfreds Futterkiste	11011	1998-04-09 00:00:00.000
2	1	ALFKI	Alfreds Futterkiste	11078	1999-05-01 00:00:00.000

Continued

Tag	Parent	Customer!1!CustomerID	Customer!1!CompanyName	Order!2!OrderID	Order!2!OrderDate
2	1	ALFKI	Alfreds Futterkiste	11079	NULL
2	1	ALFKI	Alfreds Futterkiste	11080	2000-07-22 16:48:00.000
2	1	ALFKI	Alfreds Futterkiste	11081	2000-07-22 00:00:00.000
2	1	ALFKI	Alfreds Futterkiste	11087	2000-08-05 17:37:52.520
1	NULL	ANTON	Antonio Moreno Taquería	NULL	NULL
2	1	ANTON	Antonio Moreno Taquería	10365	1996-11-27 00:00:00.000
2	1	ANTON	Antonio Moreno Taquería	10507	1997-04-15 00:00:00.000
2	1	ANTON	Antonio Moreno Taquería	10535	1997-05-13 00:00:00.000
2	1	ANTON	Antonio Moreno Taquería	10573	1997-06-19 00:00:00.000
2	1	ANTON	Antonio Moreno Taquería	10677	1997-09-22 00:00:00.000
2	1	ANTON	Antonio Moreno Taquería	10682	1997-09-25 00:00:00.000
2	1	ANTON	Antonio Moreno Taquería	10856	1998-01-28 00:00:00.000

EXPLICIT is only used on extremely detailed situations. Many of the things you might want to do with EXPLICIT can now be more easily performed using the PATH option. In general, you'll want to look at all other options first, and consider EXPLICIT an option of last resort — it's very advanced in nature, difficult to understand, and, as such, we will consider further discussion of EXPLICIT to be beyond the scope of this book.

PATH

Now let's switch gears just a little bit and get down to a more "real" XML approach to getting data.

While EXPLICIT has not been deprecated as yet, make no mistake — PATH is really *meant* to be a better way of doing what EXPLICIT originally was the only way of doing. PATH makes a lot of sense in a lot of ways, and it is how I recommend that you do complex XML output in most cases.

> *This is a more complex recommendation than it might seem. The Microsoft party line on this is that PATH is easier. Well, PATH is easier is many ways, but, as we're going to see, it has its own set of "Except for this, and except for that, and except for this other thing" that can twist your brain into knots trying to understand exactly what to do. In short, in some cases, EXPLICIT is actually easier if you don't know XPath. The thing is, if you're dealing with XML, then XPath should be on your learn list anyway, so, if you're going to know it, you should find the XPath-based approach more usable.*

> *Note, however, that if you're needing backward compatibility to SQL Server 2000, then you're going to need to stick with EXPLICIT.*

In its most straightforward sense, the PATH option isn't that bad at all. So, let's start by getting our feet wet by focusing in on just the basics of using PATH. From there, we'll get a bit more complex and show off some of what PATH has to offer.

PATH 101

With PATH, you have a model that molds an existing standard to get at your data — XPath. XPath has an accepted standard, and provides a way of pointing at specific points in your XML schema. For PATH, we're just utilizing a lot of the same rules and ideas in order to say how data should be treated in a native XML sort of way.

How PATH treats the data you refer to depends on a number of rules including whether the column is named or unnamed (like EXPLICIT, the alias is the name if you use an alias). If the column does have a name, then a number of additional rules are applied as appropriate.

Let's look at some of the possibilities.

> *XPath is its own thing, and there are entire books dedicated to just that topic. PATH utilizes a wide variety of what's available in XPath, and so there really is too much to cover here for a single chapter in a beginning text. That said, we're going to touch on the basics here, and give you a taste of the more advanced stuff in the next section. From there, it's really up to you whether you want to learn XPath more fully, and from there, what pieces of it are understood by PATH. More advanced coverage of this is also supplied in the next book in this series: Professional SQL Server 2008 Programming.*

Unnamed Columns

Data from a column that is not named will be treated as raw text within the row's element. To demonstrate this, let's take a somewhat modified version of the example we used for XML RAW. What we're doing here is listing the two customers we're interested in and the number of orders they have placed:

```
SELECT CustomerID, COUNT(*)
FROM Sales.SalesOrderHeader Orders
WHERE CustomerID = 29890 OR CustomerID = 30067
GROUP BY CustomerID
FOR XML PATH;
```

Check the output from this:

```
<row><CustomerID>29890</CustomerID>8</row>
<row><CustomerID>30067</CustomerID>12</row>
```

What it created is a row element for each row in the query — much as we had with RAW — but notice the difference in how it treated our column data.

Since the `CustomerID` column was named, it was placed in its own element (we'll explore this more in our next section) — notice, however, the number 8 in my results. This is just loose embedded text for the row element — it isn't even associated directly with the `CustomerID` since it is outside the `CustomerID` element.

> *I feel like I'm repeating myself for the five thousandth time by saying this, but, again, remember that the exact counts (4 and 8 in my case) that come back may vary on your system depending on how much you have been playing with the data in the* `SalesOrderHeader` *table. The key thing is to see how the counts are not associated with the* `CustomerID`, *but are instead just raw text associated with the row.*

My personal slant on this is that the situations where loose text at the level of the top element is a valid way of doing things is pretty limited. The rules do say you can do it, but I believe it makes for data that is not very clear. Still, this is how it works — use it as it seems to fit the needs of your particular system.

Named Columns

This is where things get considerably more complex rather quickly. In their most simple form, named columns are just as easy as unnamed were — indeed, we saw one of them in our previous example. If a column is a simple named column using PATH, then it is merely added as an additional element to the row.

```
<CustomerID>30067</CustomerID>12</row>
```

Our `CustomerID` column was a simple named column.

We can, however, add special characters into our column name to indicate that we want special behaviors for this column. Let's look at a few of the most important.

@

No, that's not a typo — the @ symbol is really the heading to this section. If we add an @ sign to our column name, then SQL Server will treat that column as an attribute of the previous column. Note that we also have to delimit the alias in single quotes to hide the @ sign (which is usually an indicator of a variable). Let's move the `CustomerID` to be an attribute of the top element for the row:

```
SELECT CustomerID AS '@CustomerID', COUNT(*)
FROM Sales.SalesOrderHeader Orders
WHERE CustomerID = 29890 OR CustomerID = 30067
GROUP BY CustomerID
FOR XML PATH;
```

This yields:

```
<row CustomerID="29890">8</row>
<row CustomerID="30067">12</row>
```

Notice that our order count remained a text element of the row — only the column that we identified as an attribute moved in. We could take this to the next step by naming our count and prefixing it to make it an attribute also:

```
SELECT CustomerID AS '@CustomerID',
       COUNT(*) AS '@OrderCount'
FROM Sales.SalesOrderHeader Orders
WHERE CustomerID = 29890 OR CustomerID = 30067
GROUP BY CustomerID
FOR XML PATH;
```

With this, we no longer have our loose text for the element:

```
<row CustomerID="29890" OrderCount="8"/>
<row CustomerID="30067" OrderCount="12"/>
```

Also notice that SQL Server was smart enough to realize that everything was contained in attributes — with no lower level elements or simple text, it chose to make it a self-closing tag (see the "/" at the end of the element).

So, why did I indicate that this stuff was tricky? Well, there are a lot of different "it only works if . . ." kind of rules here. To demonstrate this, let's make a simple modification to our original query. This one seems like it should work, but SQL Server will throw a hissy fit if you try to run it:

```
SELECT CustomerID,
       COUNT(*) AS '@OrderCount'
FROM Sales.SalesOrderHeader Orders
WHERE CustomerID = 29890 OR CustomerID = 30067
GROUP BY CustomerID
FOR XML PATH;
```

What I've done here is to go back to `CustomerID` as its own element. What, at first glance, you would expect to happen is to get a `CustomerID` element with `OrderCount` as an attribute, but it doesn't quite work that way:

```
Msg 6852, Level 16, State 1, Line 1
Attribute-centric column '@OrderCount' must not come after a non-attribute-centric
sibling in XML hierarchy in FOR XML PATH.
```

The short rendition of the "What's wrong?" answer is that it doesn't really know what it's supposed to be an attribute of. Is it an attribute of the row, or an attribute of the `CustomerID`?

/

Yes, a forward slash.

Much like @, this special character indicates special things you want done. Essentially, you use it to define something of a path — a hierarchy that relates an element to those things that belong to it. It can exist anywhere in the column name except as the first character. To demonstrate this, we're going to utilize our last (failed) example, and build into it what we were looking for when we got the error.

First, we need to alter the `OrderID` to have information on what element it belongs to:

```
SELECT CustomerID,
       COUNT(*) AS 'CustomerID/OrderCount'
FROM Sales.SalesOrderHeader Orders
WHERE CustomerID = 29890 OR CustomerID = 30067
GROUP BY CustomerID
FOR XML PATH;
```

By adding the "/", and then placing `CustomerID` before the slash, we are telling SQL Server that `OrderCount` is below `CustomerID` in a hierarchy. Now, there are many ways an XML hierarchy can be structured, so let's see what SQL Server does with this:

```
<row><CustomerID>29890<OrderCount>8</OrderCount></CustomerID></row>
<row><CustomerID>30067<OrderCount>12</OrderCount></CustomerID></row>
```

Now, if you recall, we wanted to make `OrderCount` an attribute of `CustomerID`, so, while we have `OrderCount` below `CustomerID` in the hierarchy, it's still not quite in the place we wanted it. To do that, we can combine / and @, but we need to fully define all the hierarchy. Now, since I suspect this is a bit confusing, let's take it in two steps — first, the way we might be tempted to do it, but that will yield a similar error to the earlier example:

```
SELECT CustomerID,
       COUNT(*) AS 'CustomerID/@OrderCount'
FROM Sales.SalesOrderHeader Orders
WHERE CustomerID = 29890 OR CustomerID = 30067
GROUP BY CustomerID
FOR XML PATH;
```

Error time:

```
Msg 6852, Level 16, State 1, Line 1
Attribute-centric column 'CustomerID/@OrderCount' must not come after a
non-attribute-centric sibling in XML hierarchy in FOR XML PATH.
```

To fix this, we need to understand a bit about how things are constructed when building the XML tags. The key is that the tags are essentially built in the order you list them. So, if you are wanting to add attributes to an element, you need to keep in mind that they are part of the element tag — that means you need to define any attributes before you define any other content of that element (sub elements or raw text).

In our case, we are presenting the `CustomerID` as being raw text, but the `OrderCount` as being an attribute (OK, backwards of what would be likely in real life, but hang with me here). This means we are telling SQL Server things backwards. By the time it sees the `OrderCount` information it is already done with attributes for `CustomerID` and can't go back.

So, to fix things for us, we simply need to tell it about the attributes before we tell it about any more elements or raw text:

```
SELECT COUNT(*) AS 'CustomerID/@OrderCount',
       CustomerID
```

```
FROM Sales.SalesOrderHeader Orders
WHERE CustomerID = 29890 OR CustomerID = 30067
GROUP BY CustomerID
FOR XML PATH;
```

This probably seems counterintuitive, but, again, think of the order things are being written in. The attributes are written first, and then, and only then, can we write the lower-level information for the CustomerID element. Run it, and you'll see we get what we were after:

```
<row><CustomerID OrderCount="8">29890</CustomerID></row>
<row><CustomerID OrderCount="12">30067</CustomerID></row>
```

OrderCount has now been moved into the attribute position just as we desired, and the actual CustomerID is still raw text embedded in the element.

Follow the logic of the ordering of what you ask for a bit, because it works for most everything. So, if we wanted CustomerID to also be an attribute rather than raw text, but wanted it to be after Order-Count, we can do that — we just need to make sure that it comes after the OrderCount definition.

But Wait, There's More . . .

As I said earlier, XPath has its own complexity and is a book's worth to itself, but I don't want to leave you with just the preceding text and say that's all there is.

@ and / will give you a great deal of flexibility in building the XML output just the way you want it, and probably meet the need well for most beginning applications. If, however, you need something more, then there is still more out there waiting for you. For example, you can:

❑　"Wildcard" data such that it's all run together as text data without being treated as separate columns.

❑　Embed native XML data from XML data type columns.

❑　Use XPath node tests — these are special XPath directives that change the behavior of your data.

❑　Use the data() directive to allow multiple values to be run together as one data point in the XML.

❑　Utilize namespaces.

OPENXML

Many of the concepts we've covered in this chapter up to this point stray towards what I would call advanced SQL Server topics. OPENXML strays even farther, and thus we will not delve too deep into it here. I do, however, want to make sure you understand what it does and some of the situations it can be useful for. Keep in mind that many of the things OPENXML was created for are now handled in a more native way by simply placing your XML into a native XML data type and using the XML type methods we discussed earlier in the chapter.

When the original XML feature set was first introduced back in SQL Server 2000, the native XML data type did not yet exist. We had FOR XML, and thus significant power for turning relational data into XML, but we needed something to make XML addressable in a relational formal — that something was OPENXML.

OPENXML is a rowset function that opens your string much as other rowset functions (such as OPENQUERY and OPENROWSET) work. This means that you can join to an XML document, or even use it as the source of input data by using an INSERT..SELECT or a SELECT INTO. The major difference is that it requires you to use a couple of system stored procedures to prepare your document and clear the memory after you're done using it.

To set up your document, you use sp_xml_preparedocument. This moves the string into memory and pre-parses it for optimal query performance. The XML document will stay in memory until you explicitly say to remove it or you terminate the connection that sp_xml_preparedocument was called on. The syntax is pretty simple:

```
sp_xml_preparedocument @hdoc = <integer variable> OUTPUT,
[, @xmltext = <character data>]
[, @xpath_namespaces = <url to a namespace>]
```

> Note that, if you are going to provide a namespace URL, you need to wrap it in the
> < and > symbols at both ends (for example, <root xmlns:sql ="run: schemas-
> microsoft-com:xml-sql>).

The parameters of this sproc are fairly self-describing:

- ❑ @hdoc: If you've ever programmed to the Windows API (and to tons of other things, but this is a common one), then you've seen the h before — it's Hungarian notation for a handle. A handle is effectively a pointer to a block of memory where something (could be about anything) resides. In our case, this is the handle to the XML document that we've asked SQL Server to parse and hold onto for us. This is an output variable — the variable you reference here will, after the sproc returns, contain the handle to your XML — be sure to store it away, as you will need it when you make use of OPENXML.

- ❑ @xmltext: Is what it says it is — the actual XML that you want to parse and work with.

- ❑ @xpath_namespaces: Any namespace reference(s) your XML needs to operate correctly.

After calling this sproc and saving away the handle to your document, you're ready to make use of OPENXML. The syntax for it is slightly more complex:

```
OPENXML(<handle>,<XPath to base node>[, <mapping flags>])
[WITH (<Schema Declaration>|<Table Name>)]
```

We have pretty much already discussed the handle — this is going to be an integer value that you received as an output parameter for your sp_xml_preparedocument call.

When you make your call to OPENXML, you must supply a path to a node that will serve as a starting point for all your queries. The schema declaration can refer to all parts of the XML document by navigating relative to the base node you set here.

Next up are the mapping flags. These assist you in deciding whether you want to favor elements or attributes in your OPENXML results. The options are:

Byte Value	Description
0	Same as 1 except that you can't combine it with 2 or 8 (2 + 0 is still 2). This is the default.
1	Unless combined with 2 below, only attributes will be used. If there is no attribute with the name specified, then a NULL is returned. This can also be added to either 2 or 8 (or both) to combine behavior, but this option takes precedence over option 2. If XPath finds both an attribute and an element with the same name, the attribute wins.
2	Unless combined with 1 above, only elements will be used. If there is no element with the name specified, then a NULL is returned. This can also be added to either 1 or 8 (or both) to combine behavior. If combined with 1, then the attribute will be mapped if it exists. If no attribute exists, then the element will be used. If no element exists, then a NULL is returned.
8	Can be combined with 1 or 2 above. Consumed data should not be copied to the overflow property @mp:xmltext (you would have to use the MetaProperty schema item to retrieve this). If you're not going to use the MetaProperties — and most of the time you won't be — I recommend this option. It cuts a small (OK, *very* small) amount of overhead out of the operation.

Finally comes the schema or table. If you're defining a schema and are not familiar with XPath, this part can be a bit tricky. Fortunately, this particular XPath use isn't very complex and should become second nature fairly quickly (it works a lot like directories do in Windows).

The schema can vary somewhat in the way you declare it. The definition is declared as:

```
WITH (
<Column Name> <data type> [{<Column XPath>|<MetaProperty>}]
[,<Column Name> <data type> [{<Column XPath>|<MetaProperty>}]
  ...
```

❑   The column name is just that — the name of the attribute or element you are retrieving. This will also serve as the name you refer to when you build your SELECT list, perform JOINs, and so on.

❑   The data type is any valid SQL Server data type. Because XML can have data types that are not equivalents of those in SQL Server, an automatic coercion will take place if necessary, but this is usually predictable.

❑   The column XPath is the XPath pattern (relative to the node you established as the starting point for your OPENXML function) that gets you to the node you want for your column — whether an element or attribute gets used is dependent on the flags parameter as described earlier. If this is left off, then SQL Server assumes you want the current node as defined as the starting point for your OPENXML statement.

❑ MetaProperties are a set of special variables that you can refer to in your OPENXML queries. They describe various aspects of whatever part of the XML DOM you're interested in. To use them, just enclose them in single quotes and put them in the place of the column XPath. Available MetaProperties include:

 ❑ @mp:id: Don't confuse this with the XML id that we looked at with EXPLICIT. While this property serves a similar function, it is a unique identifier (within the scope of the document) of the DOM node. The difference is that this value is system generated — as such, you can be sure it is there. It is guaranteed to refer to the same XML node as long as the document remains in memory. If the id is zero, it is the root node (its @mp:parentid property, as referred to below, will be NULL).

 ❑ @mp:parentid: This is the same as above, only for the parent.

 ❑ @mp:localname: Provides the non-fully qualified name of the node. It is used with prefix and namespace URI (Uniform Resource Identifier — you'll usually see it starting with URN) to name element or attribute nodes.

 ❑ @mp:parentlocalname: This is the same as above, only for the parent.

 ❑ @mp:namespaceuri: Provides the namespace URI of the current element. If the value of this attribute is NULL, no namespace is present.

 ❑ @mp:parentnamespaceuri: This is the same as above, only for the parent.

 ❑ @mp:prefix: Stores the namespace prefix of the current element name.

 ❑ @mp:prev: Stores the mp:id of the previous sibling relative to a node. Using this, you can tell something about the ordering of the elements at the current level of the hierarchy. For example, if the value of @mp:prev is NULL, then you are at the first node for this level of the tree.

 ❑ @mp:xmltext: This MetaProperty is used for processing purposes, and contains the actual XML for the current element.

Of course, you can always save yourself a ton of work by bypassing all these parameters. You get to do this if you have a table that directly relates (names and data types) to the XPath starting point that you've specified in your XML. If you do have such a table, you can just name it and SQL Server will make the translation for you!

OK, that's a lot to handle, but we're not quite finished yet. You see, when you're all done with your XML, you need to call sp_xml_removedocument to clean up the memory where your XML document was stored. Thankfully, the syntax is incredibly easy:

```
sp_xml_removedocument [hdoc = ]<handle of XML doc>
```

I can't stress enough how important it is to get in the habit of always cleaning up after yourself. I know that, in saying that, I probably sound like your mother. Well, like your mother, SQL Server will clean up after you some, but, like your mother, SQL Server won't clean up after you every time. SQL Server will clean things up when you terminate the connection, but what if you are using connection pooling? Some connections may never go away if your system is under load. It's an easy sproc to implement, so do it — every time!

OK, I'm sure you've been bored waiting for me to get to how you really make use of this — so now it's time for the all-important example.

Imagine that you are merging with another company and need to import some of their data into your system. For this example, we'll say that we're working on importing a few `shippers` that they have and our company doesn't. For our example, we're going to import the rows into the Accounting database that we created back in Chapter 5 (you can find the create syntax for the table with the Chapter 5 code — only the `Shippers` table should be required for this to work). A sample of what our script might look like to import these from an XML document might be:

```
USE Accounting;

DECLARE @idoc      int;
DECLARE @xmldoc    nvarchar(4000);

-- define the XML document
SET @xmldoc = '
<ROOT>
<Shipper ShipperID="100" CompanyName="Billy Bob&apos;s Great Shipping"/>
<Shipper ShipperID="101" CompanyName="Fred&apos;s Freight"/>
</ROOT>
';

--Load and parse the XML document in memory
EXEC sp_xml_preparedocument @idoc OUTPUT, @xmldoc;

--List out what our shippers table looks like before the insert
SELECT * FROM Shippers;

-- ShipperID is an IDENTITY column, so we need to allow direct updates
SET IDENTITY_INSERT Shippers ON

--See our XML data in a tabular format
SELECT * FROM OPENXML (@idoc, '/ROOT/Shipper', 0) WITH (
    ShipperID           int,
    CompanyName         nvarchar(40));

--Perform and insert based on that data
INSERT INTO Shippers
(ShipperID, ShipperName)
SELECT * FROM OPENXML (@idoc, '/ROOT/Shipper', 0) WITH (
    ShipperID           int,
    CompanyName         nvarchar(40));

--Set things back to normal
SET IDENTITY_INSERT Shippers OFF;

--Now look at the Shippers table after our insert
SELECT * FROM Shippers;

--Now clear the XML document from memory
EXEC sp_xml_removedocument @idoc;
```

The final result set from this looks just like what we wanted:

```
ShipperID    ShipperName                     DateInSystem
-----------  ------------------------------  -----------------------
1            United Parcel Service           2008-11-05 18:51:42.673

(1 row(s) affected)

ShipperID    CompanyName
-----------  --------------------------------------
100          Billy Bob's Great Shipping
101          Fred's Freight

(2 row(s) affected)

(2 row(s) affected)

ShipperID    ShipperName                     DateInSystem
-----------  ------------------------------  -----------------------
1            United Parcel Service           2008-11-05 18:51:42.673
100          Billy Bob's Great Shipping      2008-11-09 20:56:29.177
101          Fred's Freight                  2008-11-09 20:56:29.177

(3 row(s) affected)
```

We now have one more way to get XML query results, and a way to get XML turned into relational data. Keep in mind that OPENXML has other parameters and features for you to explore as you continue on your SQL Server journey.

A Brief Word on XSLT

Well now, this takes us to the last, but far and away the most complex of the things we're dealing with in this chapter. The Extensible Stylesheet Language Transformations side of things is something of a little extra toss into the XML world that increases the power of XML multifold. You see, using XSLT, we can transform our XML document into other forms.

To get us going on a quick start here, let's take a look at an XML document produced from Microsoft's old Northwind database example:

```xml
<?xml version="1.0" encoding="UTF-8"?>
<root>
 <Customer CustomerID="ALFKI" CompanyName="Alfreds Futterkiste">
        <Products ProductID="28" ProductName="Rössle Sauerkraut"/>
        <Products ProductID="39" ProductName="Chartreuse verte"/>
        <Products ProductID="46" ProductName="Spegesild"/>
 </Customer>
 <Customer CustomerID="BLONP" CompanyName="Blondesddsl père et fils">
        <Products ProductID="28" ProductName="Rössle Sauerkraut"/>
        <Products ProductID="29" ProductName="Thüringer Rostbratwurst"/>
        <Products ProductID="31" ProductName="Gorgonzola Telino"/>
        <Products ProductID="38" ProductName="Côte de Blaye"/>
        <Products ProductID="39" ProductName="Chartreuse verte"/>
        <Products ProductID="41" ProductName="Jack&apos;s New England Clam Chowder"/>
        <Products ProductID="46" ProductName="Spegesild"/>
        <Products ProductID="49" ProductName="Maxilaku"/>
 </Customer>
</root>
```

What we have here is something XML does very well — hierarchies. In this case, we have a situation where customers have ordered different products. What our XML document is laid out to tell us is what products our customers have purchased. It seems like a reasonable question — doesn't it?

Note that this is a purely visual example — you do not need to load the Northwind samples here as this was purely an "in book" example.

Now, time for me to twist things on you a bit — what if I change the question to be more along the lines of "Which customers have ordered each product?" Now our perspective has changed dramatically. At this point, a much better hierarchy would be one that had the products on the outside and the customers on the inside. Under that scenario, it would be our customers (rather than our products) that were repeated multiple times (once for each product), but it would get more to the root of our question.

With XML coupled with XSL transformations, this is no big deal. You see, I don't want to change the data that I'm looking at at all — I just need to *transform* my XML document so that I can *look* at it differently.

Don't confuse my saying "The way I look at the data" to mean how I visually look at it — what I'm talking about is more of how the data is perceived. Part of that is just how ready the data is to be used in a particular fashion. With our customers at the top of the hierarchy, our data doesn't seem very ready for use to answer questions that are product focused. What I need is to change the data to be product-focused — just like my questions.

So let's look back at the same exact data, but transformed into another look:

```xml
<?xml version="1.0" encoding="UTF-8"?>
<root>
 <Products ProductID="28" ProductName="Rössle Sauerkraut">
        <Customer CustomerID="ALFKI" CompanyName="Alfreds Futterkiste"/>
        <Customer CustomerID="BLONP" CompanyName="Blondesddsl père et fils"/>
 </Products>
 <Products ProductID="29" ProductName="Thüringer Rostbratwurst">
        <Customer CustomerID="BLONP" CompanyName="Blondesddsl père et fils"/>
 </Products>
 <Products ProductID="31" ProductName="Gorgonzola Telino">
        <Customer CustomerID="BLONP" CompanyName="Blondesddsl père et fils"/>
 </Products>
 <Products ProductID="38" ProductName="Côte de Blaye">
        <Customer CustomerID="BLONP" CompanyName="Blondesddsl père et fils"/>
 </Products>
 <Products ProductID="39" ProductName="Chartreuse verte">
        <Customer CustomerID="ALFKI" CompanyName="Alfreds Futterkiste"/>
        <Customer CustomerID="BLONP" CompanyName="Blondesddsl père et fils"/>
 </Products>
 <Products ProductID="41" ProductName="Jack&apos;s New England Clam Chowder">
        <Customer CustomerID="BLONP" CompanyName="Blondesddsl père et fils"/>
 </Products>
 <Products ProductID="46" ProductName="Spegesild">
        <Customer CustomerID="ALFKI" CompanyName="Alfreds Futterkiste"/>
        <Customer CustomerID="BLONP" CompanyName="Blondesddsl père et fils"/>
 </Products>
 <Products ProductID="49" ProductName="Maxilaku">
        <Customer CustomerID="BLONP" CompanyName="Blondesddsl père et fils"/>
 </Products>
 </root>
```

Again, this is the same data — just a different perspective.

But hang on a sec — why limit ourselves to just XML? While going over every type of transformation you could do is well outside the scope of this book, it is important to understand that XSL transforms are possible to and from a wide variety of formats. You can transform to other XML layouts, but you can also transform to other formats entirely such as CSV files or even a Word document.

> Note that I've presented XSLT here just as a concept. SQL Server does very little with XSLT — focusing on the data rather than how the data is presented. The key thing to take from this is the understanding that what is fundamentally the same data may be formatted in XML many different ways, and that XSLT provides a means for transforming XML into alternative layouts within XML as well as to non-XML formats.

Summary

Well, there you have an extreme whirlwind tour of XML, DTDs, schemas, and a bit of XPath to boot. It is impossible in one chapter to address a topic as broad as XML and its related technologies; however, I hope this chapter has at least provided insight into what XML is all about and what is involved in making use of it at the most basic level.

XML is one of the most important technologies to hit the industry in the last 10 or more years. It provides a flexible, very transportable way of describing data. This ease of description will help to facilitate not only the website development that you hear so much about, but also the kind of behind-the-scenes information exchange that businesses have longed for for a very long time indeed.

Reporting for Duty, Sir!
A Look At Reporting Services

After all the queries have been written, after all the stored procedures have been run, there remains a rather important thing we need to do in order to make our data useful — make it available to end users.

Reporting is one of those things that seems incredibly simple, but turns out to be rather tricky. You see, you can't simply start sticking numbers in front of people's faces; the numbers must make sense and, if at all possible, capture the attention of the person for whom you're reporting. To produce reports that actually get used and, therefore, are useful, there are a few things to keep in mind:

❑   **Use just the right amount of data:** Do not try to do too much in one report; nor should you do too little. A report that is a jumble of numbers is going to quickly lose a reader's attention, and you'll find that it doesn't get utilized after the first few times it is generated. Likewise, a barren report will get just a glance and get tossed without any real thought. Find a balance of mixing the right amount of data with the right data.

❑   **Make it appealing:** Sad as it is to say, another important element in reporting is what one of my daughters would call making it "prettiful" — which is to say, making it look nice and pleasing to the eye. An ugly report is a dead report.

In this chapter, we're going to be taking a look at the Reporting Services tools that first appeared as a downloadable web add-on in SQL Server 2000, and became a core part of the product in SQL Server 2005. As with all the "add-on" features of SQL Server that we cover in this book, you'll find the coverage here to be largely something of "a taste of what's possible" — there is simply too much to cover to get it all in one chapter of a much larger book. If you find that this "taste" whets your appetite, I cover some of the more advanced topics a bit more in depth in *Professional SQL Server 2008 Programming*; or consider reading a book dedicated specifically to Reporting Services such as *Professional SQL Server Reporting Services*.

Reporting Services 101

Odds are that you've already generated some reports in your day. They may have been paper reports off a printer (perhaps in something as rudimentary as Access's reporting area — which is actually one of the best parts of Access to me). They may have been off a rather robust reporting engine such as Crystal Reports. Even if you haven't used tools that fancy, one can argue that handing your boss the printout from a stored procedure is essentially a very simple (and not necessarily nice looking) report — I would tend to agree with that argument.

The reality, however, is that our managers and coworkers today expect something more. This is where Reporting Services comes in. Reporting Services really has two different varieties of operation:

❑ **Report Models:** This is making use of a relatively simple, web-driven interface that is meant to allow end users to create their own simple reports.

❑ **Reports generated in Visual Studio:** While this doesn't necessarily mean you have to write code (you can actually create simple reports using drag-and-drop functionality — something we'll do in this chapter as an example — you can design fairly robust reports.

Note that, while your users can eventually access these reports from the same Reporting Services Web host, they are based on somewhat different architectures (and, as you will see, are created in much different fashions).

In addition, Reporting Services provides features for pre-generating reports (handy if the queries that underlie the report take a while to run) as well as distributing the report via e-mail.

Building Simple Report Models

To create a simple model, start by opening the Business Intelligence Studio.

Note that this is entirely different from the SQL Server Management Studio that we've been working with thus far. The Business Intelligence Studio is a different work area that is highly developer- (rather than administrator-) focused; indeed, it is a form of Visual Studio that just has project templates oriented around many of the "extra" services that SQL Server offers. In addition to the work we'll do with the Business Intelligence Studio in this chapter, we will also visit it some to work with Integration Services in Chapter 18.

Choose File ➪ New Project, and you should bring up the dialog shown in Figure 17-1.

Choose an appropriate name (I've gone with the rather descript ReportModelProject), and click OK. This will bring you to what should look like an everyday, run-of-the-mill Visual Studio development environment.

> **Note that the exact appearance of the dialog shown in Figure 17-1 may vary somewhat depending on whether you have Visual Studio installed and, if so, which specific languages and templates you've installed. The image is of the most generic SQL Server–only installation.**

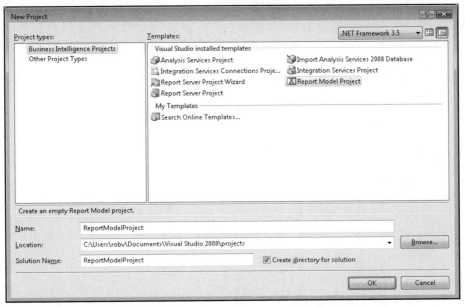

Figure 17-1

If your Visual Studio environment is still in its default configuration, you should see the Solution Explorer on the top-right side. Right-click Data Sources and choose Add New Data Source, as shown in Figure 17-2.

Figure 17-2

This will probably (unless you've already been here before and checked the "Don't show me this page again" box) bring you up to a Welcome dialog box for the Data Source Wizard. Click Next to get to the start of the meaty stuff — the data source selection page of the Data Source Wizard. There is, however, one problem; we don't have any data sources as yet (as we see in Figure 17-3).

It probably goes without saying that, without any existing data connections to choose from, we really have no choice but to click New.

> *The first time I saw this next dialog, I was mildly surprised to see that it was a different new connection dialog than had been used repeatedly in the Management Studio; nonetheless, it does contain the same basic elements, just in a slightly different visual package. (In short, don't worry if it looks a little different.)*

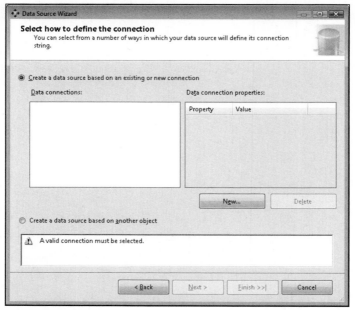

Figure 17-3

This brings us up to the Connection Manager shown in Figure 17-4.

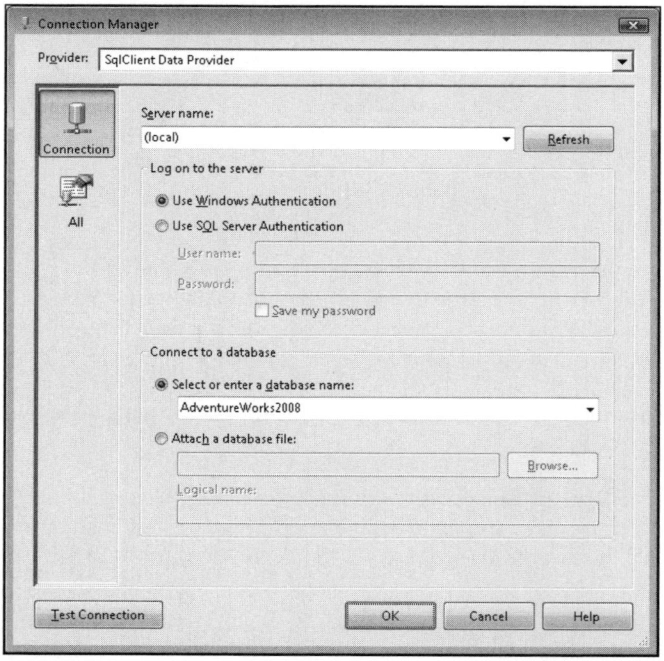

Figure 17-4

While the concepts are the same as we've seen in a few other places in the book, there are one or two new things here, so let's take a look at several key elements to this dialog.

- **Server name:** This one is what it sounds like and is the same as we've seen before. Name the server you want to connect to for this connection, or, if you're wanting to connect to the default instance of SQL Server for the local server, you can also use the aliases of "(local)" or "." (a simple period).

- **Windows/SQL Server Authentication:** Choose the authentication type to connect to your server. Microsoft (and, I must admit, me too) would rather you used Windows Authentication, but if your server is not in your domain or if your administrator is not granting rights directly to your Windows login, then you can use an administrator-supplied SQL Server–specific username and password (we've used MyLogin and MyPassword on several occasions elsewhere in the book).

- **Connect to a database:** Now things get even more interesting. Here you can either continue down the logical path of selecting a database on the server you have chosen, or you can choose to connect directly to an mdf file (in which case the SQL Server Express engine takes care of translating for you).

In my case, I've selected the local server and our old friend, the AdventureWorks2008 database.

Go ahead and click OK, and we see a different Data Source Wizard dialog than we did the first time. (See Figure 17-5.)

Our example only had the connection we just created, but we could, if desired, actually create several connections, and then choose between them. Note also the summary of the data connection properties on the right-hand side of the dialog.

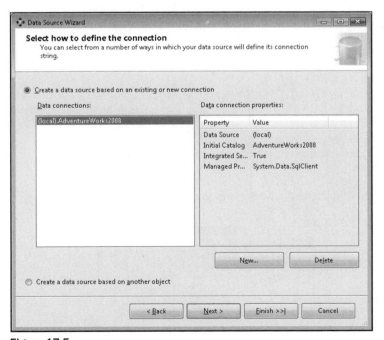

Figure 17-5

Click Next, and it brings you to the final dialog of the Wizard, as shown in Figure 17-6.

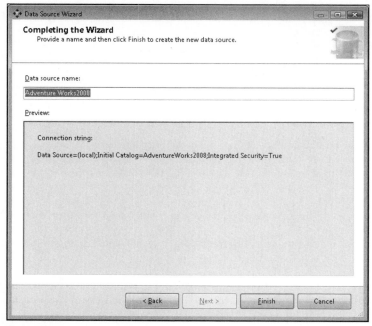

Figure 17-6

Note that the default name happens to be the database we chose, but this is truly just a name for the data source — we can call this data source whatever we want and it would still be connecting to the AdventureWorks2008 database on the local server.

> *Also take note of how it has built a connection string for us. Connection strings are a fundamental concept in all modern forms of database connectivity — virtually every connectivity model (.NET managed providers, OLE DB, ODBC, for example) uses a connection string at some level. If we had chosen some different options — for example, used a SQL Server username and password instead of Windows security — then our connection string would use a few different parameters and, of course, pass some different values.*

Go ahead and click Finish, and we have our data source for our project, as shown in Figure 17-7.

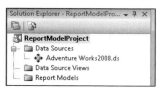

Figure 17-7

If you ponder Figure 17-7 for a moment, you'll notice that there is a bit more to our Report Model project than just data sources; indeed, we now need to take the next step and create a *Data Source view*.

Data Source Views

A Data Source view has a slight similarity to the views we learned about in Chapter 10. In particular, it can be used to provide users access to data, but can filter what data they actually see. If we give them access to the entire data source, then they are able to see all data available to that data source. Data Source views allow us to filter the data source down to just a subset of its original list of available objects.

To add our Data Source view, simply right-click Data Source View and select Add New Data Source View (tricky, isn't it?), as shown in Figure 17-8.

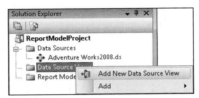

Figure 17-8

We get another of those silly "Welcome to the Wizard" dialogs, so just click Next and you'll arrive at a dialog that you've essentially already seen before — one that is basically identical (only one or two very subtle cosmetic differences) to one we had partway through creating our data source — Figure 17-5.

Accept the default, and then click through to the Select Tables and Views dialog shown in Figure 17-9. This one, as the name suggests, allows us to specify which tables and views are going to be available to end users of the Report Model we're building.

Start by selecting SalesOrderDetail and then use the > button to move that into the Selected Objects column. Next, click the Add Related Tables button and see what happens. SQL Server will use the rules that it knows about the relationships between the tables (based on defined foreign keys) to figure out what tables are related to the one or more tables we had already selected. In this case, it chose SalesOrderHeader (the parent of our SalesOrderDetail table) and SpecialOfferProduct (to which SalesOrderDetail also has a foreign key). For the report we'll be building, we don't need the SpecialOfferProduct table, so remove that by selecting that table and using the < button. Finally, add the Customer, Person and Product tables to finish catching up with the tables I have selected in Figure 17-9.

> *Don't worry about the Filter or "Show system objects" options in this table; both are pretty harmless. The short rendition is that the filter just filters down the object list to make it easy to deal with databases that have a very large number of objects to show. The "Show system objects" option is just that — it allows you to include system objects in the Report Model (which seems pretty silly to me for the vast, vast majority of applications out there).*

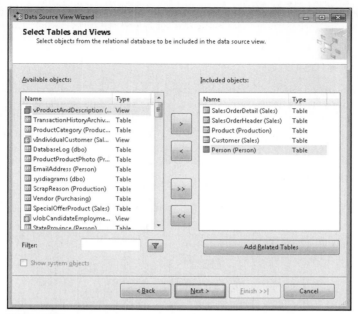

Figure 17-9

Click Next, and we're finally at the Completing the Wizard dialog shown in Figure 17-10. This dialog is pretty much just synopsizing what's to be included in this Data Source view before you finalize it and essentially tell SQL Server "Yeah, that's really what I mean!"

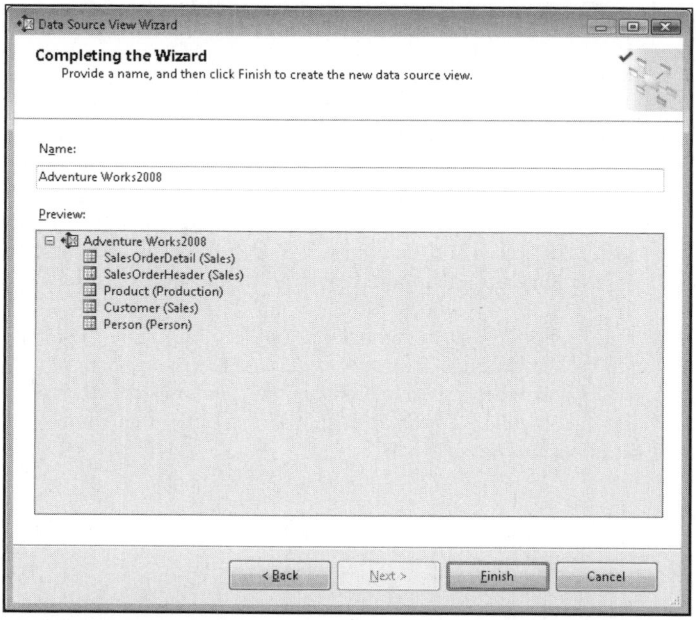

Figure 17-10

Now click Finish and the Data Source view is actually constructed and added to our Report Model Project. While we now have a workable view, the view has some issues we need to deal with prior to using it in our data model; there are no formal relationships between the `Product` table and the other tables in the Data Source view. Let's fix that....

Manipulating Relationships Between Objects In Data Source Views

While the wizard tries to put information together about our Data Source view, it has to base its information on the column names, types, and foreign key references in the table. While foreign keys are great for giving us a well-defined description of the relationship between two tables, there are often cases where there is, for some reason, a relationship that does not have a formal foreign key defined on it. In the case of the Data Source view we just created, we have no formal foreign key between `Products` and `SalesOrderHeader` (`ProductSpecialOffer` joins to both, and that is the only formal way they are related). The ProductID is, however, a viable join item between the two tables, so we need to add that reference to the Data Source view.

Start by right clicking on our new Data Source view in the Project Explorer, and select View Designer as shown in Figure 17-11.

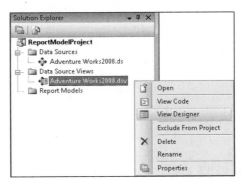

Figure 17-11

Visual Studio brings us up a visual representation of the tables involved in our Data Source view, and, as you can see in Figure 17-12, it is unaware of the relationship between `SalesOrderDetail` and `Product`.

Click and drag ProductID from the `SalesOrderDetail` table onto the ProductID in the `Product` table, and SQL Server will bring up a dialog to confirm the relationship. Click OK and the relationship should now be shown (as it is in Figure 17-13).

> Note that the click-and-drag order to relate tables is the opposite of what is used in most diagramming tools where you establish foreign keys. In most diagramming environments, you drag from the parent table to the child; the Data Source view designer works just the opposite.

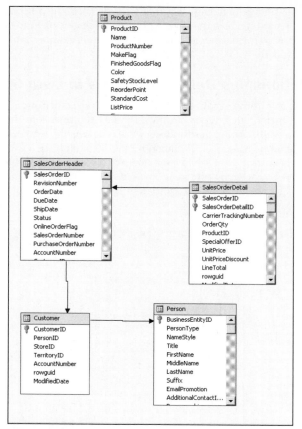

Figure 17-12

Building the Data Model

At this point, we're ready to create the actual Report Model. As we did with data source and Data Source view, simply right-click the Report Model node of the Solution Explorer tree and select Add New Report Model, as shown in Figure 17-14.

At the start of defining a Report Model, we get yet another one of those "welcome" dialogs. Click through that and you'll be at the relatively meaty Select Data Source View dialog shown in Figure 17-15. Not surprisingly, the only one that shows is the one just created (still called AdventureWorks2008).

Go ahead and select our one Data Source view and click Next to move on to the next dialog (shown in Figure 17-16), the report model generation rules.

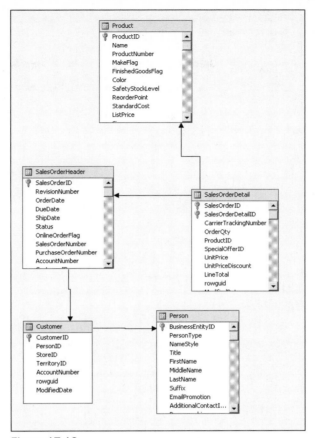

Figure 17-13

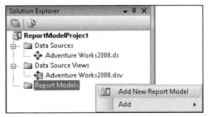

Figure 17-14

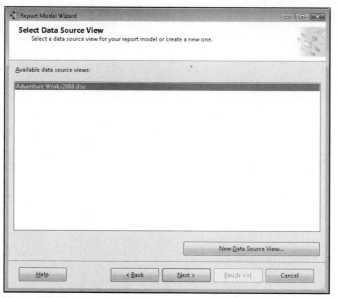

Figure 17-15

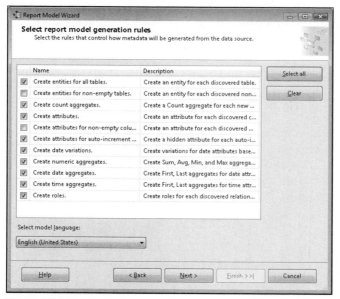

Figure 17-16

The report model generation rules determine things like what rollups are available in your Report Model, as well as other guides to assist the generation of end-user reports. Also make note of your ability to control the default language for your Report Model (handy for multinational companies or companies where you want to generate reporting for languages beyond the base install for your server).

Go ahead and accept the defaults here by clicking Next, and we move on to the Collect Model Statistics dialog. The Collect Model Statistics dialog gives us two options:

❑ **Update statistics before generating:** This will cause all statistics for the Data Source view to be updated prior to the Report Model actually being built. Each Data Source view keeps a set of statistics on the underlying data (such as how wide columns are, what data types are used, and such), and these statistics are utilized to make decisions on how exactly to best build the Report Model. You'll want to choose this option if it is the first time you're utilizing the Data Source view (as is true for us since we just created it) or if significant changes have happened since the last time the Data Source view was utilized.

❑ **Use current model statistics in the data source view:** This just makes use of what's already there. Depending on how many tables and indexes are involved, this can save a lot of time in getting the report generated (since you don't have to wait on all the statistics to be updated), but it runs the risk of the Report Model making assumptions that are out of date regarding the makeup of your data.

Whether you rely on existing statistics vs. going ahead and updating your statistics is a somewhat advanced concept. As such, I'm going to recommend that you go with the default here and always update your statistics unless you know exactly why you are skipping that and believe you understand the ramifications of doing so. For most installations, not updating the statistics in this scenario is not going to be a big deal, but it is one of those things that can very subtly reach out and bite you, so better safe than sorry.

The next (and final) dialog is the Completing the Wizard dialog. Name your Report Model (I've chosen AdventureWorks2008 Report Model — original, eh?) and click Run, and your Report Model will be generated as shown in Figure 17-17.

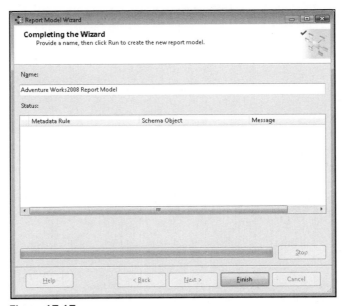

Figure 17-17

Note that other than some messages that flash by while the report is generating, there will be very little to see in this dialog unless something has gone wrong (in which case, you'll see related messages reflected in the dialog). Click Finish, and we can begin to see the results of what we just created, which should look something like Figure 17-18.

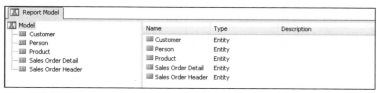

Figure 17-18

Be sure to take the time to explore the Report Model. SQL Server will make assumptions about what you do and do not want to have shown, and it will not always make the right choice for your particular database usage. Look at what it has included, what it has added, and what it has generated in the way of derived attributes (rollups and such).

Let's take a quick look at an example of a value that will default to hidden when the wizard is done building the model, but that is sometimes useful in our reports. Start by navigating to the SalesOrder-Header table. Notice how the Sales Order ID column is grayed out. If you click on it and check the property window shown in Figure 17-19, you should notice that this possibly important field has been defined as being hidden.

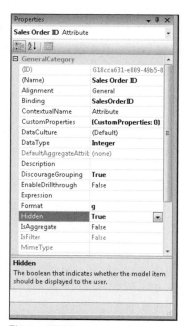

Figure 17-19

One could spend an entire chapter just going over the nuances of each entity of the model and all the attributes within it. Take particular note of how SQL Server automatically breaks down well understood attributes (such as dates) to smaller attributes (say, month, day, and year) based on well understood common uses of the underlying data type.

As it happens, we probably do want this field hidden, but you often see instances where something like the Sales Order ID, although system generated, would be the order number a customer would see on an invoice. Many identity values are artificial, "under the covers" constructs, and thus why SQL Server assumes you wouldn't want to show this in the report.

Deploying Our Model

Well, building a Report Model is all well and good, but if no one can get at it, it serves little purpose (much like designing a stored procedure, but never actually adding it to your database). To make our report usable to end users, we must *deploy* it.

Fortunately deploying our model couldn't get much easier. Indeed, the hard part is knowing that you need to and then finding the command to do so. To deploy, simply right-click in a white space area of the Solution Explorer (or on our actual report), or right-click the project name and choose Deploy. You can watch the progress of the deploy in the output window of Visual Studio:

```
Build complete -- 0 errors, 0 warnings
------ Build started: Project: ReportModelProject, Configuration: Production ------
Build complete -- 0 errors, 0 warnings
------ Deploy started: Project: ReportModelProject, Configuration: Production
------
Deploying to http://localhost/ReportServer
Deploying data source 'http://localhost/ReportServer/Data Sources/Adventure
Works2008'.
Deploying model 'AdventureWorks2008 Report Model.smdl'.
Deploy complete -- 0 errors, 0 warnings
========== Build: 1 succeeded, 0 failed, 0 up-to-date, 0 skipped ==========
========== Deploy: 1 succeeded, 0 failed, 0 skipped ==========
```

Report Creation

Our Report Model is, of course, not itself a report. Instead, it merely facilitates reports (and, considering there are lots of business type people who understand reports, but not databases, facilitating reports can be a powerful thing). Now that it is deployed, we can generate many reports from just the one model.

To see and generate reports, you need to leave the Business Intelligence Studio and actually visit the reporting user interface — which is basically just a Website. Navigate to http://<your reporting server host>/reports — in my case, I have it right on my local system, so I can get there by navigating to http://localhost/reports, as shown in Figure 17-20.

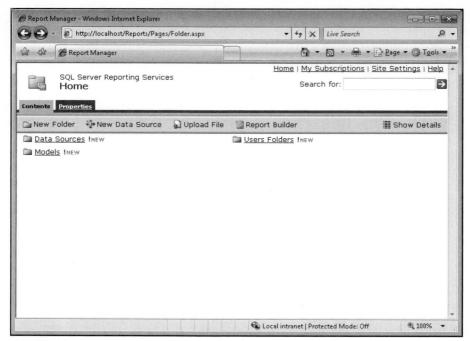

Figure 17-20

This is essentially the home page for user reports and such. Notice right away the "New!" icons next to our data sources and models (a strong hint that our deploy actually worked — amazing!). Go ahead and click on Report Builder.

> The Report Builder relies on a small applet that will try to install on your system the first time you navigate to the Report Builder. You must accept the installation of the applet if you want to use the Report Builder.

On the right-hand side of the applet that comes up, you are asked to select the source of your report data. Go ahead and select the model you just created, and click OK to get the default report template. This is a fairly robust drag-and-drop design environment that will let you explore between the tables you made available in your Report Model and choose columns you can then drag into your report. Also take note of the far right of the report layout pane. This allows you to select between a few common layouts from which to start your report.

We're going to stick with a table report (the default as it happens), and build a relatively simple report listing all orders that paid with some method other than a credit card.

Start by navigating to each table and dragging the relevant columns into the table:

- ❏ SalesOrderHeader.SalesOrderNumber
- ❏ Person.LastName
- ❏ Person.FirstName
- ❏ Product.ProductNumber
- ❏ Product.Name
- ❏ SalesOrderHeader.OrderDate
- ❏ SalesOrderHeader.DueDate

Also go ahead and click in the title area and add the title, Non Credit Card Orders. When you're done, you should wind up with something that looks like Figure 17-21 (note that I've resized columns a bit to help them fit on a page). Notice also how the fields you have used are bolded in the Fields pane of the Explorer window.

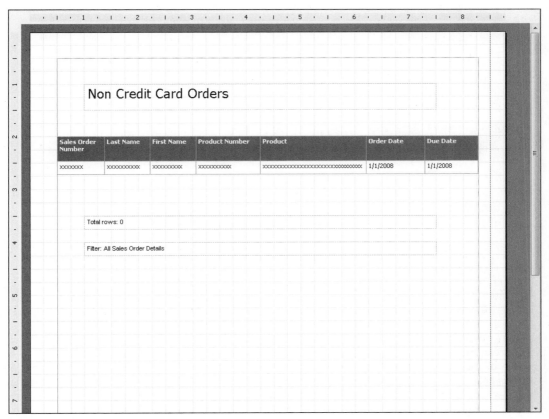

Figure 17-21

> Depending on how your report server is configured, the report may be runnable just with what we've put in thus far. For most systems, however, there is likely to be a restriction that requires you to filter your results in some manner (to avoid excessive loads) before executing the report.

To add a filter, click on the Filter icon at the top of the Report Designer window. This brings up the Filter Data dialog. Drag the Credit Card ID field into the main pane of the dialog. This sets us up to use the Credit Card ID as a filter, but we still need to set the exact filter criteria. The default comparison is an equals, which doesn't meet our need, so click on the word equals and select the Is Empty option as shown in Figure 17-22, then click OK.

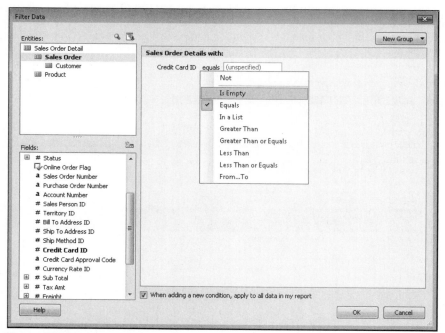

Figure 17-22

When you have this done, click Run Report, and you'll see the fruits of our labor, as shown in Figure 17-23.

We, do, however, have a minor problem — the report has quite a few pages (it will not show how many for sure until we navigate to the end), and the information isn't very useful the way it is currently sorted. No problem! The Report Builder makes this easy as cake to deal with by simply clicking the up/down arrows next to the columns of the report. In my case, I'm going to sort based on the person's last name, as shown in Figure 17-24. Notice how the report is automatically grouped where it makes sense (avoiding repeating values).

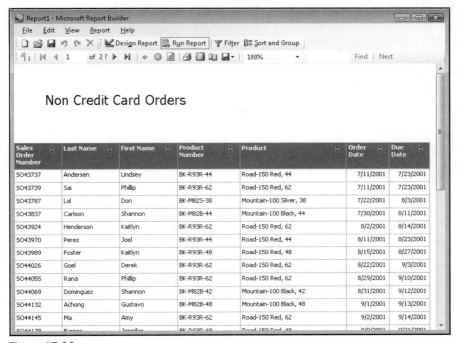

Figure 17-23

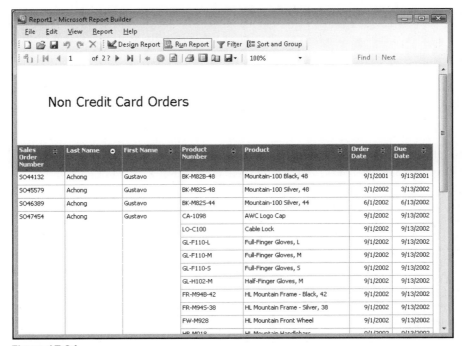

Figure 17-24

Play around with the report some, and you'll find that you can easily re-sort the result in other ways. Note that we also could have defined a default sort order — for example, sorting those with the soonest due date — by setting it in the Sort and Group dialog (next to Filter in the toolbar).

A Few Last Words on Report Models

Report Models are certainly not the catch-all, end-all of reporting. It is, however, a very cool feature in the sense that you can expose data to your end users in a somewhat controlled fashion (they don't see any more than you put in the data source, and access to the data source is secured such that you can control which users see which data sources), but still allow them to create specific reports of their own. Report models offer a very nice option for "quick and dirty" reports.

Finally, keep in mind that we generated only one very simple report for just the most simplistic of layouts. Report Models also allow for basic graphing and matrix reporting as well.

Report Server Projects

Report Models can be considered to be "scratching the surface" of things — Reporting Services has much more flexibility than that. (Indeed, I'm sure there are entire books around just on Reporting Services; there is that much to it.) In addition to what we've already seen, the Business Intelligence Development Studio will allow you to create Report Server Projects.

As I mentioned before, there are entire books around just this subject, so the approach we're going to take here is to give you something of a little taste of the possibilities through another simple example. (Indeed, we're just going to do the same example using the project method.)

At this point, you should be fairly comfortable with several of the concepts we're going to use here, so I'll spare you the copious screenshots such as those you've already endured, and get to the nitty-gritty of what needs to be done to get us up to the point of new stuff:

1. Open a new project using the Report Server Project template in the Business Intelligence Development Studio (note that this is different from the Report *Model* project we used earlier).

2. Create a new data source against our AdventureWorks2008 database. (Right-click the Shared Data Source folder and fill in the dialog — use the Edit button if you want the helpful dialog to build your connection string, or you can just copy the connection string from earlier in the chapter). Note that, to deploy this new data source, you're going to need to name it something other than the name you used earlier in the chapter (assuming you did that example).

3. Right-click the Reports folder and choose Add New Report. This takes you to the Report Wizard — click Next to move on to the Data Source Selection screen. Select the data source you just created. Then click Next.

This should bring you to the query dialog shown in Figure 17-25.

I have, of course, added the query in myself; this one should roughly duplicate the report we built in the Report Model section including the filter to just unshipped orders. I could have also entered the query builder and, while in the builder, even executed the query to verify that my query returned the expected data. Note that we also could have executed a stored procedure at this point or gone directly against a specific table.

Figure 17-25

Click next and accept the Tabular report type, and we come to the Table Design Wizard shown in Figure 17-26.

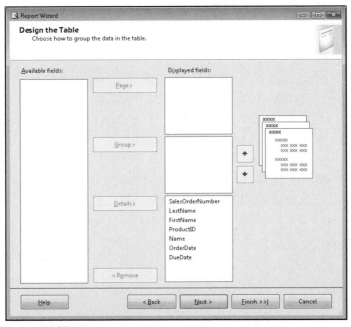

Figure 17-26

Because the query has already trimmed things down to just the columns we need (and, as it happens, even grabbed them in proper order, but we could reorder things if we wanted to), I just selected everything and moved everything into the details box.

The Page and Group fields here would allow us to set up sort hierarchies. For example, if we wanted everything to go onto separate pages based on individual customers (say, for the sales person to understand the status of their particular customers) we could move Company Name up to the Page level. Likewise, we might instead do groupings (instead of pages) based on product name so that our people pulling the orders from inventory can grab all the product needed to fill all outstanding orders in one trip.

Again, click Next, and we are presented with a Table Style dialog. Choose whatever is of your liking (I'm just going to stick with Slate) and again click Next to be greeted with the summary of what your report selections were. Change the name to "Non Credit Card Orders", and click finish to create the report definition, as shown in Figure 17-27 (yours may look a tad different if you chose a different style than I did).

The Toolbox and Report Data panes may be located slightly differently depending on your particular configuration of Visual Studio. Both have been made visible and docked here for demonstration purposes.

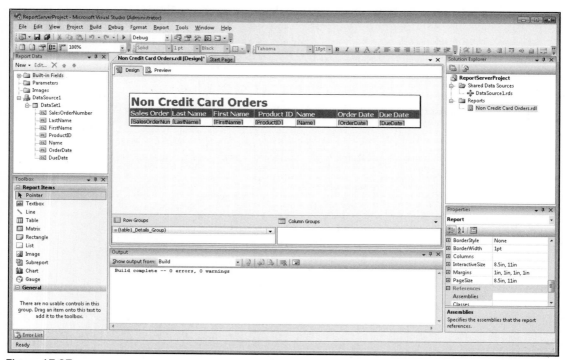

Figure 17-27

If you're familiar with other report designers, this will seem mildly familiar, as the WYSIWYG editor we're presented with here is somewhat standard fare for report designers (certainly some are more robust, but the presentation of the basics is pretty typical). Notice, however, that the name we selected for the report became the default header for the report.

If you go ahead and click the preview tab for the report, you'll find that it is largely the same as the report we generated using the Report Model notion. There are, however, some formatting areas where the defaults of the report modeler are perhaps a tad better than we have here — in particular, it makes no sense for us to report the time as part of the date if the time is always going to be midnight. With that in mind, let's make some alterations to the Wizard-generated report.

Try It Out   Altering Report Projects

We have a really great start to our report generated in seconds by the wizard. It is not, however, perfect. We want to format our dates more appropriately.

1. Right-click the first date field (Order Date) and select Text Box Properties to bring up the dialog shown in Figure 17-28.

2. Click on the fx to indicate that we want to change the output to be that of a function result, bringing up our function dialog, as shown in Figure 17-29.

3. Add in the use of the FormatDateTime function. Note that I've expanded the function helper down below. You can double-click functions and it will insert the base function name into the window above. Also, it will provide context-sensitive tooltips similar to other parts of Visual Studio as you are filling in the function. Also note that this particular function does have an optional parameter that would allow us to specify a particular date representation style (say, European or Japanese), but we're going to allow the function to format it based on whatever the localized settings are on the server.

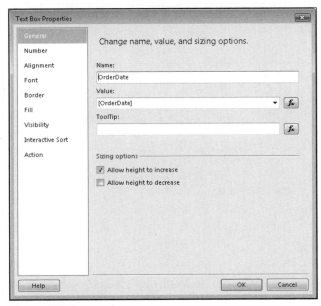

Figure 17-28

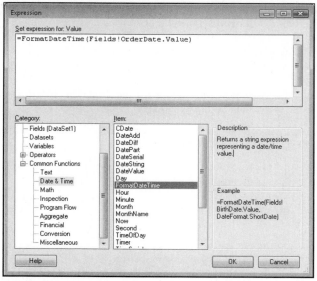

Figure 17-29

4. Click OK, and move to the Format tab. Change the "Direction" option to RTL (right to left) to cause the field to be right justified (typical for most reports).

5. Click OK, and repeat the process for RequiredDate.

6. Preview the report again, and it should look something like Figure 17-30.

Note that I've played around with column sizes a bit (try it!) to use the page efficiently.

Non Credit Card Orders

Sales Order Number	Last Name	First Name	Product ID	Name	Order Date	Due Date
SO47454	Achong	Gustavo	707	Sport-100 Helmet, Red	9/1/2002	9/13/2002
SO48395	Achong	Gustavo	707	Sport-100 Helmet, Red	12/1/2002	12/13/2002
SO50756	Achong	Gustavo	707	Sport-100 Helmet, Red	6/1/2003	6/13/2003
SO51181	Henderson	Kaitlyn	707	Sport-100 Helmet, Red	7/1/2003	7/13/2003
SO51232	Navarro	Dwayne	707	Sport-100 Helmet, Red	7/4/2003	7/16/2003
SO51234	Xu	Peter	707	Sport-100 Helmet, Red	7/4/2003	7/16/2003
SO51374	Raji	Lindsey	707	Sport-100 Helmet, Red	7/13/2003	7/25/2003
SO51407	Suri	Ronald	707	Sport-100 Helmet, Red	7/15/2003	7/27/2003

Figure 17-30

How It Works

Under the covers, there is what is called Report Definition Language — or RDL. RDL is actually an XML implementation. As we make our changes, the RDL is changed behind the scenes so the report generator will know what to do.

To see what the RDL looks like, right-click the report in the Solution Explorer and choose View Code. It's wordy stuff, but here's an excerpt from one of the fields we just edited in our report:

```
<TablixCell>
  <CellContents>
    <Textbox Name="OrderDate">
      <CanGrow>true</CanGrow>
      <KeepTogether>true</KeepTogether>
      <Paragraphs>
        <Paragraph>
          <TextRuns>
            <TextRun>
              <Value>=FormatDateTime(Fields!OrderDate.Value)</Value>
              <Style>
                <FontFamily>Tahoma</FontFamily>
              </Style>
            </TextRun>
          </TextRuns>
          <Style>
            <TextAlign>Right</TextAlign>
          </Style>
        </Paragraph>
      </Paragraphs>
      <rd:DefaultName>OrderDate</rd:DefaultName>
      <Style>
        <Border>
          <Color>LightGrey</Color>
          <Style>Solid</Style>
        </Border>
        <PaddingLeft>2pt</PaddingLeft>
        <PaddingRight>2pt</PaddingRight>
        <PaddingTop>2pt</PaddingTop>
        <PaddingBottom>2pt</PaddingBottom>
      </Style>
    </Textbox>
  </CellContents>
</TablixCell>
```

Were you to become an expert, you could, if desired, edit the RDL directly.

Deploying the Report

The thing left to do is to deploy the report. As with the Report Model approach, you can right-click the report in the Solution Explorer and choose Deploy. There is, however, a minor catch; you need to define the target to deploy to in the project definition.

1. Right-click the Report Server Project and choose Properties.

2. In the TargetServerURL field, enter the URL to your ReportServer. In my case, this may be as simple as `http://localhost/ReportServer`, but the server name could be any server you have appropriate rights to deploy to. (The Virtual Directory may also be something other than ReportServer if you defined it that way at install.)

After you've deployed, you'll want to view the report. Navigate to your report server (if on the local host and using the default directory, it would be `http://localhost/Reports`, just as it was for the Report Model examples earlier). Click on your report project, and choose your Non Credit Card Orders report. It will take a bit to come up the first time you load it. (If you navigate back to it again, the report definition will be cached and thus come up fairly quickly.) You should see your report just as we defined it in our project.

Summary

Reporting Services has had a major impact on many SQL Server installations. For many companies, having a relatively robust reporting server built right into their central data store has been liberating, making it much easier to disseminate information to data consumers. For other organizations, Reporting Services has provided an adequate solution to replace long-standing reporting packages such as Crystal Reports. SQL Server 2008 adds several new features and controls to allow for more elegant and powerful reports, plus the engine has been redesigned to allow for much higher scalability.

In this chapter, we've really only scratched the surface of what's possible. Reports can be parameterized, you can embed charts, integrate with other products (such as Microsoft SharePoint Services or Microsoft Office SharePoint Services), drill through from one report to another, and even embed reports inside of other reports.

For more information on reporting, I'd suggest a book specific to Reporting Services.

Getting Integrated with Integration Services

If you're running a mixed environment with SQL Server 2005 or migrating from that version, do not fear. SQL Server 2008 Integration Services will run old DTS packages with the installation of Legacy Services in the Installation Wizard when you install SQL Server 2008.

Use the SSIS Package Migration Wizard to help upgrade old DTS packages.

In the previous chapter, we got our first serious taste of the Business Intelligence Development Studio (also sometimes referred to as BIDS). In case you skipped again, BIDS is the Visual Studio 2008 development environment with some special SQL Server–oriented project templates and tools. The very different ways we use that environment for just SQL Server development gives something of a taste for just how flexible the Visual Studio development environment is — as we'll see, Integration Services has a pretty different feel than Reporting Services does.

In this chapter, we'll be looking at how to utilize SQL Server Integration Services (often simply called SSIS) to perform basic import and export of data, and we'll briefly discuss some of the other things possible with tools like Integration Services.

Understanding the Problem

The problems being addressed by Integration Services exist in at least some form in a large percentage of systems — how to get data into or out of our system from or to foreign data sources. It can be things like importing data from the old system into the new, or a list of available items from a vendor — or who knows what. The common thread in all of it, however, is that we need to get data that doesn't necessarily fit our tables into them anyway.

What we need is a tool that will let us *Extract*, *Transform*, and *Load* data into our database — a tool that does this is usually referred to simply as an "ETL" tool. Just how complex of a problem this kind of tool can handle varies, but Integration Services can handle nearly every kind of situation you may have.

This may bring about the question "Well, why doesn't everybody use it then since it's built in?" The answer is one of how intuitive it is in a cross-platform environment. There are third-party packages out there that are much more seamless and have fancier UI environments. These are really meant to allow unsophisticated users to move data around relatively easily — they are also outrageously expensive. Under the old DTS product, I actually had customers that were Oracle- or other DBMS-oriented, but purchased a full license for SQL Server just to make use of DTS (what SQL Server's ETL was called prior to SQL Server 2005).

Using the Import/Export Wizard to Generate Basic Packages

An SSIS package is essentially the SSIS equivalent to a program. It bundles up a set of instructions (potentially including limited conditional branch logic) such that it can be moved around, cloned, edited, and so on. The Import/Export Wizard is a tool to automate building such a package for a relatively simple import or export.

To use the Import/Export Wizard, you need to start the SQL Server Business Intelligence Suite tool from the programs menu on your system, and start a new Integration Services project (as shown in Figure 18-1).

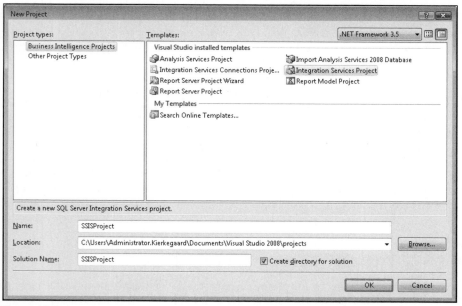

Figure 18-1

On the far right (assuming you haven't moved any of the dockable windows around), you should find a node in the Solution Explorer called SSIS Packages. Right-click this, and choose the SSIS Import and Export Wizard as shown in Figure 18-2.

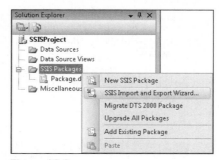

Figure 18-2

This brings up an introduction dialog that is pretty useless (that same Welcome dialog we grew tired of in the chapter on Reporting Services), but click Next and we move on to a far more fundamental dialog to help us set up a connection to a data source. (See Figure 18-3.)

> *Microsoft continues to make the mistake of using the same term — data source — in two different ways in this dialog. The first is the overarching concept of a source of data — complete with all of the information that goes into making a connection string (server, authentication, database, and the like). The second way is a sub-element of the first — the data source as an OLE DB driver type.*

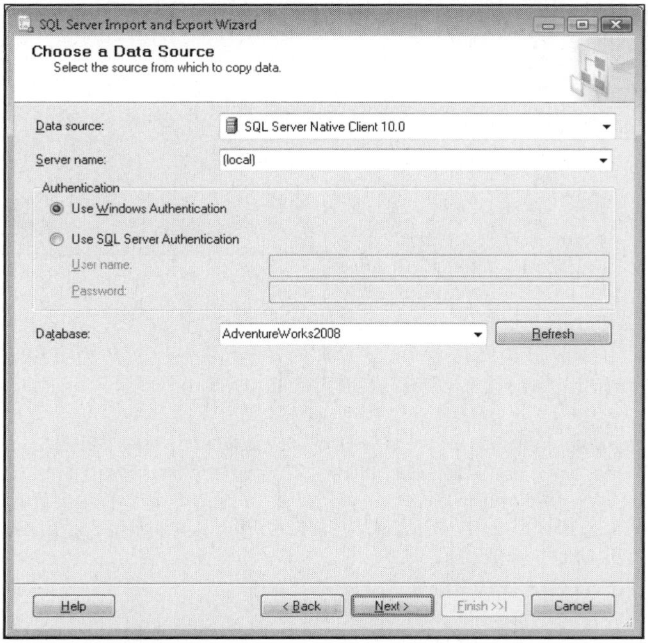

Figure 18-3

For now, leave the actual Data Source drop-down box as SQL Native Client — this is generally the preferred method for accessing SQL Server. From there, set up your authentication information (I've used Windows Authentication in the preceding example) and choose AdventureWorks2008 as your database.

You're now ready to click Next, where you'll see what is, at first glance, essentially the same dialog. This time, however, we're going to make a bit of a change in things. Change the Destination field to be Flat File Destination and, as shown in Figure 18-4, the rest of the options change to something more suitable to a file system–based destination instead of a table in our SQL Server.

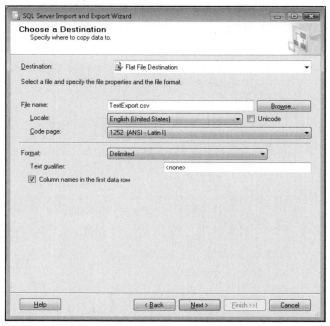

Figure 18-4

As you can see, I've chosen to name my output file `TextExport.csv`, and filled out the other information in a manner appropriate for a typical comma-delimited file.

Let me digress long enough to warn you to be very careful about using comma-delimited files. While this is something of a "tried and true" method of exporting and importing data, consider your delimiter very carefully; does your data potentially already have commas in it? What is that going to do to your exported (or imported) data? Just something to keep in mind when deciding formats (if the choice is yours — most of the time it won't be).

We're not going to go into real detail on this, because the options available will vary widely depending on the particular OLE DB data source you've selected. Indeed, the real point of the moment is just that: SSIS will alter the dialog to give you contextual choices that are relevant to the particular OLE DB data source you're using. In the preceding example, I've simply clicked the "Column names in the first data row" option, and it's time to click Next again. This takes us to choices for selecting what data we want out of our source database. We have two choices here:

❑ **Copy:** This has us do a straight copy out of a table or view.

❑ **Query:** This allows us to select out of pretty much any operation that's going to yield a result set.

Let's start by taking a look at the Query option. If you choose this option and click Next, you get yet another dialog; this one pretty boring in the sense that all it does is give you a box where you can enter in the text of your query. (See Figure 18-5.)

Figure 18-5

In my example here, I've shown where we could be setting up to export a list of employees that we hired in our first month of business. If you want to test this, you can type the query, and then try testing it with the Parse button to make sure that the query you want to run is syntactically valid, or you can copy it into a query window in the Management Studio and test it there. Then click Next to get to the dialog box shown in Figure 18-6.

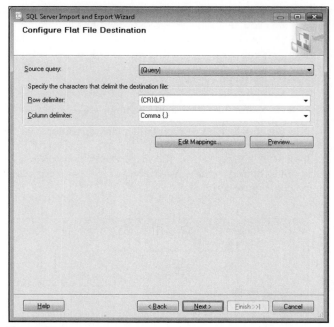

Figure 18-6

For starters, this sets us up to decide what we want our flat file to look like. I can easily change the row delimiter. (For example, if you're exporting for use in a Linux or UNIX based system, you may want to choose just a line feed rather than the line feed/carriage return option.) You can click Preview to see whether your query looks like it's going to return the data that you expect. (See Figure 18-7.)

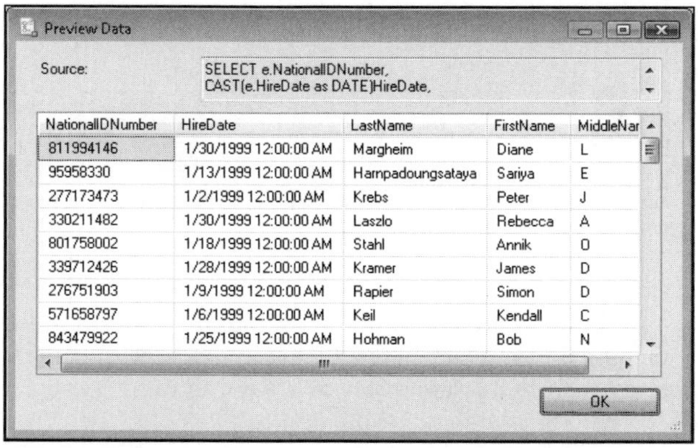

Figure 18-7

Click OK, and you're back to the Configure Flat File dialog.

Next, try clicking on the Edit Mappings… button, which takes you to the dialog box shown in Figure 18-8.

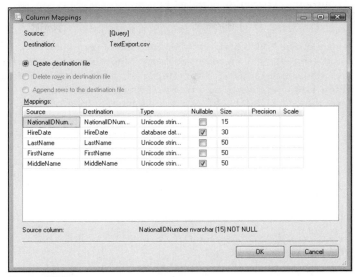

Figure 18-8

At first, things will probably appear pretty mundane here, but, actually, things are getting a lot more interesting.

Try clicking on any of the Destination column values. You'll see a drop-down option appear, and that will include the option to ignore that column, essentially omitting a source column from the destination when you output the file.

This should bring up the question of "Why would I have even put the column in the original query if I was just going to ignore it at output?" The reasons are multifold. First, you may have wanted the column there primarily for preview purposes to verify that the data is what you expected — for example, including the names to verify that it seems like the right people when you only intend to output the EmployeeID. Also, you may be using a query that is copied from some other source and want to avoid risking editing it (for example, if it is particularly complex).

One other point: This dialog is shared with the direct table choice. (Back when we chose Query, we had the option of a table, remember?) So the option is even more applicable in direct table copy scenarios, where there may be many columns in the table that you don't want in the end output.

Next, try clicking on the Type column values, and you'll see a number of choices.

I highly recommend resizing the columns in this dialog so you can see what the Type column is really trying to show you. Just hover your mouse over the right side of the column header much as you would if you were using Excel, and then click and drag the column divider to the right to enlarge the column.

Most of the time you'll stick with whatever the default conversion was, based on the source data type, but sometimes you may want to change the output type in some way, for example, treating integer data as a string to deal with some expectation of the end destination of your data. (Not all systems treat what is seemingly the same data the same way.)

Finally, you can mess with the nullability and scale/precision of your data. It's pretty rare that you would want to do this, and it's something of an advanced concept, but suffice to say that if you were to use more advanced transformations (instead of the default Import/Export Wizard), then this might be an interesting option to facilitate error trapping of data that isn't going to successfully go into your destination system. In most cases, however, you would want to do that with WHERE clauses in your original query.

Now, let's click Cancel to go back to our Configure Flat File dialog, and then click Next to move onto the next dialog.

At this point, you'll get a simple confirmation dialog. It will synopsize all the things that you've asked the wizard to do — in this case:

- ❑ Copy rows from [Query] to `C:\Documents and Settings\xxx\My Documents\TestExport.txt`.
- ❑ The new target table will be created.
- ❑ The package will be saved to the package file `C:\Documents and Settings\xxxx\My Documents\Visual Studio 2005\Projects\Integration Services Project1\Integration Services Project1\Package1.dtsx`.
- ❑ The package will not be run immediately.

Most of this is self-explanatory, but I want to stress a couple of things.

First, it will create the file for us with the name specified; if, when we designed the package, the file had been detected as already existing, then we would have been given some options on whether to overwrite the existing file or just append our data onto the end of it.

Perhaps more importantly, notice that a *package* is being created for you. This package is what amounts to an SSIS program. You can have SSIS execute that package over and over again (including scheduling it), and it will perform the defined export for you each time.

Finally, note that it says that your package will *not* be run immediately; you need either to execute this package manually or schedule it to run.

Click Next, and your package is created.

> Let me stress again that this is just something of a preparation step; your package has not run, and your data is not yet exported. You still need to execute or schedule the package to get your actual exported file. That side of things — the execution of the package — is the same for all SSIS packages though, and isn't Import/Export Wizard-specific, so we'll hold that side of things until the next section.

Examining Package Basics

Fully examining all the parts of an SSIS package and the uses of each piece can fill up the entire book on its own. (Indeed, there are many books dedicated to the subject.) But understanding at least the fundamentals is important to be able to make even the most basic use of Integration Services, so let's take a look at the package that the Import/Export Wizard just created for us.

Assuming you still have the Development Studio open (including the package we just created — if not, open that back up), you should have a fairly standard looking Visual Studio window up similar to Figure 18-9, with the exception of having some fairly Integration Services-oriented stuff in the main pane (as well as in the Connection Managers pane just below the main pane).

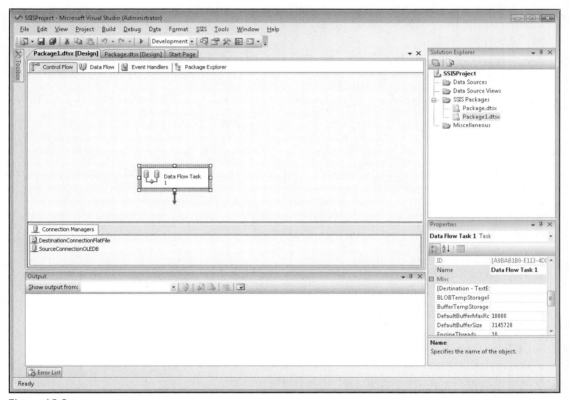

Figure 18-9

Before we explore the Integration Services panes, let's focus first on the standard Visual Studio Solutions Explorer pane (by default, in the upper right. It was what we right-clicked to start the Import/Export Wizard). You should see two packages there. The first — simply titled `Package.dtsx` — was a default package created when we first chose the Integration Services template when we first created our new package. It should be empty, and can be deleted. `Package1.dtsx` will be the one you want to select (you can rename it if you choose) in order to follow the remaining discussion in this section.

With that out of the way, let's look at a few of the key panes…

Connection Managers

I know… I know…. You expected me to go top down! Well, besides my sadistic nature coming forward, I have a more logical reason to get the Connection Managers pane out of the way. First, it's simple, and we'll be a while on the main pane, so let's get it out of the way.

By this point, you may well already have a solid idea as to what the Connection Managers pane (featured in Figure 18-10) is all about. It's about allowing you quick access to all the connections that are used in our package.

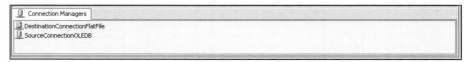

Figure 18-10

If you double-click on either of the two connection managers, you should see a dialog that will look pretty similar to the dialogs that you worked with earlier in the previous section. (Refer to Figures 18-3 and 18-4.) Notice, however, that they are not quite the same. Indeed, the FlatFileConnection Manager has a lot of the same information, but has a somewhat different editing format. For example, Figure 18-11 shows the part of the dialog oriented around editing the data types we want output.

That said, there really isn't anything new here. The connection managers area is just a path to allow us to edit our connection information (both for input and output) after we've exited the wizard.

The Package Editor Pane

This is something of the "meat and potatoes" section of the package. While we obviously couldn't move much data around without the connections we discussed in the previous section, you'll find that the connection side of things won't look all that different from package to package. The actual flow and handler side of things will, however, often vary a great deal.

As you can see along the top of Figure 18-12, the package editor has four tables to it, so let's explore each of these in turn.

Control Flow

This does pretty much what its title would indicate. It controls flow between different logical constructs, or "tasks," in our package. In our case, we have only one task defined, the Data Flow Task visible in Figure 18-12, but if you select that task (as I have in Figure 18-13), you'll see that it will show an arrow coming out of it.

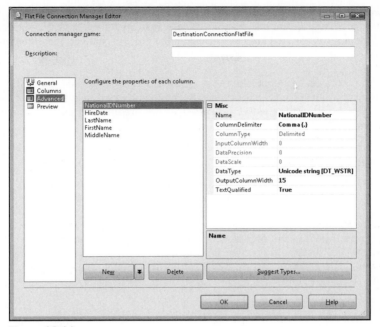

Figure 18-11

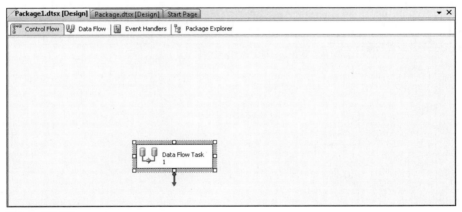

Figure 18-12

Figure 18-13

The arrow is representative of possible flow. We could, for example, add an FTP or external process task to our package to deal with elements of our Extract, Transform, and Load processes that can't be handled within the one data flow task that we have. This control flow aspect is critical to many packages in several ways:

❑   The flow outlined in this part of the package establishes precedence. Think about this for a moment: If we need to FTP our data export to some external system after we've created it, then we need to be sure that the FTP process does not fire until the export portion of the package is complete; control of flow does this for us.

❑   If multiple tasks are available that do not have precedence on earlier tasks (or are dependent on the same task), the package can allow the tasks to branch and run simultaneously.

❑   Further branching can take place depending on specific return conditions from the previous task (for example, retrieving a file if our FTP succeeds, but notifying an operator if it doesn't).

What, exactly, there is to potentially edit, varies widely depending on the specific type of task you have. It might range from things as complex as connection and login information (as would be needed in something like the FTP task mentioned earlier) to something as simple as there being nothing to edit at all. (Indeed, were we to edit our data flow task, it would actually take us to the Data Flow tab, with nothing specific to control flow.)

Data Flow

Well, since our example is based around a data flow task, it's probably not surprising to find a little bit more meat in this area. We can edit the data flow by either double-clicking our data flow task in the Control Flow tab, or selecting the data flow tab, and then selecting the data flow you're interested in from the drop-down in the top of the pane (as shown in Figure 18-14).

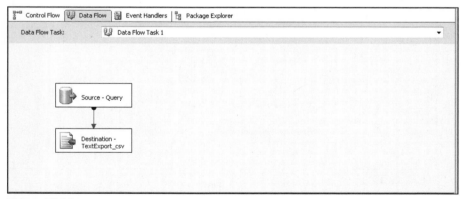

Figure 18-14

Our wizard has populated these data flow items for us, but let's take a quick look inside so we can relate to the various pieces; either double-click the Source – Query flow item, or right-click it and choose Edit.

This brings up the OLE DB Source Editor shown in Figure 18-15. The default option for editing is called the Connection Manager, but notice that, while there is overlap, there are several differences versus the dialog that we looked at earlier. If we were using a parameterized query, this would be where we could edit the properties of those parameters.

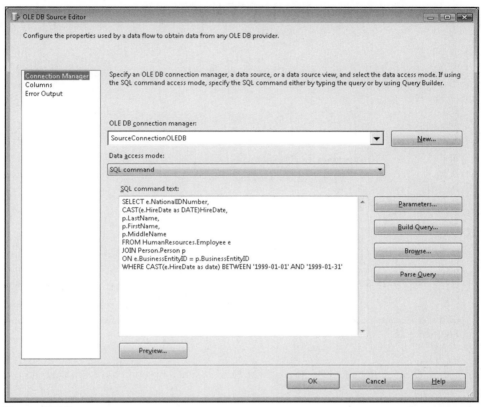

Figure 18-15

Before we leave the Data Flow section, select the Error Output option for this dialog, as shown in Figure 18-16. The key thing to draw out of this dialog is that you have different options on how to handle data flow errors. For this simple wizard-generated data flow item, all errors will be considered fatal for the package, and the package will close with a fail return to whatever called the flow item. (In this case, the data flow task in the control flow area, which will in turn pass the failure on and cause the package to terminate.) Other options would include ignoring the error (and skipping the row) or redirecting the row (perhaps to a holding table where the row can be manually or programmatically repaired before reattempting to import). Consider these options as you graduate into more advanced packages.

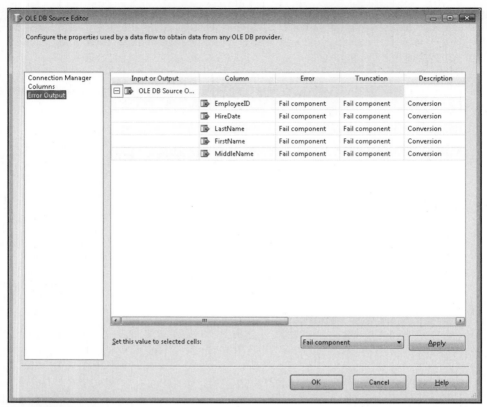

Figure 18-16

Cancel out of all the dialogs to leave things as they were when we completed the wizard.

Event Handlers

Moving over to the Event Handlers tab, we can see the many events that we can supply code for. Activate the drop-down (as I have in Figure 18-17). While the default is OnError, we can deal with a very wide range of scenarios. Let's examine how a few of these might be used:

- ❏ **OnError:** Well, I would hope that this is the most obvious one. As you would expect, this event is fired in the event an error is detected. It allows you to address the error in some fashion.

- ❏ **OnWarning:** Basically the same as OnError, but it allows you to examine and possibly address warnings too.

- ❏ **OnProgress:** For long running processes, this can be handy for updating some form of progress indicator (perhaps a status table somewhere).

- ❏ **OnPreExecute:** Allows for things like preparation code to run prior to starting the main part of the task.

And this is, of course, just a taste. What events to use will vary by need.

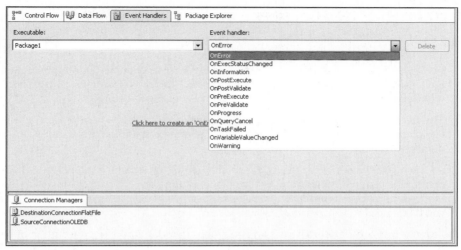

Figure 18-17

Package Explorer

This is, again, one of those things that is what it sounds like. Much like Windows Explorer is a way to explore your file system in a folder-based paradigm, the Package Explorer allows you to explore the package in a similar paradigm. In Figure 18-18, I've expanded a few of the folders to give you a feel.

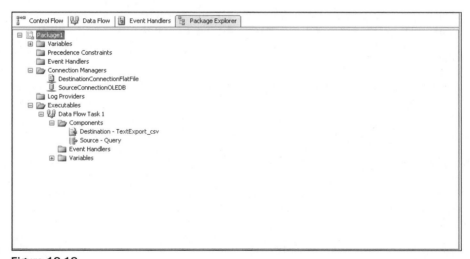

Figure 18-18

Executing Packages

There are a few different ways to execute an SSIS package:

❏ **From within the Development Studio:** The Business Intelligence Development Studio, just like any other instance of Visual Studio, allows for the idea of you running your packages from within the development environment (you gotta be able to debug!).

❏ **The Execute Package Utility:** This is essentially an executable where you can specify the package you want to execute, set up any required parameters, and have the utility run it for you on demand.

❏ **As a scheduled task using the SQL Server Agent:** We'll talk more about the SQL Server Agent in our next chapter, but for now, realize that executing an SSIS package is one of the many types of jobs that the agent understands. You can specify a package name and time and frequency to run it in, and the SQL Server agent will take care of it.

❏ **From within a program:** There is an entire object model supporting the notion of instantiating SSIS objects within your programs, setting properties for the packages, and executing them. This is fairly detailed stuff — so much so that Wrox has an entire book on the subject (*Professional SQL Server 2005 Integrations Services* by Knight et. al, Wiley 2006). As such, we're going to consider it outside the scope of this book other than letting you know it's there for advanced study when you're ready.

Executing a Package Inside the Development Studio

This works just like debugging most any Visual Studio project. Simply press F5, click the green arrow on the toolbar, or choose Start Debugging from the Debug menu. As it builds (assuming it builds successfully), you should see the Data Flow Task first turn yellow, and then green (indicating it ran successfully). If there were multiple steps to our package, then you would see each task fire in turn until the overall package was complete.

Go ahead and run the package this way, and then check out the produced text file. (Its exact location will depend on whether you specified a full path in your file definition or how Visual Studio is configured.)

Using the Execute Package Utility

The Execute Package Utility comes in two forms: A UI-driven application by the name of DTExecUI.exe, and a command-line version simply called DTExec.exe. For our exploration here, we'll fire up DTExecUI.exe. You can also navigate using Windows Explorer and find a package in the file system (they end in .DTSX) and then double-click it to execute it. Do that to our original export package, and you should get the execute dialog shown in Figure 18-19.

As you can see, there are a number of different dialogs that you can select by clicking on the various options to the left. Coverage of this could take up a book all to itself, but let's look at a few of the important things on several key dialogs within this utility.

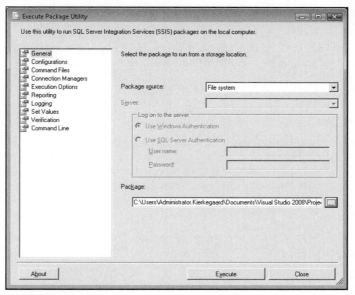

Figure 18-19

General

Many fields on this first dialog are fairly self-explanatory, but let's pay particular attention to the Package Source field. We can store SSIS packages in one of three places:

❑ **The File System:** This is what we did on our Import/Export Wizard package. This option is really nice for mobility; you can easily save the package off and move it to another system.

❑ **SQL Server:** This model stores the package in SQL Server. Under this approach, your package will be backed up whenever you back up your MSDB database (which is a system database in every SQL Server installation).

❑ **SSIS Package Store:** This storage model provides the idea of an organized set of "folders" where you can store your package along with other packages of the same general type or purpose. The folders can be stored in either MSDB or the file system.

Configurations

SSIS allows you to define configurations for your packages. These are essentially a collection of settings to be used, and you can actually combine more than one of them into a suite of settings.

Command Files

These are batch files that you wish to run as part of your package. You can use these to do system-level things such as copying files around to places you need them. (They will run under whatever account the Integration Services Service is running under, so any required access on your network will need to be granted to that account.)

Connection Managers

This is a bit of misnomer. This isn't so much a list of connection managers as it is a list of connections. By taking a look at the Description column, you'll see many of the key properties for each connection your package uses. Notice that in our example package, we have two connections, and if you look closely, you'll see how one relates to file information (for our connection to the flat file we're using) and there is another that specifically relates to SQL Server (the export source connection).

Execution Options

Do not underestimate the importance of this one. Not only does it allow you to specify how, at a high level, you want things to happen if something goes wrong (if there's an error), but it also allows you to establish checkpoint tracking — making it easy to see when and where your package is getting to different execution points. This can be critical in performance tuning and debugging.

Reporting

This one is all about letting you know what is happening. You can set up for feedback: exactly how much feedback is based on which events you decide to track and the level of information you establish.

Logging

This one is fairly complex to set up and get going, but has a very high "coolness" factor in terms of giving you a very flexible architecture of tracking even the most complex of packages.

Using this area, you can configure your package to write log information to a number of preconfigured "providers" (essentially, well understood destinations for your log data). In addition to the preinstalled providers such as text files and even a SQL Server table, you can even create your own custom providers (not for the faint of heart). You can log at the package level, or you can get very detailed levels of granularity and write to different locations for different tasks within your package.

Set Values

This establishes the starting value of any run-time properties your package uses. (There are none in our simple package.)

Verification

Totally different packages can have the same file name (just be in a different spot in the file system, for example). In addition, packages have the ability to retain different versions of themselves within the same file or package store. The Verification dialog is all about filtering or verifying what package/version you want to execute.

Command Line

You can execute SSIS packages from the command line (handy when, for example, you're trying to run DTS packages out of a batch file). This option within the SSIS Package Execution Utility is about specifying parameters you would have used if you had run the package from the command line.

The utility will establish most of this for you; the option here is just to allow you to perform something of an override on the options used when you tell the utility to execute.

Executing the Package

If you simply click Execute in the Package Execution Utility, your package will be off and running. After it runs, you should find a text file in whatever location you told your package to store it; open it up, take a look, and verify that it was what you expected.

Executing Using the SQL Server Agent

We haven't really discussed the SQL Server Agent up to this point, but, from an SSIS point of view, think of the SQL Server Agent as a job scheduler that allows you to do the same thing as running DTExec.exe, but doing so on a specific time and frequency basis with very robust job and task scheduling systems to integrate your package into a larger set of system jobs.

We will discuss the agent in a bit more detail in our next chapter.

Executing a Package from Within a Program

SQL Server offers a very rich object model that is usable from within any .NET language. The programmability object model is well beyond the scope of this book, but suffice to say that you can not only programmatically execute packages, but dynamically build packages to meet a certain need before executing them.

A Final Word on Packages

I want to take a moment and reiterate how much we've really only touched the surface of what's possible. As I've said before, there are entire books (rather large ones actually) written around Integration Services as the sole topic.

The package we focused on here was generated by the Import/Export Wizard, but the end product was a typical SSIS package. Not only could we edit it, but we could well have built it from scratch ourselves. We could easily add other tasks to deal with things like "scrubbing" data after importing it to some form of "staging" area and then perform additional tasks. We can add complex branching to deal with errors or perform several tasks in parallel; the possibilities go on and on.

Summary

SQL Server Integration Services is a robust Extract, Transform, and Load tool. You can utilize Integration Services to provide one-off or repeated import and export of data to and from your databases — mixing a variety of data sources while you're at it.

While becoming expert in all that Integration Services has to offer is a positively huge undertaking, getting basic imports and exports up and running is a relative piece of cake. I encourage you to start out simple, and then add to it as you go. As you push yourself further and further with what SSIS can do, take a look at other books that are specific to what SSIS has to offer.

Playing Administrator

And so, here we are. The relative "end of the road," and yet, it's really just the beginning. It's time to talk a bit about maintenance and administration of the databases you develop.

As a developer, I can just hear it now: "Isn't that the Database Administrator's job?" If you did indeed say something like that, then step back, and smack yourself — *hard* (and no, I'm not kidding). If there is anything I hope to instill in you in your database development efforts, it's to avoid the "Hey, I just build 'em, now it's your problem" attitude that is all too common out there.

A database-driven application is a wildly different animal than most stand-alone applications. Most stand-alone applications are either self-maintaining, or deal with single files that are relatively easy for a user to copy somewhere for backup purposes. Likewise, they usually have no "maintenance" issues the way that a database does.

In this chapter, we're going to take a look at some of the tasks that are necessary to make sure that your end users can not only recover from problems and disasters, but also perform some basic maintenance that will help things keep running smoothly.

Among the things we'll touch on are:

- ❏   Scheduling jobs
- ❏   Backing up and restoring
- ❏   Performing basic defragmentation and index rebuilding
- ❏   Using alerts
- ❏   Using Policy Based Management
- ❏   Archiving

While these are far from the only administration tasks available, these do represent something of "the minimum" you should expect to address in the deployment plans for your application.

For purposes of this book, we're going to largely stay with the GUI tools that are included in SQL Server Management Studio (we will touch very briefly on the new Policy Based Management). Be aware, however, that there are more robust options available for the more advanced user that can allow you to programmatically control many of the administration features via the SQL Server Management Objects (SMO) object model.

Scheduling Jobs

Many of the tasks that we'll go over in the remainder of the chapter can be *scheduled*. Scheduling jobs allows you to run tasks that place a load on the system at off-peak hours. It also ensures that you don't forget to take care of things. From index rebuilds to backups, you'll hear of horror stories over and over about shops that "forgot" to do that, or thought they had set up a scheduled job but never checked on it.

> *If your background is in Windows Server, and you have scheduled other jobs using the Windows Scheduler service, you could utilize that scheduling engine to support SQL Server. Doing things all in the Windows Scheduler allows you to have everything in one place, but SQL Server has some more robust branching options.*

There are basically two terms to think about: Jobs and Tasks.

- ❑ **Tasks:** These are single processes that are to be executed or a batch of commands that are to be run. Tasks are not independent. They exist only as members of jobs.

- ❑ **Jobs:** These are a grouping of one or more tasks that should be run together. You can, however, set up dependencies and branching depending on the success or failure of individual tasks. (For example, Task A runs if the previous task succeeds, but Task B runs if the previous task fails.)

Jobs can be scheduled based on the following criteria:

- ❑ Daily, weekly, or monthly basis
- ❑ A specific time of the day
- ❑ A specific frequency (say, every 10 minutes, or every hour)
- ❑ When the CPU becomes idle for a period of time
- ❑ When the SQL Server Agent starts
- ❑ In response to an alert

Tasks are run by virtue of being part of a job and based on the branching rules you define for your job. Just because a job runs doesn't mean that all the tasks that are part of that job will run; some may be executed and others not depending on the success or failure of previous tasks in the job and what *branching rules* you have established. SQL Server not only allows one task to fire automatically when another finishes, it also allows for doing something entirely different (such as running some sort of recovery task) if the current task fails.

In addition to branching you can, depending on what happens, also tell SQL Server to perform the following:

- ❑ Provide notification of the success or failure of a job to an operator. You're allowed to send a separate notification for a network message (which would pop up on a user's screen as long as they are logged in), a pager, and an e-mail address to one operator each.

❑ Write the information to the event log.

❑ Automatically delete the job (to prevent executing it later and generally "clean up").

Let's take a quick look at how to create operators in Management Studio.

Creating an Operator

If you're going to make use of the notification features of the SQL Agent, then you must have an operator set up to define the specifics for who is notified. This side of things — the creation of operators — isn't typically done through any kind of automated process or as part of the developed code; these are usually created manually by the DBA. We'll go ahead and take a rather brief look at it here just to understand how it works in relation to the scheduling of tasks.

Creating an Operator Using Management Studio

To create an operator using Management Studio, you need to navigate to the SQL Server Agent node of the server for which you're creating the operator. Expand the SQL Server Agent node, right-click the Operators member, and choose New Operator.

> *Be aware that, depending on your particular installation, the SQL Server Agent Service may not start automatically by default. If you run into any issues or if you notice the SQL Server Agent icon in Management Studio has a little red square in it, the service is probably set to manual or even disabled; you will probably want to change the service to start automatically. Regardless, make sure that it is running for the examples, Try It Out, and Exercises found in this chapter. You can do this by right-clicking the Agent node and selecting Manage Service.*

You should be presented with the dialog box shown in Figure 19-1. (Mine is partially filled in.)

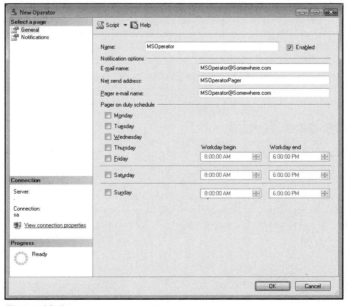

Figure 19-1

You can then fill out a schedule indicating what times this operator is to receive e-mail notifications for certain kinds of errors that you'll see on the Notifications tab.

Speaking of that Notifications tab, go ahead and click over to that tab. It should appear as in Figure 19-2.

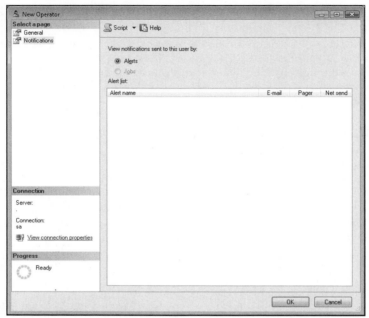

Figure 19-2

Until you have more alerts in your system (we'll get to those later in this chapter), this page may not make a lot of sense. What it is about is setting up which notifications you want this operator to receive depending on which defined alerts get triggered. Again, hard to understand this concept before we've gotten to alerts, but suffice to say that alerts are triggered when certain things happen in your database, and this page defines which alerts this particular operator receives.

Creating Jobs and Tasks

As I mentioned earlier, jobs are a collection of one or more tasks. A task is a logical unit of work, such as backing up one database or running a T-SQL script to meet a specific need such as rebuilding all your indexes.

Even though a job can contain several tasks, this is no guarantee that every task in a job will run. They will either run or not run depending on the success or failure of other tasks in the job and what you've defined to be the response for each case of success or failure. For example, you might cancel the remainder of the job if one of the tasks fails.

Just like operators, jobs can be created in Management Studio as well as through programmatic constructs. For purposes of this book, we'll stick to the Management Studio method. (Even among highly advanced SQL Server developers, programmatic construction of jobs and tasks is very rare indeed.)

Creating Jobs and Tasks Using Management Studio

SQL Server Management Studio makes it very easy to create scheduled jobs. Just navigate to the SQL Server Agent node of your server. Then right-click the Jobs member and select New Job. You should get a multimode dialog box, shown in Figure 19-3, that will help you build the job one step at a time:

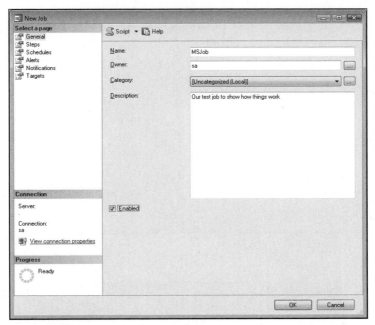

Figure 19-3

The name can be whatever you like as long as it adheres to the SQL Server rules for naming as discussed early in the book.

Most of the rest of the information is, again, self-explanatory with the exception of Category, which is just one way of grouping jobs. Many of your jobs that are specific to your application are going to be Uncategorized, although you will probably on occasion run into instances where you want to create Web Assistant, Database Maintenance, Full Text, or Replication jobs; those each go into their own category for easy identification.

We can then move on to Steps, as shown in Figure 19-4. This is the place where we tell SQL Server to start creating our new tasks that will be part of this job.

To add a new step to our job, we just click the New button and fill in the new dialog box, shown in Figure 19-5. We'll use a T-SQL statement to raise a bogus error just so we can see that things are really happening when we schedule this job. Note, however, that there is an Open button to the left of the command box; you can use this to import SQL scripts that you have saved in files.

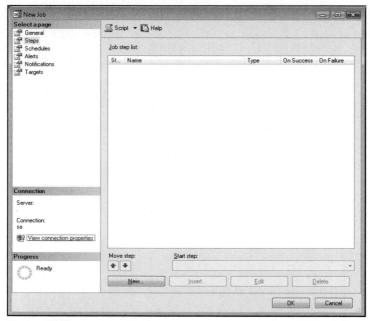

Figure 19-4

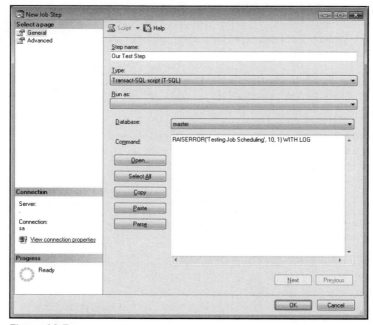

Figure 19-5

Let's go ahead and move on to the Advanced tab for this dialog box, shown in Figure 19-6; it's here that we really start to see some of the cool functionality that our job scheduler offers.

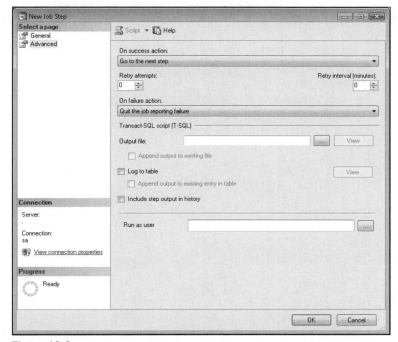

Figure 19-6

Notice several things in this dialog box:

- ❑ You can automatically set the job to retry at a specific interval if the task fails.
- ❑ You can choose what to do if the job succeeds or fails. For each result (success or failure), you can:
  - ❑ Quit reporting success
  - ❑ Quit reporting failure
  - ❑ Move on to the next step
- ❑ You can output results to a file. (This is very nice for auditing.)
- ❑ You can impersonate another user (for rights purposes). Note that you have to have the rights for that user. Since we're logged in as a sysadmin, we can run the job as the dbo or just about anyone. The average user would probably only have the guest account available (unless they were the dbo) but, hey, in most cases a general user shouldn't be scheduling their own jobs this way anyway. (Let your client application provide that functionality.)

Okay, so there's little chance that our RAISERROR statement is going to fail, so we'll just take the default of Quit the job reporting failure on this one. (We'll see other possibilities later in the chapter when we come to backups.)

That moves us back to the main New Job dialog box, and we're now ready to move on to the Schedules node, shown in Figure 19-7.

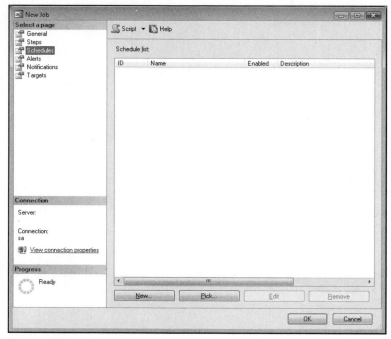

Figure 19-7

In this dialog box, we can manage one or more scheduled times for this job to run. To actually create a new scheduled time for the job to run, we need to click the New button. That brings up yet another dialog box, shown in Figure 19-8.

I've largely filled this one out already (lest you get buried in a sea of screenshots), but it is from this dialog box that we create a new schedule for this job. Recurrence and frequency are set here.

The frequency side of things can be a bit confusing because of the funny way that they've worded things. If you want something to run at multiple times every day, then you need to set the job to Occur Daily every 1 day. This seems like it would run only once a day, but then you also have the option of setting whether it runs once or at an interval. In our case, we want to set our job to run every 5 minutes.

Now we're ready to move on to the next node of our job properties: alerts, shown in Figure 19-9.

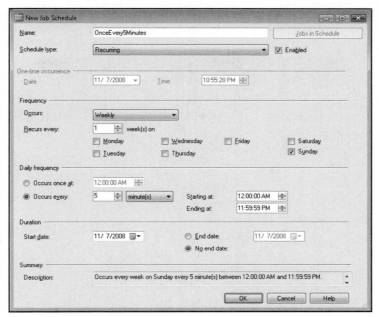

Figure 19-8

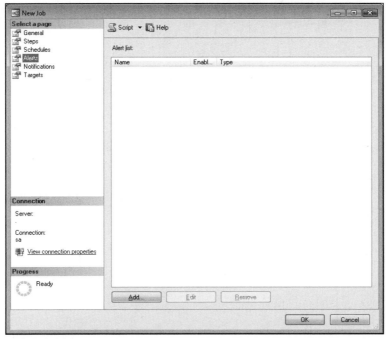

Figure 19-9

From here, we can select which alerts we want to make depending on what happens. Choose Add and we get yet another rich dialog box, shown in Figure 19-10.

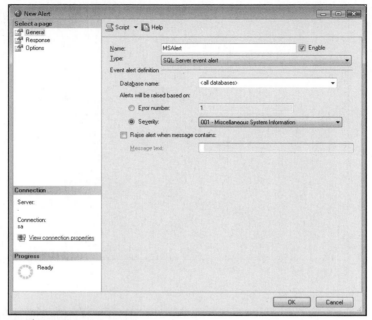

Figure 19-10

Our first node — General — is going to let us fill out some of the basics. We can, for example, limit this notification to one particular database. We also define just how severe the condition needs to be before the alert will fire (in terms of severity of the error).

From there, it is on to the Response node, shown in Figure 19-11.

Notice that I am able to choose the operator that we created earlier in the chapter. It is through the definitions of these operators that the SQL Server Agent knows what e-mail address or net send address to make the notification to. Also notice that we have control, on the right side, over how our operator is notified.

Last, but not least, we have the Options node, shown in Figure 19-12.

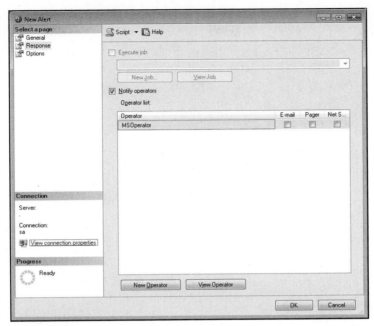

Figure 19-11

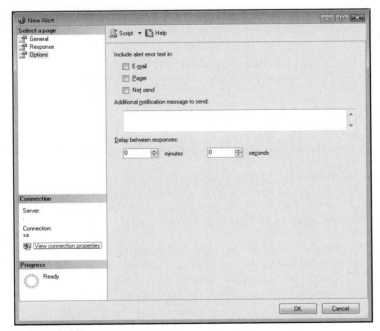

Figure 19-12

Finally, we can go back to the Notifications node of the main New Job dialog box, shown in Figure 19-13.

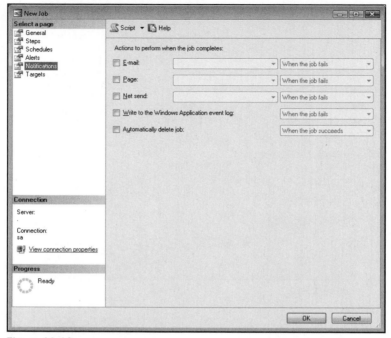

Figure 19-13

This window lets you bypass the older alerts model and define a response that is specific to this one job; we'll just stick with what we already have for now, but you could define specific additional notifications in this dialog box.

The last node in the list is the Targets node. This one generally falls in both the administrator and advanced realms, as it is based on the idea of one SQL Server scheduling jobs onto other SQL Servers. Be aware that it's there for special needs, but we will otherwise save that topic for an advanced-level text.

At this point, you are ready to say OK and exit the dialog box. You'll need to wait a few minutes before the task will fire, but you should start to see log entries appear every five minutes in the *Windows event log*. You can look at this by navigating to Start ➪ Programs ➪ Administrative Tools ➪ Event Viewer. You'll need to switch the view to use the Application log rather than the default System log.

> *Don't forget that, if you're going to be running scheduled tasks like this one, you need to have the SQL Server Agent running for them to be executed. You can check the status of the SQL Server Agent by running the SQL Server Configuration Manager and selecting the SQL Server Agent service, or by navigating to the SQL Server Agent node of the Object Explorer in Management Studio.*

> *Also, don't forget to disable this job. (Right-click the job in Management Studio after you've seen that it's working the way you expect. Otherwise, it will just continue to sit there and create entries in your Application log; eventually, the Application log will fill up and you can have problems with your system!)*

Backup and Recovery

No database-driven application should ever be deployed or sold to a customer without a mechanism for dealing with backup and recovery. As I've probably told people at least 1,000 times: You would truly be amazed at the percentage of database operations that I've gone into that do not have any kind of reliable backup. In a word: EEEeeeeeek!

There is one simple rule to follow regarding backups; do it early and often. The follow up to this to not just back up to a file on the same disk and forget it; you need to make sure that a copy moves to a completely separate place (ideally off-site) to be sure that it's safe. I've personally seen servers catch fire. (The stench was terrible, as were all the freaked out staff.) You don't want to find out that your backups went up in the same smoke that your original data did.

For applications being done by the relative beginner, you're probably going to stick with referring the customer or onsite administrator to SQL Server's own backup and recovery tools, but, even if you do, you should be prepared to support them as they come up to speed in their use. In addition, there is no excuse for not understanding what it is the customer needs to do.

Creating a Backup: a.k.a. "A Dump"

Creating a backup file of a given database is actually pretty easy. Simply navigate in Object Explorer to the database you're interested in, and right-click.

Now choose Tasks and Back up, as shown in Figure 19-14.

Figure 19-14

And you'll get a dialog box that lets you define pretty much all of the backup process as in Figure 19-15.

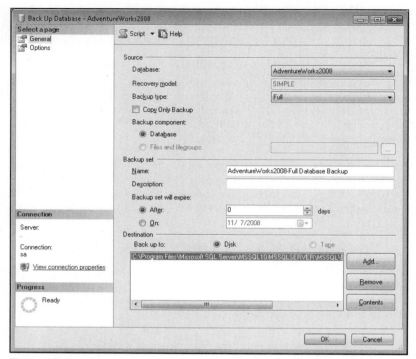

Figure 19-15

The first setting here is pretty self-explanatory — what database you want to back up. From there, however, things get a bit trickier.

Getting into the items that may not yet make sense, first up is the recovery model. The Recovery Model field here is just notifying you what the database you've selected for backup is set to; it is actually a database-level setting. We're going to defer discussion of what this is for a bit; we'll get to it in the next section when we talk about backing up transaction logs.

Now, those are the simple parts, but let's break down some of the rest of the options that are available.

Backup Type

First of the choices to be made is the backup type. Depending on the recovery model for your database (again, be patient with me, we'll get there on what this is), you'll have either two or three types of back-ups available:

❑ **Full:** This is just what it sounds like: a full backup of your actual database file as it is as of the last transaction that was committed prior to you issuing the Backup command.

❑ **Differential:** This might be referred to as a "backup *since*" backup. When you take a differential backup, it only writes out a copy of the extents (see Chapter 9 if you've forgotten) that have changed since you did the last full backup. These typically run much faster than a full backup does and will take up less space. How much less? Well, that depends on how much your data actually changes. For very large databases where backups can take a very long time to run, it is very common to have a strategy where you take a full backup only once a week or even only once a month, and then take differential backups in between to save both space and time.

❑ **Transaction Log:** This is again just what it sounds like: a copy of the transaction log. This option will show up only if your database is set to Full or Bulk logging. (This option is hidden if you are using simple logging.) Again, full discussion of what these are is coming up shortly.

A subtopic of the backup type is the backup component, which applies only to full and differential backups.

For purposes of this book, we should pretty much just be focused on backing up the whole database. That said, you'll notice another option titled Files and Filegroups. Back in our chapters on database objects and creating databases, we touched briefly on the idea of filegroups and individual files for data to be stored in. This option lets you select just one file or filegroup to participate in for this backup; I highly recommend avoiding this option until you have graduated to the "expert" class of SQL Server user.

> *Again, I want to stress that you should avoid this particular option until you've got yourself something just short of a doctorate in SQL Server Backups. The option is for special use, designed to help with very large database installations (figure terabytes) that are in high-availability scenarios. There are major consistency issues to be considered when taking and restoring from this style of backup, and they are not for the faint of heart.*

Backup Set

A backup set is basically a single name used to refer to one or more destinations for your backup.

SQL Server allows for the idea that your backup may be particularly large or that you may otherwise have reason to back up across multiple devices — be it drives or tapes. When you do this, however, you need to have all the devices you used as a destination available to recover from any of them — that is, they are a "set." The backup set essentially holds the definition of what destinations were involved in your particular backup. In addition, a backup set contains some property information for your backup. You can, for example, identify an expiration date for the backup.

Destination

This is where your data is going to be backed up to. Here is where you define one or more destinations to be utilized for one backup set. For most installations this will be a file location (which later will be moved to tape), but you can also define a backup device that would let you go directly to tape or similar backup device.

Options

In addition to those items we just covered from the General node of the dialog box, you also have a node that lets you set other miscellaneous options. Most of these are fairly self-describing. Of particular note, however, is the Transaction Log area.

Schedule

With all this setup, wouldn't it be nice to set up a job to run this backup on a regular basis? Well, the Script button up at the top of the dialog box provides a means to do just that. Click it, and you'll get a list of options. Choose "Script Action to Job…" and it will bring up the Job Schedule dialog box we saw earlier in the chapter, but with the job steps already completed. You can then define a regular schedule to run the backup you just defined by selecting the Schedules tab and filling it out as you desire.

> Note that there are several more options for backups that are only addressable via issuing actual T-SQL commands or using the .NET programmability object model SMO. These are fairly advanced use, and further coverage of them can be found in *Profession SQL Server 2008 Programming.*

Recovery Models

Well, I spent most of the last section promising that we would discuss them, so it's time to ask: What is a recovery model?

Well, back in our chapter on transactions (see Chapter 14), we talked about the transaction log. In addition to keeping track of transactions to deal with transaction rollback and atomicity of data, transaction logs are also critical to being able to recover data right up to the point of system failure.

Imagine for a moment that you're running a bank. Let's say you've been taking deposits and withdrawals for the last six hours — the time since your last full backup was done. Now, if your system went down, I'm guessing you're not going to like the idea of going to last night's backup and losing track of all the money that went out the door or came in during the interim. See where I'm going here? You really need every moment's worth of data.

Keeping the transaction log around gives us the ability to "roll forward" any transactions that happened since the last full or differential backup was done. Assuming both the data backup *and* the transaction logs are available, you should be able to recover right up to the point of failure.

The recovery model determines for how long and what type of log records are kept; there are three options:

❑ **Full:** This is what it says; everything is logged. Under this model, you should have no data loss in the event of system failure assuming you had a backup of the data available and have all transaction logs since that backup. If you are missing a log or have one that is damaged, then you'll be able to recover all data up through the last intact log you have available. Keep in mind, however, that as keeping everything suggests, this can take up a fair amount of space in a system that receives a lot of changes or new data.

❑ **Bulk-Logged:** This is like "full recovery light." Under this option, regular transactions are logged just as they are with the full recovery method, but bulk operations are not. The result is that, in the event of system failure, a restored backup will contain any changes to data pages that did not participate in bulk operations (bulk import of data or index creation, for example), but any bulk operations must be redone. The good news on this one is that bulk operations perform *much* better. This performance comes with risk attached, so your mileage may vary.

❑ **Simple:** Under this model, the transaction log essentially exists merely to support transactions as they happen. The transaction log is regularly truncated, with any completed or rolled back transactions essentially being removed from the log (not quite that simple, but that is the effect). This gives us a nice tight log that is smaller and often performs a bit better, but the log is of zero use for recovery from system failure.

For most installations, full recovery is going to be what you want to have for a production-level database. End of story.

Recovery

This is something of the reverse of the backup side of things. You've done your backups religiously, and now you want to restore one, either for recovery purposes or merely to make a copy of a database somewhere.

Once you have a backup of your database, it's fairly easy to restore it to the original location. To get started, it works much as it did for backup: Navigate to the database you want to restore to and right-click; then select Tasks ➪ Restore and up comes your Restore dialog box, as shown in Figure 19-16.

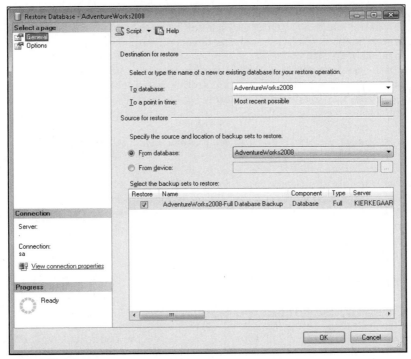

Figure 19-16

As long as what you're after is to take your old backup and slam it over the top of the database you made the backup of, this is pretty straightforward; simply say OK, and it should restore for you without issue.

Restoring to a Different Location

Things get tricky when you want to change something about where you're restoring to. As part of the backup process, the backup knows what the name of the database that was backed up, and, perhaps more importantly, it knows the path(s) to the physical files that it was supposed to be using.

Changing the destination database name is right there — no biggie — the problem is that changing the destination database name does nothing to change which physical files (the MDF and LDF files) it's going to try and store to. To deal with this, go to the Options node of the Restore dialog box.

Again, most of the options here are self-describing, but, in particular, notice the Restore As column. In this part of the dialog box, you can replace every original file's destination location and name, providing you with the way to deal with restoring multiple copies of a database to the same server (perhaps for test purposes) or installing your database to a new volume or even a new system.

Recovery Status

This one is merely about the state you want to have the database be in when you are done with this restore. This has particular relevance when you are restoring a database and still have logs to apply to the database later.

If you go with the default option (which translates to using the `WITH RECOVERY` option if you were using T-SQL), the database would immediately be in a full online status when the restore operation is complete. If, for example, you wanted to restore logs after your initial restore was done, you would want to select one of the two other options. Both of these prevent updates from happening to the database, and leave it in a state where more recovery can be done; the difference is merely one of whether users are allowed to access the database in a "read only" mode or whether the database should be appear as still being offline.

> *The issue of availability is a larger one than you probably think it is. As big of a deal as I'm sure it already seems, it's really amazing how quickly users will find their way into your system when the restore operation suddenly marks the database as available. Quite often, even if you know that you will be "done" after the current restore is completed, you'd like a chance to look over the database prior to actual users being in there. If this is the case, then be sure and use the* `NO RECOVERY` *method of restoring. You can later run a restore that is purely for a* `WITH RECOVERY` *option and get the database fully back online once you're certain you have things just as you want them.*

Index Maintenance

Back in Chapter 9, we talked about the issue of how indexes can become fragmented. This can become a major impediment to the performance of your database over time, and it's something that you need to have a strategy in place to deal with. Fortunately, SQL Server has commands that will reorganize your data and indexes to clean things up. Couple that with the job scheduling that we've already learned about, and you can automate routine defragmentation.

> *You may still run into maintenance scripts that use the old* `DBCC DBREINDEX` *or* `DBCC INDEXDE-FRAG` *commands. Both of these have been replaced by functionality within the* `ALTER INDEX` *command.*

The older DBCC *commands are still supported for backward compatibility, but Microsoft may remove them at any time, so you should be proactive about updating those scripts should you come across any.*

ALTER INDEX is the workhorse of database maintenance. We addressed this somewhat back in Chapter 9, but let's revisit this one, and then look at how to get it scheduled.

ALTER INDEX

The command ALTER INDEX is somewhat deceptive in what it does. While most ALTER commands have been about changing the definition of our object — we ALTER tables to add or disable constraints and columns, for example — ALTER INDEX is different; it is all about maintenance and zero about structure. If you need to change the makeup of your index, you still need to either DROP and CREATE it, or you need to CREATE and use the with the DROP_EXISTING=ON option.

An abbreviated version of the ALTER INDEX syntax looks like this:

```
ALTER INDEX { <name of index> | ALL }
    ON <table or view name>
    { REBUILD
        [ [ WITH ( <rebuild index option> [ ,...n ] ) ]
            | [ PARTITION = <partition number>
                [ WITH ( <partition rebuild index option>
                        [ ,...n ] ) ] ] ]
    | DISABLE
    | REORGANIZE
        [ PARTITION = <partition number> ]
        [ WITH ( LOB_COMPACTION = { ON | OFF } ) ]
    | SET ( <set_index_option> [ ,...n ] )
    }
[ ; ]
```

A fair amount on this is fairly detailed "Realm of the advanced DBA" stuff — usually used on an ad hoc basis to deal with very specific problems, but there are some core elements here that should be part of our regular maintenance planning. We'll start by looking at a couple of top parameters and then look at the options that are part of our larger maintenance planning needs.

Index Name

You can name a specific index if you want to maintain one specific index, or use ALL to indicate that you want to perform this maintenance on every index associated with the named table.

Table or View Name

Pretty much just what it sounds like: the name of the specific object (table or view) that you want to perform the maintenance on. Note that it needs to be one specific table. (You can feed it a list and say "do all of these please!")

REBUILD

This is the "industrial strength" approach to fixing an index. If you run ALTER INDEX with this option, the old index is completely thrown away and reconstructed from scratch. The result is a truly optimized index, where every page in both the leaf and non-leaf levels of the index have been reconstructed as you have defined them, either the defaults, or using switches to change things like the fill factor.

> *Careful on this one. By default, as soon as you kick off a* REBUILD, *the index you are working on is essentially gone until the rebuild is complete. Any queries that relied on that index may become exceptionally slow (potentially by orders of magnitude). This is the sort of thing you want to test on an offline system first to have an idea how long it's going to take, and then schedule to run in off hours, preferably with someone monitoring it to be sure it's back online when peak hours come along.*

The Enterprise version of SQL Server does include a special ONLINE version of this option that will keep the index alive and build the new one parallel to the old, but realize that non-Enterprise versions are not going to have that option available, and, even if it is, the creation of the index is going to be a significant load on the system; tread carefully when rebuilding. In general, treat this one as though it can have major side effects while it runs, and leave its use squarely in the domain of the database administrator.

DISABLE

This one does what it says, only in somewhat drastic fashion. It would be nice if all this command did was take your index offline until you decided what you want to do, but instead it essentially marks the index as unusable. Once an index has been disabled, it must be rebuilt (not reorganized, but rebuilt) before it will be active again.

This is one you're very, very rarely going to do yourself. (You would more likely just drop the index.) It is far more likely to happen during a SQL Server upgrade or some other oddball situation.

> *Yet another BE CAREFUL!!! warning on this one. If you disable the clustered index for your table, it has the effect of disabling the table. The data will remain, but will be inaccessible by all indexes, since they all depend on the clustered index — the entire table is effectively offline until you rebuild the clustered index.*

REORGANIZE

BINGO!!! from the developer perspective. With REORGANIZE we hit a happy medium in life. When you reorganize your index, you get a slightly less complete optimization than you get with a full rebuild, but one that occurs online. (Users can still utilize the index.)

This should, if you're paying attention, bring about the question "What exactly do you mean by '*slightly less complete*'?" Well, REORGANIZE works only on the leaf level of your index; non-leaf levels of the index go untouched. This means that we're not quite getting a full optimization, but, for the lion's share of indexes, that is not where your real cost of fragmentation is, although it can happen and your mileage may vary.

Given its much lower impact on users, this is usually the tool you'll want to use as part of your regular maintenance plan; let's take a look at running a index reorganization command.

Try It Out	Index Reorganization

To run this through its paces, we're going to do a reorg on a table in the AdventureWorks2008 database. The Production.TransactionHistory table is an excellent example of a table that is likely to have many rows inserted over time and then have rows purged back out of it as the transactions become old enough to delete. In this case, we'll reorganize all the indexes on the table in one simple command:

```
ALTER INDEX ALL
ON Production.TransactionHistory
REORGANIZE;
```

You should get back essentially nothing from the database — just a simple message: `Command(s) completed successfully`.

How It Works

The `ALTER INDEX` command sees that `ALL` was supplied instead of a specific index name and looks up which indexes are available for our `Production.TransactionHistory` table (leaving out any that are disabled since a reorganization will do nothing for them). It then enumerates each index behind the scenes and performs the reorganization on each, reorganizing just the leaf level of each index (including reorganizing the actual data since the clustered index on this table will also be reorganized).

Archiving Data

Ooh — here's a tricky one. There are as many ways of archiving data as there are database engineers. If you're building an OLAP database, for example, to utilize with Analysis Services, then that will often address what you need to know as far as archiving for long-term reporting goes. Regardless of how you're making sure the data you need long term is available, there will likely come a day when you need to deal with the issue of your data becoming simply too voluminous for your system to perform well.

As I said, there are just too many ways to go about archiving because every database is a little bit different. The key is to think about archiving needs at the time that you create your database. Realize that, as you start to delete records, you're going to be hitting referential integrity constraints and/or orphaning records; design in a logical path to delete or move records at archive time. Here are some things to think about as you write your archive scripts:

❑   If you already have the data in an OLAP database, then you probably don't need to worry about saving it anywhere else; talk to your boss and your attorney on that one.

❑   How often is the data really used? Is it worth keeping? Human beings are natural born pack rats — just a bit larger than the rodent version. Simply put, we hate giving things up; that includes our data. If you're only worried about legal requirements, think about just saving a copy of never or rarely used data to tape (I'd suggest multiple backups for archive data) and reducing the amount of data you have online; your users will love you for it when they see improved performance.

❑   Don't leave orphans. As you start deleting data, your referential integrity constraints should keep you from leaving that many orphans, but you'll wind up with some where referential integrity didn't apply. This situation can lead to serious system errors.

❑   Realize that your archive program will probably need a long time to run. The length of time it runs and the number of rows affected may create concurrency issues with the data your online users are trying to get at; plan on running it at a time where your system will have not be used.

❑   TEST! TEST! TEST!

Policy Based Management

This is a relatively advanced feature that is new with SQL Server 2008. The idea is fairly simple: Modern relational systems are all about proactive management of your data — why not proactively manage the objects and rules applied to the server?

With Policy Based Management, you establish a set of rules to govern your server or even all servers in your domain. There is a wide list of items that can have policies attached to them, for example:

❑ Object names: Want to enforce that all stored procedures begin with "sp"? No problem. You can establish such a rule using Policy Based Management.

❑ All databases should have the ANSI ARITHABORT option set to true by default.

How exactly these are enforced is set by rule — treatment options include:

❑ **On Demand:** Only check for violations of policy when an administrator has specifically requested the policy audit.

❑ **Scheduled:** Run an audit of policy violations according to some schedule (creating a list of violations, but not changing anything).

❑ **On Change: Prevent:** This proactively prevents the policy violation from being allowed. Under our earlier example, any stored procedure that didn't start with sp would fail during creation.

❑ **On Change – Log:** This notes the violation, but simply logs it (facilitating later reporting).

Most installations will not need the power behind Policy Based Management, but it is a tremendous leap forward in manageability for larger, multi-server environments.

Summary

Well, that gives you a few things to think about. It's really easy to, as a developer, think about many administrative tasks and establish what the increasingly inaccurately named *Hitchhiker's Guide to the Galaxy* trilogy called an "SEP" field. That's something that makes things like administration seem invisible because it's "somebody else's problem." Don't go there!

> A project I'm familiar with from several years ago is a wonderful example of taking responsibility for what can happen. A wonderful system was developed for a non-profit group that operates in the Northwestern United States. After about eight months of operation, an emergency call was placed to the company that developed the software (it was a custom job.) After some discussion, it was determined that the database had somehow become corrupted, and it was recommended to the customer that the database be restored from a backup. The response? "Backup?" The development company in question missed something very important. They knew they had an inexperienced customer that would have no administration staff — who was going to tell the customer to do backups and help set it up if the development company didn't? I'm happy to say that the development company in question learned from that experience, and so should you.

Think about administration issues as you're doing your design and especially in your deployment plan. If you plan ahead to simplify the administration of your system, you'll find that your system is much more successful; that usually translates into rewards for the developer (that is, you!).

Exercises

1. Take the command that we made to reorganize our `Production.TransactionHistory` table, and schedule it to run as a weekend job Sunday mornings at 2AM.

2. Perform a full backup of the AdventureWorks2008 database. Save the backup to `C:\MyBackup.bak` (or alter slightly if you don't have enough disk space on that volume).

3. Restore the backup you created in Exercise 2 to a new database name — NewAdventures.

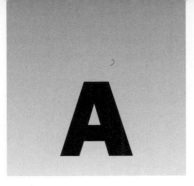

A

System Functions

SQL Server includes a number of "System Functions" as well as more typical functions with the product. Some of these are used often and are fairly clear right from the beginning in terms of how to use them. Others, though, are both rarer in use and more cryptic in nature.

In this appendix, we'll try to clarify the use of most of these functions in a short, concise manner.

> *Just as an FYI, in prior releases, many system functions were often referred to as "Global Variables."*
> *This was a misnomer, and Microsoft has striven to fix it over the last few releases — changing*
> *the documentation to refer to them by the more proper "system function" name. Just keep the old*
> *terminology in mind in case any old fogies (such as myself) find themselves referring to them as*
> *Globals.*

The T-SQL functions available in SQL Server 2008 fall into the following categories:

- ❑ Legacy "system" functions
- ❑ Aggregate functions
- ❑ Configuration functions
- ❑ Cryptographic functions
- ❑ Cursor functions
- ❑ Date and time functions
- ❑ Mathematical functions
- ❑ Metadata functions
- ❑ Ranking functions
- ❑ Rowset functions
- ❑ Security functions
- ❑ String functions
- ❑ System functions
- ❑ Text and image functions

In addition, we have the OVER *operator, which, while largely working as a ranking tool, can be applied to other forms of T-SQL functions (most notably aggregates). While I only discuss it as part of the ranking functions, you may see it referenced several other places in this appendix.*

Legacy System Functions (a.k.a. Global Variables)

@@CONNECTIONS

Returns the number of connections attempted since the last time your SQL Server was started.

This one is the total of all connection *attempts* made since the last time your SQL Server was started. The key thing to remember here is that we are talking about attempts, not actual connections, and that we are talking about connections as opposed to users.

Every attempt made to create a connection increments this counter regardless of whether that connection was successful or not. The only catch with this is that the connection attempt has to have made it as far as the server. If the connection failed because of NetLib differences or some other network issue, then your SQL Server wouldn't even know that it needed to increase the count — it only counts if the server saw the connection attempt. Whether the attempt succeeded or failed does not matter.

It's also important to understand that we're talking about connections instead of login attempts. Depending on your application, you may create several connections to your server, but you'll probably only ask the user for information once. Indeed, even Query Analyzer does this. When you click for a new window, it automatically creates another connection based on the same login information.

This, like a number of other system functions, is often better served by a system stored procedure, sp_monitor. *This procedure, in one command, produces the information from the number of connections, CPU busy, through to the total number of writes by SQL Server. So, if basic information is what you're after, then* sp_monitor *may be better — if you need discrete data that you can manipulate, then* @@CONNECTIONS *provides a nice, neat, scalar piece of data.*

@@CPU_BUSY

Returns the time in milliseconds that the CPU has been actively doing work since SQL Server was last started. This number is based on the resolution of the system timer — which can vary — and can therefore vary in accuracy.

This is another of the "since the server started" kind of functions. This means that you can't always count on the number going up as your application runs. It's possible, based on this number, to figure out a CPU percentage that your SQL Server is taking up. Realistically though, I'd rather tap right into the Performance Monitor for that if I had some dire need for it. The bottom line is that this is one of those really cool things from a "gee, isn't it swell to know that" point of view, but doesn't have all that many practical uses in most applications.

@@IDLE

Returns the time in milliseconds (based on the resolution of the system timer) that SQL Server has been idle since it was last started.

You can think of this one as being something of the inverse of @@CPU_BUSY. Essentially, it tells you how much time your SQL Server has spent doing nothing. If anyone finds a programmatic use for this one, send me an e-mail — I'd love to hear about it (I can't think of one).

@@IO_BUSY

Returns the time in milliseconds (based on the resolution of the system timer) that SQL Server has spent doing input and output operations since it was last started. This value is reset every time SQL Server is started.

This one doesn't really have any rocket science to it, and it is another one of those that I find falls into the "no real programmatic use" category.

@@PACK_RECEIVED and @@PACK_SENT

Respectively return the number of input packets read/written from/to the network by SQL Server since it was last started.

Primarily, these are network troubleshooting tools.

@@PACKET_ERRORS

Returns the number of network packet errors that have occurred on connections to your SQL Server since the last time the SQL Server was started.

Primarily a network troubleshooting tool.

@@TIMETICKS

Returns the number of microseconds per tick. This varies by machines and is another of those that falls under the category of "no real programmatic use."

@@TOTAL_ERRORS

Returns the number of disk read/write errors encountered by the SQL Server since it was last started.

Don't confuse this with runtime errors or as having any relation to @@ERROR. This is about problems with physical I/O. This one is another of those of the "no real programmatic use" variety. The primary use here would be more along the lines of system diagnostic scripts. Generally speaking, I would use Performance Monitor for this instead.

@@TOTAL_READ and @@TOTAL_WRITE

Respectively return the total number of disk reads/writes by SQL Server since it was last started.

The names here are a little misleading, as these do not include any reads from cache — they are only physical I/O.

@@TRANCOUNT

Returns the number of active transactions — essentially the transaction nesting level — for the current connection.

This is a very big one when you are doing transactioning. I'm not normally a big fan of nested transactions, but there are times where they are difficult to avoid. As such, it can be important to know just where you are in the transaction-nesting side of things (for example, you may have logic that only starts a transaction if you're not already in one).

If you're not in a transaction, then @@TRANCOUNT is 0. From there, let's look at a brief example:

```
SELECT @@TRANCOUNT As TransactionNestLevel       --This will be zero
                                                 --at this point

BEGIN TRAN
SELECT @@TRANCOUNT As TransactionNestLevel       --This will be one
                                                 --at this point

  BEGIN TRAN
    SELECT @@TRANCOUNT As TransactionNestLevel   --This will be two
                                                 --at this point
  COMMIT TRAN
SELECT @@TRANCOUNT As TransactionNestLevel       --This will be back to one
                                                 --at this point
ROLLBACK TRAN
SELECT @@TRANCOUNT As TransactionNestLevel       --This will be back to zero
                                                 --at this point
```

Note that, in this example, the @@TRANCOUNT at the end would also have reached zero if we had a COMMIT as our last statement.

Aggregate Functions

Aggregate functions are applied to sets of records rather than a single record. The information in the multiple records is processed in a particular manner and then is displayed in a single record answer. Aggregate functions are often used in conjunction with the GROUP BY clause.

The aggregate functions are:

❑ AVG

❑ CHECKSUM

- ❏ CHECKSUM_AGG
- ❏ COUNT
- ❏ COUNT_BIG
- ❏ GROUPING
- ❏ MAX
- ❏ MIN
- ❏ STDEV
- ❏ STDEVP
- ❏ SUM
- ❏ VAR
- ❏ VARP

In most aggregate functions, the ALL or DISTINCT keywords can be used. The ALL argument is the default and will apply the function to all the values in the expression, even if a value appears numerous times. The DISTINCT argument means that a value will only be included in the function once, even if it occurs several times.

Aggregate functions cannot be nested. The expression cannot be a subquery.

AVG

AVG returns the average of the values in expression. The syntax is as follows:

```
AVG([ALL | DISTINCT] <expression>)
```

The expression must contain numeric values. NULL values are ignored. This function supports the OVER operator described in the ranking functions section of this appendix.

CHECKSUM

This is a basic hash algorithm usually used to detect changes or consistency in data. This particular function accepts either an expression as an argument or a * (which implies that you want all columns in all the joined tables to be included). The basic syntax is:

```
CHECKSUM(<expression>, [...n] | * )
```

Note that the order of your expression — or in the case of a *, the join order — will affect the checksum value, so, for example:

```
CHECKSUM(SalesOrderID, OrderDate)
```

would not give the same result as:

```
CHECKSUM(OrderDate, SalesOrderID )
```

This function is *NOT* compatible with the OVER operator.

CHECKSUM_AGG

Like CHECKSUM, this is a basic hash algorithm usually used to detect changes or consistency in data. The primary difference is that CHECKSUM is oriented around rows, whereas CHECKSUM_AGG is oriented around columns. The basic syntax is:

```
CHECKSUM_AGG( [ALL | DISTINCT] <expression>)
```

The expression value can be virtually anything, including, if you wish, concatenation of columns (just remember to cast as necessary); however, remember that expression order does matter, so if you're concatenating, Col1 + Col2 does not equal Col2 + Col1.

COUNT

COUNT returns the number of items in expression. The data type returned is of type int. The syntax is as follows:

```
COUNT
(
    [ALL | DISTINCT] <expression> | *
)
```

The expression cannot be of the uniqueidentifier, text, image, or ntext data types. The * argument returns the number of rows in the table; it does not eliminate duplicate or NULL values.

This function supports the OVER operator described in the ranking functions section of this appendix.

COUNT_BIG

COUNT_BIG returns the number of items in a group. This is very similar to the COUNT function just described, with the exception that the return value has a data type of bigint. The syntax is as follows:

```
COUNT_BIG
(
    [ALL | DISTINCT ] <expression> | *
)
```

Like COUNT, this function supports the OVER operator described in the ranking functions section of this appendix.

GROUPING

GROUPING adds an extra column to the output of a SELECT statement. The GROUPING function is used in conjunction with CUBE or ROLLUP to distinguish between normal NULL values and those added as a result of CUBE and ROLLUP operations. Its syntax is:

```
GROUPING (<column name>)
```

GROUPING is only used in the SELECT list. Its argument is a column that is used in the GROUP BY clause and that is to be checked for NULL values.

This function supports the OVER operator described in the ranking functions section of this appendix.

MAX

The MAX function returns the maximum value from expression. The syntax is as follows:

```
MAX([ALL | DISTINCT] <expression>)
```

MAX ignores any NULL values.

This function supports the OVER operator described in the ranking functions section of this appendix.

MIN

The MIN function returns the smallest value from expression. The syntax is as follows:

```
MIN([ALL | DISTINCT] <expression>)
```

MIN ignores NULL values.

This function supports the OVER operator described in the ranking functions section of this appendix.

STDEV

The STDEV function returns the standard deviation of all values in expression. The syntax is as follows:

```
STDEV(<expression>)
```

STDEV ignores NULL values.

This function supports the OVER operator described in the ranking functions section of this appendix.

STDEVP

The STDEVP function returns the standard deviation for the population of all values in expression. The syntax is as follows:

```
STDEVP(<expression>)
```

STDEVP ignores NULL values and supports the OVER operator described in the ranking functions section of this appendix.

SUM

The SUM function will return the total of all values in expression. The syntax is as follows:

```
SUM([ALL | DISTINCT] <expression>)
```

SUM ignores NULL values. This function supports the OVER operator described in the ranking functions section of this appendix.

VAR

The VAR function returns the variance of all values in expression. The syntax is as follows:

```
VAR(<expression>)
```

VAR ignores NULL values. This function supports the OVER operator described in the ranking functions section of this appendix.

VARP

The VARP function returns the variance for the population of all values in expression. The syntax is as follows:

```
VARP(<expression>)
```

VARP ignores NULL values. This function supports the OVER operator described in the ranking functions section of this appendix.

Configuration Functions

Well, I'm sure it will come as a complete surprise (ok, not really…), but configuration functions are those functions that tell us about options as they are set for the current server or database (as appropriate).

@@DATEFIRST

Returns the numeric value that corresponds to the day of the week that the system considers the first day of the week.

The default in the United States is 7, which equates to Sunday. The values convert as follows:

- ❑ 1 — Monday (the first day for most of the world)
- ❑ 2 — Tuesday
- ❑ 3 — Wednesday

- ❑   4 — Thursday
- ❑   5 — Friday
- ❑   6 — Saturday
- ❑   7 — Sunday

This can be really handy when dealing with localization issues, so you can properly layout any calendar or other day-of-week-dependent information you have.

> *Use the* SET DATEFIRST *function to alter this setting.*

@@DBTS

Returns the last used timestamp for the current database.

At first look, this one seems to act an awful lot like @@IDENTITY in that it gives you the chance to get back the last value set by the system (this time, it's the last timestamp instead of the last identity value). The things to watch out for on this one include:

- ❑   The value changes based on any change in the database, not just the table you're working on.
- ❑   *Any* timestamp change in the database is reflected, not just those for the current connection.

Because you can't count on this value truly being the last one that you used (someone else may have done something that would change it), I personally find very little practical use for this one.

@@LANGID and @@LANGUAGE

Respectively return the ID and the name of the language currently in use.

These can be handy for figuring out if your product has been installed in a localization situation or not, and if so, what language is the default.

For a full listing of the languages currently supported by SQL Server, use the system stored procedure, sp_helplanguage.

@@LOCK_TIMEOUT

Returns the current amount of time in milliseconds before the system will time out waiting for a blocked resource.

If a resource (a page, a row, a table, whatever) is blocked, your process will stop and wait for the block to clear. This determines just how long your process will wait before the statement is canceled.

The default time to wait is 0 (which equates to indefinitely) unless someone has changed it at the system level (using sp_configure). Regardless of how the system default is set, you will get a value of −1 from this global unless you have manually set the value for the current connection using SET LOCK_TIMEOUT.

@@MAX_CONNECTIONS

Returns the maximum number of simultaneous user connections allowed on your SQL Server.

Don't mistake this one to mean the same thing as you would see under the Maximum Connections property in the Management Console. This one is based on licensing and will show a very high number if you have selected "per seat" licensing.

Note that the actual number of user connections allowed also depends on the version of SQL Server you are using and the limits of your application(s) and hardware.

@@MAX_PRECISION

Returns the level of precision currently set for decimal and numeric data types.

The default is 38 places, but the value can be changed by using the /p option when you start your SQL Server. The /p can be added by starting SQL Server from a command line or by adding it to the Startup parameters for the MSSQLServer service in the Windows 2000, 2003, XP, or 2008 services applet.

@@NESTLEVEL

Returns the current nesting level for nested stored procedures.

The first stored procedure (sproc) to run has an @@NESTLEVEL of 0. If that sproc calls another, then the second sproc is said to be nested in the first sproc (and @@NESTLEVEL is incremented to a value of 1). Likewise, the second sproc may call a third, and so on up to maximum of 32 levels deep. If you go past the level of 32 levels deep, not only will the transaction be terminated, but you should revisit the design of your application.

@@OPTIONS

Returns information about options that have been applied using the SET command.

Since you only get one value back, but can have many options set, SQL Server uses binary flags to indicate what values are set. In order to test whether the option you are interested in is set, you must use the option value together with a bitwise operator. For example:

```
IF (@@OPTIONS & 2)
```

If this evaluates to `True`, then you would know that `IMPLICIT_TRANSACTIONS` had been turned on for the current connection. The values are:

Bit	SET Option	Description
1	DISABLE_ DEF_CNST_CHK	Interim vs. deferred constraint checking.
2	IMPLICIT_ TRANSACTIONS	A transaction is started implicitly when a statement is executed.
4	CURSOR_CLOSE ON_COMMIT	Controls behavior of cursors after a COMMIT operation has been performed.
8	ANSI_WARNINGS	Warns of truncation and NULL in aggregates.
16	ANSI_PADDING	Controls padding of fixed-length variables.
32	ANSI_NULLS	Determines handling of nulls when using equality operators.
64	ARITHABORT	Terminates a query when an overflow or divide-by-zero error occurs during query execution.
128	ARITHIGNORE	Returns NULL when an overflow or divide-by-zero error occurs during a query.
256	QUOTED_ IDENTIFIER	Differentiates between single and double quotation marks when evaluating an expression.
512	NOCOUNT	Turns off the row(s) affected message returned at the end of each statement.
1024	ANSI_NULL_ DFLT_ON	Alters the session's behavior to use ANSI compatibility for nullability. Columns created with new tables or added to old tables without explicit null option settings are defined to allow nulls. Mutually exclusive with ANSI_NULL_DFLT_OFF.
2048	ANSI_NULL_ DFLT_OFF	Alters the session's behavior not to use ANSI compatibility for nullability. New columns defined without explicit nullability are defined not to allow nulls. Mutually exclusive with ANSI_NULL_DFLT_ON.
4096	CONCAT_NULL_ YIELDS_NULL	Returns a NULL when concatenating a NULL with a string.
8192	NUMERIC_ ROUNDABORT	Generates an error when a loss of precision occurs in an expression.

@@REMSERVER

Returns the value of the server (as it appears in the login record) that called the stored procedure.

Used only in stored procedures. This one is handy when you want the sproc to behave differently depending on what remote server (often a geographic location) the sproc was called from.

@@SERVERNAME

Returns the name of the local server that the script is running from.

If you have multiple instances of SQL Server installed (a good example would be a web hosting service that uses a separate SQL Server installation for each client), then @@SERVERNAME returns the following local server name information if the local server name has not been changed since setup:

Instance	Server Information
Default instance	`<servername>`
Named instance	`<servername\instancename>`
Virtual server — default instance	`<virtualservername>`
Virtual server — named instance	`<virtualservername\instancename>`

@@SERVICENAME

Returns the name of the registry key under which SQL Server is running. This will be MSSQLService if it is the default instance of SQL Server, or the instance name if applicable.

@@SPID

Returns the server process ID (SPID) of the current user process.

This equates to the same process ID that you see if you run sp_who. What's nice is that you can tell the SPID for your current connection, which can be used by the DBA to monitor, and if necessary terminate, that task.

@@TEXTSIZE

Returns the current value of the TEXTSIZE option of the SET statement, which specifies the maximum length, in bytes, returned by a SELECT statement when dealing with text or image data.

The default is 4096 bytes (4KB). You can change this value by using the SET TEXTSIZE statement.

@@VERSION

Returns the current version of SQL Server as well as the processor type and OS architecture.

For example:

```
SELECT @@VERSION
```

gives:

```
--------------------------------------------------------------------------
Microsoft SQL Server 2008 (RTM) - 10.0.1600.22 (X64)
 Jul  9 2008 14:17:44
 Copyright (c) 1988-2008 Microsoft Corporation
 Developer Edition (64-bit) on Windows NT 6.0 <X64> (Build 6001: Service Pack 1)


 (1 row(s) affected)
```

Unfortunately, this doesn't return the information into any kind of structured field arrangement, so you have to parse it if you want to use it to test for specific information.

Consider using the xp_msver system sproc instead — it returns information in such a way that you can more easily retrieve specific information from the results.

Cryptographic Functions

These are functions that help support the encryption, decryption, digital signing, and digital signature validation. Some of these are new with SQL Server 2008, and some came with SQL Server 2005. Notice that there are duplicates of most functions from a general use point of view, but that they are different in that one supports a symmetric key and the duplicate (usually with an "Asym" in the name) supports an asymmetrical key.

Now, you may ask "why would I need these?" The answer is as varied as the possible applications for SQL Server. The quick answer though is this: Any time you're sending or accepting data that you want to protect during transport. For example, since SQL Server supports HTTP endpoints, and, from that, hosting of its own web services, you may want to accept or return encrypted information with a client of your web service. Perhaps a more basic example is simply that you've chosen to encrypt the data in your database, and now you need to get it back out in a useful manner.

AsymKey_ID

Given the name of an asymmetric key, this function returns an int that corresponds to the related ID from the database. The syntax is simple:

```
AsymKey_ID('<Asymmetric Key Name>')
```

You must have permissions to the key in question to use this function.

Cert_ID

Similar to `AsymKey_ID`, this returns an ID that relates to the name of a certificate name. The syntax is simple:

```
Cert_ID('<Certificate Name>')
```

You must have permissions to the certificate in question to use this function.

CertProperty

Allows you to fetch various properties of a given certificate (as identified by the certificate's ID). Valid properties include the start date, expiration date, certificate issuer's name, serial number, security ID (the "SID," which can also be returned as a string), and the subject of the certificate (who or what is being certified). The syntax looks like this:

```
CertProperty ( <Cert_ID> ,
     '<Expiry Date>' | '<Start Date>' | '<Issuing Authority>' | '<Certificate
     Serial Number>' | '<Subject>' | '<Security ID>' | '<SID as a String>'  )
```

The data type returned will vary depending on the specific property you're looking for (datetime, nvarchar, or varbinary as appropriate).

DecryptByAsmKey

As you can imagine by the name, this one decrypts a chunk of data utilizing an asymmetric key. It requires the key (by ID), the encrypted data (either as a literal string or a string coercible variable), and the password used to encrypt the asymmetric key (if one was used when the key was created). The syntax is straightforward enough:

```
DecryptByAsymKey(<Asymmetric Key ID>, {'<encrypted string>'|<string variable>}
     [, '<password>'])
```

Keep in mind that, if a password was utilized when creating the asymmetric key, the same password is going to be required to properly decrypt data utilizing that key.

DecryptByCert

This is basically the same as `DecryptByAsmKey`, except that it expects a certificate rather than an asymmetric key. Like `DecryptByAsmKey`, this one decrypts a chunk of data utilizing a key. It requires the certificate (by ID), the encrypted data (either as a literal string or a string coercible variable), and the password used to further encrypt the data (if one was used). The syntax looks almost just like `DecryptByAsymKey`:

```
DecryptByCert(<Certificate ID>, {'<encrypted string>'|<string variable>}
     [, '<password>'])
```

Again, any password utilized when encrypting the data will be needed to properly decrypt it.

DecryptByKey

Like its asymmetric and certificate based brethren, this one decrypts a chunk of data utilizing a key. What's different is that this one not only expects a symmetric key (instead of the other types of key), but it also expects that key to already be "open" (using the OPEN SYMMETRIC KEY command). Other than that, it is fairly similar in use, with the encrypted data (either as a literal string or a string coercible variable) fed in as a parameter and, in this case, a hash key optionally accepted as an authenticator:

```
DecryptByKey({'<encrypted string>'|<string variable>},
    [<add authenticator value>, '<authentication hash>'|<string variable>])
```

Note that if you provide an add authenticator value (in the form of an int), that value must match the value supplied when the string was encrypted, and you must also supply a hash value that matches the hash supplied at encryption time.

DecryptByPassPhrase

Like the name says, this one decrypts data that was encrypted not by a formal key, but by a passphrase. Other than accepting a passphrase parameter instead of assuming an open key, DecryptByPassPhrase works almost exactly like DecryptByKey:

```
DecryptByPassPhrase({'<passphrase>'|<string variable>},
    {'<encrypted string>'|<string variable>},
    [<add authenticator value>, '<authentication hash>'|<string variable>])
```

As with DecryptByKey, if you provide an add authenticator value (in the form of an int), that value must match the value supplied when the string was encrypted, and you must also supply a hash value that matches the hash supplied at encryption time.

EncryptByAsmKey

Encrypts a chunk of data utilizing an asymmetric key. It requires the key (by ID) and the data to be encrypted (either as a literal string or a string coercible variable). The syntax is straightforward enough:

```
EncryptByAsmKey(<Asymmetric Key ID>, {'<string to encrypt>'|<string variable>})
```

Keep in mind that if a password was utilized when the asymmetric key was added to the database, the same password will be required to properly decrypt any data encrypted using that key.

EncryptByCert

This is basically the same as EncryptByAsmKey, except that it expects a certificate rather than an asymmetric key. Like EncryptByAsmKey, this one encrypts a chunk of data utilizing the provided key. It requires the certificate (by ID), the data to be encrypted (either as a literal string or a string coercible variable), and optionally, the password to be used to further encrypt the data. The syntax looks almost just like EncryptByAsmKey:

```
EncryptByCert(<Certificate ID>, {'<string to be encrypted>'|<string variable>}
    [, '<password>'])
```

Again, any password utilized when encrypting the data will be needed to properly decrypt it.

EncryptByKey

This one not only expects a symmetric key (instead of the other types of key), but it also expects that key to already be "open" (using the OPEN SYMMETRIC KEY command) and a GUID to be available to reference that key by. Other than that, it is fairly similar in use, with the data to be encrypted (either as a literal string or a string coercible variable) fed in as a parameter and, in this case, a hash key optionally accepted as an authenticator):

```
EncryptByKey({<Key GUID>, '<string to be encrypted>'|<string variable>},
    [<add authenticator value>, '<authentication hash>'|<string variable>])
```

Note that if you provide an add authenticator value (in the form of an int), that value must be supplied when the string is decrypted, and you must also supply a hash value (which again will be needed at decryption time).

EncryptByPassPhrase

This one encrypts data not by using a formal key, but by a passphrase. Other than accepting a passphrase parameter instead of assuming an open key, EncryptByPassPhrase works almost exactly like EncryptByKey:

```
EncryptByPassPhrase({'<passphrase>'|<string variable>},
    {'<string to be encrypted>'|<string variable>},
    [<add authenticator value>, '<authentication hash>'|<string variable>])
```

As with EncryptByKey, if you provide an add authenticator value (in the form of an int), that value must be supplied when the string is decrypted, and you must also supply a hash value.

Key_GUID

Fetches the GUID for a given symmetric key in the current database:

```
Key_GUID('<Key Name>')
```

Key_ID

Fetches the GUID for a given symmetric key in the current database:

```
Key_ID('<Key Name>')
```

SignByAsymKey

Adds an asymmetric key signature to a given plain text value:

```
SignByAsymKey(<Asymmetric Key ID>, <string variable> [, '<password>'])
```

SignByCert

Returns a varbinary(8000) containing the resulting signature provided a given certificate and plain text value:

```
SignByCert(<Certificate ID>, <string variable> [, '<password>'])
```

VerifySignedByAsymKey

Returns an int (again, I think this odd since it is functionally a bit) indicating successful or failed validation of a signature against a given asymmetric key and plain text value:

```
VerifySignedByAsymKey(<Asymmetric Key ID>, <plain text> , <signature>)
```

VerifySignedByCert

Returns an int (though, personally I think this odd since it is functionally a bit) indicating successful or failed validation of a signature against a given asymmetric key and plain text value:

```
VerifySignedByCert(<Certificate ID>, <signed plain text> , <signature>)
```

Cursor Functions

These provide various information on the status or nature of a given cursor.

@@CURSOR_ROWS

Returns how many rows are currently in the last cursor set opened on the current connection. Note that this is for cursors, not temporary tables.

Keep in mind that this number is reset every time you open a new cursor. If you need to open more than one cursor at a time, and you need to know the number of rows in the first cursor, then you'll need to move this value into a holding variable before opening subsequent cursors.

It's possible to use this to set up a counter to control your WHILE loop when dealing with cursors, but I strongly recommend against this practice — the value contained in @@CURSOR_ROWS can change depending on the cursor type and whether SQL Server is populating the cursor asynchronously or not. Using @@FETCH_STATUS is going to be far more reliable and at least as easy to use.

If the value returned is a negative number larger than –1, then you must be working with an asynchronous cursor, and the negative number is the number of records so far created in the cursor. If, however, the value is –1, then the cursor is a dynamic cursor, in that the number of rows is constantly changing. A returned value of 0 informs you that either no cursor opened has been opened, or the last cursor opened is no longer open. Finally, any positive number indicates the number of rows within the cursor.

To create an asynchronous cursor, set sp_configure cursor threshold *to a value greater than 0. Then, when the cursor exceeds this setting, the cursor is returned, while the remaining records are placed into the cursor asynchronously.*

@@FETCH_STATUS

Returns an indicator of the status of the last cursor FETCH operation.

If you're using cursors, you're going to be using @@FETCH_STATUS. This one is how you know the success or failure of your attempt to navigate to a record in your cursor. It will return a constant depending on whether SQL Server succeeded in your last FETCH operation or not, and, if the FETCH failed, why. The constants are:

❑   0 — Success

❑   -1 — Failed. Usually because you are beyond either the beginning or end of the cursorset.

❑   -2 — Failed. The row you were fetching wasn't found, usually because it was deleted between the time when the cursorset was created and when you navigated to the current row. Should only occur in scrollable, non-dynamic cursors.

For purposes of readability, I often will set up some constants prior to using @@FETCH_STATUS.

For example:

```
DECLARE @NOTFOUND int
DECLARE @BEGINEND int

SELECT @NOTFOUND = -2
SELECT @BEGINEND = -1
```

I can then use these in my conditional in the WHILE statement of my cursor loop instead of just the row integer. This can make the code quite a bit more readable.

CURSOR_STATUS

The CURSOR_STATUS function allows the caller of a stored procedure to determine if that procedure has returned a cursor and result set. The syntax is as follows:

```
CURSOR_STATUS
    (
        {'<local>', '<cursor name>'}
        | {'<global'>, '<cursor name>'}
        | {'<variable>', '<cursor variable>'}
    )
```

local, global, and variable all specify constants that indicate the source of the cursor. local equates to a local cursor name, global to a global cursor name, and variable to a local variable.

If you are using the cursor name form then there are four possible return values:

❑   1 — The cursor is open. If the cursor is dynamic, its result set has zero or more rows. If the cursor is not dynamic, it has one or more rows.

❑   0 — The result set of the cursor is empty.

❑   -1 — The cursor is closed.

❑   -3 — A cursor of cursor name does not exist.

If you are using the `cursor variable` form, there are five possible return values:

❑ 1 — The cursor is open. If the cursor is dynamic, its result set has zero or more rows. If the cursor is not dynamic, it has one or more rows.

❑ 0 — The result set is empty.

❑ -1 — The cursor is closed.

❑ -2 — There is no cursor assigned to the `cursor variable`.

❑ -3 — The variable with name `cursor variable` does not exist, or if it does exist, has not had a cursor allocated to it yet.

Date and Time Functions

This is an area with several new items in SQL Server 2008. In addition to working with timestamp data (which is actually more oriented toward versioning than anything to do with a clock or calendar), date and time functions perform operations on values that have any of the various date and time data types supported by SQL Server.

When working with many of these functions, SQL Server recognizes eleven "dateparts" and their abbreviations, as shown in the following table:

Datepart	Abbreviations
year	yy, yyyy
quarter	qq, q
month	mm, m
dayofyear	dy, y
day	dd, d
week	wk, ww
weekday	dw
hour	hh
minute	mi, n
second	ss, s
millisecond	ms

CURRENT_TIMESTAMP

The CURRENT_TIMESTAMP function simply returns the current date and time as a datetime type. It is equivalent to GETDATE(). The syntax is as follows:

```
CURRENT_TIMESTAMP
```

DATEADD

The DATEADD function adds an interval to a date and returns a new date. The syntax is as follows:

```
DATEADD(<datepart>, <number>, <date>)
```

The *datepart* argument specifies the time scale of the interval (day, week, month, and so on) and may be any of the dateparts recognized by SQL Server. The number argument is the number of dateparts that should be added to the date.

DATEDIFF

The DATEDIFF function returns the difference between two specified dates in a specified unit of time (for example: hours, days, weeks). The syntax is as follows:

```
DATEDIFF(<datepart>, <startdate>, <enddate>)
```

The datepart argument may be any of the dateparts recognized by SQL Server and specifies the unit of time to be used.

DATENAME

The DATENAME function returns a string representing the name of the specified datepart (for example: 1999, Thursday, July) of the specified date. The syntax is as follows:

```
DATENAME(<datepart>, <date>)
```

DATEPART

The DATEPART function returns an integer that represents the specified datepart of the specified date. The syntax is as follows:

```
DATEPART(<datepart>, <date>)
```

The DAY function is equivalent to DATEPART(dd, <date>); MONTH is equivalent to DATEPART(mm, <date>); YEAR is equivalent to DATEPART(yy, <date>).

DAY

The DAY function returns an integer representing the day part of the specified date. The syntax is as follows:

```
DAY(<date>)
```

The DAY function is equivalent to DATEPART(dd, <date>).

GETDATE

The GETDATE function returns the current system date and time. The syntax is as follows:

```
GETDATE()
```

GETUTCDATE

The GETUTCDATE function returns the current UTC (Universal Time Coordinate) time. In other words, this returns GMT (Greenwich Mean Time). The value is derived by taking the local time from the server, and the local time zone, and calculating GMT from this. Daylight saving is included. GETUTCDATE cannot be called from a user-defined function. The syntax is as follows:

```
GETUTCDATE()
```

ISDATE

The ISDATE function determines whether an input expression is a valid date. The syntax is as follows:

```
ISDATE(<expression>)
```

MONTH

The MONTH function returns an integer that represents the month part of the specified date. The syntax is as follows:

```
MONTH(<date>)
```

The MONTH function is equivalent to DATEPART(mm, <date>).

SYSDATETIME

Much like the more venerable GETDATE function, SYSDATETIME returns the current system date and time. The differences are twofold: First, SYSDATETIME returns a higher level of precision. Second, the newer function returns the newer datetime2 data type (to support the higher precision — a precision of 7 in this case). The syntax is as follows:

```
SYSDATETIME()
```

SYSDATETIMEOFFSET

Similar to SYSDATETIME, this returns the current system date and time. Instead of the simple datetime2 data type, however, SYSDATETIMEOFFSET returns the time in the new datetimeoffset data type (with a precision of 7), thus providing offset information versus universal time. The syntax is as follows:

```
SYSDATETIMEOFFSET()
```

SYSUTCDATETIME

Much like the more venerable GETUTCDATE function, SYSDATETIME returns the current UTC date and time. SYSDATETIME, however, returns the newer datetime2 data type (to a precision of 7). The syntax is as follows:

```
SYSUTCDATETIME()
```

SWITCHOFFSET

Returns a datetimeoffset value that is changed from the stored time zone offset to a specified new time zone offset.

So, for example, we can see how the offset gets applied in an example:

```
SWITCHOFFSET ( <datetime to offset>, <time zone offset amount> )
CREATE TABLE dbo.test
   (
   ColDatetimeoffset datetimeoffset
   );
GO
INSERT INTO dbo.test
VALUES ('1998-09-20 7:45:50.71345 -5:00');
GO
SELECT SWITCHOFFSET (ColDatetimeoffset, '-08:00')
FROM dbo.test;
GO
--Returns: 1998-09-20 04:45:50.7134500 -08:00
SELECT ColDatetimeoffset
FROM dbo.test;
--Returns: 1998-09-20 07:45:50.7134500 -05:00
```

TODATETIMEOFFSET

Accepts a given piece of date/time information and adds a provided time offset to produce a datetimeoffset data type. The syntax is:

```
TODATETIMEOFFSET(<data that resolves to datetime>, <time zone>)
```

So, for example:

```
DECLARE @OurDateTimeTest datetime;
SELECT @OurDateTimeTest = '2008-01-01 12:54';
```

```
SELECT TODATETIMEOFFSET(@OurDateTimeTest, '-07:00');
```

Yields:

```
---------------------------------
1/1/2008 12:54:00 PM -07:00

(local)(sa): (1 row(s) affected)
```

YEAR

The YEAR function returns an integer that represents the year part of the specified date. The syntax is as follows:

```
YEAR(<date>)
```

The YEAR function is equivalent to DATEPART(yy, <date>).

Hierarchy Functions

As mentioned before, the new implementation of hierarchyIDs is somewhat beyond the scope of this title. For detailed explanations on the use of the following functions please refer to the professional version of this book. For now we will just list, and briefly describe, the functions provided by SQL Server 2008 to assist in working with the hierarchyIDs and the trees associated with them.

GetAncestor

The GetAncestor function returns the hierarchyID of nth ancestor of the item in question. The syntax is as follows:

```
GetAncestor(<numeric expression>)
```

The parameter passed in determines how many levels up the hierarchy chain you wish to retrieve descendants from. For example, 1 would return children of the item in question, 2 would return the grandchildren, and 0 would return the hierarchyID of the item in question itself.

GetDescendant

Returns a child node of the parent.

GetLevel

Returns an integer that represents the depth of the node in the tree.

GetRoot

Returns the root of the hierarchy tree.

IsDescendantOf

Returns true if child is a descendant of the item in question.

Parse

Parse converts the canonical string representation of a hierarchyID to a hierarchyID value. Parse is called implicitly when a conversion from a string type to hierarchyID occurs.

GetReparentedValue

Returns a node whose path from the root is the path to the newRoot, followed by the path from the oldRoot to the current item.

ToString

The functional equivalent of using a CAST function, this returns a string typed value of the hierarchy node you apply the function to.

Mathematical Functions

The mathematical functions perform calculations. They are:

- ABS
- ACOS
- ASIN
- ATAN
- ATN2
- CEILING
- COS
- COT
- DEGREES
- EXP
- FLOOR
- LOG

❑   LOG10

❑   PI

❑   POWER

❑   RADIANS

❑   RAND

❑   ROUND

❑   SIGN

❑   SIN

❑   SQRT

❑   SQUARE

❑   TAN

ABS

The ABS function returns the positive, absolute value of numeric expression. The syntax is as follows:

```
ABS(<numeric expression>)
```

ACOS

The ACOS function returns the angle in radians for which the cosine is the expression (in other words, it returns the arccosine of expression). The syntax is as follows:

```
ACOS(<expression>)
```

The value of expression must be between –1 and 1 and be of the float data type.

ASIN

The ASIN function returns the angle in radians for which the sine is the expression (in other words, it returns the arcsine of expression). The syntax is as follows:

```
ASIN(<expression>)
```

The value of expression must be between –1 and 1 and be of the float data type.

ATAN

The ATAN function returns the angle in radians for which the tangent is expression (in other words, it returns the arctangent of expression). The syntax is as follows:

```
ATAN(<expression>)
```

The expression must be of the float data type.

ATN2

The ATN2 function returns the angle in radians for which the tangent is between the two expressions provided (in other words, it returns the arctangent of the two expressions). The syntax is as follows:

```
ATN2(<expression1>, <expression2>)
```

Both expression1 and expression2 must be of the float data type.

CEILING

The CEILING function returns the smallest integer that is equal to or greater than the specified expression. The syntax is as follows:

```
CEILING(<expression>)
```

COS

The COS function returns the cosine of the angle specified in expression. The syntax is as follows:

```
COS(<expression>)
```

The angle given should be in radians and expression must be of the float data type.

COT

The COT function returns the cotangent of the angle specified in expression. The syntax is as follows:

```
COT(<expression>)
```

The angle given should be in radians and expression must be of the float data type.

DEGREES

The DEGREES function takes an angle given in radians (expression) and returns the angle in degrees. The syntax is as follows:

```
DEGREES(<expression>)
```

EXP

The EXP function returns the exponential value of the value given in expression. The syntax is as follows:

```
EXP(<expression>)
```

The expression must be of the float data type.

FLOOR

The FLOOR function returns the largest integer that is equal to or less than the value specified in expression. The syntax is as follows:

```
FLOOR(<expression>)
```

LOG

The LOG function returns the natural logarithm of the value specified in expression. The syntax is as follows:

```
LOG(<expression>)
```

The expression must be of the float data type.

LOG10

The LOG10 function returns the base10 logarithm of the value specified in expression. The syntax is as follows:

```
LOG10(<expression>)
```

The expression must be of the float data type.

PI

The PI function returns the value of the constant. The syntax is as follows:

```
PI()
```

POWER

The POWER function raises the value of the specified expression to the specified power. The syntax is as follows:

```
POWER(<expression>, <power>)
```

RADIANS

The RADIANS function returns an angle in radians corresponding to the angle in degrees specified in expression. The syntax is as follows:

```
RADIANS(<expression>)
```

RAND

The RAND function returns a random value between 0 and 1. The syntax is as follows:

```
RAND([<seed>])
```

The optional seed value is an integer expression, which specifies a start value to be used in random number generation. You can allow SQL Server to generate its own random seed value each time you call it, or you can specify your own.

Be careful when specifying a literal seed value. Given a specific seed value, SQL Server will always return the same result (meaning your RAND is suddenly not random at all). If you truly need a random number generated, then either allow SQL Server to select a random seed for you, or use a constantly changing seed such as the number of nanoseconds since a particular point in time.

ROUND

The ROUND function takes a number specified in expression and rounds it to the specified length:

```
ROUND(<expression>, <length> [, <function>])
```

The length parameter specifies the precision to which expression should be rounded. The length parameter should be of the tinyint, smallint, or int data type. The optional function parameter can be used to specify whether the number should be rounded or truncated. If a function value is omitted or is equal to 0 (the default), the value in expression will be rounded. If any value other than 0 is provided, the value in expression will be truncated.

SIGN

The SIGN function returns the sign of the expression. The possible return values are +1 for a positive number, 0 for zero, and -1 for a negative number. The syntax is as follows:

```
SIGN(<expression>)
```

SIN

The SIN function returns the sine of an angle. The syntax is as follows:

```
SIN(<angle>)
```

The angle should be in radians and must be of the float data type. The return value will also be of the float data type.

SQRT

The SQRT function returns the square root of the value given in expression. The syntax is as follows:

```
SQRT(<expression>)
```

The expression must be of the float data type.

SQUARE

The SQUARE function returns the square of the value given in expression. The syntax is as follows:

```
SQUARE(<expression>)
```

The expression must be of the float data type.

TAN

The TAN function returns the tangent of the value specified in expression. The syntax is as follows:

```
TAN(<expression>)
```

The expression parameter specifies the number of radians and must be of the float or real data type.

Basic Metadata Functions

The metadata functions provide information about the database and database objects. They are:

- ❏ COL_LENGTH
- ❏ COL_NAME
- ❏ COLUMNPROPERTY
- ❏ DATABASEPROPERTY
- ❏ DATABASEPROPERTYEX
- ❏ DB_ID
- ❏ DB_NAME
- ❏ FILE_ID
- ❏ FILE_NAME
- ❏ FILEGROUP_ID
- ❏ FILEGROUP_NAME
- ❏ FILEGROUPPROPERTY
- ❏ FILEPROPERTY
- ❏ FULLTEXTCATALOGPROPERTY
- ❏ FULLTEXTSERVICEPROPERTY
- ❏ INDEX_COL

- ❏   INDEXKEY_PROPERTY
- ❏   INDEXPROPERTY
- ❏   OBJECT_ID
- ❏   OBJECT_NAME
- ❏   OBJECTPROPERTY
- ❏   OBJECTPROPERTYEX
- ❏   @@PROCID
- ❏   SCHEMA_ID
- ❏   SCHEMA_NAME
- ❏   SQL_VARIANT_PROPERTY
- ❏   TYPE_ID
- ❏   TYPE_NAME
- ❏   TYPEPROPERTY

COL_LENGTH

The COL_LENGTH function returns the defined length of a column. The syntax is as follows:

```
COL_LENGTH('<table>', '<column>')
```

The column parameter specifies the name of the column for which the length is to be determined. The table parameter specifies the name of the table that contains that column.

COL_NAME

The COL_NAME function takes a table ID number and a column ID number and returns the name of the database column. The syntax is as follows:

```
COL_NAME(<table_id>, <column_id>)
```

The column_id parameter specifies the ID number of the column. The table_id parameter specifies the ID number of the table that contains that column.

COLUMNPROPERTY

The COLUMNPROPERTY function returns data about a column or procedure parameter. The syntax is as follows:

```
COLUMNPROPERTY(<id>, <column>, <property>)
```

The id parameter specifies the ID of the table/procedure. The column parameter specifies the name of the column/parameter. The property parameter specifies the data that should be returned for the column or procedure parameter. The property parameter can be one of the following values:

❑ AllowsNull — Allows NULL values.

❑ IsComputed — The column is a computed column.

❑ IsCursorType — The procedure is of type CURSOR.

❑ IsFullTextIndexed — The column has been full-text indexed.

❑ IsIdentity — The column is an IDENTITY column.

❑ IsIdNotForRepl — The column checks for IDENTITY NOT FOR REPLICATION.

❑ IsOutParam — The procedure parameter is an output parameter.

❑ IsRowGuidCol — The column is a ROWGUIDCOL column.

❑ Precision — The precision for the data type of the column or parameter.

❑ Scale — The scale for the data type of the column or parameter.

❑ UseAnsiTrim — The ANSI padding setting was ON when the table was created.

The return value from this function will be 1 for True, 0 for False, and NULL if the input was not valid — except for Precision (where the precision for the data type will be returned) and Scale (where the scale will be returned).

DATABASEPROPERTY

The DATABASEPROPERTY function returns the setting for the specified database and property name. The syntax is as follows:

```
DATABASEPROPERTY('<database>', '<property>')
```

The database parameter specifies the name of the database for which data on the named property will be returned. The property parameter contains the name of a database property and can be one of the following values:

❑ IsAnsiNullDefault — The database follows the ANSI-92 standard for NULL values.

❑ IsAnsiNullsEnabled — All comparisons made with a NULL cannot be evaluated.

❑ IsAnsiWarningsEnabled — Warning messages are issued when standard error conditions occur.

❑ IsAutoClose — The database frees resources after the last user has exited.

❑ IsAutoShrink — Database files can be shrunk automatically and periodically.

❑ IsAutoUpdateStatistics — The autoupdate statistics option has been enabled.

❑ IsBulkCopy — The database allows nonlogged operations (such as those performed with the Bulk Copy Program).

❑ IsCloseCursorsOnCommitEnabled — Any cursors that are open when a transaction is committed will be closed.

❑ IsDboOnly — The database is only accessible to the dbo.

❑ IsDetached — The database was detached by a detach operation.

❑ IsEmergencyMode — The database is in emergency mode.

❑ IsFulltextEnabled — The database has been full-text enabled.

❑ IsInLoad — The database is loading.

❑ IsInRecovery — The database is recovering.

❑ IsInStandby — The database is read-only and restore log is allowed.

❑ IsLocalCursorsDefault — Cursor declarations default to LOCAL.

❑ IsNotRecovered — The database failed to recover.

❑ IsNullConcat — Concatenating to a NULL results in a NULL.

❑ IsOffline — The database is offline.

❑ IsQuotedIdentifiersEnabled — Identifiers can be delimited by double quotation marks.

❑ IsReadOnly — The database is in a read-only mode.

❑ IsRecursiveTriggersEnabled — The recursive firing of triggers is enabled.

❑ IsShutDown — The database encountered a problem during startup.

❑ IsSingleUser — The database is in single-user mode.

❑ IsSuspect — The database is suspect.

❑ IsTruncLog — The database truncates its logon checkpoints.

❑ Version — The internal version number of the SQL Server code with which the database was created.

The return value from this function will be 1 for true, 0 for false, and NULL if the input was not valid — except for Version (where the function will return the version number if the database is open and NULL if the database is closed).

DATABASEPROPERTYEX

The DATABASEPROPERTYEX function is basically a superset of DATABASEPROPERTY, and also returns the setting for the specified database and property name. The syntax is pretty much just the same as DATABASEPROPERTY and is as follows:

```
DATABASEPROPERTYEX('<database>', '<property>')
```

DATABASEPROPERTYEX just has a few more properties available, including:

❑ Collation — Returns the default collation for the database (remember, collations can also be overridden at the column level).

- ❏ ComparisonStyle — Indicates the Windows comparison style (for example, case sensitivity) of the particular collation.

- ❏ IsAnsiPaddingEnabled — Whether strings are padded to the same length before comparison or insert.

- ❏ IsArithmaticAbortEnabled — Whether queries are terminated when a data overflow or divide-by-zero error occurs.

The database parameter specifies the name of the database for which data on the named property will be returned. The property parameter contains the name of a database property and can be one of the following values:

DB_ID

The DB_ID function returns the database ID number. The syntax is as follows:

```
DB_ID(['<database name>'])
```

The optional database_name parameter specifies which database's ID number is required. If the database_name is not given, the current database will be used instead.

DB_NAME

The DB_NAME function returns the name of the database that has the specified ID number. The syntax is as follows:

```
DB_NAME([<database id>])
```

The optional database_id parameter specifies which database's name is to be returned. If no database_id is given, the name of the current database will be returned.

FILE_ID

The FILE_ID function returns the file ID number for the specified file name in the current database. The syntax is as follows:

```
FILE_ID('<file name>')
```

The file_name parameter specifies the name of the file for which the ID is required.

FILE_NAME

The FILE_NAME function returns the filename for the file with the specified file ID number. The syntax is as follows:

```
FILE_NAME(<file id>)
```

The file_id parameter specifies the ID number of the file for which the name is required.

FILEGROUP_ID

The `FILEGROUP_ID` function returns the filegroup ID number for the specified filegroup name. The syntax is as follows:

```
FILEGROUP_ID('<filegroup name>')
```

The `filegroup_name` parameter specifies the filegroup name of the required filegroup ID.

FILEGROUP_NAME

The `FILEGROUP_NAME` function returns the filegroup name for the specified filegroup ID number. The syntax is as follows:

```
FILEGROUP_NAME(<filegroup id>)
```

The `filegroup_id` parameter specifies the filegroup ID of the required filegroup name.

FILEGROUPPROPERTY

The `FILEGROUPPROPERTY` returns the setting of a specified filegroup property, given the filegroup and property name. The syntax is as follows:

```
FILEGROUPPROPERTY(<filegroup name>, <property>)
```

The `filegroup_name` parameter specifies the name of the filegroup that contains the property being queried. The `property` parameter specifies the property being queried and can be one of the following values:

- ❑ `IsReadOnly` — The filegroup name is read-only.
- ❑ `IsUserDefinedFG` — The filegroup name is a user-defined filegroup.
- ❑ `IsDefault` — The filegroup name is the default filegroup.

The return value from this function will be 1 for `True`, 0 for `False`, and `NULL` if the input was not valid.

FILEPROPERTY

The `FILEPROPERTY` function returns the setting of a specified filename property, given the filename and property name. The syntax is as follows:

```
FILEPROPERTY(<file_name>, <property>)
```

The `file_name` parameter specifies the name of the filegroup that contains the property being queried. The `property` parameter specifies the property being queried and can be one of the following values:

- ❑ `IsReadOnly` — The file is read-only.
- ❑ `IsPrimaryFile` — The file is the primary file.

❑   `IsLogFile` — The file is a log file.

❑   `SpaceUsed` — The amount of space used by the specified file.

The return value from this function will be 1 for `True`, 0 for `False`, and `NULL` if the input was not valid, except for `SpaceUsed` (which will return the number of pages allocated in the file).

FULLTEXTCATALOGPROPERTY

The `FULLTEXTCATALOGPROPERTY` function returns data about the full-text catalog properties. The syntax is as follows:

```
FULLTEXTCATALOGPROPERTY(<catalog name>, <property>)
```

The `catalog_name` parameter specifies the name of the full-text catalog. The `property` parameter specifies the property that is being queried. The properties that can be queried are:

❑   `PopulateStatus` — For which the possible return values are: 0 (idle), 1 (population in progress), 2 (paused), 3 (throttled), 4 (recovering), 5 (shutdown), 6 (incremental population in progress), 7 (updating index).

❑   `ItemCount` — Returns the number of full-text indexed items currently in the full-text catalog.

❑   `IndexSize` — Returns the size of the full-text index in megabytes.

❑   `UniqueKeyCount` — Returns the number of unique words that make up the full-text index in this catalog.

❑   `LogSize` — Returns the size (in bytes) of the combined set of error logs associated with a full-text catalog.

❑   `PopulateCompletionAge` — Returns the difference (in seconds) between the completion of the last full-text index population and 01/01/1990 00:00:00.

FULLTEXTSERVICEPROPERTY

The `FULLTEXTSERVICEPROPERTY` function returns data about the full-text service-level properties. The syntax is as follows:

```
FULLTEXTSERVICEPROPERTY(<property>)
```

The `property` parameter specifies the name of the service-level property that is to be queried. The `property` parameter may be one of the following values:

❑   `ResourceUsage` — Returns a value from 1 (background) to 5 (dedicated).

❑   `ConnectTimeOut` — Returns the number of seconds that the Search Service will wait for all connections to SQL Server for full-text index population before timing out.

❑   `IsFulltextInstalled` — Returns 1 if Full-Text Service is installed on the computer and a 0 otherwise.

INDEX_COL

The INDEX_COL function returns the indexed column name. The syntax is as follows:

```
INDEX_COL('<table>', <index id>, <key id>)
```

The table parameter specifies the name of the table, index_id specifies the ID of the index, and key_id specifies the ID of the key.

INDEXKEY_PROPERTY

This function returns information about the index key.

```
INDEXKEY_PROPERTY(<table id>, <index id>, <key id>, <property>)
```

The table_id parameter is the numerical ID of data type int, which defines the table you wish to inspect. Use OBJECT_ID to find the numerical table_id. index_id specifies the ID of the index, and is also of data type int. key_id specifies the index column position of the key; for example, with a key of three columns, setting this value to 2 will determine that you are wishing to inspect the middle column. Finally, the property is the character string identifier of one of two properties you wish to find the setting of. The two possible values are ColumnId, which will return the physical column ID, and IsDescending, which returns the order that the column is sorted (1 is for descending and 0 is ascending).

INDEXPROPERTY

The INDEXPROPERTY function returns the setting of a specified index property, given the table ID, index name, and property name. The syntax is as follows:

```
INDEXPROPERTY(<table ID>, <index>, <property>)
```

The property parameter specifies the property of the index that is to be queried. The property parameter can be one of these possible values:

- ❏ IndexDepth — The depth of the index.
- ❏ IsAutoStatistic — The index was created by the autocreate statistics option of sp_dboption.
- ❏ IsClustered — The index is clustered.
- ❏ IsStatistics — The index was created by the CREATE STATISTICS statement or by the auto-create statistics option of sp_dboption.
- ❏ IsUnique — The index is unique.
- ❏ IndexFillFactor — The index specifies its own fill factor.
- ❏ IsPadIndex — The index specifies space to leave open on each interior node.
- ❏ IsFulltextKey — The index is the full-text key for a table.
- ❏ IsHypothetical — The index is hypothetical and cannot be used directly as a data access path.

The return value from this function will be 1 for True, 0 for False, and NULL if the input was not valid, except for IndexDepth (which will return the number of levels the index has) and IndexFillFactor (which will return the fill factor used when the index was created or last rebuilt).

OBJECT_ID

The OBJECT_ID function returns the specified database object's ID number. The syntax is as follows:

```
OBJECT_ID('<object>')
```

OBJECT_NAME

The OBJECT_NAME function returns the name of the specified database object. The syntax is as follows:

```
OBJECT_NAME(<object id>)
```

OBJECTPROPERTY

The OBJECTPROPERTY function returns data about objects in the current database. The syntax is as follows:

```
OBJECTPROPERTY(<id>, <property>)
```

The id parameter specifies the ID of the object required. The property parameter specifies the information required on the object. The following property values are allowed:

CnstIsClustKey	ExecIsInsteadOfTrigger
CnstIsColumn	ExecIsLastDeleteTrigger
CnstIsDeleteCascade	ExecIsLastInsertTrigger
CnstIsDisabled	ExecIsLastUpdateTrigger
CnstIsNonclustKey	ExecIsQuotedIdentOn
CnstIsNotRepl	ExecIsStartup
CnstIsNotTrusted	ExecIsTriggerDisabled
CnstIsUpdateCascade	ExecIsTriggerNotForRepl
ExecIsAfterTrigger	ExecIsUpdateTrigger
ExecIsAnsiNullsOn	HasAfterTrigger
ExecIsDeleteTrigger	HasDeleteTrigger
ExecIsFirstDeleteTrigger	HasInsertTrigger
ExecIsFirstInsertTrigger	HasInsteadOfTrigger
ExecIsFirstUpdateTrigger	HasUpdateTrigger
ExecIsInsertTrigger	IsAnsiNullsOn

IsCheckCnst

IsConstraint

IsDefault

IsDefaultCnst

IsDeterministic

IsExecuted

IsExtendedProc

IsForeignKey

IsIndexable

IsIndexed

IsInlineFunction

IsMSShipped

IsPrimaryKey

IsProcedure

IsQueue

IsQuotedIdentOn

IsReplProc

IsRule

IsScalarFunction

IsSchemaBound

IsSystemTable

IsTable

IsTableFunction

IsTrigger

IsUniqueCnst

IsUserTable

IsView

OwnerId

TableDeleteTrigger

TableDeleteTriggerCount

TableFullTextBackgroundUpdateIndexOn

TableFulltextCatalogId

TableFullTextChangeTrackingOn

TableFulltextDocsProcessed

TableFulltextFailCount

TableFulltextItemCount

TableFulltextKeyColumn

TableFulltextPendingChanges

TableFulltextPopulateStatus

TableHasActiveFulltextIndex

TableHasCheckCnst

TableHasClustIndex

TableHasDefaultCnst

TableHasDeleteTrigger

TableHasForeignKey

TableHasForeignRef

TableHasIdentity

TableHasIndex

TableHasInsertTrigger

TableHasNonclustIndex

TableHasPrimaryKey

TableHasRowGuidCol

TableHasTextImage

TableHasTimestamp

TableHasUniqueCnst

TableHasUpdateTrigger

TableInsertTrigger

TableInsertTriggerCount

TableIsFake

TableIsLockedOnBulkLoad

TableIsPinned

TableTextInRowLimit

TableUpdateTrigger

TableUpdateTriggerCount

The return value from this function will be 1 for True, 0 for False, and NULL if the input was not valid, except for:

❑ OwnerId — Returns the database user ID of the owner of that object — note that this is different from the SchemaID of the object and will likely not be that useful in SQL Server 2005 and beyond.

❑ TableDeleteTrigger, TableInsertTrigger, TableUpdateTrigger — Return the ID of the first trigger with the specified type. Zero is returned if no trigger of that type exists.

❑ TableDeleteTriggerCount, TableInsertTriggerCount, TableUpdateTriggerCount — Return the number of the specified type of trigger that exists for the table in question.

❑ TableFulltextCatalogId — Returns the ID of the full-text catalog if there is one, and zero if no full-text catalog exists for that table.

❑ TableFulltextKeyColumn — Returns the ColumnID of the column being utilized as the unique index for that full-text index.

❑ TableFulltextPendingChanges — The number of entries that have changed since the last full-text analysis was run for this table. Change tracking must be enabled for this function to return useful results.

❑ TableFulltextPopulateStatus — This one has multiple possible return values:

   ❑ 0 — Indicates that the full-text process is currently idle.

   ❑ 1 — A full population run is currently in progress.

   ❑ 2 — An incremental population is currently running.

   ❑ 3 — Changes are currently being analyzed and added to the full-text catalog.

   ❑ 4 — Some form of background update (such as that done by the automatic change tracking mechanism) is currently running.

   ❑ 5 — A full-text operation is in progress, but has either been throttled (to allow other system requests to perform as needed) or has been paused.

   You can use the feedback from this option to make decisions about what other full-text-related options are appropriate (to check whether a population is in progress so you know whether other functions, such as TableFulltextDocsProcessed, are valid).

❑ TableFulltextDocsProcessed — Valid only while full-text indexing is actually running, this returns the number of rows processed since the full-text index processing task started. A zero result indicates that full-text indexing is not currently running (a null result means full-text indexing is not configured for this table).

❑ TableFulltextFailCount — Valid only while full-text indexing is actually running, this returns the number of rows that full-text indexing has, for some reason, skipped (no indication of reason). As with TableFulltextDocsProcessed, a zero result indicates the table is not currently being analyzed for full text, and a null indicates that full text is not configured for this table.

❑ TableIsPinned — This is left in for backward compatibility only and will always return "0" in SQL Server 2005 and beyond.

OBJECTPROPERTYEX

OBJECTPROPERTYEX is an extended version of the OBJECTPROPERTY function.

```
OBJECTPROPERTYEX(<id>, <property>)
```

Like OBJECTPROPERTY, the id parameter specifies the ID of the object required. The property parameter specifies the information required on the object. OBJECTPROPERTYEX supports all the same property values as OBJECTPROPERTY but adds the following property values as additional options:

❑ BaseType — Returns the base data type of an object.

❑ IsPrecise — Indicates that your object does not contain any imprecise computations. For example, an int or decimal is precise, but a float is not — computations that utilize imprecise data types must be assumed to return imprecise results. Note that you can specifically mark any .NET assemblies you produce as being precise or not.

❑ IsSystemVerified — Indicates whether the IsPrecise and IsDeterministic properties can be verified by SQL Server itself (as opposed to just having been set by the user).

❑ SchemaId — Just what it sounds like — returns the internal system ID for a given object. You can then use SCHEMA_NAME to put a more user-friendly name on the schema ID.

❑ SystemDataAccess — Indicates whether the object in question relies on any system table data.

❑ UserDataAccess — Indicates whether the object in question utilizes any of the user tables or system user data.

@@PROCID

Returns the stored procedure ID of the currently running procedure.

Primarily a troubleshooting tool when a process is running and using up a large amount of resources. Is used mainly as a DBA function.

SCHEMA_ID

Given a schema name, returns the internal system ID for that schema. Utilizes the syntax:

```
SCHEMA_ID( <schema name> )
```

SCHEMA_NAME

Given an internal schema system ID, returns the user-friendly name for that schema. The syntax is:

```
SCHEMA_NAME( <schema id> )
```

SQL_VARIANT_PROPERTY

SQL_VARIANT_PROPERTY is a powerful function and returns information about an sql_variant. This information could be from BaseType, Precision, Scale, TotalBytes, Collation, or MaxLength. The syntax is:

```
SQL_VARIANT_PROPERTY (expression, property)
```

Expression is an expression of type sql_variant. Property can be any one of the following values:

Value	Description	Base Type of sql_variant Returned
BaseType	Data types include: char, int, money, nchar, ntext, numeric, nvarchar, real, smalldatetime, smallint, smallmoney, text, timestamp, tinyint, uniqueidentifier, varbinary, varchar	sysname
Precision	The precision of the numeric base data type: datetime = 23 smalldatetime = 16 float = 53 real = 24 decimal (p,s) and numeric (p,s) = p money = 19 smallmoney = 10 int = 10 smallint = 5 tinyint = 3 bit = 1 All other types = 0	int
Scale	The number of digits to the right of the decimal point of the numeric base data type: decimal (p,s) and numeric (p,s) = s money and smallmoney = 4 datetime = 3 All other types = 0	int
TotalBytes	The number of bytes required to hold both the metadata and data of the value. If the value is greater than 900, index creation will fail.	int
Collation	The collation of the particular sql_variant value.	sysname
MaxLength	The maximum data type length, in bytes.	int

TYPEPROPERTY

The TYPEPROPERTY function returns information about a data type. The syntax is as follows:

```
TYPEPROPERTY(<type>, <property>)
```

The type parameter specifies the name of the data type. The property parameter specifies the property of the data type that is to be queried; it can be one of the following values:

- ❑   Precision — Returns the number of digits/characters.
- ❑   Scale — Returns the number of decimal places.
- ❑   AllowsNull — Returns 1 for True and 0 for False.
- ❑   UsesAnsiTrim — Returns 1 for True and 0 for False.

Rowset Functions

The rowset functions return an object that can be used in place of a table reference in a T-SQL statement. The rowset functions are:

- ❑   CHANGETABLE
- ❑   CONTAINSTABLE
- ❑   FREETEXTTABLE
- ❑   OPENDATASOURCE
- ❑   OPENQUERY
- ❑   OPENROWSET
- ❑   OPENXML

CHANGETABLE

Returns change tracking information for a table. You can use this statement to return all changes for a table or change tracking information for a specific row. The syntax is as follows:

```
CHANGETABLE (
        { CHANGES table , last_sync_version
        | VERSION table , <primary_key_values> } )
[AS] table_alias [ ( column_alias [ ,...n ] )
```

CONTAINSTABLE

The CONTAINSTABLE function is used in full-text queries. Please refer to Chapter 21 for an example of its usage. The syntax is as follows:

```
CONTAINSTABLE (<table>, {<column> | *}, '<contains_search_condition>')
```

FREETEXTTABLE

The FREETEXTTABLE function is used in full-text queries. The syntax is as follows:

```
FREETEXTTABLE (<table>, {<column> | *}, '<freetext_string>')
```

OPENDATASOURCE

The OPENDATASOURCE function provides ad hoc connection information. The syntax is as follows:

```
OPENDATASOURCE (<provider_name>, <init_string>)
```

The provider_name is the name registered as the ProgID of the OLE DB provider used to access the data source. The init_string should be familiar to VB programmers, as this is the initialization string to the OLE DB provider. For example, the init_string could look like:

```
"User Id=wonderison;Password=JuniorBlues;DataSource=MyServerName"
```

OPENQUERY

The OPENQUERY function executes the specified pass-through query on the specified linked_server. The syntax is as follows:

```
OPENQUERY(<linked_server>, '<query>')
```

OPENROWSET

The OPENROWSET function accesses remote data from an OLE DB data source. The syntax is as follows:

```
OPENROWSET('<provider_name>'
    {
     '<datasource>';'<user id>';'<password>'
     | '<provider_string>'
    },
    {
       [<catalog.>][<schema.>]<object>
       | '<query>'
    })
```

The provider_name parameter is a string representing the friendly name of the OLE DB provided as specified in the registry. The data_source parameter is a string corresponding to the required OLE DB data source. The user_id parameter is a relevant username to be passed to the OLE DB provider. The password parameter is the password associated with the user_id.

The provider_string parameter is a provider-specific connection string and is used in place of the datasource, user_id, and password combination.

The catalog parameter is the name of catalog/database that contains the required object. The schema parameter is the name of the schema or object owner of the required object. The object parameter is the object name.

The `query` parameter is a string that is executed by the provider and is used instead of a combination of `catalog`, `schema`, and `object`.

OPENXML

By passing in an XML document as a parameter, or by retrieving an XML document and defining the document within a variable, `OPENXML` allows you to inspect the structure and return data, as if the XML document were a table. The syntax is as follows:

```
OPENXML(<idoc int> [in],<rowpattern> nvarchar[in],[<flags> byte[in]])
[WITH (<SchemaDeclaration> | <TableName>)]
```

The `idoc_int` parameter is the variable defined using the `sp_xml_prepareddocument` system sproc. `Rowpattern` is the node definition. The `flags` parameter specifies the mapping between the XML document and the rowset to return within the `SELECT` statement. `SchemaDeclaration` defines the XML schema for the XML document; if there is a table defined within the database that follows the XML schema, then `TableName` can be used instead.

Before being able to use the XML document, it must be prepared by using the `sp_xml_preparedocument` system procedure.

Security Functions

The security functions return information about users and roles. They are:

- ❏ HAS_DBACCESS
- ❏ IS_MEMBER
- ❏ IS_SRVROLEMEMBER
- ❏ SUSER_ID
- ❏ SUSER_NAME
- ❏ SUSER_SID
- ❏ USER
- ❏ USER_ID
- ❏ USER_NAME

HAS_DBACCESS

The `HAS_DBACCESS` function is used to determine whether the user that is logged in has access to the database being used. A return value of 1 means the user does have access, and a return value of 0 means that he or she does not. A `NULL` return value means the `database_name` supplied was invalid. The syntax is as follows:

```
HAS_DBACCESS ('<database name>')
```

IS_MEMBER

The IS_MEMBER function returns whether the current user is a member of the specified Windows NT group/SQL Server role. The syntax is as follows:

```
IS_MEMBER ({'<group>' | '<role>'})
```

The group parameter specifies the name of the NT group and must be in the form domain\group. The role parameter specifies the name of the SQL Server role. The role can be a database fixed role or a user-defined role but cannot be a server role.

This function will return a 1 if the current user is a member of the specified group or role, a 0 if the current user is not a member of the specified group or role, and NULL if the specified group or role is invalid.

IS_SRVROLEMEMBER

The IS_SRVROLEMEMBER function returns whether a user is a member of the specified server role. The syntax is as follows:

```
IS_SRVROLEMEMBER ('<role>' [,'<login>'])
```

The optional login parameter is the name of the login account to check — the default is the current user. The role parameter specifies the server role and must be one of the following possible values:

- ❑ sysadmin
- ❑ dbcreator
- ❑ diskadmin
- ❑ processadmin
- ❑ serveradmin
- ❑ setupadmin
- ❑ securityadmin

This function returns a 1 if the specified login account is a member of the specified role, a 0 if the login is not a member of the role, and a NULL if the role or login is invalid.

SUSER_ID

The SUSER_ID function returns the specified user's login ID number. The syntax is as follows:

```
SUSER_ID(['<login>'])
```

The login parameter is the specified user's login ID name. If no value for login is provided, the default of the current user will be used instead.

The SUSER_ID *system function has long since been replaced by* SUSER_SID, *and remains in the product purely for backward compatibility purposes. Avoid using* SUSER_ID, *as the internal value it returns may change from server to server (the SID is much more reliable when you consider a database may be restored to a new server where a given login may have a different* SUSER_ID).*

SUSER_NAME

The SUSER_NAME function returns the specified user's login ID name. The syntax is as follows:

```
SUSER_NAME([<server user id>])
```

The server_user_id parameter is the specified user's login ID number. If no value for server_user_id is provided, the default of the current user will be used instead.

The SUSER_NAME *system function is included in SQL Server 2000 for backward compatibility only, so if possible you should use* SUSER_SNAME *instead.*

SUSER_SID

The SUSER_SID function returns the security identification number (SID) for the specified user. The syntax is as follows:

```
SUSER_SID(['<login>'])
```

The login parameter is the user's login name. If no value for login is provided, the current user will be used instead.

SUSER_SNAME

The SUSER_SNAME function returns the login ID name for the specified security identification number (SID). The syntax is as follows:

```
SUSER_SNAME([<server user sid>])
```

The server_user_sid parameter is the user's SID. If no value for the server_user_sid is provided, the current user's will be used instead.

USER

The USER function allows a system-supplied value for the current user's database username to be inserted into a table if no default has been supplied. The syntax is as follows:

```
USER
```

USER_ID

The USER_ID function returns the specified user's database ID number. The syntax is as follows:

```
USER_ID(['<user>'])
```

The user parameter is the username to be used. If no value for user is provided, the current user is used.

USER_NAME

The USER_NAME function is the functional reverse of USER_ID, and returns the specified user's username in the database given a database ID number. The syntax is as follows:

```
USER_NAME(['<user id>'])
```

The user id parameter is the id of the user you want the name for. If no value for user id is provided, the current user is assumed.

String Functions

The string functions perform actions on string values and return strings or numeric values. The string functions are:

- ❑ ASCII
- ❑ CHAR
- ❑ CHARINDEX
- ❑ DIFFERENCE
- ❑ LEFT
- ❑ LEN
- ❑ LOWER
- ❑ LTRIM
- ❑ NCHAR
- ❑ PATINDEX
- ❑ QUOTENAME
- ❑ REPLACE
- ❑ REPLICATE
- ❑ REVERSE
- ❑ RIGHT
- ❑ RTRIM
- ❑ SOUNDEX
- ❑ SPACE
- ❑ STR
- ❑ STUFF
- ❑ SUBSTRING

❏   UNICODE

❏   UPPER

ASCII

The ASCII function returns the ASCII code value of the leftmost character in character_expression. The syntax is as follows:

```
ASCII(<character expression>)
```

CHAR

The CHAR function converts an ASCII code (specified in expression) into a string. The syntax is as follows:

```
CHAR(<expression>)
```

The expression can be any integer between 0 and 255.

CHARINDEX

The CHARINDEX function returns the starting position of an expression in a character_string. The syntax is as follows:

```
CHARINDEX(<expression>, <character string> [, <start location>])
```

The expression parameter is the string, which is to be found. The character_string is the string to be searched, usually a column. The start_location is the character position to begin the search, if this is anything other than a positive number, the search will begin at the start of character_string.

DIFFERENCE

The DIFFERENCE function returns the difference between the SOUNDEX values of two expressions as an integer. The syntax is as follows:

```
DIFFERENCE(<expression1>, <expression2>)
```

This function returns an integer value between 0 and 4. If the two expressions sound identical (for example, blue and blew) a value of 4 will be returned. If there is no similarity, a value of 0 is returned.

LEFT

The LEFT function returns the leftmost part of an expression, starting a specified number of characters from the left. The syntax is as follows:

```
LEFT(<expression>, <integer>)
```

The expression parameter contains the character data from which the leftmost section will be extracted. The integer parameter specifies the number of characters from the left to begin — it must be a positive integer.

LEN

The LEN function returns the number of characters in the specified expression. The syntax is as follows:

```
LEN(<expression>)
```

LOWER

The LOWER function converts any uppercase characters in the expression into lowercase characters. The syntax is as follows:

```
LOWER(<expression>)
```

LTRIM

The LTRIM function removes any leading blanks from a character_expression. The syntax is as follows:

```
LTRIM(<character expression>)
```

NCHAR

The NCHAR function returns the Unicode character that has the specified integer_code. The syntax is as follows:

```
NCHAR(<integer code>)
```

The integer_code parameter must be a positive whole number from 0 to 65,535.

PATINDEX

The PATINDEX function returns the starting position of the first occurrence of a pattern in a specified expression or zero if the pattern was not found. The syntax is as follows:

```
PATINDEX('<%pattern%>', <expression>)
```

The pattern parameter is a string that will be searched for. Wildcard characters can be used, but the % characters must surround the pattern. The expression parameter is character data in which the pattern is being searched for — usually a column.

QUOTENAME

The QUOTENAME function returns a Unicode string with delimiters added to make the specified string a valid SQL Server delimited identifier. The syntax is as follows:

```
QUOTENAME('<character string>'[, '<quote character>'])
```

The `character_string` parameter is a Unicode string. The `quote_character` parameter is a one-character string that will be used as a delimiter. The `quote_character` parameter can be a single quotation mark (`'`), a left or a right bracket (`[]`), or a double quotation mark (`"`) — the default is for brackets to be used.

REPLACE

The `REPLACE` function replaces all instances of second specified string in the first specified string with a third specified string. The syntax is as follows:

```
REPLACE('<string expression1>', '<string expression2>', '<string expression3>')
```

The `string_expression1` parameter is the expression in which to search. The `string_expression2` parameter is the expression to search for in `string_expression1`. The `string_expression3` parameter is the expression with which to replace all instances of `string_expression2`.

REPLICATE

The `REPLICATE` function repeats a `character_expression` a specified number of times. The syntax is as follows:

```
REPLICATE(<character expression>, <integer>)
```

REVERSE

The `REVERSE` function returns the reverse of the specified `character_expression`. The syntax is as follows:

```
REVERSE(<character expression>)
```

RIGHT

The `RIGHT` function returns the rightmost part of the specified `character_expression`, starting a specified number of characters (given by `integer`) from the right. The syntax is as follows:

```
RIGHT(<character expression>, <integer>)
```

The `integer` parameter must be a positive whole number.

RTRIM

The `RTRIM` function removes all the trailing blanks from a specified `character_expression`. The syntax is as follows:

```
RTRIM(<character expression>)
```

SOUNDEX

The SOUNDEX function returns a four-character (SOUNDEX) code, which can be used to evaluate the similarity of two strings. The syntax is as follows:

```
SOUNDEX(<character expression>)
```

SPACE

The SPACE function returns a string of repeated spaces, the length of which is indicated by integer. The syntax is as follows:

```
SPACE(<integer>)
```

STR

The STR function converts numeric data into character data. The syntax is as follows:

```
STR(<numeric expression>[, <length>[, <decimal>]])
```

The numeric_expression parameter is a numeric expression with a decimal point. The length parameter is the total length including decimal point, digits, and spaces. The decimal parameter is the number of places to the right of the decimal point.

STUFF

The STUFF function deletes a specified length of characters and inserts another set of characters in their place. The syntax is as follows:

```
STUFF(<expression>, <start>, <length>, <characters>)
```

The expression parameter is the string of characters in which some will be deleted and new ones added. The start parameter specifies where to begin deletion and insertion of characters. The length parameter specifies the number of characters to delete. The characters parameter specifies the new set of characters to be inserted into the expression.

SUBSTRING

The SUBSTRING function returns part of an expression. The syntax is as follows:

```
SUBSTRING(<expression>, <start>, <length>)
```

The expression parameter specifies the data from which the substring will be taken, and can be a character string, binary string, text, or an expression that includes a table. The start parameter is an integer that specifies where to begin the substring. The length parameter specifies how long the substring is.

UNICODE

The UNICODE function returns the Unicode number that represents the first character in character_expression. The syntax is as follows:

```
UNICODE('<character expression>')
```

UPPER

The UPPER function converts all the lowercase characters in character_expression into uppercase characters. The syntax is as follows:

```
UPPER(<character expression>)
```

System Functions

The system functions – the more longstanding way of referring to what Microsoft is now referring to simply as "other" – can be used to return information about values, objects and settings with SQL Server. The functions are as follows:

- ❑ APP_NAME
- ❑ CASE
- ❑ CAST and CONVERT
- ❑ COALESCE
- ❑ COLLATIONPROPERTY
- ❑ CURRENT_TIMESTAMP
- ❑ CURRENT_USER
- ❑ DATALENGTH
- ❑ FORMATMESSAGE
- ❑ GETANSINULL
- ❑ HOST_ID
- ❑ HOST_NAME
- ❑ IDENT_CURRENT
- ❑ IDENT_INCR
- ❑ IDENT_SEED
- ❑ IDENTITY
- ❑ ISDATE
- ❑ ISNULL
- ❑ ISNUMERIC

- ❑   NEWID
- ❑   NULLIF
- ❑   PARSENAME
- ❑   PERMISSIONS
- ❑   ROWCOUNT_BIG
- ❑   SCOPE_IDENTITY
- ❑   SERVERPROPERTY
- ❑   SESSION_USER
- ❑   SESSIONPROPERTY
- ❑   STATS_DATE
- ❑   SYSTEM_USER
- ❑   USER_NAME

APP_NAME

The APP_NAME function returns the application name for the current session if one has been set by the application as an nvarchar type. It has the following syntax:

```
APP_NAME()
```

CASE

The CASE function evaluates a list of conditions and returns one of multiple possible results. It also has two formats:

- ❑   The simple CASE function compares an expression to a set of simple expressions to determine the result.
- ❑   The searched CASE function evaluates a set of Boolean expressions to determine the result.

Both formats support an optional ELSE argument.

Simple CASE function:

```
CASE <input expression>
    WHEN <when expression> THEN <result expression>
    ELSE <else result expression>
END
```

Searched CASE function:

```
CASE
    WHEN <Boolean expression> THEN <result expression>
    ELSE <else result expression>
END
```

CAST and CONVERT

These two functions provide similar functionality in that they both convert one data type into another type.

Using CAST:

```
CAST(<expression> AS <data type>)
```

Using CONVERT:

```
CONVERT (<data type>[(<length>)], <expression> [, <style>])
```

Where `style` refers to the style of date format when converting to a character data type.

COALESCE

The COALESCE function is passed an undefined number of arguments and it tests for the first non-null expression among them. The syntax is as follows:

```
COALESCE(<expression> [,...n])
```

If all arguments are NULL then COALESCE returns NULL.

COLLATIONPROPERTY

The COLLATIONPROPERTY function returns the property of a given collation. The syntax is as follows:

```
COLLATIONPROPERTY(<collation name>, <property>)
```

The collation_name parameter is the name of the collation you wish to use, and property is the property of the collation you wish to determine. This can be one of three values:

Property Name	Description
CodePage	The non-Unicode code page of the collation.
LCID	The Windows LCID of the collation. Returns NULL for SQL collations.
ComparisonStyle	The Windows comparison style of the collation. Returns NULL for binary or SQL collations.

CURRENT_USER

The CURRENT_USER function simply returns the current user as a sysname type. It is equivalent to USER_NAME(). The syntax is as follows:

```
CURRENT_USER
```

DATALENGTH

The DATALENGTH function returns the number of bytes used to represent expression as an integer. It is especially useful with varchar, varbinary, text, image, nvarchar, and ntext data types because these data types can store variable-length data. The syntax is as follows:

```
DATALENGTH(<expression>)
```

@@ERROR

Returns the error code for the last T-SQL statement that ran on the current connection. If there is no error, then the value will be zero.

If you're going to be writing stored procedures or triggers, this is a bread-and-butter kind of system function — you pretty much can't live without it.

> *The thing to remember with @@ERROR is that its lifespan is just one statement. This means that, if you want to use it to check for an error after a given statement, then you either need to make your test the very next statement, or you need to move it into a holding variable. In general, I recommend using ERROR_NUMBER() in a TRY...CATCH block unless you need to support pre-SQL Server 2005 code.*

A listing of all the system errors can be viewed by using the sys.messages system table in the master database.

To create your own custom errors, use sp_addmessage.

FORMATMESSAGE

The FORMATMESSAGE function uses existing messages in sysmessages to construct a message. The syntax is as follows:

```
FORMATMESSAGE(<msg number>, <param value>[,...n])
```

Where msg_number is the ID of the message in sysmessages.

> FORMATMESSAGE *looks up the message in the current language of the user. If there is no localized version of the message, the U.S. English version is used.*

GETANSINULL

The GETANSINULL function returns the default nullability for a database as an integer. The syntax is as follows:

```
GETANSINULL(['<database>'])
```

The database parameter is the name of the database for which to return nullability information.

When the nullability of the given database allows NULL values and the column or data type nullability is not explicitly defined, GETANSINULL returns 1. This is the ANSI NULL default.

HOST_ID

The HOST_ID function returns the ID of the workstation. The syntax is as follows:

```
HOST_ID()
```

HOST_NAME

The HOST_NAME function returns the name of the workstation. The syntax is as follows:

```
HOST_NAME()
```

IDENT_CURRENT

The IDENT_CURRENT function returns the last identity value created for a table, within any session or scope of that table. This is exactly like @@IDENTITY and SCOPE_IDENTITY; however, this has no limit to the scope of its search to return the value.

The syntax is as follows:

```
IDENT_CURRENT('<table name>')
```

The table_name is the table for which you wish to find the current identity.

IDENT_INCR

The IDENT_INCR function returns the increment value specified during the creation of an identity column in a table or view that has an identity column. The syntax is as follows:

```
IDENT_INCR('<table or view>')
```

The table_or_view parameter is an expression specifying the table or view to check for a valid identity increment value.

IDENT_SEED

The IDENT_SEED function returns the seed value specified during the creation of an identity column in a table or a view that has an identity column. The syntax is as follows:

```
IDENT_SEED('<table or view>')
```

The table_or_view parameter is an expression specifying the table or view to check for a valid identity increment value.

@@IDENTITY

Returns the last identity value created by the current connection.

If you're using identity columns and then referencing them as a foreign key in another table, you'll find yourself using this one all the time. You can create the parent record (usually the one with the identity you need to retrieve), then select @@IDENTITY to know what value you need to relate child records to.

If you perform inserts into multiple tables with identity values, remember that the value in @@IDENTITY will only be for the *last* identity value inserted — anything before that will have been lost, unless you move the value into a holding variable after each insert. Also, if the last column you inserted into didn't have an identity column, then @@IDENTITY will be set to NULL.

IDENTITY

The IDENTITY function is used to insert an identity column into a new table. It is used only with a SELECT statement with an INTO table clause. The syntax is as follows:

```
IDENTITY(<data type>[, <seed>, <increment>]) AS <column name>
```

Where:

❑   data type is the data type of the identity column.

❑   seed is the value to be assigned to the first row in the table. Each subsequent row is assigned the next identity value, which is equal to the last IDENTITY value plus the increment value. If neither seed nor increment is specified, both default to 1.

❑   increment is the increment to add to the seed value for successive rows in the table.

❑   column name is the name of the column that is to be inserted into the new table.

ISNULL

The ISNULL function checks an expression for a NULL value and replaces it with a specified replacement value. The syntax is as follows:

```
ISNULL(<check expression>, <replacement value>)
```

ISNUMERIC

The ISNUMERIC function determines whether an expression is a valid numeric type. The syntax is as follows:

```
ISNUMERIC(<expression>)
```

NEWID

The NEWID function creates a unique value of type uniqueidentifier. The syntax is as follows:

```
NEWID()
```

NULLIF

The NULLIF function compares two expressions and returns a NULL value. The syntax is as follows:

```
NULLIF(<expression1>, <expression2>)
```

PARSENAME

The PARSENAME function returns the specified part of an object name. The syntax is as follows:

```
PARSENAME('<object name>', <object piece>)
```

The object_name parameter specifies the object name from the part that is to be retrieved. The object_piece parameter specifies the part of the object to return. The object_piece parameter takes one of these possible values:

- ❑   1 — Object name
- ❑   2 — Owner name
- ❑   3 — Database name
- ❑   4 — Server name

PERMISSIONS

The PERMISSIONS function returns a value containing a bitmap, which indicates the statement, object, or column permissions for the current user. The syntax is as follows:

```
PERMISSIONS([<objectid> [, '<column>']])
```

The object_id parameter specifies the ID of an object. The optional column parameter specifies the name of the column for which permission information is being returned.

@@ROWCOUNT

Returns the number of rows affected by the last statement.

One of the most used globals, my most common use for this one is to check for non–run-time errors — that is, items that are logically errors to your program but that SQL Server isn't going to see any problem with. An example is a situation where you are performing an update based on a condition, but you find that it affects zero rows. Odds are that, if your client submitted a modification for a particular row, then it was expecting that row to match the criteria given — zero rows affected is indicative of something being wrong.

However, if you test this system function on any statement that does not return rows, then you will also return a value of 0.

ROWCOUNT_BIG

The ROWCOUNT_BIG function is very similar to @@ROWCOUNT in that it returns the number of rows from the last statement. However, the value returned is of a data type of bigint. The syntax is as follows:

```
ROWCOUNT_BIG()
```

SCOPE_IDENTITY

The SCOPE_IDENTITY function returns the last value inserted into an identity column in the same scope (that is, within the same sproc, trigger, function, or batch). This is similar to IDENT_CURRENT, discussed earlier, although that was not limited to identity insertions made in the same scope.

This function returns a sql_variant data type, and the syntax is as follows:

```
SCOPE_IDENTITY()
```

SERVERPROPERTY

The SERVERPROPERTY function returns information about the server you are running on. The syntax is as follows:

```
SERVERPROPERTY('<propertyname>')
```

The possible values for propertyname are:

Property Name	Values Returned
Collation	The name of the default collation for the server.
Edition	The edition of the SQL Server instance installed on the server. Returns one of the following nvarchar results: 'Desktop Engine' 'Developer Edition' 'Enterprise Edition' 'Enterprise Evaluation Edition' 'Personal Edition' 'Standard Edition'
Engine tEdition	The engine edition of the SQL Server instance installed on the server: 1 — Personal or Desktop Engine 2 — Standard 3 — Enterprise (returned for Enterprise, Enterprise Evaluation, and Developer)
InstanceName	The name of the instance to which the user is connected.
IsClustered	Will determine if the server instance is configured in a failover cluster: 1 — Clustered 0 — Not clustered NULL — Invalid input or error
IsFullText Installed	To determine if the full-text component is installed with the current instance of SQL Server: 1 — Full-text is installed. 0 — Full-text is not installed. NULL — Invalid input or error

Continued

Property Name	Values Returned
IsIntegrated SecurityOnly	To determine if the server is in integrated security mode: 1 — Integrated security 0 — Not integrated security NULL — Invalid input or error
IsSingleUser	To determine if the server is a single-user installation: 1 — Single user 0 — Not single user NULL — Invalid input or error
IsSync WithBackup	To determine if the database is either a published database or a distribution database, and can be restored without disrupting the current transactional replication: 1 — True 0 — False
LicenseType	What type of license is installed for this instance of SQL Server: PER_SEAT — Per-seat mode PER_PROCESSOR — Per-processor mode DISABLED — Licensing is disabled
MachineName	Returns the Windows NT computer name on which the server instance is running. For a clustered instance (an instance of SQL Server running on a virtual server on Microsoft Cluster Server), it returns the name of the virtual server.
NumLicenses	Number of client licenses registered for this instance of SQL Server, if in per-seat mode. Number of processors licensed for this instance of SQL Server, if in per-processor mode.
ProcessID	Process ID of the SQL Server service. (The ProcessID is useful in identifying which sqlservr.exe belongs to this instance.)
ProductVersion	Very much like Visual Basic projects, in that the version details of the instance of SQL Server are returned, in the form of 'major.minor.build'.
ProductLevel	Returns the value of the version of the SQL Server instance currently running. Returns: 'RTM' — Shipping version 'SPn' — Service pack version 'Bn' — Beta version
ServerName	Both the Windows NT server and instance information associated with a specified instance of SQL Server.

The SERVERPROPERTY *function is very useful for multi-sited corporations where developers need to find out information from a server.*

SESSION_USER

The SESSION_USER function allows a system-supplied value for the current session's username to be inserted into a table if no default value has been specified. The syntax is as follows:

```
SESSION_USER
```

SESSIONPROPERTY

The SESSIONPROPERTY function is used to return the SET options for a session. The syntax is as follows:

```
SESSIONPROPERTY (<option>)
```

This function is useful when there are stored procedures that are altering session properties in specific scenarios. This function should rarely be used, as you should not alter too many of the SET options during run time.

STATS_DATE

The STATS_DATE function returns the date that the statistics for the specified index were last updated. The syntax is as follows:

```
STATS_DATE(<table id>, <index id>)
```

SYSTEM_USER

The SYSTEM_USER function allows a system-supplied value for the current system username to be inserted into a table if no default value has been specified. The syntax is as follows:

```
SYSTEM_USER
```

USER_NAME

The USER_NAME returns a database username. The syntax is as follows:

```
USER_NAME([<id>])
```

The id parameter specifies the ID number of the required username; if no value is given the current user is assumed.

Text and Image Functions

The text and image functions perform operations on text or image data. They are:

❑ PATINDEX (This was covered in the "String Functions" section earlier in the appendix.)

❑ TEXTPTR

❑ TEXTVALID

TEXTPTR

The TEXTPTR function checks the value of the text pointer that corresponds to a text, ntext, or image column and returns a varbinary value. The text pointer should be checked to ensure that it points to the first text page before running READTEXT, WRITETEXT, and UPDATE statements. The syntax is as follows:

```
TEXTPTR(<column>)
```

TEXTVALID

The TEXTVALID function checks whether a specified text pointer is valid. The syntax is as follows:

```
TEXTVALID('<table.column>', <text pointer>)
```

The table.column parameter specifies the name of the table and column to be used. The text_ptr parameter specifies the text pointer to be checked.

This function will return 0 if the pointer is invalid and 1 if the pointer is valid.

Very Simple Connectivity Examples

Entire books are written around the subject of connectivity. For the first several books I put out, I deliberately avoided the topic entirely in the basic belief that it is a simply huge topic — one that is difficult to do justice to in less than a full book. That said, having a SQL Server but not allowing programs to connect to it is the same as not having a SQL Server at all. Sure, we may log into Management Studio and write queries directly, but the reality is that the vast majority of our users out there never actually see the database directly.

For this *"Beginning"* title, I'm still going to touch on the subject only in a very limited fashion that is purely meant for quick reference once you've looked at other sources, or perhaps to give you an inkling of what is involved. If you're serious about displaying excellence in working with SQL Server or any other connectivity-based data solution, I highly recommend you purchase a book specifically on data access and connectivity.

This appendix is a collection of extremely simple connectivity examples utilizing a couple of client languages and a few features in two different connectivity models. We're going to stick a few basic examples of connecting within each language/model mix and leave the discussion of the whys and hows to books that are focused solely on connectivity.

> *I can't stress enough how these examples are truly the basics. You can make many, many choices and optimizations for connectivity. Each connectivity model has its own quirks, and different languages sometimes bring their own flair. If you're trying to get more out of this than just a basic feel for how it's done (or perhaps an "Oh yeah, I forgot that part"), check out the connectivity coverage I offer in* Professional SQL Server 2008 Programming *or perhaps another connectivity-specific book. (There are likely entire books just for your particular language and connectivity model mix.)*

> *Connectivity models covered here include:*

- ❑ ADO.NET
- ❑ ADO

Within the ADO.NET example, we'll look at a couple of different approaches to how to utilize the features provided.

> **All code examples provided here were created with Visual Studio 2008. The basic principles provided here should work just fine under other versions of Visual Studio or other editors for the languages provided, but it's conceivable that I've thrown in a .NET Framework 3.5 quirk and not noticed it. (If so, apologies to those operating under different .NET Framework versions.)**

Some General Concepts

Before we get going too deep with "just code," there are a few key constructs that we need to understand. There are several different connectivity models that have come and gone over time; you'll hear about such names as OLE-DB, ODBC, and, of course, ADO, among others. The connectivity model of the day these days tends to be ADO.NET or LINQ. Given the life span of these things, I wouldn't be surprised at all if there were yet a different one by the time the next version of SQL Server comes out.

Even with all the different models that have come and gone, some concepts seem to always exist in every object model — let's take a look at these real quick:

❑ **Connection:** The connection object is pretty much what it sounds like — the object that defines and establishes your actual communications link to your database. The kinds of parameter information that will exist for a connection object include such things as the username, password, database, and server you wish to connect to. Some of the methods that will exist include such things as connect and disconnect.

❑ **Command:** This object is the one that carries information about what it is you want to do. Some object models will not include this object, or at least not feature it, but the concept is always there. (It is sometimes hidden as a method of the connection object.)

❑ **Data set:** This is the result of a query — that is, if the query returns data. Some queries in which you execute, for example, a simple INSERT statement, will not return results, but, if results are returned, there will be some sort of data set (sometimes called a result set or recordset) that the query returns them into. Data set objects will generally allow for you to iterate through the records in them (often forward only in direction but usually settable to allow for more robust positioning). They will also generally allow for data to be updated, inserted, and deleted.

Connectivity Examples

What we're going to do in this section is provide some hyper (and I do mean in the extreme) examples of how to get connected in the two most common languages of the day — C# and VB.NET. For each language, we'll show a couple of examples — one for each of two different kinds of operations (fetching a simple data set and executing a query that does not return a data set).

Connecting in C#

C# is a fairly clean language and is relatively easy to learn, much like VB, but it has the extra benefit of providing some C-based concepts and also being much closer in syntax (making it easier to transition between the two).

Returning a Data Set

```csharp
using System;
using System.Data.SqlClient;

class Program
{
    static void Main()
    {
        //Create some base strings so you can look at these
        // separately from the commands they run in

        // Integrated Security - next line should be uncommented to use
        string strConnect = "Data Source=(local);Initial Catalog=master;Integrated
Security=SSPI";
        // SQL Security - next line should be uncommented to use
        //string strConnect = "Data Source=(local);Initial Catalog=master;User
Id=sa;Password=MyPass";

        string strCommand = "SELECT Name, database_id as ID FROM sys.databases";

        SqlDataReader rsMyRS = null;

        SqlConnection cnMyConn = new SqlConnection(strConnect);

        try
        {
            // "Open" the connection (this is the first time it actually
            // contacts the database server)
            cnMyConn.Open();

            // Create the command object now
            SqlCommand sqlMyCommand = new SqlCommand(strCommand, cnMyConn);

            // Create the result set
            rsMyRS = sqlMyCommand.ExecuteReader();

            //Output what we got
            while (rsMyRS.Read())
            {
                // Write out the first (ordinal numbers here)
                // column. We can also refer to the column by name
                Console.WriteLine(rsMyRS["Name"]);
            }
            Console.WriteLine();
            Console.WriteLine("Press any key to continue...");
            Console.ReadKey();
        }
```

```
            finally
            {
                // Clean up
                if (rsMyRS != null)
                {
                    rsMyRS.Close();
                }

                if (cnMyConn != null)
                {
                    cnMyConn.Close();
                }
            }
        }
    }
}
```

Executing Commands with No Data Set

```
using System;
using System.Data.SqlClient;

class Program
{
    static void Main()
    {
        //Create some base strings so you can look at these
        // separately from the commands they run in

        // Integrated Security - next line should be uncommented to use
        string strConnect = "Data Source=(local);Initial Catalog=master;Integrated
Security=SSPI";
        // SQL Security - next line should be uncommented to use
        //string strConnect = "Data Source=(local);Initial Catalog=master;User
Id=sa;Password=MyPass";

        string strCommand = "CREATE TABLE Foo(Column1    INT NOT NULL PRIMARY KEY)";
        string strCommand2 = "DROP TABLE Foo";

        SqlConnection cnMyConn = new SqlConnection(strConnect);

        try
        {
            // "Open" the connection (this is the first time it actually
            // contacts the database server)
            cnMyConn.Open();

            // Create the command object now
            SqlCommand sqlMyCommand = new SqlCommand(strCommand, cnMyConn);

            // Execute the command
            sqlMyCommand.ExecuteNonQuery();

            Console.WriteLine("Table Created");
            Console.WriteLine("Press enter to continue (you can go check to make
sure that it's there first) ");
```

```
            Console.ReadLine();

            // Change the command
            sqlMyCommand.CommandText = strCommand2;

            sqlMyCommand.ExecuteNonQuery();

            Console.WriteLine("It's gone");

            Console.WriteLine();
            Console.WriteLine("Press any key to continue...");
            Console.ReadKey();
        }
        finally
        {
            // Clean up
            if (cnMyConn != null)
            {
                cnMyConn.Close();
            }
        }
    }
}
```

Connecting in VB.NET

VB.NET continues replacing the venerable Visual Basic. While I'm increasingly favoring C# for my own efforts, VB remains the code of choice for many.

Returning a Data Set

```
Imports System
Imports System.Data
Imports System.Data.SqlClient

Module Program

    Sub Main()

        'Create some base strings so you can look at these
        'separately from the commands they run in

        ' Integrated Security - next 2 lines should be uncommented to use
        '      Windows authentication
        Dim strConnect As String = _
            "Data Source=(local);Initial Catalog=master;Integrated Security=SSPI"
        ' SQL Security - next 2 lines should be uncommented to use
        '      SQL Server authentication
        'Dim strConnect As String = _
        '      "Data Source=(local);Initial Catalog=master;User Id=sa;Password=MyPass"

        Dim strCommand As String = _
            "SELECT Name, database_id as ID FROM sys.databases"
```

```
                Dim rsMyRS As SqlClient.SqlDataReader

                Dim cnMyConn As New SqlClient.SqlConnection(strConnect)

                ' "Open" the connection (this is the first time it actually
                ' contacts the database server)
                cnMyConn.Open()

                ' Create the command object now
                Dim sqlMyCommand As New SqlClient.SqlCommand(strCommand, cnMyConn)

                ' Create the result set
                rsMyRS = sqlMyCommand.ExecuteReader()

                'Output what we got
                Do While rsMyRS.Read
                    ' Write out the first (ordinal numbers here)
                    ' column. We can also refer to the column by name
                    Console.WriteLine(rsMyRS("Name"))
                Loop

                Console.WriteLine()
                Console.WriteLine("Press any key to continue...")
                Console.ReadKey()

                ' Clean up
                rsMyRS.Close()
                cnMyConn.Close()

            End Sub

        End Module
```

Executing Commands with No Data Set

```
        Imports System
        Imports System.Data
        Imports System.Data.SqlClient

        Module Program

            Sub Main()

                'Create some base strings so you can look at these
                'separately from the commands they run in

                ' Integrated Security - next 2 lines should be uncommented to use
                Dim strConnect As String = _
                    "Data Source=(local);Initial Catalog=master;Integrated Security=SSPI"
                ' SQL Security - next 2 lines should be uncommented to use
                'Dim strConnect As String = _
                '    "Data Source=(local);Initial Catalog=master;User Id=sa;Password=MyPass"

                Dim strCommand As String = "CREATE TABLE Foo(Column1   INT NOT NULL PRIMARY KEY)"
```

```vb
        Dim strCommand2 As String = "DROP TABLE Foo"

        Dim cnMyConn As New SqlClient.SqlConnection(strConnect)

        ' "Open" the connection (this is the first time it actually
        ' contacts the database server)
        cnMyConn.Open()

        ' Create the command object now
        Dim sqlMyCommand As New SqlClient.SqlCommand(strCommand, cnMyConn)

        ' Execute the command
        sqlMyCommand.ExecuteNonQuery()

        Console.WriteLine("Table Created")
        Console.WriteLine("Press enter to continue (you can go check to make sure
that it's there first)")
        Console.ReadLine()

        ' Change the command
        sqlMyCommand.CommandText = strCommand2

        sqlMyCommand.ExecuteNonQuery()

        Console.WriteLine("It's gone")

        Console.WriteLine()
        Console.WriteLine("Press any key to continue...")
        Console.ReadKey()

        ' Clean up
        cnMyConn.Close()

    End Sub

End Module
```

A Brief Word on LINQ

LINQ is, as I write this, "all the rage" so to speak. For the rare few that haven't heard of LINQ, it is a new (or, more accurately, a new attempt at an) access method based on the notion of homogeneous data sources. LINQ has its own query language — one that is very similar to SQL, and yet different enough to create no small degree of work when trying to convert between the two.

While LINQ certainly has, and will likely continue for at least a while to have a lot of momentum as the new way of accessing data, I remain something of a skeptic. Don't get me wrong. LINQ has some cool things to offer, but I've seen LINQ-type data access notions come and go many times over the years, so I've been trained to question the staying power of such models.

Appendix B: Very Simple Connectivity Examples

A full discussion of LINQ is well beyond the scope of this book, and the query syntax is different enough that I am going to avoid confusing the beginner here with the new twist on things. That said, it is worth noting some things about what LINQ is and isn't.

LINQ uses a strongly typed model to allow queries to a wide variety of data. While access to SQL Server is what is most relevant to this book, it's important to note that LINQ is very capable of connectivity with non-tabular data sources. LINQ can be used to access XML (XPath is generally the better choice, but you may want to use LINQ for consistency with other data access you're doing), and it can be used to access things such as object collections. In short, it is wildly flexible about what kind of data it is returning.

Beyond the flexibility, the primary advantage I see to LINQ is that it is strongly typed. Previous access models used a binding model where your program didn't really have any assurances of what data type it was getting back until runtime. LINQ utilizes a far more early binding to the data, and therefore is able to catch many types of type mismatch or similar errors earlier in the coding process. This is, of course, not entirely foolproof, but it is an advance in terms of the particular area it is addressing.

If you're thinking that you're going to use LINQ for all your data access, all I can do is to encourage you to make sure that you understand *why* LINQ is your choice prior to making it. Don't use it because it's the latest "cool" thing, but rather because it fits your particular need better than the other options available to you.

Index

E